America's Top White-Collar Jobs

Detailed Information on 110 Major Office, Management, Sales, and Professional Jobs

FIFTH EDITION

J. M

- Thorough, up-to-
  top white-collar

- Information on s
  and training req
  potential, and m

- Special section o

- Resume example
  writers for some
  ment, sales, and

- Helpful informat
  trends

America's Top White-Collar Jobs, *Fifth Edition*
Detailed Information on 110 Major Office, Management, Sales, and Professional Jobs

© 2001 by J. Michael Farr

Published by JIST Works, an imprint of JIST Publishing, Inc.
8902 Otis Avenue
Indianapolis, IN 46216-1033
Phone: 800-648-JIST   Fax: 800-JIST-FAX   E-mail: editorial@jist.com
Visit our Web site at **www.jist.com** for more details on JIST, free job search information and book chapters, and ordering information on our many products!

Some other books by J. Michael Farr:
The Very Quick Job Search
The Quick Resume & Cover Letter Book
America's Top Resumes for America's Top Jobs
Getting the Job You Really Want
Best Jobs for the 21st Century (LaVerne L.
    Ludden, coauthor)

Other books in the America's Top Jobs® series:
America's Top 300 Jobs
America's Top Jobs for College Graduates
America's Fastest Growing Jobs
America's Top Medical, Education & Human Services Jobs
America's Top Jobs for People Without a Four-Year Degree
America's Top Military Careers

For other career-related materials, turn to the back of this book. Some of JIST's many publications are described there. You may also request a free JIST catalog using the order form.

Quantity discounts are available for JIST books. Please call our Sales Department at 1-800-648-5478 for more information and a free catalog.

Editors: Susan Pines, Audra McFarland, Veda Dickerson
Cover and Interior Designer: Aleata Howard
Interior Layout: Carolyn J. Newland

Printed in the United States of America

03 02 01 00   9 8 7 6 5 4 3 2 1

We have been careful to provide accurate information throughout this book, but it is possible that errors and omissions have been introduced. Please consider this in making any career plans or other important decisions. Trust your own judgment above all else and in all things.

Trademarks: All brand names and product names used in this book are trade names, service marks, trademarks, or registered trademarks of their respective owners.

ISBN 1-56370-719-5

Relax–You Don't Have to Read This Whole Book!

*T*his is a big book, but you don't need to read it all. I've organized it into easy-to-use sections so you can browse just the information you want. To get started, simply scan the table of contents, where you'll find brief explanations of the major sections plus a list of the jobs described in Section One. Really, this book is easy to use, and I hope that it helps you.

White-Collar Jobs Are Growing Rapidly

Many jobs in America are called white-collar jobs. They are called this because, in the past, people doing these jobs often wore white shirts. (People in factories and other jobs often wore blue shirts or uniforms, and the jobs they do are called blue-collar jobs.) In many offices today, attire is less formal than white-collar. But the term is still used because it accurately enough describes many office, management, sales, and professional jobs.

The white-collar jobs I emphasize in this book are among the most rapidly growing jobs, and they provide an enormous range of opportunities. Many of these jobs require advanced education or substantial experience, but many do not. Some jobs, such as those in sales, may not require lengthy training and yet offer the potential for unlimited earnings. Others offer entry-level and part-time opportunities that can lead to more responsibility later.

Who Should Use This Book?

This is more than a book of job descriptions. I've spent quite a bit of time thinking about how to make its contents useful for a variety of situations, including the following:

- **For exploring career options.** The descriptions give a wealth of information on many of the most desirable jobs in the labor market.

- **For considering more education or training.** The information here can help you avoid costly mistakes in choosing a career or deciding on additional training or education—and increase your chances of planning a bright future.

- **For job seeking.** This book will help you identify new job targets, prepare for interviews, and write targeted resumes. The advice in Section Two has been proven to cut job search time in half!

- **For counseling.** This is a valuable source of information on jobs and trends. Section One provides thorough job descriptions, and Section Three gives data on trends in jobs and industries.

Credits: The occupational descriptions in this book come from the good people at the U.S. Department of Labor, as published in the most recent edition of the *Occupational Outlook Handbook*. The *OOH* is the best source of career information available, and the descriptions include the latest data on earnings and other details. The information in Section Three on labor market trends is also from various sources at the U.S. Department of Labor. Thank you to all the people at the Labor Department who toil on gathering, compiling, analyzing, and making sense of this information. It's good stuff, and I hope you can make good use of it.

Mike Farr

Mike Farr

Table of Contents

Summary of Major Sections

Introduction. The introduction explains each job description element, gives tips on using the book for career exploration and job seeking, and provides other details. *The introduction begins on page 1.*

Section One: Descriptions of 110 Major White-Collar Jobs. This is the book's major section, with thorough descriptions of 110 office (including clerical), management, sales, and professional jobs. Each description gives information on working conditions, skills required, growth projections, training or education needed, typical earnings, and much more. The jobs are presented in alphabetic order. They are listed with their page numbers beginning at right. *Section One begins on page 9.*

Section Two: The Quick Job Search—Advice on Planning Your Career and Getting a Good Job in Less Time. This brief but important section offers results-oriented career planning and job search techniques, including tips on exploring career options, defining your ideal job, writing resumes, getting interviews, answering problem questions, and surviving unemployment. The second part of this section features professionally written and designed resumes for some of America's top office, management, sales, and professional jobs. *Section Two begins on page 299.*

Section Three: Important Trends in Jobs and Industries. This section includes two well-written articles on labor market trends, plus tables with information on hundreds of major jobs. The articles are short and worth your time. *Section Three begins on page 347.*

Titles of the articles and tables are as follows:

- "Tomorrow's Jobs: Important Labor Market Trends Through the Year 2008," *page 349*

- "Employment Trends in Major Industries," *page 356*

- Details on 500 Major Jobs: Earnings, Projected Growth, Education Required, Unemployment Rates, and Other Details, *page 366*

- 252 Major Jobs, Sorted by Percent of Projected Growth, *page 396*

The 110 Jobs Described in Section One

The titles for the 110 jobs described in Section One are listed below in alphabetic order, with the page number where each description begins. Find jobs that seem interesting to you and read those descriptions. The descriptions are easy to understand, but the introduction provides additional information to help you interpret them.

Accountants and Auditors 11

Actors, Directors, and Producers 14

Actuaries 17

Adjusters, Investigators, and Collectors 19

Administrative Services and Facility Managers 25

Adult and Vocational Education Teachers 27

Advertising, Marketing, and Public Relations Managers 29

Aircraft Pilots and Flight Engineers 32

Air Traffic Controllers 35

Announcers 38

Architects, Except Landscape and Naval 40

Archivists, Curators, Museum Technicians, and Conservators 43

Armed Forces 46

Bank Tellers 53

Billing Clerks and Billing Machine Operators 55

Blue-Collar Worker Supervisors 57

Bookkeeping, Accounting, and Auditing Clerks 59

Brokerage Clerks and Statement Clerks 60

Budget Analysts 62

Cashiers 64

Chiropractors 66

D.E. Gavit Jr. Sr. High School
1670- 175th Street
Hammond, IN 46324

Clergy 68

College and University Faculty 73

Computer Operators 76

Computer Programmers 78

Construction and Building Inspectors ... 81

Construction Managers 84

Cost Estimators 86

Counselors 89

Counter and Rental Clerks 92

Court Reporters, Medical Transcriptionists, and Stenographers 94

Dentists 96

Designers 98

Dietitians and Nutritionists 101

Dispatchers 103

Drafters 105

Economists and Marketing Research Analysts 107

Education Administrators 110

Employment Interviewers, Private or Public Employment Service 113

Engineering, Natural Science, and Computer and Information Systems Managers ... 116

Farmers and Farm Managers 119

File Clerks 122

Financial Managers 123

Funeral Directors and Morticians 126

General Managers and Top Executives ... 129

Government Chief Executives and Legislators 131

Health Services Managers 133

Home Health and Personal Care Aides ... 135

Hotel Managers and Assistants 137

Hotel, Motel, and Resort Desk Clerks ... 139

Human Resources Clerks, except Payroll and Timekeeping 141

Human Resources, Training, and Labor Relations Specialists and Managers ... 142

Industrial Production Managers 147

Information Clerks 149

Inspectors and Compliance Officers, Except Construction 154

Insurance Sales Agents 157

Insurance Underwriters 160

Interviewing and New Accounts Clerks ... 162

Landscape Architects 164

Lawyers and Judicial Workers 167

Librarians 172

Library Assistants and Bookmobile Drivers ... 175

Library Technicians 177

Loan Clerks and Credit Authorizers, Checkers, and Clerks 178

Loan Officers and Counselors 180

Mail Clerks and Messengers 182

Management Analysts 184

Manufacturers' and Wholesale Sales Representatives 187

Material Recording, Scheduling, Dispatching, and Distributing Occupations 189

Office and Administrative Support Supervisors and Managers 195

Office Clerks, General 197

Operations Research Analysts 198

Opticians, Dispensing 200

Optometrists 201

Order Clerks 203

Paralegals 205

Payroll and Timekeeping Clerks 207

Pharmacists 209

Physicians 211

Podiatrists 214

Police and Detectives 216

Postal Clerks and Mail Carriers 220

Private Detectives and Investigators ... 222

Property, Real Estate, and Community Association Managers 225

Psychologists 227

Public Relations Specialists 230

Purchasing Managers, Buyers, and Purchasing Agents 233

©2001 • JIST Works • Indianapolis, IN

Real Estate Agents and Brokers 236

Receptionists 239

Records Processing Occupations 241

Reservation and Transportation Ticket
Agents and Travel Clerks 251

Restaurant and Food Service Managers 253

Retail Salespersons 256

Retail Sales Worker Supervisors and
Managers 258

School Teachers—Kindergarten, Elementary,
and Secondary 260

Secretaries 264

Securities, Commodities, and Financial
Services Sales Representatives 266

Services Sales Representatives 270

Shipping, Receiving, and Traffic Clerks 272

Social Workers 274

Special Education Teachers 277

Speech-Language Pathologists and
Audiologists 279

Statisticians 282

Stock Clerks 284

Surveyors, Cartographers, Photogrammetrists,
and Surveying Technicians 285

Travel Agents 287

Urban and Regional Planners 289

Veterinarians 291

Word Processors, Typists, and Data Entry
Keyers 294

Writers and Editors, including Technical
Writers 296

INTRODUCTION

This book is about improving your life, not just about selecting a job. The right job will have an enormous impact on how you live your life.

While a huge amount of information is available on occupations, most people don't know where to find accurate, reliable facts to help them make good career decisions—or they don't take the time to look. Important choices such as what to do with your career or whether to get additional training or education deserve your time.

This book provides information on jobs often called "white collar." Included in this category are clerical, administrative, management, sales, and professional jobs. People in these jobs usually work in an office. White-collar jobs present an enormous range of opportunities, taking in a variety of pay, educational requirements, and types of work. Many white-collar jobs have been among the most rapidly growing jobs, and this trend is projected to continue.

If you are considering a job change, this book will likely help you identify one or more interesting possibilities. If you are considering more training or education, this book will help with solid information. More training and education is typically required to get better jobs now, but some jobs, such as those in sales, have high pay but do not require advanced education. This book is designed to give you facts to help you explore your options.

A certain type of work or workplace may interest you as much as a certain type of job. If your interests and values are to work with children, for example, you can do this in a variety of work environments, in a variety of industries, and in a variety of jobs. For this reason, I suggest you begin exploring alternatives by following your interests—and finding a career path that allows you to use your talents doing something you enjoy.

Also remember that money is not everything. The time you spend in career planning can pay off in more than higher earnings. Being satisfied with your work—and your life—is often more important than how much you earn. This book can help you find the work that suits you best.

Keep in Mind That Your Situation Is *Not* "Average"

While the employment growth and earnings trends for many occupations and industries are quite positive, the averages in this book will not be true for many individuals. Within any field, some earn much more and some much less.

My point is, your situation is probably not average. Some people do better than others, and others are willing to accept less pay for a more desirable work environment. Earnings vary enormously in different parts of the country, in different occupations, and in different industries. But this book's solid information is a great place to start. Good information will give you a strong foundation for good decisions.

Four Important Labor Market Trends That Will Affect Your Career

Our economy has changed in dramatic ways over the past 10 years, with profound effects on how we work and live. Section Three provides more information on labor market trends but, in case you don't read it, here are four trends that you simply *must* consider.

I. Education and Earnings Are Related

It should come as no surprise that people with higher education and training levels have higher average earnings. The data that follows comes from the Department of Labor's Internet site. The site presents the median earnings for people with various levels of education (median is the point where half earn more and half less) as well as the average percentage unemployed. Based on this information, I computed the earnings advantage at various levels of education compared to those with a high school diploma.

Earnings and Unemployment Rate for Year-Round, Full-Time Workers Age 25 and Over, by Educational Attainment			
Level of Education	**Median Annual Earnings**	**Premium Over High School Grads**	**Unem- ployment Rate**
Professional degree	$72,700	180%	1.3%
Doctoral degree	$62,400	140%	1.4%
Master's degree	$50,000	92%	1.6%
Bachelor's degree	$40,100	54%	1.9%
Associate degree	$31,700	22%	2.5%
Some college, no degree	$30,400	17%	3.2%
High school graduate	$26,000	—	4.0%
Less than a high school diploma	$19,700	-24%	7.1%

Source: Unemployment rate—Bureau of Labor Statistics, 1998 data; Earnings—Bureau of the Census, 1997 data

The earnings difference between a college graduate and someone with a high school education is $14,100 a year—enough to buy a nice car, make a down payment on a house, or even take a month's vacation for two to Europe. As you see, over a lifetime, this earnings difference will make an enormous difference in lifestyle.

And there is more. Jobs that require a four-year college degree are projected to grow about twice as fast as jobs that do not. People with higher levels of education also tend to be unemployed at lower rates and for shorter periods. Overall, the data on earnings and other criteria indicate that those with more education and training do better than those with less. There are exceptions, of course, but the facts are quite clear.

Many jobs can be obtained without a college degree, but most better paying jobs require training beyond high school or substantial work experience. Still, some workers without college degrees earn more than those with degrees. According to the U.S. Department of Labor, two out of five workers without college degrees earned more than the average for all workers. One in six earned as much—or more—than the average for those with four-year college degrees.

2. Knowledge of Computer and Other Technologies Is Increasingly Important

As you looked over the list of jobs on the contents page, you may have noticed that many require computer or technical

skills. Even jobs that do not appear to be technical often call for computer literacy. Clerical workers without basic computer skills will have limited job options, since most clerical jobs now require such skills. Librarians, paralegals, and many others often need technical training to handle increasingly technical jobs.

In all fields, those without job-related technical and computer skills will have a more difficult time finding good opportunities since they are competing with those who have these skills. Older workers, by the way, often do not have the computer skills that younger workers do. Employers tend to hire the skills they need, and people without these abilities won't get the best jobs.

3. Ongoing Education and Training Are Essential

School and work once were separate activities, and most people did not go back to school when they began working. But with rapid changes in technology, most people will be or are required to learn throughout their work lives. Jobs are constantly upgraded, and today's jobs often cannot be handled with the knowledge and skills that workers had just a few years ago. To remain competitive, those without technical or computer skills must get them. Those who do not will face increasingly limited job options.

What this means is that you should plan to upgrade your job skills throughout your working life. This can include taking formal courses—or it could mean reading work-related magazines at home, signing up for on-the-job training, and participating in other forms of education. Continuously upgrading your work-related skills is no longer optional for most jobs, and you ignore doing so at your peril.

4. Good Career Planning Has Increased in Importance

Most people spend more time watching TV during a week than they spend on career planning during an entire year. Yet most people will change their jobs many times and make major career changes five to seven times. It just makes sense to spend more time on career planning.

While you probably picked up this book for its information on jobs, it also provides a great deal of information on career planning. For example, Section Two gives career and job search advice, and Section Three has good information on labor market trends and other important topics. I urge you to read these and related materials because career planning and job-seeking skills are survival skills for this new economy.

Information on the Major Sections of This Book

It should be easy to understand how to use this book. I offered some brief comments on each section in the table of contents, and that may be all you need. If you want more, here are some additional details that you may find useful.

Section One: Descriptions of 110 Major White-Collar Jobs

Section One is the main part of the book and probably the reason you picked it up. It contains brief, well-written descriptions for 110 major white-collar jobs. These jobs are presented in alphabetic order. To make the job descriptions easy to find, I created a table of contents that shows where each one begins.

Together, the jobs in Section One provide enormous variety at all levels of earnings and training. One way to explore career options is to go to the table of contents and identify those jobs that seem interesting. You can quickly spot jobs you want to learn more about, and you may see other jobs that you had not considered before.

Your next step would be to read the descriptions for the jobs that interest you and, based on what you learn, identify those that *most* interest you. These are the jobs you should consider, and Sections Two and Three will give you additional information on how you might best do so.

Each occupational description in this book follows a standard format, making it easier for you to compare jobs. This overview explains how the occupational descriptions are organized. It highlights information presented in each part of a description, gives examples of specific occupations in some cases, and offers some hints on how to interpret the information provided.

Job Title

This is the title used for the job in the *Occupational Outlook Handbook*, published by the U.S. Department of Labor.

Those Numbers at the Beginning of Each Description

The numbers in parentheses that appear just below the title of most occupational descriptions are from the new Occupational Information Network (O*NET). The O*NET was developed by the U.S. Department of Labor to replace the older *Dictionary of Occupational Titles* (*DOT*). Like the *DOT* in the past, the O*NET is used by state employment service offices to classify applicants and job openings, and by some career information centers and libraries to file occupational information.

Significant Points

The bullet points under "Significant Points" highlight key characteristics for each job.

Nature of the Work

This segment discusses what workers do. Individual job duties may vary by industry or employer. For instance, workers in larger firms tend to be more specialized, whereas those in smaller firms often have a wider variety of duties. Most occupations have several levels of skills and responsibilities through which workers may progress. Beginners may start as trainees performing routine tasks under close supervision. Experienced workers usually undertake more difficult tasks and are expected to perform with less supervision.

The influence of technological advancements on the way work is done is mentioned. For example, the Internet allows purchasers to acquire supplies with a click of the mouse, saving time and money. This part also discusses emerging specialties. For instance, sales engineers comprise a new specialty within manufacturers' and wholesale sales representatives.

Working Conditions

This part identifies the typical hours worked, the workplace environment, susceptibility to injury, special equipment, physical activities, and the extent of travel required. In many occupations people work regular business hours—40 hours a week, Monday through Friday—but many do not. For example, clergy and restaurant and food service managers often work evenings and weekends.

The work setting can range from a hospital, to a mall, to an off-shore oil rig. Police and detectives might be susceptible to injury, while paralegals have high job-related stress. Veterinarians may wear protective clothing or equipment; mail carriers do physically demanding work; and aircraft pilots are frequently away from home overnight.

Employment

This part reports the number of jobs the occupation provided in 1998 and the key industries where these jobs are found. When significant, the geographic distribution of jobs and the proportion of part-time (less than 35 hours a week) and self-employed workers in the occupation are mentioned. Self-employed workers accounted for nearly 9 percent of the workforce in 1998; however, they were concentrated in a small number of occupations, such as dentists and farmers.

Training, Other Qualifications, and Advancement

After knowing what a job is all about, it is important to understand how to train for it. This part describes the most significant sources of training, including the training preferred by employers, the typical length of training, and advancement possibilities. The jobs included in this book do not require college, postgraduate, or professional education. In addition to training requirements, the descriptions also mention desirable skills, aptitudes, and personal characteristics.

Some occupations require certification or licensing to enter the field, to advance, or to practice independently. Certification or licensing generally involves completing courses and passing examinations. Many occupations increasingly have continuing education or skill improvement requirements to keep up with the changing economy or to improve advancement opportunities.

Job Outlook

In planning for the future, an individual should consider potential job opportunities. This part describes the factors that will result in growth or decline in the number of jobs. In some cases, this book mentions the relative number of job openings an occupation is likely to provide. Occupations that are large and have high turnover rates generally provide the most job openings—reflecting the need to replace workers who transfer to other occupations or stop working.

Some descriptions discuss the relationship between the number of job seekers and job openings. In some occupations, there is a rough balance between job seekers and openings, whereas other occupations are characterized by shortages or surpluses. Limited training facilities, salary regulations, or undesirable aspects of the work can cause shortages of entrants. On the other hand, glamorous or potentially high-paying occupations, such as actors or lawyers, generally have surpluses of job seekers. Variation in job opportunities by industry, size of firm, or geographic location also may be discussed. Even in crowded fields, job openings do exist. Good students or well-qualified individuals should not be deterred from undertaking training or seeking entry.

Susceptibility to layoffs due to imports, slowdowns in economic activity, technological advancements, or budget cuts are also addressed in this part.

Key Phrases Used in the Descriptions	
This box explains how to interpret the key phrases used to describe projected changes in employment. It also explains the terms used to describe the relationship between the number of job openings and the number of job seekers. The descriptions of this relationship in a particular occupation reflect the knowledge and judgment of economists in the Bureau's Office of Employment Projections.	

Changing Employment Between 1998 and 2008

If the statement reads:	Employment is projected to:
Grow much faster than average	Increase 36 percent or more
Grow faster than average	Increase 21 to 35 percent
Grow about as fast as average	Increase 10 to 20 percent
Grow more slowly than average or little or no change	Increase 0 to 9 percent
Decline	Decrease 1 percent or more

Opportunities and Competition for Jobs

If the statement reads:	Job openings compared to job seekers may be:
Very good to excellent opportunities	More numerous
Good or favorable opportunities	In rough balance
May face keen competition or can expect keen competition	Fewer

Earnings

This part discusses typical earnings and how workers are compensated—annual salaries, hourly wages, commissions, piece rates, tips, or bonuses. Within every occupation, earnings vary by experience, responsibility, performance, tenure, and geographic area. Earnings data from the Bureau of Labor Statistics and, in some cases, from outside sources are included. Data may cover the entire occupation or a specific group within the occupation.

Benefits account for more than a quarter of total compensation costs to employers. Benefits such as paid vacation, health insurance, and sick leave generally are not mentioned because they are so widespread. Less common benefits include child care, tuition for dependents, housing assistance, summers off, and free or discounted merchandise or services. In addition, employers increasingly offer flexible hours and profit-sharing plans to attract and retain highly qualified workers.

Related Occupations

Occupations involving similar aptitudes, interests, education, and training are listed.

Sources of Additional Information

No single publication can completely describe all aspects of an occupation. Thus, this book lists mailing addresses for associations, government agencies, unions, and other organizations that can provide occupational information. In some cases, toll-free phone numbers and Internet addresses are listed. Free or relatively inexpensive publications offering more information may be mentioned; some of these may also be available in libraries, school career centers, guidance offices, or on the Internet.

Section Two: The Quick Job Search—Advice on Planning Your Career and Getting a Good Job in Less Time

For the past 20 years, I've been interested in helping people find better jobs in less time. If you have ever experienced unemployment, you know it is not pleasant. Unemployment is something most people want to get over quickly, and the quicker the better. Section Two will give you some techniques to help.

I know that most people who read this book want to improve themselves. You want to look at career and training options that lead to a better job and life in whatever way you define this—better pay, more flexibility, more enjoyable or more meaningful work, to prove to your mom that you really can do anything you set your mind to, and so on. That is why I included advice on career planning and job search in Section Two. It's a short section, but it includes the basics that are most important in planning your career and in reducing the time it takes to get a job. I hope it will get you thinking about what is important to you in the long run.

I know you will resist completing the activities in Section Two, but consider this: It is often not the best person who gets the job, it is the best job seeker. Those who do their career planning and job search homework often get jobs over those with better credentials.

The reason is that those who have spent time planning their careers and who know how to conduct an effective job search have distinct advantages over those who do not:

1. They get more interviews, including many for jobs that will never be advertised.

2. They do better in interviews.

People who understand what they want and what they have to offer employers will present their skills more convincingly and are much better at answering problem questions. And, because they have learned more about job search techniques, they are likely to get more interviews with employers who need the skills they have.

Doing better in interviews will often make the difference between getting a job offer or sitting at home. And spending some time on planning your career can make an enormous difference to your happiness and lifestyle over time. So please consider reading Section Two and completing its activities. Go ahead and schedule a time right now to at least read Section Two. An hour or so spent there can help you do just enough better in your career planning, job seeking, or interviewing to make the difference. Go ahead—get out your schedule book and get it over with (nag, nag, nag).

The second part of Section Two showcases professionally written resumes for some of America's top white-collar jobs. Use these examples when creating your resume.

One other thing: If you work through Section Two, and it helps you in some significant way, I'd like to hear from you. Please write or e-mail me via the publisher, whose contact information appears elsewhere in this book.

Section Three: Important Trends in Jobs and Industries

This section is made up of two very good articles on labor market trends and additional data on hundreds of major jobs. The information comes directly from various U.S. Department of Labor sources. The articles are interesting, well written, and short. I know this section sounds boring, but the articles are quick reads and will give you a good idea of the trends that will impact your career in the years to come.

The first article is titled "Tomorrow's Jobs: Important Labor Market Trends Through the Year 2008." It highlights the many important trends in employment and includes information on the fastest growing jobs, jobs with high pay at various levels of education, and other details.

The second article is titled "Employment Trends in Major Industries." I included this information because you can often use your skills or training in industries you may not have

considered. It provides a good review of major trends with an emphasis on helping you make good employment decisions. This information can help you seek jobs in industries with higher pay or that are more likely to interest you. Also, the industry you work in, while often overlooked, is often as important as the occupation you choose.

After the two articles comes a table titled "Details on 500 Major Jobs." Tables on various jobs are, I admit, boring. This one provides growth projections and other information on 500 jobs that employ over 90 percent of the labor force. This table covers many more jobs than described in this book, and reviewing it can help you identify possibilities you might not otherwise consider.

The final part of Section Three includes a list I created that arranges a group of major jobs in order of percentage growth projected through 2008. This is an interesting list, and it includes all the jobs described in Section One as well as many others. Use the details to be the life of the next party you attend.

Tips on Using This Book

This book is based on information provided by government sources, so it includes the most up-to-date and accurate data available anywhere. The entries are well written and pack a lot of information into short descriptions. The information in *America's Top White-Collar Jobs* is used in many ways, but this discussion will provide tips on the four most frequent uses:

- For exploring career, education, or training alternatives
- For job seekers
- For employers and business people
- For counselors, instructors, and other career specialists

Tips for Exploring Career, Education, or Training Alternatives

America's Top White-Collar Jobs is an excellent resource for anyone exploring career, education, or training alternatives. While many people take career interest tests to identify career options, using this book can perform a similar function.

Many people do not have a good idea of what they want to do in their careers. They may be considering additional training or education—but don't know what sort they should get. If you are one of these people, *America's Top White-Collar Jobs* can help in several ways. Here are a few pointers.

Review the list of jobs. Trust yourself. Many research studies indicate that most people have a good sense of their interests. Your interests can be used to guide you to career options to consider in more detail.

Begin by looking over the occupations listed in the table of contents. If others will be using this book, please don't mark in it. Instead, on a separate sheet of paper, list the jobs that interest you. Or make a photocopy of the table of contents and mark the jobs that interest you. Look at all the jobs, because you may identify previously overlooked possibilities.

The next step is to read the job descriptions that most interest you. A quick review will often eliminate one or more of these jobs based on pay, working conditions, education required, or other considerations. Once you have identified the three or four jobs that seem most interesting, research each one more thoroughly before making any important decisions.

Study the jobs and their training and education requirements. Too many people decide to obtain additional training or education without knowing much about the jobs the training will lead to. Reviewing the descriptions in *America's Top White-Collar Jobs* is one way to learn more about an occupation before you enroll in an education or training program. If you are currently a student, the job descriptions in this book can also help you decide on a major course of study or learn more about the jobs for which your studies are preparing you.

Do not too quickly eliminate a job that interests you. If a job requires more education or training than you currently have, you can obtain this training in many ways.

Don't abandon your past experience and education too quickly. If you have significant work experience, training, or education, these should not be abandoned too quickly. Many skills you have learned and used in previous jobs or other settings can apply to related jobs. Many people have changed careers after carefully considering what they wanted to do and found that the skills they have can still be used.

America's Top White-Collar Jobs can help you explore career options in several ways. First, carefully review descriptions for jobs you have held in the past. On a separate sheet of paper, write the words used to describe the skills needed in those jobs. Then do the same with jobs that interest you now. You will be able to identify skills used in previous jobs that are needed in the jobs that interest you for the future. These "transferable" skills form the basis for transferring to a new career.

You can also identify skills you have developed or used in nonwork activities, such as hobbies, family responsibilities, volunteer work, school, military, and extracurricular activities.

The descriptions in *America's Top White-Collar Jobs* can even be used if you want to stay with the same employer. For example, you may identify jobs within your organization that offer more rewarding work, higher pay, or other advantages over your present job. Read the descriptions related to these jobs, and you may be able to transfer into another job rather than leave the organization.

Tips for Job Seekers

You can use the descriptions in this book to give you an edge in finding job openings and in getting job offers over those with better credentials. Here are some ways *America's Top White-Collar Jobs* can help you in the job search.

Identify related job targets. You are probably limiting your job search to a small number of jobs that you feel qualified for. But this approach eliminates many jobs that you could do and could enjoy. Your search for a new job should be broadened to include more possibilities.

Go through the entire list of jobs in the table of contents and check any that require skills similar to those you have. Look over all jobs, since doing so will sometimes help you identify targets that you would have otherwise overlooked.

Many people are also not aware of the many specialized jobs related to their training or experience. The descriptions in *America's Top White-Collar Jobs* are for major job titles, but a variety of more specialized jobs may require similar skills. Reference books that list more specialized job titles include the *Enhanced Occupational Outlook Handbook* and *The O*NET Dictionary of Occupational Titles*. Both are published by JIST. Similar information is available in software form.

The descriptions can also point out job prospects related to the jobs that interest you but that have higher responsibility or compensation levels. While you may not consider yourself qualified for such jobs now, you should think about seeking jobs that are above your previous levels but within your ability to handle.

Prepare for interviews. This book's job descriptions are an essential source of information to help you prepare for interviews. Before an interview, carefully review the description for the job, and you will be much better prepared to emphasize your key skills. You should also review descriptions for past jobs and identify skills needed in the new job.

Negotiate pay. The job descriptions in this book will help you know what pay range to expect. Note that local pay and other details can differ substantially from the national averages in the descriptions.

Tips for Employers and Business People

Employers, human resource personnel, and other business people can use this book's information in a variety of ways. The material can help you write job descriptions, study pay ranges, and set criteria for new employees. The information can also help you conduct more effective interviews by providing a list of key skills needed by new hires.

Tips for Counselors, Instructors, and Other Career Specialists

Suggestions for using this book to help people explore career options or find jobs are mostly self-explanatory or contained in the previous tips. My best suggestion to professionals is to get this book off the bookshelf and into the hands of those who need it. Leave it on a table or desk and show people how the information can help them. Wear this book out! Its real value is as a tool used often and well.

Additional Information About the Projections

Readers interested in more information about projections and details on the labor force, economic growth, industry and occupational employment, or the methods and assumptions used in this book's projections should consult the November 1999 edition of the *Monthly Labor Review,* published by the Bureau of Labor Statistics, or the Winter 1999–2000 *Occupational Outlook Quarterly,* also published by BLS. Information on the limitations inherent in economic projections also can be found in these publications.

For more information about employment change, job openings, earnings, unemployment rates, and training requirements by occupation, consult *Occupational Projections and Training Data,* 2000–01 Edition, published by the BLS.

For occupational information from an industry perspective, including some occupations and career paths that *America's Top White-Collar Jobs* does not cover, consult another BLS publication—the *Career Guide to Industries,* 2000–2001 Edition. This book is also available from JIST.

SECTION ONE

DESCRIPTIONS OF 110 MAJOR WHITE-COLLAR JOBS

This is the book's major section. It contains descriptions for 110 major occupations arranged in alphabetic order. Refer to the table of contents for a list of the jobs and the page numbers where their descriptions begin.

A good way to identify job descriptions you want to explore is to use the table of contents as a checklist. If you are interested in technical jobs, for example, you can go through the list and quickly identify those you want to learn more about. If you look at all the titles, you may spot other jobs that might be interesting, and you should consider these as well.

While the descriptions are easy to understand, the introduction provides additional information that will help you interpret them. If you are not the sort of person to read introductions, feel free to jump right in and begin reading the descriptions that interest you. When reading the descriptions, keep in mind that they present information that is the average for the country. Conditions in your area and with specific employers may be quite different. For example, pay may be higher or lower than stated in the descriptions, and the same jobs are often in great demand in one location and hard to obtain in another. People just entering a job will typically earn less than the average pay for more experienced workers. these are just several examples of how the typical situation may not fit your own.

Of course, there is more to learning about and selecting career options than simply reading job descriptions. For this reason, I suggest you read Section Two, which provides advice on planning your career and on getting a good job. Section Three also offers information to help you weigh your options and make good decisions. For example, the article titled "Tomorrow's Jobs: Important Labor Market Trends Through the Year 2008" discusses rapidly growing jobs and trends in all major occupational groups.

Accountants and Auditors

(O*NET 21114A and 21114B)

Significant Points

- Most jobs require at least a bachelor's degree in accounting or a related field.

- Jobseekers who obtain professional recognition through certification or licensure, a master's degree, proficiency in accounting and auditing computer software, or specialized expertise will have an advantage in the job market.

- Competition will remain keen for the most prestigious jobs in major accounting and business firms.

Nature of the Work

Accountants and auditors help to ensure that the Nation's firms are run more efficiently, its public records are kept more accurately, and its taxes are paid properly and on time. They perform these vital functions by offering an increasingly wide array of business and accounting services to their clients. Broadly, these services include public, management, and government accounting, as well as internal auditing. In each of these major fields, however, accountants and auditors continue to carry out the fundamental tasks of the occupation—prepare, analyze, and verify financial documents in order to provide information to clients.

Specific job duties vary widely in the four major fields of accounting. Public accountants perform a broad range of accounting, auditing, tax, and consulting activities for their clients, who may be corporations, governments, nonprofit organizations, or individuals. For example, some public accountants concentrate on tax matters, such as advising companies of the tax advantages and disadvantages of certain business decisions and preparing individual income tax returns. Others are consultants who offer advice in areas such as compensation or employee health care benefits; the design of accounting and data processing systems; and the selection of controls to safeguard assets. Some specialize in forensic accounting—investigating and interpreting bankruptcies and other complex financial transactions. Still others audit a client's financial statements and report to investors and authorities that they have been prepared and reported correctly. Public accountants, many of whom are Certified Public Accountants (CPAs), generally have their own businesses or work for public accounting firms.

Management accountants—also called industrial, corporate, or private accountants—record and analyze the financial information of the companies for which they work. Other responsibilities include budgeting, performance evaluation, cost management, and asset management. They are usually part of executive teams involved in strategic planning or new product development. Management accountants analyze and interpret the financial information corporate executives need to make sound business decisions. They also prepare financial reports for non-management groups, including stockholders, creditors, regulatory agencies, and tax authorities. Within accounting departments, they may work in areas including financial analysis, planning and budgeting, and cost accounting.

Many persons with an accounting background work in the public sector. Government accountants and auditors maintain and examine the records of government agencies and audit private businesses and individuals whose activities are subject to government regulations or taxation. Accountants employed by Federal, State, and local governments guarantee that revenues are received and expenditures are made in accordance with laws and regulations. Those who are employed by the Federal government may work as Internal Revenue Service agents or in financial management, financial institution examination, or budget analysis and administration.

An increasingly important area of accounting and auditing is internal auditing. Internal auditors verify the accuracy of their organization's records and check for mismanagement, waste, or fraud. Specifically, they examine and evaluate their firms' financial and information systems, management procedures, and internal controls to ensure that records are accurate and controls are adequate to protect against fraud and waste. They also review company operations—evaluating their efficiency, effectiveness, and compliance with corporate policies and procedures, laws, and government regulations. There are many types of highly specialized auditors, such as electronic data processing, environmental, engineering, legal, insurance premium, bank, and health care auditors. As computer systems make information more timely, internal auditors help managers to base their decisions on actual data, rather than personal observation. Internal auditors may also recommend controls for their organization's computer system to ensure the reliability of the system and the integrity of the data.

Computers are rapidly changing the nature of the work for most accountants and auditors. With the aid of special software packages, accountants summarize transactions in standard formats for financial records and organize data in special formats for financial analysis. These accounting packages greatly reduce the amount of tedious manual work associated with data and record keeping. Personal and laptop computers enable accountants and auditors to be more mobile and to use their clients' computer systems to extract information from large mainframe computers. As a result of these trends, a growing number of accountants and auditors have extensive computer skills and specialize in correcting problems with software or developing software to meet unique data needs.

Working Conditions

Most accountants and auditors work in a typical office setting. Self-employed accountants may be able to do part of their work at home. Accountants and auditors employed by public accounting firms and government agencies may travel frequently to perform audits at clients' places of business, branches of their firm, or government facilities.

Most accountants and auditors generally work a standard 40-hour week, but many work longer hours, particularly if they are self-employed and have numerous clients. Tax specialists often work long hours during the tax season.

Employment

Accountants and auditors held over 1,080,000 jobs in 1998. They worked throughout private industry and government, but about 1 out of 4 worked for accounting, auditing, and bookkeeping firms. Approximately 1 out of 10 accountants or auditors were self-employed.

Many accountants and auditors are unlicensed management accountants, internal auditors, or government accountants and auditors. However, a large number are licensed Certified Public Accountants, Public Accountants (PAs), Registered Public Accountants (RPAs), and Accounting Practitioners (APs). Most accountants and auditors work in urban areas, where public accounting firms and central or regional offices of businesses are concentrated.

Some individuals with backgrounds in accounting and auditing are full-time college and university faculty; others teach part time while working as self-employed accountants or as salaried accountants for private industry or government.

Training, Other Qualifications, and Advancement

Most accountant and internal auditor positions require at least a bachelor's degree in accounting or a related field. Beginning accounting and auditing positions in the Federal government, for example, usually require 4 years of college (including 24 semester hours in accounting or auditing) or an equivalent combination of education and experience. Some employers prefer applicants with a master's degree in accounting or a master's degree in business administration with a concentration in accounting.

Previous experience in accounting or auditing can help an applicant get a job. Many colleges offer students an opportunity to gain experience through summer or part-time internship programs conducted by public accounting or business firms. In addition, practical knowledge of computers and their applications in accounting and internal auditing is a great asset for jobseekers in the accounting field.

Professional recognition through certification or licensure provides a distinct advantage in the job market. All CPAs must have a certificate, and the partners in their firm must have licenses issued by a State Board of Accountancy. The vast majority of States require CPA candidates to be college graduates, but a few States substitute a number of years of public accounting experience for the college degree. Based on recommendations made by the American Institute of Certified Public Accountants, 17 States currently require CPA candidates to complete 150 semester hours of college coursework—an additional 30 hours beyond the usual 4-year bachelor's degree. Most States have adopted similar legislation that will become effective in the future. Many schools have altered their curricula accordingly, and prospective accounting majors should carefully research accounting curricula and the requirements for any States in which they hope to become licensed.

All States use the four-part Uniform CPA Examination prepared by the American Institute of Certified Public Accountants. The two-day CPA examination is rigorous, and only about one-quarter of those who take it each year pass every part they attempt. Candidates are not required to pass all four parts at once, but most States require candidates to pass at least two parts for partial credit and all four sections within a certain period of time. Most States also require applicants for a CPA certificate to have some accounting experience.

The designations PA and RPA are also recognized by most States, and several States continue to issue these licenses. With the growth in the number of CPAs, however, the majority of States are phasing out non-CPA designations (PA, RPA, and AP) by not issuing new licenses. Accountants who hold PA and RPA designations have legal rights, duties, and obligations similar to those of CPAs, but their qualifications for licensure are less stringent. AP designation requires less formal training and covers a more limited scope of practice than the CPA.

Nearly all States require CPAs and other public accountants to complete a certain number of hours of continuing professional education before their licenses can be renewed. The professional associations representing accountants sponsor numerous courses, seminars, group study programs, and other forms of continuing education. Professional societies bestow other forms of credentials on a voluntary basis. Voluntary certification can attest to professional competence in a specialized field of accounting and auditing. It can also certify that a recognized level of professional competence has been achieved by accountants and auditors who acquired some skills on the job, without the formal education or public accounting work experience needed to meet the rigorous standards required to take the CPA examination.

The Institute of Management Accountants (IMA) confers the Certified Management Accountant (CMA) designation upon applicants who complete a bachelor's degree or attain a minimum score on specified graduate school entrance exams. Applicants must also pass a four-part examination, agree to meet continuing education requirements, comply with standards of professional conduct, and have worked at least 2 years in management accounting. The CMA program is administered through the Institute of Certified Management Accountants, an affiliate of the IMA.

Graduates from accredited colleges and universities who have worked for two years as internal auditors and have passed a four-part examination may earn the designation Certified Internal Auditor (CIA) from the Institute of Internal Auditors. Similarly, the Information Systems Audit and Control Association confers the designation Certified Information Systems Auditor (CISA) upon candidates who pass an examination and have 5 years of experience in auditing electronic data processing systems. Auditing or data processing experience and college education may be substituted for up to 3 years of work experience in this program. The Accreditation Council for Accountancy and Taxation, a satellite organization of the National Society of Public Accountants, confers three designations—Accredited in Accountancy (AA), Accredited Tax Advisor (ATA), and Accredited Tax Preparer (ATP). Candidates for the AA must pass an exam, while candidates for the ATA and ATP must complete the required coursework and pass an exam. Other organizations, such as the National Association of Certified Fraud Examiners and the Bank Administration Institute, confer specialized auditing designations. Often a practitioner will hold multiple licenses and designations. For instance, an internal auditor might be a CPA, CIA, and CISA.

Persons planning a career in accounting should have an aptitude for mathematics and be able to analyze, compare, and interpret facts and figures quickly. They must be able to clearly communicate the results of their work to clients and managers. Accountants and auditors must be good at working with people as well as with business systems and computers. Because millions of financial statement users rely on their services, accountants and auditors should have high standards of integrity.

Capable accountants and auditors may advance rapidly; those having inadequate academic preparation may be assigned routine jobs and find promotion difficult. Many graduates of junior colleges and business and correspondence schools, as well as bookkeepers and accounting clerks who meet the education and experience requirements set by their employers, can obtain junior accounting positions and advance to positions with more responsibilities by demonstrating their accounting skills on the job.

Beginning public accountants usually start by assisting with work for several clients. They may advance to positions with more responsibility in 1 or 2 years, and to senior positions within another few years. Those who excel may become supervisors, managers, or partners, open their own public accounting firms, or transfer to executive positions in management accounting or internal auditing in private firms.

Management accountants often start as cost accountants, junior internal auditors, or trainees for other accounting positions. As they rise through the organization, they may advance to accounting manager, chief cost accountant, budget director, or manager of internal auditing. Some become controllers, treasurers, financial vice presidents, chief financial officers, or corporation presidents. Many senior corporation executives have a background in accounting, internal auditing, or finance.

In general, there is a large degree of mobility among public accountants, management accountants, and internal auditors. Practitioners often shift into management accounting or internal auditing from public accounting, or between internal auditing and management accounting. However, it is less common for accountants and auditors to move from either management accounting or internal auditing into public accounting.

Job Outlook

Employment of accountants and auditors is expected to grow about as fast as the average for all occupations through the year 2008. In addition to openings resulting from growth, the need to replace accountants and auditors who retire or transfer to other occupations will produce thousands of job openings annually in this large occupation.

As the economy grows, the number of business establishments will increase, requiring more accountants and auditors to set up books, prepare taxes, and provide management advice. As these businesses grow, the volume and complexity of information developed by accountants and auditors regarding costs, expenditures, and taxes will increase as well. More complex requirements for accountants and auditors also arise from changes in legislation related to taxes, financial reporting standards, business investments, mergers, and other financial matters. In addition, businesses will increasingly need quick, accurate, and individually tailored financial informa-

tion due to the demands of growing international competition. These trends will positively affect the employment of accountants and auditors.

The changing role of accountants and auditors also will spur job growth. In response to market demand, these professionals will offer more management and consulting services as they take on a greater advisory role and develop more sophisticated and flexible accounting systems. By focusing more on analyzing operations rather than just providing financial data, accountants will help to increase the demand for their services. Also, internal auditors will increasingly be needed to discover and eliminate waste and fraud.

However, this trend will be counteracted somewhat by a decrease in the demand for traditional services and growing use of accounting software. Accountants will spend less time performing audits due to potential liability and relatively low profits, and will shift away from tax preparation due to the increasing popularity of tax preparation firms. As computer programs continue simplifying some accounting-related tasks, clerical staff will increasingly handle many routine calculations.

Accountants and auditors who have earned professional recognition through certification or licensure should have the best job prospects. For example, CPAs should continue to enjoy a wide range of job opportunities, especially as more States enact the 150-hour requirement, making it more difficult to obtain this certification. Similarly, CMAs should be in demand as their management advice is increasingly sought. Applicants with a master's degree in accounting, or a master's degree in business administration with a concentration in accounting, will also have an advantage in the job market.

Proficiency in accounting and auditing computer software, or expertise in specialized areas such as international business, specific industries, or current legislation, may also be helpful in landing certain accounting and auditing jobs. In addition, employers increasingly seek applicants with strong interpersonal and communication skills. Regardless of one's qualifications, however, competition will remain keen for the most prestigious jobs in major accounting and business firms.

Earnings

In 1998, the median annual earnings of accountants and auditors were $37,860. The middle half of the occupation earned between $29,840 and $49,460. The top 10 percent of accountants and auditors earned more than $76,160, and the bottom decile earned less than $23,800. Accountants and auditors earn slightly more in urban areas. In 1997, median annual earnings in the industries employing the largest numbers of accountants and auditors were:

Accounting, auditing, and bookkeeping $38,100

State government, except education and hospitals 35,900

Federal government 43,100

Local government, except education and hospitals 36,400

Commercial banks 35,700

According to a salary survey conducted by the National Association of Colleges and Employers, bachelor's degree candidates in accounting received starting offers averaging $34,500 a year in 1999; master's degree candidates in accounting averaged $36,800.

According to a salary survey conducted by Robert Half International, a staffing services firm specializing in accounting and finance, accountants and auditors with up to 1 year of experience earned between $26,000-$36,250 in 1999. Those with 1 to 3 years of experience earned between $29,250-$41,250. Senior accountants and auditors earned between $34,750-$51,000; managers earned between $41,750-$68,500; and directors of accounting and auditing earned between $56,250-$91,000 a year. The variation in salaries reflects differences in size of firm, location, level of education, and professional credentials.

In the Federal government, the starting annual salary for junior accountants and auditors was about $20,600 in 1999. Candidates who had a superior academic record might start at $25,500, while applicants with a master's degree or 2 years of professional experience usually began at $31,200. Beginning salaries were slightly higher in selected areas where the prevailing local pay level was higher. Accountants employed by the Federal government in nonsupervisory, supervisory, and managerial positions averaged about $58,200 a year in 1999; auditors averaged $62,500.

Related Occupations

Accountants and auditors design internal control systems and analyze financial data. Others for whom training in accounting is invaluable include appraisers, budget officers, loan officers, financial analysts and managers, bank officers, actuaries, underwriters, tax collectors and revenue agents, FBI special agents, securities sales representatives, and purchasing agents.

Sources of Additional Information

Information about careers in certified public accounting and about CPA standards and examinations may be obtained from:

- American Institute of Certified Public Accountants, Harborside Financial Center, 201 Plaza III, Jersey City, NJ 07311-3881. Internet: http://www.aicpa.org

Information on careers in management accounting and the CMA designation may be obtained from:

- Institute of Management Accountants, 10 Paragon Dr., Montvale, NJ 07645-1760. Internet: http://www.imanet.org

Information on the Accredited in Accountancy/Accredited Business Accountant, Accredited Tax Advisor, or Accredited Tax Preparer designations may be obtained from:

- National Society of Accountants and the Accreditation Council for Accountancy and Taxation, 1010 North Fairfax St., Alexandria, VA 22314. Internet: http://www.acatcredentials.org

Information on careers in internal auditing and the CIA designation may be obtained from:

- The Institute of Internal Auditors, 249 Maitland Ave., Altamonte Springs, FL 32701-4201. Internet: http://www.theiia.org

Information on careers in information systems auditing and the CISA designation may be obtained from:

- The Information Systems Audit and Control Association, 3701 Algonquin Rd., Suite 1010, Rolling Meadows, IL 60008. Internet: http://www.isaca.org

For information on accredited programs in accounting and business, contact:

- American Assembly of Collegiate Schools of Business—The International Association for Management Education, 605 Old Ballas Rd., Suite 220, St. Louis, MO 63141. Internet: http://www.aacsb.edu

Actors, Directors, and Producers

(O*NET 34047F, 34056A, 34056B, 34056D, 34056E, 34056F, 34056G, 34056H, 34056J, and 34056K)

Significant Points

- Aspiring actors face frequent rejections in auditions and long periods of unemployment; competition for roles is often intense.

- While formal training is helpful, experience and talent are more important for success in this field.

- Because of erratic employment, earnings for actors are relatively low.

Nature of the Work

Although most people associate actors, directors, and producers with the screens of Hollywood or stages of Broadway, these workers are more likely to be found in a local theatre, television studio, circus, or comedy club. Actors, directors, and producers include workers as diverse as narrators; clowns; comedians; acrobats; jugglers; stunt, rodeo, and aquatic performers; casting, stage, news, sports, and public service directors; production, stage, artist and repertoire managers; and producers and their assistants. In essence, actors, directors, and producers express ideas and create images in theaters, film, radio, television, and a variety of other media. They "make the words come alive" for their audiences.

Actors entertain and communicate with people through their interpretation of dramatic roles. However, only a few actors ever achieve recognition as stars—whether on stage, in motion pictures, or on television. A few others are well-known, experienced performers who frequently are cast in supporting roles. Most actors struggle for a toehold in the profession and pick up parts wherever they can. Although actors often prefer a certain type of role, experience is so important to success in this field that even established actors continue to accept small roles, including commercials and product endorsements. Other actors work as background performers, or "extras," with small parts and no lines to deliver; still others work for theater companies, teaching acting courses to the public.

Directors interpret plays or scripts. In addition, they audition and select cast members, conduct rehearsals, and direct the work of the cast and crew. Directors use their knowledge of acting, voice, and movement to achieve the best possible performance, and they usually approve the scenery, costumes, choreography, and music.

Producers are entrepreneurs. They select plays or scripts, arrange financing, and decide on the size, cost, and content of a production. They hire directors, principal members of the cast, and key production staff members. Producers also negotiate contracts with artistic personnel, often in accordance with collective bargaining agreements. Producers work on a project from beginning to end, coordinating the activities of writers, directors, managers, and other personnel. Increasingly, producers who work on motion pictures must have a working knowledge of the new technology needed to create special effects.

Working Conditions

Acting demands patience and total commitment, because actors are often rejected in auditions and must endure long periods of unemployment between jobs. Actors typically work long, irregular hours, sometimes under adverse weather conditions that may exist "on location." They also must travel when shows are "on the road." Coupled with the heat of stage or studio lights and heavy costumes, these factors require stamina. Actors working on Broadway productions often work long hours during rehearsals, but generally work about 30 hours a week once the show opens. Evening work is a regular part of a stage actor's life, as several performances are often held on one day. Flawless performances require tedious memorization of lines and repetitive rehearsals. On television, actors must deliver a good performance with very little preparation.

Directors and producers often work under stress as they try to meet schedules, stay within budgets, and resolve personnel problems while putting together a production. Directors must be aware of union rules and how they affect production schedules. For example, actors must be paid a minimum salary and can work no more than a set number of hours, depending on their contract. Additional restrictions are placed on productions using child actors and animals.

Employment

In 1998, actors, directors, and producers held about 160,000 jobs in motion pictures, stage plays, television, and radio. Many others were between jobs, so the total number of actors, directors, and producers employed at some time during the year was higher. In winter, most employment opportunities on stage are in New York and other large cities, many of which have established professional regional theaters. In summer, stock companies in suburban and resort areas also provide employment. Actors, directors, and producers also find work on cruise lines and in amusement parks. In addition, many cities have small nonprofit professional companies such as "little theaters," repertory companies, and dinner theaters, which provide opportunities for local amateur talent as well as for professional entertainers. Normally, casts are selected in New York City for shows that go on the road.

Employment in motion pictures and films for television is centered in Hollywood and New York City. However, small studios are located throughout the country. In addition, many films are shot on location and may employ local professional and nonprofessional day players and extras. In television, opportunities are concentrated in the network centers of New York, Los Angeles, and Atlanta, but local television stations around the country also employ a substantial number of these workers.

Training, Other Qualifications, and Advancement

Although many people have the technical skills to enter this industry, few receive the opportunity to display their talent. To gain experience, most aspiring actors and directors take part in high school and college plays, or they work with little theaters and other acting groups. The best way to start is to use local opportunities and build on them. Local and regional theater experience may help in obtaining work in New York or Los Angeles. Actors and directors try to work their way up to major productions. Intense competition, however, ensures that few succeed.

Formal dramatic training or acting experience is generally necessary, although some people enter the field without it. Most people take college courses in theater, arts, drama, and dramatic literature. Many experienced actors pursue additional formal training to learn new skills and improve old ones. An actor often researches his character's lifestyle and history, as well as information about the location of the story. Sometimes actors learn a foreign language or develop an accent to make the character more realistic.

Training can be obtained at dramatic arts schools in New York and Los Angeles and at colleges and universities throughout the country that offer bachelor or higher degrees in dramatic and theater arts. College drama curriculums usually include courses in liberal arts, stage speech and movement, directing, playwriting, play production, design, and the history of the drama, as well as practical courses in acting.

Actors need talent, creative ability, and training that will enable them to portray different characters. Training in singing and dancing is especially useful for stage work. Actors must have poise, stage presence, the capability to affect an audience, and the ability to follow directions. Modeling experience may also be helpful. Physical appearance is often a deciding factor in being selected for particular roles.

Many professional actors rely on agents or managers to find work, negotiate contracts, and plan their careers. Agents generally earn a percentage of an actor's contract. Other actors rely solely on attending open auditions for parts. Trade publications list the time, date, and location of these auditions. Many of these auditions are only open to union members, and union membership requires work experience.

To become a movie extra, one must usually be listed by a casting agency, such as Central Casting, a no-fee agency that supplies extras to the major movie studios in Hollywood. Applicants are accepted only when the number of persons of a particular type on the list—for example, athletic young women, old men, or small children—is below the foreseeable need. In recent years, only a very small proportion of applicants has succeeded in being listed.

There are no specific training requirements for directors and producers, so they come from many different backgrounds. Talent, experience, and business acumen are very important determinants of success for directors and producers. Actors, writers, film editors, and business managers commonly enter these fields. Producers often start in the industry working behind the scenes with successful directors. Additionally, formal training in directing and producing is available at a number of colleges and universities.

As the reputations of actors, directors, and producers grow, they are able to work on larger productions or in more prestigious theaters. Actors may also advance to lead or specialized roles. A few actors move into acting-related jobs, as drama coaches or directors of stage, television, radio, or motion picture productions. Some teach drama in colleges and universities.

The length of a performer's working life depends largely on training, skill, versatility, and perseverance. Although some actors, directors, and producers continue working throughout their lives, many leave the occupation after a short time because they cannot find enough work to make a living. In fact, many who stay with the occupation must take a second job to support themselves.

Job Outlook

Employment of actors, directors, and producers is expected to grow faster than the average for all occupations through 2008. In addition, an even greater number of job openings is expected to arise from the need to replace workers who leave the field. Nevertheless, competition for these jobs will be stiff, as the glamour of actor, director, and producer jobs, coupled with the lack of formal entry requirements, will attract many people to these occupations. As in the past, only the most talented will find regular employment.

Rising foreign demand for American productions, combined with a growing domestic market, should stimulate demand for actors and other production personnel. An increasing population, a greater desire to attend live performances, and the growth of cable and satellite television, television syndication, home movie rentals, and music videos will fuel this demand. In addition to the increasing demand for these media, attendance at stage productions is expected to grow, and touring productions of Broadway plays and other large shows are providing new opportunities for actors and directors. However, employment may be affected by government funding for the arts—a decline in funding could dampen future employment growth.

Earnings

Median annual earnings of actors, directors, and producers were $27,400 in 1998. Minimum salaries, hours of work, and other conditions of employment are covered in collective bargaining agreements between producers of shows and unions representing workers in this field. The Actors' Equity Association represents stage actors; Screen Actors Guild covers actors in motion pictures, including television, commercials, and films; and the American Federation of Television and Radio Artists (AFTRA) represents television and radio performers. Most stage directors belong to the Society of Stage Directors and Choreographers, and film and television directors belong to the Directors Guild of America. While these unions generally determine minimum salaries, any actor or director may negotiate for a salary higher than the minimum.

On July 1, 1998, the members of Screen Actors Guild and AFTRA approved a new joint contract covering all unionized employment. Under the contract, motion picture and television actors with speaking parts earned a minimum daily rate of $576, or $2,000 for a five-day week, in 1998. Actors also receive contributions to their health and pension plans and additional compensation for reruns and foreign telecasts.

According to Actors Equity Association, the minimum weekly salary for actors in Broadway stage productions was $1,135 per week in 1998. Those in small "off-Broadway" theaters received minimums ranging from $450 to $600 a week, depending on the seating capacity of the theater. Smaller regional theaters pay $400-$600 per week. For shows on the road, actors receive about an additional $100 per day for living expenses. However, less than 15 percent of dues-paying members work during any given week. In 1998, less than half worked on a stage production. Average earnings for those able to find employment was less than $10,000 in 1998.

Some well-known actors have salary rates well above the minimums, and the salaries of the few top stars are many times the figures cited, creating the false impression that all actors are highly paid. In reality, earnings for most actors are low because employment is so erratic. Screen Actors Guild reports that the average income its members earn from acting is less than $5,000 a year. Therefore, most actors must supplement their incomes by holding jobs in other fields.

Many actors who work more than a set number of weeks per year are covered by a union health, welfare, and pension fund, including hospitalization insurance, to which employers contribute. Under some employment conditions, Actors' Equity and AFTRA members have paid vacations and sick leave.

Earnings of stage directors vary greatly. According to the Society of Stage Directors and Choreographers, summer theaters offer compensation, including "royalties" (based on the number of performances), usually ranging from $2,500 to $8,000 for a three- to four-week run of a production. Directing a production at a dinner theater will usually pay less than a summer theater but has more potential for royalties. Regional theaters may hire directors for longer periods of time, increasing compensation accordingly. The highest paid directors work on Broadway productions, commonly earning $100,000 plus royalties per show.

Producers seldom get a set fee; instead, they get a percentage of a show's earnings or ticket sales.

Related Occupations

People who work in occupations requiring acting skills include dancers, choreographers, disc jockeys, drama teachers or coaches, and radio and television announcers. Others working in occupations related to acting are playwrights, scriptwriters, stage managers, costume designers, makeup artists, hair stylists, lighting designers, and set designers. Workers in occupations involved with the business aspects of theater productions include managing directors, company managers, booking managers, publicists, and agents for actors, directors, and playwrights.

Sources of Additional Information

Information about opportunities in regional theaters may be obtained from:

- Theatre Communications Group, Inc., 355 Lexington Ave., New York, NY 10017.

A directory of theatrical programs may be purchased from:

- National Association of Schools of Theater, 11250 Roger Bacon Dr., Suite 21, Reston, VA 22090.

For general information on actors, directors, and producers, contact:

- Screen Actors Guild, 5757 Wilshire Blvd., Los Angeles, CA 90036-3600.
- Association of Independent Video and Filmmakers, 304 Hudson St., 6th Floor, New York, NY 10013.
- American Federation of Television and Radio Artists—Screen Actors Guild, 4340 East-West Hwy., Suite 204, Bethesda, MD 20814-4411.

Actuaries

(O*NET 25313)

Significant Points

- A strong background in mathematics is essential for an actuary.
- About 2 out of 3 actuaries are employed in the insurance industry.
- Employment opportunities will be good despite the limited number of openings in this small occupation because stringent qualifying requirements induced by the examination system limit the number of new entrants.

Nature of the Work

Actuaries are essential employees because they determine future risk, make price decisions, and formulate investment strategies. Some actuaries also design insurance, financial, and pension plans and ensure that these plans are maintained on a sound financial basis. Most actuaries specialize in life and health or property and casualty insurance; others work primarily in finance or employee benefits. Some use a broad knowledge of business and mathematics in investment, risk classification, or pension planning.

Regardless of specialty, actuaries assemble and analyze data to estimate probabilities of an event taking place, such as death, sickness, injury, disability, or property loss. They also address financial questions, including the level of pension contributions required to produce a certain retirement income level or the projected future return on investments. Moreover, actuaries may help determine company policy and sometimes explain complex technical matters to company executives, government officials, shareholders, policyholders, or the public in general. They may testify before public agencies on proposed legislation affecting their businesses or explain changes in contract provisions to customers. They also may help companies develop plans to enter new lines of business.

Most actuaries are employed in the insurance industry, in which they estimate the amount a company will pay in claims. For example, property/casualty actuaries calculate the expected amount of claims resulting from automobile accidents, which varies depending on the insured person's age, sex, driving history, type of car, and other factors. Actuaries ensure that the price, or premium, charged for such insurance will enable the company to cover claims and other expenses. This premium must be profitable, yet competitive with other insurance companies.

Actuaries employed in other industries perform several different functions. The small but growing group of actuaries in the financial services industry, for example, manages credit and helps price corporate security offerings. Because banks now offer their customers investment products such as annuities and asset management services, actuaries increasingly help financial institutions manage the substantial risks associated with these products. Actuaries employed as pension actuaries enrolled under the provisions of the Employee Retirement Income Security Act of 1974 (ERISA) evaluate pension plans covered by that act and report on their financial soundness to plan members, sponsors, and Federal regulators.

In addition to salaried actuaries, numerous consulting actuaries provide advice to clients on a contract basis. Their clients include insurance companies, corporations, health maintenance organizations, health care providers, government agencies, and attorneys. The duties of most consulting actuaries are similar to those of other actuaries. For example, some design pension plans by calculating the future value of current deductions from earnings and determining the amount of employer contributions. Others provide advice to health care plans or financial services firms. Consultants sometimes testify in court regarding the value of potential lifetime earnings of a person who is disabled or killed in an accident, the current value of future pension benefits in divorce cases, or other complex calculations. Many consulting actuaries work in reinsurance, where one insurance company arranges to share a large prospective liability policy with another insurance company in exchange for a percentage of the premium.

Working Conditions

Actuaries have desk jobs, and their offices are usually comfortable and pleasant. They often work at least 40 hours a week. Some actuaries, particularly consulting actuaries, may travel to meet with clients. Consulting actuaries may also experience more erratic employment and be expected to work more than 40 hours per week.

Employment

Actuaries held about 16,000 jobs in 1998. Almost one-half of the actuaries who were wage and salary workers were employed in the insurance industry. Some had jobs in life and health insurance companies, while property and casualty insurance companies, pension funds, or insurance agents and brokers employed others. Most of the remaining actuaries worked for firms providing services, especially management and public relations, or for actuarial consulting services. A relatively small number of actuaries were employed by security and commodity brokers or government agencies. Some developed computer software for actuarial calculations. In 1998, 2,300 actuaries were self-employed.

Training, Other Qualifications, and Advancement

Applicants for beginning actuarial jobs usually have a bachelor's degree in mathematics, actuarial science, statistics, or a business-related discipline, such as economics, finance, or accounting. About 55 colleges and universities offer an actuarial science program, and most colleges and universities offer a degree in mathematics or statistics. Some companies hire applicants without specifying a major, provided that the applicant has a working knowledge of mathematics, including calculus, probability, and statistics, and has demonstrated this ability by passing at least the beginning few actuarial exams required for professional designation. Courses in economics, accounting, computer science, finance, and insurance are also useful. Companies increasingly prefer well-rounded individuals who, in addition to a strong technical background, have some training in liberal arts and business.

Two professional societies sponsor programs leading to full professional status in their specialty. The first, the Society of Actuaries (SOA), administers a series of actuarial examinations for the life and health insurance, pension, and finance and investment fields. The Casualty Actuarial Society (CAS), on the other hand, gives a series of examinations for the property and casualty field, which includes fire, accident, medical malpractice, workers compensation, and personal injury liability.

The first parts of the SOA and CAS examination series are jointly sponsored by the two societies and cover the same material. For this reason, students do not need to commit themselves to a specialty until they have taken the initial examinations. These examinations test an individual's competence in probability, calculus, statistics, and other branches of mathematics. The first few examinations help students evaluate their potential as actuaries. Those who pass one or more examinations have better opportunities for employment at higher starting salaries than those who do not.

Actuaries are encouraged to complete the entire series of examinations as soon as possible, advancing first to the Associate level and then to the Fellowship level. Advanced casualty topics include investment and assets, dynamic financial analysis, and valuation of insurance topics. Completion of the examination process usually takes from five to ten years. Examinations are given twice a year, in May and November. Although many companies allot time to their employees for study, extensive home study is required to pass the examinations, and many actuaries study for months to prepare for each examination. It is likewise common for employers to pay the hundreds of dollars for fees and study materials. Most reach the Associate level within four to six years and the Fellowship level a few years later.

Specific requirements apply for pension actuaries, who verify the financial status of defined benefit pension plans to the Federal government. These actuaries must be enrolled by the Joint Board for the Enrollment of Actuaries. To qualify for enrollment, applicants must meet certain experience and examination requirements, as stipulated by the Joint Board.

To perform their duties effectively, actuaries must keep up with current economic and social trends and legislation, as well as developments in health, business, finance, and economics that could affect insurance or investment practices. Good communication and interpersonal skills are also important, particularly for prospective consulting actuaries.

Beginning actuaries often rotate among different jobs in an organization to learn various actuarial operations and phases of insurance work, such as marketing, underwriting, and product development. At first, they prepare data for actuarial projects or perform other simple tasks. As they gain experience, actuaries may supervise clerks, prepare correspondence, draft reports, and conduct research. They may move from one company to another early in their careers as they move up to higher positions.

Advancement depends largely on job performance and the number of actuarial examinations passed. Actuaries with a broad knowledge of the insurance, pension, investment, or employee benefits fields can advance to administrative and executive positions in their companies. Actuaries with supervisory ability may advance to management positions in other areas, such as underwriting, accounting, data processing, marketing, or advertising. Some actuaries assume faculty positions in the Nation's colleges and universities.

Job Outlook

Employment of actuaries is expected to grow more slowly than the average for all occupations through 2008. Although expected growth in managed health plans in the health services industry should provide good prospects for actuaries, anticipated downsizing and merger activity in the insurance agent and broker industry will adversely affect the outlook for these workers. Prospective actuaries who pass several beginning actuarial exams will find relatively few job openings. The number of openings to replace those who leave the occupation each year is limited, and new openings are restricted by the relatively small size of the occupation.

Actuarial employment is projected to grow in property and casualty insurance as this sector experiences growth in terms of employment and billing. Actuaries will continue to be involved in the development of product liability insurance, medical malpractice, and workers' compensation coverage. The development of new financial tools such as dynamic financial analysis has increased the demand for property and casualty actuaries. The growing need to evaluate catastrophic risks such as earthquakes and calculate prices for insuring facilities against such risks is another source of increasing demand for property and casualty actuaries. Planning for the systematic financing of environmental risks, such as toxic waste clean-up, will further lift demand for actuaries in this specialty.

Employment of consulting actuaries is expected to grow faster than employment of actuaries among life insurance carriers—traditionally the leading employer of actuaries. As many life insurance carriers seek to boost profitability by streamlining operations, actuarial employment may be cut back. Investment firms and large corporations may increasingly turn to consultants to provide actuarial services formerly performed in-house.

Earnings

Median annual earnings of actuaries were $65,560 in 1998. The middle 50 percent earned between $45,560 and $89,860. The lowest 10 percent had earnings of less than $36,000, while the top 10 percent earned more than $123,810. The average salary for actuaries employed by the Federal government was $72,800 in early 1999. According to the National Association of Colleges and Employers, annual starting salaries for bachelor's degree graduates in mathematics/actuarial science averaged about $37,300 in 1999.

Insurance companies and consulting firms give merit increases to actuaries as they gain experience and pass examinations. Some companies also offer cash bonuses for each professional designation achieved. A 1998 salary survey of insurance and financial services companies, conducted by the Life Office Management Association, Inc., indicated that the average base salary for an entry-level actuary with the largest U. S. companies was about $41,500. Associate Actuaries with the largest U. S. companies, who direct and provide leadership in the design, pricing, and implementation of insurance products, received an average salary of $88,000. Actuaries at the highest technical level without managerial responsibilities in the same size companies earned an average of $101,600.

Related Occupations

Actuaries determine the probability of income or loss from various risk factors. Other workers whose jobs involve related skills include accountants, economists, financial analysts, mathematicians, and statisticians.

Sources of Additional Information

For facts about actuarial careers, contact:

- American Academy of Actuaries, 1100 17th St. NW., 7th Floor, Washington, DC 20036. Internet: http://www.actuary.org/index.htm

For information about actuarial careers in life and health insurance, employee benefits and pensions, and finance and investments, contact:

- Society of Actuaries, 475 N. Martingale Rd., Suite 800, Schaumburg, IL 60173-2226. Internet: http://www.soa.org

For information about actuarial careers in property and casualty insurance, contact:

- Casualty Actuarial Society, 1100 N. Glebe Rd., Suite 600, Arlington, VA 22201. Internet: http://www.casact.org

Career information on actuaries specializing in pensions is available from:

- American Society of Pension Actuaries, 4350 N. Fairfax Dr., Suite 820, Arlington, VA 22203. Internet: http://www.aspa.org

Adjusters, Investigators, and Collectors

(O*NET 21921, 53123, 53302, 533113, 53314, 53502, and 53508)

Significant Points

- A high school education is sufficient to qualify for most positions, but employers prefer to hire college graduates as claim representatives.

- Projected employment change varies by occupation—the number of adjustment clerks is expected to grow faster than average as businesses emphasize good customer re-

lations, whereas welfare eligibility clerks will likely decline in number because of welfare reform legislation.

Nature of the Work

Adjusters, investigators, and collectors perform a wide range of functions, but their most important role is acting as intermediaries with the public. Insurance companies, department stores, banks, and social services agencies employ adjusters, investigators, and collectors to deal with the challenges they face such as handling complaints, interpreting and explaining policies or regulations, resolving billing disputes, collecting delinquent accounts, and determining eligibility for governmental assistance. The variety of titles and responsibilities in this grouping of occupations can be categorized into claim representatives, insurance processing clerks, adjustment clerks, bill and account collectors, and welfare eligibility workers and interviewers.

Claim Representatives. Insurance companies investigate claims, negotiate settlements, and authorize payments to claimants. *Claim representatives* do this work. When a policyholder files a claim for property damage or a hospital stay, for example, the claim representative must initially determine whether the customer's insurance policy covers the loss and the amount of the loss covered. They then must determine the amount to pay the claimant.

In life and health insurance companies, claim representatives are typically called *claim examiners*. Claim examiners usually specialize in group or individual insurance plans and in hospital, dental, or prescription drug claims. Examiners review health-related claims to see if the costs are reasonable based on the diagnosis. They check with guides that provide information on the average period of disability for various causes, expected treatments, and average hospital stay. Examiners will then either authorize the appropriate payment or refer the claim to an investigator for a more thorough review. Claim investigators look into any contestable claims.

Claim representatives working in life insurance review the causes of death, particularly in the case of an accident, as most life insurance companies pay additional benefits if the death is due to an accident. They may also review new applications for life insurance to make sure applicants have no serious illnesses that would prevent them from qualifying for insurance.

In the property and casualty insurance area, claim representatives handle minor claims filed by automobile or homeowner policyholders. These workers (also called "inside adjusters" or "telephone adjusters") contact claimants by telephone or mail to obtain information on repair costs, medical expenses, or other details the company requires. Many companies centralize this operation through a drive-in claims center, where the cost of repair is determined and a check is issued immediately. More complex cases, usually involving bodily injury, are referred to senior representatives, adjusters, or claim examiners. Cases may also be referred to "independent adjusters" who work for independent adjusting firms not affiliated with a particular insurance company. Some adjusters work with multiple types of insurance. Others specialize in homeowner claims, business losses, automotive damage, product liability, or workers' compensation. Material damage adjusters inspect automobile damage and use the latest computerized estimating equipment to prepare estimates of the damage.

In all of these specialties, claim adjusters primarily plan and schedule the work required to process a claim. They investigate claims by interviewing the claimant and witnesses, consulting police and hospital records, and inspecting property damage to determine the extent of the company's liability. The information from this work, including photographs and written or taped statements, is included in a report that is used to evaluate a claim. When the policyholder's claim is legitimate, the claim adjuster negotiates with the claimant and settles the claim. When claims are contested, adjusters may testify in court.

Claim representatives, adjusters, and examiners are making more use of computers to keep records of clients and actions taken in various claims. Most work on desktop computers, and many use portable laptop computers to enter or access information when they are on assignment away from their offices.

Insurance Processing Clerks. Processing new insurance policies, modifying existing policies, and recording claims is the work of *policy processing clerks*. Using computers, they process new policies by first reviewing the insurance application to ensure that all the questions have been answered. After underwriters have reviewed an application and the company determines that it will issue a policy, a policy processing clerk prepares the necessary forms and informs the insurance sales agent of the application's status. Policy processing clerks also update existing policies—such as a change in beneficiary, amount of coverage, or type of insurance—and recalculate premiums. They then mail correspondence notices regarding changes to the sales agent and policyholder. Policy processing clerks maintain computer files for each policyholder, including policies that are to be reinstated or canceled.

The majority of policy processing clerks work for insurance agencies, where they are usually referred to as customer service representatives. In this capacity, they perform a number of duties in addition to processing policies for customers. Customer service representatives also take calls from clients, answer questions, process changes to the policies, submit applications to the insurance carriers, and obtain information on claims.

Most of the remaining policy processing clerks work for large insurance companies. For many of them, the job is becoming more customer service related as more carriers deal directly with the public. These clerks usually work in call centers, in which they take policy information from current customers and enter it directly into the computer. Other policy processors handle policy changes initiated primarily by the insurance company.

Another type of insurance processing clerk is the claims clerk, also called claims interviewer or claims processor. These clerks obtain information from policyholders regarding claims from fire damage, personal injury or illness, or an automobile accident, for example. They are primarily responsible for getting the necessary information on a claim, such as specific details of an accident. This is usually done over the telephone while the claims clerk simultaneously enters the information into a computer. If information regarding the claim is missing, a claims clerk will call or write the insured or other party for the missing information. Once the information is entered, the claims clerk forwards the claim for payment or to a claim representative, who will further examine the claim. In addition to taking information, some claims clerks can pay small claims, direct insureds to auto repair facilities or local contractors to make home repairs, and may give limited direction to insureds on how to proceed with the claim in emergencies.

Adjustment Clerks. Investigating and resolving customers' complaints about merchandise, service, billing, or credit rating is done by *adjustment clerks*. They may work for banks, department stores, insurance companies, and other large organizations that sell products and services to the public. They are more commonly referred to as customer service representatives or customer complaint clerks.

Adjustment clerks examine all pertinent information to determine if a customer's complaint is valid. In department stores, this may mean checking sales slips, warranties, or the merchandise in question. In banks, these clerks might review records and videotapes of automated teller machine transactions. For insurance carriers, they may review the terms of the policies to see if a particular loss is covered. Regardless of the setting, these clerks get information—in person, by telephone, or through written correspondence—from all parties involved.

After evaluating the facts, adjustment clerks attempt to remedy the situation by exchanging merchandise, refunding money, crediting customers' accounts, or adjusting customers' bills. Adjustment clerks ensure that the appropriate changes are set in motion and follow up on the recommendations to ensure customer satisfaction. To prevent similar complaints in the future, they may recommend improvements in product, packaging, shipping, service, or billing methods and procedures. Adjustment clerks keep records of all relevant matters, using them to prepare reports for their supervisors.

In many organizations, adjustment clerks investigate billing errors and other customer complaints. They also respond to many types of inquiries from customers, including taking orders, canceling accounts, or simply providing information on the company's products and services. These requests may be handled immediately over the phone or may require the adjustment clerk to send a letter to the customer.

Bill and Account Collectors. Sometimes called collection agents, *bill and account collectors* ensure that customers pay their overdue accounts. Some are employed by third-party collection agencies, while others, known as "in-house collectors," work directly for the original creditors, such as department stores, hospitals, or banks.

The duties of bill and account collectors are similar in the many different organizations in which they are employed. First, collectors attempt to locate and notify customers of delinquent accounts, usually over the telephone, but sometimes by letter. When customers move without leaving a forwarding address, collectors may check with the post office, telephone companies, credit bureaus, or former neighbors to obtain their new address. This is called "skiptracing."

Once collectors find the debtors, they inform them of the overdue account and solicit payment. If necessary, they review the terms of the sale, service, or credit contract with the customer. Collectors also may attempt to learn the cause of the delay in payment. Where feasible, they offer the customer advice on how to pay off the debts, such as by taking out a bill consolidation loan. However, the collector's objective is always to ensure that the customer first pays the debt in question.

If a customer agrees to pay, collectors record this commitment and check later to verify that the payment was indeed made. Collectors may have authority to grant an extension of time if customers ask for one. If a customer fails to respond, collectors prepare a statement indicating this for the credit department of the establishment. In more extreme cases, collectors may initiate repossession proceedings or service disconnections or may hand the account over to an attorney for legal action. Most collectors handle other administrative functions for the accounts assigned to them. This may include recording changes of addresses and purging the records of the deceased.

Collectors use computers and a variety of automated systems to keep track of overdue accounts. Collectors usually work at video display terminals that are linked to computers. In sophisticated predicted dialer systems, a computer dials the telephone automatically and the collector speaks only when a connection has been made. Such systems eliminate time spent calling busy or non-answering numbers. Many collectors use regular telephones, but others wear headsets like those used by telephone operators.

Welfare Eligibility Workers and Interviewers. *Welfare eligibility workers and interviewers*—sometimes referred to as intake workers, eligibility specialists, family investment counselors, or income maintenance specialists—determine who may receive welfare and other types of social assistance. Welfare eligibility workers and interviewers work with various public assistance programs. The best known are Aid to Families with Dependent Children, Medicaid, and Food Stamps. Depending on local circumstances, they may also work with other programs, such as those for public housing, refugee assistance, and fuel assistance. Although the majority work for State and local governments, a number of eligibility workers work in hospitals and physician offices where they interview patients regarding their eligibility for government assistance.

Many welfare eligibility workers and interviewers specialize in an area such as housing, but most are responsible for several areas. They also may assist social workers by informing them of pertinent information they have gathered during their interviews with applicants.

The primary task of these workers is interviewing and investigating applicants and recipients of public assistance. Based on the personal and financial information they obtain and the rules and regulations of each program, they initiate procedures to grant, modify, deny, or terminate individuals' eligibility for various aid programs. This information is recorded and evaluated to determine the amounts of the grants.

These workers often provide information to applicants and current recipients. For example, they may explain and interpret eligibility rules and regulations or identify other resources available in the community for financial or social welfare assistance. Eligibility workers also keep track of those on welfare, making sure recipients attend job training classes and seek employment. More experienced eligibility workers may help train new workers. In addition, they may be assigned to special fraud-detection units.

The authority of welfare eligibility workers and interviewers varies from one jurisdiction to another. In some places, senior workers are authorized to decide on an applicant's eligibility, subject to review by their supervisor. In other places, they can only make recommendations to their supervisors, who in turn make the ultimate decision.

An increasing number of jurisdictions are using computers to improve worker productivity and to reduce the incidence of welfare fraud. In these settings, welfare eligibility workers enter information into a computer as they interview applicants and recipients. In the most advanced systems, the computer terminal prompts them with a variety of questions to ask during an interview.

Although these workers usually interview applicants and recipients who visit their offices, they may make occasional home visits, especially if the applicant or recipient is elderly or disabled. They may also check with employers or other references to verify answers and get further information.

Working Conditions

Although adjusters, investigators, and collectors share many working conditions, differences exist in the various segments of this grouping of workers. Most claim representatives work a standard five-day, 40-hour week and work in a typical office environment. However, many others work evening shifts and on weekends. As insurance companies place more emphasis on customer service, they are providing more claim services around the clock. This means that a growing number of claim representatives may work evenings and weekends staffing claims centers, many of which are open 24 hours a day, 7 days a week. Many claim adjusters, on the other hand, work outside the office, inspecting damaged buildings and automobiles. Occasionally, experienced adjusters are away from home for days when they travel to the scene of a disaster—such as a tornado, hurricane, or flood—to work with local adjusters and government officials. Some adjusters are on emergency call in the case of such incidents. Material damage adjusters can work at local claim centers where policyholders take their cars for estimates of damage. In general, adjusters are able to arrange their work schedule to accommodate evening and weekend appointments with clients. This accommodation may result in adjusters working 50 or 60 hours a week. Some report to the office every morning to get their assignments, while others simply call from home and spend their days traveling to claim sites. This enables some adjusters to work independently.

Most insurance processing clerks work 40 hours a week in an office. Many of these workers sit at video display terminals and enter or access information while the customer is on the telephone. Because most companies provide 24-hour claim service to their policyholders, some claim clerks work evenings and weekends. Many claim clerks work part time.

Adjustment clerks or customer service representatives are increasingly available in the evenings and on weekends, particularly the growing number of clerks who work for catalog and Internet retailers. These clerks usually work in call-center environments, taking calls from customers 24 hours a day, 7 days a week. Other adjustment clerks work in the offices of businesses and work standard business hours.

Bill and account collectors and welfare eligibility workers and interviewers work in offices, usually during regular business hours. However, some collectors work evenings and weekends when clients can be more easily reached. Some bill and account collectors work part time, while others can work as temporaries for collection agencies. Dealing with upset or angry clients is often part of the daily routine in these jobs, making the work stressful at times.

Employment

Adjusters, investigators, and collectors held about 1.5 million jobs in 1998. The following tabulation shows the percent distribution of employment by detailed occupation:

Adjustment clerks 33

Bill and account collectors 21

Insurance policy processing clerks 12

Insurance adjusters, examiners, and investigators 12

Insurance claim clerks 11

Welfare eligibility workers and interviewers 7

Claims examiners, property and casualty insurance 3

All other adjusters and investigators 1

Insurance companies employ the vast majority of claim adjusters, examiners, investigators, policy processing clerks, and claim clerks. Hospitals and physician offices and independent adjusting and claims processing firms employ the remainder.

Adjustment clerks are found throughout the economy; however, they are concentrated in the wholesale and retail sectors. Wholesalers, department stores, or catalog and Internet retailers employ nearly 1 out of 4 adjustment clerks. Insurance companies, airlines, hospitals, and telephone companies are other major employers of these workers.

About 1 in 5 bill and account collectors works for a collection agency. Many others work in banks, department stores, governments, and other institutions that lend money and extend credit.

Around 3 of every 4 welfare eligibility workers and interviewers work for Federal, State, or local government agencies. Most of those not employed by government work for private social service agencies and medical facilities.

Training, Other Qualifications, and Advancement

Training and entry requirements vary widely for adjuster, investigator, and collector jobs. A high school education is sufficient to qualify for most insurance processing clerk, adjustment clerk, and bill and account collector positions, while a bachelor's degree is preferred for most claim representative positions. While some college education is preferred for adjuster or welfare eligibility worker or interviewer positions, many people qualify for these positions on the strength of related prior work experience. Because a significant and growing proportion of adjusters, investigators, and collectors use computers, word processing and other computer skills are helpful.

Claim Representatives. Most companies prefer to hire college graduates for claim representative positions. Entry-level workers may be hired without college coursework, however, if they have specialized experience. For example, people with knowledge of automobile mechanics or body repair may qualify as material damage adjusters, and those with extensive clerical experience might be hired as inside adjusters. Both adjusters and examiners should be problem solvers and enjoy working with details.

No specific college major is recommended for these occupations. An adjuster, though, who has a business or an accounting background might specialize in claims of financial loss due to strikes, breakdowns in equipment, or damage to merchandise. College training in engineering is helpful in adjusting industrial claims, such as damage from fires and other accidents. A legal background is helpful in handling workers' compensation and product liability cases. Knowledge of computer applications is also extremely important for all claim representatives.

Six States require independent or public adjusters to be licensed. Applicants in these States usually must comply with one or more of the following: pass a licensing examination covering the fundamentals of adjusting; complete an approved course in insurance or loss adjusting; furnish character references; be at least 20 or 21 years of age and a resident of the State; and file a surety bond.

Because they often work closely with claimants, witnesses, and other insurance professionals, claim representatives must be able to communicate effectively with others. Some companies require applicants to pass a series of written aptitude tests designed to measure communication, analytical, and general mathematical skills. They must also understand Federal and State insurance laws and regulations.

Most large insurance companies provide classroom training for entry-level claim adjusters and examiners. For example, material damage adjusters may be offered classes about automobile body construction, analysis of collision data, repair cost estimation, and computerized estimating equipment.

Workers also may receive training through courses offered by the Insurance Institute of America, a nonprofit organization offering educational programs and professional certification to persons in the property-liability insurance industry. The Insurance Institute of America offers an Associate in Claims designation upon successful completion of four essay examinations. Adjusters can prepare for the examination through independent home study or company and public classes. The Institute also offers a certificate upon successful completion of the Introduction to Claims program and an examination. In addition, the International Claim Association offers a program on life and health insurance claim administration. Completion of the six-examination program leads to the professional Associate, Life, and Health Claims designation.

Beginning adjusters and examiners work on small claims under the supervision of an experienced worker. As they learn more about claim investigation and settlement, they are assigned larger, more complex claims. Trainees are promoted as they demonstrate competence in handling assignments and as they progress in their coursework. Employees who demonstrate competence in claim work or administrative skills may be promoted to claims approver or claims manager. Other claim representatives are promoted to claim investigators.

Insurance Processing Clerks. A high school education is sufficient for most policy processing and customer service positions. For customer service jobs, applicants must possess excellent communication and customer service skills. All candidates should be familiar with computers and be able to type well. Previous office or customer service experience is also an asset.

A few experienced insurance processing clerks may be promoted to a clerical supervisor position. Advancement to a claim representative or an underwriting technician position is possible for clerks who demonstrate potential, have college coursework, or have taken specialized courses in insurance. Many companies offer training for their employees so they can acquire the knowledge necessary to advance.

Policy processing clerks working in customer service jobs can advance their careers by obtaining the Certified Insurance Service Representative (CISR) designation administered by the Society of Certified Insurance Service Representatives. To earn the designation, applicants must attend five one-day classes and pass an examination at the end of each class.

Adjustment Clerks. Many employers do not require any formal education for adjustment clerk positions. Instead, they look for people who can read and write well and who possess good communication and interpersonal skills. Computer skills are also important. Foreign language skills are an asset for those adjustment clerks working in call centers handling a variety of callers from throughout the country.

Adjustment clerk is an entry-level position in some, but not all, organizations. Depending on their assignment, new adjustment clerks may receive training on the job from a supervisor or an experienced coworker, or they may enter a formal training course offered by the organization. As companies strive for better customer service, training is becoming more important, covering such topics as how to use the company's computers, what standard forms to use, whom to contact in other departments of the organization, and how to deal with customers.

Bill and Account Collectors. While a high school diploma is sometimes required for bill and account collector positions, formal education beyond high school is not stressed. Prior experience in the field of telemarketing or as a telephone operator is helpful, as is knowledge of the billing process. Employers seek individuals who speak clearly and who are persistent and detail-oriented.

Employers normally provide training to new bill and account collectors. This training, which may last up to a couple of months, is usually conducted in a classroom or on the job. Although not required by law, many employers also require their collectors to get certified through the American Collectors Association (ACA). ACA seminars concentrate on current State and Federal compliance laws. Since most States recognize these credentials, ACA-certified collectors have greater career mobility. In training seminars, employers use videotapes, computer programs, role-playing, and hands-on experience. New collectors learn about locating customers, billing procedures, and most importantly, communications and negotiation. Learning to use the firm's computer and telephone systems is also an integral part of their training. Successful bill and account collectors may become supervisors. Some even start their own collection agencies.

Welfare Eligibility Workers and Interviewers. Hiring requirements for welfare eligibility workers and interviewers vary widely. Depending on the jurisdiction, applicants may need a high school diploma, associate degree, or bachelor's degree. Work experience in a closely related field—such as employment interviewing, social work, or insurance claims—may also qualify one for this job. In parts of the country with a high concentration of non-English speaking people, fluency in a foreign language may be an advantage.

Because they deal with people who are in difficult economic circumstances, welfare eligibility workers and interviewers should be compassionate and empathetic. They must be detail-oriented and able to follow the numerous procedures and regulations regarding eligibility. Welfare eligibility workers also must be very organized because they work under tight deadlines and often have large caseloads.

After they are hired, eligibility workers are given training, sometimes in a formal classroom setting, other times in a more informal manner. They are taught the policies, procedures, and program regulations that they are expected to use to determine eligibility. If a formal training program is selected, a supervisor or senior eligibility worker usually provides follow-up on-the-job training.

In some jurisdictions, advancement can result in being given the authority to determine eligibility or additional responsibilities. Senior eligibility workers may train new personnel and can advance to a supervisory position. Some workers can advance to the job of social worker, although additional formal education, such as a bachelor's or master's degree, usually is needed.

Job Outlook

Overall employment of adjusters, investigators, and collectors is expected to grow faster than the average for all occupations over the 1998-2008 period. Most job openings, however, will result from the need to replace workers who transfer to other occupations or leave the labor force.

Projected growth rates vary considerably by occupation. Employment of insurance claim representatives is expected to grow about as fast as average as an increasing volume of insurance will result in more insurance claims. The need for life, health, home, and automobile insurance will increase as the population expands and people accumulate assets and take on family responsibilities. Also, new or expanding businesses will need protection for new plants and equipment and for insurance covering their employees' health and safety. Growth in the insurance industry will translate into job growth because many of the duties of claim representatives are not easily automated. Opportunities should be particularly good for claim representatives who specialize in complex business insurance such as marine cargo, workers' compensation, and product liability. Also, representatives with some medical knowledge will be in demand by health insurers and health maintenance organizations as these companies seek additional claim examiners to improve public relations.

Insurance processing occupations are expected to grow about as fast as average, with claim clerks growing faster than policy processing clerks. Unlike other clerical jobs that are declining in number, many policy processors have transformed into customer service representatives with a wider range of responsibilities. Because policy changes can now be entered directly into the computer as the policy change is being requested, the customer service representative is the best person to perform this service. Agencies, in particular, are hiring more customer service representatives to essentially run the office while the agents spend more time soliciting clients. Also, the growing number of insurance companies that sell policies directly to the public are hiring more customer service representatives to handle policy changes directly from clients. Although the job has become highly automated and the changes can be made

more easily, a person is still required to enter the data. However, policy processors who perform mostly clerical duties and have no customer service role will decline as their job becomes increasingly automated and the industry strives for paperless transactions.

Medical facilities and independent claims processing companies are increasingly hiring claims clerks to handle routine medical claims. This will keep the number of claims clerks growing at an average rate through 2008. However, claims clerks working for insurance companies—particularly health insurance—will grow more slowly as their job becomes increasingly automated through the implementation of electronic claims processing software that minimizes claims handling. However, in property and casualty insurance, the job still requires contact with policyholders and is less subject to automation than other clerical positions.

Employment of adjustment clerks is expected to grow faster than average as business establishments place an increased emphasis on maintaining good customer relations. An important aspect of good customer service is resolving customers' complaints and inquiries in a friendly and timely fashion. Because much of their work involves direct communication with customers, demand for adjustment clerks is expected to keep pace with growth in the number of customers. In particular, catalog and Internet retailers, whose growth is expected to skyrocket over the next 10 years, will demand more adjustment clerks acting as customer service representatives to handle an increasing number of requests.

Bill and account collector jobs also are expected to grow much faster than average as the level of consumer debt rises and as more companies seek to improve their debt collection by contracting with third-party collection agencies. Government agencies are increasingly using third-party collection agencies to collect on everything from parking tickets to child support payments and overdue taxes. Contrary to the pattern in most occupations, employment of bill and account collectors tends to rise during recessions, reflecting the difficulty that many people have in meeting their financial obligations.

Employment of welfare eligibility workers and interviewers is expected to decline as many people move from welfare to work, and as State and local governments attempt to curb growth in their expenditures for public assistance. The need to replace workers who leave this occupation will be large, however, as this job has a high turnover rate.

Earnings

Earnings of adjusters, investigators, and collectors vary significantly. The median annual earnings for selected occupations in 1998 were as follows:

Insurance adjusters, examiners, and investigators $38,290
Welfare eligibility workers and interviewers 33,100
Insurance claims clerks 24,010
Insurance policy processing clerks 23,960
Bill and account collectors 22,540
Adjustment clerks 22,040

Workers in some occupations receive additional bonuses or benefits as part of their job. Adjusters are often furnished a cellular telephone and a company car or are reimbursed for use of their own vehicle for business purposes. Although many receive only a salary, some bill and account collectors receive commissions or bonuses in addition to salary, depending on how many cases they close.

Welfare eligibility workers and interviewers are twice as likely to belong to unions than workers in all occupations. In 1997, about 23 percent of all welfare eligibility workers and interviewers were union members, compared to 13 percent for all occupations. The two principal unions representing these workers are the American Federation of State, County, and Municipal Employees, and the Service Employees International Union.

Related Occupations

Insurance adjusters and examiners investigate, analyze, and determine the validity of their firm's liability concerning disability, illness, casualty, or property loss or damages. Workers in other occupations that require similar skills include cost estimators, budget analysts, and private investigators.

The work of bill and account collectors, adjustment clerks, and insurance processing clerks is similar to that of customer service representatives, telemarketers, telephone interviewers, and other workers who deal with the public over the telephone.

The work of welfare eligibility workers is similar to that of social and human service assistants, financial aid counselors, loan and credit counselors, probation officers, and other workers who interview customers or clients.

Sources of Additional Information

General information about a career as a claim representative or an insurance processing clerk is available from the home offices of many life and property and liability insurance companies. Information about career opportunities in these occupations also may be obtained from:

● Insurance Information Institute, 110 William St., New York, NY 10038. Internet: http://www.iii.org

Information about licensing requirements for claim adjusters may be obtained from the department of insurance in each State.

For information about the Associate in Claims (AIC) designation, or the Introduction to Claims program, contact:

● Insurance Institute of America, 720 Providence Rd., P.O. Box 3016, Malvern, PA 19355-0716. Internet: http://www.aicpcu.org

Information on the Associate, Life, and Health Claims designation can be obtained from:

● Life Office Management Association, 2300 Windy Ridge Pkwy., Atlanta, GA 30327-4308. Internet: http://www.loma.org

Information on the Certified Insurance Service Representative designation can be obtained from:

● The Society of Certified Insurance Service Representatives, P.O. Box 27028, Austin, TX 78755. Internet: http://www.scic.com

Career information on bill and account collectors is available from:

- American Collectors Association, Inc., P.O. Box 39106, Minneapolis, MN 55439-0106. Internet: http://www.collector.com

Employment information on welfare eligibility workers and interviewers is available at social service offices of municipal, county, and State governments.

Administrative Services and Facility Managers

(O*NET 13014B)

Significant Points

- Administrative services and facility managers work in private industry and government and have varied responsibilities, experience, earnings, and education.

- Despite projected employment growth, especially among facility managers, competition should remain keen due to the substantial supply of competent, experienced workers seeking managerial jobs.

Nature of the Work

Administrative services and facility managers perform a broad range of duties in virtually every sector of the economy. *Administrative services managers,* for example, coordinate and direct support services to organizations as diverse as insurance companies, computer manufacturers, and government offices. These workers manage the many services that allow organizations to operate efficiently, such as secretarial and reception; administration; payroll; conference planning and travel; information and data processing; mail; materials scheduling and distribution; printing and reproduction; records management; telecommunications management; personal property procurement, supply, and disposal; security; and parking.

Specific duties for these managers vary by degree of responsibility and authority. First-line administrative services managers directly supervise a staff that performs various support services. Mid-level managers, on the other hand, develop departmental plans, set goals and deadlines, implement procedures to improve productivity and customer service, and define the responsibilities of supervisory-level managers. Some mid-level administrative services managers oversee first-line supervisors from various departments, including the clerical staff. Mid-level managers also may be involved in the hiring and dismissal of employees, but they generally have no role in the formulation of personnel policy. Some of these managers advance to upper-level positions such as vice president of administrative services.

In small organizations, a single administrative services manager may oversee all support services. In larger ones, however, first-line administrative services managers often report to mid-level managers who, in turn, report to owners or top-level managers. As the size of the firm increases, administrative services managers are more likely to specialize in specific support activities. For example, some administrative services managers work primarily as office managers, contract administrators, or unclaimed property officers. In many cases, the duties of these administrative services managers are similar to those of other managers and supervisors.

Because of the range of administrative services required by organizations, the nature of many of these managers' jobs also varies significantly. Administrative services managers who work as contract administrators, for instance, oversee the preparation, analysis, negotiation, and review of contracts related to the purchase or sale of equipment, materials, supplies, products, or services. In addition, some administrative services managers acquire, distribute, and store supplies, while others dispose of surplus property or oversee the disposal of unclaimed property.

Facility managers are assigned a wide range of tasks in planning, designing, and managing facilities. They are responsible for coordinating the physical workplace with the people and work of an organization. This task requires integrating the principles of business administration and architecture, as well as the behavioral and engineering sciences. Although the specific tasks assigned to facility managers vary substantially depending on the organization, the duties fall into several categories. They include operations and maintenance, real estate, project planning and management, communication, finance, quality assessment, facility function, and human and environmental factors. Tasks within these broad categories may include space and workplace planning, budgeting, the purchase and sale of real estate, lease management, renovations, or architectural planning and design. Facility managers may suggest and oversee renovation projects for a variety of reasons, ranging from improving efficiency to ensuring that facilities meet government regulations and environmental, health, and security standards. Additionally, facility managers continually monitor the facility to ensure that it remains safe, secure, and well-maintained. Often, the facility manager is responsible for directing staff including maintenance, grounds, and custodial workers.

Working Conditions

Administrative services and facility managers generally work in comfortable offices. However, managers involved in contract administration and personal property procurement, use, and disposal may travel extensively between their home office, branch offices, vendors' offices, and property sales sites. Also, facility managers who are responsible for the design of workspaces may spend time at construction sites and may travel between different facilities while monitoring the work of maintenance, grounds, and custodial staffs.

Most administrative services and facility managers work a standard 40-hour week. However, uncompensated overtime is often required to resolve problems and meet deadlines. Facility managers are often on call to address a variety of problems that can arise in a facility during non-work hours. Because of frequent deadlines and the challenges of managing staff and resources, the work of administrative services and facility managers can be stressful.

Employment

Administrative services and facility managers held about 364,000 jobs in 1998. Over half worked in service industries, including management, business, social, and health services. The remaining workers were widely dispersed throughout the economy.

Training, Other Qualifications, and Advancement

Educational requirements for these managers vary widely, depending on the size and complexity of the organization. In small organizations, experience may be the only requirement needed to enter a position as office manager. When an opening in administrative services management occurs, the office manager may be promoted to the position based on past performance. In large organizations, however, administrative services managers are normally hired from outside, and each position has formal education and experience requirements. Some administrative services managers have advanced degrees.

Specific requirements vary by job responsibility. For first-line administrative services managers of secretarial, mailroom, and related support activities, many employers prefer an associate degree in business or management, although a high school diploma may suffice when combined with appropriate experience. For managers of audiovisual, graphics, and other technical activities, post-secondary technical school training is preferred. Managers of highly complex services such as contract administration generally need a bachelor's degree in business, human resources, or finance. Regardless of major, the curriculum should include courses in office technology, accounting, business mathematics, computer applications, human resources, and business law. Most facility managers have an undergraduate or graduate degree in engineering, architecture, business administration, or facility management. Many have a background in real estate, construction, or interior design, in addition to managerial experience. Whatever the manager's educational background, it must be accompanied by related work experience reflecting demonstrated ability. For this reason, many administrative services managers have advanced through the ranks of their organization, acquiring work experience in various administrative positions before assuming first-line supervisory duties. All managers who oversee departmental supervisors should be familiar with office procedures and equipment. Managers of personal property acquisition and disposal need experience in purchasing and sales, as well as knowledge of a variety of supplies, machinery, and equipment. Managers concerned with supply, inventory, and distribution should be experienced in receiving, warehousing, packaging, shipping, transportation, and related operations. Contract administrators may have worked as contract specialists, cost analysts, or procurement specialists. Managers of unclaimed property often have experience in insurance claims analysis and records management.

Persons interested in becoming administrative services or facility managers should have good communication skills and be able to establish effective working relationships with many different people, ranging from managers, supervisors, and professionals, to clerks and blue-collar workers. They should be analytical, detail oriented, flexible, and decisive. The ability to coordinate several activities at once, quickly analyze and resolve specific problems, and cope with deadlines is also important.

Most administrative services managers in small organizations advance by moving to other management positions or to a larger organization. Advancement is easier in large firms that employ several levels of administrative services managers. Attainment of the Certified Administrative Manager (CAM) designation offered by the Institute of Certified Professional Managers through work experience and successful completion of examinations can increase a manager's advancement potential. In addition, a bachelor's degree enhances a first-level manager's opportunities to advance to a mid-level management position, such as director of administrative services, and eventually to a top-level management position, such as executive vice president for administrative services. Those with the required capital and experience can establish their own management consulting firm.

Advancement of facility managers is based on the practices and size of individual companies. Some facility managers transfer from other departments within the organization or work their way up from technical positions. Others advance through a progression of facility management positions that offer additional responsibilities. Completion of the competency-based professional certification program offered by the International Facility Management Association can give prospective candidates an advantage. In order to qualify for this Certified Facility Manager (CFM) designation, applicants must meet certain educational and experience requirements.

Job Outlook

Employment of administrative services and facility managers is expected to grow about as fast as the average for all occupations through 2008. Demand should be especially strong for facility managers and for administrative services managers in management services and management consulting as public and private organizations continue to contract out and streamline administrative services in an effort to cut costs. Many additional job openings will stem from the need to replace workers who transfer to other jobs, retire, or stop working for other reasons. Nevertheless, competition should remain keen due to the large number of competent, experienced workers seeking managerial jobs.

Continuing corporate restructuring and increasing utilization of office technology should result in a flatter organizational structure with fewer levels of the management, reducing the need for some middle management positions. This should adversely affect administrative services managers who oversee first-line managers. Because many administrative managers have a variety of functions, however, the effects of these changes on employment should be less severe than for other middle managers who specialize in certain functions.

Earnings

Earnings of administrative services and facility managers vary greatly depending on their employer, specialty, and geographic area in which they work. In general, however, median annual earnings of administrative services and facility managers in 1998 were $44,370. The middle 50 percent earned between $31,980 and

$68,840. The lowest 10 percent earned less than $24,100, and the highest 10 percent earned more than $89,850. Median annual earnings in the industries employing the largest numbers of these workers in 1997 were as follows:

Hospitals	$49,000
Commercial banks	47,500
Colleges and universities	44,500
Local government, except education and hospitals	40,900
Management and public relations	36,900

In the Federal government, contract specialists in nonsupervisory, supervisory, and managerial positions averaged $55,300 a year in early 1999; facilities managers, $53,100; industrial property managers, $52,100; property disposal specialists, $48,000; administrative officers, $53,100, and support services administrators, $43,900.

According to the International Facility Management Association, facility managers had annual earnings of approximately $66,000 in 1998. Entry-level positions in facility management offered salaries ranging from $27,000 to $42,000 a year. However, facility directors can earn more than $80,000 per year, and top facility executives can earn in excess of $160,000. These salaries vary depending on level of education, exact position, company size, and geographic location.

Related Occupations

Administrative services and facility managers direct and coordinate support services and oversee the purchase, use, and disposal of personal property. Occupations with similar functions include appraisers, buyers, office and administrative support supervisors, contract specialists, cost estimators, procurement services managers, property and real estate managers, purchasing managers, and personnel managers.

Sources of Additional Information

For information about careers in facility management, facility management education and degree programs, as well as the Certified Facility Manager (CFM) designation, contact:

- International Facility Management Association, 1 East Greenway Plaza, Suite 1100, Houston, TX 77046-0194. Internet: http://www.ifma.org

General information regarding facility management and a list of facility management educational and degree programs may be obtained from:

- The Association of Higher Education Facilities Officers, 1643 Prince St., Alexandria, VA 22314-2818. Internet: http://www.appa.org

For information about the Certified Administrative Manager designation, contact:

- Institute of Certified Professional Managers, James Madison University, College of Business, Harrisonburg, VA 22807. Internet: http://www.cob.jmu.edu/icpm

Adult and Vocational Education Teachers

(O*NET 31314 and 31317)

Significant Points

- More than one-third works part time; many also hold other jobs—often involving work related to the subject they teach.

- Practical experience is often all that is needed to teach vocational courses, but a graduate degree may be required to teach nonvocational courses.

- Opportunities should be best for part-time positions.

Nature of the Work

Adult and vocational education teachers work in four main areas: adult vocational-technical education, adult remedial education, adult continuing education, and prebaccalaureate training. *Adult vocational-technical education teachers* provide instruction for occupations that do not require a college degree, such as welder, dental hygienist, x-ray technician, auto mechanic, and cosmetologist. Other instructors help people update their job skills or adapt to technological advances. For example, an *adult education teacher* may train students how to use new computer software programs. *Adult remedial education teachers* provide instruction in basic education courses for school dropouts or others who need to upgrade their skills to find a job. *Adult continuing education teachers* teach courses that students take for personal enrichment, such as cooking, dancing, writing, exercise and physical fitness, photography, and personal finance.

Adult and vocational education teachers may lecture in classrooms or work in an industry or laboratory setting to give students hands-on experience. Increasingly, adult vocational-technical education teachers integrate academic and vocational curriculums so students obtain a variety of skills that can be applied to the "real world." For example, an electronics student may be required to take courses in principles of mathematics and science in conjunction with hands-on electronics skills. Generally, teachers demonstrate techniques, have students apply them, and critique the students' work. For example, welding instructors show students various welding techniques, watch them use tools and equipment, and have them repeat procedures until they meet the specific standards required by the trade.

Increasingly, minimum standards of proficiency are being established for students in various vocational-technical fields. Adult and vocational education teachers must be aware of new standards and develop lesson plans to ensure that students meet basic criteria. Also, adult and vocational education teachers and community col-

leges are assuming a greater role in students' transition from school to work by helping establish internships and providing information about prospective employers.

Businesses also are increasingly providing their employees with work-related training to keep up with changing technology. Training is often provided through contractors, professional associations, or community colleges.

Adult education teachers who instruct in adult basic education programs may work with students who do not speak English; teach adults reading, writing, and mathematics up to the 8th-grade level; or teach adults through the 12th-grade level in preparation for the General Educational Development tests (GED). The GED offers the equivalent of a high school diploma. These teachers may refer students for counseling or job placement. Because many people who need adult basic education are reluctant to seek it, teachers also may recruit participants.

Adult and vocational education teachers also prepare lessons and assignments, grade papers and do related paperwork, attend faculty and professional meetings, and stay abreast of developments in their field.

Working Conditions

Since adult and vocational education teachers work with adult students, they do not encounter some of the behavioral or social problems sometimes found with younger students. The adults attend by choice, are highly motivated, and bring years of experience to the classroom—attributes that can make teaching these students rewarding and satisfying. However, teachers in adult basic education deal with students at different levels of development who may lack effective study skills and self-confidence and who may require more attention and patience than other students.

More than 1 in 3 adult and vocational education teachers work part time. To accommodate students who may have job or family responsibilities, many institutions offer courses at night or on weekends, which range from two- to four-hour workshops and from one-day mini-sessions to semester-long courses. Some adult and vocational education teachers have several part-time teaching assignments or work a full-time job in addition to their part-time teaching job, leading to long hours and a hectic schedule.

Although most adult and vocational education teachers work in classroom settings, some are consultants to businesses and teach classes at job sites.

Employment

Adult and vocational education teachers held about 588,000 jobs in 1998. About one-fifth were self-employed.

A variety of establishments employed adult and vocational education teachers in 1998: public school systems; community and junior colleges; universities; businesses that provide formal education and training for their employees; schools and institutes that teach automotive repair, bartending, business, computer skills, electronics, medical technology, and other subjects; dance studios; job training centers; community organizations; labor unions; and religious organizations.

Training, Other Qualifications, and Advancement

Training requirements vary by State and by subject. In general, teachers need work or other experiences in their field, and a license or certificate in fields where these usually are required for full professional status. In some cases, particularly at educational institutions, a master's or doctoral degree is required to teach nonvocational courses, which can be applied towards a 4-year degree program. Many vocational teachers in junior or community colleges do not have a master's or doctoral degree but draw on their work experience and knowledge, bringing practical experience to the classroom. For general adult education classes, an acceptable portfolio of work is required. For example, to secure a job teaching a photography course, an applicant would need to show examples of previous work.

Most States and the District of Columbia require adult basic education teachers and adult literacy instructors to have a bachelor's degree from an approved teacher training program, and some States require teacher certification.

Adult and vocational education teachers update their skills through continuing education to maintain certification—requirements vary among institutions. Teachers may take part in seminars, conferences, or graduate courses in adult education or training and development, or may return to work in business or industry for a limited time. Businesses are playing a growing role in adult education, forming consortiums with training institutions and junior colleges and providing input to curriculum development. Adult and vocational education teachers maintain an ongoing dialogue with businesses to determine the most current skills needed in the workplace.

Adult and vocational education teachers should communicate and relate well with students, enjoy working with them, and be able to motivate them. Adult basic education instructors, in particular, must be patient, understanding, and supportive in order to make students comfortable, develop trust, and help them better understand concepts.

Some teachers advance to administrative positions in departments of education, colleges and universities, and corporate training departments. These positions often require advanced degrees, such as a doctorate in adult and continuing education.

Job Outlook

Employment of adult and vocational education teachers is expected to grow about as fast as the average for all occupations through 2008 as the demand for adult education programs continues to rise. Opportunities should be best for part-time positions, especially in fields such as computer technology, automotive mechanics, and medical technology, which offer attractive—and often higher-paying—job opportunities outside of teaching.

According to the National Center for Education Statistics, an estimated 4 out of 10 adults participated in some form of adult education in 1997. Participation in continuing education grows as the educational attainment of the population increases. To keep abreast of changes in their fields and advances in technology, an increasing number of adults are taking courses—often subsidized or funded entirely by employers—for career advancement or to upgrade their skills. In addition, an increasing number of adults are participating in classes for personal enrichment and enjoyment. Enrollment in adult basic education and literacy programs is increasing because of changes in immigration policy that require basic competency in English and civics. And, more employers are demanding higher levels of basic academic skills—reading, writing, and arithmetic—which is increasing enrollment in remedial education and GED preparation classes.

Employment growth of adult vocational-technical education teachers will result from the need to train young adults for entry-level jobs. Experienced workers who want to switch fields or whose jobs have been eliminated due to changing technology or business reorganization also require training. Businesses are finding it essential to provide training to their workers to remain productive and globally competitive. Cooperation between businesses and educational institutions continues to increase to ensure that students are taught the skills employers desire. This should result in greater demand for adult and vocational education teachers, particularly at community and junior colleges. Since adult education programs receive State and Federal funding, employment growth may be affected by government budgets.

Additional job openings for adult and vocational education teachers will stem from the need to replace persons who leave the occupation. Many teach part time and move into and out of the occupation for other jobs, family responsibilities, or retirement.

Earnings

Median annual earnings of adult education teachers were $24,800 in 1998. The middle 50 percent earned between $18,170 and $34,140. The lowest 10 percent earned less than $13,080, and the highest 10 percent earned more than $47,430. Median annual earnings in the industries employing the largest numbers of adult education teachers in 1997 were as follows:

Elementary and secondary schools	$29,900
Colleges and universities	25,900
Schools and educational services, not elsewhere classified	24,600
Dance studios, schools, and halls	23,600
Individual and family services	19,400

Median annual earnings of vocational education teachers were $34,430 in 1998. The middle 50 percent earned between $24,890 and $45,230. The lowest 10 percent earned less than $18,010, and the highest 10 percent earned more than $63,850. Median annual earnings in the industries employing the largest numbers of vocational education teachers in 1997 were as follows:

State government, except education and hospitals	$37,200
Elementary and secondary schools	37,000
Colleges and universities	34,800
Vocational schools	32,600
Schools and educational services, not elsewhere classified	24,700

Earnings varied widely by subject, academic credentials, experience, and region of the country. Part-time instructors usually are paid hourly wages and do not receive benefits or pay for preparation time outside of class.

Related Occupations

Adult and vocational education teaching requires a wide variety of skills and aptitudes, including the ability to influence, motivate, train, and teach; organizational, administrative, and communication skills; and creativity. Workers in other occupations that require these aptitudes include other teachers, counselors, school administrators, public relations specialists, employee development specialists, and social workers.

Sources of Additional Information

Information on adult basic education programs and teacher certification requirements is available from State departments of education and local school districts.

For information about adult vocational-technical education teaching positions, contact State departments of vocational-technical education.

For information on adult continuing education teaching positions, contact departments of local government, State adult education departments, schools, colleges and universities, religious organizations, or a wide range of businesses that provide formal training for their employees.

General information on adult and vocational education is available from:

- Association for Career and Technical Education, 1410 King St., Alexandria, VA 22314. Internet: http://www.acteonline.org
- ERIC Clearinghouse on Adult, Career, and Vocational Education, 1900 Kenny Rd., Columbus, OH 43210-1090. Internet: http://www.ericacve.org

Advertising, Marketing, and Public Relations Managers

(O*NET 13011A, 13011B, 13011C, and 13011D)

Significant Points

- Employment is projected to increase rapidly, but competition for jobs is expected to be intense.
- Advertising, marketing, and public relations managers have high earnings, but substantial travel and long hours, including evenings and weekends, are common.

● A college degree with almost any major is suitable for entering this occupation, but most people enter these jobs after acquiring experience in related positions.

Nature of the Work

The objective of any firm is to market its products or services profitably. In small firms, the owner or chief executive officer might assume all advertising, promotions, marketing, sales, and public relations responsibilities. In large firms, which may offer numerous products and services nationally or even worldwide, an executive vice president directs overall advertising, promotions, marketing, sales, and public relations policies. Advertising, marketing, and public relations managers coordinate the market research, marketing strategy, sales, advertising, promotion, pricing, product development, and public relations activities. Middle and supervisory managers oversee and supervise staffs of professionals and technicians.

Advertising and promotion staffs usually are small except in the largest firms. In a small firm, they may serve as a liaison between the firm and the advertising or promotion agency to which many advertising or promotional functions are contracted out. In larger firms, advertising managers oversee in-house account services, creative services, and media services departments. The *account executive* manages the account services department, assesses the need for advertising, and in advertising agencies, maintains the accounts of clients. The creative services department develops the subject matter and presentation of advertising. The *creative director* oversees the copy chief, art director, and their respective staffs. The *media director* oversees planning groups that select the communication media—for example, radio, television, newspapers, magazines, Internet, or outdoor signs—to disseminate the advertising.

Promotion managers supervise staffs of promotion specialists. They direct promotion programs combining advertising with purchase incentives to increase sales. In an effort to establish closer contact with purchasers—dealers, distributors, or consumers—promotion programs may involve direct mail, telemarketing, television or radio advertising, catalogs, exhibits, inserts in newspapers, Internet advertisements or websites, in-store displays or product endorsements, and special events. Purchase incentives may include discounts, samples, gifts, rebates, coupons, sweepstakes, and contests.

Marketing managers develop the firm's detailed marketing strategy. With the help of subordinates, including *product development managers* and *market research managers,* they determine the demand for products and services offered by the firm and its competitors. In addition, they identify potential markets—for example, business firms, wholesalers, retailers, government, or the general public. Marketing managers develop pricing strategy with an eye toward maximizing the firm's share of the market and its profits while ensuring that the firm's customers are satisfied. In collaboration with sales, product development, and other managers, they monitor trends that indicate the need for new products and services and oversee product development. Marketing managers work with advertising and promotion managers to promote the firm's products and services and to attract potential users.

Public relations managers supervise public relations specialists. These managers direct publicity programs to a targeted public. They often specialize in a specific area, such as crisis management—or in a specific industry, such as healthcare. They use every available communication media in their effort to maintain the support of the specific group upon whom their organization's success depends, such as consumers, stockholders, or the general public. For example, public relations managers may clarify or justify the firm's point of view on health or environmental issues to community or special interest groups.

Public relations managers also evaluate advertising and promotion programs for compatibility with public relations efforts and serve as the eyes and ears of top management. They observe social, economic, and political trends that might ultimately have an effect upon the firm, and they make recommendations on how to enhance the firm's image based on those trends.

Public relations managers may confer with labor relations managers to produce internal company communications—such as news about employee-management relations—and with financial managers to produce company reports. They assist company executives in drafting speeches, arranging interviews, and handling other forms of public contact; oversee company archives; and respond to information requests. In addition, some handle special events such as sponsorship of races, parties introducing new products, or other activities the firm supports in order to gain public attention through the press without advertising directly.

Sales managers direct the firm's sales program. They assign sales territories, set goals, and establish training programs for the sales representatives. Managers advise the sales representatives on ways to improve their sales performance. In large, multiproduct firms, they oversee regional and local sales managers and their staffs. Sales managers maintain contact with dealers and distributors. They analyze sales statistics gathered by their staffs to determine sales potential and inventory requirements and monitor the preferences of customers. Such information is vital to develop products and maximize profits.

Working Conditions

Advertising, marketing, and public relations managers are provided with offices close to top managers. Long hours, including evenings and weekends, are common. Almost 40 percent of advertising, marketing, and public relations managers worked 50 hours or more a week, compared to 15 percent for all occupations. Working under pressure is unavoidable when schedules change and problems arise, but deadlines and goals must still be met.

Substantial travel may be involved. For example, attendance at meetings sponsored by associations or industries is often mandatory. Sales managers travel to national, regional, and local offices and to various dealers and distributors. Advertising and promotion managers may travel to meet with clients or representatives of communications media. At times, public relations managers travel to meet with special interest groups or government officials. Job transfers between headquarters and regional offices are common, particularly among sales managers.

Employment

Advertising, marketing, and public relations managers held about 485,000 jobs in 1998. They are found in virtually every industry. Industries employing them in significant numbers include wholesale trade, manufacturing firms, advertising, computer and data processing services, and management and public relations.

Training, Other Qualifications, and Advancement

A wide range of educational backgrounds are suitable for entry into advertising, marketing, and public relations managerial jobs, but many employers prefer a broad liberal arts background. A bachelor's degree in sociology, psychology, literature, or philosophy, among other subjects, is acceptable. However, requirements vary depending upon the particular job.

For marketing, sales, and promotion management positions, some employers prefer a bachelor's or master's degree in business administration with an emphasis on marketing. Courses in business law, economics, accounting, finance, mathematics, and statistics are advantageous. In highly technical industries, such as computer and electronics manufacturing, a bachelor's degree in engineering or science combined with a master's degree in business administration is preferred.

For advertising management positions, some employers prefer a bachelor's degree in advertising or journalism. A course of study should include marketing, consumer behavior, market research, sales, communication methods and technology, and visual arts—for example, art history and photography.

For public relations management positions, some employers prefer a bachelor's or master's degree in public relations or journalism. The individual's curriculum should include courses in advertising, business administration, public affairs, political science, and creative and technical writing.

For all these specialties, courses in management and completion of an internship while in school are highly recommended. Familiarity with word processing and database applications also is important for many advertising, marketing, and public relations management positions. Today, interactive marketing, product promotion, and advertising are increasingly prevalent, and computer skills are vital.

Most advertising, marketing, and public relations management positions are filled by promoting experienced staff or related professional or technical personnel. For example, many managers are former sales representatives, purchasing agents, buyers, product or brand specialists, advertising specialists, promotion specialists, and public relations specialists. In small firms, where the number of positions is limited, advancement to a management position usually comes slowly. In large firms, promotion may occur more quickly.

Although experience, ability, and leadership are emphasized for promotion, advancement can be accelerated by participation in management training programs conducted by many large firms. Many firms also provide their employees with continuing education opportunities, either in-house or at local colleges and universities, and encourage employee participation in seminars and conferences, often provided by professional societies. In collaboration with colleges and universities, numerous marketing and related associations sponsor national or local management training programs. Courses include brand and product management, inter-

national marketing, sales management evaluation, telemarketing and direct sales, promotion, marketing communication, market research, organizational communication, and data processing systems procedures and management. Many firms pay all or part of the cost for those who successfully complete courses.

Some associations (listed under sources of additional information) offer certification programs for advertising, marketing, and public relations managers. Certification is a sign of competence and achievement in this field that is particularly important in a competitive job market. While relatively few advertising, marketing, and public relations managers currently are certified, the number of managers who seek certification is expected to grow. For example, Sales and Marketing Executives International offers a management certification program based on education and job performance. The Public Relations Society of America offers an accreditation program for public relations practitioners based on years of experience and an examination.

Persons interested in becoming advertising, marketing, and public relations managers should be mature, creative, highly motivated, resistant to stress, flexible, and decisive. The ability to communicate persuasively, both orally and in writing, with other managers, staff, and the public is vital. Advertising, marketing, and public relations managers also need tact, good judgment, and exceptional ability to establish and maintain effective personal relationships with supervisory and professional staff members and client firms.

Because of the importance and high visibility of their jobs, advertising, marketing, and public relations managers often are prime candidates for advancement to the highest ranks. Well-trained, experienced, successful managers may be promoted to higher positions in their own or other firms. Some become top executives. Managers with extensive experience and sufficient capital may open their own businesses.

Job Outlook

Advertising, marketing, and public relations manager jobs are highly coveted and will be sought by other managers or highly experienced professional and technical personnel, resulting in substantial competition. College graduates with extensive experience, a high level of creativity, and strong communication skills should have the best job opportunities. Those who have new media and interactive marketing skills will be particularly sought after.

Employment of advertising, marketing, and public relations managers is expected to increase faster than the average for all occupations through 2008. Increasingly intense domestic and global competition in products and services offered to consumers should require greater marketing, promotional, and public relations efforts by managers. Management and public relations firms may experience particularly rapid growth as businesses increasingly hire contractors for these services rather than support additional full-time staff.

Projected employment growth varies by industry. For example, employment of advertising, marketing, and public relations managers is expected to grow much faster than average in most business services industries, such as computer and data processing, and in management and public relations firms, while little or no change is projected in manufacturing industries.

Earnings

Median annual earnings of advertising, marketing, promotions, public relations, and sales managers in 1998 were $57,300. The middle 50 percent earned between $38,230 and $84,950 a year. The lowest 10 percent earned less than $28,190, and the highest 10 percent earned more than $116,160 a year. Median annual earnings in the industries employing the largest number of advertising, marketing, promotions, public relations, and sales managers in 1997 were as follows:

Professional and commercial equipment	$69,800
Telephone communications	64,100
Computer and data processing services	60,800
Advertising	54,300
Management and public relations	51,100

According to a National Association of Colleges and Employers survey, starting salaries for marketing majors graduating in 1999 averaged about $31,900; advertising majors averaged about $26,600.

Salary levels vary substantially depending upon the level of managerial responsibility, length of service, education, firm size, location, and industry. For example, manufacturing firms usually pay advertising, marketing, and public relations managers higher salaries than nonmanufacturing firms do. For sales managers, the size of their sales territory is another important determinant of salary. Many managers earn bonuses equal to 10 percent or more of their salaries.

Related Occupations

Advertising, marketing, and public relations managers direct the sale of products and services offered by their firms and the communication of information about their firms' activities. Other personnel involved with advertising, marketing, and public relations include art directors, artists and commercial artists, copy chiefs, copywriters, writers and editors, lobbyists, marketing research analysts, public relations specialists, promotion specialists, and sales representatives.

Sources of Additional Information

For information about careers and certification in sales and marketing, contact:

- Sales and Marketing Executives International, 5500 Interstate North Pkwy., No. 545, Atlanta, GA 30328-4662. Internet: http://www.smei.org

For information about careers in advertising management, contact:

- American Association of Advertising Agencies, 405 Lexington Ave., New York, NY 10174-1801. Internet: http://www.aaaa.org
- American Advertising Federation, Education Services Department, 1101 Vermont Ave. NW., Suite 500, Washington, DC 20005. Internet: http://www.aaf.org

Information about careers and certification in public relations management is available from:

- Public Relations Society of America, 33 Irving Place, New York, NY 10003-2376. Internet: http://www.prsa.org

Aircraft Pilots and Flight Engineers

(O*NET 97702B, 97702C, 97702D, 97702E, 97702H, and 97702J)

Significant Points

- Competition is expected for jobs because aircraft pilots have very high earnings, especially those employed by national airlines.

- Pilots usually start with smaller commuter and regional airlines to acquire the experience needed to qualify for higher paying jobs with national airlines.

- Most pilots have traditionally learned to fly in the military, but growing numbers are entering from civilian FAA certified pilot training schools.

Nature of the Work

Pilots are highly trained professionals who fly airplanes and helicopters to carry out a wide variety of tasks. Although most pilots transport passengers and cargo, others are involved in more unusual tasks, such as dusting crops, spreading seed for reforestation, testing aircraft, directing fire fighting efforts, tracking criminals, monitoring traffic, and rescuing and evacuating injured persons.

Except on small aircraft, two pilots usually make up the cockpit crew. Usually, the most experienced pilot, the *captain*, is in command and supervises all other crew members. The pilot and copilot share flying and other duties, such as communicating with air traffic controllers and monitoring the instruments. Some large aircraft have a third pilot—*the flight engineer*—who assists the other pilots by monitoring and operating many of the instruments and systems, making minor in-flight repairs, and watching for other aircraft. New technology can perform many flight tasks, however, and virtually all new aircraft now fly with only two pilots, who rely more heavily on computerized controls. As older, less technologically sophisticated aircraft continue to retire from airline fleets, flight engineer jobs will diminish.

Before departure, pilots plan their flights carefully. They thoroughly check their aircraft to make sure the engines, controls, instruments, and other systems are functioning properly. They also make sure that baggage or cargo has been loaded correctly. They confer with flight dispatchers and aviation weather forecasters to find out about weather conditions en-route and at their destination. Based on this information, they choose a route, altitude, and speed that will provide the fastest, safest, and smoothest flight. When flying under instrument flight rules—procedures governing the operation of the aircraft when there is poor visibility—the pilot in command, or the company dispatcher, normally files an instrument flight plan with air traffic control so that the flight can be coordinated with other air traffic.

Takeoff and landing are the most difficult parts of the flight and require close coordination between the pilot and first officer. For example, as the plane accelerates for takeoff, the pilot concentrates on the runway while the first officer scans the instrument panel. To calculate the speed they must attain to become airborne, pilots consider the altitude of the airport, outside temperature, weight of the plane, and speed and direction of the wind. The moment the plane reaches takeoff speed, the first officer informs the pilot, who then pulls back on the controls to raise the nose of the plane.

Unless the weather is bad, the actual flight is relatively easy. Airplane pilots, with the assistance of autopilot and the flight management computer, steer the plane along their planned route and are monitored by the air traffic control stations they pass along the way. They regularly scan the instrument panel to check their fuel supply, the condition of their engines, and the air-conditioning, hydraulic, and other systems. Pilots may request a change in altitude or route if circumstances dictate. For example, if the ride is rougher than expected, they may ask air traffic control if pilots flying at other altitudes have reported better conditions. If so, they may request a change. This procedure also may be used to find a stronger tailwind or a weaker headwind to save fuel and increase speed.

In contrast, helicopters are used for short trips at relatively low altitude, so pilots must be constantly on the lookout for trees, bridges, power lines, transmission towers, and other dangerous obstacles. Regardless of the type of aircraft, all pilots must monitor warning devices designed to help detect sudden shifts in wind conditions that can cause crashes.

Pilots must rely completely on their instruments when visibility is poor. Using the altimeter readings, they know how high above ground they are and whether or not they can fly safely over mountains and other obstacles. Special navigation radios give pilots precise information which, with the help of special maps, tell them their exact position. Other very sophisticated equipment provides directions to a point just above the end of a runway and enables pilots to land completely "blind."

Once on the ground, pilots must complete records about their flight for their organization and the Federal Aviation Administration (FAA).

The number of nonflying duties a pilot has depends on the employment setting. Airline pilots have the services of large support staffs, and consequently, they perform few nonflying duties. Pilots employed by other organizations, such as charter operators or businesses, have many other duties. They may load the aircraft, handle all passenger luggage to ensure a balanced load, and supervise refueling; other nonflying responsibilities include keeping records, scheduling flights, arranging for major maintenance, and performing minor aircraft maintenance and repair work.

Some pilots are instructors. They teach their students the principles of flight in ground-school classes and demonstrate how to operate aircraft in dual-controlled planes and helicopters. A few specially trained pilots are "examiners" or "check pilots." They periodically fly with other pilots or pilot's license applicants to make sure they are proficient.

Working Conditions

By law, airline pilots cannot fly more than 100 hours a month or more than 1,000 hours a year. Most airline pilots fly an average of 75 hours a month and work an additional 75 hours a month performing nonflying duties. About one-fifth of all pilots work more than 40 hours a week. Most spend a considerable amount of time away from home because the majority of flights involve overnight layovers. When pilots are away from home, the airlines provide hotel accommodations, transportation between the hotel and airport, and an allowance for meals and other expenses. Airlines operate flights at all hours of the day and night, so work schedules often are irregular. Flight assignments are based on seniority.

Those pilots not employed by the airlines often have irregular schedules as well; they may fly 30 hours one month and 90 hours the next. Because these pilots frequently have many nonflying responsibilities, they have much less free time than airline pilots. Except for business pilots, most do not remain away from home overnight. They may work odd hours. Flight instructors may have irregular and seasonal work schedules depending on their students' available time and the weather. Instructors frequently work at night or on weekends.

Airline pilots, especially those on international routes, often suffer jet lag—fatigue caused by many hours of flying through different time zones. The work of test pilots, who check the flight performance of new and experimental planes, may be dangerous. And pilots who are crop dusters may be exposed to toxic chemicals and seldom have the benefit of a regular landing strip. Helicopter pilots involved in police work may be subject to personal injury.

Although flying does not involve much physical effort, the mental stress of being responsible for a safe flight, no matter what the weather, can be tiring. Pilots must be alert and quick to react if something goes wrong, particularly during takeoff and landing.

Employment

Civilian pilots held about 94,000 jobs in 1998. About 84 percent worked for airlines. Others worked as flight instructors at local airports or for large businesses that fly company cargo and executives in their own airplanes or helicopters. Some pilots flew small planes for air taxi companies, usually to or from lightly traveled airports not served by major airlines. Others worked for a variety of businesses performing tasks such as crop dusting, inspecting pipelines, or conducting sightseeing trips. Federal, State, and local governments also employed pilots. A few pilots were self-employed.

The employment of airplane pilots is not distributed like the population. Pilots are more concentrated in California, Texas, Georgia, Washington, Nevada, Hawaii, and Alaska, which have a high amount of flying activity relative to their population.

Training, Other Qualifications, and Advancement

All pilots who are paid to transport passengers or cargo must have a commercial pilot's license with an instrument rating issued by the FAA. Helicopter pilots must hold a commercial pilot's certificate with a helicopter rating. To qualify for these licenses, applicants must be at least 18 years old and have at least 250 hours of flight experience. The time can be reduced through participation in certain flight school curricula approved by the FAA. They also must pass a strict physical examination to make sure that they are in good health and have 20/20 vision with or without glasses, good hearing, and no physical handicaps that could impair their performance. Applicants must pass a written test that includes questions on the principles of safe flight, navigation techniques, and FAA regulations. They also must demonstrate their flying ability to FAA or designated examiners.

To fly in periods of low visibility, pilots must be rated by the FAA to fly by instruments. Pilots may qualify for this rating by having 105 hours of flight experience, including 40 hours of experience in flying by instruments; they also must pass a written examination on procedures and FAA regulations covering instrument flying and demonstrate to an examiner their ability to fly by instruments.

Airline pilots must fulfill additional requirements. Pilots must have an airline transport pilot's license. Applicants for this license must be at least 23 years old and have a minimum of 1,500 hours of flying experience, including night and instrument flying, and pass FAA written and flight examinations. Usually they also have one or more advanced ratings, such as multi-engine aircraft or aircraft type ratings depending upon the requirements of their particular flying jobs. Because pilots must be able to make quick decisions and accurate judgments under pressure, many airline companies reject applicants who do not pass required psychological and aptitude tests.

All licenses are valid as long as a pilot can pass the periodic physical examinations and tests of flying skills required by Federal government and company regulations.

The Armed Forces have always been an important source of trained pilots for civilian jobs. Military pilots gain valuable experience on jet aircraft and helicopters, and persons with this experience are usually preferred for civilian pilot jobs. This primarily reflects the extensive flying time military pilots receive. Persons without Armed Forces training also become pilots by attending flight schools. The FAA has certified about 600 civilian flying schools, including some colleges and universities that offer degree credit for pilot training. Over the projection period, Federal budget reductions are expected to reduce military pilot training. As a result, FAA certified schools will train a larger share of pilots than in the past. Prospective pilots may also learn to fly by taking lessons from individual FAA-certified flight instructors.

Although some small airlines will hire high school graduates, most airlines require at least two years of college and prefer to hire college graduates; about 90 percent of all pilots have completed some college. In fact, most entrants to this occupation have a college degree. If the number of college-educated applicants continues to increase, employers may make a college degree an educational requirement.

Depending on the type of aircraft, new airline pilots start as first officers or flight engineers. Although some airlines favor applicants who already have a flight engineer's license, they may provide flight engineer training for those who have only the commercial license. Many pilots begin with smaller regional or commuter airlines where they obtain experience flying passengers on scheduled flights into busy airports in all weather conditions. These jobs often lead to higher paying jobs with bigger national airlines.

Initial training for airline pilots includes a week of company indoctrination, three to six weeks of ground school and simulator training, and 25 hours of initial operating experience, including a check-ride with an FAA aviation safety inspector. Once trained and "on the line," pilots are required to attend recurrent training and simulator checks twice a year throughout their career.

Organizations other than airlines usually require less flying experience. However, a commercial pilot's license is a minimum requirement, and employers prefer applicants who have experience in the type of craft they will be flying. New employees usually start as first officers or fly less sophisticated equipment. Test pilots often are required to have an engineering degree.

Advancement for all pilots usually is limited to other flying jobs. Many pilots start as flight instructors, building up their flying hours while they earn money teaching. As they become more experienced, these pilots occasionally fly charter planes or perhaps get jobs with small air transportation firms, such as air taxi companies. Some advance to business flying jobs. A small number get flight engineer jobs with the airlines.

In the airlines, advancement usually depends on seniority provisions of union contracts. After one to five years, flight engineers advance according to seniority to first officer and, after 5 to 15 years, to captain. Seniority also determines which pilots get the more desirable routes. In a non-airlines job, a first officer may advance to pilot and, in large companies, to chief pilot or director of aviation in charge of aircraft scheduling, maintenance, and flight procedures.

Job Outlook

Pilots are expected to face considerable competition for jobs through the year 2008 because the number of applicants for new positions is expected to exceed the number of job openings. Competition will be especially keen early in the projection period due to a temporary increase in the pool of qualified pilots seeking jobs. Mergers and bankruptcies during the recent restructuring of the industry caused a large number of airline pilots to lose their jobs. Also, Federal budget reductions resulted in many pilots leaving the Armed Forces. These and other qualified pilots seek jobs in this occupation because it offers very high earnings, glamour, prestige, and free or low-cost travel benefits. As time passes, some pilots will fail to maintain their qualifications, and the number of applicants competing for each opening should decline. Factors affecting demand, however, are not expected to ease that competition.

Relatively few jobs will be created from rising demand for pilots because employment is expected to increase more slowly than the average for all occupations through 2008. The expected growth in airline passenger and cargo traffic will create a need for more airliners, pilots, and flight instructors. However, computerized flight management systems on new aircraft will eliminate the need for flight engineers on those planes, thus restricting the growth of pilot employment. In addition, the trend toward using larger planes in the airline industry will increase pilot productivity. Future business travel could also be adversely affected by the growing use of teleconferencing; facsimile mail; and electronic communications, such as e-mail; as well as the elimination of many middle management positions in corporate downsizing. Employment of business pilots is expected to grow slower than in the past as more businesses opt to fly with regional and smaller airlines serving their area rather than buy and operate their own aircraft. On the other hand, the number of helicopter pilots is expected to increase more rapidly as the demand expands for the type of services that helicopters can offer, such as police and rescue operations.

Job openings resulting from the need to replace pilots who retire or leave the occupation traditionally have been very low. Aircraft pilots usually have a strong attachment to their occupation because it requires a substantial investment in specialized training that is not transferable to other fields, and it commonly offers very high earnings. However, many of the pilots who were hired in the late 1960s are approaching the age for mandatory retirement, so retirements of pilots are expected to increase and generate several thousand job openings each year.

Pilots who have logged the greatest number of flying hours in the more sophisticated equipment typically have the best prospects. This is the reason military pilots usually have an advantage over other applicants. Jobseekers with the most FAA licenses will also have a competitive advantage. Opportunities for pilots in the regional commuter airlines and international service are expected to be more favorable because these segments are expected to grow faster than other segments of the industry.

Employment of pilots is sensitive to cyclical swings in the economy. During recessions when a decline in the demand for air travel forces airlines to curtail the number of flights, airlines may temporarily furlough some pilots. Commercial and corporate flying, flight instruction, and testing of new aircraft also decline during recessions, adversely affecting pilots in those areas.

Earnings

Earnings of airline pilots are among the highest in the Nation and depend on factors such as the type, size, and maximum speed of the plane and the number of hours and miles flown. For example, pilots who fly jet aircraft usually earn higher salaries than turbo-prop pilots do. In 1998, median annual earnings of aircraft pilots and flight engineers were $91,750. Pilots and flight engineers may earn extra pay for night and international flights.

Airline pilots usually are eligible for life and health insurance plans financed by the airlines. They also receive retirement benefits, and if they fail the FAA physical examination at some point in their careers, they get disability payments. In addition, pilots receive an expense allowance, or "per diem," for every hour they are away from home. Per diem can represent up to $500 each month in addition to their salary. Some airlines also provide allowances to pilots for purchasing and cleaning their uniforms. As an additional benefit, pilots and their immediate families usually are entitled to free or reduced fare transportation on their own and other airlines.

More than one-half of all aircraft pilots are members of unions. Most of the pilots who fly for the major airlines are members of the Airline Pilots Association, International, but those employed by one major airline are members of the Allied Pilots Association. Some flight engineers are members of the Flight Engineers' International Association.

Related Occupations

Although they are not in the cockpit, air traffic controllers and flight dispatchers also play an important role in making sure flights are safe and on schedule, and they participate in many of the decisions pilots must make.

Sources of Additional Information

Information about job opportunities, salaries for a particular airline, and the qualifications required may be obtained by writing to the personnel manager of the airline.

For information on airline pilots, contact:

- Airline Pilots Association, 1625 Massachusetts Ave. NW., Washington, DC 20036.
- Air Transport Association of America, 1301 Pennsylvania Ave. NW., Suite 1110, Washington, DC 20006.

For information on helicopter pilots, contact:

- Helicopter Association International, 1619 Duke St., Alexandria, VA 22314.

For a copy of List of Certificated Pilot Schools, write to:

- Superintendent of Documents, U.S. Government Printing Office, Washington, DC 20402. There is a $2.75 charge for this publication.

For information about job opportunities in companies other than airlines, consult the classified section of aviation trade magazines and apply to companies that operate aircraft at local airports.

Air Traffic Controllers

(O*NET 39002)

Significant Points

- Nearly all air traffic controllers are employed and trained by the Federal government.
- Keen competition is expected in this occupation.
- Aircraft controllers earn relatively high pay and have good benefits.

Nature of the Work

The air traffic control system is a vast network of people and equipment that ensures the safe operation of commercial and private aircraft. Air traffic controllers coordinate the movement of air traffic to make certain that planes stay a safe distance apart. Their immediate concern is safety, but controllers also must direct planes efficiently to minimize delays. Some regulate airport traffic; others regulate flights between airports.

Although *airport tower* or *terminal controllers* watch over all planes traveling through the airport's airspace, their main responsibility is to organize the flow of aircraft in and out of the airport. Relying on radar and visual observation, they closely monitor each plane to ensure a safe distance between all aircraft and to guide pilots between the hangar or ramp and the end of the airport's airspace. In addition, controllers keep pilots informed about changes in weather conditions such as wind shear (a sudden change in the velocity or direction of the wind that can cause the pilot to lose control of the aircraft).

During arrival and departure, several controllers direct each plane. As a plane approaches an airport, the pilot radios ahead to inform the terminal of its presence. The controller in the radar room, just beneath the control tower, has a copy of the plane's flight plan and already has observed the plane on radar. If the path is clear, the controller directs the pilot to a runway; if the airport is busy, the plane is fitted into a traffic pattern with other aircraft waiting to land. As the plane nears the runway, the pilot is asked to contact the tower. There, another controller, who also is watching the plane on radar, monitors the aircraft the last mile or so to the runway, delaying any departures that would interfere with the plane's landing. After the plane has landed, a ground controller in the tower directs it along the taxiways to its assigned gate. The ground controller usually works entirely by sight, but may use radar if visibility is very poor.

The procedure is reversed for departures. The ground controller directs the plane to the proper runway. The local controller then informs the pilot about conditions at the airport, such as weather, speed and direction of wind, and visibility. The local controller also issues runway clearance for the pilot to take off. Once in the air, the plane is guided out of the airport's airspace by the departure controller.

After each plane departs, airport tower controllers notify *enroute controllers* who take charge next. There are 21 enroute control centers located around the country, each employing 300 to 700 controllers, with more than 150 on duty during peak hours at the busier facilities. Airplanes usually fly along designated routes; each center is assigned a certain airspace containing many different routes. Enroute controllers work in teams of up to three members, depending on how heavy traffic is; each team is responsible for a section of the center's airspace. A team, for example, might be responsible for all planes that are 30 to 100 miles north of an airport and flying at an altitude between 6,000 and 18,000 feet.

To prepare for planes about to enter the team's airspace, the radar associate controller organizes flight plans coming off a printer. If two planes are scheduled to enter the team's airspace at nearly the same time, location, and altitude, this controller may arrange with the preceding control unit for one plane to change its flight path. The previous unit may have been another team at the same or an adjacent center, or a departure controller at a neighboring terminal. As a plane approaches a team's airspace, the radar controller accepts responsibility for the plane from the previous controlling unit. The controller also delegates responsibility for the plane to the next controlling unit when the plane leaves the team's airspace.

The radar controller, who is the senior team member, observes the planes in the team's airspace on radar and communicates with the pilots when necessary. Radar controllers warn pilots about nearby planes, bad weather conditions, and other potential hazards. Two planes on a collision course will be directed around each other. If a pilot wants to change altitude in search of better flying conditions, the controller must check to determine that no other planes will be along the proposed path. As the flight progresses, the team responsible for the aircraft notifies the next team in charge. Through team coordination, the plane arrives safely at its destination.

Both airport tower and enroute controllers usually control several planes at a time; often, they have to make quick decisions about completely different activities. For example, a controller might direct a plane on its landing approach and at the same time provide pilots entering the airport's airspace with information about conditions at the airport. While instructing these pilots, the controller also would observe other planes in the vicinity, such as those in a holding pattern waiting for permission to land, to ensure that they remain well separated.

In addition to airport towers and enroute centers, air traffic controllers also work in flight service stations operated at more than 100 locations. These *flight service specialists* provide pilots with information on the station's particular area, including terrain, preflight and inflight weather information, suggested routes, and other information important to the safety of a flight. Flight service station specialists help pilots in emergency situations and initiate and coordinate searches for missing or overdue aircraft. However, they are not involved in actively managing air traffic.

Some air traffic controllers work at the Federal Aviation Administration's (FAA) Air Traffic Control Systems Command Center in Herndon, Virginia, where they oversee the entire system. They look for situations that will create bottlenecks or other problems in the system, and they respond with a management plan for traffic into and out of the troubled sector. The objective is to keep traffic levels in the trouble spots manageable for the controllers working at enroute centers.

Currently, the FAA is in the midst of developing and implementing a new automated air traffic control system. As a result, more powerful computers will help controllers deal with the demands of increased air traffic. Some traditional air traffic controller tasks—like determining how far apart planes should be kept—will be done by computer. Present separation standards call for a 2,000-foot vertical spacing between two aircraft operating above 29,000 feet and flying the same ground track. With the aid of new technologies, the FAA will be able to reduce this vertical separation standard to 1,000 feet. Improved communication between computers on airplanes and those on the ground also is making the controller's job a little easier.

At present controllers sit at consoles with green-glowing screens that display radar images generated by a computer. In the future, controllers will work at a modern workstation computer that depicts air routes in full-color on a 20- by 20-inch screen. The controllers will select radio channels simply by touching on-screen buttons instead of turning dials or switching switches. The new technology will also enable controllers to zoom in on selected corners of the air space that is their responsibility and get better images of moving traffic than is possible with today's machines. However, the new automated air traffic control system will not be fully operational until at least 2003.

The FAA is also considering implementing a system called "free flight" which would give pilots much more freedom in operating their aircraft. The change will require new concepts of shared responsibility between controllers and pilots. Air traffic controllers will still be central to the safe operation of the system, but their responsibilities will eventually shift from controlling to monitoring flights. At present, controllers assign routes, altitudes, and speeds. Under the new system, airlines and pilots would choose them. Controllers would intervene only to ensure that aircraft remained at safe distances from one another, to prevent congestion in terminal areas and entry into closed airspace, or to otherwise ensure safety. Today's practices often result in planes zigzagging from point to point along corridors instead of flying from city to city in a straight line. This results in lost time and fuel. However, it may be several years before a free flight system is implemented, despite its potential advantages. For the system to work, new equipment must be added for pilots and controllers, and new procedures must be developed to accommodate both the tightly controlled and flexible aspects of free flight. Budget constraints within the Federal government may delay or slow implementation.

Working Conditions

Controllers work a basic 40-hour week; however, they may work additional hours for which they receive overtime pay or equal time off. Because most control towers and centers operate 24 hours a day, 7 days a week, controllers rotate night and weekend shifts.

During busy times, controllers must work rapidly and efficiently. This requires total concentration to keep track of several planes at the same time and make certain all pilots receive correct instructions. The mental stress of being responsible for the safety of several aircraft and their passengers can be exhausting for some persons.

Employment

Air traffic controllers held about 30,000 jobs in 1998. They were employed by the Federal government at airports—in towers and flight service stations—and in enroute traffic control centers. The overwhelming majority worked for the FAA. Some professional controllers conduct research at the FAA's national experimental center near Atlantic City, New Jersey. Others serve as instructors at the FAA Academy in Oklahoma City, Oklahoma. A small number of civilian controllers worked for the Department of Defense. In addition to controllers employed by the Federal government, some worked for private air traffic control companies providing service to non-FAA towers.

Training, Other Qualifications, and Advancement

Air traffic controller trainees are selected through the competitive Federal Civil Service system. Applicants must pass a written test that measures their ability to learn the controller's duties. Applicants with experience as a pilot, navigator, or military controller can improve their rating by scoring well on the occupational knowledge portion of the examination. Abstract reasoning and three-dimensional spatial visualization are among the aptitudes the exam

measures. In addition, applicants usually must have three years of general work experience or four years of college, or a combination of both. Applicants also must survive a week of screening at the FAA Academy in Oklahoma City, which includes aptitude tests using computer simulators and physical and psychological examinations. Successful applicants receive drug screening tests. For airport tower and enroute center positions, applicants must be less than 31 years old. Those 31 years old and over are eligible for positions at flight service stations.

Controllers must be articulate because pilots must be given directions quickly and clearly. Intelligence and a good memory also are important because controllers constantly receive information that they must immediately grasp, interpret, and remember. Decisiveness is also required because controllers often have to make quick decisions. The ability to concentrate is crucial because controllers must make these decisions in the midst of noise and other distractions.

Trainees learn their jobs through a combination of formal and on-the-job training. They receive seven months of intensive training at the FAA academy, where they learn the fundamentals of the airway system, FAA regulations, controller equipment, aircraft performance characteristics, as well as more specialized tasks. To receive a job offer, trainees must successfully complete the training and pass a series of examinations, including a controller skills test that measures speed and accuracy in recognizing and correctly solving air traffic control problems. The test requires judgments on spatial relationships and requires application of the rules and procedures contained in the Air Traffic Control Handbook. Based on aptitude and test scores, trainees are selected to work at either an enroute center or a tower.

After graduation, it takes several years of progressively more responsible work experience, interspersed with considerable classroom instruction and independent study, to become a fully qualified controller. This training includes instruction in the operation of the new, more automated air traffic control system—including the automated Microwave Landing System that enables pilots to receive instructions over automated data links—that is being installed in control sites across the country.

Controllers who fail to complete either the academy or the on-the-job portion of the training are usually dismissed. Controllers must pass a physical examination each year and a job performance examination twice each year. Failure to become certified in any position at a facility within a specified time may also result in dismissal. Controllers also are subject to drug screening as a condition of continuing employment.

At airports, new controllers begin by supplying pilots with basic flight data and airport information. They then advance to ground controller, then local controller, departure controller, and finally, arrival controller. At an enroute traffic control center, new controllers first deliver printed flight plans to teams and gradually advance to radar associate controller and then radar controller.

Controllers can transfer to jobs at different locations or advance to supervisory positions, including management or staff jobs in air traffic control and top administrative jobs in the FAA. However, there are only limited opportunities for a controller to switch from a position in an enroute center to a tower.

Job Outlook

Extremely keen competition is expected for air traffic controller jobs because the occupation attracts many more qualified applicants than the small number of job openings that result from replacement needs. Turnover is very low because of the relatively high pay and liberal retirement benefits, and controllers have a very strong attachment to the occupation. Most of the current work force was hired as a result of the controller's strike during the 1980s, so the average age of current controllers is fairly young. Relatively few controllers will be eligible to retire over the 1998-2008 period.

Employment of air traffic controllers is expected to show little or no change through the year 2008. Employment growth is not expected to keep pace with growth in the number of aircraft flying because of the implementation of a new air traffic control system over the next 10 years. This computerized system will assist the controller by automatically making many of the routine decisions. Automation will allow controllers to handle more traffic, thus increasing their productivity.

Air traffic controllers who continue to meet the proficiency and medical requirements enjoy more job security than most workers. The demand for air travel and the workloads of air traffic controllers decline during recessions, but controllers seldom are laid off.

Earnings

Median annual earnings of air traffic controllers in 1998 were $64,880. The middle 50 percent earned between $50,980 and $78,840. The lowest 10 percent earned less than $36,640, and the highest 10 percent earned more than $87,210.

The average annual salary for air traffic controllers in the Federal government—which employs 86 percent of the total—in nonsupervisory, supervisory, and managerial positions was $48,300 in 1999. Both the worker's job responsibilities and the complexity of the particular facility determine a controller's pay. For example, controllers who work at the FAA's busiest air traffic control facilities earn higher pay.

Depending on length of service, air traffic controllers receive 13 to 26 days of paid vacation and 13 days of paid sick leave each year, life insurance, and health benefits. In addition, controllers can retire at an earlier age and with fewer years of service than other Federal employees. Air traffic controllers are eligible to retire at age 50 with 20 years of service as an active air traffic controller or after 25 years of active service at any age. There is a mandatory retirement age of 56 for controllers who manage air traffic.

Related Occupations

Other occupations that involve the direction and control of traffic in air transportation are airline-radio operator and airplane dispatcher.

Sources of Additional Information

Information on acquiring a job as an air traffic controller with the Federal government may be obtained from the Office of Personnel Management (OPM) through a telephone-based system. Consult your telephone directory under U.S. Government for a local number or call (912) 757-3000; TDD (912) 744-2299. That number is not toll free, and charges may result. Information also is available from their Internet site: http://www.usajobs.opm.gov.

Announcers

(O*NET 34017 and 34021)

Significant Points

- Competition for announcer jobs will continue to be keen.

- Jobs at small stations usually have low pay, but they offer the best opportunities for beginners.

- Related work experience at a campus radio station or as an intern at a commercial station can be helpful for breaking into the occupation.

Nature of the Work

Announcers in radio and television perform a variety of tasks on and off the air. They announce station program information such as program schedules and station breaks for commercials or public service information, and they introduce and close programs. Announcers read prepared scripts or ad-lib commentary on the air when presenting news, sports, weather, time, and commercials. If a written script is required, they may do the research and writing. Announcers also interview guests and moderate panels or discussions. Some provide commentary for the audience during sporting events, parades, and other events. Announcers are often well known to radio and television audiences and may make promotional appearances and remote broadcasts for their stations.

Radio announcers are often called disc jockeys. Some disc jockeys specialize in one kind of music. They announce music selections and may decide what music to play. While on the air, they comment on the music, weather, and traffic. They may take requests from listeners, interview guests, and manage listener contests.

Newscasters or anchors work at large stations and specialize in news, sports, or weather. Show hosts may specialize in a certain area of interest such as politics, personal finance, sports, or health. They contribute to the preparation of the program content; interview guests; and discuss issues with viewers, listeners, or an in-studio audience.

Announcers at smaller stations may cover all of these areas and tend to have more off-air duties as well. They may operate the control board, monitor the transmitter, sell commercial time to advertisers, keep a log of the station's daily programming, and do production work. Consolidation and automation make it possible for announcers to do some work previously performed by broadcast technicians. Announcers use the control board to broadcast programming, commercials, and public service announcements according to schedule. Public radio and television announcers are involved with station fundraising efforts.

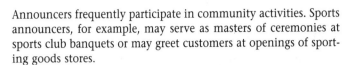

Announcers frequently participate in community activities. Sports announcers, for example, may serve as masters of ceremonies at sports club banquets or may greet customers at openings of sporting goods stores.

Although most announcers are employed in radio and television broadcasting, some are employed in the cable television or motion picture production industries. Other announcers may use a public address system to provide information to the audience at sporting and other events. Some disc jockeys announce and play music at clubs, dances, restaurants, and weddings.

Working Conditions

Announcers usually work in well-lighted, air-conditioned, sound-proof studios.

The broadcast day is long for radio and TV stations—some are on the air 24 hours a day—so announcers can expect to work unusual hours. Many present early morning shows, when most people are getting ready for work or commuting, while others do late night programs.

Announcers often work within tight schedule constraints, which can be physically and mentally stressful. For many announcers, the intangible rewards—creative work, many personal contacts, and the satisfaction of becoming widely known—far outweigh the disadvantages of irregular and often unpredictable hours, work pressures, and disrupted personal lives.

Employment

Announcers held about 60,000 jobs in 1998. Nearly all were staff announcers employed in radio and television broadcasting, but some were freelance announcers who sold their services for individual assignments to networks and stations or to advertising agencies and other independent producers. Many announcing jobs are part time.

Training, Other Qualifications, and Advancement

Entry to this occupation is highly competitive. Formal training in broadcasting from a college or technical school (private broadcasting school) is valuable. Station officials pay particular attention to taped auditions that show an applicant's delivery and—in television—appearance and style on commercials, news, and interviews. Those hired by television stations usually start out as production assistants, researchers, or reporters and are given a chance to move into announcing if they show an aptitude for "on-air" work. Newcomers to TV broadcasting also may begin as news camera operators. A beginner's chance of landing an on-air job is remote, except possibly for a small radio station. In radio, newcomers usually start out taping interviews and operating equipment.

Announcers usually begin at a station in a small community and, if qualified, may move to a better paying job in a large city. They also may advance by hosting a regular program as a disc jockey, sportscaster, or other specialist. Competition is particularly intense for employment by networks, and employers look for college graduates with at least several years of successful announcing experience.

Announcers must have a pleasant and well-controlled voice, good timing, and excellent pronunciation, and must know correct grammar usage. Television announcers need a neat, pleasing appearance as well. Knowledge of theater, sports, music, business, politics, and other subjects likely to be covered in broadcasts improves chances for success. Announcers also must be computer-literate because programming is created and edited by computer. In addition, they should be able to ad-lib all or part of a show and to work under tight deadlines. The most successful announcers attract a large audience by combining a pleasing personality and voice with an appealing style.

High school and college courses in English, public speaking, drama, foreign languages, and computer science are valuable, and hobbies such as sports and music are additional assets. Students may gain valuable experience at campus radio or TV facilities and at commercial stations while serving as interns. Paid or unpaid internships provide students with hands-on training and the chance to establish contacts in the industry. Unpaid interns often receive college credit and are allowed to observe and assist station employees. Although the Fair Labor Standards Act limits the work unpaid interns may perform in a station, unpaid internships are the rule; sometimes they lead to paid internships. Paid internships are valuable because interns do work ordinarily done by regular employees and may even go on the air.

Persons considering enrolling in a broadcasting school should contact personnel managers of radio and television stations as well as broadcasting trade organizations to determine the school's reputation for producing suitably trained candidates.

Job Outlook

Competition for jobs as announcers will be keen because the broadcasting field attracts many more jobseekers than there are jobs. Small radio stations are more inclined to hire beginners, but the pay is low. Interns usually receive preference for available positions. Because competition for ratings is so intense in major metropolitan areas, large stations will continue to seek announcers who have proven that they can attract and retain a large audience.

Announcers who are knowledgeable in business, consumer, and health news may have an advantage over others. While specialization is more common at large stations and the networks, many small stations also encourage it.

Employment of announcers is expected to decline slightly through 2008 due to the lack of growth of new radio and television stations. Openings in this relatively small field will arise from the need to replace those who transfer to other kinds of work or leave the labor force. Job openings also arise because of high turnover within the occupation. Changes in station ownership, format, and ratings frequently cause periods of unemployment for many announcers. Many announcers leave the field because they cannot advance to better paying jobs.

Increasing consolidation of radio and television stations, new technology, and the growth of alternative media sources will contribute to the expected decline in employment of announcers.

Consolidation in broadcasting may lead to increased use of syndicated programming and programs originating outside a station's viewing or listening area. Digital technology will increase the productivity of announcers, reducing the time spent on off-air technical and production work. In addition, all traditional media, including radio and television, may suffer losses in audience as the American public increases its use of personal computers.

Employment in this occupation is not significantly affected by downturns in the economy. If recessions cause advertising revenues to fall, stations tend to cut "behind-the-scenes" workers rather than announcers and broadcasters.

Earnings

Salaries in broadcasting vary widely but in general are relatively low except for announcers in large stations in major markets or who work for a network. They are higher in television than in radio and higher in commercial than in public broadcasting.

Median hourly earnings of announcers in 1998 were $8.62. The middle 50 percent earned between $6.17 and $12.76. The lowest 10 percent earned less than $5.63, and the highest 10 percent earned more than $21.28. Median hourly earnings of announcers in 1997 were $8.20 in the radio and television broadcasting industry.

Related Occupations

The success of announcers depends upon how well they communicate. Others who must be skilled at oral communication include interpreters, sales workers, public relations specialists, and teachers. Many announcers also must entertain their audience, so their work is similar to other entertainment-related occupations such as actors, directors and producers, dancers, and musicians.

Sources of Additional Information

General information on the broadcasting industry is available from:

- National Association of Broadcasters, 1771 N St. NW., Washington, DC 20036. Internet: http://www.nab.org

Architects, Except Landscape and Naval

(O*NET 22302)

Significant Points

- About 30 percent were self-employed; that's more than three times the proportion for all professionals.

- Licensing requirements include a professional degree in architecture, a period of practical training or internship, and passing all divisions of the Architect Registration Examination.

- Beginners may face competition, especially for jobs in the most prestigious firms; summer internship experience and knowledge of computer-aided design and drafting technology are advantages.

Nature of the Work

Architects design buildings and other structures. The design of a building involves far more than its appearance. Buildings must also be functional, safe, and economical, and must suit the needs of the people who use them. Architects take all these things into consideration when they design buildings and other structures.

Architects provide professional services to individuals and organizations planning a construction project. They may be involved in all phases of development, from the initial discussion with the client through the entire construction process. Their duties require specific skills: designing, engineering, managing, supervising, and communicating with clients and builders.

The architect and client discuss the objectives, requirements, and budget of a project. In some cases, architects provide various predesign services, such as conducting feasibility and environmental impact studies, selecting a site, or specifying the requirements the design must meet. For example, they may determine space requirements by researching the number and type of potential users of a building. The architect then prepares drawings and a report presenting ideas for the client to review.

After the initial proposals are discussed and accepted, architects develop final construction plans. These plans show the building's appearance and details for its construction. Accompanying these are drawings of the structural system; air-conditioning, heating, and ventilating systems; electrical systems; plumbing; and possibly site and landscape plans. They also specify the building materials and, in some cases, the interior furnishings. In developing designs, architects follow building codes, zoning laws, fire regulations, and other ordinances, such as those requiring easy access by disabled persons. Throughout the planning stage, they make necessary changes. Although they have traditionally used pencil and paper to produce design and construction drawings, architects are increasingly turning to computer-aided design and drafting (CADD) technology for these important tasks.

Architects may also assist the client in obtaining construction bids, selecting a contractor, and negotiating the construction contract. As construction proceeds, they may visit the building site to ensure the contractor is following the design, adhering to the schedule, using the specified materials, and meeting quality work standards. The job is not complete until all construction is finished, required tests are performed, and construction costs are paid. Sometimes, architects also provide post-construction services, such as facilities management. They advise on energy efficiency measures, evaluate how well the building design adapts to the needs of occupants, and make necessary improvements.

Architects design a wide variety of buildings, such as office and apartment buildings, schools, churches, factories, hospitals, houses, and airport terminals. They also design complexes such as urban centers, college campuses, industrial parks, and entire communities. They may also advise on the selection of building sites, prepare cost analysis and land-use studies, and do long-range planning for land development.

Architects sometimes specialize in one phase of work. Some specialize in the design of one type of building—for example, hospitals, schools, or housing. Others focus on planning and predesign services or construction management, and do little design work. They often work with engineers, urban planners, interior designers, landscape architects, and others. In fact, architects spend a great deal of their time coordinating information from, and the work of, other professionals engaged in the same project. Consequently, architects are now using the Internet to update designs and communicate changes for the sake of speed and cost savings.

During a training period leading up to licensing as architects, entry-level workers are called intern-architects. This training period, which generally lasts three years, gives them practical work experience while they prepare for the Architect Registration Examination (ARE). Typical duties may include preparing construction drawings on CADD or assisting in the design of one part of a project.

Working Conditions

Architects usually work in a comfortable environment. Most of their time is spent in offices consulting with clients, developing reports and drawings, and working with other architects and engineers. However, they often visit construction sites to review the progress of projects.

Architects may occasionally be under stress, working nights and weekends to meet deadlines. In 1998, almost 2 out of 5 architects worked more than 40 hours a week, in contrast to 1 in 4 workers in all occupations combined.

Employment

Architects held about 99,000 jobs in 1998. The majority of jobs were in architectural firms—most of which employ fewer than 5 workers. A few worked for general building contractors, and for government agencies responsible for housing, planning, or community development, such as the U.S. Departments of Defense and Interior, and the General Services Administration. About 3 in 10 architects were self-employed.

Training, Other Qualifications, and Advancement

All States and the District of Columbia require individuals to be licensed (registered) before they may call themselves architects or contract to provide architectural services. Many architecture school graduates work in the field even though they are not licensed. However, a licensed architect is required to take legal responsibility for all work. Licensing requirements include a professional degree in architecture, a period of practical training or internship, and passage of all sections of the ARE.

In many States, the professional degree in architecture must be from one of the 105 schools of architecture with programs accredited by the National Architectural Accrediting Board (NAAB). However, State architectural registration boards set their own standards, so graduation from a non NAAB-accredited program may meet the educational requirement for licensing in some States. Several types of professional degrees in architecture are available through colleges and universities. The majority of all architectural degrees are from five-year Bachelor of Architecture programs, intended for students entering from high school or with no previous architectural training. Some schools offer a two-year Master of Architecture program for students with a preprofessional undergraduate degree in architecture or a related area or a three- or four-year Master of Architecture program for students with a degree in another discipline. In addition, there are many combinations and variations of these programs.

The choice of degree type depends upon each individual's preference and educational background. Prospective architecture students should consider the available options before committing to a program. For example, although the 5-year Bachelor of Architecture program offers the fastest route to the professional degree, courses are specialized and, if the student does not complete the program, moving to a nonarchitectural program may be difficult. A typical program includes courses in architectural history and theory, building design, professional practice, math, physical sciences, and liberal arts. Central to most architectural programs is the design studio, where students put into practice the skills and concepts learned in the classroom. During the final semester of many programs, students devote their studio time to creating an architectural project from beginning to end, culminating in a three-dimensional model of their design.

Many schools of architecture also offer graduate education for those who already have a bachelor's or master's degree in architecture or other areas. Although graduate education beyond the professional degree is not required for practicing architects, it is for research, teaching, and certain specialties.

Architects must be able to visually communicate their ideas to clients. Artistic and drawing ability is very helpful in doing this, but not essential. More important are a visual orientation and the ability to conceptualize and understand spatial relationships. Good communication skills, the ability to work independently or as part of a team, and creativity are important qualities for anyone interested in becoming an architect. Computer literacy is also required as most firms use computers for writing specifications, two- and three-dimensional drafting, and financial management. A knowledge of computer-aided design and drafting (CADD) is helpful and will become essential as architectural firms continue to adopt this technology. Recently, the profession recognized National CAD Standards (NCS); architecture students who master NCS will have an advantage in the job market.

All State architectural registration boards require a training period before candidates may sit for the ARE and become licensed. Many States have adopted the training standards established by the Intern Development Program, a branch of the American Institute of Architects and the National Council of Architectural Registration Boards. These standards stipulate broad and diversified training under the supervision of a licensed architect over a three-year period. New graduates usually begin as intern-architects in architectural firms, where they assist in preparing architectural documents or drawings. They may also do research on building codes and materials or write specifications for building materials, installation criteria, the quality of finishes, and other related details. Graduates with degrees in architecture also enter related fields such as graphic, interior, or industrial design; urban planning; real estate development; civil engineering; or construction management. In such cases, an architectural license (and thus the internship period) is not required.

After completing the internship period, intern-architects are eligible to sit for the ARE. The examination tests candidates on architectural knowledge, and is given in sections throughout the year. Candidates who pass the ARE and meet all standards established by their State board are licensed to practice in that State.

After becoming licensed and gaining experience, architects take on increasingly responsible duties, eventually managing entire projects. In large firms, architects may advance to supervisory or managerial positions. Some architects become partners in established firms; others set up their own practice.

Several States require continuing education to maintain a license, and many more States are expected to adopt mandatory continuing education. Requirements vary by State, but they usually involve the completion of a certain number of credits every year or two through seminars, workshops, formal university classes, conferences, self-study courses, or other sources.

Job Outlook

Prospective architects may face competition for entry-level jobs, especially if the number of architectural degrees awarded remains at current levels or increases. Employment of architects is projected to grow about as fast as the average for all occupations through 2008, and additional job openings will stem from the need to replace architects who retire or leave the labor force for other reasons. However, many individuals are attracted to this occupation, and the number of applicants often exceeds the number of available jobs, especially in the most prestigious firms. Prospective architects who complete at least one summer internship—either paid or unpaid—while in school and who know CADD technology (especially that which conforms to the new national standards) will have a distinct advantage in obtaining an intern-architect position after graduation.

Employment of architects is strongly tied to the level of local construction, particularly nonresidential structures such as office buildings, shopping centers, schools, and healthcare facilities. After a boom in non-residential construction during the 1980s, building slowed significantly during the first half of the 1990s. Despite slower labor force growth and increases in telecommuting and flexiplace work, however, non-residential construction is expected to grow more quickly between 1998 and 2008 than during the previous decade, driving demand for more architects.

As the stock of buildings ages, demand for remodeling and repair work should grow considerably. The needed renovation and rehabilitation of old buildings, particularly in urban areas where space for new buildings is becoming limited, is expected to provide many job opportunities for architects. In addition, demographic trends and changes in health care delivery are influencing the demand for certain institutional structures, and should also provide more jobs for architects in the future. For example, increases in the school-age population have resulted in new school construction. Addi-

tions to existing schools (especially colleges and universities), as well as overall modernization, will continue to add to demand for architects through 2008. Growth is expected in the number of adult care centers, assisted-living facilities, and community health clinics, all of which are preferable, less costly alternatives to hospitals and nursing homes.

Because construction—particularly office and retail—is sensitive to cyclical changes in the economy, architects will face particularly strong competition for jobs or clients during recessions, and layoffs may occur. Those involved in the design of institutional buildings such as schools, hospitals, nursing homes, and correctional facilities, will be less affected by fluctuations in the economy.

Even in times of overall good job opportunities, however, there may be areas of the country with poor opportunities. Architects who are licensed to practice in one State must meet the licensing requirements of other States before practicing elsewhere. These requirements are becoming more standardized, however, facilitating movement to other States.

Earnings

Median annual earnings of architects were $47,710 in 1998. The middle 50 percent earned between $37,380 and $68,920. The lowest 10 percent earned less than $30,030, and the highest 10 percent earned more than $87,460.

According to the American Institute of Architects, the median compensation, including bonuses, for intern-architects in architectural firms was $35,200 in 1999. Licensed architects with 3 to 5 of years experience had median earnings of $41,100; licensed architects with 8 to 10 years of experience, but who were not managers or principals of a firm, earned $54,700. Principals or partners of firms had median earnings of $132,500 in 1999, although partners in some large practices earned considerably more. Similar to other industries, small architectural firms (fewer than five employees) are less likely than larger firms to provide employee benefits.

Earnings of partners in established architectural firms may fluctuate because of changing business conditions. Some architects may have difficulty establishing their own practices and may go through a period when their expenses are greater than their income, requiring substantial financial resources.

Related Occupations

Architects design and construct buildings and related structures. Others who engage in similar work are landscape architects, building contractors, civil engineers, urban planners, interior designers, industrial designers, and graphic designers.

Sources of Additional Information

Information about education and careers in architecture can be obtained from:

- Careers in Architecture Program, The American Institute of Architects, 1735 New York Ave. NW., Washington, DC 20006. Internet: http://www.aiaonline.com

Archivists, Curators, Museum Technicians, and Conservators

(O*NET 31511A, 31511B, 31511C, and 31511D)

Significant Points

- Employment usually requires graduate education and related work experience.

- Keen competition is expected because qualified applicants outnumber the most desirable job openings.

Nature of the Work

Archivists, curators, museum and archives technicians, and conservators search for, acquire, appraise, analyze, describe, arrange, catalogue, restore, preserve, exhibit, maintain, and store valuable items that can be used by researchers or for exhibitions, publications, broadcasting, and other educational programs. Depending on the occupation, these items include historical documents, audiovisual materials, institutional records, works of art, coins, stamps, minerals, clothing, maps, living and preserved plants and animals, buildings, computer records, or historic sites.

Archivists and curators plan and oversee the arrangement, cataloguing, and exhibition of collections and, along with technicians and conservators, maintain collections. Archivists and curators may coordinate educational and public outreach programs, such as tours, workshops, lectures, and classes, and may work with the boards of institutions to administer plans and policies. They also may research topics or items relevant to their collections. Although some duties of archivists and curators are similar, the types of items they deal with differ. Curators usually handle objects found in cultural, biological, or historical collections, such as sculptures, textiles, and paintings, while archivists mainly handle valuable records, documents, or objects that are retained because they originally accompanied and relate specifically to the document.

Archivists determine what portion of the vast amount of records maintained by various organizations, such as government agencies, corporations, or educational institutions, or by families and individuals, should be made part of permanent historical holdings, and which of these records should be put on exhibit. They maintain records in their original arrangement according to the creator's organizational scheme and describe records to facilitate retrieval. Records may be saved on any medium, including paper, film, video tape, audio tape, electronic disk, or computer. They also may be copied onto some other format in order to protect the original and to make them more accessible to researchers who use the records. As computers and various storage media evolve, archivists must keep abreast of technological advances in electronic information storage.

Archives may be part of a library, museum, or historical society, or they may exist as a distinct unit within an organization or company. Archivists consider any medium containing recorded information as documents, including letters, books, and other paper documents, photographs, blueprints, audiovisual materials, and computer records. Any document that reflects organizational transactions, hierarchy, or procedures can be considered a record. Archivists often specialize in an area of history or technology so they can better determine what records in that area qualify for retention and should become part of the archives. Archivists also may work with specialized forms of records, such as manuscripts, electronic records, photographs, cartographic records, motion pictures, and sound recordings.

Computers are increasingly used to generate and maintain archival records. Professional standards for use of computers in handling archival records are still evolving. However, computers are expected to transform many aspects of archival collections as computer capabilities, including multimedia and World Wide Web use, expand and allow more records to be stored and exhibited electronically.

Curators oversee collections in museums, zoos, aquariums, botanical gardens, nature centers, and historic sites. They acquire items through purchases, gifts, field exploration, inter-museum exchanges, or (in the case of some plants and animals) reproduction. Curators also plan and prepare exhibits. In natural history museums, curators collect and observe specimens in their natural habitat. Their work involves describing and classifying species, while specially trained collection managers and technicians provide hands-on care of natural history collections. Most curators use computer databases to catalogue and organize their collections. Many also use the Internet to make information available to other curators and the public. Increasingly, curators are expected to participate in grant writing and fundraising to support their projects.

Most curators specialize in a field, such as botany, art, paleontology, or history. Those working in large institutions may be highly specialized. A large natural history museum, for example, would employ specialists in birds, fishes, insects, and mollusks. Some curators maintain the collection, others do research, and others perform administrative tasks. Registrars, for example, keep track of and move objects in the collection. In small institutions with only one or a few curators, one curator may be responsible for multiple tasks, from maintaining collections to directing the affairs of the museum.

Conservators manage, care for, preserve, treat, and document works of art, artifacts, and specimens. This may require substantial historical, scientific, and archaeological research. They use x-rays, chemical testing, microscopes, special lights, and other laboratory equipment and techniques to examine objects and determine their condition, the need for treatment or restoration, and the appropriate method for preservation. They then document their findings and treat items to minimize deterioration or restore items to their original state. Conservators usually specialize in a particular material or group of objects, such as documents and books, paintings, decorative arts, textiles, metals, or architectural material.

Museum directors formulate policies, plan budgets, and raise funds for their museums. They coordinate activities of their staff to establish and maintain collections. As their role has evolved, mu-

seum directors increasingly need business backgrounds in addition to an understanding of the subject matter of their collections.

Museum technicians assist curators and conservators by performing various preparatory and maintenance tasks on museum items. Some museum technicians may also assist curators with research. Archives technicians help archivists organize, maintain, and provide access to historical documentary materials.

Working Conditions

The working conditions of archivists and curators vary. Some spend most of their time working with the public, providing reference assistance and educational services. Others perform research or process records, which often means working alone or in offices with only a few people. Those who restore and install exhibits or work with bulky, heavy record containers may climb, stretch, or lift. Those in zoos, botanical gardens, and other outdoor museums or historic sites frequently walk great distances.

Curators who work in large institutions may travel extensively to evaluate potential additions to the collection, organize exhibitions, and conduct research in their area of expertise. However, travel is rare for curators employed in small institutions.

Employment

Archivists, curators, museum technicians, and conservators held about 23,000 jobs in 1998. About a quarter were employed in museums, botanical gardens, and zoos, and approximately 2 in 10 worked in educational services, mainly in college and university libraries. More than one-third worked in Federal, State, and local government. Most Federal archivists work for the National Archives and Records Administration; others manage military archives in the Department of Defense. Most Federal government curators work at the Smithsonian Institute, in the military museums of the Department of Defense, and in archaeological and other museums managed by the Department of Interior. All State governments have archival or historical records sections employing archivists. State and local governments have numerous historical museums, parks, libraries, and zoos employing curators.

Some large corporations have archives or records centers, employing archivists to manage the growing volume of records created or maintained as required by law or necessary to the firms' operations. Religious and fraternal organizations, professional associations, conservation organizations, major private collectors, and research firms also employ archivists and curators.

Conservators may work under contract to treat particular items, rather than as a regular employee of a museum or other institution. These conservators may work on their own as private contractors, or as employees of conservation laboratories or regional conservation centers that contract their services to museums.

Training, Other Qualifications, and Advancement

Employment as an archivist, conservator, or curator usually requires graduate education and related work experience. Many archivists

and curators work in archives or museums while completing their formal education, to gain the "hands-on" experience that many employers seek when hiring.

Employers usually look for archivists with undergraduate and graduate degrees in history or library science who have courses in archival science. Some positions may require knowledge of the discipline related to the collection, such as business or medicine. An increasing number of archivists have a double master's degree in history and library science. Currently no programs offer bachelor's or master's degrees in archival science. However, approximately 65 colleges and universities offer courses or practical training in archival science as part of history, library science, or another discipline. The Academy of Certified Archivists offers voluntary certification for archivists. Certification requires the applicant to have experience in the field and to pass an examination offered by the Academy.

Archivists need research and analytical ability to understand the content of documents and the context in which they were created and to decipher deteriorated or poor quality printed matter, handwritten manuscripts, or photographs and films. A background in preservation management is often required of archivists because they are responsible for taking proper care of their records. Archivists also must be able to organize large amounts of information and write clear instructions for its retrieval and use. In addition, computer skills and the ability to work with electronic records and databases are increasingly important.

Many archives are very small, including one-person shops, with limited promotion opportunities. Archivists typically advance by transferring to a larger unit with supervisory positions. A doctorate in history, library science, or a related field may be needed for some advanced positions, such as director of a State archive.

For employment as a curator, most museums require a master's degree in an appropriate discipline of the museum's specialty—art, history, or archaeology—or museum studies. Many employers prefer a doctoral degree, particularly for curators in natural history or science museums. Earning two graduate degrees—in museum studies (museology) and a specialized subject—gives a candidate a distinct advantage in this competitive job market. In small museums, curatorial positions may be available to individuals with a bachelor's degree. For some positions, an internship of full-time museum work supplemented by courses in museum practices is needed.

Curatorial positions often require knowledge in a number of fields. For historic and artistic conservation, courses in chemistry, physics, and art are desirable. Because curators—particularly those in small museums—may have administrative and managerial responsibilities, courses in business administration, public relations, marketing, and fundraising also are recommended. Similar to archivists, curators need computer skills and the ability to work with electronic databases. Curators also need to be familiar with digital imaging, scanning technology, and copyright infringement, because many are responsible for posting information on the Internet.

Curators must be flexible because of their wide variety of duties. They need to design and present exhibits and, in small museums, they need the manual dexterity to build exhibits or restore objects. Leadership ability and business skills are important for museum directors, and marketing skills are valuable for increasing museum attendance and fundraising.

In large museums, curators may advance through several levels of responsibility, eventually to museum director. Curators in smaller museums often advance to larger ones. Individual research and publications are important for advancement in larger institutions.

Museum technicians usually need a bachelor's degree in an appropriate discipline of the museum's specialty, museum studies training, or previous museum work experience, particularly in exhibit design. Similarly, archives technicians usually need a bachelor's degree in library science or history, or relevant work experience. Technician positions often serve as a stepping stone for individuals interested in archival and curatorial work. With the exception of small museums, a master's degree is needed for advancement.

When hiring conservators, employers look for a master's degree in conservation or a closely related field, as well as substantial experience. There are only a few graduate programs in museum conservation techniques in the United States. Competition for entry to these programs is keen; to qualify, a student must have a background in chemistry, archaeology or studio art, and art history, as well as work experience. For some programs, knowledge of a foreign language is also helpful. Conservation apprenticeships or internships as an undergraduate can also enhance one's admission prospects. Graduate programs last two to four years; the latter years include internship training. A few individuals enter conservation through apprenticeships with museums, nonprofit organizations, and conservators in private practice. Apprenticeships should be supplemented with courses in chemistry, studio art, and history. Apprenticeship training, although accepted, usually is a more difficult route into the conservation profession.

Relatively few schools grant a bachelor's degree in museum studies. More common are undergraduate minors or tracks of study that are part of an undergraduate degree in a related field, such as art history, history, or archaeology. Students interested in further study may obtain a master's degree in museum studies. Colleges and universities throughout the country offer master's degrees in museum studies. However, many employers feel that, while museum studies are helpful, a thorough knowledge of the museum's specialty and museum work experience are more important.

Continuing education, which enables archivists, curators, conservators, and museum technicians to keep up with developments in the field, is available through meetings, conferences, and workshops sponsored by archival, historical, and museum associations. Some larger organizations, such as the National Archives, offer such training in-house.

Job Outlook

Competition for jobs as archivists, curators, museum technicians, and conservators is expected to be keen because qualified applicants outnumber job openings. Graduates with highly specialized training, such as master's degrees in both library science and history, with a concentration in archives or records management, and extensive computer skills should have the best opportunities for jobs as archivists. A curator job is attractive to many people, and many applicants have the necessary training and subject knowledge; but there are only a few openings. Consequently, candidates may have to work part time, as an intern, or even as a volunteer assistant curator or research associate after completing their formal education. Substantial work experience in collection manage-

ment, exhibit design, or restoration, as well as database management skills, will be necessary for permanent status. Job opportunities for curators should be best in art and history museums, which are the largest employers in the museum industry.

The job outlook for conservators may be more favorable, particularly for graduates of conservation programs. However, competition is stiff for the limited number of openings in these programs, and applicants need a technical background. Students who qualify and successfully complete the program, have knowledge of a foreign language, and are willing to relocate, will have an advantage over less qualified candidates.

Employment of archivists, curators, museum technicians, and conservators is expected to increase about as fast as the average for all occupations through 2008. Jobs are expected to grow as public and private organizations emphasize establishing archives and organizing records and information, and as public interest in science, art, history, and technology increases. However, museums and other cultural institutions are often subject to funding cuts during recessions or periods of budget tightening, reducing demand for archivists and curators during these times. Although the rate of turnover among archivists and curators is relatively low, the need to replace workers who leave the occupation or stop working will create some additional job openings.

Earnings

Median annual earnings of archivists, curators, museum technicians, and conservators in 1998 were $31,750. The middle 50 percent earned between $23,090 and $43,840. The lowest 10 percent earned less than $16,340, and the highest 10 percent earned more than $63,580. Median annual earnings of archivists, curators, museum technicians, and conservators in 1997 were $28,400 in museums and art galleries.

Earnings of archivists and curators vary considerably by type and size of employer, and often by specialty. Average salaries in the Federal government, for example, are usually higher than those in religious organizations. Salaries of curators in large, well-funded museums can be several times higher than those in small ones.

The average annual salary for all museum curators in the Federal government in nonsupervisory, supervisory, and managerial positions was about $59,200 in 1999. Archivists averaged $57,500; museum specialists and technicians, $40,400; and archives technicians, $40,000.

Related Occupations

The skills that archivists, curators, museum technicians, and conservators use to preserve, organize, and display objects or information of historical interest are shared by anthropologists, arborists, archaeologists, botanists, ethnologists, folklorists, genealogists, historians, horticulturists, information specialists, librarians, paintings restorers, records managers, and zoologists.

Sources of Additional Information

For information on archivists and on schools offering courses in archival studies, contact:

● Society of American Archivists, 527 South Wells St., 5th floor, Chicago, IL 60607-3922. Internet: http://www.archivists.org

For general information about careers as a curator and schools offering courses in museum studies, contact:

● American Association of Museums, 1575 I St. NW., Suite 400, Washington, DC 20005. Internet: http://www.aam-us.org

For information about conservation and preservation careers and education programs, contact:

● American Institute for Conservation of Historic and Artistic Works, 1717 K St. NW., Suite 301, Washington, DC 20006. Internet: http://palimpsest.stanford.edu/aic

Armed Forces

(O*NET 99003)

Significant Points

● Opportunities should be good in all branches of the Armed Forces for applicants who meet designated standards.

● Enlisted personnel need at least a high school diploma; officers need a bachelor's or advanced degree.

● Hours and working conditions can be arduous and vary substantially.

● Some training and duty assignments are hazardous, even in peacetime.

Nature of the Work

Maintaining a strong national defense encompasses such diverse activities as running a hospital, commanding a tank, programming computers, operating a nuclear reactor, and repairing and maintaining a helicopter. The military provides training and work experience in these fields and many others for more than 1.2 million people who serve in the active Army, Navy, Marine Corps, Air Force, and Coast Guard, their Reserve components, and the Air and Army National Guard.

The military distinguishes between enlisted and officer careers. Enlisted personnel comprise about 85 percent of the Armed Forces and carry out the fundamental operations of the military in areas such as combat, administration, construction, engineering, health care, and human resources. Officers, who make up the remaining 15 percent of the Armed Forces, are the leaders of the military. They supervise and manage activities in every occupational specialty in the military.

The following sections discuss the major occupational groups for enlisted personnel and officers.

Enlisted occupational groups:

Administrative careers include a wide variety of positions. The military must keep accurate information for planning and managing its operations. Paper and electronic records are kept on equipment, funds, personnel, supplies, and other property of the military. Enlisted administrative personnel record information, type reports, and maintain files to assist military offices. Personnel may work in a specialized area such as finance, accounting, legal, maintenance, or supply.

Combat specialty occupations refer to those enlisted specialties, such as infantry, artillery, and special forces, that operate weapons or execute special missions during combat situations. They normally specialize by the type of weapon system or combat operation. These personnel maneuver against enemy forces, and they position and fire artillery, guns, and missiles to destroy enemy positions. They may also operate tanks and amphibious assault vehicles in combat or scouting missions. When the military has difficult and dangerous missions to perform, they call upon special operations teams. These elite combat forces stay in a constant state of readiness to strike anywhere in the world on a moment's notice. Special operations forces team members conduct offensive raids, demolitions, intelligence, search and rescue, and other missions from aboard aircraft, helicopters, ships, or submarines.

Construction occupations in the military include personnel who build or repair buildings, airfields, bridges, foundations, dams, bunkers, and the electrical and plumbing components of these structures. Enlisted personnel in construction occupations operate bulldozers, cranes, graders, and other heavy equipment. Construction specialists may also work with engineers and other building specialists as part of military construction teams. Some personnel specialize in areas such as plumbing or electrical wiring. Plumbers and pipe fitters install and repair the plumbing and pipe systems needed in buildings, on aircraft, and on ships. Building electricians install and repair electrical wiring systems in offices, airplane hangars, and other buildings on military bases.

Electronic and electrical equipment repair personnel repair and maintain electronic and electrical equipment used in the military today. Repairers normally specialize by type of equipment being repaired, such as avionics, computer, communications, or weapons systems. For example, avionics technicians install, test, maintain, and repair a wide variety of electronic systems including navigational and communications equipment on aircraft. Weapons maintenance technicians maintain and repair weapons used by combat forces, most of which have electronic components and systems that assist in locating targets, aiming weapons, and firing them.

The military has many *engineering, science, and technical* occupations that require specific knowledge to operate technical equipment, solve complex problems or to provide and interpret information. Enlisted personnel normally specialize in an area such as information technology, space operations, environmental health and safety, or intelligence. Information technology specialists, for example, develop software programs and operate computer systems. Space operations specialists use and repair spacecraft ground control command equipment, including electronic systems that track spacecraft location and operation. Environmental health and safety specialists inspect military facilities and food supplies for the presence of disease, germs, or other conditions hazardous to health and the environment. Intelligence specialists gather and study information using aerial photographs and various types of radar and surveillance systems.

Health care personnel assist medical professionals in treating and providing services for patients. They may work as part of a patient service team in close contact with doctors, dentists, nurses, and physical therapists to provide the necessary support functions within a hospital or clinic. Health care specialists normally specialize in a particular area. They may provide emergency medical treatment, operate diagnostic equipment such as x-ray and ultrasound equipment, conduct laboratory tests on tissue and blood samples, maintain pharmacy supplies, or maintain patient records.

Human resource development specialists recruit and place qualified personnel and provide the training programs necessary to help people perform their jobs effectively. Personnel in this career area normally specialize by activity. Recruiting specialists, for example, provide information about military careers to young people, parents, schools, and local communities. They explain service employment and training opportunities, pay and benefits, and the nature of service life. Personnel specialists collect and store information about people's careers in the military, including training, job assignment, promotion, and health information. Training specialists and instructors provide military personnel with the knowledge needed to perform their jobs.

Machine operator and production careers include occupations that require the operation of industrial equipment, machinery, and tools to fabricate and repair parts for a variety of items and structures. They may operate boilers, turbines, nuclear reactors, and portable generators aboard ships and submarines. Personnel often specialize by type of work performed. Welders, for instance, work with various types of metals to repair or form the structural parts of ships, submarines, buildings, or other equipment. Other specialists inspect, maintain, and repair survival equipment such as parachutes and aircraft life support equipment.

Media and public affairs careers include those occupations that are involved in the public presentation and interpretation of military information and events. Enlisted media and public affairs personnel take and develop photographs; film, record, and edit audio and video programs; present news and music programs; and produce graphic artwork, drawings, and other visual displays. Other public affairs specialists act as interpreters and translators to convert written or spoken foreign languages into English or other languages.

Protective service personnel enforce military laws and regulations and provide emergency response to natural and man-made disasters. Personnel normally specialize by function. Specialists in emergency management implement response procedures for all types of disasters, such as floods, earthquakes, hurricanes, or enemy attack. Military police control traffic, prevent crime, and respond to emergencies. Other law enforcement and security specialists investigate crimes committed on military property and guard inmates in military correctional facilities. Firefighters put out, control, and help prevent fires in buildings, aircraft, and aboard ships.

Support services occupations include subsistence services and occupations that support the morale and well-being of military personnel and their families. Food service specialists prepare all types of food in dining halls, hospitals, and ships. Counselors help military personnel and their families to overcome social problems. They work as part of a team that may include social workers, psychologists, medical officers, chaplains, personnel specialists, and commanders. The military also provides chaplains and religious program specialists to help meet the spiritual needs of its personnel. Religious program specialists assist chaplains with religious services, religious education programs, and administrative duties.

Transportation and material handling specialists ensure the safe transport of people and cargo. Most personnel within this occupational group are classified according to mode of transportation (i.e. aircraft, automotive vehicle, or ship). Air crew members operate equipment on board aircraft during operations. Vehicle drivers operate all types of heavy military vehicles including fuel or water tank trucks, semi-tractor trailers, heavy troop transports, and passenger buses. Boat operators navigate and pilot many types of small water craft, including tugboats, gunboats, and barges. Cargo specialists load and unload military supplies and material using equipment such as forklifts and cranes.

Vehicle and machinery mechanics conduct preventive and corrective maintenance on aircraft, automotive and heavy equipment, heating and cooling systems, marine engines, and powerhouse station equipment. They typically specialize by the type of equipment they maintain. Aircraft mechanics inspect, service, and repair helicopters and airplanes. Automotive and heavy equipment mechanics maintain and repair vehicles such as jeeps, cars, trucks, tanks, self-propelled missile launchers, and other combat vehicles. They also repair bulldozers, power shovels, and other construction equipment. Heating and cooling mechanics install and repair air conditioning, refrigeration, and heating equipment. Marine engine mechanics repair and maintain gasoline and diesel engines on ships, boats, and other water craft. They also repair shipboard mechanical and electrical equipment. Powerhouse mechanics install, maintain, and repair electrical and mechanical equipment in power-generating stations.

Officer occupational groups:

Combat specialty officers plan and direct military operations, oversee combat activities, and serve as combat leaders. This category includes officers in charge of tanks and other armored assault vehicles, artillery systems, special forces, and infantry. They normally specialize by type of unit that they lead. Within the unit, they may specialize by the type of weapon system. Artillery and missile system officers, for example, direct personnel as they target, launch, test, and maintain various types of missiles and artillery. Special forces officers lead their units in offensive raids, demolitions, intelligence gathering, and search and rescue missions.

Engineering, science, and technical officers have a wide range of responsibilities based on their area of expertise. They lead or perform activities in areas such as information technology, environmental health and safety, and engineering. These officers may direct the operations of communications centers or the development of complex computer systems. Environmental health and safety officers study the air, ground, and water to identify and analyze sources of pollution and its effects. They also direct programs to control safety and health hazards in the workplace. Other personnel work as aerospace engineers to design and direct the development of military aircraft, missiles, and spacecraft.

Executive, administrative, and managerial officers oversee and direct military activities in key functional areas such as finance, accounting, health administration, logistics, and supply. Health services administrators, for instance, are responsible for the overall quality of care provided at the hospitals and clinics they operate. They

must ensure that each department works together to provide the highest quality of care. As another example, the military buys billions of dollars worth of equipment, supplies, and services from private industry each year. Purchasing and contracting managers negotiate and monitor contracts for purchasing equipment, materials, and services.

Health care officers provide health services at military facilities based on their area of specialization. Officers who examine, diagnose, and treat patients with illness, injury, or disease include physicians, registered nurses, and dentists. Other health care officers provide therapy, rehabilitative treatment, and other services for patients. Physical and occupational therapists plan and administer therapy to help patients adjust to disabilities, regain independence, and return to work. Speech therapists evaluate and treat patients with hearing and speech problems. Dietitians manage food service facilities and plan meals for hospital patients and outpatients who need special diets. Pharmacists manage the purchasing, storing, and dispensing of drugs and medicines.

Human resource development officers manage recruitment, placement, and training strategies and programs in the military. Personnel in this area normally specialize by activity. Recruiting managers direct recruiting efforts and provide information about military careers to young people, parents, schools, and local communities. Personnel managers direct military personnel functions such as job assignment, staff promotion, and career counseling. Training and education directors identify training needs and develop and manage educational programs designed to keep military personnel current in the skills they need to perform their jobs.

Support services officers include personnel who manage food service activities and perform services in support of the morale and well being of military personnel and their families. Food service managers oversee the preparation and delivery of food services within dining facilities located on military installations and vessels. Social workers focus on improving conditions that cause social problems, such as drug and alcohol abuse, racism, and sexism. Chaplains conduct worship services for military personnel and perform other spiritual duties covering beliefs and practices of all religious faiths.

Media and public affairs officers oversee the development, production, and presentation of information or events for the public. These officers may produce and direct motion pictures, videotapes, and TV and radio broadcasts that are used for training, news, and entertainment. Some plan, develop, and direct the activities of military bands. Public affairs officers respond to inquiries about military activities and prepare news releases and reports to keep the public informed.

Protective service officers are responsible for the safety and protection of individuals and property on military bases and vessels. Emergency management officers plan and prepare for all types of natural and man-made disasters. They develop warning, control, and evacuation plans to be used in the event of a disaster. Law enforcement and security officers enforce applicable laws on military bases and investigate crimes when the law has been transgressed.

Officers in *transportation* occupations manage and perform activities related to the safe transport of military personnel and material by air, road, rail, and water. Officers normally specialize by mode of transportation or area of expertise because, in many cases, there are licensing and certification requirements. Pilots in the military fly various types of specialized airplanes and helicopters to carry troops and equipment and execute combat missions. Navigators use radar, radio, and other navigation equipment to determine their positions and plan their routes of travel. Officers on ships and submarines work as a team to manage the various departments aboard their vessels. Transportation officers must also direct the maintenance of transportation equipment.

Employment

In 1999, more than 1.2 million individuals were on active duty in the Armed Forces—about 445,000 in the Army, 272,000 in the Navy, 343,000 in the Air Force, 143,000 in the Marine Corps, and 26,000 in the Coast Guard. Table 1 shows the occupational composition of enlisted personnel in 1999; table 2 presents similar information for officer personnel.

TABLE 1
Military enlisted personnel by broad occupational category and branch of military service, 1999

Occupational Group—Enlisted	Army	Air Force	Coast Guard	Marine Corps	Navy	Total, all services
Administrative occupations	17,124	16,599	1,834	11,078	13,569	60,204
Combat specialty occupations	105,811	214	—	30,009	1,926	137,960
Construction occupations	4,214	5,732	2,181	3,972	2,775	18,874
Electronic and electrical repair occupations	25,431	51,900	3,075	12,876	43,879	137,161
Engineering, science, and technical occupations	39,362	47,091	2,193	15,705	34,726	139,077
Health care occupations	28,933	21,770	688	0[1]	23,090	74,481
Support services occupations	12,994	7,210	1,158	3,109	8,654	33,125
Machine operator and precision work occupations	2,295	7,066	1,501	1,940	18,807	31,609
Media and public affairs occupations	8,001	6,393	125	1,831	2,985	19,335
Protective service occupations	24,562	18,602	180	6,315	7,038	56,697

Occupational Group—Enlisted	Army	Air Force	Coast Guard	Marine Corps	Navy	Total, all services
Transportation and material handling occupations..............	53,556	31,582	4,244	27,876	28,524	145,782
Vehicle machinery mechanic occupations	46,783	47,807	2,392	15,796	39,541	152,319
Human resource development occupations	14,504	10,376	348	1,672	12,459	39,359
Total, by service[2]	383,570	272,342	19,919	132,179	237,973	1,045,983

[1] The Marine Corps employs no medical personnel. Their medical services are provided by the Navy.
[2] Sum of individual items may not equal totals because personnel on temporary assignment are not included in these occupational classifications.
SOURCE: U.S. Department of Defense, Defense Manpower Data Center East

TABLE 2
Military officer personnel by broad occupational category and branch of service, 1999

Occupational Group—Officer	Army	Air Force	Coast Guard	Marine Corps	Navy	Total, all services
Combat specialty occupations	19,470	5,951	42	1,102	2,232	28,797
Engineering, science, and technical occupations	16,106	15,840	1,392	1,706	7,924	42,968
Executive, administrative, and managerial occupations	8,259	8,905	349	1,290	6,321	25,124
Health care occupations	11,055	11,073	8	0[1]	7,332	29,468
Support services occupations	1,211	1,636	—	45	1,155	4,047
Media and public affairs occupations	50	1,570	18	142	335	2,115
Protective service occupations	1,671	1,446	374	330	786	4,607
Transportation occupations	1,851	19,890	3,341	5,017	13,140	43,239
Human resource development occupations	1,256	4,093	265	1,673	4,136	11,423
Total, by service[2]	60,929	70,404	5,789	11,305	43,361	191,788
Total (Enlisted and Officer)[2]	444,499	342,746	25,708	143,484	281,334	1,237,771

[1] The Marine Corps employs no medical personnel. Their medical services are provided by the Navy.
[2] Sum of individual items may not equal totals because personnel on temporary assignment are not included in these occupational classifications.
SOURCE: U.S. Department of Defense, Defense Manpower Data Center East

Military personnel are stationed throughout the United States and in many countries around the world. More than one-third of military jobs are located in California, Texas, North Carolina, and Virginia. About 258,000 individuals were stationed outside the United States in 1998, including those assigned to ships at sea. More than 116,000 of these were stationed in Europe, mainly in Germany, and another 96,000 were assigned to East Asia and the Pacific area, mostly in Japan and the Republic of Korea.

Training, Other Qualifications, and Advancement

Enlisted personnel. In order to join the services, enlisted personnel must sign a legal agreement called an enlistment contract, which usually involves a commitment to eight years of service. Depending on the terms of the contract, two to six years are spent on active duty, and the balance are spent in the reserves. The enlistment contract obligates the service to provide the agreed-upon job, rating, pay, cash bonuses for enlistment in certain occupations, medical and other benefits, occupational training, and continuing education. In return, enlisted personnel must serve satisfactorily for the specified period of time.

Requirements for each service vary, but certain qualifications for enlistment are common to all branches. In order to enlist, one must be between the ages of 17 and 35, be a U.S. citizen or immigrant alien holding permanent resident status, not have a felony record, and possess a birth certificate. Applicants who are 17 must have the consent of a parent or legal guardian before entering the service. Air Force enlisted personnel must enter active duty before their 28th birthday. Applicants must pass both a written examination—the Armed Services Vocational Aptitude Battery—and meet certain minimum physical standards such as height, weight, vision, and overall health. All branches require high school graduation or its equivalent for certain enlistment options. In 1999, more than 9 out of 10 volunteers were high school graduates. Single parents are generally not eligible to enlist.

People thinking about enlisting in the military should learn as much as they can about military life before making a decision. This is especially important if you are thinking about making the military a career. Speaking to friends and relatives with military experience is a good idea. Determine what the military can offer you and what it will expect in return. Then talk to a recruiter, who can determine if you qualify for enlistment, explain the various enlistment options, and tell you which military occupational specialties currently have openings. Bear in mind that the recruiter's job is to recruit promising applicants into their branch of military service, so the information he or she gives you is likely to stress the positive aspects of military life in the branch in which the recruiter serves.

Ask the recruiter for the branch you have chosen to assess your chances of being accepted for training in the occupation or occupations of your choice, or, better still, take the aptitude exam to see how well you score. The military uses the aptitude exam as a placement exam, and test scores largely determine an individual's chances of being accepted into a particular training program. Selection for a particular type of training depends on the needs of the service, your general and technical aptitudes, and your personal preference. Because all prospective recruits are required to take the exam, those who do so before committing themselves to enlist have the advantage of knowing in advance whether they stand a good chance of being accepted for training in a particular specialty. The recruiter can schedule you for the Armed Services Vocational Aptitude Battery without any obligation. Many high schools offer the exam as an easy way for students to explore the possibility of a military career, and the test also provides insight into career areas where the student has demonstrated aptitudes and interests.

If you decide to join the military, the next step is to pass the physical examination and sign an enlistment contract. This involves choosing, qualifying, and agreeing on a number of enlistment options such as length of active duty time, which may vary according to the enlistment option. Most active duty programs have enlistment options ranging from three to six years, although there are some two-year programs. The contract will also state the date of enlistment and other options such as bonuses and types of training to be received. If the service is unable to fulfill its part of the contract, such as providing a certain kind of training, the contract may become null and void.

All services offer a "delayed entry program" by which an individual can delay entry into active duty for up to one year after enlisting. High school students can enlist during their senior year and enter a service after graduation. Others choose this program because the job training they desire is not currently available but will be within the coming year or because they need time to arrange personal affairs.

Women are eligible to enter most military specialties. Although many women serve in medical and administrative support positions, women also work as mechanics, missile maintenance technicians, heavy equipment operators, fighter pilots, and intelligence officers. Only occupations involving direct exposure to combat are excluded.

People planning to apply the skills gained through military training to a civilian career should first determine how good the prospects are for civilian employment in jobs related to the military specialty that interests them. Second, they should know the prerequisites for the related civilian job. Many occupations require a license, certification, or minimum level of education. In such cases, it is important to determine whether military training is sufficient

to enter the civilian equivalent and, if not, what additional training will be required. Such information often can be obtained from school counselors.

Following enlistment, new members of the Armed Forces undergo recruit training, which is better known as "basic" training. Recruit training provides a 6- to 11-week introduction to military life with courses in military skills and protocol. Days and nights are carefully structured and include rigorous physical exercises designed to improve strength and endurance and build unit cohesion.

Following basic training, most recruits take additional training at technical schools that prepare them for a particular military occupational specialty. The formal training period generally lasts from 10 to 20 weeks, although training for certain occupations—nuclear power plant operator, for example—may take as long as a year. Recruits not assigned to classroom instruction receive on-the-job training at their first duty assignment.

Many service people get college credit for the technical training they receive on duty, which, combined with off-duty courses, can lead to an associate's degree through community college programs such as the Community College of the Air Force. In addition to on-duty training, military personnel may choose from a variety of educational programs. Most military installations have tuition assistance programs for people wishing to take courses during off-duty hours. These may be correspondence courses or degree programs offered by local colleges or universities. Tuition assistance pays up to 75 percent of college costs. Also available are courses designed to help service personnel earn high school equivalency diplomas. Each service branch provides opportunities for full-time study to a limited number of exceptional applicants. Military personnel accepted into these highly competitive programs receive full pay, allowances, tuition, and related fees. In return, they must agree to serve an additional amount of time in the service. Other very selective programs enable enlisted personnel to qualify as commissioned officers through additional military training.

Warrant officers. Warrant officers are technical and tactical leaders who specialize in a specific technical area; for example, one group of warrant officers is Army aviators. The Army Warrant Officer Corps comprises less than 3 percent of the total Army. Although small in size, their level of responsibility is high. They receive extended career opportunities, worldwide leadership assignments, and increased pay and retirement benefits. Selection to attend the Warrant Officer Candidate School is highly competitive and restricted to those with the rank of E5 or higher (see table 3).

Officers. Officer training in the Armed Forces is provided through the Federal service academies (Military, Naval, Air Force, and Coast Guard); the Reserve Officers Training Corps (ROTC) offered at many colleges and universities; Officer Candidate School (OCS) or Officer Training School (OTS); the National Guard (State Officer Candidate School programs); the Uniformed Services University of Health Sciences; and other programs. All are very selective and are good options for those wishing to make the military a career.

Federal service academies provide a four-year college program leading to a Bachelor of Science degree. Midshipmen or cadets are provided free room and board, tuition, medical care, and a monthly allowance. Graduates receive regular or reserve commissions and have a five-year active duty obligation, or longer if entering flight training.

To become a candidate for appointment as a cadet or midshipman in one of the service academies, most applicants obtain a nomination from an authorized source (usually a member of Congress). Candidates do not need to know a member of Congress personally to request a nomination. Nominees must have an academic record of the requisite quality, college aptitude test scores above an established minimum, and recommendations from teachers or school officials; they must also pass a medical examination. Appointments are made from the list of eligible nominees. Appointments to the Coast Guard Academy, however, are made strictly on a competitive basis. A nomination is not required.

ROTC programs train students in about 950 Army, 60 Navy and Marine Corps, and 550 Air Force units at participating colleges and universities. Trainees take two to five hours of military instruction a week in addition to regular college courses. After graduation, they may serve as officers on active duty for a stipulated period of time. Some may serve their obligation in the Reserves or Guard. In the last two years of a ROTC program, students receive a monthly allowance while attending school and additional pay for summer training. ROTC scholarships for two, three, and four years are available on a competitive basis. All scholarships pay for tuition and have allowances for subsistence, textbooks, supplies, and other fees.

College graduates can earn a commission in the Armed Forces through OCS or OTS programs in the Army, Navy, Air Force, Marine Corps, Coast Guard, and National Guard. These officers generally must serve their obligation on active duty. Those with training in certain health professions may qualify for direct appointment as officers. In the case of health professions students, financial assistance and internship opportunities are available from the military in return for specified periods of military service. Prospective medical students can apply to the Uniformed Services University of Health Sciences, which offers free tuition in a program leading to a Doctor of Medicine (M.D.) degree. In return, graduates must serve for seven years in either the military or the Public Health Service. Direct appointments also are available for those qualified to serve in other special duties, such as the judge advocate general (legal) or chaplain corps. Flight training is available to commissioned officers in each branch of the Armed Forces. In addition, the Army has a direct enlistment option to become a warrant officer aviator.

Each service has different criteria for promoting personnel. Generally, the first few promotions for both enlisted and officer personnel come easily; subsequent promotions are much more competitive. Criteria for promotion may include time in service and grade, job performance, a fitness report (supervisor's recommendation), and written examinations. People who are passed over for promotion several times generally must leave the military. The following table shows the officer, warrant officer, and enlisted ranks by service.

TABLE 3
Military rank and employment for active duty personnel, March 1999

Grade	Rank and title				
	Army	**Navy and Coast Guard**	**Air Force**	**Marine Corps**	**Total DOD Employment**
Commissioned officers:					
O-10	General	Admiral	General	General	38
O-9	Lieutenant General	Vice Admiral	Lieutenant General	Lieutenant General	114
O-8	Major General	Rear Admiral Upper	Major General	Major General	287
O-7	Brigadier General	Rear Admiral Lower	Brigadier General	Brigadier General	446
O-6	Colonel	Captain	Colonel	Colonel	11,423
O-5	Lieutenant Colonel	Commander	Lieutenant Colonel	Lieutenant Colonel	28,428
O-4	Major	Lieutenant Commander	Major	Major	43,027
O-3	Captain	Lieutenant	Captain	Captain	69,358
O-2	1st Lieutenant	Lieutenant (JG)	1st Lieutenant	1st Lieutenant	28,096
O-1	2nd Lieutenant	Ensign	2nd Lieutenant	2nd Lieutenant	22,038
Warrant officers:					
W-5	Chief Warrant Officer	Chief Warrant Officer	—	Chief Warrant Officer	459
W-4	Chief Warrant Officer	Chief Warrant Officer	—	Chief Warrant Officer	2,123
W-3	Chief Warrant Officer	Chief Warrant Officer	—	Chief Warrant Officer	4,019
W-2	Chief Warrant Officer	Chief Warrant Officer	—	Chief Warrant Officer	6,455
W-1	Warrant Officer	Warrant Officer	—	Warrant Officer	2,402

(continues)

	Army	Navy and Coast Guard	Air Force	Marine Corps	Total DOD Employment
Enlisted personnel:					
E-9	Sergeant Major	Master Chief Petty Officer	Chief Master Sergeant	Sergeant Major	10,241
E-8	1st Sergeant/Master Sergeant	Sr. Chief Petty Officer	Senior Master Sergeant	Master Sergeant/1st Sergeant	26,014
E-7	Sergeant First Class	Chief Petty Officer	Master Sergeant	Gunnery Sergeant	99,201
E-6	Staff Sergeant	Petty Officer 1st Class	Technical Sergeant	Staff Sergeant	163,075
E-5	Sergeant	Petty Officer 2nd Class	Staff Sergeant	Sergeant	232,854
E-4	Corporal/Specialist	Petty Officer 3rd Class	Senior Airman	Corporal	264,757
E-3	Private First Class	Seaman	Airman 1st Class	Lance Corporal	186,647
E-2	Private	Seaman Apprentice	Airman	Private 1st Class	98,115
E-1	Private	Seaman Recruit	Airman Basic	Private	57,961

SOURCE: U.S. Department of Defense

Job Outlook

Opportunities should be good for qualified individuals in all branches of the Armed Forces through 2008. Many military personnel retire after 20 years of service with a pension while still young enough to start a new career. About 365,000 enlisted personnel and officers must be recruited each year to replace those who complete their commitment or retire. Since the end of the draft in 1973, the military has met its personnel requirements through volunteers. When the economy is good, it is more difficult for all the services to meet their quotas; it is much easier to do so in times of recession.

America's strategic position is stronger than it has been in decades. Although there were reductions in personnel due to the reduction in the threat from Eastern Europe and Russia, the number of active duty personnel is now expected to remain about constant through 2008. The Armed Forces' goal is to maintain a sufficient force to fight and win two major regional conflicts occurring at the same time. Political events, however, could cause these plans to change.

Educational requirements will continue to rise as military jobs become more technical and complex. High school graduates and applicants with a college background will be sought to fill the ranks of enlisted personnel, while virtually all officers will need at least a bachelor's degree and, in some cases, an advanced degree as well.

Earnings

The earnings structure for military personnel are shown in table 4. Most enlisted personnel started as recruits at Grade E-1 in 1999; however, those with special skills or above-average education started as high as Grade E-4. Most warrant officers started at Grade W-1 or W-2, depending upon their occupational and academic qualifications and the branch of service, but these individuals all had previous military service, and this is not an entry-level occupation. Most commissioned officers started at Grade O-1, while some highly trained officers (for example, physicians, engineers, and scientists) started as high as Grade O-3 or O-4.

In addition to basic pay, military personnel receive free room and board (or a tax-free housing and subsistence allowance), medical and dental care, a military clothing allowance, military supermarket and department store shopping privileges, 30 days of paid vacation a year (referred to as leave), and travel opportunities. Other allowances are paid for foreign duty, hazardous duty, submarine and flight duty, and employment as a medical officer. Athletic and other recreational facilities such as libraries, gymnasiums, tennis courts, golf courses, bowling centers, and movies are available on many military installations. Military personnel are eligible for retirement benefits after 20 years of service.

The Veterans Administration (VA) provides numerous benefits to those who have served at least two years in the Armed Forces. Veterans are eligible for free care in VA hospitals for all service-related disabilities regardless of time served; those with other medical problems are eligible for free VA care if they are unable to pay the cost of hospitalization elsewhere. Admission to a VA medical center depends on the availability of beds, however. Veterans are also eligible for certain loans, including home loans. Veterans, regardless of health, can convert a military life insurance policy to an individual policy with any participating company in the veteran's State of residence. In addition, job counseling, testing, and placement services are available.

Veterans who participate in the New Montgomery GI Bill Program receive educational benefits. Under this program, Armed Forces personnel may elect to deduct from their pay up to $100 a month to put toward their future education for the first 12 months of active duty. Veterans who serve on active duty for three years or more, or two years active duty plus four years in the Selected Reserve or National Guard, will receive $427.87 a month in basic benefits for 36 months. Those who enlist and serve for less than three years will receive $347.65 a month. In addition, each service provides its own additional contributions for future education. This sum becomes the service member's educational fund. Upon separation from active duty, the fund can be used to finance educational costs at any VA-approved institution. VA-approved schools include many vocational, correspondence, business, technical, and flight training schools; community and junior colleges; and colleges and universities.

TABLE 4
Military basic monthly pay by grade for active duty personnel, January 1, 1999

Grade	Years of service					
	Less than 2	Over 4	Over 8	Over 12	Over 16	Over 20
O-9	6,947.10	7,281.00	7,466.10	7,776.90	8,425.80	8,892.60
O-8	6,292.20	6,634.50	7,129.20	7,466.10	7,776.90	8,425.80
O-7	5,228.40	5,583.90	5,834.40	6,172.50	7,129.20	7,619.70
O-6	3,875.10	4,536.60	4,536.60	4,536.60	5,432.40	5,834.40
O-5	3,099.60	3,891.00	3,891.00	4,224.30	4,845.00	5,277.90
O-4	2,612.40	3,393.30	3,608.70	4,071.90	4,444.80	4,566.60
O-3	2,427.60	3,210.60	3,484.80	3,855.30	3,949.50	3,949.50
O-2	2,117.10	2,871.30	2,930.40	2,930.40	2,930.40	2,930.40
O-1	1,838.10	2,312.10	2,312.10	2,312.10	2,312.10	2,312.10
W-5	—	—	—	—	—	4,221.30
W-4	2,473.20	2,714.10	2,962.80	3,303.00	3,577.80	3,792.00
W-3	2,247.90	2,469.90	2,681.70	2,930.40	3,114.00	3,335.70
W-2	1,968.90	2,192.10	2,438.40	2,623.80	2,809.50	2,993.10
W-1	1,640.40	2,037.90	2,221.50	2,407.20	2,591.70	2,777.70
E-8	—	—	2,412.60	2,547.30	2,682.90	2,811.30
E-7	1,684.80	1,952.10	2,082.90	2,216.70	2,382.60	2,480.40
E-6	1,449.30	1,715.40	1,844.10	2,010.00	2,140.20	2,172.60
E-5	1,271.70	1,514.70	1,680.30	1,811.10	1,844.10	1,844.10
E-4	1,185.90	1,428.60	1,485.30	1,485.30	1,485.30	1,485.30
E-3	1,179.80	1,274.70	1,274.70	1,274.70	1,274.70	1,274.70
E-2	1,075.80	1,075.80	1,075.80	1,075.80	1,075.80	1,075.80
E-1 >4mos	959.40	959.40	959.40	959.40	959.40	959.40

SOURCE: U.S. Department of Defense—Defense Finance and Accounting Service

Sources of Additional Information

Each of the military services publishes handbooks, fact sheets, and pamphlets describing entrance requirements, training and advancement opportunities, and other aspects of military careers. These publications are widely available at all recruiting stations, at most State employment service offices, and in high schools, colleges, and public libraries. Information on educational and other veterans' benefits is available from VA offices located throughout the country.

In addition, the *Military Career Guide Online* is a compendium of military occupational, training, and career information presented by the Defense Manpower Data Center, a Department of Defense agency which is designed for use by students and jobseekers. This information is available on the Internet at http://www.militarycareers.com.

Bank Tellers

(O*NET 53102)

Significant Points

- The projected decline in employment of tellers reflects cost cutting by banks and the growing use of banking technology to perform routine banking services.

- Many job openings will arise from replacement needs in this large occupation because turnover is high, little formal education is required, and the position offers relatively low pay.

- Applicants trained to provide a variety of financial services, along with those seeking part-time work, should have the best job prospects.

Nature of the Work

The bank teller is the person most people associate with a bank. Tellers make up 28 percent of bank employees, and they conduct most of a bank's routine transactions. Among their responsibilities are cashing checks, accepting deposits and loan payments, and processing withdrawals. They may also sell savings bonds, accept payment for customers' utility bills and charge cards, process necessary paperwork for certificates of deposit, and sell travelers' checks. Some tellers specialize in handling foreign currencies or commercial or business accounts.

Being a teller requires a great deal of attention to detail. Before cashing a check, a teller must verify the date, bank name, identification of the person to receive payment, and legality of the document. They must also make sure that written and numerical amounts agree and that the account has sufficient funds to cover the check. The teller then must carefully count cash to avoid errors. Sometimes a customer withdraws money in the form of a cashier's check, which the teller prepares and verifies. When accepting a deposit, tellers must check the accuracy of the deposit slip before processing the transaction.

Before starting a shift, tellers receive and count an amount of working cash for their drawers. A supervisor, usually the head teller, verifies this amount. Tellers use this cash for payments during the day and are responsible for its safe and accurate handling. Before leaving, tellers count cash on hand, list the currency-received tickets on a balance sheet, make sure the accounts balance, and sort checks and deposit slips. Over the course of a work day, tellers may also process numerous mail transactions. Some tellers replenish cash drawers and corroborate deposits and payments to automated teller machines (ATMs).

In most banks, head tellers are responsible for the teller line. In addition to the typical duties of a teller, a head teller's responsibilities include preparing work schedules, accessing the vault, ensuring the correct cash balance in the vault, and overseeing shipments of cash to and from the Federal Reserve.

Technology continues to play a large role in the job duties of all tellers. In most banks, for example, tellers use computer terminals to record deposits and withdrawals. These terminals often give tellers quick access to detailed information on customer accounts. Tellers can use this information to tailor services to fit a customer's needs or to recommend an appropriate bank product or service.

Because banks offer more and increasingly complex financial services, tellers in many banks are being trained to perform some functions of customer service representatives, in addition to their other duties. These tellers are required to learn about the various financial products and services the bank offers so they can briefly explain them to customers and refer interested customers to appropriate specialized sales personnel.

Working Conditions

Tellers generally work weekdays, although some evening and weekend work may be required. The job offers ample opportunity to work part time with flexible hours; in some banks, 90 percent of tellers work part time. Banks often hire part-time, or "peak-time," tellers for busy banking periods, such as lunch hours and Saturday mornings. An increasing number of tellers work outside a traditional bank setting, as more branches are established in shopping malls and grocery stores. These tellers usually work more evening and weekend hours and have more varied responsibilities than other tellers.

Continual communication with customers, repetitive tasks, long periods of standing within a small area, and a high level of attention to security characterize the job. Tellers wishing to provide more personalized service in a less hectic environment often choose to work for a small bank. Full-time employment and a full range of benefits are also more common in small banks, leading to lower turnover rates.

Employment

Bank tellers held about 560,000 jobs in 1998; about 1 out of 3 worked part time. The overwhelming majority worked in commercial banks, savings institutions, or credit unions. The remaining were employed in a variety of other financial service companies.

Training, Other Qualifications, and Advancement

When hiring tellers, banks seek applicants who have excellent communication skills, enjoy working with the public, and possess a strong math aptitude. Tellers must feel comfortable handling large amounts of cash and working with computers and video terminals. In general, banks prefer applicants with some sales and cash handling experience. In some metropolitan areas, employers seek multilingual tellers.

Although tellers work independently, their record keeping is closely supervised. Accuracy and attention to detail are vital. Tellers should be courteous, attentive, and patient in dealing with the public, because customers often judge a bank by the way they are treated at the teller window. Maturity, tact, and the ability to quickly explain bank procedures and services are important in helping customers complete transactions or make financial decisions.

Many new tellers transfer from other occupations, and virtually all tellers have at least a high school education. Usually, new tellers in large banks receive at least one week of formal classroom training. Classes are followed by several weeks of on-the-job training, in which tellers observe experienced workers before doing the work themselves. Smaller banks rely primarily upon on-the-job training. In addition to instruction in basic duties, many banks now include extensive training in the bank's products and services, communication and sales skills, and instruction on equipment, such as ATMs and on-line video terminals.

In large banks, beginners usually start for a few days as limited-transaction tellers, cashing checks and processing simple transactions, before becoming full-service tellers. Often, banks simultaneously train tellers for other clerical duties as well.

Advancement opportunities are good for well-trained, motivated employees. Experienced tellers may advance to head teller, customer service representative, or new accounts clerk. Outstanding tellers who have had some college or specialized training offered by the banking industry may be promoted to a managerial position. Banks encourage this upward mobility by providing access to education and other sources of additional training.

Tellers can prepare for better jobs by taking courses offered or accredited by the American Institute of Banking (an educational affiliate of the American Bankers Association) or the Institute of Financial Education. These organizations have several hundred chapters in cities across the country and numerous study groups in small communities. They also offer correspondence courses and work closely with local colleges and universities in preparing courses of study. Most banks use the facilities of these organizations to conduct cooperative training programs or develop independent training programs. In addition, many banks refund employees' college tuition fees upon successful completion of courses. Although most courses are meant for employed tellers, some community colleges offer pre-employment training programs. These programs can help prepare applicants for a job in banking and can give them an advantage over other jobseekers.

Tellers who are trained to sell insurance products must receive a State license to sell insurance. This requires passing an examination, usually after taking a pre-licensing course.

Job Outlook

Employment of bank tellers is expected to decline through 2008. Nevertheless, many job openings will arise from replacement needs, because turnover is high—a characteristic typical of large occupations that normally require little formal education and offer relatively low pay. Applicants for part-time jobs should fare better than applicants for full-time positions.

The banking industry will continue to undergo many changes that will impact employment of traditional tellers, who perform only routine transactions. Principal among these are technology, bank mergers, and changing employment needs. For example, ATMs and the increased use of direct deposit of paychecks and benefit checks have reduced the need for bank customers to interact with tellers for routine transactions. In addition, electronic banking is spreading rapidly throughout the banking industry. This type of banking, conducted over the telephone or through computer networks, will also reduce the number of tellers over the long run.

Bank mergers, particularly those involving competing banks, have reduced the number of branches as the newly formed banks cut costs and eliminate duplicate services. This has adversely affected employment of tellers who work primarily in branch offices. Bank mergers are expected to continue as banks seek to further reduce costs and offer more services that only large banks can provide, such as numerous ATM locations, more types of loans, and securities brokerage and insurance services.

Teller employment is also being impacted by the increasing use of 24-hour phone centers by many large banks. These telephone centers allow a customer to interact with a bank representative at a distant location, either by telephone or video terminal. Customer service representatives, who can handle a wider variety of transactions than tellers, including loan applications and credit card issuance, usually staff such centers.

Even though some banks have streamlined their branches, the total number of bank branches is expected to increase to meet the needs of a growing population. Branches are being added in non-traditional locations, such as grocery stores, malls, and mobile trailers designed to reach people who do not have easy access to banks. Often, these branches are open longer hours and offer greater customer convenience. Many of these nontraditional branch offices are small and are staffed by tellers who are trained as customer service representatives. As a result, tellers who can provide a variety of financial services will be in greater demand in the future.

Earnings

Median annual earnings of full-time bank tellers were $17,200 in 1998. The middle 50 percent earned between $14,660 and $20,180. The lowest 10 percent earned less than $12,970, while the top 10 percent earned more than $23,000. Some banks offer incentives that reward tellers for inducing customers to use other financial products and services offered by the bank. In general, greater responsibilities result in a higher salary. Experience, length of service, and, especially, the location and size of the bank also are important. Full-time tellers generally receive a full range of benefits, from life and health insurance to pension benefits, whereas part-time tellers often do not.

Median annual earnings in the industries employing the largest number of bank tellers in 1997 were:

Savings institutions	$16,800
Commercial banks	16,600
Credit unions	16,500

Related Occupations

Tellers combine customer service and knowledge of bank procedures with quickness and accuracy to process money, checks, and other financial items for customers. Other workers with similar duties include new accounts clerks, cashiers, toll collectors, post office clerks, auction clerks, and ticket sellers.

Sources of Additional Information

General information about tellers and other banking occupations, training opportunities, and the banking industry is available from:

● American Bankers Association, 1120 Connecticut Ave. NW, Washington, DC 20036. Internet: http://www.aba.com

State bankers' associations can furnish specific information about job opportunities in their States. Individual banks can provide detailed information about job openings and the activities, responsibilities, and preferred qualifications of tellers.

Billing Clerks and Billing Machine Operators

(O*NET 55344 and 56002)

Significant Points

- Most jobs require only a high school diploma.
- Numerous job opportunities should arise due to high turnover in this occupation.

Nature of the Work

Billing clerks keep records, calculate charges, and maintain files of payments made for goods or services. Billing machine operators run machines that generate bills, statements, and invoices.

Billing clerks review purchase orders, bills of lading, sales tickets, hospital records, or charge slips to calculate the total amount due from a customer. Calculating the charges for an individual's hospital stay may require a letter to an insurance company; a clerk computing trucking rates for machine parts may consult a rate book. In accounting, law, consulting, and similar firms, billing clerks calculate client fees based on the actual time required to perform the task. They keep track of the accumulated hours and dollar amounts to charge to each job, the type of job performed for a customer, and the percentage of work completed.

After billing clerks review all necessary information, they compute the charges using calculators or computers. They then prepare itemized statements, bills, or invoices used for billing and record keeping purposes, depending on the organization's needs. In one organization, the clerk might prepare a bill containing the amount due and date and type of service; in another, the clerk would produce a detailed invoice with codes for all goods and services provided. This latter form might list items sold, credit terms, date of shipment or dates services were provided, a salesperson's or doctor's identification if necessary, and the sales total.

After entering all information, *billing machine operators* run off the bill to send to the customer. Computers and specialized billing software allow many clerks to calculate charges and prepare bills in one step. Computer packages prompt clerks to enter data from hand-written forms and manipulate the necessary entries of quantities, labor, and rates to be charged. Billing clerks verify the entry of information and check for errors before the computer prints the bill. After the bills are printed, billing clerks check them again for accuracy.

Working Conditions

Billing clerks and billing machine operators typically are employed in an office environment. Most work alongside other clerical workers, but some work in centralized units away from the front office.

Because the majority of billing clerks and billing machine operators use computers on a daily basis, these workers may experience eye and muscle strain, backaches, headaches, and repetitive motion injuries. Also, clerks who review detailed data may have to sit for extended periods of time.

Most billing clerks and billing machine operators work regular business hours. Billing clerks in hotels, restaurants, and stores may work overtime during peak holiday and vacation seasons.

Employment

In 1998, billing clerks held about 342,000 jobs, and billing machine operators held about 107,000 jobs. One-third of the billing clerks' jobs were in health services, mostly in physicians' offices. Transportation and wholesale trade industries each accounted for 1 out of 10 jobs. Most of the remaining jobs were found in manufacturing or retail trade.

Wholesale and retail trade establishments provided about one-third of all billing machine operator jobs; service establishments, including health services, provided another third. Of the remaining jobs, most were found in banks and other financial institutions.

Training, Other Qualifications, and Advancement

Employers typically require applicants to have at least a high school diploma or its equivalent. Most employers prefer workers who are computer-literate. Knowledge of word processing and spreadsheet software is especially valuable, as are experience working in an office and good interpersonal skills.

Billing clerks and billing machine operators often learn the skills they need in high schools, business schools, and community colleges. Business education programs offered by these institutions typically include courses in typing, word processing, shorthand, business communications, records management, and office systems and procedures.

Some entrants are college graduates with degrees in business, finance, or liberal arts. Although a degree is rarely required, many graduates accept entry-level clerical positions to get into a particular company or to enter the finance or accounting field with the hope of being promoted to professional or managerial positions. Workers with college degrees are likely to start at higher salaries and advance more easily than those without degrees.

Once hired, billing clerks and billing machine operators usually receive on-the-job training. Under the guidance of a supervisor or other senior worker, new employees learn company procedures. Some formal classroom training may also be necessary, such as training in specific computer software.

Billing clerks and billing machine operators must be careful, orderly, and detail-oriented in order to avoid making errors and to recognize errors made by others. These workers should also be discreet and trustworthy because they frequently come in contact with confidential material. Additionally, clerks should have a strong aptitude for numbers.

Billing clerks and billing machine operators usually advance by taking on more duties in the same occupation for higher pay or transferring to a closely related occupation. Most companies fill office and administrative support supervisory and managerial positions by promoting individuals from within their organizations, so those who acquire additional skills, experience, and training improve their advancement opportunities.

Job Outlook

Job openings for those seeking work as billing clerks or billing machine operators are expected to be numerous through the year 2008. Despite the lack of rapid employment growth, many job openings will occur as workers transfer to other occupations or leave the labor force. Turnover in this occupation is relatively high, which is characteristic of an entry-level occupation requiring only a high school diploma.

Employment of billing clerks is expected to grow about as fast as the average for all occupations through the year 2008. A growing economy and increased demand for billing services will result in more business transactions. Rising worker productivity as computers manage more account information will not keep employment from rising. More complex billing applications will increasingly require workers with greater technical expertise.

Employment of billing machine operators, on the other hand, is expected to decline through the year 2008. More advanced machines and computers will continue to replace billing machines, enabling billing clerks to perform the jobs formerly done by billing machine operators. In some organizations, productivity gains from billing software will increasingly allow accounting clerks to take over the responsibilities of billing clerks and billing machine operators.

Earnings

Salaries of billing clerks and billing machine operators vary considerably. The region of the country, size of city, and type and size of establishment all influence salary levels. The level of industry or technical expertise required and the complexity and uniqueness of responsibilities may also affect earnings. Median annual earnings for those working full time in 1998 were as follows:

Billing clerks $22,670

Billing machine operators 20,560

Related Occupations

Today, most clerks enter data into a computer system and perform basic analysis of the data. Other clerical workers who enter and manipulate data include bank tellers, statistical clerks, receiving clerks, medical records clerks, hotel and motel clerks, credit clerks, and reservation and transportation ticket agents.

Sources of Additional Information

State employment service offices can provide information about job openings for the occupation.

Blue-Collar Worker Supervisors

(O*NET 81002, 81005A, 81005B, 81008, 81011, and 81017)

Significant Points

- Although many workers with high school diplomas still rise through the ranks, employers increasingly seek applicants with post-secondary training.

- Employment in manufacturing is expected to decline, reflecting the increasing use of computers, the implementation of self-directed work teams, and leaner management structures.

- In construction and most other nonmanufacturing industries, employment of managers and the workers they supervise is expected to increase.

- Supervisors in the highly cyclical construction industry may be laid off when construction activity declines.

Nature of the Work

For the millions of workers who assemble manufactured goods, service electronics equipment, work in construction, load trucks, or perform thousands of other activities, a blue-collar worker supervisor is the boss. In addition to "the boss," blue-collar worker supervisors go by many other titles. The most common are first-line supervisor and foreman or forewoman, but titles vary according to the industry in which these workers are employed. In the textile industry, for example, these supervisors may be referred to as second hands; on ships, they may be called boatswains. In the construction industry, supervisors can be referred to as superintendents, crew chiefs, or foremen and forewomen, depending upon the type and size of their employer. Toolpushers or gang pushers are common terms used to describe blue-collar supervisors in the oil drilling business.

Although the responsibilities of blue-collar worker supervisors are as varied as the titles they hold, their primary task is to ensure that workers, equipment, and materials are used properly to maximize productivity. To accomplish this, they perform many duties. Supervisors make sure machinery is set up correctly, schedule or perform repairs and maintenance work, create work schedules, keep production and employee records, monitor employees, and ensure that work is done correctly and on time. In addition, they organize workers' activities, make necessary adjustments to ensure that work continues uninterrupted, train new workers, and ensure the existence of a safe working environment.

The means by which supervisors perform these duties have changed dramatically in recent years as companies have restructured their operations for maximum efficiency. Supervisors now use computers to schedule work flow, monitor the quality of workers' output, keep track of materials, update the inventory control system, and perform other supervisory tasks. In addition, new management philosophies that emphasize fewer levels of management and greater employee power in decision making have altered the role of these supervisors. In the past, supervisors exercised their authority to direct the efforts of blue-collar workers; increasingly, supervisors are assuming the role of a facilitator for groups of workers, aiding in group decision making and conflict resolution.

Because they serve as the main conduit of information between management and blue-collar workers, supervisors have many interpersonal tasks related to their job. They inform workers about company plans and policies; recommend good performers for wage increases, awards, or promotions; and deal with poor performers by outlining expectations, counseling workers in proper methods, issuing warnings, or recommending disciplinary action. They also meet on a regular basis with their managers, reporting any problems and discussing possible solutions. Supervisors may often meet among themselves to discuss goals, company operations, and performance. In companies with labor unions, supervisors must follow all provisions of labor-management contracts.

Working Conditions

Blue-collar worker supervisors work in a range of settings based on the industry in which they are employed. Many supervisors work on the shop floor. This can be tiring if they are on their feet most of their shift or working near loud and dangerous machinery. Other supervisors, such as those in construction and oil exploration and production, sometimes work outdoors in severe weather conditions.

Supervisors may be on the job before other workers arrive and often stay after others leave. Some supervisors work in plants that operate around the clock, so they may work any one of three shifts, as well as weekends and holidays. In some cases, supervisors work all three shifts on a rotating basis; in others, shift assignments are made on the basis of seniority.

Because organizational restructuring and downsizing have required many blue-collar worker supervisors to oversee more workers and departments in recent years, longer hours and added responsibilities have increased on-the-job stress for many supervisors.

Employment

Blue-collar worker supervisors held about 2.3 million jobs in 1998. Although salaried supervisors are found in almost all industries, 2 of every 5 work in manufacturing. Other industries employing blue-collar worker supervisors include wholesale and retail trade, public utilities, repair shops, transportation, and government. The vast majority of the 230,000 self-employed workers in this occupation are employed in construction.

Training, Other Qualifications, and Advancement

When choosing supervisors, employers generally look for experience, job knowledge, organizational skills, and leadership qualities. Employers also emphasize the ability to motivate employees, maintain high morale, and command respect. In addition, well-rounded applicants who are able to deal with different situations

and a diverse work force are desired. Communication and interpersonal skills are also extremely important attributes in this occupation.

Completion of high school is often the minimum educational requirement to become a blue-collar worker supervisor, but workers generally receive training in human resources, computer software, and management before they advance to these positions. Although many workers with high school diplomas still rise through the ranks, employers increasingly seek applicants with post-secondary technical degrees. In high-technology industries, such as aerospace and electronics, employers may require a bachelor's degree or technical school training. Large companies usually offer better opportunities for promotion to blue-collar worker supervisor positions than do smaller companies.

In most manufacturing companies, a degree in business or engineering, combined with in-house training, is needed to advance from supervisor to department head or production manager. In the construction industry, supervisors increasingly need a degree in construction management or engineering if they expect to advance to project manager, operations manager, or general superintendent. Some use their skills and experience to start their own construction contracting firms. Supervisors in repair shops may open their own businesses.

Job Outlook

Employment of blue-collar worker supervisors is expected to grow more slowly than the average for all occupations through 2008. As the number of workers in the economy increases, so will the need to supervise these workers. Organizational restructuring and new developments in technology, however, will moderate employment growth. In addition to growth, many openings will arise from the need to replace workers who transfer to other occupations or leave the labor force.

Projected job growth varies by industry. In manufacturing, employment of supervisors is expected to show little to no change despite an increase in manufacturing jobs as each supervisor is expected to oversee more workers. This trend reflects the increasing use of computers to meet supervisory responsibilities, such as production analysis and scheduling, greater involvement of production workers in decision making, and the formation of self-directed work teams. These developments are not as prevalent in construction and most other nonmanufacturing industries, where the employment of blue-collar worker supervisors is expected to rise along with employment of the workers they supervise.

Because of their skill and seniority, blue-collar worker supervisors often are protected from layoffs during a recession. However, some supervisors in the highly cyclical construction industry may be laid off when construction activity declines.

Earnings

Median annual earnings for blue-collar worker supervisors were $37,180 in 1998. The middle 50 percent earned between $28,210 and $48,290. The lowest 10 percent earned less than $21,910, and the highest 10 percent earned over $71,320. Most supervisors earn significantly more than the workers they supervise. Although most blue-collar workers are paid by the hour, the majority of supervisors receive an annual salary. Some supervisors receive extra pay when they work overtime. Median annual earnings in the industries employing the largest number of blue-collar worker supervisors in 1997 were:

Nonresidential building construction	$39,700
Motor vehicle dealers	37,500
Local government, except education and hospitals	36,500
Residential building construction	35,800
Miscellaneous plastics products (manufacturing)	31,500

Related Occupations

Other workers with supervisory duties include those who supervise professional, technical, sales, clerical, and service workers. Some of these are retail store or department managers, sales managers, clerical supervisors, bank officers, head tellers, hotel managers, postmasters, head cooks, head nurses, and surveyors.

Sources of Additional Information

For information on management development programs for blue-collar worker supervisors, contact:

- American Management Association, 1601 Broadway, New York, NY 10019. Internet: http://www.amanet.org
- National Management Association, 2210 Arbor Blvd., Dayton, OH 45439. Internet: http://www.nma1.org
- American Institute of Constructors, 1300 N. 17th St., Suite 830, Rosslyn, VA 22209.
- AIC Constructor Certification Commission, 466 94th Ave. North, St. Petersburg, FL 33702. Internet: http://www.aicnet.org

Bookkeeping, Accounting, and Auditing Clerks

(O*NET 49023B, 55338A, and 55338B)

Significant Points

- Most jobs require only a high school diploma.
- Numerous job opportunities should arise due to high turnover in this occupation.

Nature of the Work

Bookkeeping, accounting, and auditing clerks are an organization's financial record keepers. They compute, classify, record, and verify numerical data to develop and maintain financial records.

In small establishments, *bookkeeping clerks* handle all aspects of financial transactions. They record debits and credits, compare current and past balance sheets, summarize details of separate ledgers, and prepare reports for supervisors and managers. They may also prepare bank deposits by compiling data from cashiers, verifying and balancing receipts, and sending cash, checks, or other forms of payment to the bank.

In large offices and accounting departments, *accounting clerks* have more specialized tasks. Their titles often reflect the type of accounting they do, such as accounts payable clerk or accounts receivable clerk. In addition, responsibilities vary by level of experience. Entry-level accounting clerks post details of transactions, total accounts, and compute interest charges. They may also monitor loans and accounts to ensure that payments are up to date.

More advanced accounting clerks may total, balance, and reconcile billing vouchers; ensure completeness and accuracy of data on accounts; and code documents according to company procedures. They post transactions in journals and on computer files and update these files when needed. Senior clerks also review computer printouts against manually maintained journals and make necessary corrections. They may also review invoices and statements to ensure that all information is accurate and complete, and reconcile computer reports with operating reports.

Auditing clerks verify records of transactions posted by other workers. They check figures, postings, and documents for correct entry, mathematical accuracy, and proper codes. They also correct or note errors for accountants or other workers to adjust.

As organizations continue to computerize their financial records, many bookkeeping, accounting, and auditing clerks use specialized accounting software on personal computers. They increasingly post charges to accounts on computer spreadsheets and databases, as manual posting to general ledgers is becoming obsolete. These workers now enter information from receipts or bills into computers, which is then stored either electronically, as computer printouts, or both. Widespread use of computers has also enabled bookkeeping, accounting, and auditing clerks to take on additional responsibilities, such as payroll, timekeeping, and billing.

Working Conditions

Most clerks typically are employed in an office environment. Most work alongside other clerical workers, but some clerks work in centralized units away from the front office.

Because the majority of clerks use computers on a daily basis, these workers may experience eye and muscle strain, backaches, headaches, and repetitive motion injuries. Also, clerks who review detailed data may have to sit for extended periods of time.

Most clerks work regular business hours. Accounting clerks may work longer hours to meet deadlines at the end of the fiscal year, during tax time, or when monthly and yearly accounting audits are performed. Billing, bookkeeping, and accounting clerks in hotels, restaurants, and stores may work overtime during peak holiday and vacation seasons.

Employment

Bookkeeping, accounting, and auditing clerks held about 2.1 million jobs in 1998. About 25 percent worked in wholesale and retail

trade, and 16 percent were in organizations providing business, health, and social services. Approximately 1 out of 3 of bookkeeping, accounting, and auditing clerks worked part time in 1998.

Training, Other Qualifications, and Advancement

Employers typically require applicants to have at least a high school diploma or its equivalent, although many employers prefer to hire clerks with a higher level of education. Most employers prefer clerks who are computer-literate. Knowledge of word processing and spreadsheet software is especially valuable, as are experience working in an office and good interpersonal skills.

Clerks often learn the skills they need in high schools, business schools, and community colleges. Business education programs offered by these institutions typically include courses in typing, word processing, shorthand, business communications, records management, and office systems and procedures.

Some entrants into the occupation are college graduates with degrees in business, finance, or liberal arts. Although a degree is rarely required, many graduates accept entry-level clerical positions to get into a particular company or to enter the finance or accounting field with the hope of being promoted to professional or managerial positions. Some companies, such as accounting firms, have a set plan of advancement that tracks college graduates from entry-level clerical jobs into managerial positions. Workers with college degrees are likely to start at higher salaries and advance more easily than those without degrees.

Once hired, clerks usually receive on-the-job training. Under the guidance of a supervisor or other senior worker, new employees learn company procedures. Some formal classroom training may also be necessary, such as training in specific computer software.

Clerks must be careful, orderly, and detail-oriented to avoid making errors and to recognize errors made by others. These workers should also be discreet and trustworthy because they frequently come in contact with confidential material. Additionally, bookkeeping, accounting, and auditing clerks should have a strong aptitude for numbers.

Clerks usually advance by taking on more duties in the same occupation for higher pay or transferring to a closely related occupation. Most companies fill office and administrative support supervisory and managerial positions by promoting individuals from within their organizations, so clerks who acquire additional skills, experience, and training improve their advancement opportunities. With appropriate experience and education, some clerks may become accountants.

Job Outlook

Virtually all job openings for bookkeeping, accounting, and auditing clerks through 2008 will stem from replacement needs. Each year, numerous jobs will become available, as these clerks transfer to other occupations or leave the labor force. Although turnover is lower than among other record clerks, the large size of the occupation ensures plentiful job openings, including many opportunities for temporary and part-time work.

Employment of bookkeeping, accounting, and auditing clerks is expected to decline through 2008. Although a growing economy will result in more financial transactions and other activities that require these clerical workers, the continuing spread of office automation will lift worker productivity and contribute to employment decline. In addition, organizations of all sizes will continue to consolidate various record keeping functions, thus reducing the demand for these clerks.

Earnings

Salaries of clerks vary. The region of the country, size of city, and type and size of establishment all influence salary levels. The level of industry or technical expertise required and the complexity and uniqueness of a clerk's responsibilities may also affect earnings. Median annual earnings of full-time bookkeeping, accounting, and auditing clerks in 1998 were $23,190.

Related Occupations

Today, most clerks enter data into a computer system and perform basic analysis of the data. Other clerical workers who enter and manipulate data include bank tellers, statistical clerks, receiving clerks, medical record clerks, hotel and motel clerks, credit clerks, and reservation and transportation ticket agents.

Sources of Additional Information

State employment service offices can provide information about job openings for this occupation.

Brokerage Clerks and Statement Clerks

(O*NET 53126 and 53128)

Significant Points

- Some of these jobs require only a high school diploma, while others are considered entry-level positions for which a bachelor's degree is needed.

- Employment of brokerage clerks is expected to increase faster than the average for all occupations.

Nature of the Work

Brokerage clerks perform a number of different jobs with wide ranging responsibilities, but all involve computing and recording data on securities transactions. Brokerage clerks may also contact customers, take orders, and inform clients of changes to their accounts. Some of these jobs are more clerical and require only a high school diploma, while others are considered entry-level positions for which a bachelor's degree is needed. Brokerage clerks, who work in the operations departments of securities firms, on trading floors, and in branch offices, are also called margin clerks, dividend clerks, transfer clerks, and broker's assistants.

The broker's assistant, also called sales assistant, is the most common type of brokerage clerk. These workers typically assist two brokers, for whom they take calls from clients, write up order tickets, process the paperwork for opening and closing accounts, record a client's purchases and sales, and inform clients of changes in their accounts. All brokers' assistants must be knowledgeable about investment products so they can clearly communicate with clients. Those with a "Series 7" license can make recommendations to clients at the instruction of the broker. The Series 7 license is issued to securities and commodities sales representatives by the National Association of Securities Dealers and allows them to provide advice on securities to the public.

Brokerage clerks in the operations areas of securities firms perform many duties to facilitate the sale and purchase of stocks, bonds, commodities, and other kinds of investments. These clerks produce the necessary records of all transactions that occur in their area of the business. Job titles for many of these clerks depend upon the type of work they perform. Purchase-and-sale clerks, for example, match orders to buy with orders to sell. They balance and verify stock trades by comparing the records of the selling firm to those of the buying firm. Dividend clerks ensure timely payments of stock or cash dividends to clients of a particular brokerage firm. Transfer clerks execute customer requests for changes to security registration and examine stock certificates for adherence to banking regulations. Receive-and-deliver clerks facilitate the receipt and delivery of securities among firms and institutions. Margin clerks post accounts and monitor activity in customers' accounts to ensure that clients make payments and stay within legal boundaries concerning stock purchases.

Technology is changing the nature of many of these workers' jobs. A significant and growing number of brokerage clerks use custom-designed software programs to process transactions more quickly. Only a few customized accounts are still handled manually.

Statement clerks assemble, verify, and send bank statements every month. In many banks, statement clerks are called statement operators because they spend much of their workday running sophisticated, high-speed machines. These machines fold computer-printed statements, collate those longer than one page, insert statements and canceled checks into envelopes, and seal and weigh them for postage. Statement clerks load the machine with statements, canceled checks, and envelopes. They then monitor the equipment and correct minor problems. For more serious problems, they call repair personnel.

In banks that do not have such machines, statement clerks perform all operations manually. They may also be responsible for verifying signatures and checking for missing information on checks, placing canceled checks into trays, and retrieving them to send with the statements. In a growing number of banks, only the statement is printed and sent to the account holder. The canceled checks are not returned; this is known as check truncation.

Statement clerks are employed primarily by large banks. In smaller banks, a teller or bookkeeping clerk, who performs other duties during the rest of the month, usually handles the statement clerk's function. Some small banks send their statement information to larger banks for processing, printing, and mailing.

Working Conditions

Brokerage and statement clerks typically are employed in an office environment. Most work alongside other clerical workers, but some records processing clerks work in centralized units away from the front office.

Because the majority of clerks use computers on a daily basis, these workers may experience eye and muscle strain, backaches, headaches, and repetitive motion injuries. Also, clerks who review detailed data may have to sit for extended periods of time.

Most clerks work regular business hours. Brokerage clerks may have to work overtime if there is a high volume of activity in the stock or bond market.

Employment

Brokerage clerks held about 77,000 jobs in 1998, and statement clerks held about 16,000 jobs. Brokerage clerks work in firms that sell securities and commodities. Banking institutions employed almost all statement clerks.

Training, Other Qualifications, and Advancement

Employers typically require applicants to have at least a high school diploma or its equivalent, and brokerage firms usually seek college graduates for brokerage clerk jobs. Most employers prefer workers who are computer-literate. Knowledge of word processing and spreadsheet software is especially valuable, as are experience working in an office and good interpersonal skills.

Clerks often learn the skills they need in high schools, business schools, and community colleges. Business education programs offered by these institutions typically include courses in typing, word processing, shorthand, business communications, records management, and office systems and procedures.

Some entrants are college graduates with degrees in business, finance, or liberal arts. Many graduates accept entry-level clerical positions to get into a particular company or to enter the finance or accounting field with the hope of being promoted to professional or managerial positions. Some companies, such as brokerage firms, have a set plan of advancement that tracks college graduates from entry-level clerical jobs into managerial positions. Workers with college degrees are likely to start at higher salaries and advance more easily than those without degrees.

Once hired, clerks usually receive on-the-job training. Under the guidance of a supervisor or other senior worker, new employees learn company procedures. Some formal classroom training may also be necessary, such as training in specific computer software.

Clerks must be careful, orderly, and detail-oriented in order to avoid making errors and to recognize errors made by others. These workers should also be discreet and trustworthy because they frequently

come in contact with confidential material. Additionally, clerks should have a strong aptitude for numbers. Because statement clerks have access to confidential financial information, these workers must be bonded.

Clerks usually advance by taking on more duties in the same occupation for higher pay or transferring to a closely related occupation. Most companies fill office and administrative support supervisory and managerial positions by promoting individuals from within their organizations, so clerks who acquire additional skills, experience, and training improve their advancement opportunities. With appropriate experience and education, some clerks may become securities, commodities, and financial services sales representatives.

Job Outlook

Employment of brokerage clerks is expected to increase faster than the average for all occupations, while employment of statement clerks should decline. With people increasingly investing in securities, demand for brokerage clerks will climb to meet the needs of processing larger volumes of transactions. Because most back office operations are now computerized, employment growth among brokerage clerks is not expected to keep pace with overall employment growth in the securities and commodities industry; however, brokerage clerks will still be needed to update records, enter changes to customer's accounts, and verify securities transfers.

Broker's assistants will also increase in number along with the number of full-service brokers. Because these clerks spend much of their day answering telephone calls, placing orders, and often running the office, their jobs are not readily subject to automation.

The number of statement clerks is declining rapidly due to increasing technology in the Nation's banks. With the job of producing statements almost completely automated, the mailing of checks and statements is now done mostly by machine. In addition, the further spread of check truncation and the increased use of automated teller machines and other electronic money transfers should result in significantly fewer checks being written and processed.

Earnings

Salaries of clerks vary considerably. The region of the country, size of city, and type and size of establishment all influence salary levels. The level of industry or technical expertise required and the complexity and uniqueness of a clerk's responsibilities may also affect earnings. Median annual earnings of full-time workers in 1998 were as follows:

Brokerage clerks	$27,920
Statement clerks	18,640

Related Occupations

Today, most clerks enter data into a computer system and perform basic analysis of the data. Other clerical workers who enter and manipulate data include bank tellers, statistical clerks, receiving clerks, medical records clerks, hotel and motel clerks, credit clerks, and reservation and transportation ticket agents.

Sources of Additional Information

State employment service offices can provide information about job openings for the occupation.

Budget Analysts

(O*NET 21117)

Significant Points

- One out of three budget analysts work in Federal, State, and local governments.

- A bachelor's degree generally is the minimum educational requirement; however, some employers require a master's degree.

- Competition for jobs should remain keen due to the substantial number of qualified applicants; those with a master's degree should have the best job prospects.

Nature of the Work

Deciding how to distribute limited financial resources efficiently is an important challenge in all organizations. In most large and complex organizations, this task would be nearly impossible were it not for budget analysts. These professionals play the primary role in the development, analysis, and execution of budgets, which are used to allocate current resources and estimate future requirements. Without effective analysis and feedback about budgetary problems, many private and public organizations could become bankrupt.

Budget analysts can be found in private industry, nonprofit organizations, and the public sector. In private sector firms, a budget analyst examines, analyzes, and seeks new ways to improve efficiency and increase profits. Although analysts working in nonprofit and governmental organizations usually are not concerned with profits, they still try to find the most efficient distribution of funds and other resources among various departments and programs.

Budget analysts have many responsibilities in these organizations, but their primary task is providing advice and technical assistance in the preparation of annual budgets. At the beginning of each budget cycle, managers and department heads submit proposed operating and financial plans to budget analysts for review. These plans outline expected programs, including proposed program increases and new initiatives, estimated costs and expenses, and capital expenditures needed to finance these programs.

Analysts examine the budget estimates or proposals for completeness, accuracy, and conformance with established procedures, regulations, and organizational objectives. Sometimes they employ cost-benefit analysis to review financial requests, assess program tradeoffs, and explore alternative funding methods. They also examine past and current budgets and research economic and financial developments that affect the organization's spending. This process enables analysts to evaluate proposals in terms of the organization's priorities and financial resources.

After this initial review process, budget analysts consolidate the individual departmental budgets into operating and capital budget summaries. These summaries contain comments and supporting statements that support or argue against funding requests. Budget summaries are then submitted to senior management, or as is often the case in local and State governments, to appointed or elected officials. Budget analysts then help the chief operating officer, agency head, or other top managers analyze the proposed plan and devise possible alternatives if the projected results are unsatisfactory. The final decision to approve the budget, however, is usually made by the organization head in a private firm or elected officials in government, such as the State legislative body.

Throughout the remainder of the year, analysts periodically monitor the budget by reviewing reports and accounting records to determine if allocated funds have been spent as specified. If deviations appear between the approved budget and actual performance, budget analysts may write a report explaining the causes of the variations along with recommendations for new or revised budget procedures. In order to avoid or alleviate deficits, they may recommend program cuts or reallocation of excess funds. They also inform program managers and others within their organization of the status and availability of funds in different budget accounts. Before any changes are made to an existing program or a new one is implemented, a budget analyst assesses its efficiency and effectiveness. Analysts also may also be involved in long-range planning activities such as projecting future budget needs.

The budget analyst's role has broadened as limited funding has led to downsizing and restructuring throughout private industry and government. Not only do they develop guidelines and policies governing the formulation and maintenance of the budget, but they also measure organizational performance, assess the effect of various programs and policies on the budget, and help draft budget-related legislation. In addition, budget analysts sometimes conduct training sessions for company or government agency personnel regarding new budget procedures.

Working Conditions

Budget analysts usually work in a comfortable office setting. Long hours are common among these workers, especially during the initial development and mid-year and final reviews of budgets. The pressure of deadlines and tight work schedules during these periods can be extremely stressful, and analysts are usually required to work more than the routine 40 hours a week.

Budget analysts spend the majority of their time working independently, compiling and analyzing data and preparing budget proposals. Nevertheless, their schedule is sometimes interrupted by special budget requests, meetings, and training sessions. Some budget analysts travel to obtain budget details and explanations of various programs from coworkers or to personally observe funding allocation.

Employment

Budget analysts held about 59,000 jobs throughout private industry and government in 1998. Federal, State, and local governments are major employers, accounting for one-third of all budget analyst jobs. The Department of Defense employed 7 of every 10 budget analysts working for the Federal government. Other major employers include schools, hospitals, and banks.

Training, Other Qualifications, and Advancement

Private firms and government agencies generally require candidates for budget analyst positions to have at least a bachelor's degree. Within the Federal government, a bachelor's degree in any field is sufficient for an entry-level budget analyst position. State and local governments have varying requirements, but a bachelor's degree in one of many areas (accounting, finance, business or public administration, economics, political science, statistics, or a social science such as sociology) may qualify one for entry into the occupation. Sometimes, a field closely related to the employing industry or organization, such as engineering, may be preferred. An increasing number of States and other employers require a candidate to possess a master's degree to ensure adequate analytical and communication skills. Some firms prefer candidates with backgrounds in business because business courses emphasize quantitative and analytical skills. Occasionally, budget and financial experience can be substituted for formal education.

Because developing a budget involves manipulating numbers and requires strong analytical skills, courses in statistics or accounting are helpful, regardless of the prospective budget analyst's major field of study. Financial analysis is automated in almost every organization, and therefore familiarity with word processing and the financial software packages used in budget analysis is often required. Software packages commonly used by budget analysts include electronic spreadsheets and database and graphics software. Employers usually prefer job candidates who already possess these computer skills.

In addition to analytical and computer skills, those seeking a career as a budget analyst must also be able to work under strict time constraints. Strong oral and written communication skills are essential for analysts because they must prepare, present, and defend budget proposals to decision makers.

Entry-level budget analysts may receive some formal training when they begin their jobs, but most employers feel that the best training is obtained by working through one complete budget cycle. During the cycle, which is typically one year, analysts become familiar with the various steps involved in the budgeting process. The Federal government, on the other hand, offers extensive on-the-job and classroom training for entry-level trainees. In addition to on-the-job training, budget analysts are encouraged to participate in the various classes offered throughout their careers.

Budget analysts start their careers with limited responsibilities. In the Federal government, for example, beginning budget analysts compare projected costs with prior expenditures; consolidate and enter data prepared by others; and assist higher grade analysts by doing research. As analysts progress, they begin to develop and formulate budget estimates and justification statements; perform in-depth analyses of budget requests; write statements supporting funding requests; advise program managers and others on the status and availability of funds in different budget activities; and present and defend budget proposals to senior managers.

Beginning analysts usually work under close supervision. Capable entry-level analysts can be promoted into intermediate level positions within one to two years and then into senior positions within a few more years. Progressing to a higher level means added budgetary responsibility and can lead to a supervisory role. Because of the importance and high visibility of their jobs, senior budget analysts are prime candidates for promotion to management positions in various parts of the organization.

Job Outlook

Employment of budget analysts is expected to grow about as fast as the average for all occupations through 2008. Employment growth will be driven by the continuing demand of the Nation's public and private sector organizations for sound financial analysis. In addition to employment growth, many job openings will result from the need to replace experienced budget analysts who transfer to other occupations or leave the labor force.

Despite the increase in demand for budget analysts, competition for jobs should remain keen due to the substantial number of qualified applicants. Candidates with a master's degree should have the best job opportunities. Familiarity with computer financial software packages should also enhance a jobseeker's employment prospects in this field.

Expanding automation is playing a complex role in the job outlook for budget analysts. Computers allow budget analysts to process more data in less time, enabling them to be more productive. However, because analysts now have a greater supply of data available to them, their jobs are becoming more complicated. In addition, as businesses become increasingly complex and specialization within organizations becomes more common, planning and financial control increasingly demand attention. These factors should offset any adverse computer-induced effects on employment of budget analysts.

In coming years, companies will continue to rely heavily on budget analysts to examine, analyze, and develop budgets. Because the financial analysis performed by budget analysts is an important function in every large organization, the employment of budget analysts has remained relatively unaffected by downsizing in the Nation's workplaces. In addition, because financial and budget reports must be completed during periods of economic growth and slowdowns, budget analysts usually are less subject to layoffs during economic downturns than many other workers.

Earnings

Salaries of budget analysts vary widely by experience, education, and employer. Median annual earnings of budget analysts in 1998 were $44,950. The middle 50 percent earned between $36,190 and $61,410. The lowest 10 percent earned less than $30,000, and the highest 10 percent earned more than $81,160.

According to a survey conducted by Robert Half International, a staffing services firm specializing in accounting and finance, starting salaries of budget and other financial analysts in small firms ranged from $27,000 to $30,500 in 1998; in large organizations, they ranged from $29,500 to $33,750. In small firms, analysts with one to three years of experience earned from $30,750 to $36,750;

in large companies, such analysts earned from $34,000 to $44,750. Senior analysts in small firms earned from $36,500 to $42,000; in large firms, they earned from $41,750 to $53,750. Earnings of managers in this field ranged from $42,750 to $54,750 a year in small firms, while managers in large organizations earned between $51,750 and $69,500.

In the Federal government, budget analysts usually started as trainees earning $20,600 or $25,500 a year in 1999. Candidates with a master's degree might begin at $31,200. Beginning salaries were slightly higher in selected areas where the prevailing local pay level was higher. The average annual salary in 1999 for budget analysts employed by the Federal government in nonsupervisory, supervisory, and managerial positions was $52,000.

Related Occupations

Budget analysts review, analyze, and interpret financial data; make recommendations for the future; and assist in the implementation of new ideas. Workers who use these skills in other occupations include accountants and auditors, economists, financial analysts, financial managers, and loan officers.

Sources of Additional Information

Information about career opportunities as a budget analyst may be available from your State or local employment service.

Information on acquiring a job as a budget analyst with the Federal government may be obtained from the Office of Personnel Management through a telephone-based system. Consult your telephone directory under U.S. government for a local number, or call (912) 757-3000; TDD (912) 744-2299. That number is not toll free and charges may result. Information also is available from their Internet site: http://www.usajobs.opm.gov.

Cashiers

(O*NET 49023A)

Significant Points

- Good employment opportunities are expected due to the large number of workers who leave this occupation each year.
- The occupation offers plentiful opportunities for part-time work.

Nature of the Work

Supermarkets, department stores, gasoline service stations, movie theaters, restaurants, and many other businesses employ cashiers to register the sale of their merchandise. Most cashiers total bills, receive money, make change, fill out charge forms, and give receipts.

Although specific job duties vary by employer, cashiers are usually assigned to registers at the beginning of their shifts and given drawers containing "banks" of money. They must count their banks to ensure they contain the correct amount of money and adequate supplies of change. At the end of their shifts, they once again count the drawers' contents and compare the totals with sales data. An occasional shortage of small amounts may be overlooked, but in many establishments, repeated shortages are grounds for dismissal.

In addition to counting the contents of their drawers at the end of their shifts, cashiers usually separate and total charge forms, return slips, coupons, and any other noncash items. Cashiers also handle returns and exchanges. They must ensure that merchandise is in good condition and determine where and when it was purchased and what type of payment was used.

After entering charges for all items and subtracting the value of any coupons or special discounts, cashiers total the bill and take payment. Acceptable forms of payment include cash, personal check, charge, and debit cards. Cashiers must know the store's policies and procedures for each type of payment the store accepts. For checks and charges, they may request additional identification from the customer or call in for an authorization. They must verify the age of customers purchasing alcohol or tobacco. When the sale is complete, cashiers issue receipts to the customers and return the appropriate change. They may also wrap or bag the purchases.

Cashiers traditionally have totaled customers' purchases using cash registers—manually entering the price of each product. However, most establishments are now using more sophisticated equipment, such as scanners and computers. In a store with scanners, a cashier passes a product's Universal Product Code over the scanning device, which transmits the code number to a computer. The computer identifies the item and its price. In other establishments, cashiers manually enter codes into computers, and descriptions of the items and their prices appear on the screen.

Depending on the type of establishment, cashiers may have other duties as well. In many supermarkets, for example, cashiers weigh produce and bulk food as well as return unwanted items to the shelves. In convenience stores, cashiers may be required to know how to use a variety of machines other than cash registers and how to furnish money orders. Operating ticket-dispensing machines and answering customers' questions are common duties for cashiers who work at movie theaters and ticket agencies. Counter and rental clerks, who perform many similar duties, are discussed elsewhere.

Working Conditions

About one-half of all cashiers work part time. Hours of work often vary depending on the needs of the employer. Generally, cashiers are expected to work weekends, evenings, and holidays to accommodate customers' needs. However, many employers offer flexible schedules. For example, full-time workers who work on weekends may receive time off during the week. Because the holiday season is the busiest time for most retailers, many employers restrict the use of vacation time from Thanksgiving through the beginning of January.

Most cashiers work indoors, usually standing in booths or behind counters. In addition, they are often unable to leave their workstations without supervisory approval because they are responsible for large sums of money. The work of cashiers can be very repetitious, but improvements in workstation design are being made to combat problems caused by repetitive motion. In addition, the work can sometimes be dangerous. In 1998, cashiers were victims of 6.5 percent of all workplace homicides, although they made up less than 2.5 percent of the total workforce.

Employment

Cashiers held about 3.2 million jobs in 1998. Although employed in almost every industry, nearly one third of all jobs were in supermarkets and other food stores. Restaurants, department stores, gasoline service stations, drug stores, and other retail establishments also employed large numbers of these workers. Outside of retail establishments, many cashiers worked in hotels, schools, and motion picture theaters. Because cashiers are needed in businesses and organizations of all types and sizes, job opportunities are found throughout the country.

Training, Other Qualifications, and Advancement

Cashier jobs tend to be entry-level positions requiring little or no previous work experience. Although there are no specific educational requirements, employers filling full-time jobs often prefer applicants with high school diplomas.

Nearly all cashiers are trained on the job. In small businesses, an experienced worker often trains beginners. The first day is usually spent observing the operation and becoming familiar with the store's equipment, policies, and procedures. After this, trainees are assigned to a register—frequently under the supervision of a more experienced worker. In larger businesses, before being placed at cash registers, trainees spend several days in classes. Topics typically covered include a description of the industry and the company, store policies and procedures, equipment operation, and security.

Training for experienced workers is not common, except when new equipment is introduced or when procedures change. In these cases, the employer or a representative of the equipment manufacturer trains workers on the job.

Persons who want to become cashiers should be able to do repetitious work accurately. They also need basic mathematics skills and good manual dexterity. Because cashiers deal constantly with the public, they should be neat in appearance and able to deal tactfully and pleasantly with customers. In addition, some businesses prefer to hire persons who can operate specialized equipment or who have business experience, such as typing, selling, or handling money.

Advancement opportunities for cashiers vary. For those working part time, promotion may be to a full-time position. Others advance to head cashier or cash office clerk. In addition, this job offers a good opportunity to learn about an employer's business and can serve as a stepping stone to a more responsible position.

Job Outlook

As in the past, opportunities for cashiers are expected to continue to be good, due to rapid employment growth and the need to re-

place the large number of workers who transfer to other occupations or leave the labor force.

Cashier employment is expected to increase as fast as the average for all occupations through the year 2008 due to expanding demand for goods and services by a growing population. Traditionally, workers under the age of 25 have filled many of the openings in this occupation—in 1998, about half of all cashiers were 24 years of age or younger. Some establishments have begun hiring elderly and disabled persons as well to fill some of their job openings. Opportunities for part-time work are expected to continue to be excellent.

Earnings

The starting wage for many cashiers is the Federal minimum wage, which was $5.15 an hour in 1999. In some States, State law sets the minimum wage higher, and establishments must pay at least that amount. Wages tend to be higher in areas where there is intense competition for workers.

Median hourly earnings of cashiers in 1998 were $6.58. The middle 50 percent earned between $5.95 and $8.22 an hour. The lowest 10 percent earned less than $5.66, and the highest 10 percent earned more than $9.82 an hour. Median hourly earnings in the industries employing the largest number of cashiers in 1997 were as follows:

Department stores	$6.70
Grocery stores	6.30
Gasoline service stations	6.10
Drug stores and proprietary stores	5.80
Eating and drinking places	5.70

Benefits for full-time cashiers tend to be better than for those working part time. Cashiers often receive health and life insurance and paid vacations. In addition, those working in retail establishments often receive discounts on purchases, and cashiers in restaurants may receive free or low-cost meals. Some employers also offer employee stock option plans and education reimbursement plans.

Related Occupations

Cashiers accept payment for the purchase of goods and services. Other workers with similar duties include food and beverage service workers, bank tellers, counter and rental clerks, postal clerks and mail carriers, and retail salespersons.

Sources of Additional Information

General information on retailing is available from:

- National Retail Federation, 325 7th St. NW., Suite 1100, Washington, DC 20004. Internet: http://www.nrf.com

For information about employment opportunities as a cashier, contact:

- National Association of Convenience Stores, 1605 King St., Alexandria, VA 22314-2792.

- United Food and Commercial Workers International Union, Education Office, 1775 K St. NW., Washington, DC 20006-1502.

- Retail, Wholesale, and Department Store Union, 30 East 29th St., 4th Floor, New York, NY 10016.

Chiropractors

(O*NET 32113)

Significant Points

- Employment of chiropractors is expected to increase rapidly, and job prospects should be good.

- Chiropractic care of back, neck, extremities, and other joint damage has become more accepted as a result of recent research and changing attitudes.

- In chiropractic, as in other types of independent practice, earnings are relatively low in the beginning, but they increase as the practice grows.

Nature of the Work

Chiropractors, also known as doctors of chiropractic or chiropractic physicians, diagnose and treat patients whose health problems are associated with the body's muscular, nervous, and skeletal systems, especially the spine. Chiropractors believe interference with these systems impairs normal functions and lowers resistance to disease. They also hold that spinal or vertebral dysfunction alters many important body functions by affecting the nervous system, and that skeletal imbalance through joint or articular dysfunction, especially in the spine, can cause pain.

The chiropractic approach to health care is holistic, stressing the patient's overall health and wellness. It recognizes that many factors affect health, including exercise, diet, rest, environment, and heredity. Chiropractors use natural, drugless, nonsurgical health treatments, and rely on the body's inherent recuperative abilities. They also recommend lifestyle changes—in eating, exercise, and sleeping habits, for example—to their patients. When appropriate, chiropractors consult with and refer patients to other health practitioners.

Like other health practitioners, chiropractors follow a standard routine to secure the information needed for diagnosis and treatment. They take the patient's medical history; conduct physical, neurological, and orthopedic examinations; and may order laboratory tests. X-rays and other diagnostic images are important tools because of the emphasis on the spine and its proper function. Chiropractors also employ a postural and spinal analysis common to chiropractic diagnosis.

In cases in which difficulties can be traced to involvement of musculoskeletal structures, chiropractors manually adjust the spinal column. Many chiropractors use water, light, massage, ultrasound, electric, and heat therapy. They may also apply supports such as straps, tapes, and braces. Chiropractors counsel patients about wellness concepts such as nutrition, exercise, lifestyle changes, and stress management, but do not prescribe drugs or perform surgery.

Some chiropractors specialize in sports injuries, neurology, orthopedics, nutrition, internal disorders, or diagnostic imaging.

Many chiropractors are solo or group practitioners who also have the administrative responsibilities of running a practice. In larger offices, chiropractors delegate these tasks to office managers and chiropractic assistants. Chiropractors in private practice are responsible for developing a patient base, hiring employees, and keeping records.

Working Conditions

Chiropractors work in clean, comfortable offices. The average workweek is about 40 hours, although longer hours are not uncommon. Solo practitioners set their own hours, but may work evenings or weekends to accommodate patients.

Chiropractors, like other health practitioners, are sometimes on their feet for long periods of time. Chiropractors who take x-rays employ appropriate precautions against the dangers of repeated exposure to radiation.

Employment

Chiropractors held about 46,000 jobs in 1998. Most chiropractors are in solo practice, although some are in group practice or work for other chiropractors. A small number teach, conduct research at chiropractic institutions, or work in hospitals and clinics.

Many chiropractors are located in small communities. There are geographic imbalances in the distribution of chiropractors, in part because many establish practices close to chiropractic institutions.

Training, Other Qualifications, and Advancement

All States and the District of Columbia regulate the practice of chiropractic and grant licenses to chiropractors who meet educational and examination requirements established by the State. Chiropractors can only practice in States where they are licensed. Some States have agreements permitting chiropractors licensed in one State to obtain a license in another without further examination, provided that educational, examination, and practice credentials meet State specifications.

Most State boards require at least two years of undergraduate education, and an increasing number require a four-year bachelor's degree. All boards require completion of a four-year chiropractic college course at an accredited program leading to the Doctor of Chiropractic degree.

For licensure, most State boards recognize either all or part of the four-part test administered by the National Board of Chiropractic Examiners. State examinations may supplement the National Board tests, depending on State requirements.

To maintain licensure, almost all States require completion of a specified number of hours of continuing education each year. Continuing education programs are offered by accredited chiropractic programs and institutions and chiropractic associations. Special councils within some chiropractic associations also offer programs leading to clinical specialty certification, called "diplomate" certification, in areas such as orthopedics, neurology, sports injuries, occupational and industrial health, nutrition, diagnostic imaging, thermography, and internal disorders.

In 1998, there were 16 chiropractic programs and institutions in the United States accredited by the Council on Chiropractic Education. All required applicants to have at least 60 semester hours of undergraduate study leading toward a bachelor's degree, including courses in English, the social sciences or humanities, organic and inorganic chemistry, biology, physics, and psychology. Many applicants have a bachelor's degree, which may eventually become the minimum entry requirement. Several chiropractic colleges offer prechiropractic study, as well as a bachelor's degree program. Recognition of prechiropractic education offered by chiropractic colleges varies among the State boards.

During the first two years, most chiropractic programs emphasize classroom and laboratory work in basic science subjects such as anatomy, physiology, public health, microbiology, pathology, and biochemistry. The last two years stress courses in manipulation and spinal adjustments and provide clinical experience in physical and laboratory diagnosis, neurology, orthopedics, geriatrics, physiotherapy, and nutrition. Chiropractic programs and institutions grant the degree of Doctor of Chiropractic (D.C.).

Chiropractic requires keen observation to detect physical abnormalities. It also takes considerable hand dexterity to perform adjustments, but not unusual strength or endurance. Chiropractors should be able to work independently and handle responsibility. As in other health-related occupations, empathy, understanding, and the desire to help others are good qualities for dealing effectively with patients.

Newly licensed chiropractors can set up a new practice, purchase an established one, or enter into partnership with an established practitioner. They may also take a salaried position with an established chiropractor, a group practice, or a health care facility.

Job Outlook

Job prospects are expected to be good for persons who enter the practice of chiropractic. Employment of chiropractors is expected to grow faster than the average for all occupations through the year 2008 as consumer demand for alternative medicine grows. Chiropractors emphasize the importance of healthy lifestyles and do not prescribe drugs or perform surgery. As a result, chiropractic care is appealing to many health-conscious Americans. Chiropractic treatment of back, neck, extremities, and other joint damage has become more accepted as a result of recent research and changing attitudes about alternative health care practices. The rapidly expanding older population, with their increased likelihood of mechanical and structural problems, will also increase demand.

Demand for chiropractic treatment is also related to the ability of patients to pay, either directly or through health insurance. Although more insurance plans now cover chiropractic services, the extent of such coverage varies among plans. Increasingly, chiropractors must educate communities about the benefits of chiropractic care in order to establish a successful practice.

In this occupation, replacement needs arise almost entirely from retirements. Chiropractors usually remain in the occupation until they retire; few transfer to other occupations. Establishing a new practice will be easiest in areas with a low concentration of chiropractors.

Earnings

Median annual earnings of salaried chiropractors were $63,930 in 1998. The middle 50 percent earned between $36,820 and $110,820 a year.

Self-employed chiropractors usually earn more than salaried chiropractors. According to the American Chiropractic Association, average income for all chiropractors, including the self-employed, was about $86,500 (after expenses) in 1997. In chiropractic, as in other types of independent practice, earnings are relatively low in the beginning and increase as the practice grows. Earnings are also influenced by the characteristics and qualifications of the practitioner and geographic location. Self-employed chiropractors must provide for their own health insurance and retirement.

Related Occupations

Chiropractors treat and work to prevent bodily disorders and injuries. So do physicians, dentists, optometrists, podiatrists, veterinarians, occupational therapists, and physical therapists.

Sources of Additional Information

General information on chiropractic as a career is available from:

- American Chiropractic Association, 1701 Clarendon Blvd., Arlington, VA 22209. Internet: http://www.amerchiro.org
- International Chiropractors Association, 1110 North Glebe Rd., Suite 1000, Arlington, VA 22201. Internet: http://www.chiropractic.org
- World Chiropractic Alliance, 2950 N. Dobson Rd., Suite 1, Chandler, AZ 85224-1802.
- Dynamic Chiropractic, P.O. Box 6100, Huntington, CA 92615. Internet: http://www.chiroweb.com

For a list of chiropractic programs and institutions, as well as general information on chiropractic education, contact:

- Council on Chiropractic Education, 7975 North Hayden Rd., Suite A-210, Scottsdale, AZ 85258.

For information on State education and licensure requirements, contact:

- Federation of Chiropractic Licensing Boards, 901 54th Ave., Suite 101, Greeley, CO 80634. Internet: http://www.fclb.org/fclb

For information on requirements for admission to a specific chiropractic college, as well as scholarship and loan information, contact the admissions office of the individual college.

Clergy

Nature of the Work

Religious beliefs—such as Buddhist, Christian, Jewish, or Moslem—are significant influences in the lives of millions of Americans, and they prompt many believers to participate in organizations that reinforce their faith. Even within a religion, many denominations may exist, with each group having unique traditions and responsibilities assigned to its clergy. For example, Christianity has more than 70 denominations, while Judaism has four major branches, as well as groups within each branch, with diverse customs.

Clergy are religious and spiritual leaders and teachers and interpreters of their traditions and faith. Most members of the clergy serve in a pulpit. They organize and lead regular religious services and officiate at special ceremonies, including confirmations, weddings, and funerals. They may lead worshipers in prayer, administer the sacraments, deliver sermons, and read from sacred texts such as the Bible, Torah, or Koran. When not conducting worship services, clergy organize, supervise, and lead religious education programs for their congregations. Clergy visit the sick or bereaved to provide comfort, and they counsel persons who are seeking religious or moral guidance or who are troubled by family or personal problems. They also may work to expand the membership of their congregations and solicit donations to support their activities and facilities.

Clergy who serve large congregations often share their duties with associates or more junior clergy. Senior clergy may spend considerable time on administrative duties. They oversee the management of buildings, order supplies, contract for services and repairs, and supervise the work of staff and volunteers. Associate or assistant members of the clergy sometimes specialize in an area of religious service, such as music, education, or youth counseling. Clergy also work with committees and officials, elected by the congregation, who guide the management of the congregation's finances and real estate.

Some members of the clergy serve their religious communities in ways that do not call for them to hold positions in congregations. Some serve as chaplains in the Armed Forces and in hospitals, while others help to carry out the missions of religious community and social services agencies. A few members of the clergy serve in administrative or teaching posts in schools at all grade levels, including seminaries.

Working Conditions

Members of the clergy typically work long and irregular hours. Those who do not work in congregational settings may have more routine schedules. In 1998, almost one-fifth of full-time clergy worked 60 or more hours a week, three times that of all workers in professional specialty occupations. Although many of their activities are sedentary and intellectual in nature, clergy frequently are called upon on short notice to visit the sick, comfort the dying and their families, and provide counseling to those in need. Involvement in community, administrative, and educational activities sometimes requires clergy to work evenings, early mornings, holidays, and weekends.

Because of their roles as leaders regarding spiritual and moral issues, some members of the clergy often feel obligated to address and resolve both societal problems and the personal problems of their congregations' members, which can lead to stress.

Training and Other Qualifications

Educational requirements for entry into the clergy vary greatly. Similar to other professional occupations, about 3 out of 4 members of the clergy have completed at least a bachelor's degree. Many denominations require that clergy complete a bachelor's degree and a graduate-level program of theological study; others will admit anyone who has been "called" to the vocation. Some faiths do not allow women to become clergy; however, those that do are experiencing increases in the numbers of women seeking ordination. Men and women considering careers in the clergy should consult their religious leaders to verify specific entrance requirements.

Individuals considering a career in the clergy should realize they are choosing not only a career but also a way of life. In fact, most members of the clergy remain in their chosen vocation throughout their lives; in 1998, 12 percent of clergy were 65 or older, compared to only 3 percent of workers in all professional specialty occupations.

Religious leaders must exude confidence and motivation, yet remain tolerant and able to listen to the needs of others. They should be capable of making difficult decisions, working under pressure, and living up to the moral standards set by their faith and community.

The following statements provide more detailed information on Protestant ministers, rabbis, and Roman Catholic priests.

Protestant Ministers

(O*NET 27502)

Significant Points

- Entry requirements vary greatly; many denominations require a bachelor's degree followed by study at a theological seminary, whereas others have no formal educational requirements.

- Competition for positions is generally expected because of the large number of qualified candidates, but it will vary among denominations and geographic regions.

Nature of the Work

Protestant ministers lead their congregations in worship services and administer the various rites of the church, such as baptism, confirmation, and Holy Communion. The services that ministers conduct differ among the numerous Protestant denominations and even among congregations within a denomination. In many denominations, ministers follow a traditional order of worship; in others, they adapt the services to the needs of youth and other groups within the congregation. Most services include Bible readings, hymn singing, prayers, and a sermon. In some denominations, Bible readings by members of the congregation and individual testimonials constitute a large part of the service. In addition to these duties, ministers officiate at weddings, funerals, and other occasions.

Each Protestant denomination has its own hierarchical structure. Some ministers are responsible only to the congregation they serve, whereas others are assigned duties by elder ministers or by the bishops of the diocese they serve. In some denominations, ministers are reassigned to a new pastorate by a central governing body or diocese every few years.

Ministers who serve small congregations usually work personally with parishioners. Those who serve large congregations may share specific aspects of the ministry with one or more associates or assistants, such as a minister of education or a minister of music.

Employment

According to the National Council of Churches, there were more than 400,000 Protestant ministers in 1998, including those who served without a regular congregation or those who worked in closely related fields, such as chaplains working in hospitals, the Armed Forces, universities, and correctional institutions. Although there are many denominations, most ministers are employed by the five largest Protestant bodies: Baptist, Episcopalian, Lutheran, Methodist, and Presbyterian.

Although most ministers are located in urban areas, many serve two or more smaller congregations in less densely populated areas. Some small churches increasingly employ part-time ministers who are seminary students, retired ministers, or holders of secular jobs. Unpaid pastors serve other churches with meager funds. In addition, some churches employ specially trained members of the laity to conduct nonliturgical functions.

Training and Other Qualifications

Educational requirements for entry into the Protestant ministry vary greatly. Many denominations require, or at least strongly prefer, a bachelor's degree followed by study at a theological seminary. However, some denominations have no formal educational requirements, and others ordain persons having various types of training from Bible colleges or liberal arts colleges. Many denominations now allow women to be ordained, but others do not. Persons considering a career in the ministry should first verify the ministerial requirements with their particular denomination.

In general, each large denomination has its own schools of theology that reflect its particular doctrine, interests, and needs. However, many of these schools are open to students from other denominations. Several interdenominational schools associated with universities give both undergraduate and graduate training covering a wide range of theological points of view.

In 1998-99, the Association of Theological Schools in the United States and Canada accredited 135 Protestant denominational theological schools. These schools admit only students who have received a bachelor's degree or its equivalent from an accredited college. After college graduation, many denominations require a three-year course of professional study in one of these accredited schools, or seminaries, for the degree of Master of Divinity.

The standard curriculum for accredited theological schools consists of four major categories: Biblical studies, history, theology, and practical theology. Courses of a practical nature include pastoral care, preaching, religious education, and administration. Many accredited schools require that students work under the supervision of a faculty member or experienced minister. Some institutions offer Doctor of Ministry degrees to students who have completed additional study—usually two or more years—and served at least two years as a minister. Scholarships and loans often are available for students of theological institutions.

Persons who have denominational qualifications for the ministry usually are ordained after graduation from a seminary or after serving a probationary pastoral period. Denominations that do not require seminary training ordain clergy at various appointed times. Some churches ordain ministers with only a high school education.

Women and men entering the clergy often begin their careers as pastors of small congregations or as assistant pastors in large churches. Pastor positions in large metropolitan areas or in large congregations often require many years of experience.

Job Outlook

Competition is expected to continue for paid Protestant ministers through the year 2008, reflecting slow growth of church membership and the large number of qualified candidates. Graduates of theological schools should have the best prospects. The degree of competition for paid positions will vary among denominations and geographic regions. For example, relatively favorable prospects are expected for ministers in evangelical churches. Competition, however, will be keen for responsible positions serving large urban congregations. Ministers willing to work part time or for small, rural congregations should have better opportunities. Most job openings will stem from the need to replace ministers who retire, die, or leave the ministry.

For newly ordained Protestant ministers who are unable to find parish positions, employment alternatives include working in youth counseling, family relations, and social welfare organizations; teaching in religious educational institutions; or serving as chaplains in the Armed Forces, hospitals, universities, and correctional institutions.

Earnings

Salaries of Protestant clergy vary substantially, depending on experience, denomination, size and wealth of the congregation, and geographic location. For example, some denominations tie a minister's pay to the average pay of the congregation or the community. As a result, ministers serving larger, wealthier congregations often earned significantly higher salaries than those in smaller,

less affluent areas or congregations. Ministers with modest salaries sometimes earn additional income from employment in secular occupations.

Sources of Additional Information

Persons who are interested in entering the Protestant ministry should seek the counsel of a minister or church guidance worker. Theological schools can supply information on admission requirements. Prospective ministers also should contact the ordination supervision body of their particular denomination for information on special requirements for ordination.

Rabbis

(O*NET 27502)

Significant Points

- Ordination usually requires completion of a college degree followed by a four- or five-year program at a Jewish seminary.

- Graduates of Jewish seminaries have excellent job prospects, reflecting current unmet needs for rabbis and the need to replace the many rabbis approaching retirement age.

Nature of the Work

Rabbis serve Orthodox, Conservative, Reform, and Reconstructionist Jewish congregations. Regardless of the branch of Judaism they serve or their individual points of view, all rabbis preserve the substance of Jewish religious worship. Congregations differ in the extent to which they follow the traditional form of worship—for example, in the wearing of head coverings, in the use of Hebrew as the language of prayer, and in the use of instrumental music or a choir. Additionally, the format of the worship service and, therefore, the ritual that the rabbi uses may vary even among congregations belonging to the same branch of Judaism.

Rabbis have greater independence in religious expression than other clergy, because of the absence of a formal religious hierarchy in Judaism. Instead, rabbis are responsible directly to the board of trustees of the congregation they serve. Those serving large congregations may spend considerable time in administrative duties, working with their staffs and committees. Large congregations frequently have associate or assistant rabbis, who often serve as educational directors. All rabbis play a role in community relations. For example, many rabbis serve on committees, alongside business and civic leaders in their communities to help find solutions to local problems.

Rabbis also may write for religious and lay publications and teach in theological seminaries, colleges, and universities.

Employment

Based on information from organizations representing the four major branches of Judaism, there were approximately 1,800 Reform, 1,175 Conservative, 1,800 Orthodox, and 250 Reconstructionist rabbis in 1999. Although the majority served congregations, many rabbis functioned in other settings. Some taught in Jewish studies programs at colleges and universities, and others served as chaplains in hospitals, colleges, or the military. Additionally, some rabbis held positions in one of the many social service or Jewish community agencies.

Although rabbis serve Jewish communities throughout the Nation, they are concentrated in major metropolitan areas with large Jewish populations.

Training and Other Qualifications

To become eligible for ordination as a rabbi, a student must complete a course of study in a seminary. Entrance requirements and the curriculum depend upon the branch of Judaism with which the seminary is associated. Most seminaries require applicants to be college graduates.

Jewish seminaries typically take five years for completion of studies, with an additional preparatory year required for students without sufficient grounding in Hebrew and Jewish studies. In addition to the core academic program, training generally includes fieldwork and internships providing hands-on experience and, in some cases, study in Jerusalem. Seminary graduates are awarded the title Rabbi and earn the Master of Arts in Hebrew Letters degree. After more advanced study, some earn the Doctor of Hebrew Letters degree.

In general, the curricula of Jewish theological seminaries provide students with a comprehensive knowledge of the Bible, the Torah, rabbinic literature, Jewish history, Hebrew, theology, and courses in education, pastoral psychology, and public speaking. Students receive extensive practical training in dealing with social problems in the community. Training for alternatives to the pulpit, such as leadership in community services and religious education, is increasingly stressed. Some seminaries grant advanced academic degrees in such fields as biblical and Talmudic research. All Jewish theological seminaries make scholarships and loans available.

Major rabbinical seminaries include the Jewish Theological Seminary of America, which educates rabbis for the Conservative branch; the Hebrew Union College—Jewish Institute of Religion, which educates rabbis for the Reform branch; and the Reconstructionist Rabbinical College, which educates rabbis in the newest branch of Judaism. About 35 seminaries educate and ordain Orthodox rabbis. Although the number of Orthodox seminaries is relatively high, the number of students attending each seminary is low. The Orthodox movement, as a whole, constitutes only about 10 percent of the American Jewish community. The Rabbi Isaac Elchanan Theological Seminary and the Beth Medrash Govoha Seminary are representative Orthodox seminaries. In all cases, rabbinic training is rigorous. When students have become sufficiently learned in the Torah, the Bible, and other religious texts, they may be ordained with the approval of an authorized rabbi, acting either independently or as a representative of a rabbinical seminary.

Newly ordained rabbis usually begin as spiritual leaders of small congregations, assistants to experienced rabbis, directors of Hillel Foundations on college campuses, teachers in educational institutions, or chaplains in the Armed Forces. As a rule, experienced rabbis fill the pulpits of large well-established Jewish congregations.

Job Outlook

Job opportunities for rabbis are expected to be excellent in all four of the major branches of Judaism through the year 2008, reflecting current unmet needs for rabbis, together with the need to replace the many rabbis approaching retirement age. Rabbis willing to work in small, underserved communities should have particularly good prospects.

Graduates of Orthodox seminaries who seek pulpits should have good opportunities as growth in enrollments slows and as many graduates seek alternatives to the pulpit. Reconstructionist rabbis are expected to have very good employment opportunities as membership expands rapidly. Conservative and Reform rabbis are expected to have excellent job opportunities serving congregations or in other settings because job prospects will be numerous in these two largest Jewish movements.

Earnings

Based on limited information, annual average earnings of rabbis generally ranged from $50,000 to $100,000 in 1998, including benefits. Benefits may include housing, health insurance, and a retirement plan. Income varies widely, depending on the size and financial status of the congregation, as well as denominational branch and geographic location. Rabbis may earn additional income from gifts or fees for officiating at ceremonies such as bar or bat mitzvahs and weddings.

Sources of Additional Information

Persons who are interested in becoming rabbis should discuss with a practicing rabbi their plans for this vocation. Information on the work of rabbis and allied occupations can be obtained from:

- Rabbinical Council of America, 305 7th Ave., New York, NY 10001. (Orthodox) Internet: http://www.rabbis.org
- The Jewish Theological Seminary of America, 3080 Broadway, New York, NY 10027. (Conservative) Internet: http://www.jtsa.edu
- Hebrew Union College-Jewish Institute of Religion, One West 4th St., New York, NY 10012. (Reform) Internet: http://www.huc.edu
- Reconstructionist Rabbinical College, 1299 Church Rd., Wyncote, PA 19095. (Reconstructionist) Internet: http://www.rrc.edu

Roman Catholic Priests

(O*NET 27502)

Significant Points

- Preparation generally requires eight years of study beyond high school, usually including a college degree followed by four or more years of theology study at a seminary.

- The shortage of Roman Catholic priests is expected to continue, resulting in a very favorable outlook.

Nature of the Work

Priests in the Catholic Church belong to one of two groups: diocesan or religious. Both types of priests have the same powers, acquired through ordination by a bishop. Differences lie in their way of life, type of work, and the Church authority to which they are responsible. *Diocesan priests* commit their lives to serving the people of a diocese, a church administrative region, and generally work in parishes assigned by the bishop of their diocese. Diocesan priests take oaths of celibacy and obedience. *Religious priests* belong to a religious order, such as the Jesuits, Dominicans, or Franciscans. In addition to the vows taken by diocesan priests, religious priests take a vow of poverty.

Diocesan priests attend to the spiritual, pastoral, moral, and educational needs of the members of their church. A priest's day usually begins with morning meditation and mass and may end with an individual counseling session or an evening visit to a hospital or home. Many priests direct and serve on church committees, work in civic and charitable organizations, and assist in community projects. Some counsel parishioners preparing for marriage or the birth of a child.

Religious priests receive duty assignments from their superiors in their respective religious orders. Some religious priests specialize in teaching, whereas others serve as missionaries in foreign countries, where they may live under difficult and primitive conditions. Other religious priests live a communal life in monasteries, where they devote their lives to prayer, study, and assigned work.

Both religious and diocesan priests hold teaching and administrative posts in Catholic seminaries, colleges and universities, and high schools. Priests attached to religious orders staff many of the Church's institutions of higher education and many high schools, whereas diocesan priests usually are concerned with the parochial schools attached to parish churches and with diocesan high schools. Members of religious orders do much of the missionary work conducted by the Catholic Church in this country and abroad.

Employment

According to *The Official Catholic Directory*, there were approximately 47,000 priests in 1998; about two-thirds were diocesan priests. There are priests in nearly every city and town and in many rural communities; however, the most work in metropolitan areas, where most Catholics reside.

Training and Other Qualifications

Men exclusively are ordained as priests. Women may serve in church positions that do not require priestly ordination. Preparation for the priesthood generally requires eight years of study beyond high school, usually including a college degree followed by four or more years of theology study at a seminary.

Preparatory study for the priesthood may begin in the first year of high school, at the college level, or in theological seminaries after college graduation. Nine high-school seminaries provided a college preparatory program in 1998. Programs emphasize English grammar, speech, literature, and social studies, as well as religious formation. Latin may be required, and modern languages are encouraged. In Hispanic communities, knowledge of Spanish is mandatory.

Those who begin training for the priesthood in college do so in one of 87 priesthood formation programs offered either through Catholic colleges or universities or in freestanding college seminaries. Preparatory studies usually include training in philosophy, religious studies, and prayer.

Today, most candidates for the priesthood have a four-year degree from an accredited college or university and then attend one of 47 theological seminaries (also called theologates) and earn either the Master of Divinity or the Master of Arts degree. Thirty-five theologates primarily train diocesan priests; the other 12 theologates mostly educate priests for religious orders. (Slight variations in training reflect the differences in their expected duties.) Theology coursework includes sacred scripture; dogmatic, moral, and pastoral theology; homiletics (art of preaching); Church history; liturgy (sacraments); and canon (church) law. Fieldwork experience usually is required.

Young men are never denied entry into seminaries because of lack of funds. In seminaries for diocesan priests, scholarships or loans are available, and contributions of benefactors and the Catholic Church finance those in religious seminaries—who have taken a vow of poverty and are not expected to have personal resources.

Graduate work in theology beyond that required for ordination is also offered at a number of American Catholic universities or at ecclesiastical universities around the world, particularly in Rome. Also, many priests do graduate work in fields unrelated to theology. Priests are encouraged by the Catholic Church to continue their studies, at least informally, after ordination. In recent years, the Church has stressed continuing education for ordained priests in the social sciences, such as sociology and psychology.

A newly ordained diocesan priest usually works as an assistant pastor. Newly ordained priests of religious orders are assigned to the specialized duties for which they have been trained. Depending on the talents, interests, and experience of the individual, many opportunities for additional responsibility exist within the Church.

Job Outlook

The shortage of Roman Catholic priests is expected to continue, resulting in a very favorable job outlook through the year 2008. Many priests will be needed in the years ahead to provide for the spiritual, educational, and social needs of the increasing number of Catholics. In recent years, the number of ordained priests has been insufficient to fill the needs of newly established parishes and other Catholic institutions and to replace priests who retire, die, or leave the priesthood. This situation is likely to continue, as seminary enrollments remain below the levels needed to overcome the current shortfall of priests.

In response to the shortage of priests, permanent deacons and teams of clergy and laity increasingly are performing certain traditional functions within the Catholic Church. The number of ordained deacons has increased five-fold over the past 20 years, and this trend should continue. Throughout most of the country, permanent deacons have been ordained to preach and perform liturgical functions, such as baptisms, marriages, and funerals, and to provide service to the community. Deacons are not authorized to celebrate Mass, nor are they allowed to administer the Sacraments of

Reconciliation and the Anointing of the Sick. Teams of clergy and laity undertake some liturgical and nonliturgical functions, such as hospital visits and religious teaching.

Earnings

Diocesan priests' salaries vary from diocese to diocese. According to the National Federation of Priests' Council, low-end cash only salaries averaged $12,936 per year in 1998; high-end salaries averaged $15,483 per year. Average salaries, including in-kind earnings, were $30,713 per year in 1998. In addition to a salary, diocesan priests receive a package of benefits that may include a car allowance, room and board in the parish rectory, health insurance, and a retirement plan.

Diocesan priests who do special work related to the church, such as teaching, usually receive a salary which is less than a lay person in the same position would receive. The difference between the usual salary for these jobs and the salary the priest receives is called "contributed service." In some situations, housing and related expenses may be provided; in other cases, the priest must make his own arrangements. Some priests doing special work receive the same compensation a lay person would receive.

Religious priests take a vow of poverty and are supported by their religious order. Any personal earnings are given to the order. Their vow of poverty is recognized by the Internal Revenue Service, which exempts them from paying Federal income tax.

Sources of Additional Information

Young men interested in entering the priesthood should seek the guidance and counsel of their parish priests and diocesan vocational office. For information regarding the different religious orders and the diocesan priesthood, as well as a list of the seminaries that prepare students for the priesthood, contact the diocesan director of vocations through the office of the local pastor or bishop.

Individuals seeking additional information about careers in the Catholic Ministry should contact their local diocese.

For information on training programs for the Catholic ministry, contact:

- Center for Applied Research in the Apostolate (CARA), Georgetown University, Washington, DC 20057.

College and University Faculty

(O*NET 31202, 31204, 31206, 31209, 31210, 31212, 31114, 31216, 31218, 31222, 31224, 31226, and 31299)

Significant Points

- A Ph.D. is usually required for full-time, tenure-track positions in four-year colleges and universities.

- Applicants for full-time college faculty positions should expect to face keen competition.

- Job prospects will continue to be better in certain fields—computer science, engineering, and business, for example—that offer attractive nonacademic job opportunities and attract fewer applicants for academic positions.

Nature of the Work

College and university faculty teach and advise nearly 15 million full- and part-time college students and perform a significant part of our Nation's research. Faculty also keep up with developments in their fields and consult with government, business, nonprofit, and community organizations.

Faculty usually are organized into departments or divisions based on subject or field. They usually teach several different courses—algebra, calculus, and statistics, for example. They may instruct undergraduate or graduate students or both. College and university faculty may give lectures to several hundred students in large halls, lead small seminars, or supervise students in laboratories. They prepare lectures, exercises, and laboratory experiments; grade exams and papers; and advise and work with students individually. In universities, they also supervise graduate students' teaching and research. College faculty work with an increasingly varied student population made up of growing shares of part-time, older, and culturally and racially diverse students.

Faculty keep abreast of developments in their field by reading current literature, talking with colleagues, and participating in professional conferences. They also do their own research to expand knowledge in their field. They perform experiments; collect and analyze data; and examine original documents, literature, and other source material. From this process, they arrive at conclusions and publish their findings in scholarly journals, books, and electronic media.

College and university faculty increasingly use technology in all areas of their work. In the classroom, they may use computers—including the Internet, electronic mail, software programs such as statistical packages, and CD-ROMs—as teaching aids. Some faculty use closed-circuit and cable television, satellite broadcasts, and video, audio, and Internet teleconferencing to teach courses to students at remote sites. Faculty post course content, class notes, class schedules, and other information on the Internet. They also use computers to do research, participate in discussion groups, or publicize professional research papers. Faculty will use these technologies more as quality and affordability improve.

Most faculty members serve on academic or administrative committees that deal with the policies of their institution, departmental matters, academic issues, curricula, budgets, equipment purchases, and hiring. Some work with student and community organizations. Department chairpersons are faculty members who usually teach some courses but usually have heavier administrative responsibilities.

The proportion of time spent on research, teaching, administrative, and other duties varies by individual circumstance and type of institution. Faculty members at universities normally spend a significant part of their time doing research; those in four-year col-

leges, somewhat less; and those in two-year colleges, relatively little. The teaching load, however, often is heavier in two-year colleges and somewhat lower at four-year institutions. Full professors at all types of institutions usually spend a larger portion of their time conducting research than do assistant professors, instructors, and lecturers.

Working Conditions

College faculty usually have flexible schedules. They must be present for classes, usually 12 to 16 hours per week, and for faculty and committee meetings. Most establish regular office hours for student consultations, usually 3 to 6 hours per week. Otherwise, faculty are free to decide when and where they will work and how much time to devote to course preparation, grading, study, research, graduate student supervision, and other activities.

Initial adjustment to these responsibilities can be challenging as new faculty adapt to switching roles from student to teacher. This adjustment may be even more difficult should class sizes grow in response to faculty and budget cutbacks, increasing an instructor's workload. Also, many institutions are increasing their reliance on part-time faculty, who usually have limited administrative and student advising duties, which leaves the declining number of full-time faculty with a heavier workload. To ease the transition from student to teacher, some institutions offer career development programs.

Some faculty members work staggered hours and teach night and weekend classes. This is particularly true for faculty who teach at two-year community colleges or institutions with large enrollments of older students with full-time jobs or family responsibilities. Most colleges and universities require faculty to work nine months of the year, which allows them the time to teach additional courses, do research, travel, or pursue nonacademic interests during the summer and school holidays. Colleges and universities usually have funds to support faculty research or other professional development needs, including travel to conferences and research sites.

Faculty may experience a conflict between their responsibilities to teach students and the pressure to do research and to publish their findings. This may be a particular problem for young faculty seeking advancement in four-year research universities. However, increasing emphasis on undergraduate teaching performance in tenure decisions may alleviate some of this pressure.

Part-time faculty usually spend little time on campus because they do not have offices. In addition, they may teach at more than one college, requiring travel between places of employment, earning the name "gypsy faculty." Part-time faculty are usually not eligible for tenure. For those seeking full-time employment in academia, dealing with this lack of job security can be stressful.

Employment

College and university faculty held about 865,000 jobs in 1998, mostly in public institutions.

About 3 out of 10 college and university faculty worked part time in 1998. Some part-timers, known as "adjunct faculty," have primary jobs outside of academia—in government, private industry, or in nonprofit research—and teach "on the side." Others prefer to work part-time hours or seek full-time jobs but are unable to obtain them due to intense competition for available openings. Some work part time in more than one institution. Many adjunct faculty are not qualified for tenure-track positions because they lack a doctoral degree.

Training, Other Qualifications, and Advancement

Most college and university faculty are in four academic ranks: professor, associate professor, assistant professor, and instructor. These positions are usually considered to be tenure-track positions. A small number of faculty, called lecturers, usually are not on the tenure track.

Most faculty members are hired as instructors or assistant professors. Four-year colleges and universities usually consider doctoral degree holders for full-time tenure-track positions, but may hire master's degree holders or doctoral candidates for certain disciplines, such as the arts, or for part-time and temporary jobs. In two-year colleges, master's degree holders fill most full-time positions. However, with increasing competition for available jobs, institutions can be more selective in their hiring practices. Master's degree holders may find it increasingly difficult to obtain employment as they are passed over in favor of candidates holding a Ph.D.

Doctoral programs, including time spent completing a master's degree and a dissertation, take an average of six to eight years of full-time study beyond the bachelor's degree. Some programs, such as the humanities, take longer to complete; others, such as engineering, usually are shorter. Candidates specialize in a subfield of a discipline—for example, organic chemistry, counseling psychology, or European history—but also take courses covering the entire discipline. Programs include 20 or more increasingly specialized courses and seminars plus comprehensive examinations on all major areas of the field. Candidates also must complete a dissertation—a written report on original research in the candidate's major field of study. The dissertation sets forth an original hypothesis or proposes a model and tests it. Students in the natural sciences and engineering usually do laboratory work; in the humanities, they study original documents and other published material. The dissertation, done under the guidance of one or more faculty advisors, usually takes one or two years of full-time work.

In some fields, particularly the natural sciences, some students spend an additional two years on postdoctoral research and study before taking a faculty position. Some Ph.D.s extend or take new postdoctoral appointments if they are unable to find a faculty job. Most of these appointments offer a nominal salary.

A major step in the traditional academic career is attaining tenure. New tenure-track faculty are usually hired as instructors or assistant professors and must serve a certain period (usually seven years) under term contracts. At the end of the contract period, their record of teaching, research, and overall contribution to the institution is reviewed; tenure is granted if the review is favorable. According to the American Association of University Professors, in 1998-99 about 65 percent of all full-time faculty held tenure, and about 86 percent were in tenure-track positions. Those denied tenure usually must leave the institution. Tenured professors cannot be fired without just cause and due process. Tenure protects the faculty's academic freedom—the ability to teach and conduct research without fear of being fired for advocating unpopular ideas. It also gives both faculty and institutions the stability needed for effective research and teaching and provides financial security for faculty. Some institutions have adopted post-tenure review policies to encourage ongoing evaluation of tenured faculty.

The number of tenure-track positions is expected to decline as institutions seek flexibility in dealing with financial matters and changing student interests. Institutions will rely more heavily on limited term contracts and part-time faculty, shrinking the total pool of tenured faculty. Some institutions offer limited term contracts to prospective faculty—typically two-, three-, or five-year full-time contracts. These contracts may be terminated or extended at the end of the period. Institutions are not obligated to grant tenure to these contract holders. In addition, some institutions have limited the percentage of faculty who can be tenured.

Some faculty—based on teaching experience, research, publication, and service on campus committees and task forces—move into administrative and managerial positions, such as departmental chairperson, dean, and president. At four-year institutions, such advancement requires a doctoral degree. At two-year colleges, a doctorate is helpful but not usually required, except for advancement to some top administrative positions.

College faculty should have inquiring and analytical minds and a strong desire to pursue and disseminate knowledge. They must be able to communicate clearly and logically, both orally and in writing. They should be able to establish rapport with students and, as models for them, be dedicated to the principles of academic integrity and intellectual honesty. Additionally, they must be self-motivated and able to work in an environment where they receive little direct supervision.

Job Outlook

Employment of college and university faculty is expected to increase faster than the average for all occupations through 2008 as enrollments in higher education increase. Many additional openings will arise as faculty members retire. Nevertheless, prospective job applicants should expect to face competition, particularly for full-time tenure-track positions at four-year institutions.

Between 1998 and 2008, the traditional college-age (18-24) population will grow again after several years of decline. This population increase, along with a higher proportion of 18- to 24-year-olds attending college and a growing number of part-time, female, minority, and older students, will spur college enrollments. Enrollment is projected to rise from 14.6 million in 1998 to 16.1 million in 2008, an increase of about 10 percent.

Growing numbers of students will necessitate hiring more faculty to teach. At the same time, many faculty will be retiring, opening up even more positions. Also, the number of doctoral degrees is expected to grow more slowly than in the past, somewhat easing the competition for some faculty positions.

Despite expected job growth and the need to replace retiring faculty, many in the academic community are concerned that institutions will increasingly favor the hiring of adjunct faculty over full-time, tenure-track faculty. For many years, keen competition for faculty jobs forced some applicants to accept part-time academic appointments that offered little hope of tenure and forced others to seek nonacademic positions. Many colleges, faced with reduced State funding for higher education and growing numbers of part-time and older students, increased the hiring of part-time faculty to save money on pay and benefits and to accommodate the needs of nontraditional-age students. If funding remains tight over the projection period, this trend of hiring adjunct or part-time faculty is likely to continue. Because of uncertainty about future funding sources, some colleges and universities are also controlling costs by changing the mix of academic programs offered, eliminating some programs altogether, and increasing class size.

Even if the proportion of full-time positions does not shrink, job competition will remain keen for coveted tenure-track jobs. Some institutions are expected to increasingly hire full-time faculty on limited-term contracts, reducing the number of tenure-track positions available. Overall, job prospects will continue to be better in certain

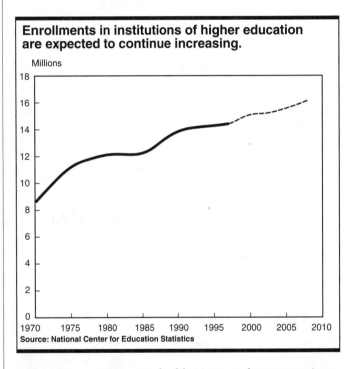

Enrollments in institutions of higher education are expected to continue increasing.

Source: National Center for Education Statistics

fields—business, engineering, health science, and computer science, for example—that offer attractive nonacademic job opportunities and attract fewer applicants for academic positions. Also, excellent job prospects in a field—for example, computer science—result in higher student enrollments, increasing faculty needs in that field. On the other hand, poor job prospects in a field, such as history in recent years, discourages students and reduces demand for faculty.

Earnings

Median annual earnings of college and university faculty in 1998 were $46,630. The middle 50 percent earned between $33,390 and $71,360. The lowest 10 percent earned less than $23,100; the highest 10 percent earned more than $90,360.

Earnings vary according to faculty rank and type of institution, geographic area, and field. According to a 1998-99 survey by the American Association of University Professors, salaries for full-time faculty averaged $56,300. By rank, the average for professors was $72,700;

associate professors, $53,200; assistant professors, $43,800; instructors, $33,400; and lecturers, $37,200. Faculty in four-year institutions earn higher salaries, on the average, than those in two-year schools. Average salaries for faculty in public institutions ($55,900) were lower in 1998-99 than those for private independent institutions ($63,500) but higher than those for religiously affiliated private colleges and universities ($49,400). In fields with high-paying nonacademic alternatives (notably medicine and law but also engineering and business, among others) earnings exceed these averages. In others, such as the humanities and education, they are lower.

Most faculty members have significant earnings in addition to their base salary, from consulting, teaching additional courses, researching, writing for publication, or other employment.

Most college and university faculty enjoy some unique benefits, including access to campus facilities, tuition waivers for dependents, housing and travel allowances, and paid sabbatical leaves. Part-time faculty usually have fewer benefits (including health insurance, retirement benefits, and sabbatical leave) than full-time faculty do.

Related Occupations

College and university faculty function both as teachers and as researchers. They communicate information and ideas. Related occupations include elementary and secondary school teachers, librarians, writers, consultants, lobbyists, trainers and employee development specialists, and policy analysts. Faculty research activities often are similar to those of scientists, as well as managers and administrators in industry, government, and nonprofit research organizations.

Sources of Additional Information

Professional societies generally provide information on academic and nonacademic employment opportunities in their fields.

Special publications on higher education, such as *The Chronicle of Higher Education*, are available in libraries and list specific employment opportunities for faculty.

Computer Operators

(O*NET 56011 and 56014)

Significant Points

- Employment is expected to decline sharply due to advances in technology.

- Opportunities will be best for operators who are familiar with a variety of operating systems and who keep up to date with the latest technology.

Nature of the Work

Computer operators oversee the operation of computer hardware systems, ensuring that these machines are used as efficiently as possible. They may work with mainframes, minicomputers, or networks of personal computers. Computer operators must anticipate problems and take preventive action, as well as solve problems that occur during operations.

The duties of computer operators vary with the size of the installation, the type of equipment used, and the policies of the employer. Generally, operators control the console of either a mainframe digital computer or a group of minicomputers. Working from operating instructions prepared by programmers, users, or operations managers, computer operators set controls on the computer and on peripheral devices required to run a particular job.

Computer operators load equipment with tapes, disks, and paper, as needed. While the computer is running—which may be 24 hours a day for large computers—computer operators monitor the control console and respond to operating and computer messages. Messages indicate the individual specifications of each job being run. If an error message occurs, operators must locate and solve the problem or terminate the program. Operators also maintain logbooks or operating records, listing each job that is run and events such as machine malfunctions that occur during their shift. In addition, computer operators may help programmers and systems analysts test and debug new programs.

As the trend toward networking computers accelerates, a growing number of computer operators are working on personal computers (PCs) and minicomputers. In many offices, factories, and other work settings, PCs and minicomputers are connected in networks, often referred to as local area networks (LANs) or multi-user systems. Whereas users in the area operate some of these computers, many require the services of full-time operators. The tasks performed are very similar to those performed on large computers.

As organizations continue to look for opportunities to increase productivity, automation is expanding into additional areas of computer operations. Sophisticated software, coupled with robotics, enable a computer to perform many routine tasks formerly done by computer operators. Scheduling, loading and downloading programs, mounting tapes, rerouting messages, and running periodic reports can be done without the intervention of an operator. Consequently, these improvements will change what computer operators do in the future. As technology advances, the responsibilities of many computer operators are shifting to areas such as network operations, user support, and database maintenance.

Working Conditions

Computer operating personnel generally work in well-lighted, well-ventilated, comfortable rooms. Because many organizations use their computers 24 hours a day, 7 days a week, computer operators may be required to work evening or night shifts and weekends. Shift assignments usually are made based on seniority. However, increasingly automated operations will lessen the need for shift work because many companies let the computer take over operations during less desirable working hours. In addition, advances in telecommuting technologies (such as faxes, modems, and e-mail) and data center automation (such as automated tape libraries) enable some operators to monitor batch processes, check systems performance, and record problems for the next shift.

Because computer operators generally spend a lot of time in front of a computer monitor, as well as performing repetitive tasks such as loading and unloading printers, they may be susceptible to eyestrain, back discomfort, and hand and wrist problems.

Employment

In 1998, computer operators held about 251,000 jobs. The majority of jobs for computer operators are found in organizations such as wholesale trade establishments, manufacturing companies, data processing service firms, financial institutions, and government agencies that have data processing needs requiring large computer installations. A large number of computer operators are employed by service firms in the computer and data processing services industry, as more companies contract out the operation of their data processing centers.

Training, Other Qualifications, and Advancement

Workers usually receive on-the-job training in order to become acquainted with their employer's equipment and routines. The length of training varies with the job and the experience of the worker. However, previous work experience is the key to obtaining an operator job in many large establishments. Employers generally look for specific hands-on experience with the type of equipment and related operating systems they use. Additionally, formal computer-related training, perhaps through a community college or technical school, is recommended. Related training can also be obtained through the Armed Forces and from some computer manufacturers. As computer technology changes and data processing centers become more automated, increasingly more employers will require candidates to have formal training and experience for operator jobs.

Because computer technology changes so rapidly, operators must be adaptable and willing to learn. Analytical and technical expertise are also needed, particularly by operators who work in automated data centers, to deal with the unique or high-level problems a computer is not programmed to handle. Operators must be able to communicate well and to work effectively with programmers or users, as well as with other operators. Additionally, computer operators must be able to work independently because they may have little or no direct supervision.

A few computer operators may advance to supervisory jobs, although most management positions within data processing or computer operations centers require advanced formal education, such as a bachelor's (or higher) degree. Through on-the-job experience and additional formal education, some computer operators may advance to jobs in areas such as network operations or support. As they gain experience in programming, some operators may advance to jobs as programmers or analysts. A move into these types of jobs is becoming much more difficult, as employers increasingly require candidates for more skilled computer jobs to possess at least a bachelor's degree.

Job Outlook

Employment of computer operators is expected to decline sharply through the year 2008. Experienced operators are expected to compete for the small number of openings that will arise each year to replace workers who transfer to other occupations or leave the labor force. Opportunities will be best for operators who are familiar with a variety of operating systems and who keep up to date with the latest technology.

Advances in technology have reduced both the size and cost of computer equipment, while increasing the capacity for data storage and processing automation. These improvements in technology have fueled an expansion in the use of sophisticated computer hardware and software in practically every industry in such areas as factory and office automation, telecommunications, medicine, education, and administration. The expanding use of software that automates computer operations gives companies the option of making systems user-friendly, greatly reducing the need for operators. These new technologies will require operators to monitor a greater number of operations at the same time and be capable of solving a broader range of problems that may arise. The result is that fewer and fewer operators will be needed to perform more highly skilled work.

Computer operators who are displaced by automation may be reassigned to support staffs that maintain personal computer networks or assist other members of the organization. Operators who keep up with changing technology by updating their skills and enhancing their training should have the best prospects of moving into other areas such as network administration and technical support. Others may be retrained to perform different job duties, such as supervising an operations center, maintaining automation packages, or analyzing computer operations to recommend ways to increase productivity. In the future, operators who wish to work in the computer field will need to know more about programming, automation software, graphics interface, client/server environments, and open systems in order to take advantage of changing opportunities.

Earnings

Median annual earnings of computer operators, except peripheral equipment operators were $25,030 in 1998. The middle 50 percent earned between about $20,410 and $31,610 a year. The lowest 10 percent earned less than $16,260; the highest 10 percent earned more than $39,130. Median annual earnings in the industries employing the largest numbers of computer operators, except peripheral equipment operators in 1997 are shown below:

Computer and data processing services	$24,300
Hospitals	23,600
Personnel supply services	22,600
Federal government	22,500
Commercial banks	20,200

In the Federal government, computer operators with a high school diploma started at about $21,600 a year in 1999; those with one year of college started at $23,000. Applicants with operations experience started at higher salaries.

Median annual earnings of peripheral equipment operators were $22,860 in 1998. The middle 50 percent earned between $18,240 and $29,370 a year. The lowest 10 percent earned less than $14,870; the highest 10 percent earned more than $37,220.

According to Robert Half International, the average starting salaries for console operators ranged from $26,000 to $35,500 in 1999. Salaries generally are higher in large organizations than in small ones.

Related Occupations

Other occupations involving work with computers include computer scientists, engineers, and systems analysts; computer programmers, and computer service technicians. Other occupations in which workers operate electronic office equipment include data entry keyers, secretaries, typists and word processors, and typesetters and compositors.

Sources of Additional Information

For information about work opportunities in computer operations, contact firms that use computers such as banks, manufacturing and insurance firms, colleges and universities, and data processing service organizations. The local office of the State employment service can supply information about employment and training opportunities.

Computer Programmers

(O*NET 25105)

Significant Points

- The level of education and experience required by employers has been rising, due to the increasing complexity of programming.

- A growing number of computer programmers are employed on a temporary or contract basis.

- Job prospects should be best for college graduates who are up to date with the latest skills and technologies.

Nature of the Work

Computer programmers write, test, and maintain the detailed instructions, called programs or software, that computers must follow to perform their functions. They also conceive, design, and test logical structures for solving problems by computer. Many technical innovations in programming—advanced computing technologies and sophisticated new languages and programming tools—have redefined the role of a programmer and elevated much of the programming work done today. As a result, it is becoming more difficult to distinguish different computer specialists—including programmers—since job titles shift so rapidly, reflecting new areas of specialization or changes in technology. Job titles and descriptions also may vary, depending on the organization. In this occupational statement, computer programmer refers to individuals whose main job function is programming; this group has a wide range of responsibilities and educational backgrounds.

Computer programs tell the computer what to do, such as which information to identify and access, how to process it, and what equipment to use. Programs vary widely depending upon the type of information to be accessed or generated. For example, the instructions involved in updating financial records are very different from those required to duplicate conditions on board an aircraft for pilots training in a flight simulator. Although simple programs can be written in a few hours, programs that use complex mathematical formulas, whose solutions can only be approximated, or that draw data from many existing systems, may require more than a year of work. In most cases, several programmers work together as a team under a senior programmer's supervision.

Programmers write specific programs by breaking down each step into a logical series of instructions the computer can follow. They then code these instructions in a conventional programming language, such as COBOL; an artificial intelligence language, such as Prolog; or one of the most advanced function-oriented or object-oriented languages, such as Java, C++, or Visual Basic. Programmers usually know more than one programming language; and since many languages are similar, they can often learn new languages relatively easily. In practice, programmers are often referred to by the language they know, such as Java programmers, or by the type of function they perform or environment in which they work, such as database programmers, mainframe programmers, or Internet programmers. In many large organizations, programmers follow descriptions that have been prepared by software engineers or systems analysts. These descriptions list the input required, the steps the computer must follow to process data, and the desired arrangement of the output.

Many programmers are involved in updating, repairing, modifying and expanding existing programs. When making changes to a section of code, called a *routine*, programmers need to make other users aware of the task the routine is to perform. They do this by inserting comments in the coded instructions, so others can understand the program. Innovations such as computer-aided software engineering (CASE) tools enable a programmer to concentrate on writing the unique parts of the program, because the tools automate various pieces of the program being built. CASE tools generate whole sections of code automatically, rather than line by line. This also yields more reliable and consistent programs and increases programmers' productivity by eliminating some routine steps.

Programmers test a program by running it to ensure the instructions are correct and it produces the desired information. If errors do occur, the programmer must make the appropriate change and recheck the program until it produces the correct results, a process called debugging. Programmers working in a mainframe environment may prepare instructions for a computer operator who will run the program. They may also contribute to a manual for users.

Programmers often are grouped into two broad types: applications programmers and systems programmers. *Applications programmers* usually focus on business, engineering, or science. They write software to handle a specific job, such as a program to track inventory, within an organization. They may also revise existing packaged software. *Systems programmers*, on the other hand, maintain and control computer systems software, such as operating systems, networked systems, and database systems. These workers make changes in the sets of instructions that determine how the network, workstations, and central processing unit of the system handle the various jobs they have been given and how they communicate with peripheral equipment, such as terminals, printers, and disk drives. Because of their knowledge of the entire computer system, systems programmers often help applications programmers determine the source of problems that may occur with their programs.

Programmers in software development companies may work directly with experts from various fields to create software (either programs designed for specific clients or packaged software for general use) ranging from games and educational software to programs for desktop publishing, financial planning, and spreadsheets. Much of this type of programming is in the preparation of packaged software, which comprises one of the most rapidly growing segments of the computer services industry.

In some organizations, particularly small ones, workers commonly referred to as *programmer-analysts* are responsible for both the systems analysis and the actual programming work. Advanced programming languages and new object-oriented programming capabilities are increasing the efficiency and productivity of both programmers and users. The transition from a mainframe environment to one that is primarily personal computer (PC) based has blurred the once rigid distinction between the programmer and the user. Increasingly, adept end-users are taking over many of the tasks previously performed by programmers. For example, the growing use of packaged software, like spreadsheet and database management software packages, allows users to write simple programs to access data and perform calculations.

Working Conditions

Programmers generally work in offices in comfortable surroundings. Many programmers may work long hours or weekends to meet deadlines or fix critical problems that occur during off hours. Given the technology available, telecommuting is becoming common for a wide range of computer professionals—including computer programmers. Programmers can access a system from remote locations to make corrections or fix problems.

Like other workers who spend long periods of time in front of a computer terminal typing at a keyboard, programmers are susceptible to eyestrain, back discomfort, and hand and wrist problems, such as carpal tunnel syndrome.

Employment

Computer programmers held about 648,000 jobs in 1998. Programmers are employed in almost every industry, but the largest concentration is in the computer and data processing services industry, which includes firms that write and sell software. Large numbers of programmers can also be found working for firms that provide engineering and management services, telecommunications companies, manufacturers of computer and office equipment, financial institutions, insurance carriers, educational institutions, and government agencies.

A growing number of computer programmers are employed on a temporary or contract basis or work as independent consultants, as companies demand expertise with new programming languages or specialized areas of application. Rather than hiring programmers as permanent employees and then laying them off after a job

is completed, employers can contract with temporary help agencies, consulting firms, or directly with programmers themselves. A marketing firm, for example, may only require the services of several programmers to write and debug the software necessary to get a new database management system running. This practice also enables companies to bring in people with a specific set of skills—usually in one of the latest technologies—as it applies to their business needs. Bringing in an independent contractor or consultant with a certain level of experience in a new or advanced programming language, for example, enables an establishment to complete a particular job without having to retrain existing workers. Such jobs may last anywhere from several weeks to a year or longer. There were 31,000 self-employed computer programmers in 1998, and this number is expected to increase.

Training, Other Qualifications, and Advancement

While there are many training paths available for programmers, mainly because employers' needs are so varied, the level of education and experience employers seek has been rising due to the growing number of qualified applicants and the increasing complexity of some programming tasks. Bachelor's degrees are now commonly required, although some programmers may qualify for certain jobs with two-year degrees or certificates. College graduates who are interested in changing careers or developing an area of expertise also may return to a two-year community college or technical school for additional training. In the absence of a degree, substantial specialized experience or expertise may be needed. Even for those with a degree, employers appear to be placing more emphasis on previous experience for all types of programmers.

About 3 out of 5 computer programmers had a bachelor's degree or higher in 1998 (see Table 1). Of these, some hold a degree in computer science, mathematics, or information systems, whereas others have taken special courses in computer programming to supplement their study in fields such as accounting, inventory control, or other areas of business. As the level of education and training required by employers continues to rise, this percentage should increase in the future.

TABLE 1

Highest level of school completed or degree received, computer programmers, 1998

	Percent
High school graduate or equivalent or less	10.6
Some college, no degree	20.5
Associate degree	10.2
Bachelor's degree	45.3
Graduate degree	13.4

Required skills vary from job to job, but the demand for various skills is generally driven by changes in technology. Employers using computers for scientific or engineering applications usually prefer college graduates who have degrees in computer or informa-

tion science, mathematics, engineering, or the physical sciences. Graduate degrees in related fields are required for some jobs. Employers who use computers for business applications prefer to hire people who have had college courses in information systems (MIS) and business and who possess strong programming skills. Although knowledge of traditional languages is still important, increasing emphasis is placed on newer, object-oriented programming languages and tools, such as C++, Visual Basic, and Java. Additionally, employers are seeking persons familiar with fourth and fifth generation languages that involve graphic user interface (GUI) and systems programming. Employers also prefer applicants who have general business skills and experience related to the operations of the firm. Students can improve their employment prospects by participating in a college work-study program or by undertaking an internship.

Most systems programmers hold a four-year degree in computer science. Extensive knowledge of a variety of operating systems is essential. This includes being able to configure an operating system to work with different types of hardware and adapting the operating system to best meet the needs of a particular organization. Programmers must also be able to work with database systems, such as DB2, Oracle, or Sybase, for example.

When hiring programmers, employers look for people with the necessary programming skills who can think logically and pay close attention to detail. The job calls for patience, persistence, and the ability to work on exacting analytical work, especially under pressure. Ingenuity and imagination are also particularly important, when programmers design solutions and test their work for potential failures. The ability to work with abstract concepts and to do technical analysis is especially important for systems programmers, because they work with the software that controls the computer's operation. Since programmers are expected to work in teams and interact directly with users, employers want programmers who are able to communicate with nontechnical personnel.

Entry-level or junior programmers may work alone on simple assignments after some initial instruction or on a team with more experienced programmers. Either way, beginning programmers generally must work under close supervision. Because technology changes so rapidly, programmers must continuously update their training, by taking courses sponsored by their employer or software vendors.

For skilled workers who keep up to date with the latest technology, the prospects for advancement are good. In large organizations, programmers may be promoted to lead programmer and be given supervisory responsibilities. Some applications programmers may move into systems programming after they gain experience and take courses in systems software. With general business experience, programmers may become programmer analysts or systems analysts or be promoted to a managerial position. Other programmers, with specialized knowledge and experience with a language or operating system, may work in research and development areas, such as multimedia or Internet technology. As employers increasingly contract out programming jobs, more opportunities should arise for experienced programmers with expertise in a specific area to work as consultants.

Technical or professional certification is a way to demonstrate a level of competency or quality. Product vendors or software firms also offer certification and may require professionals who work with their products to be certified. Many are widely sought and considered industry standards. Voluntary certification is also available through other organizations. Professional certification may provide a jobseeker a competitive advantage.

Job Outlook

Employment of programmers is expected to grow faster than the average for all occupations through 2008. Jobs for both systems and applications programmers should be plentiful in data processing service firms, software houses, and computer consulting businesses. These types of establishments are part of computer and data processing services, which is projected to be the fastest growing industry in the economy. As organizations attempt to control costs and keep up with changing technology, they will maintain a need for programmers to assist in conversions to new computer languages and systems. In addition, numerous job openings will result from the need to replace programmers who leave the labor force or transfer to other occupations such as manager or systems analyst.

Despite numerous openings, a number of factors will continue to moderate employment growth. The consolidation and centralization of systems and applications, developments in packaged software, advanced programming languages and tools, and the growing ability of users to design, write, and implement more of their own programs means more of the programming functions can be transferred to other types of workers. Furthermore, completion of Year 2000 work will mean that many programmers will need to be retrained and redeployed in other areas. And, as the level of technological innovation and sophistication increases, programmers should continue to face increasing competition from programming businesses overseas where much routine work can be outsourced at a lower cost.

Nevertheless, employers will continue to need programmers with strong technical skills who understand an employer's business and its programming needs. Given the importance of networking and the expansion of client/server environments, organizations will look for programmers who can support data communications and help implement electronic commerce and intranet strategies. Demand for programmers with strong object-oriented programming capabilities and technical specialization in areas such as client/server programming, multimedia technology, and graphic user interface (GUI), should arise from the expansion of intranets, extranets, and World Wide Web applications. Programmers will also be needed to create and maintain expert systems and embed these technologies in more and more products.

As programming tasks become increasingly sophisticated and an additional level of skill and experience is demanded by employers, graduates of two-year programs and people with less than a two-year degree or its equivalent in work experience should face strong competition for programming jobs. Competition for entry-level positions, however, can also affect applicants with a bachelor's degree. Prospects should be best for college graduates with knowledge of and experience working with a variety of programming languages and tools, including C++ and other object-oriented languages like Visual Basic and Java, as well as newer domain-specific languages that apply to computer networking, database management, and Internet application development. Because demand fluctuates with employers' needs, job seekers should keep up to date with the latest skills and technologies. Individuals who want to become programmers can enhance their prospects by combining the appropriate formal training with practical work experience.

Earnings

Median annual earnings of computer programmers were $47,550 in 1998. The middle 50 percent earned between $36,020 and $70,610 a year. The lowest 10 percent earned less than $27,670; the highest 10 percent earned more than $88,730. Median annual earnings in the industries employing the largest numbers of computer programmers in 1997 were:

Personnel supply services	$53,700
Computer and data processing services	48,900
Telephone communications	48,800
Professional and commercial equipment	47,700
Management and public relations	46,400

According to the National Association of Colleges and Employers, starting salary offers for graduates with a bachelor's degree in computer programming averaged about $40,800 a year in 1999.

Programmers working in the West or Northeast earned somewhat more than those working in the South or Midwest. On average, systems programmers earn more than applications programmers.

According to Robert Half International, average annual starting salaries in 1999 ranged from $38,000 to $50,500 for applications development programmers and from $49,000 to $63,000 for systems programmers. Average starting salaries for Internet programmers ranged from $48,800 to $68,300.

Related Occupations

Other professional workers who must be detail-oriented include computer scientists, computer engineers, systems analysts, database administrators, statisticians, mathematicians, engineers, financial analysts, accountants, actuaries, and operations research analysts.

Sources of Additional Information

State employment service offices can provide information about job openings for computer programmers. Also check with your city's chamber of commerce for information on the area's largest employers.

For information about certification as a computing professional, contact:

- Institute for Certification of Computing Professionals (ICCP), 2200 East Devon Ave., Suite 268, Des Plaines, IL 60018. Internet: http://www.iccp.org

Further information about computer careers is available from:

- The Association for Computing Machinery (ACM), 1515 Broadway, New York, NY 10036. Internet: http://www.acm.org

- Institute of Electrical and Electronics Engineers—United States of America, 1828 L St. NW., Suite 1202, Washington, DC 20036. Internet: http://www.ieee.org

Construction and Building Inspectors

(O*NET 21908A, 21908B, and 83005B)

Significant Points

- Local governments, primarily municipal or county building departments, employed nearly 60 percent of these workers.

- Construction and building inspectors tend to be older, more experienced workers who have spent years working in related occupations.

Nature of the Work

Construction and building inspectors examine the construction, alteration, or repair of buildings, highways and streets, sewer and water systems, dams, bridges, and other structures to ensure compliance with building codes and ordinances, zoning regulations, and contract specifications. Building codes and standards are the primary means by which building construction is regulated in the United States to assure the health and safety of the general public. Inspectors make an initial inspection during the first phase of construction, and follow-up inspections throughout the construction project to monitor compliance with regulations. However, no inspection is ever exactly the same. In areas where certain types of severe weather or natural disasters are more common, inspectors monitor compliance with additional safety regulations designed to protect structures and occupants in these events.

Building inspectors inspect the structural quality and general safety of buildings. Some specialize—for example, in structural steel or reinforced concrete structures. Before construction begins, *plan examiners* determine whether the plans for the building or other structure comply with building code regulations, and if they are suited to the engineering and environmental demands of the building site. Inspectors visit the work site before the foundation is poured to inspect the soil condition and the positioning and depth of the footings. Later, they return to the site to inspect the foundation after it has been completed. The size and type of structure, as well as the rate of completion, determine the number of other site visits they must make. Upon completion of the project, they make a final comprehensive inspection.

In addition to structural characteristics, a primary concern of building inspectors is fire safety. They inspect structures' fire sprinklers, alarms, and smoke control systems, as well as fire exits. Inspectors assess the type of construction, building contents, adequacy of fire protection equipment, and risks posed by adjoining buildings.

There are many types of inspections and inspectors. *Electrical inspectors* examine the installation of electrical systems and equipment to ensure they function properly and comply with electrical codes and standards. They visit work sites to inspect new and existing sound and security systems, wiring, lighting, motors, and generating equipment. They also inspect the installation of the electrical wiring for heating and air-conditioning systems, appliances, and other components.

Elevator inspectors examine lifting and conveying devices such as elevators, escalators, moving sidewalks, lifts and hoists, inclined railways, ski lifts, and amusement rides.

Mechanical inspectors inspect the installation of the mechanical components of commercial kitchen appliances, heating and air-conditioning equipment, gasoline and butane tanks, gas and oil piping, and gas-fired and oil-fired appliances. Some specialize in boilers or ventilating equipment as well.

Plumbing inspectors examine plumbing systems, including private disposal systems, water supply and distribution systems, plumbing fixtures and traps, and drain, waste, and vent lines.

Public works inspectors ensure that Federal, State, and local government construction of water and sewer systems, highways, streets, bridges, and dams conforms to detailed contract specifications. They inspect excavation and fill operations, the placement of forms for concrete, concrete mixing and pouring, asphalt paving, and grading operations. They record the work and materials used so that contract payments can be calculated. Public works inspectors may specialize in highways, structural steel, reinforced concrete, or ditches. Others specialize in dredging operations required for bridges and dams or for harbors.

Home inspectors generally conduct inspections of newly built or previously owned homes. Increasingly, prospective home buyers hire home inspectors to inspect and report the condition of a home's major systems, components, and structure. They are typically hired either immediately prior to a purchase offer on a home, or as a contingency to a sales contract. In addition to structural quality, home inspectors must be able to inspect all home systems and features, from plumbing, electrical, and heating or cooling systems to roofing.

The owner of a building or structure under construction employs *specification inspectors* to ensure work is done according to design specifications. They represent the owners' interests, not the general public. Insurance companies and financial institutions also may use specification inspectors.

Details concerning construction projects, building and occupancy permits, and other documentation are generally stored on computers so they can easily be retrieved, kept accurate, and updated. For example, inspectors may use laptop computers to record their findings while inspecting a site. Most inspectors use computers to help them monitor the status of construction inspection activities and keep track of issued permits.

Although inspections are primarily visual, most inspectors (except home inspectors) may use tape measures, survey instruments, metering devices, and test equipment such as concrete strength measurers. They keep a log of their work, take photographs, file reports, and, if necessary, act on their findings. For example, construction inspectors notify the construction contractor, superintendent, or supervisor when they discover a code or ordinance violation or something that does not comply with the contract specifications or approved plans. If the problem is not corrected within a reasonable or specified period of time, government inspectors have authority to issue a "stop-work" order.

Many inspectors also investigate construction or alterations being done without proper permits. Inspectors who are employees of municipalities enforce laws pertaining to the proper design, construction, and use of buildings. They direct violators of permit laws to obtain permits and submit to inspection.

Working Conditions

Construction and building inspectors usually work alone. However, several may be assigned to large, complex projects, particularly because inspectors tend to specialize in different areas of construction. Though they spend considerable time inspecting construction work sites, inspectors also spend time in a field office reviewing blueprints, answering letters or telephone calls, writing reports, and scheduling inspections.

Inspection sites are dirty and may be cluttered with tools, materials, or debris. Inspectors may have to climb ladders or many flights of stairs, or crawl around in tight spaces. Although their work is not generally considered hazardous, inspectors, like other construction workers, wear hard hats and adhere to other safety requirements while at a construction site.

Inspectors normally work regular hours. However, they may work additional hours during periods when a lot of construction is taking place. Also, if an accident occurs at a construction site, inspectors must respond immediately and may work additional hours to complete their reports.

Employment

Construction and building inspectors held about 68,000 jobs in 1998. Local governments, primarily municipal or county building departments, employed nearly 60 percent. Employment of local government inspectors is concentrated in cities and in suburban areas undergoing rapid growth. Local governments employ large inspection staffs, including many plan examiners or inspectors who specialize in structural steel, reinforced concrete, boiler, electrical, and elevator inspection.

Another 17 percent of construction and building inspectors worked for engineering and architectural services firms, conducting inspections for a fee or on a contract basis. Most of the remaining inspectors were employed by the Federal and State governments. Many construction inspectors employed by the Federal government work for the U.S. Army Corps of Engineers. Other Federal employers include the Tennessee Valley Authority and the Departments of Agriculture, Housing and Urban Development, and Interior.

Training, Other Qualifications, and Advancement

Although requirements vary considerably depending upon where one is employed, individuals who want to become construction and building inspectors should have a thorough knowledge of construction materials and practices in either a general area, such as structural or heavy construction, or in a specialized area, such as electrical or plumbing systems, reinforced concrete, or structural steel. Construction or building inspectors need several years of experience as a manager, supervisor, or craft worker before becoming inspectors. Many previously worked as carpenters, electricians, plumbers, or pipefitters.

Because inspectors need to possess the right mix of technical knowledge, experience and education, employers prefer to hire inspectors who have formal training as well as experience. Most require at least a high school diploma or equivalent, even for those with considerable experience. More often, employers look for persons who have studied engineering or architecture or who have a degree from a community or junior college with courses in construction technology, drafting, mathematics, and building inspection. Many community colleges offer certificate or associate degree programs in building inspection technology. Courses in blueprint reading, algebra, geometry, and English are also useful.

Construction and building inspectors must be in good physical condition in order to walk and climb about construction sites. They must also have a driver's license. In addition, Federal, State, and many local governments may require that inspectors pass a civil service exam.

Construction and building inspectors usually receive much of their training on the job, although they must learn building codes and standards on their own. Working with an experienced inspector, they learn about inspection techniques; codes, ordinances, and regulations; contract specifications; and record keeping and reporting duties. They may begin by inspecting less complex types of construction, such as residential buildings, and then progress to more difficult assignments. An engineering or architectural degree is often required for advancement to supervisory positions.

Because they advise builders and the general public on building codes, construction practices, and technical developments, construction and building inspectors must keep abreast of changes in these areas. Continuing education is imperative in this field. Many employers provide formal training programs to broaden inspectors' knowledge of construction materials, practices, and techniques. Inspectors who work for small agencies or firms that do not conduct training programs can expand their knowledge and upgrade their skills by attending State-sponsored training programs, by taking college or correspondence courses, or by attending seminars sponsored by various related organizations such as model code organizations.

Most States and cities require some type of certification for employment and, even if not required, certification can enhance an inspector's opportunities for employment and advancement to more responsible positions. To become certified, inspectors with substantial experience and education must pass stringent examinations on code requirements, construction techniques, and materials. The three major model code organizations offer voluntary certification as do other professional membership associations. In most cases, there are no education or experience prerequisites, and certification consists of passing an examination in a designated field. Many categories of certification are awarded for inspectors and plan examiners in a variety of disciplines, including the designation "CBO," Certified Building Official.

Job Outlook

Employment of construction and building inspectors is expected to grow as fast as the average for all occupations through 2008. Growing concern for public safety and improvements in the quality of construction should continue to stimulate demand for construction and building inspectors. Despite the expected employment growth, most job openings will arise from the need to replace inspectors who transfer to other occupations or leave the labor force. Construction and building inspectors tend to be older, more experienced workers who have spent years working in other occupations.

Opportunities should be best for highly experienced supervisors and craft workers who have some college education, engineering or architectural training, or who are certified as inspectors or plan examiners. Thorough knowledge of construction practices and skills in areas such as reading and evaluating blueprints and plans are essential. However, inspectors are involved in all phases of construction, including maintenance and repair work, and are therefore less likely to lose jobs during recessionary periods when new construction slows. As the population grows and the volume of real estate transactions increases, greater emphasis on home inspections should result in rapid growth in employment of home inspectors. In addition, there should be good opportunities in engineering, architectural, and management services firms due to the tendency of governments—particularly the Federal and State—to contract out inspection work, as well as expected growth in private inspection services.

Earnings

Median annual earnings of construction and building inspectors were $37,540 in 1998. The middle 50 percent earned between $29,540 and $47,040. The lowest 10 percent earned less than $22,770, and the highest 10 percent earned more than $61,820. Median annual earnings in the industries employing the largest numbers of construction and building inspectors in 1997 were:

Engineering and architectural services $36,500

Local government, except education and hospitals 36,300

State government, except education and hospitals 32,700

Generally, building inspectors, including plan examiners, earn the highest salaries. Salaries in large metropolitan areas are substantially higher than those in small local jurisdictions.

Related Occupations

Construction and building inspectors combine knowledge of construction principles and law with an ability to coordinate data, diagnose problems, and communicate with people. Workers in other occupations using a similar combination of skills include engineers, drafters, estimators, industrial engineering technicians, surveyors, architects, and construction managers.

Sources of Additional Information

Information about certification and a career as a construction or building inspector is available from the following model code organizations:

- International Conference of Building Officials, 5360 Workman Mill Rd., Whittier, CA 90601-2298. Internet: http://www.icbo.org
- Building Officials and Code Administrators International, Inc., 4051 West Flossmoor Rd., Country Club Hills, IL 60478. Internet: http://www.bocai.org
- Southern Building Code Congress International, Inc., 900 Montclair Rd., Birmingham, AL 35213.

Information about a career as a home inspector is available from:

- American Society of Home Inspectors, Inc., 932 Lee St., Suite 101, Des Plaines, IL 60016. Internet: http://www.ashi.com

For information about a career as a State or local government construction or building inspector, contact your State or local employment service.

Construction Managers

(O*NET 15017B)

Significant Points

- Construction managers must be available, often 24 hours a day, to deal with delays, bad weather, or emergencies at the site.

- The increasing level and complexity of construction activity should spur demand for managers.

- Individuals who combine industry work experience with a bachelor's degree in construction or building science or construction management should have the best job prospects.

Nature of the Work

Construction managers plan and direct construction projects. They may have job titles, such as *constructor, construction superintendent, general superintendent, project engineer, project manager, general construction manager, or executive construction manager.* Construction managers may be owners or salaried employees of a construction management or contracting firm, or they may work under contract or as a salaried employee of the owner, developer, contractor, or management firm overseeing the construction project. This book uses the term "construction manager" to describe salaried or self-employed managers who oversee construction supervisors and workers.

In contrast with the definition used in this book, "construction manager" is defined more narrowly within the construction industry to denote a management firm, or an individual employed by such a firm, who is involved in management oversight of a construction project. Under this definition, construction managers usually represent the owner or developer with other participants throughout the project. Although they usually play no direct role in the actual construction of a structure, they typically schedule and coordinate all design and construction processes including the selection, hiring, and oversight of specialty trade contractors.

Managers and professionals who work in the construction industry, such as general managers, project engineers, cost estimators, and others, are increasingly called *constructors*. Through education and past work experience, this broad group of professionals manages, coordinates, and supervises the construction process from the conceptual development stage through final construction on a timely and economical basis. Given designs for buildings, roads, bridges, or other projects, constructors oversee the organization, scheduling, and implementation of the project to execute those designs. They are responsible for coordinating and managing people, materials, and equipment; budgets, schedules, and contracts; and the safety of employees and the general public.

On large projects, construction managers may work for a *general contractor*—the firm with overall responsibility for all activities. There they oversee the completion of all construction in accordance with the engineer or architect's drawings and specifications and prevailing building codes. They arrange for *trade contractors* to perform specialized craft work or other specified construction work. On small projects, such as remodeling a home, a self-employed construction manager or skilled trades worker who directs and oversees employees is often referred to as the construction "contractor."

Large construction projects, such as an office building or industrial complex, are too complicated for one person to manage. These projects are divided into many segments: site preparation, including land clearing and earth moving; sewage systems; landscaping and road construction; building construction, including excavation and laying foundations, erection of structural framework, floors, walls, and roofs; and building systems, including fire protection, electrical, plumbing, air-conditioning, and heating. Construction managers may work as part of a team or be in charge of one or more of these activities.

Construction managers evaluate various construction methods and determine the most cost-effective plan and schedule. They determine the appropriate construction methods and schedule all required construction site activities into logical, specific steps, budgeting the time required to meet established deadlines. This may require sophisticated estimating and scheduling techniques and the use of computers with specialized software. This also involves the selection and coordination of trade contractors hired to complete specific pieces of the project—which could include everything from structural metalworking and plumbing to painting and carpet installation. Construction managers determine the labor requirements and, in some cases, supervise or monitor the hiring and dismissal of workers. They oversee the performance of all trade contractors and are responsible for ensuring all work is completed on schedule.

Construction managers direct and monitor the progress of construction activities, at times through other construction supervisors. This includes the delivery and use of materials, tools, and equipment, as well as the quality of construction, worker productivity, and safety. They are responsible for obtaining all necessary permits and licenses and, depending upon the contractual arrangements, they direct or monitor compliance with building and safety codes and other regulations. They may have several subordinates, such as assistant managers or superintendents, field engineers, or crew supervisors, reporting to them.

Construction managers regularly review engineering and architectural drawings and specifications to monitor progress and ensure compliance with plans and specifications. They track and control construction costs to avoid cost overruns. Based upon direct observation and reports by subordinate supervisors, managers may prepare daily reports of progress and requirements for labor, material, and machinery and equipment at the construction site. They meet regularly with owners, trade contractors, architects, and other design professionals to monitor and coordinate all phases of the construction project.

Working Conditions

Construction managers work out of a main office from which the overall construction project is monitored, or out of a field office at the construction site. Management decisions regarding daily construction activities are usually made at the job site. Managers usually travel when the construction site is in another State or when they are responsible for activities at two or more sites. Management of overseas construction projects usually entails temporary residence in another country.

Construction managers must be "on call," often 24 hours a day, to deal with delays, bad weather, or emergencies at the site. Most work more than a standard 40-hour week because construction may proceed around-the-clock. This type of work schedule can go on for days, even weeks, to meet special project deadlines, especially if there are delays.

Although the work usually is not considered inherently dangerous, construction managers must be careful while touring construction sites. Managers must establish priorities and assign duties. They need to observe job conditions and be alert to changes and potential problems, particularly involving safety on the job site and adherence to regulations.

Employment

Construction managers held about 270,000 jobs in 1998. Around 45,000 were self-employed. About 85 percent of salaried construction managers were employed in the construction industry, about 36 percent by specialty trade contractors—for example, plumbing, heating and air-conditioning, and electrical contractors—and about 38 percent by general building contractors. Engineering, architectural, and construction management services firms, as well as local governments, educational institutions, and real estate developers employed others.

Training, Other Qualifications, and Advancement

Persons interested in becoming a construction manager need a solid background in building science, business, and management, as well as related work experience within the construction industry. They need to understand contracts, plans, and specifications and to be knowledgeable about construction methods, materials, and regulations. Familiarity with computers and software programs for job costing, scheduling, and estimating is increasingly important.

Traditionally, persons advance to construction management positions after having substantial experience as construction craft workers—carpenters, masons, plumbers, or electricians, for example—or after having worked as construction supervisors or as owners of independent specialty contracting firms overseeing workers in one or more construction trades. However, more and more employers—particularly, large construction firms—hire individuals who combine industry work experience with a bachelor's degree in construction or building science or construction management. Practical industry experience is very important, whether through internships, cooperative education programs, or tenure in the industry.

Construction managers should be flexible and work effectively in a fast-paced environment. They should be decisive and work well under pressure, particularly when faced with unexpected occurrences or delays. The ability to coordinate several major activities at once, while analyzing and resolving specific problems, is essential, as is understanding engineering, architectural, and other construction drawings. Good oral and written communication skills are also important, as are leadership skills. Managers must be able to establish a good working relationship with many different people, including owners, other managers, design professionals, supervisors, and craft workers.

Advancement opportunities for construction managers vary depending upon an individual's performance and the size and type of company for which they work. Within large firms, managers may eventually become top-level managers or executives. Highly experienced individuals may become independent consultants; some serve as expert witnesses in court or as arbitrators in disputes. Those with the required capital may establish their own construction management services or specialty contracting or general contracting firm.

In 1998, over 100 colleges and universities offered four-year degree programs in construction management or construction science. These programs include courses in project control and development, site planning, design, construction methods, construction materials, value analysis, cost estimating, scheduling, contract administration, accounting, business and financial management, building codes and standards, inspection procedures, engineering and architectural sciences, mathematics, statistics, and information technology. Graduates from four-year degree programs are usually hired as assistants to project managers, field engineers, schedulers, or cost estimators. An increasing number of graduates in related fields—engineering or architecture, for example—also enter construction management, often after having had substantial experience on construction projects or after completing graduate studies in construction management or building science.

Around 30 colleges and universities offer a master's degree program in construction management or construction science, and at least two offer a Ph.D. in the field. Master's degree recipients, especially those with work experience in construction, typically become construction managers in very large construction or construction management companies. Often, individuals who hold a bachelor's degree in an unrelated field seek a master's degree in order to work in the construction industry. Doctoral degree recipients usually become college professors or conduct research.

Many individuals also attend training and educational programs sponsored by industry associations, often in collaboration with postsecondary institutions. A number of two-year colleges throughout the country offer construction management or construction technology programs.

Both the American Institute of Constructors (AIC) and the Construction Management Association of America (CMAA) have established voluntary certification programs for construction professionals. Requirements combine written examinations with verification of professional experience. AIC awards the designations Associate Constructor (AC) and Certified Professional Constructor (CPC) to candidates who meet the requirements and pass appropriate construction examinations. CMAA awards the designation Certified Construction Manager (CCM) to practitioners who meet the requirements in a construction management firm, complete a professional construction management "capstone" course, and pass a technical examination. Although certification is not required to work in the construction industry, voluntary certification can be valuable because it provides evidence of competence and experience.

Job Outlook

Employment of construction managers is expected to increase about as fast as the average for all occupations through 2008, as the level and complexity of construction activity continues to grow. Prospects in construction management, engineering and architectural services, and construction contracting firms should be best for persons who have a bachelor's or higher degree in construction science, construction management, or construction engineering as well as practical experience working in construction. Employers prefer applicants with previous construction work experience who can combine a strong background in building technology with proven supervisory or managerial skills. In addition to job growth, many openings should result annually from the need to replace workers who transfer to other occupations or leave the labor force.

The increasing complexity of construction projects should increase demand for management level personnel within the construction industry, because sophisticated technology and the proliferation of laws setting standards for buildings and construction materials, worker safety, energy efficiency, and environmental protection have further complicated the construction process. Advances in building materials and construction methods and the growing number of multipurpose buildings, electronically operated "smart" buildings, and energy-efficient structures will further add to the demand for more construction managers. However, employment of construction managers can be sensitive to the short-term nature of many construction projects and cyclical fluctuations in construction activity.

Earnings

Earnings of salaried construction managers and self-employed independent construction contractors vary depending upon the size and nature of the construction project, its geographic location, and economic conditions. In addition to typical benefits, many salaried construction managers receive benefits such as bonuses and use of company motor vehicles.

Median annual earnings of construction managers in 1998 were $47,610. The middle 50 percent earned between $36,360 and $70,910. The lowest 10 percent earned less than $28,970, and the highest 10 percent earned more than $89,480. Median annual earnings in the industries employing the largest numbers of managers in 1997 were:

Nonresidential building construction	$47,700
Plumbing, heating, and air conditioning	47,000
Heavy construction, except highway	45,700
Miscellaneous special trade contractors	44,200
Residential building construction	40,600

According to a 1999 salary survey by the National Association of Colleges and Employers, candidates with a bachelor's degree in construction management received offers averaging $34,300 a year. Bachelor's degree candidates with degrees in construction science received offers averaging $36,600.

Related Occupations

Construction managers participate in the conceptual development of a construction project and oversee its organization, scheduling, and implementation. Occupations in which similar functions are performed include architects, civil engineers, construction supervisors, cost engineers, cost estimators, real estate developers, electrical engineers, industrial engineers, landscape architects, and mechanical engineers.

Sources of Additional Information

For information about career opportunities in the construction industry, contact:

- Associated Builders and Contractors, 1300 North 17th St., Rosslyn, VA 22209. Internet: http://www.abc.org
- Associated General Contractors of America, 1957 E St. NW, Washington, DC 20006-5199. Internet: http://www.agc.org

For information about constructor certification and professional career opportunities in the construction industry, contact:

- American Institute of Constructors, 466 94th Ave. North. Petersburg, FL 33702. Internet: http://www.aicnet.org

For information about construction management and construction manager certification, contact:

- Construction Management Association of America, 7918 Jones Branch Dr., Suite 540, McLean, VA 22102. Internet: http://www.access.digex.net/~cmaa

Information on accredited construction science and management programs and accreditation requirements is available from:

- American Council for Construction Education, 1300 Hudson Lane, Suite 3, Monroe, LA 71201-6054. Internet: http://www.acce.org

Cost Estimators

(O*NET 21902 and 85305D)

Significant Points

- Growth of the construction industry, where about 58 percent of all cost estimators are employed, will be the driving force behind the demand for these workers.

• Job prospects in construction should be best for those workers with a degree in construction management or construction science, engineering, or architecture, and who have practical experience in various phases of construction or in a specialty craft area.

Nature of the Work

Accurately forecasting the cost of future projects is vital to the survival of any business. Cost estimators develop cost information for owners or managers to use in determining resource and material quantities, making bids for contracts, determining if a new product will be profitable, or determining which products are making a profit for a firm.

Regardless of the industry in which they work, estimators compile and analyze data on all the factors that can influence costs—such as materials, labor, location, and special machinery requirements, including computer hardware and software. Job duties vary widely depending on the type and size of the project. *Cost engineers* usually have an engineering background and apply scientific principles and methods to undertake feasibility studies, value engineering, and life-cycle costing.

The methods of and motivations for estimating costs can vary greatly, depending on the industry. On a construction project, for example, the estimating process begins with the decision to submit a bid. After reviewing various drawings and specifications, the estimator visits the site of the proposed project. The estimator needs to gather information on access to the site and availability of electricity, water, and other services, as well as surface topography and drainage. The information developed during the site visit usually is recorded in a signed report that is made part of the final project estimate.

After the site visit is completed, the estimator determines the quantity of materials and labor the firm will have to furnish. This process, called the quantity survey or "takeoff," involves completing standard estimating forms by filling in dimensions, number of units, and other information. A cost estimator working for a general contractor, for example, will estimate the costs of all items the contractor must provide. Although subcontractors will estimate their costs as part of their own bidding process, the general contractor's cost estimator often analyzes bids made by subcontractors as well. Also during the takeoff process, the estimator must make decisions concerning equipment needs, sequence of operations, and crew size. Allowances for the waste of materials, inclement weather, shipping delays, and other factors that may increase costs must also be incorporated in the estimate.

On completion of the quantity surveys, the estimator prepares a total project cost summary, including the costs of labor, equipment, materials, subcontracts, overhead, taxes, insurance, markup, and any other costs that may affect the project. The chief estimator then prepares the bid proposal for submission to the owner.

Construction cost estimators may also be employed by the project's architect or owner to estimate costs or track actual costs relative to bid specifications as the project develops. In large construction companies employing more than one estimator, it is common practice for estimators to specialize. For instance, one may estimate only electrical work, and another may concentrate on excavation, concrete, and forms.

In manufacturing and other firms, cost estimators usually are assigned to the engineering, cost, or pricing departments. The estimator's goal in manufacturing is to accurately estimate the costs associated with making products. The job may begin when management requests an estimate of the costs associated with a major redesign of an existing product or the development of a new product or production process. When estimating the cost of developing a new product, for example, the estimator works with engineers, first reviewing blueprints or conceptual drawings to determine the machining operations, tools, gauges, and materials that would be required for the job. The estimator then prepares a parts list and determines whether it is more efficient to produce or to purchase the parts. To do this, the estimator must initiate inquiries for price information from potential suppliers. The next step is to determine the cost of manufacturing each component of the product. Some high technology products require a tremendous amount of computer programming during the design phase. The cost of software development is one of the fastest growing and most difficult activities to estimate. Some cost estimators now specialize in estimating only computer software development and related costs.

The cost estimator then prepares time-phase charts and learning curves. Time-phase charts indicate the time required for tool design and fabrication, tool "debugging" (finding and correcting all problems) manufacturing of parts, assembly, and testing. Learning curves graphically represent the rate at which performance improves with practice. These curves are commonly called "cost reduction" curves because many problems—such as engineering changes, rework, parts shortages, and lack of operator skills—diminish as the number of parts produced increases, resulting in lower unit costs.

Using all this information, the estimator then calculates the standard labor hours necessary to produce a predetermined number of units. Standard labor hours are then converted to dollar values, to which are added factors for waste, overhead, and profit to yield the unit cost in dollars. The estimator then compares the cost of purchasing parts with the firm's cost of manufacturing them to determine which is cheaper.

Computers play an integral role in cost estimating today, because estimating may involve complex mathematical calculations and require advanced mathematical techniques. For example, to undertake a parametric analysis (a process used to estimate project costs on a per-unit basis subject to the specific requirements of a project), cost estimators use a computer database containing information on costs and conditions of many other similar projects. Although computers cannot be used for the entire estimating process, they can relieve estimators of much of the drudgery associated with routine, repetitive, and time-consuming calculations. Computers are also used to produce all the necessary documentation with the help of word processing and spreadsheet software. This leaves estimators with more time to study and analyze projects and can lead to more accurate estimates.

Working Conditions

Although estimators spend most of their time in an office, construction estimators must make visits to project work sites that can

be dusty, dirty, and occasionally hazardous environments. Likewise, estimators in manufacturing must spend time on the factory floor where it also can be noisy and dirty. In some industries, frequent travel between a firm's headquarters and its subsidiaries or subcontractors also may be required.

Although estimators normally work a 40-hour week, overtime is common. Cost estimators often work under pressure and stress, especially when facing bid deadlines. Inaccurate estimating can cause a firm to lose out on a bid or lose money on a job that was not accurately estimated.

Employment

Cost estimators held about 152,000 jobs in 1998, about 58 percent of which were in the construction industry. Another 26 percent of salaried cost estimators were employed in manufacturing industries. The remainder worked for engineering and architectural services firms, business services firms, and throughout a wide range of other industries. Operations research, production control, cost, and price analysts who work for government agencies may also do significant amounts of cost estimating in the course of their regular duties. In addition, the duties of construction managers may also include estimating costs.

Cost estimators work throughout the country, usually in or near major industrial, commercial, and government centers, and in cities and suburban areas undergoing rapid change or development.

Training, Other Qualifications, and Advancement

Entry requirements for cost estimators vary by industry. In the construction industry, employers increasingly prefer individuals with a degree in building construction, construction management, construction science, engineering, or architecture. However, most construction estimators also have considerable construction experience, gained through tenure in the industry, internships, or cooperative education programs. Applicants with a thorough knowledge of construction materials, costs, and procedures in areas ranging from heavy construction to electrical work, plumbing systems, or masonry work have a competitive edge.

In manufacturing industries, employers prefer to hire individuals with a degree in engineering, physical science, operations research, mathematics, or statistics, or in accounting, finance, business, economics, or a related subject. In most industries, great emphasis is placed on experience involving quantitative techniques.

Cost estimators should have an aptitude for mathematics; be able to quickly analyze, compare, and interpret detailed and sometimes poorly defined information; and be able to make sound and accurate judgments based on this knowledge. Assertiveness and self-confidence in presenting and supporting their conclusions are important, as are strong communications and interpersonal skills, because estimators may work as part of a project team alongside managers, owners, engineers, and design professionals. Cost estimators also need knowledge of computers, including word processing and spreadsheet packages. In some instances, familiarity with special estimation software or programming skills may also be required.

Regardless of their background, estimators receive much training on the job; almost every company has its own way of handling estimates. Working with experienced estimators, they become familiar with each step in the process. Those with no experience reading construction specifications or blueprints first learn that aspect of the work. They then may accompany an experienced estimator to the construction site or shop floor where they observe the work being done, take measurements, or perform other routine tasks. As they become more knowledgeable, estimators learn how to tabulate quantities and dimensions from drawings and how to select the appropriate material prices.

For most estimators, advancement takes the form of higher pay and prestige. Some move into management positions, such as project manager for a construction firm or manager of the industrial engineering department for a manufacturer. Others may go into business for themselves as consultants, providing estimating services for a fee to government or construction and manufacturing firms.

Many colleges and universities include cost estimating as part of bachelor's and associate degree curriculums in civil engineering, industrial engineering, and construction management or construction engineering technology. In addition, cost estimating is a significant part of many master's degree programs in construction science or construction management. Organizations representing cost estimators, such as American Association of Cost Engineers (AACE) International and the Society of Cost Estimating and Analysis, also sponsor educational and professional development programs. These programs help students, estimators-in-training, and experienced estimators stay abreast of changes affecting the profession. Specialized courses and programs in cost estimating techniques and procedures are also offered by many technical schools, community colleges, and universities.

Voluntary certification can be valuable to cost estimators because it provides professional recognition of the estimator's competence and experience. In some instances, individual employers may even require professional certification for employment. Both AACE International and the Society of Cost Estimating and Analysis administer certification programs. To become certified, estimators usually must have between three and seven years of estimating experience and must pass both a written and an oral examination. In addition, certification requirements may include publication of at least one article or paper in the field.

Job Outlook

Overall employment of cost estimators is expected to grow about as fast as average for all occupations through the year 2008. No new projects in construction, manufacturing, or other industries are undertaken without careful analysis and estimation of the costs involved. In addition to openings created by growth, some job openings will also arise from the need to replace workers who transfer to other occupations or leave the labor force.

Growth of the construction industry, where about 58 percent of all cost estimators are employed, will be the driving force behind the demand for these workers. The fastest growing sectors of the construction industry are expected to be special trade contractors and those associated with heavy construction and spending on the Nation's infrastructure. Construction and repair of highways and streets, bridges, and construction of more subway systems, airports, water and sewage systems, and electric power plants and transmission lines will stimulate demand for many more cost estimators. Job prospects in construction should be best for cost estimators with a degree in construction management or construction science, engineering, or architecture, who have practical experience in various phases of construction or in a specialty craft area.

Employment of cost estimators in manufacturing should remain relatively stable as firms continue to use their services to identify and control their operating costs. Experienced estimators with degrees in engineering, science, mathematics, business administration, or economics and who have computer expertise should have the best job prospects in manufacturing.

Earnings

Salaries of cost estimators vary widely by experience, education, size of firm, and industry. Median annual earnings of cost estimators in 1998 were $40,590. The middle 50 percent earned between $31,270 and $53,490. The lowest 10 percent earned less than $24,330, and the highest 10 percent earned more than $79,400. Median annual earnings in the industries employing the largest numbers of managers in 1997 were:

Nonresidential building construction	$43,400
Electrical work	40,800
Plumbing, heating, and air conditioning	40,700
Miscellaneous special trade contractors	39,200
Residential building construction	35,300

College graduates with degrees in fields such as engineering or construction management that provide a strong background in cost estimating could start at a higher level. According to a 1999 salary survey by the National Association of Colleges and Employers, bachelor's degree candidates with degrees in construction science received offers averaging about $36,600 a year. Bachelor's degree candidates with degrees in construction management received offers averaging $34,300 a year.

Related Occupations

Other workers who quantitatively analyze information include appraisers, cost accountants, auditors, budget analysts, cost engineers, economists, financial analysts, loan officers, operations research analysts, underwriters, and value engineers. In addition, the duties of production managers and construction managers may also involve analyzing costs.

Sources of Additional Information

Information about career opportunities, certification, educational programs, and cost estimating techniques may be obtained from:

- AACE International, 209 Prairie Ave., Suite 100, Morgantown, WV 26505. Internet: http://www.aacei.org
- Professional Construction Estimators Association of America, P.O. Box 11626, Charlotte, NC 28220-1626. Internet: http://www.pcea.org
- Society of Cost Estimating and Analysis, 101 S. Whiting St., Suite 201, Alexandria, VA 22304. Internet: http://www.erols.com/scea

Counselors

(O*NET 31514)

Significant Points

- About 6 out of 10 counselors have a master's degree.
- Most States require some form of counselor credentialing, licensure, certification, or registry for practice outside schools; all States require school counselors to hold a State school counseling certification.

Nature of the Work

Counselors assist people with personal, family, educational, mental health, and career decisions and problems. Their duties depend on the individuals they serve and the settings in which they work.

School and college counselors in elementary, secondary, and post-secondary schools help students evaluate their abilities, interests, talents, and personality characteristics to develop realistic academic and career goals. Counselors use interviews, counseling sessions, tests, or other methods when evaluating and advising students. They operate career information centers and career education programs. High school counselors advise on college majors, admission requirements, entrance exams, and financial aid and on trade, technical school, and apprenticeship programs. They help students develop job search skills such as resume writing and interviewing techniques. College career planning and placement counselors assist alumni or students with career development and job hunting techniques.

Elementary school counselors observe younger children during classroom and play activities and confer with their teachers and parents to evaluate their strengths, problems, or special needs. They also help students develop good study habits. They do less vocational and academic counseling than secondary school counselors.

School counselors at all levels help students understand and deal with their social, behavioral, and personal problems. They emphasize preventive and developmental counseling to provide students with the life skills needed to deal with problems before they occur, and to enhance personal, social, and academic growth. Counselors provide special services, including alcohol and drug prevention programs, and classes that teach students to handle conflicts without resorting to violence. Counselors also try to identify cases involving domestic abuse and other family problems that can affect a student's development. Counselors work with students individually, in small groups, or with entire classes. They consult and work with parents, teachers, school administrators, school psychologists, school nurses, and social workers.

Rehabilitation counselors help people deal with the personal, social, and vocational effects of disabilities. They counsel people with disabilities resulting from birth defects, illness or disease, accidents, or the stress of daily life. They evaluate the strengths and limitations of individuals, provide personal and vocational counseling,

and arrange for medical care, vocational training, and job placement. Rehabilitation counselors interview individuals with disabilities and their families, evaluate school and medical reports, and confer and plan with physicians, psychologists, occupational therapists, and employers to determine the capabilities and skills of the individual. Conferring with the client, they develop a rehabilitation program, which often includes training to help the person develop job skills. They also work toward increasing the client's capacity to live independently.

Employment, or *vocational*, *counselors* help individuals make career decisions. They explore and evaluate the client's education, training, work history, interests, skills, and personal traits and arrange for aptitude and achievement tests. They also work with individuals to develop job search skills and assist clients in locating and applying for jobs.

Mental health counselors emphasize prevention and work with individuals and groups to promote optimum mental health. They help individuals deal with addictions and substance abuse; suicide; stress management; problems with self-esteem; issues associated with aging; job and career concerns; educational decisions; issues of mental and emotional health; and family, parenting, and marital problems. Mental health counselors work closely with other mental health specialists, including psychiatrists, psychologists, clinical social workers, psychiatric nurses, and school counselors.

Other counseling specialties include marriage and family, multicultural, and gerontological counseling. A gerontological counselor provides services to elderly persons who face changing lifestyles because of health problems and helps families cope with these changes. A multicultural counselor helps employers adjust to an increasingly diverse workforce.

Working Conditions

Most school counselors work the traditional 9- to 10-month school year with a 2- to 3-month vacation, although an increasing number are employed on 10 1/2- or 11-month contracts. They usually have the same hours as teachers. College career planning and placement counselors work long and irregular hours during recruiting periods.

Rehabilitation and employment counselors usually work a standard 40-hour week. Self-employed counselors and those working in mental health and community agencies often work evenings to counsel clients who work during the day.

Counselors must possess high physical and emotional energy to handle the array of problems they address. Dealing with these problems daily can cause stress.

Since privacy is essential for confidential and frank discussions with clients, counselors usually have private offices.

Employment

Counselors held about 182,000 jobs in 1998. (This employment estimate only includes vocational and educational counselors; employment data are not available for other counselors discussed in this statement, such as rehabilitation and mental health counselors.)

In addition to elementary and secondary schools and colleges and universities, counselors work in a wide variety of public and private establishments. These include health care facilities; job training, career development, and vocational rehabilitation centers; social agencies; correctional institutions; and residential care facilities, such as halfway houses for criminal offenders and group homes for children, the aged, and the disabled. Counselors also work in organizations engaged in community improvement and social change, as well as drug and alcohol rehabilitation programs and State and local government agencies. A growing number of counselors work in health maintenance organizations, insurance companies, group practice, and private practice. This growth has been spurred by laws allowing counselors to receive payments from insurance companies and requiring employers to provide rehabilitation and counseling services to employees.

Training, Other Qualifications, and Advancement

Formal education is necessary to gain employment as a counselor. About 6 out of 10 counselors have a master's degree; fields of study include college student affairs, elementary or secondary school counseling, education, gerontological counseling, marriage and family counseling, substance abuse counseling, rehabilitation counseling, agency or community counseling, clinical mental health counseling, counseling psychology, career counseling, and related fields.

Graduate-level counselor education programs in colleges and universities usually are in departments of education or psychology. Courses are grouped into eight core areas: Human growth and development; social and cultural foundations; helping relationships; group work; career and lifestyle development; appraisal; research and program evaluation; and professional orientation. In an accredited program, 48 to 60 semester hours of graduate study, including a period of supervised clinical experience in counseling, are required for a master's degree. In 1999, 133 institutions offered programs in counselor education, including career, community, gerontological, mental health, school, student affairs, and marriage and family counseling that were accredited by the Council for Accreditation of Counseling and Related Educational Programs (CACREP). Another organization, the Council on Rehabilitation Education (CORE), accredits graduate programs in rehabilitation counseling. Accredited master's degree programs include a minimum of two years of full-time study, including 600 hours of supervised clinical internship experience.

In 1999, 45 States and the District of Columbia had some form of counselor credentialing, licensure, certification, or registry legislation governing practice outside schools. Requirements vary from State to State. In some States, credentialing is mandatory; in others, it is voluntary.

All States require school counselors to hold State school counseling certification; however, certification requirements vary from State to State. Some States require public school counselors to have both counseling and teaching certificates. Depending on the State, a master's degree in counseling and two to five years of teaching experience could be required for a school counseling certificate.

Counselors must be aware of educational and training requirements that are often very detailed and that vary by area and by counseling specialty. Prospective counselors should check with State and local governments, employers, and national voluntary certification organizations in order to determine which requirements apply.

Many counselors elect to be nationally certified by the National Board for Certified Counselors (NBCC), which grants the general practice credential, "National Certified Counselor." To be certified, a counselor must hold a graduate degree in counseling from a regionally accredited institution, have at least two years of supervised field experience in a counseling setting (graduates from counselor education programs accredited by the above-mentioned CACREP are exempted), and pass NBCC's National Counselor Examination for Licensure and Certification (NCE). This national certification is voluntary and distinct from State certification. However, in some States those who pass the national exam are exempt from taking a State certification exam. NBCC also offers specialty certification in school, clinical mental health, and addictions counseling. To maintain their certification, counselors must repeat and pass the NCE or complete 100 hours of acceptable continuing education credit every five years.

Another organization, the Commission on Rehabilitation Counselor Certification, offers voluntary national certification for rehabilitation counselors. Many employers require rehabilitation counselors to be nationally certified. To become certified, rehabilitation counselors usually must graduate from an accredited educational program, complete an internship, and pass a written examination. (Certification requirements vary according to an applicant's educational history. Employment experience, for instance, is required for those without a counseling degree other than the rehabilitation specialty.) They are then designated as "Certified Rehabilitation Counselors." To maintain their certification, counselors must re-take the certification exam or complete 100 hours of acceptable continuing education credit every five years.

Vocational and related rehabilitation agencies usually require a master's degree in rehabilitation counseling, counseling and guidance, or counseling psychology for rehabilitation counselor jobs. Some, however, accept applicants with a bachelor's degree in rehabilitation services, counseling, psychology, sociology, or related fields. A bachelor's degree often qualifies a person to work as a counseling aide, rehabilitation aide, or social service worker. Experience in employment counseling, job development, psychology, education, or social work is helpful.

Some States require counselors in public employment offices to have a master's degree; others accept a bachelor's degree with appropriate counseling courses.

Clinical mental health counselors usually have a master's degree in mental health counseling, another area of counseling, or psychology or social work. Voluntary certification is available through the National Board for Certified Counselors, Inc. Generally, to receive certification as a clinical mental health counselor, a counselor must have a master's degree in counseling, two years of post-master's experience, a period of supervised clinical experience, a taped sample of clinical work, and a passing grade on a written examination.

Some employers provide training for newly hired counselors. Many have work-study programs so those employed counselors can earn graduate degrees. Counselors must participate in graduate studies, workshops, and personal studies to maintain their certificates and licenses.

Persons interested in counseling should have a strong interest in helping others and the ability to inspire respect, trust, and confidence. They should be able to work independently or as part of a team. Counselors follow the code of ethics associated with their respective certifications and licenses.

Prospects for advancement vary by counseling field. School counselors can move to a larger school; become directors or supervisors of counseling, guidance, or pupil personnel services; or, usually with further graduate education, become counselor educators, counseling psychologists, or school administrators. Some counselors choose to work at the State department of education.

Rehabilitation, mental health, and employment counselors can become supervisors or administrators in their agencies. Some counselors move into research, consulting, or college teaching or go into private or group practice.

Job Outlook

Overall employment of counselors is expected to grow faster than the average for all occupations through 2008. In addition, numerous job openings will occur as many counselors reach retirement age. (This employment projection applies only to vocational and educational counselors. Future job market conditions for rehabilitation and mental health counselors are discussed later in this section.)

Employment of school and vocational counselors is expected to grow as a result of increasing enrollments, particularly in secondary and post-secondary schools, State legislation requiring counselors in elementary schools, and the expanded responsibilities of counselors. Counselors are becoming more involved in crisis and preventive counseling, helping students deal with issues ranging from drug and alcohol abuse to death and suicide. Also, the growing diversity of student populations is presenting challenges to counselors in dealing with multicultural issues. Budgetary constraints, however, can dampen job growth of school counselors. When funding is tight, schools usually prefer to hire new teachers before adding counselors in an effort to keep classroom sizes at acceptable levels. If this happens, student-to-counselor ratios in many schools could increase as student enrollments grow.

As with other government jobs, the number of employment counselors who work primarily for State and local government could be limited by budgetary constraints. However, demand for government employment counseling could grow as new welfare laws require welfare recipients to find jobs. Opportunities for employment counselors working in private job training services should grow as counselors provide training and other services to laid-off workers, experienced workers seeking new or second careers, full-time homemakers seeking to enter or reenter the work force, and workers who want to upgrade their skills.

Demand is expected to be strong for rehabilitation and mental health counselors. Under managed care systems, insurance companies increasingly provide for reimbursement of counselors, enabling many counselors to move from schools and government agencies to private practice. Counselors are also forming group prac-

tices to receive expanded insurance coverage. The number of people who need rehabilitation services will rise as advances in medical technology continue to save lives that only a few years ago would have been lost. In addition, legislation requiring equal employment rights for people with disabilities will spur demand for counselors. Counselors not only will help individuals with disabilities with their transition into the work force, but also will help companies comply with the law. Employers are also increasingly offering employee assistance programs that provide mental health and alcohol and drug abuse services. A growing number of people are expected to use these services as the elderly population grows, and as society focuses on ways of developing mental well-being, such as controlling stress associated with job and family responsibilities.

Earnings

Median annual earnings of vocational and educational counselors in 1998 were $38,650. The middle 50 percent earned between $28,400 and $49,960. The lowest 10 percent earned less than $21,230, and the highest 10 percent earned more than $73,920. Median annual earnings in the industries employing the largest numbers of vocational and educational counselors in 1997 are shown below:

Elementary and secondary schools	$42,100
State government, except education and hospitals	35,800
Colleges and universities	34,700
Job training and related services	24,100
Individual and family services	22,300

School counselors can earn additional income working summers in the school system or in other jobs.

Self-employed counselors who have well-established practices, as well as counselors employed in group practices, usually have the highest earnings, as do some counselors working for private firms, such as insurance companies and private rehabilitation companies.

Related Occupations

Counselors help people evaluate their interests, abilities, and disabilities and deal with personal, social, academic, and career problems. Others who help people in similar ways include college and student affairs workers, teachers, personnel workers and managers, human services workers, social workers, psychologists, psychiatrists, psychiatric nurses, members of the clergy, occupational therapists, training and employee development specialists, and equal employment opportunity/affirmative action specialists.

Sources of Additional Information

For general information about counseling, as well as information on specialties such as school, college, mental health, rehabilitation, multicultural, career, marriage and family, and gerontological counseling, contact:

- American Counseling Association, 5999 Stevenson Ave., Alexandria, VA 22304-3300. Internet: http://www.counseling.org

For information on accredited counseling and related training programs, contact:

- Council for Accreditation of Counseling and Related Educational Programs, American Counseling Association, 5999 Stevenson Ave., 4th floor, Alexandria, VA 22304. Internet: http://www.counseling.org/cacrep

For information on national certification requirements for counselors, contact:

- National Board for Certified Counselors, Inc., 3 Terrace Way, Suite D, Greensboro, NC 27403-3660. Internet: http://www.nbcc.org

For information on certification requirements for rehabilitation counselors and a list of accredited rehabilitation education programs, contact:

- Commission on Rehabilitation Counselor Certification, 1835 Rohlwing Rd., Suite E, Rolling Meadows, IL 60008.

State departments of education can supply information on colleges and universities that offer approved guidance and counseling training for State certification and licensure requirements.

State employment service offices have information about job opportunities and entrance requirements for counselors.

Counter and Rental Clerks

(O*NET 49017)

Significant Points

- Jobs are primarily entry level and require little or no experience and little formal education.
- Part-time employment opportunities are expected to be plentiful.

Nature of the Work

Whether renting video tapes or air compressors, dropping off clothes to be dry-cleaned or appliances to be serviced, we rely on counter and rental clerks to handle these transactions efficiently. Although specific duties vary by establishment, counter and rental clerks answer questions involving product availability, cost, and rental provisions. Counter and rental clerks also take orders, calculate fees, receive payments, and accept returns. (Cashiers and retail salespersons, occupations with similar duties, are discussed elsewhere in this book.)

Regardless of where they work, counter and rental clerks must be knowledgeable about the company's services, policies, and procedures.

Depending on the type of establishment, counter and rental clerks use their special knowledge to give advice on a wide variety of products and services, which may range from hydraulic tools to shoe repair. For example, in the car rental industry, they inform customers about the features of different types of automobiles as well as daily and weekly rental costs. They also ensure that customers meet age and other requirements for rental cars and indicate when and in what condition cars must be returned. Those in the equipment rental industry have similar duties, but they must also know how to operate and care for the machinery rented. In dry-cleaning establishments, counter clerks inform customers when items will be ready. In video rental stores, they advise customers about the length of rental, scan returned movies, restock the shelves, handle money, and log daily reports.

When taking orders, counter and rental clerks use various types of equipment. In some establishments, they write out tickets and order forms, although most use computers or bar code scanners. Most of these computer systems are user friendly, require very little data entry, and are customized for the firm. Scanners "read" the product code and display a description of the item on a computer screen. However, clerks must ensure that the data on the screen accurately matches the product.

Working Conditions

Firms employing counter and rental clerks usually operate nights and weekends for the convenience of their customers. However, many employers offer flexible schedules. Some counter and rental clerks work 40-hour weeks, but about one-half are on part-time schedules—usually during rush periods, such as weekends, evenings, and holidays.

Working conditions are usually pleasant; most stores and service establishments are clean, well-lighted, and temperature controlled. However, clerks are on their feet much of the time and may be confined behind a small counter area. This job requires constant interaction with the public and can be taxing—especially during busy periods.

Employment

Counter and rental clerks held 469,000 jobs in 1998. About 1 of every 4 clerks worked for a video tape rental store. Other large employers included dry cleaners, automobile rental firms, equipment rental firms, and miscellaneous amusement and recreation establishments.

Counter and rental clerks are employed throughout the country but are concentrated in metropolitan areas, where personal services and renting and leasing services are in greater demand.

Training, Other Qualifications, and Advancement

Counter and rental clerk jobs are primarily entry level and require little or no experience and little formal education. However, many employers prefer those with at least a high school diploma.

In most companies, counter and rental clerks are trained on the job, sometimes through the use of video tapes, brochures, and pamphlets. Clerks usually learn how to operate the equipment and become familiar with the establishment's policies and procedures under the observation of a more experienced worker. However, some employers have formal classroom training programs lasting from a few hours to a few weeks. Topics covered in this training include a description of the industry, the company and its policies and procedures, equipment operation, sales techniques, and customer service. Counter and rental clerks must also become familiar with the different products and services rented or provided by their company in order to give customers the best possible service.

Counter and rental clerks should enjoy working with people and have the ability to deal tactfully with difficult customers. They should be able to handle several tasks at once, while continuing to provide friendly service. In addition, good oral and written communication skills are essential.

Advancement opportunities depend on the size and type of company. Many establishments that employ counter or rental clerks tend to be small businesses, making advancement difficult. But in larger establishments with a corporate structure, jobs as counter and rental clerks offer good opportunities for workers to learn about their company's products and business practices. These jobs can be stepping stones to more responsible positions, because it is common in many establishments to promote counter and rental clerks into assistant manager positions.

In certain industries, such as equipment repair, counter and rental jobs may be an additional or alternate source of income for workers who are unemployed or entering semi-retirement. For example, retired mechanics could prove invaluable at tool rental centers because of their relevant knowledge.

Job Outlook

Employment in this occupation is expected to increase faster than the average for all occupations through the year 2008 due to businesses' desire to improve customer service. Industries employing counter and rental clerks that are expected to grow rapidly include equipment rental and leasing, automotive rentals, and amusement and recreation services. The number of new jobs created in other industries, such as video tape rental stores, will also be significant. Nevertheless, most job openings will arise from the need to replace experienced workers who transfer to other occupations or leave the labor force. Part-time employment opportunities are expected to be plentiful.

Earnings

Counter and rental clerks typically start at the minimum wage, which, in establishments covered by Federal law, was $5.15 an hour in 1999. In some States, State law sets the minimum wage higher, and establishments must pay at least that amount. Wages also tend to be higher in areas where there is intense competition for workers. In addition to wages, some counter and rental clerks receive commissions based on the number of contracts they complete or services they sell.

Median hourly earnings of counter and rental clerks in 1998 were $6.97. The middle 50 percent earned between $6.03 and $8.79 an hour. The lowest 10 percent earned less than $5.70, and the highest 10 percent earned more than $11.12 an hour. Median hourly earnings in the industries employing the largest number of counter and rental clerks in 1997 were as follows:

Miscellaneous equipment rental and leasing $8.20

Automotive rentals, no drivers 8.10

Miscellaneous amusement and recreation services 6.30

Laundry, cleaning, and garment services 6.20

Video tape rental 5.70

Full-time workers typically receive health and life insurance, paid vacation, and sick leave. Benefits for counter and rental clerks who work part time tend to be significantly less than for those who work full time. Many companies offer discounts to both full- and part-time employees on the services they provide.

Related Occupations

Counter and rental clerks take orders and receive payment for services rendered. Other workers with similar duties include bank tellers, cashiers, food and beverage service occupations, postal clerks, and retail salespersons.

Sources of Additional Information

For general information on employment in the equipment rental industry contact:

- American Rental Association, 1900 19th St., Moline, IL 61265. Internet: http://www.ararental.org

For more information about the work of counter clerks in dry cleaning and laundry establishments, contact:

- International Fabricare Institute, 12251 Tech Rd., Silver Spring, MD 20904. Internet: http://www.ifi.org

Court Reporters, Medical Transcriptionists, and Stenographers

(O*NET 55302A and 55302B)

Significant Points

- A high school diploma is sufficient for stenographers; employers prefer medical transcriptionists who have completed a vocational school or community college program; and court reporters usually need a two- or four-year postsecondary school degree.

- Overall employment is projected to grow about as fast as the average, as rapid growth among medical transcriptionists is offset by the decline among stenographers.

- Because of their relatively high salaries, keen competition should exist for court reporter positions; certified court reporters and medical transcriptionists should enjoy the best job prospects.

Nature of the Work

Although court reporters, medical transcriptionists, and stenographers all transcribe spoken words, the specific responsibilities of each of these workers differ markedly. Court reporters and stenographers typically take verbatim reports of speeches, conversations, legal proceedings, meetings, and other events when written accounts of spoken words are necessary for correspondence, records, or legal proof. Medical transcriptionists, on the other hand, translate and edit recorded dictation by physicians and other health care providers regarding patient assessment and treatment.

Court reporters document all statements made in official proceedings using a stenotype machine, which allows them to press multiple keys at a time to record combinations of letters representing sounds, words, or phrases. These symbols are then recorded on computer disks or CD-ROM, which are then translated and displayed as text in a process called computer-aided transcription. Stenotype machines used for real-time captioning are linked directly to the computer. As the reporter keys in the symbols, they instantly appear as text on the screen. This is used for closed captioning for the hearing-impaired on television or in courts, classrooms, or meetings. In all of these cases, accuracy is crucial because only one person is creating an official transcript.

Although many court reporters record official proceedings in the courtroom, the majority of court reporters work outside the courtroom. Freelance reporters, for example, take depositions for attorneys in offices and document proceedings of meetings, conventions, and other private activities. Others capture the proceedings in government agencies of all levels, from the U.S. Congress to State and local governing bodies. Court reporters who specialize in captioning live television programming, commonly known as *stenocaptioners*, work for television networks or cable stations captioning news, emergency broadcasts, sporting events, and other programming.

Medical transcriptionists use headsets and transcribing machines to listen to recordings by physicians and other health care professionals. These workers transcribe a variety of medical reports about emergency room visits, diagnostic imaging studies, operations, chart reviews, and final summaries. To understand and accurately transcribe dictated reports into a format that is clear and comprehensible for the reader, the medical transcriptionist must understand the language of medicine, anatomy and physiology, diagnostic procedures, and treatment. They also must be able to translate medical jargon and abbreviations into their expanded forms. After reviewing and editing for grammar and clarity, the medical transcriptionist transcribes the dictated reports and returns them in either printed or electronic form to the dictator for review and signature, or correction. These reports eventually become a part of the patient's permanent file.

Stenographers take dictation and then transcribe their notes on a word processor or onto a computer diskette. They may take dictation using either shorthand or a stenotype machine, which prints shorthand symbols. General stenographers, including most beginners, take routine dictation and perform other office tasks such as typing, filing, answering telephones, and operating office machines. Experienced and highly skilled stenographers often supervise other stenographers, typists, and clerical workers and take more difficult dictation. For example, skilled stenographers may attend staff meetings and provide word-for-word records or summary reports of the proceedings to the participants. Some experienced stenographers take dictation in foreign languages; others work as public stenographers serving traveling business people and others. Technical stenographers must know the medical, legal, engineering, or scientific terminology used in a particular profession.

Working Conditions

The majority of these workers are employed in comfortable settings. Court reporters, for example, work in the offices of attorneys, courtrooms, legislatures, and conventions. Medical transcriptionists are found in hospitals, doctors' offices, or medical transcription services. Stenographers usually work in clean, well-lighted offices. An increasing number of court reporters and medical transcriptionists work from home-based offices as subcontractors for law firms, hospitals, and transcription services.

Work in these occupations presents few hazards, although sitting in the same position for long periods can be tiring, and workers can suffer wrist, back, neck, or eye problems due to strain and risk repetitive motion injuries such as carpal tunnel syndrome. Also, the pressure to be accurate and fast can also be stressful.

Many court reporters, medical transcriptionists, and stenographers work a standard 40-hour week, although about 1 in 4 works part time. A substantial number of court reporters and medical transcriptionists are self-employed, which may result in irregular working hours.

Employment

Court reporters, medical transcriptionists, and stenographers held about 110,000 jobs in 1998. More than 1 in 4 were self-employed. Of those who worked for a wage or salary, about one-third worked for State and local governments, a reflection of the large number of court reporters working in courts, legislatures, and various agencies. About 1 in 4 worked for hospitals and physicians' offices, reflecting the concentration of medical transcriptionists in health services. Other transcriptionists, stenographers, and court reporters worked for colleges and universities, secretarial and court reporting services, temporary help supply services, and law firms.

Training, Other Qualifications, and Advancement

The training for each of the three occupations varies significantly. Court reporters usually complete a two- or four-year training program offered by about 300 post-secondary vocational and technical schools and colleges. Currently, the National Court Reporters Association (NCRA) has approved about 110 programs, all of which offer courses in computer-aided transcription and real-time reporting. NCRA-approved programs require students to capture 225 words per minute. Court reporters in the Federal government usually must capture at least 205 words a minute.

Some States require court reporters to be Notary Publics or to be a Certified Court Reporter (CCR); reporters must pass a State certification test administered by a board of examiners to earn this designation. The National Court Reporters Association confers the designation Registered Professional Reporter (RPR) upon those who

pass a two-part examination and participate in continuing education programs. Although voluntary, the RPR designation is recognized as a mark of distinction in this field.

For medical transcriptionist positions, understanding medical terminology is essential. Good English grammar and punctuation skills are required, as well as familiarity with personal computers and word processing software. Good listening skills are also necessary, because some doctors and health care professionals speak English as a second language.

Employers prefer to hire transcriptionists who have completed post-secondary training in medical transcription, which is offered by many vocational schools and community colleges. Completion of a two-year associate's degree program—including coursework in anatomy, medical terminology, medicolegal issues, and English grammar and punctuation—is highly recommended. Many of these programs include supervised on-the-job experience. The American Association for Medical Transcription awards the voluntary designation Certified Medical Transcriptionist (CMT) to those who earn passing scores on written and practical examinations. As in many other fields, certification is recognized as a sign of competence in medical transcription.

Stenographic skills are taught in high schools, vocational schools, community colleges, and proprietary business schools. For stenographer jobs, employers prefer to hire high school graduates and seldom have a preference among the many different shorthand methods. Although requirements vary in private firms, applicants with the best speed and accuracy usually receive first consideration in hiring. To qualify for jobs in the Federal government, stenographers must be able to take dictation at a minimum of 80 words per minute and type at least 40 words per minute. Workers must achieve higher rates to advance to more responsible positions.

Stenographers, especially those with strong interpersonal and communication skills may advance to secretarial positions with more responsibilities. In addition, some stenographers complete the necessary education to become court reporters or medical transcriptionists.

Job Outlook

Overall employment of court reporters, medical transcriptionists, and stenographers is projected to grow about as fast as the average for all occupations through 2008. Employment growth among medical transcriptionists should be offset by the decline among stenographers; the number of court reporters should remain fairly constant.

Demand for medical transcriptionists is expected to increase due to rapid growth in health care industries spurred by a growing and aging population. Advancements in voice recognition technology are not projected to reduce the need for medical transcriptionists because these workers will continue to be needed to review and edit drafts for accuracy. Moreover, growing numbers of medical transcriptionists will be needed to amend patients' records, edit for grammar, and discover discrepancies in medical records. Job opportunities should be the best for those who earn an associate's degree or certification from the American Association for Medical Transcription.

There should be little or no change in employment of court reporters. Despite increasing numbers of civil and criminal cases, budget

constraints limit the ability of Federal, State, and local courts to expand. The growing number of conventions, conferences, depositions, seminars, and similar meetings in which proceedings are recorded should create limited demand for court reporters. Although many of these events are videotaped, a written transcript must still be created for legal purposes or if the proceedings are to be published. In addition, the trend to provide instantaneous written captions for the deaf and hearing-impaired should strengthen demand for stenocaptioners. Because of their relatively high salaries, keen competition should exist for court reporter positions; those with certification should enjoy the best job prospects.

The widespread use of dictation machines has greatly reduced the need for office stenographers. Audio recording equipment and the use of personal computers by managers and other professionals should continue to further decrease the demand for these workers.

Earnings

Court reporters, medical transcriptionists, and stenographers had median annual earnings of $25,430 in 1998. The middle 50 percent earned between $21,060 and $31,470; the lowest paid 10 percent earned less than $17,060; and the highest paid 10 percent earned more than $39,070. Median 1997 annual salaries in the industries employing the largest number of these workers were:

Local government, except education and hospitals $29,300

State government, except education and hospitals 29,000

Mailing, reproduction, and stenographic services 28,600

Hospitals 23,500

Offices and clinics of medical doctors 22,600

Court reporters usually earn higher salaries than stenographers or medical transcriptionists, and many supplement their income by doing additional freelance work. According to a National Court Reporters Association survey of its members, average annual earnings for court reporters were about $54,000 in 1999. According to the 1999 HayGroup survey, about three-quarters of health care institutions paid their medical transcriptionists for time worked, with average salaries ranging from $20,000 to $30,000 annually. About a fifth of those respondents used a combination of payment methods (time worked plus incentive for production), with average salaries ranging from $28,000 to $36,000 annually. Regardless of specialty, earnings depend on education, experience, and geographic location.

Related Occupations

A number of other workers type, record information, and process paperwork. Among these are administrative assistants, bookkeepers, receptionists, secretaries, and human resource clerks. Other workers who provide medical and legal support include paralegals, medical assistants, and medical record technicians.

Sources of Additional Information

For information about careers, training, and certification in court reporting, contact:

- National Court Reporters Association, 8224 Old Courthouse Rd., Vienna, VA 22182. Internet: http://www.verbatimreporters.com

For information on a career as a medical transcriptionist, contact:

- American Association for Medical Transcription, P.O. Box 576187, Modesto, CA 95357. Internet: http://www.aamt.org/aamt

For information on a career as a federal court reporter, contact:

- United States Court Reporters Association, 1904 Marvel Lane, Liberty, MO 64068. Internet: http://www.uscra.org

State employment service offices can provide information about job openings for court reporters, medical transcriptionists, and stenographers.

Dentists

(O*NET 32105A, 32105B, 32105D, 32105F, and 32105G)

Significant Points

- Most dentists have at least eight years of education beyond high school.

- Employment of dentists is expected to grow slower than the average as young people are troubled less by tooth decay.

- Dental care will focus more on prevention, including teaching people how to better care for their teeth.

Nature of the Work

Dentists diagnose, prevent, and treat teeth and tissue problems. They remove decay, fill cavities, examine x-rays, place protective plastic sealants on children's teeth, straighten teeth, and repair fractured teeth. They also perform corrective surgery on gums and supporting bones to treat gum diseases. Dentists extract teeth and make models and measurements for dentures to replace missing teeth. They provide instruction on diet, brushing, flossing, the use of fluorides, and other aspects of dental care. They also administer anesthetics and write prescriptions for antibiotics and other medications.

Dentists use a variety of equipment, including x-ray machines, drills, and instruments such as mouth mirrors, probes, forceps, brushes, and scalpels. They wear masks, gloves, and safety glasses to protect themselves and their patients from infectious diseases.

Dentists in private practice oversee a variety of administrative tasks, including bookkeeping, and buying equipment and supplies. They may employ and supervise dental hygienists, dental assistants, dental laboratory technicians, and receptionists.

Most dentists are general practitioners, handling a variety of dental needs. Other dentists practice in one of eight specialty areas. *Orthodontists*, the largest group of specialists, straighten teeth. The next largest group, *oral and maxillofacial surgeons*, operate on the mouth and jaws. The remainder may specialize as *pediatric dentists* (dentistry for children); *periodontists* (treating gums and bone supporting the teeth); *prosthodontists* (making artificial teeth or dentures); *endodontists* (root canal therapy); *public health dentists*; and *oral pathologists* (studying oral diseases).

Working Conditions

Most dentists work four or five days a week. Some work evenings and weekends to meet their patients' needs. Most full-time dentists work about 40 hours a week, but others work more. Initially, dentists may work more hours as they establish their practice. Experienced dentists often work fewer hours. A considerable number continue in part-time practice well beyond the usual retirement age.

Most dentists are "solo practitioners," meaning they own their own businesses and work alone or with a small staff. Some dentists have partners, and a few work for other dentists as associate dentists.

Employment

Dentists held about 160,000 jobs in 1998. About 9 out of 10 dentists are in private practice. Others work in private and public hospitals and clinics, for the Federal government, and in dental research.

Training, Other Qualifications, and Advancement

All 50 States and the District of Columbia require dentists to be licensed. In most States, a candidate must graduate from a dental school accredited by the American Dental Association's Commission on Dental Accreditation and pass written and practical examinations to qualify for a license. Candidates may fulfill the written part of the State licensing by passing the National Board Dental Examinations. Individual States or regional testing agencies give the written or practical examinations.

Currently, about 17 States require dentists to obtain a specialty license before practicing as a specialist. Requirements include two to four years of postgraduate education and, in some cases, completion of a special State examination. Most State licenses permit dentists to engage in both general and specialized practice. Dentists who want to teach or do research usually spend an additional two to five years in advanced dental training, in programs operated by dental schools or hospitals.

Dental schools require a minimum of two years of college-level predental education. However, most dental students have at least a bachelor's degree. Predental education emphasizes course work in the sciences.

All dental schools require applicants to take the Dental Admissions Test (DAT). When selecting students, schools consider scores earned on the DAT, the applicant's grade point average, and information gathered through recommendations and interviews.

Dental school usually lasts four academic years. Studies begin with classroom instruction and laboratory work in basic sciences including anatomy, microbiology, biochemistry, and physiology. Beginning courses in clinical sciences, including laboratory techniques, are also provided at this time. During the last two years, students

treat patients, usually in dental clinics, under the supervision of licensed dentists.

Most dental schools award the degree of Doctor of Dental Surgery (D.D.S.). The rest award an equivalent degree, Doctor of Dental Medicine (D.M.D.).

Dentistry requires diagnostic ability and manual skills. Dentists should have good visual memory, excellent judgment of space and shape, a high degree of manual dexterity, and scientific ability. Good business sense, self-discipline, and communication skills are helpful for success in private practice. High school and college students who want to become dentists should take courses in biology, chemistry, physics, health, and mathematics.

Some dental school graduates work for established dentists as associates for a year or two in order to gain experience and save money to equip an office of their own. Most dental school graduates, however, purchase an established practice or open a new practice immediately after graduation. Each year about one-fourth to one-third of new graduates enroll in postgraduate training programs to prepare for a dental specialty.

Job Outlook

Employment of dentists is expected to grow slower than the average for all occupations through 2008. Although employment growth will provide some job opportunities, most jobs will result from the need to replace the large number of dentists projected to retire. Job prospects should be good if the number of dental school graduates does not grow significantly, keeping the supply of newly qualified dentists near current levels.

Demand for dental care should grow substantially through 2008. As members of the baby-boom generation advance into middle age, a large number will need maintenance on complicated dental work, such as bridges. In addition, elderly people are more likely to retain their teeth than were their predecessors, so they will require much more care than in the past. The younger generation will continue to need preventive check-ups despite treatments such as fluoridation of the water supply, which decreases the incidence of tooth decay.

Dental care will focus more on prevention, including teaching people how to better care for their teeth. Dentists will increasingly provide care that is aimed at preventing tooth loss (rather than just providing treatments, such as fillings). Improvements in dental technology will also allow dentists to provide more effective and less painful treatment to their patients.

However, the employment of dentists is not expected to grow as rapidly as the demand for dental services. As their practices expand, dentists are likely to hire more dental hygienists and dental assistants to handle routine services.

Earnings

Median annual earnings of salaried dentists were $110,160 in 1998. Earnings vary according to number of years in practice, location, hours worked, and specialty.

Self-employed dentists in private practice tend to earn more than salaried dentists. A relatively large proportion of dentists is self-

employed. Like other business owners, these dentists must provide their own health insurance, life insurance, and retirement benefits.

Related Occupations

Dentists examine, diagnose, prevent, and treat diseases and abnormalities. So do clinical psychologists, optometrists, physicians, chiropractors, veterinarians, and podiatrists.

Sources of Additional Information

For information on dentistry as a career and a list of accredited dental schools, contact:

- American Dental Association, Commission on Dental Accreditation, 211 E. Chicago Ave., Chicago, IL 60611. Internet: http://www.ada.org
- American Association of Dental Schools, 1625 Massachusetts Ave. NW., Washington, DC 20036. Internet: http://www.aads.jhu.edu

The American Dental Association will also furnish a list of State boards of dental examiners. Persons interested in practicing dentistry should obtain the requirements for licensure from the board of dental examiners of the State in which they plan to work.

Prospective dental students should contact the office of student financial aid at the schools to which they apply, for information on scholarships, grants, and loans, including Federal financial aid.

Designers

(O*NET 34038A, 34038B, 34038C, 34038D, 34038F, 34041, 34044, and 39999H)

Significant Points

- Four out of 10 designers are self-employed; that's almost four times the proportion for all professional specialty occupations.

- Creativity is crucial in all design occupations; formal education requirements range from a high school diploma for floral designers to a bachelor's degree for industrial designers.

- Despite projected faster-than-average employment growth, keen competition is expected for most jobs, because many talented individuals are attracted to careers as designers.

Nature of the Work

Designers are people with a desire to create. They combine practical knowledge with artistic ability to turn abstract ideas into formal designs for the clothes we wear, the living and office space we inhabit, and the merchandise we buy. Designers usually specialize in a particular area of design, such as automobiles, clothing, furniture, home appliances, industrial equipment, interiors of homes or office buildings, movie and theater sets, packaging, or floral arrangements.

The first step in developing a new design or altering an existing one is to determine the needs of the client and the ultimate function for which the design is intended. When creating a design, the designer considers size, shape, weight, color, materials used, cost, ease of use, and safety.

The designer then prepares sketches—either by hand or with the aid of a computer—to illustrate the vision for the design. After consulting with the client, an art or design director, or a product development team, the designer creates a detailed design using drawings, a structural model, computer simulations, or a full-scale prototype. Many designers are increasingly using computer-aided design (CAD) tools to create and better visualize the final product. Computer models allow greater ease and flexibility in making changes to a design, thus reducing design costs and cutting the time it takes to deliver a product to market. Industrial designers use computer-aided industrial design (CAID) to create designs and to communicate them to automated production tools.

Designers sometimes supervise assistants who carry out their creations. Designers who run their own businesses also may devote a considerable amount of time to developing new business contacts and to performing administrative tasks, such as reviewing catalogues and ordering samples.

Design encompasses a number of different fields. Many designers specialize in a particular area of design, whereas others work in more than one. *Industrial designers* develop countless manufactured products, including airplanes; cars; home appliances; children's toys; computer equipment; and medical, office, and recreational equipment. They combine artistic talent with research on product use, marketing, materials, and production methods to create the most functional and appealing design and to make the product competitive with others in the marketplace. Most industrial designers concentrate in an area of sub-specialization, such as kitchen appliances.

Furniture designers design furniture for manufacture. These designers use their knowledge of design trends, competitors' products, production costs, production capability, and characteristics of a company's market to create home and office furniture that is both functional and attractive. They also may prepare detailed drawings of fixtures, forms, or tools required in the production of furniture. Some furniture designers fashion custom pieces or styles according to a specific period or country. Furniture designers must be strongly involved with the fashion industry and aware of current trends and styles.

Interior designers plan the space and furnish the interiors of private homes, public buildings, and commercial or institutional establishments such as offices, restaurants, hospitals, hotels, and theaters. They also plan the interiors for additions to and renovations of existing structures. Most interior designers specialize, and some further specialize in a related line of work. For example, some may concentrate in residential design, and others may further specialize by focusing on a particular room, such as kitchens or baths. With a client's tastes, needs, and budget in mind, interior designers prepare drawings and specifications for interior construction, furnishings, lighting, and finishes. Increasingly, designers use computers to plan layouts that can be changed easily to include ideas received from the client. Interior designers also design lighting and architectural details (such as crown molding); coordinate colors; and select furniture, floor coverings, and curtains. Interior designers must design space to conform to Federal, State, and local laws, including building codes. Design plans for public areas also must meet accessibility standards for the disabled and elderly.

Set, lighting, and costume designers create set, lighting, and costume designs for movie, television, and theater productions. They study scripts, confer with directors and other designers, and conduct research to determine the appropriate historical period, fashion, and architectural styles.

Fashion designers design clothing and accessories. Some high-fashion designers are self-employed and design for individual clients. Other high-fashion designers cater to specialty stores or high fashion department stores. These designers create original garments, as well as follow established fashion trends. Most fashion designers, however, work for apparel manufacturers, adapting designs of men's, women's, and children's fashions for the mass market.

Textile designers, using their knowledge of textile materials and fashion trends, design fabric for garments, upholstery, rugs, and other products. Computers are widely used in pattern design and grading; intelligent pattern engineering (IPE) systems enable great automation in generating patterns.

Floral designers cut and arrange live, dried, or artificial flowers and foliage into designs, according to the customer's order. They trim flowers and arrange bouquets, sprays, wreaths, dish gardens, and terrariums. They usually work from a written order indicating the occasion; customer preference for color and type of flower; price; and the date, time, and place the floral arrangement or plant is to be ready or be delivered. The variety of duties performed by a floral designer depends on the size of the shop and the number of designers employed. In a small operation, the floral designer may own the shop and do almost everything from growing and purchasing flowers to keeping financial records.

Merchandise displayers and window dressers plan and erect commercial displays, such as those in windows and interiors of retail stores and at trade exhibitions.

Working Conditions

Working conditions and places of employment vary. Designers employed by manufacturing establishments or design firms generally work regular hours in well-lighted and comfortable settings. Self-employed designers tend to work longer hours.

Designers frequently adjust their workday to suit their clients' schedules, meeting with them during evening or weekend hours when necessary. Designers may transact business in their own offices or clients' homes or offices, or they may travel to other locations, such as showrooms, design centers, and manufacturing facilities.

Industrial designers usually work regular hours but occasionally work overtime to meet deadlines. In contrast, set, lighting, and costume designers work long and irregular hours, and they often are under pressure to make rapid changes. Fashion designers may work long hours, particularly during production deadlines or before fashion shows, when overtime usually is necessary. In addi-

tion, fashion designers may be required to travel to production sites across the United States and overseas. Interior designers generally work under deadlines and may work overtime to finish a job. They regularly carry heavy and bulky sample books to meetings with clients. Floral designers usually work regular hours in a pleasant work environment, except during holidays, when overtime usually is required.

All designers face frustration at times, when their designs are rejected or when they cannot be as creative as they wish. Independent consultants, who are paid by the assignment, are under pressure to please clients and to find new ones to maintain an income.

Employment

Designers held about 423,000 jobs in 1998. Four out of 10 were self-employed.

Designers work in a number of different industries, depending on their design specialty. Most industrial designers, for example, work for engineering or architectural consulting firms or for large corporations. Interior designers usually work for furniture and home furnishings stores, interior designing services, and architectural firms. Many interior designers do freelance work—full time, part time, or in addition to a salaried job in another occupation.

Set, lighting, and costume designers work for theater companies and film and television production companies. Fashion designers generally work for textile, apparel, and pattern manufacturers, or for fashion salons, high-fashion department stores, and specialty shops. Most floral designers work for retail flower shops or in floral departments located inside grocery and department stores.

Training, Other Qualifications, and Advancement

Creativity is crucial in all design occupations. People in this field must have a strong sense of the aesthetic—an eye for color and detail, a sense of balance and proportion, and an appreciation for beauty. Sketching ability is helpful for most designers, but it is especially important for fashion designers. A good portfolio (a collection of examples of a person's best work) is often the deciding factor in getting a job. Except for floral design, formal preparation in design is necessary.

Educational requirements for entry-level positions vary. Some design occupations, notably industrial design, require a bachelor's degree. Interior designers normally need a college education, in part because few clients (especially commercial clients) are willing to entrust responsibility for designing living and working space to a designer with no formal credentials.

Interior design is the only design field subject to government regulation. According to the American Society for Interior Designers, 21 States and the District of Columbia require interior designers to be licensed. Because licensing is not mandatory in all States, an interior designer's professional standing is important. Membership in a professional association usually requires the completion of three or four years of post-secondary education in design, at least two years of practical experience in the field, and passage of the National Council for Interior Design qualification examination.

In fashion design, employers seek individuals with a two- or four-year degree who are knowledgeable in the areas of textiles, fabrics, and ornamentation, as well as trends in the fashion world. Similarly, furniture designers must keep abreast of trends in fashion and style, in addition to methods and tools used in furniture production. Several universities and schools of design offer degrees in furniture design.

Set, lighting, and costume designers typically have college degrees in their particular area of design. A Master of Fine Arts (MFA) degree from an accredited university program further establishes one's design credentials. Membership in the United Scenic Artists, Local 829, is a nationally recognized standard of achievement for scenic designers.

In contrast to the other design occupations, a high school diploma ordinarily suffices for floral design jobs. Most floral designers learn their skills on the job. When employers hire trainees, they generally look for high school graduates who have a flair for color and a desire to learn. Completion of formal training, however, is an asset for floral designers, particularly for advancement to the chief floral designer level. Vocational and technical schools offer programs in floral design, usually lasting less than a year, while two- and four-year programs in floriculture, horticulture, floral design, or ornamental horticulture are offered by community and junior colleges and colleges and universities.

Formal training for some design professions also is available in two- and three-year professional schools that award certificates or associate degrees in design. Graduates of two-year programs normally qualify as assistants to designers. The Bachelor of Fine Arts degree is granted at four-year colleges and universities. The curriculum in these schools includes art and art history, principles of design, designing and sketching, and specialized studies for each of the individual design disciplines, such as garment construction, textiles, mechanical and architectural drawing, computerized design, sculpture, architecture, and basic engineering. A liberal arts education, with courses in merchandising, business administration, marketing, and psychology, along with training in art, also is a good background for most design fields. Additionally, persons with training or experience in architecture qualify for some design occupations, particularly interior design.

Computer-aided design (CAD) increasingly is used in all areas of design (except floral design), so many employers expect new designers to be familiar with the use of the computer as a design tool. For example, industrial designers extensively use computers in the aerospace, automotive, and electronics industries. Interior designers use computers to create numerous versions of interior space designsso the client can see and choose from several designs; images can be inserted, edited, and replaced easily and without added cost. In furniture design, a chair's basic shape and structure may be duplicated and updated by applying new upholstery styles and fabrics with the use of computers.

The National Association of Schools of Art and Design currently accredits about 200 post-secondary institutions with programs in art and design; most of these schools award a degree in art. Some award degrees in industrial, interior, textile, graphic, or fashion design. Many schools do not allow formal entry into a bachelor's degree program until a student has finished a year of basic art and design courses successfully. Applicants may be required to submit sketches and other examples of their artistic ability.

The Foundation for Interior Design Education Research also accredits interior design programs and schools. Currently, there are more than 120 accredited programs in the United States and Canada, located in schools of art, architecture, and home economics.

Individuals in the design field must be creative, imaginative, persistent, and able to communicate their ideas in writing, visually, or verbally. Because tastes in style and fashion can change quickly, designers need to be well read, open to new ideas and influences, and quick to react to changing trends. Problem-solving skills and the ability to work independently and under pressure are important traits. People in this field need self-discipline to start projects on their own, to budget their time, and to meet deadlines and production schedules. Good business sense and sales ability also are important, especially for those who freelance or run their own business.

Beginning designers usually receive on-the-job training and normally need one to three years of training before they advance to higher-level positions. Experienced designers in large firms may advance to chief designer, design department head, or other supervisory positions. Some designers become teachers in design schools and colleges and universities. Some experienced designers open their own firms.

Job Outlook

Despite projected faster-than-average employment growth, designers in most fields—with the exception of floral and furniture design—are expected to face keen competition for available positions. Many talented individuals are attracted to careers as designers. Individuals with little or no formal education in design, as well as those who lack creativity and perseverance, will find it very difficult to establish and maintain a career in design. Floral design should be the least competitive of all design fields because of the relatively low pay and limited opportunities for advancement, as well as the relatively high job turnover of floral designers in retail flower shops.

Overall, the employment of designers is expected to grow faster than the average for all occupations through the year 2008. In addition to employment growth, many job openings will result from the need to replace designers who leave the field. Increased demand for industrial designers will stem from the continued emphasis on product quality and safety; the demand for new products that are easy and comfortable to use; the development of high-technology products in medicine, transportation, and other fields; and growing global competition among businesses. Rising demand for professional design of private homes, offices, restaurants and other retail establishments, and institutions that care for the rapidly growing elderly population should spur employment growth of interior designers. Demand for fashion, textile, and furniture designers should remain strong, because many consumers are concerned with fashion and style.

Earnings

Median annual earnings for designers in all specialties except interior design were $29,200 in 1998. The middle 50 percent earned between $18,420 and $43,940. The lowest 10 percent earned less than $13,780, and the highest 10 percent earned over $68,310. Median annual earnings in the industries employing the largest numbers of designers, except interior designers, in 1997 were as follows:

Engineering and architectural services.......................... $41,300

Apparel, piece goods, and notions 38,400

Mailing, reproduction, and stenographic services 36,000

Retail stores, not elsewhere classified 16,500

Median annual earnings for interior designers were $31,760 in 1998. The middle 50 percent earned between $23,580 and $42,570. The lowest 10 percent earned less than $18,360 and the highest 10 percent earned over $65,810. Median annual earnings in the industries employing the largest numbers of interior designers in 1997 were as follows:

Engineering and architectural services.......................... $33,000

Furniture and home furnishings stores 27,800

Miscellaneous business services 26,800

Median annual earnings of merchandise displayers and window dressers were $18,180 in 1998. The lowest 10 percent earned less than $12,680, and the highest 10 percent earned over $28,910.

According to the Industrial Designers Society of America, the average base salary for an industrial designer with one to two years of experience was about $31,000 in 1998. Staff designers with five years of experience earned $39,000, whereas senior designers with eight years of experience earned $51,000. Industrial designers in managerial or executive positions earned substantially more—up to $500,000 annually; however, $75,000 to $100,000 was more representative.

Related Occupations

Workers in other occupations who design or arrange objects, materials, or interiors to enhance their appearance and function include visual artists, architects, landscape architects, engineers, photographers, and interior decorators. Some computer-related occupations, including Internet page designers and webmasters, require design skills.

Sources of Additional Information

For an order form for a directory of accredited college-level programs in art and design (available for $15.00) or career information in design occupations, contact:

● National Association of Schools of Art and Design, 11250 Roger Bacon Dr., Suite 21, Reston, VA 20190.

For information on careers and a list of academic programs in industrial design, write to:

● Industrial Designers Society of America, 1142-E Walker Rd., Great Falls, VA 22066. Internet: http://www.idsa.org

For information on degree, continuing education, and licensure programs in interior design, contact:

● American Society for Interior Designers, 608 Massachusetts Ave. NE., Washington, DC 20002-6006.

For a list of schools with accredited programs in interior design, contact:

● Foundation for Interior Design Education Research, 60 Monroe Center NW., Grand Rapids, MI 49503. Internet: http://www.fider.org

For information about careers in floral design, contact:

● Society of American Florists, 1601 Duke St., Alexandria, VA 22314.

Dietitians and Nutritionists

(O*NET 32521)

Significant points

● Employment of dietitians is expected to grow about as fast as the average for all occupations through the year 2008 due to increased emphasis on disease prevention by improved health habits.

● Dietitians and nutritionists need at least a bachelor's degree in dietetics, foods and nutrition, food service systems management, or a related area.

Nature of the Work

Dietitians and nutritionists plan food and nutrition programs and supervise the preparation and serving of meals. They help prevent and treat illnesses by promoting healthy eating habits, scientifically evaluating clients' diets, and suggesting diet modifications, such as less salt for those with high blood pressure or reduced fat and sugar intake for those who are overweight.

Dietitians run food service systems for institutions such as hospitals and schools, promote sound eating habits through education, and conduct research. Major areas of practice are clinical, community, management, research, business and industry, and consultant dietetics.

Clinical dietitians provide nutritional services for patients in institutions such as hospitals and nursing homes. They assess patients' nutritional needs, develop and implement nutrition programs, and evaluate and report the results. They also confer with doctors and other health care professionals in order to coordinate medical and nutritional needs. Some clinical dietitians specialize in the management of overweight patients, care of the critically ill, or care of renal (kidney) and diabetic patients. In addition, clinical dietitians in nursing homes, small hospitals, or correctional facilities may also manage the food service department.

Community dietitians counsel individuals and groups on nutritional practices designed to prevent disease and promote good health. Working in places such as public health clinics, home health agencies, and health maintenance organizations, they evaluate individual needs, develop nutritional care plans, and instruct individuals and their families. Dietitians working in home health agencies provide instruction on grocery shopping and food preparation to the elderly, individuals with special needs, and children.

Increased interest in nutrition has led to opportunities in food manufacturing, advertising, and marketing, in which dietitians analyze foods, prepare literature for distribution, or report on issues such as the nutritional content of recipes, dietary fiber, or vitamin supplements.

Management dietitians oversee large-scale meal planning and preparation in health care facilities, company cafeterias, prisons, and schools. They hire, train, and direct other dietitians and food service workers; budget for and purchase food, equipment, and supplies; enforce sanitary and safety regulations; and prepare records and reports.

Consultant dietitians work under contract with health care facilities or in their own private practice. They perform nutrition screenings for their clients and offer advice on diet-related concerns such as weight loss or cholesterol reduction. Some work for wellness programs, sports teams, supermarkets, and other nutrition-related businesses. They may consult with food service managers, providing expertise in sanitation, safety procedures, menu development, budgeting, and planning.

Working Conditions

Most dietitians work a regular 40-hour week, although some work weekends. Many dietitians work part time.

Dietitians and nutritionists usually work in clean, well-lighted, and well-ventilated areas. However, some dietitians work in warm, congested kitchens. Many dietitians and nutritionists are on their feet for most of the workday.

Employment

Dietitians and nutritionists held about 54,000 jobs in 1998. Over half were in hospitals, nursing homes, or offices and clinics of physicians.

State and local governments provided about 1 job in 6—mostly in health departments and other public health related areas. Other jobs were in restaurants, social service agencies, residential care facilities, diet workshops, physical fitness facilities, school systems, colleges and universities, and the Federal government (mostly in the Department of Veterans Affairs). Some were employed by firms that provide food services on contract to such facilities as colleges and universities, airlines, correctional facilities, and company cafeterias.

Some dietitians were self-employed, working as consultants to facilities such as hospitals and nursing homes and seeing individual clients.

Training, Other Qualifications, and Advancement

High school students interested in becoming a dietitian or nutritionist should take courses in biology, chemistry, mathematics, health, and communications. Dietitians and nutritionists need at least a bachelor's degree in dietetics, foods and nutrition, food service systems management, or a related area. College students in these majors take courses in foods, nutrition, institution management, chemistry, biochemistry, biology, microbiology, and physi-

ology. Other suggested courses include business, mathematics, statistics, computer science, psychology, sociology, and economics.

Twenty-seven of the 41 States with laws governing dietetics require licensure, 13 require certification, and 1 requires registration. The Commission on Dietetic Registration of the American Dietetic Association (ADA) awards the Registered Dietitian credential to those who pass a certification exam after completing their academic coursework and supervised experience. Since practice requirements vary by State, interested candidates should determine the requirements of the State in which they want to work before sitting for any exam.

As of 1999, there were 235 bachelor's and master's degree programs approved by the ADA's Commission on Accreditation/Approval for Dietetics Education (CAADE). Supervised practice experience can be acquired in two ways. There are 51 ADA-accredited coordinated programs combining academic and supervised practice experience in a four- to five-year program. The second option requires completion of 900 hours of supervised practice experience, either in one of the 225 CAADE-accredited internships or in one of the 25 CAADE-approved preprofessional practice programs. Internships and preprofessional practice programs may be full-time programs lasting nine months to a year or part-time programs lasting two years. Students interested in research, advanced clinical positions, or public health may need a graduate degree.

Experienced dietitians may advance to assistant, associate, or director of a dietetic department or might become self-employed. Some dietitians specialize in areas such as renal or pediatric dietetics. Others may leave the occupation to become sales representatives for equipment, pharmaceutical, or food manufacturers.

Job Outlook

Employment of dietitians is expected to grow about as fast as the average for all occupations through 2008 due to increased emphasis on disease prevention by improved dietary habits. A growing and aging population will increase the demand for meals and nutritional counseling in nursing homes, schools, prisons, community health programs, and home health care agencies. Public interest in nutrition and the emphasis on health education and prudent lifestyles will also spur demand, especially in management. Besides employment growth, job openings will also result from the need to replace experienced workers who leave the occupation.

The number of dietitian positions in hospitals is expected to grow slowly as hospitals continue to contract out food service operations. On the other hand, employment is expected to grow fast in contract providers of food services, social services agencies, and offices and clinics of physicians.

Employment growth for dietitians and nutritionists may be somewhat constrained by some employers substituting other workers such as health educators, food service managers, and dietetic technicians. Growth also is constrained by limitations on insurance reimbursement for dietetic services.

Earnings

Median annual earnings of dietitians and nutritionists were $35,020 in 1998. The middle 50 percent earned between $28,010 and $42,720 a year. The lowest 10 percent earned less than $20,350, and the highest 10 percent earned more than $51,320 a year. Median annual earnings in the industries employing the largest number of dietitians and nutritionists in 1997 were as follows:

Hospitals	$34,900
Local government, except education and hospitals	31,200
Nursing and personal care facilities	28,400

According to the American Dietetic Association, median annual income for registered dietitians in 1997 varied by practice area as follows: clinical nutrition, $35,500; food and nutrition management, $44,900; community nutrition, $34,900; consultation and business, $46,000; and education and research, $45,200. Salaries also vary by years in practice, educational level, geographic region, and size of community.

Related Occupations

Dietitians and nutritionists apply the principles of food and nutrition in a variety of situations. Jobs similar to management dietitians' include home economists and food service managers. Nurses and health educators often provide services related to those of community dietitians.

Sources of Additional Information

For a list of academic programs, scholarships, and other information about dietetics, contact:

- The American Dietetic Association, 216 West Jackson Blvd., Suite 800, Chicago, IL 60606-6995. Internet: http://www.eatright.org

Dispatchers

(O*NET 58002 and 58005)

Significant Points

- This occupation is expected to grow about as fast as the average for all occupations.

- Duties vary, depending on the employer's needs.

Nature of the Work

The work of dispatchers varies greatly depending on the industry. Dispatchers keep records, logs, and schedules of the calls they receive, transportation vehicles they monitor and control, and actions they take. They maintain information on each call and then prepare a detailed report on all activities occurring during the shift. Many dispatchers employ computer-aided dispatch systems to accomplish these tasks.

Regardless of where they work, all dispatchers are assigned a specific territory and have responsibility for all communications within this area. Many work in teams, especially in large communications centers or companies. One person usually handles all dispatching calls to the response units or company's drivers, while the other members of the team usually receive the incoming calls and deal with the public.

Police, fire, and ambulance dispatchers, also called public safety dispatchers, monitor the location of emergency services personnel from any one or all of the jurisdiction's emergency services departments. They dispatch the appropriate type and number of units in response to calls for assistance. Dispatchers, or call takers, often are the first people the public contacts when they call for emergency assistance. If certified for emergency medical services, the dispatcher may provide medical instruction to those on the scene until the medical staff arrives.

Usually, dispatchers constitute the communications workforce on a shift. A dispatcher is responsible for communication within an assignment area, while the call takers receive calls and transfer information to the dispatchers. During the course of the shift, personnel will rotate such that the assignment responsibility of the dispatcher will be shared with those in the call taker role.

Police, fire, and ambulance dispatchers work in a variety of settings; they may work in a police station, a fire station, a hospital, or a centralized city communications center. In many cities, the police department serves as the communications center. In these situations, all 911 emergency calls go to the police department, where a dispatcher handles the police calls and screens the others before transferring them to the appropriate service.

When handling calls, dispatchers carefully question each caller to determine the type, seriousness, and location of the emergency. This information is posted either electronically by computer or, with decreasing frequency, by hand, and communicated immediately to uniformed or supervisory personnel. They quickly decide on the priority of the incident, the kind and number of units needed, and the location of the closest and most suitable units available. Typically, a team of call takers answer calls and relay the information to the dispatchers. Responsibility then shifts to the dispatchers, who send response units to the scene and monitor the activity of the public safety personnel answering the dispatch.

When appropriate, dispatchers stay in close contact with other service providers—for example, a police dispatcher would monitor the response of the fire department when there is a major fire. In a medical emergency, dispatchers not only keep in close touch with the dispatched units, but also with the caller. They may give extensive pre-arrival first aid instructions while the caller is waiting for the ambulance. They continuously give updates on the patient's condition to the ambulance personnel, and often serve as a link between the medical staff in a hospital and the emergency medical technicians in the ambulance.

Other dispatchers coordinate deliveries, service calls, and related activities for a variety of firms. Truck dispatchers, who work for local and long distance trucking companies, coordinate the movement of trucks and freight between cities. They direct the pickup and delivery activities of drivers. They receive customers' requests for pickup and delivery of freight; consolidate freight orders into truckloads for specific destinations; assign drivers and trucks; and draw up routes and pickup and delivery schedules. Bus dispatchers make sure local and long distance buses stay on schedule. They handle all problems that may disrupt service and dispatch other

buses, or arrange for repairs to restore service and schedules. Train dispatchers ensure the timely and efficient movement of trains according to train orders and schedules. They must be aware of track switch positions, track maintenance areas, and the location of other trains running on the track. Taxicab dispatchers, or starters, dispatch taxis in response to requests for service and keep logs on all road service calls. Tow truck dispatchers take calls for emergency road service. They relay the problem to a nearby service station or a tow truck service and see to it that the emergency road service is completed. Gas and water service dispatchers monitor gas lines and water mains and send out service trucks and crews to take care of emergencies.

Working Conditions

Working conditions vary considerably by employment setting. The work of dispatchers can be very hectic when many calls come in at the same time. The job of public safety dispatcher is particularly stressful, because slow or improper response to a call can result in serious injury or further harm. Also, callers who are anxious or afraid may become excited and be unable to provide necessary information; some may become abusive. Despite provocations, dispatchers must remain calm, objective, and in control of the situation.

Dispatchers sit for long periods, using telephones, computers, and two-way radios. Much of their time is spent at video display terminals, viewing monitors and observing traffic patterns. As a result of working for long stretches with computers and other electronic equipment, dispatchers can experience significant eyestrain and back discomfort. Generally, dispatchers work a 40-hour week; however, rotating shifts and compressed work schedules are common. Alternative work schedules are necessary to accommodate evening, weekend, and holiday work, as well as 24-hours-per-day, seven-days-per-week operations.

Employment

Dispatchers held 248,000 jobs in 1998. About one-third were police, fire, and ambulance dispatchers, almost all of whom worked for State and local governments—primarily for local police and fire departments. Most of the remaining dispatchers worked for local and long distance trucking companies and bus lines; telephone, electric, and gas utility companies; wholesale and retail establishments; railroads; and companies providing business services.

Although dispatching jobs are found throughout the country, most dispatchers work in urban areas where large communications centers and businesses are located.

Training, Other Qualifications, and Advancement

Many dispatching occupations are entry level and require no more than a high school diploma. Increasingly however, employers prefer to hire those familiar with computers and other electronic office and business equipment. Those who have taken business courses or have previous business, dispatching, or specific job-related experience may be preferred. Because the nature of the work is to communicate effectively with other people, good oral and written communications skills are essential. Typing, filing, record keeping, and other clerical skills are also important.

State or local government civil service regulations usually govern police, fire, emergency medical, and ambulance dispatching jobs. Candidates for these positions may have to pass written, oral, and performance tests. Also, they may be asked to attend training classes and attain the proper certification in order to qualify for advancement.

Trainees usually develop the necessary skills on the job. This informal training lasts from several days to a few months, depending on the complexity of the job. Working with an experienced dispatcher, new dispatchers monitor calls and learn how to operate a variety of communications equipment, including telephones, radios, and wireless appliances. As trainees gain confidence, they begin to handle calls themselves. Many public safety dispatchers also participate in structured training programs sponsored by their employer. Some employers offer a course designed by the Association of Public Safety Communications Officials. This course covers topics such as interpersonal communications; overview of the police, fire, and rescue functions; modern public safety telecommunications systems; basic radio broadcasting; local, State, and National crime information computer systems; and telephone complaint/report processing procedures. Other employers develop in-house programs based on their own needs. Emergency medical dispatchers often receive special training or have special skills. Increasingly, public safety dispatchers receive training in stress and crisis management, as well as family counseling. Employers are recognizing the toll this work has on daily living and the potential impact stress has on the job, on the work environment, and in the home.

Communications skills and the ability to work under pressure are important personal qualities for dispatchers. Residency in the city or county of employment frequently is required for public safety dispatchers. Dispatchers in transportation industries must be able to deal with sudden influxes of shipments and disruptions of shipping schedules caused by bad weather, road construction, or accidents.

Although there are no mandatory licensing or certification requirements, some States require that public safety dispatchers possess a certificate to work on a State network, such as the Police Information Network. The Association of Public Safety Communications Officials, the National Academy of Emergency Medical Dispatch, and the International Municipal Signal Association all offer certification programs. Many dispatchers participate in these programs to improve their prospects for career advancement.

Advancement opportunities for dispatching workers vary with the place of employment. Dispatchers who work for private firms, which are usually small, will find few opportunities for advancement. Public safety dispatchers, on the other hand, may become a shift or divisional supervisor or chief of communications or move to higher paying administrative jobs. Some go on to become police officers or firefighters.

Job Outlook

Overall employment of dispatchers is expected to grow about as fast as the average for all occupations through 2008. In addition to job growth, job openings will result from the need to replace those who transfer to other occupations or leave the labor force.

Employment of police, fire, and ambulance dispatchers is expected to grow more slowly than the average for all occupations. Intense competition for available resources among governmental units should limit the ability of many growing communities to keep pace with rapidly growing emergency services needs. To balance the increased demand for emergency services, many districts are seeking to consolidate their communications centers into a shared, areawide facility, which will further restrict opportunities in this industry. Individuals with computer skills and experience will have a greater opportunity for employment as public safety dispatchers.

Population growth and economic expansion are expected to lead to average employment growth for dispatchers not involved in public safety. Although the overall increase will be about average, not all specialties will be affected in the same way. For example, employment of taxicab, train, and truck dispatchers is sensitive to economic conditions. When economic activity falls, demand for transportation services declines. They may experience layoffs or a shortened workweek, and jobseekers may have some difficulty finding entry-level jobs. Employment of tow truck dispatchers, on the other hand, is seldom affected by general economic conditions because of the emergency nature of their business.

Earnings

Earnings of dispatching occupations vary somewhat by industry. The range of median hourly earnings in 1998 are shown in the following table.

Dispatchers, except police, fire, and ambulance $12.68

Dispatchers, police, fire, and ambulance 11.38

Workers in dispatching occupations usually receive the same benefits as most other workers.

Related Occupations

Other occupations that involve directing and controlling the movement of vehicles, freight, and personnel, as well as information and message distribution, are airline dispatchers, air traffic controllers, radio and television transmitter operators, telephone operators, customer service representatives, and transportation agents.

Sources of Additional Information

For further information on training and certification for police, fire, and emergency dispatchers, contact:

- National Academy of Emergency Medical Dispatch, 139 East South Temple, Suite 530, Salt Lake City, UT 84111. Internet: http://www.naemd.org

- Association of Public Safety Communications Officials, 2040 S. Ridgewood, South Daytona, FL 32119-2257. Internet: http://www.apcointl.org

- International Municipal Signal Association, 165 East Union St., P.O. Box 539, Newark, NY 14513-1526.Internet: http://www.imsafety.org

For general information on dispatchers, contact:

- Service Employees International Union, AFL-CIO, CLC, 1313 L St. NW., Washington, DC 20005-4100. Internet: http://www.seiu.org

- American Train Dispatchers Association, 1370 Ontario St., Cleveland, OH 44113. Internet: http://www.ble.org/atdd/dwv.html

Information on job opportunities for police, fire, and emergency dispatchers is available from personnel offices of State and local governments or police departments. Information about work opportunities for other types of dispatchers is available from local employers and State employment service offices.

Drafters

(O*NET 22514A, 22514B, 22514C, 22514D, and 22517)

Significant Points

- The type and quality of post-secondary drafting programs varies considerably; prospective students should be careful in selecting a program.

- Opportunities should be best for individuals who have at least two years of post-secondary training in drafting and considerable skill and experience using computer-aided drafting (CAD) systems.

- Demand for particular drafting specializations varies geographically, depending on the needs of local industry.

Nature of the Work

Drafters prepare technical drawings and plans used by production and construction workers to build everything from manufactured products such as spacecraft or industrial machinery to structures such as office buildings or oil and gas pipelines. Their drawings provide visual guidelines, showing the technical details of the products and structures, specifying dimensions, materials to be used, and procedures and processes to be followed. Drafters fill in technical details, using drawings, rough sketches, specifications, codes, and calculations previously made by engineers, surveyors, architects, or scientists. For example, they use their knowledge of standardized building techniques to draw in the details of a structure. Some drafters use their knowledge of engineering and manufacturing theory and standards to draw the parts of a machine in order to determine design elements such as the number and kind of fasteners needed to assemble it. They use technical handbooks, tables, calculators, and computers to do this.

Traditionally, drafters sat at drawing boards and used compasses, dividers, protractors, triangles, and other drafting devices to prepare a drawing manually. Most drafters now use computer-aided drafting (CAD) systems to prepare drawings. These systems employ computer work stations that create a drawing on a video screen. The drawings are stored electronically so that revisions or duplications can be made easily. These systems also permit drafters to easily and quickly prepare variations of a design. Although this equipment has become easier to operate, CAD is only a tool. Persons who produce technical drawings using CAD still function as a drafter, and they need most of the knowledge of traditional drafters—relating to drafting skills and standards—as well as CAD skills.

As CAD technology advances, and the cost of the systems continues to fall, it is likely that almost all drafters will use CAD systems regularly in the future. However, manual drafting may still be used in certain applications, especially in specialty firms that produce many one-of-a-kind drawings with little repetition.

Drafting work has many specialties, and titles may denote a particular discipline of design or drafting. *Architectural drafters* draw architectural and structural features of buildings and other structures. They may specialize by the type of structure (such as residential or commercial) or by material used (such as reinforced concrete, masonry, steel, or timber).

Aeronautical drafters prepare engineering drawings detailing plans and specifications used for the manufacture of aircraft, missiles, and parts.

Electrical drafters prepare wiring and layout diagrams used by workers who erect, install, and repair electrical equipment and wiring in communication centers, power plants, electrical distribution systems, and buildings.

Electronic drafters draw wiring diagrams, circuit board assembly diagrams, schematics, and layout drawings used in the manufacture, installation, and repair of electronic devices and components.

Civil drafters prepare drawings and topographical and relief maps used in major construction or civil engineering projects such as highways, bridges, pipelines, flood control projects, and water and sewage systems.

Mechanical drafters prepare detail and assembly drawings of a wide variety of machinery and mechanical devices, indicating dimensions, fastening methods, and other requirements.

Process piping or *pipeline drafters* prepare drawings used for layout, construction, and operation of oil and gas fields, refineries, chemical plants, and process piping systems.

Working Conditions

Drafters usually work in comfortable offices furnished to accommodate their tasks. They may sit at adjustable drawing boards or drafting tables when doing manual drawings, although most drafters work at computer terminals much of the time. Because they spend long periods of time in front of computer terminals doing detailed work, drafters may be susceptible to eyestrain, back discomfort, and hand and wrist problems.

Employment

Drafters held about 283,000 jobs in 1998. More than 35 percent of all drafters worked in engineering and architectural services firms that design construction projects or do other engineering work on a contract basis for organizations in other industries. Another 29 percent worked in durable goods manufacturing industries, such as machinery, electrical equipment, and fabricated metals. The remainder were mostly employed in the construction, communications, utilities, and personnel supply services industries. About 17,600 were self-employed in 1998.

Training, Other Qualifications, and Advancement

Employers prefer applicants for drafting positions who have completed post-secondary school training in drafting, which is offered by technical institutes, community colleges, and some four-year colleges and universities. Employers are most interested in applicants who have well-developed drafting and mechanical drawing skills; a knowledge of drafting standards, mathematics, science, and engineering technology; and a solid background in computer-aided drafting and design techniques. In addition, communication and problem-solving skills are important.

Individuals planning careers in drafting should take courses in math, science, computer technology, design or computer graphics, and any high school drafting courses available. Mechanical and visual aptitude are also important. Prospective drafters should be able to draw freehand, three-dimensional objects and do detailed work accurately and neatly. Artistic ability is helpful in some specialized fields, as is knowledge of manufacturing and construction methods. In addition, prospective drafters should have good interpersonal skills because they work closely with engineers, surveyors, architects, and other professionals.

Entry-level or junior drafters usually do routine work under close supervision. After gaining experience, intermediate-level drafters progress to more difficult work with less supervision. They may be required to exercise more judgment and perform calculations when preparing and modifying drawings. Drafters may eventually advance to senior drafter, designer, or supervisor. Many employers pay for continuing education, and with appropriate college degrees, drafters may go on to become engineering technicians, engineers, or architects.

Many types of publicly and privately operated schools provide some form of drafting training. The kind and quality of programs vary considerably. Therefore, prospective students should be careful in selecting a program. They should contact prospective employers regarding their preferences and ask schools to provide information about the kinds of jobs obtained by graduates, type and condition of instructional facilities and equipment, and faculty qualifications.

Technical institutes offer intensive technical training but less of the general education than do junior and community colleges. Certificates or diplomas based on completion of a certain number of course hours may be rewarded. Many offer two-year associate degree programs, which are similar to or part of the programs offered by community colleges or State university systems. Other technical institutes are run by private, often for-profit, organizations, sometimes called proprietary schools. Their programs vary considerably in both length and type of courses offered.

Community colleges offer curriculums similar to those in technical institutes but include more courses on theory and liberal arts. Often there is little or no difference between technical institute and community college programs. However, courses taken at community colleges are more likely to be accepted for credit at four-year colleges than those at technical institutes. After completing a two-year associate degree program, graduates may obtain jobs as drafters or continue their education in related fields at four-year colleges. Four-year colleges usually do not offer drafting training, but college courses in engineering, architecture, and mathematics are useful for obtaining a job as a drafter.

Area vocational-technical schools are post-secondary public institutions that serve local students and emphasize training needed by local employers. Many offer introductory drafting instruction. Most require a high school diploma or its equivalent for admission.

Technical training obtained in the Armed Forces can also be applied in civilian drafting jobs. Some additional training may be necessary, depending on the technical area or military specialty.

The American Design Drafting Association (ADDA) has established a certification program for drafters. Although drafters are not usually required to be certified by employers, certification demonstrates that nationally recognized standards have been met. Individuals who wish to become certified must pass the Drafter Certification Test, which is administered periodically at ADDA-authorized test sites. Applicants are tested on their knowledge and understanding of basic drafting concepts such as geometric construction, working drawings, and architectural terms and standards.

Job Outlook

Employment of drafters is expected to grow more slowly than the average for all occupations through 2008. Although industrial growth and increasingly complex design problems associated with new products and manufacturing will increase the demand for drafting services, greater use of CAD equipment by architects and engineers, as well as drafters, should offset this growth in demand. Many job openings, however, are expected to arise as drafters move to other occupations or leave the labor force.

Opportunities should be best for individuals who have at least two years of post-secondary training in a drafting program that provides strong technical skills and who have considerable skill and experience using CAD systems. CAD has increased the complexity of drafting applications while enhancing the productivity of drafters. It has also enhanced the nature of drafting by creating more possibilities for design and drafting. As technology continues to advance, employers will look for drafters having a strong background in fundamental drafting principles with a higher level of technical sophistication and an ability to apply this knowledge to a broader range of responsibilities.

Demand for particular drafting specialties varies throughout the country because employment is usually contingent upon the needs of local industry. Employment of drafters remains highly concentrated in industries that are sensitive to cyclical changes in the economy, such as engineering and architectural services and durable goods manufacturing. During recessions, drafters may be laid off. However, a growing number of drafters should continue to be employed on a temporary or contract basis, as more companies turn to the personnel supply services industry to meet their changing needs.

Earnings

Median hourly earnings of drafters were $15.56 in 1998. The middle 50 percent earned between $12.29 and $19.73. The lowest 10 percent earned less than $10.19, and the highest 10 percent earned

more than $24.84. Median hourly earnings in the industries employing the largest numbers of drafters in 1997 were as follows:

Motor vehicles and equipment	$21.50
Personnel supply services	16.20
Miscellaneous business services	15.60
Fabricated structural metal products	14.30

Related Occupations

Other workers who prepare or analyze detailed drawings and make precise calculations and measurements include architects, landscape architects, designers, engineers, engineering technicians, science technicians, cartographers, and surveyors.

Sources of Additional Information

Information on schools offering programs in drafting and related fields is available from:

- Accrediting Commission of Career Schools and Colleges of Technology, 2101 Wilson Blvd., Suite 302, Arlington, VA 22201.

Information about certification is available from:

- American Design Drafting Association, P.O. Box 11937, Columbia, SC 29211. Internet: http://www.adda.org.

Economists and Marketing Research Analysts

(O*NET 27102A and 27102B)

Significant Points

- Demand for qualified marketing research analysts should be strong.

- Candidates who hold a master's degree in economics have much better employment prospects than bachelor's degree holders.

Nature of the Work

Economists. Economists study how society distributes scarce resources such as land, labor, raw materials, and machinery to produce goods and services. They conduct research, collect and analyze data, monitor economic trends, and develop forecasts. They research issues such as energy costs, inflation, interest rates, imports, and employment levels.

Most economists are concerned with practical applications of economic policy. They use their understanding of economic relationships to advise businesses and other organizations, including insurance companies, banks, securities firms, industry and trade associations, labor unions, and government agencies. Economists use mathematical models to develop programs predicting answers to questions such as the nature and length of business cycles, the effects of a specific rate of inflation on the economy, or the effects of tax legislation on unemployment levels.

Economists devise methods and procedures for obtaining the data they need. For example, sampling techniques may be used to conduct a survey, and various mathematical modeling techniques may be used to develop forecasts. Preparing reports on research results is an important part of an economist's job. Relevant data must be reviewed and analyzed, applicable tables and charts prepared, and the results presented in clear, concise language that can be understood by non-economists. Presenting economic and statistical concepts in a meaningful way is particularly important for economists whose research is directed toward making policies for an organization.

Economists who work for government agencies may assess economic conditions in the United States or abroad in order to estimate the economic effects of specific changes in legislation or public policy. They may study areas such as how the dollar's fluctuation against foreign currencies affects import and export levels. The majority of government economists work in the area of agriculture, labor, or quantitative analysis; some economists work in almost every area of government. For example, economists in the U.S. Department of Commerce study production, distribution, and consumption of commodities produced overseas, while economists employed with the Bureau of Labor Statistics analyze data on the domestic economy such as prices, wages, employment, productivity, and safety and health. An economist working in State or local government might analyze data on the growth of school-aged populations, prison growth, and employment and unemployment rates, in order to project spending needs for future years.

Marketing Research Analysts. Marketing research analysts are concerned with the potential sales of a product or service. They analyze statistical data on past sales to predict future sales. They gather data on competitors and analyze prices, sales, and methods of marketing and distribution. Like economists, marketing research analysts devise methods and procedures for obtaining the data they need. They often design telephone, personal, or mail interview surveys to assess consumer preferences. Under the marketing research analyst's direction, trained interviewers usually conduct the surveys.

After compiling the data, marketing research analysts evaluate it and make recommendations to their client or employer based upon their findings. They provide a company's management with information needed to make decisions on the promotion, distribution, design, and pricing of company products or services. The information may also be used to determine the advisability of adding new lines of merchandise, opening new branches, or otherwise diversifying the company's operations. Analysts may conduct opinion research to determine public attitudes on various issues. This can help political or business leaders and others assess public support for their electoral prospects or advertising policies.

Working Conditions

Economists and marketing research analysts have structured work schedules. They often work alone, writing reports, preparing statistical charts, and using computers, but they may also be an integral part of a research team. Most work under pressure of deadlines and tight schedules, which may require overtime. Their routine may be interrupted by special requests for data, as well as by the need to attend meetings or conferences. Frequent travel may be necessary.

Employment

Economists and marketing research analysts held about 70,000 jobs in 1998. Private industry provided about 4 out of 5 jobs for salaried workers, particularly economic and marketing research firms, management consulting firms, banks, securities and commodities brokers, and computer and data processing companies. A wide range of government agencies provided the remaining jobs, primarily for economists. The Departments of Labor, Agriculture, and Commerce are the largest Federal employers of economists. A number of economists and marketing research analysts combine a full-time job in government, academia, or business with part-time or consulting work in another setting.

Employment of economists and marketing research analysts is concentrated in large cities. Some economists work abroad for companies with major international operations, for U.S. Government agencies, and for international organizations like the World Bank and the United Nations.

Besides the jobs described above, many economists and marketing research analysts held faculty positions in colleges and universities. Economics and marketing faculty have flexible work schedules, and may divide their time among teaching, research, consulting, and administration.

Training, Other Qualifications, and Advancement

Graduate training is required for many private sector economist and marketing research analyst jobs and for advancement to more responsible positions. Economics includes many specialties at the graduate level, such as advanced economic theory, econometrics, international economics, and labor economics. Students should select graduate schools strong in specialties in which they are interested. Marketing research analysts may earn advanced degrees in economics, business administration, marketing, statistics, or some closely related discipline. Some schools help graduate students find internships or part-time employment in government agencies, economic consulting firms, financial institutions, or marketing research firms prior to graduation.

Undergraduate economics majors can choose from a variety of courses, ranging from microeconomics, macroeconomics, and econometrics, to more philosophical courses, such as the history of economic thought.

In addition to courses in business, marketing, and consumer behavior, marketing majors should take other liberal arts and social science courses, including economics, psychology, English, and sociology. Because of the importance of quantitative skills to economists and marketing researchers, courses in mathematics, statistics, econometrics, sampling theory and survey design, and computer science are extremely helpful.

In the Federal government, candidates for entry-level economist positions must have a bachelor's degree with a minimum of 21 semester hours of economics and 3 hours of statistics, accounting, or calculus. Competition is keen for positions requiring only a bachelor's degree, however, and additional education or superior academic performance is likely to be required to gain employment.

A master's degree is usually the minimum requirement for a job as an instructor in junior and community colleges. In most colleges and universities, however, a Ph.D. is necessary for appointment as an instructor. A Ph.D. and extensive publications in academic journals are required for a professorship, tenure, and promotion.

Whether working in government, industry, research organizations, marketing, or consulting firms, economists and marketing research analysts with graduate degrees usually qualify for more responsible research and administrative positions. Many businesses, research and consulting firms, and government agencies seek individuals who have strong computer and quantitative skills and can perform complex research. A Ph.D. is necessary for top economist or marketing positions in many organizations. Many corporation and government executives have a strong background in economics or marketing.

A bachelor's degree with a major in economics or marketing may not be sufficient to obtain some positions as an economist or marketing analyst, but it is excellent preparation for many entry-level positions as a research assistant, administrative or management trainee, marketing interviewer, or any of a number of professional sales jobs.

Aspiring economists and marketing research analysts should gain experience gathering and analyzing data, conducting interviews or surveys, and writing reports on their findings while in college. This experience can prove invaluable later in obtaining a full-time position in the field, since much of their work, in the beginning, may center on these duties. With experience, economists and marketing research analysts eventually are assigned their own research projects.

Those considering careers as economists or marketing research analysts should be able to pay attention to details because much time is spent on precise data analysis. Patience and persistence are necessary qualities since economists and marketing research analysts must spend long hours on independent study and problem solving. At the same time, they must work well with others, especially marketing research analysts, who often oversee interviews for a wide variety of individuals. Economists and marketing research analysts must be able to present their findings, both orally and in writing, in a clear, meaningful way.

Job Outlook

Employment of economists and marketing research analysts is expected to grow about as fast as the average for all occupations through 2008. Many job openings are likely to result from the need to replace experienced workers who transfer to other occupations, retire, or leave the labor force for other reasons.

Opportunities for economists should be best in private industry, especially in research, testing, and consulting firms, as more companies contract out for economic research services. The growing complexity of the global economy, competition, and increased reliance on quantitative methods for analyzing the current value of future funds, business trends, sales, and purchasing should spur demand for economists. The growing need for economic analyses in virtually every industry should result in additional jobs for economists. Employment of economists in the Federal government should decline more slowly than other occupations in the Federal workforce. Slow employment growth is expected among economists in State and local government.

An advanced degree coupled with a strong background in economic theory, mathematics, statistics, and econometrics provides the basis for acquiring any specialty within the field. Those skilled in quantitative techniques and their application to economic modeling and forecasting, coupled with good communications skills, should have the best job opportunities.

Bachelor degree holders in economics may face competition for the limited number of economist positions for which they qualify. They will qualify for a number of other positions, however, where they can take advantage of their economic knowledge in conducting research, developing surveys, or analyzing data. Many graduates with bachelor's degrees will find good jobs in industry and business as management or sales trainees or administrative assistants. Economists with good quantitative skills are qualified for research assistant positions in a broad range of fields.

Candidates who meet State certification requirements may become high school economics teachers. The demand for secondary school economics teachers is expected to grow as economics becomes an increasingly important and popular course.

Ph.D. degree holders in economics and marketing are likely to face keen competition for teaching positions in colleges and universities. However, opportunities should be good in other areas such as industry and consulting firms.

Demand for qualified marketing research analysts should be strong due to an increasingly competitive economy. Marketing research provides organizations valuable feedback from purchasers, allowing companies to evaluate consumer satisfaction and more effectively plan for the future. As companies seek to expand their market and consumers become better informed, the need for marketing professionals will increase.

Opportunities for marketing research analysts with graduate degrees should be good in a wide range of employment settings, particularly in marketing research firms, as companies find it more profitable to contract out for marketing research services rather than support their own marketing department. Other organizations, including financial services organizations, health care institutions, advertising firms, manufacturing firms producing consumer goods, and insurance companies may offer job opportunities for marketing research analysts.

Those with a bachelor's degree who have a strong background in mathematics, statistics, survey design, and computer science, may be hired by private firms as research assistants or interviewers.

Earnings

Median annual earnings of economists and marketing research analysts were $48,330 in 1998. The middle 50 percent earned be-

tween $34,650 and $74,500 a year. The lowest 10 percent earned less than $26,540, and the highest 10 percent earned more than $94,810 a year. Median annual earnings in the industries employing the largest number of economists and marketing research analysts in 1997 were as follows:

Federal government	$65,300
Management and public relations	51,900
Research and testing services	47,500

The Federal government recognizes education and experience in certifying applicants for entry-level positions. The entrance salary for economists having a bachelor's degree was about $20,600 a year in 1999; however, those with superior academic records could begin at $25,500. Those having a master's degree could qualify for positions at an annual salary of $31,200. Those with a Ph.D. could begin at $37,700, while some individuals with experience and an advanced degree could start at $45,200. Starting salaries were slightly higher in selected areas where the prevailing local pay was higher. The average annual salary for economists employed by the Federal government was $67,800 a year in early 1999.

Related Occupations

Economists are concerned with understanding and interpreting financial matters, among other subjects. Other jobs in this area include financial managers, financial planners, insurance underwriters, actuaries, credit analysts, loan officers, and budget analysts.

Marketing research analysts do research to find out how well the market receives products or services. This may include planning, implementation, and analysis of surveys to determine people's needs and preferences. Other jobs using these skills include psychologists, sociologists, and urban and regional planners.

Sources of Additional Information

For information on careers in economics and business, contact:

- National Association for Business Economics, 1233 20th St. NW., Suite 505, Washington, DC 20036. Internet: http://www.nabe.com

For information about careers and salaries in marketing research, contact:

- Marketing Research Association, 1344 Silas Deane Hwy., Suite 306, Rocky Hill, CT 06067-0230. Internet: http://www.mra-net.org
- Council of American Survey Research Organizations, 3 Upper Devon, Port Jefferson, NY 11777. Internet: http://www.casro.org/index.htm

Information on acquiring a job as an economist with the Federal government may be obtained from the Office of Personnel Management (OPM) through a telephone-based system. Consult your telephone directory under U.S. Government for a local number or call (912) 757-3000; TDD (912) 744-2299. This number is not toll free, and charges may result. Information also is available from the OPM Internet site: http://www.usajobs.opm.gov.

Education Administrators

(O*NET 15005A and 15005B)

Significant Points

- Most jobs require experience in a related occupation, such as teacher or admissions counselor, and a master's or doctoral degree.

- Many jobs offer high earnings, considerable community prestige, and the satisfaction of working with young people.

- Competition will be keen for jobs in higher education, but opportunities should be better at the elementary and secondary school level.

Nature of the Work

Smooth operation of an educational institution requires competent administrators. Education administrators provide direction, leadership, and day-to-day management of educational activities in schools, colleges and universities, businesses, correctional institutions, museums, and job training and community service organizations. *Education administrators* set educational standards and goals and establish the policies and procedures to carry them out. They develop academic programs; monitor students' educational progress; train and motivate teachers and other staff; manage guidance and other student services; administer record keeping; prepare budgets; handle relations with parents, prospective and current students, employers, and the community; and perform many other duties.

Education administrators also supervise managers, support staff, teachers, counselors, librarians, coaches, and others. In an organization such as a small daycare center, one administrator may handle all these functions. In universities or large school systems, responsibilities are divided among many administrators, each with a specific function.

Those who manage elementary and secondary schools are called *principals*. They set the academic tone and hire, evaluate, and help improve the skills of teachers and other staff. Principals confer with staff to advise, explain, or answer procedural questions. They visit classrooms, observe teaching methods, review instructional objectives, and examine learning materials. They actively work with teachers to develop and maintain high curriculum standards, develop mission statements, and set performance goals and objectives. Principals must use clear, objective guidelines for teacher appraisals, since pay is often based on performance ratings.

Principals also meet and interact with other administrators, students, parents, and representatives of community organizations. Decision-making authority has increasingly shifted from school district central offices to individual schools. Thus, parents, teachers, and other members of the community play an important role in setting school policies and goals. Principals must pay attention to the concerns of these groups when making administrative decisions.

Principals prepare budgets and reports on various subjects, including finances and attendance, and oversee the requisitioning and allocation of supplies. As school budgets become tighter, many principals are more involved in public relations and fund raising to secure financial support for their schools from local businesses and the community.

Principals must take an active role to ensure that students meet national academic standards. Many principals develop school/business partnerships and school-to-work transition programs for students. Increasingly, principals must be sensitive to the needs of the rising number of non-English speaking and culturally diverse students. Growing enrollments, which are leading to overcrowding at many existing schools, are also a cause for concern. When addressing problems of inadequate resources, administrators serve as advocates to build new schools or repair existing ones.

Schools continue to be involved with students' emotional welfare as well as their academic achievement. As a result, principals face responsibilities outside the academic realm. For example, in response to the growing number of dual-income and single-parent families and teenage parents, schools have established before- and after-school child-care programs or family resource centers, which also may offer parenting classes and social service referrals. With the help of community organizations, some principals have established programs to combat increases in crime, drug and alcohol abuse, and sexually transmitted disease among students.

Assistant principals aid the principal in the overall administration of the school. Some assistant principals hold this position for several years to prepare for advancement to principal; others are career assistant principals. They are responsible for scheduling student classes, ordering textbooks and supplies, and coordinating transportation, custodial, cafeteria, and other support services. They usually handle discipline, attendance, social and recreational programs, and health and safety. They also may counsel students on personal, educational, or vocational matters. With site-based management, assistant principals play a greater role in developing curriculum, evaluating teachers, and building school-community relations—responsibilities previously assumed solely by the principal. The number of assistant principals a school employs may vary depending on the number of students.

Administrators in school district central offices manage public schools under their jurisdiction. This group includes those who direct subject area programs such as English, music, vocational education, special education, and mathematics. They plan, evaluate, standardize, and improve curriculums and teaching techniques and help teachers improve their skills and learn about new methods and materials. They oversee career counseling programs and testing that measures students' abilities and helps place them in appropriate classes. Central office administrators also include directors of programs such as guidance, school psychology, athletics, curriculum and instruction, and professional development. With site-based management, administrators have transferred primary responsibility for many of these programs to the principals, assistant principals, teachers, and other staff.

In colleges and universities, *academic deans, deans of faculty, provosts,* and *university deans* assist presidents and develop budgets and academic policies and programs. They also direct and coordinate the activities of deans of individual colleges and chairpersons of academic departments.

College or university department heads or *chairpersons* are in charge of departments such as English, biological science, and mathematics. In addition to teaching, they coordinate schedules of classes and teaching assignments; propose budgets; recruit, interview, and hire applicants for teaching positions; evaluate faculty members; encourage faculty development; and perform other administrative duties. In overseeing their departments, chairpersons must consider and balance the concerns of faculty, administrators, and students.

Higher education administrators provide student services. *Vice presidents of student affairs or student life, deans of students, and directors of student services* may direct and coordinate admissions, foreign student services, health and counseling services, career services, financial aid, and housing and residential life, as well as social, recreational, and related programs. In small colleges, they may counsel students. *Registrars* are custodians of students' records. They register students, prepare student transcripts, evaluate academic records, assess and collect tuition and fees, plan and implement commencement, oversee the preparation of college catalogs and schedules of classes, and analyze enrollment and demographic statistics. *Directors of admissions* manage the process of recruiting, evaluating, and admitting students and work closely with financial aid directors, who oversee scholarship, fellowship, and loan programs. Registrars and admissions officers must adapt to technological innovations in student information systems. For example, for those whose institutions present information—such as college catalogs and schedules—on the Internet, knowledge of on-line resources, imaging, and other computer skills is important. *Directors of student* activities plan and arrange social, cultural, and recreational activities, assist student-run organizations, and may conduct new student orientation. *Athletic directors* plan and direct intramural and intercollegiate athletic activities, including publicity for athletic events, preparation of budgets, and supervision of coaches.

Working Conditions

Education administrators hold management positions with significant responsibility. Coordinating and interacting with faculty, parents, and students can be fast-paced and stimulating, but also stressful and demanding. Some jobs include travel. Principals and assistant principals whose main duty often is discipline may find working with difficult students challenging and frustrating. The number of school-age children is rising, and some school systems have hired assistant principals because a school's population increased significantly. However, in other school systems, principals may manage larger student bodies, which can be stressful.

Many education administrators work more than 40 hours a week, including some nights and weekends when they oversee school activities. Most administrators work 10 or 11 months a year, but some work year round.

Employment

Education administrators held about 447,000 jobs in 1998. About 9 out of 10 were in educational services, which includes elemen-

tary, secondary, and technical schools, and colleges and universities. The rest worked in child day care centers, religious organizations, job training centers, State departments of education, and businesses and other organizations that provided training for their employees.

Training, Other Qualifications, and Advancement

Most education administrators begin their careers in related occupations and prepare for jobs in education administration by completing their master's or doctoral degrees. Because of the diversity of duties and levels of responsibility, their educational backgrounds and experience vary considerably. Principals, assistant principals, central office administrators, and academic deans usually held teaching positions before moving into administration. Some teachers move directly into principal positions; others first become assistant principals or gain experience in other central office administrative jobs at either the school or district level in positions such as department head, curriculum specialist, or subject matter advisor. In some cases, administrators move up from related staff jobs such as recruiter, guidance counselor, librarian, residence hall director, or financial aid or admissions counselor.

To be considered for education administrator positions, workers must first prove themselves in their current jobs. In evaluating candidates, supervisors look for determination, confidence, innovativeness, motivation, and leadership. The ability to make sound decisions and organize and coordinate work efficiently is essential. Since much of an administrator's job involves interacting with others—such as students, parents, and teachers—they must have strong interpersonal skills and be effective communicators and motivators. Knowledge of management principles and practices, gained through work experience and formal education, is important. A familiarity with computer technology is a plus for principals, who are becoming increasingly involved in gathering information and coordinating technical resources for their students and classrooms.

In most public schools, principals, assistant principals, and school administrators in central offices need a master's degree in education administration or educational supervision. Some principals and central office administrators have a doctorate or specialized degree in education administration. In private schools, which are not subject to State certification requirements, some principals and assistant principals hold only a bachelor's degree; however, the majority have a master's or doctoral degree. Most States require principals to be licensed as school administrators. License requirements vary by State. National standards for school leaders, including principals and supervisors, were recently developed by the Interstate School Leaders Licensure Consortium. Several States currently use these national standards as guidelines to assess beginning principals for licensure, and many more States are expected to adopt the standards for this purpose. Some States require administrators to take continuing education courses to keep their certification, thus ensuring that administrators have the most up-to-date skills. The number and type of courses required to maintain certification vary by State.

Academic deans and chairpersons usually have a doctorate in their specialty. Most have held a professorship in their department before advancing. Admissions, student affairs, and financial aid directors and registrars sometimes start in related staff jobs with bachelor's degrees (any field usually is acceptable) and obtain advanced degrees in college student affairs or higher education administration. A Ph.D. or Ed.D. usually is necessary for top student affairs positions. Computer literacy and a background in mathematics or statistics may be assets in admissions, records, and financial work.

Advanced degrees in higher education administration, educational supervision, and college student affairs are offered in many colleges and universities. The National Council for Accreditation of Teacher Education accredits these programs. Education administration degree programs include courses in school management, school law, school finance and budgeting, curriculum development and evaluation, research design and data analysis, community relations, politics in education, counseling, and leadership. Educational supervision degree programs include courses in supervision of instruction and curriculum, human relations, curriculum development, research, and advanced pedagogy courses.

Education administrators advance by moving up an administrative ladder or transferring to larger schools or systems. They also may become superintendent of a school system or president of an educational institution.

Job Outlook

Expect substantial competition for prestigious jobs as higher education administrators. Many faculty and other staff meet the education and experience requirements for these jobs and seek promotion. However, the number of openings is relatively small; only the most highly qualified are selected. Candidates who have the most formal education and who are willing to relocate should have the best job prospects.

On the other hand, it is becoming more difficult to attract candidates for some principal, vice principal, and administration jobs at the elementary and secondary school level, particularly in districts where crowded conditions and smaller budgets make the work more stressful. Many teachers no longer have a strong incentive to move into these positions. The pay is not significantly higher and does not compensate for the added workload, responsibilities, and pressures of the position. Also, site-based management has given teachers more decision-making responsibility in recent years, possibly satisfying their desire to move into administration.

Employment of education administrators is expected to grow about as fast as the average for all occupations over the 1998-2008 period. Additional openings will result from the need to replace administrators who retire or transfer to other occupations.

School enrollments at the elementary, secondary, and post-secondary level are all expected to grow over the projection period. Rather than opening new schools, many schools will enlarge to accommodate more students, increasing the need for additional assistant principals to help with the larger workload. Employment of education administrators will also grow as more services are provided to students and as efforts to improve the quality of education continue.

However, budget constraints are expected to moderate growth in this profession. At the post-secondary level, some institutions have been reducing administrative staffs to contain costs. Some colleges are consolidating administrative jobs and contracting with other providers for some administrative functions.

Earnings

Salaries of education administrators depend on several factors, including the location and enrollment size of the school or school district. Median annual earnings of education administrators in 1998 were $60,400 a year. The middle 50 percent earned between $43,870 and $80,030 a year. The lowest 10 percent earned less than $30,480; the highest 10 percent earned more than $92,680. Median annual earnings in the industries employing the largest numbers of education administrators in 1997 were as follows:

Elementary and secondary schools	$61,800
Colleges and universities	60,000
Vocational schools	43,700
Miscellaneous schools and educational services	33,800
Child day care services	25,000

According to a survey of public schools, conducted by the Educational Research Service, average salaries for principals and assistant principals in the 1997-98 school year were as follows:

Directors, managers, coordinators, and supervisors of instructional services	$73,058
Principals:	
Elementary school	$64,653
Junior high/middle school	68,740
Senior high school	74,380
Assistant principals:	
Elementary school	$53,206
Junior high/middle school	57,768
Senior high school	60,999

In 1997-98, according to the College and University Personnel Association, median annual salaries for selected administrators in higher education were as follows:

Academic deans:	
Medicine	$235,000
Law	160,400
Engineering	121,841
Business	90,745
Arts and sciences	87,293
Education	85,013
Social sciences	64,022
Mathematics	60,626
Student services directors:	
Admissions and registrar	$52,500
Student financial aid	48,448
Student activities	36,050

Related Occupations

Education administrators apply organizational and leadership skills to provide services to individuals. Workers in related occupations include medical and health services managers, social service agency administrators, recreation and park managers, museum directors, library directors, and professional and membership organization executives. Since principals and assistant principals usually have extensive teaching experience, their backgrounds are similar to those of teachers and many school counselors.

Sources of Additional Information

For information on elementary and secondary school principals, assistant principals, and central office administrators, contact:

- American Federation of School Administrators, 1729 21st St. NW., Washington, DC 20009.
- American Association of School Administrators, 1801 North Moore St., Arlington, VA 22209.

For information on elementary school principals and assistant principals, contact:

- The National Association of Elementary School Principals, 1615 Duke St., Alexandria, VA 22314-3483.

For information on collegiate registrars and admissions officers, contact:

- American Association of Collegiate Registrars and Admissions Officers, One Dupont Circle NW., Suite 520, Washington, DC 20036-1171.

For information on college and university personnel, contact:

- The College and University Personnel Association, 1233 20th St. NW., Washington, DC 20036-1250.

For information on professional development and graduate programs for college student affairs administrators, visit the National Association of Student Personnel Administrators Internet site: http://www.naspa.org

Employment Interviewers, Private or Public Employment Service

(O*NET 21508)

Significant Points

- Although employers prefer applicants with a college degree, educational requirements range from a high school diploma to a master's or doctoral degree.

- Most new jobs will arise in personnel supply firms, especially those specializing in temporary help.

Nature of the Work

Whether you are looking for a job or trying to fill one, you might need the help of an employment interviewer. These workers, sometimes called personnel consultants, human resources coordinators, personnel development specialists, or employment brokers, help jobseekers find employment and employers find qualified employees. Employment interviewers obtain information from employers as well as jobseekers and put together the best combination of applicant and job.

The majority of employment interviewers are employed in private personnel supply firms or State employment security offices. Those in personnel supply firms who place permanent employees are usually called counselors. These workers offer tips on personal appearance, suggest ways to present a positive image, provide background information on the company with which an interview is scheduled, and recommend interviewing techniques. Employment interviewers in some firms specialize in placing applicants in particular kinds of jobs—for example, secretarial, word processing, computer programming and computer systems analysis, engineering, accounting, law, or health. Counselors in such firms usually have three to five years of work experience in their field.

Some employment interviewers work in temporary help services companies, placing the company's employees in firms that need temporary help. Employment interviewers take job orders from client firms and match their requests against a list of available workers. They select the most qualified workers available and assign them to the firms requiring assistance.

Regular evaluation of employee job skills is an important part of the job for interviewers working in temporary help services companies. Initially, interviewers evaluate or test new employees' skills to determine their abilities and weaknesses. The results are kept on file and referred to when filling job orders. In some cases, the company trains employees to improve their skills, so interviewers periodically reevaluate or retest employees to identify any new skills they may have developed.

Traditionally, firms that placed permanent employees dealt with highly skilled applicants, such as lawyers or accountants, and those placing temporary employees dealt with less skilled workers, such as secretaries or data entry operators. However, temporary help services increasingly place workers with a wide range of educational backgrounds and work experience. Businesses are now turning to temporary employees to fill all types of positions—from clerical to managerial, professional, and technical—to reduce the wage and benefit costs associated with hiring permanent employees.

The duties of employment interviewers in job service centers differ somewhat from those in personnel supply firms because applicants may lack marketable skills. In these centers, jobseekers present resumes and fill out forms regarding education, job history, skills, awards, certificates, and licenses. An employment interviewer reviews these forms and asks the applicant about the type of job sought and salary range desired.

Because an applicant in these centers may have unrealistic expectations, employment interviewers must be tactful but persuasive. Some applicants are high school dropouts or have poor English skills, a history of drug or alcohol dependency, or a prison record.

The amount and nature of special help for such applicants vary from State to State. In some States, it is the employment interviewer's responsibility to counsel hard-to-place applicants and refer them elsewhere for literacy or language instruction, vocational training, transportation assistance, child care, and other services. In other States, specially trained counselors perform this task.

Applicants may also need help identifying the kind of work for which they are best suited. The employment interviewer evaluates the applicant's qualifications and either chooses an appropriate occupation or class of occupations or refers the applicant for vocational testing. After identifying an appropriate job type, the employment interviewer searches the file of job orders seeking a possible job match and refers the applicant to the employer if a match is found. If no match is found, the interviewer shows the applicant how to use listings of available jobs.

Besides helping individuals find jobs, employment interviewers help firms fill job openings. The services they provide depend on the company or type of agency they work for and the clientele it serves. In most of these agencies, employers usually pay private agencies to recruit workers. The employer places a "job order" with the agency describing the opening and listing requirements including education, licenses or credentials, and experience. Employment interviewers often contact the employer to determine their exact personnel needs. The employment interviewer then reviews the job requirements and the jobseeker qualifications to determine the best possible match of position and applicant. Although computers are increasingly used to keep records and match employers with jobseekers, personal contact with an employment interviewer remains an essential part of an applicant's job search.

A private industry employment interviewer must also be a salesperson. Counselors pool together a group of qualified applicants and try to sell them to many different companies. Often a consultant will call a company that has never been a client with the aim of filling their employment needs. Maintaining good relations with employers is an important part of the employment interviewer's job because this helps assure a steady flow of job orders. Being prepared to fill an opening quickly with a qualified applicant impresses employers most and keeps them as clients.

Working Conditions

Employment interviewers usually work in comfortable, well-lit offices, often using a computer to match information about employers and jobseekers. Some interviewers, however, may spend much of their time out of the office conducting interviews. The work can be hectic, especially in temporary help service companies that supply clients with immediate help for short periods of time. The private placement industry is competitive, and some overtime may be required.

Employment

Employment interviewers held about 66,000 jobs in 1998. Over half worked in the private sector for personnel supply services, typically for employment placement firms or temporary help services companies. About 2 out of 10 worked for State or local government. Others were employed by organizations that provide various services, such as job training and vocational rehabilitation.

Employees of career consulting or outplacement firms are not included in these estimates. Workers in these firms help clients market themselves; they do not act as job brokers, nor do they match individuals with particular vacancies.

Training, Other Qualifications, and Advancement

Although most public and private agencies prefer to hire college graduates for interviewer jobs, a degree is not always necessary. Hiring requirements in the private sector reflect a firm's management approach as well as the placements in which its interviewers specialize. Those who place highly trained individuals such as accountants, lawyers, engineers, physicians, or managers usually have some training or experience in the field in which they are placing workers. Thus, a bachelor's, master's, or even a doctoral degree may be a prerequisite for some interviewers. Even with the right education, however, sales ability is still required to succeed in the private sector.

Educational requirements play a lesser role for interviewers placing clerks or laborers; a high school diploma may be sufficient. In these positions, qualities such as energy level, telephone voice, and sales ability take precedence over educational attainment. Other desirable qualifications for employment interviewers include good communications skills, a desire to help people, office skills, and adaptability. A friendly, confidence-winning manner is an asset because personal interaction plays a large role in this occupation. Increasingly, employment interviewers use computers as a tool; thus, basic knowledge of computers is helpful.

Entry-level employment interviewer positions in the public sector are usually filled by college graduates, even though the positions do not always require a bachelor's degree. Some States allow substitution of suitable work experience for college education. Suitable experience is usually defined as working in close contact with the public or spending time in other jobs, including clerical jobs, in a job service office. In States that permit employment interviewers to engage in counseling, course work in counseling may be required.

Most States and many large city and county governments use some form of merit system for hiring interviewers. Applicants may take a written exam, undergo a preliminary interview, or submit records of their education and experience for evaluation. Those who meet the standards are placed on a list from which the top-ranked candidates are selected for later interviews and possible hiring.

Advancement as an employment interviewer in the public sector is often based on a system providing regular promotions and salary increases for those meeting established standards. Advancement to supervisory positions is highly competitive. In personnel supply firms, advancement often depends on one's success in placing workers and usually takes the form of greater responsibility and higher income. Successful individuals occasionally establish their own businesses.

Job Outlook

Employment in this occupation is expected to grow about as fast as the average for all occupations through the year 2008. The majority of new jobs will arise in personnel supply firms, especially those specializing in temporary help. Job growth is not anticipated in State job service offices because of budgetary limitations, the growing use of computerized job matching and information systems, and increased contracting out of employment services to private firms. In addition to openings resulting from growth, a small number of openings will stem from the need to replace experienced interviewers who transfer to other occupations, retire, or stop working for other reasons.

Economic expansion and new business formation should mean growing demand for the services of personnel supply firms and employment interviewers. Firms that lack the time or resources to develop their own screening procedures will continue to turn to personnel firms. Rapid expansion of firms supplying temporary help in particular will be responsible for much of the growth in this occupation. Businesses of all types are turning to temporary help services companies for additional workers to handle short-term assignments, staff one-time projects, launch new programs, and reduce wage and benefit costs associated with hiring permanent employees.

Entry into this occupation is relatively easy for college graduates and for people who have had some college courses, except in those positions specializing in placement of workers with highly specialized training, such as lawyers, doctors, and engineers.

Employment interviewers who place permanent workers may lose their jobs during recessions because employers reduce or eliminate hiring for permanent positions during downturns in the economy. State job service employment interviewers are less susceptible to layoffs than those who place permanent or temporary personnel in the private sector.

Earnings

Median annual earnings of employment interviewers in 1998 were $29,800. The middle 50 percent earned between $23,520 and $39,600. The lowest 10 percent earned less than $18,420, and the highest 10 percent earned more than $73,180. Employment interviewers earn slightly more in urban areas.

Earnings in private firms vary, in part because the basis for compensation varies. Workers in personnel supply firms tend to be paid on a commission basis; those in temporary help service companies receive a salary. When workers are paid on a commission basis, total earnings depend on the type and number of placements. In general, those who place more highly skilled or hard-to-find employees earn more. An interviewer or counselor working strictly on a commission basis often makes around 30 percent of what he or she bills the client, although this varies widely from firm to firm.

Some employment interviewers work on a salary-plus-commission basis because they fill difficult or highly specialized positions requiring long periods of search. The salary is usually small by normal standards; however, it guarantees these individuals security through slow times. The commission provides the incentive and opportunity for higher earnings.

Some personnel supply firms employ new workers for a two- to three-month probationary period during which they draw a regular salary. This gives new workers time to develop their skills and

acquire clients while simultaneously giving employers an opportunity to evaluate them. If they are hired, their earnings are then usually based on commission.

Related Occupations

Employment interviewers serve as intermediaries for jobseekers and employers. Workers in several other occupations do similar jobs. Personnel officers, for example, screen and help hire new employees, but they concern themselves mainly with the hiring needs of the firm; they never represent individual jobseekers. Personnel officers may also have additional duties in areas such as payroll or benefits management.

Career counselors help students and alumni find jobs, but they primarily emphasize career counseling and decision making, not placement. Counselors in community organizations and vocational rehabilitation facilities help clients find jobs, but they also assist with drug or alcohol dependencies, housing, transportation, child care, and other problems that stand in the way of finding and keeping a job.

Sources of Additional Information

For information on a career as an employment interviewer/counselor, contact:

- National Association of Personnel Services, 3133 Mt. Vernon Ave., Alexandria, VA 22305. Internet: http://www.napsweb.org
- American Staffing Association, 277 South Washington St., Suite 200, Alexandria, VA 22314. Internet: http://www.natss.org

For information on a career as an employment interviewer in State employment security offices, contact:

- Interstate Conference of Employment Security Agencies, 444 North Capitol St. NW., Suite 142, Washington, DC 20001. Internet: http://www.icesa.org

Engineering, Natural Science, and Computer and Information Systems Managers

(O*NET 13017A, 13017B, and 13017C)

Significant Points

- Projected job growth stems primarily from rapid growth among computer-related occupations.
- Employers prefer managers with advanced technical knowledge and strong communication and administrative skills.

Nature of the Work

Engineering, natural science, and computer and information systems managers plan, coordinate, and direct research, design, production, and computer-related activities. They may supervise engineers, scientists, technicians, computer specialists, and information technology workers, along with support personnel.

These managers use advanced technical knowledge of engineering, science, and computer and information systems to oversee a variety of activities. They determine scientific and technical goals within broad outlines provided by top management. These goals may include the redesigning of an aircraft, improvements in manufacturing processes, the development of large computer networks, or advances in scientific research. Managers make detailed plans for the accomplishment of these goals; for example, working with their staff, they may develop the overall concepts of a new product or identify technical problems standing in the way of project completion.

To perform effectively, they must also possess knowledge of administrative procedures, such as budgeting, hiring, and supervision. These managers propose budgets for projects and programs and make decisions on staff training and equipment purchases. They hire and assign scientists, engineers, computer specialists, information technology workers, and support personnel to carry out specific parts of the projects. They supervise the work of these employees, review their output, and establish administrative procedures and policies.

In addition, these managers use communication skills extensively. They spend a great deal of time coordinating the activities of their unit with other units or organizations. They confer with higher levels of management; with financial, production, marketing, and other managers; and with contractors and equipment and materials suppliers.

Engineering managers supervise people who design and develop machinery, products, systems, and processes, and they direct and coordinate production, operations, quality assurance, testing, or maintenance in industrial plants. Many are plant engineers, who direct and coordinate the design, installation, operation, and maintenance of equipment and machinery in industrial plants. Others manage research and development teams that produce new products and processes or improve existing ones.

Natural science managers oversee the work of life and physical scientists, including agricultural scientists, chemists, biologists, geologists, medical scientists, and physicists. These managers direct research and development projects and coordinate activities such as testing, quality control, and production. They may work on basic research projects or on commercial activities. Science managers sometimes conduct their own research in addition to managing the work of others.

Computer and information systems managers direct the work of systems analysts, computer programmers, and other computer-related workers. These managers plan and coordinate activities such as the installation and upgrading of hardware and software; programming and systems design; the development of computer networks; and the implementation of Internet and intranet sites. They analyze the computer and information needs of their organization and determine personnel and equipment requirements. They assign and review the work of their subordinates and purchase necessary equipment.

Working Conditions

Engineering, natural science, and computer and information systems managers spend most of their time in an office. Some managers, however, may also work in laboratories or industrial plants, where they are normally exposed to the same conditions as research scientists and may occasionally be exposed to the same conditions as production workers. Most managers work at least 40 hours a week and may work much longer on occasion to meet project deadlines. Some may experience considerable pressure in meeting technical or scientific goals within short timeframes or tight budgets.

Employment

Engineering, natural science, and computer and information systems managers held about 326,000 jobs in 1998. About 1 in 3 works in services industries, primarily for firms providing computer and data processing, engineering and architectural, or research and testing services. Manufacturing industries employ another third. Manufacturing industries with the largest employment include industrial machinery and equipment, electronic and other electrical equipment, transportation equipment, instruments, and chemicals. Other large employers include government agencies, communications and utilities companies, and financial and insurance firms.

Training, Other Qualifications, and Advancement

Strong technical knowledge is essential for engineering, natural science, and computer and information systems managers, who must understand and guide the work of their subordinates and explain the work in non-technical terms to senior management and potential customers. Therefore, these management positions usually require work experience and formal education similar to that of engineers, mathematicians, scientists, or computer professionals.

Most engineering managers begin their careers as engineers, after completing a bachelor's degree in the field. To advance to higher level positions, engineers generally must assume management responsibility. To fill management positions, employers seek engineers who possess administrative and communications skills in addition to technical knowledge in their specialty. Many engineers gain these skills by obtaining master's degrees in engineering management or business administration. Employers often pay for such training; in large firms, some courses required in these degree programs may be offered on-site.

Many science managers begin their careers as chemists, biologists, geologists, or scientists in other disciplines. Most scientists engaged in basic research have a Ph.D.; some in applied research and other activities may have a bachelor's or master's degree. Science managers must be specialists in the work they supervise. In addition, employers prefer managers with communication and administrative skills and, increasingly, familiarity with computers. Graduate programs allow scientists to augment their undergraduate training with instruction in other fields, such as management or computer technology. Given the rapid pace of scientific developments, science managers must continuously upgrade their knowledge.

Many computer and information systems managers have experience as systems analysts; others may have experience as computer engineers, programmers, or operators, or in other computer occupations. A bachelor's degree is usually required for management positions, and a graduate degree is often preferred by employers. However, a few computer and information systems managers may have only an associate degree. Employers seek managers who have experience with the specific software or technology to be used on the job. In addition to technical skills, employers also seek managers who have business and interpersonal skills.

Engineering, natural science, and computer and information systems managers may advance to progressively higher leadership positions within their discipline. Some may become managers in non-technical areas such as marketing, human resources, or sales. In high technology firms, managers in non-technical areas often must possess the same specialized knowledge as managers in technical areas. For example, employers in an engineering firm may prefer to hire experienced engineers as sales people because the complex services offered by the firm can only be marketed by someone with specialized engineering knowledge.

Job Outlook

Employment of engineering, natural science, and computer and information systems managers is expected to increase much faster than the average for all occupations through the year 2008. Technological advancements will increase the employment of engineers, scientists, and computer-related workers; as a result, the demand for managers to direct these workers will also increase. In addition, job openings will result from the need to replace managers who retire or move into other occupations. Opportunities for obtaining a management position will be best for workers with advanced technical knowledge and strong communication and administrative skills.

Underlying the growth of engineering and natural science managers are competitive pressures and advancing technologies that require companies to update and improve products and services more frequently. Investment in facilities and equipment to expand research and output should increase the need for engineering and science managers. Faster-than-average employment growth among electrical, electronics, and civil engineers will provide strong employment opportunities for engineering managers in these areas. Among scientists, faster-than-average growth in the employment of biologists and medical scientists will provide similar opportunities for natural science managers.

Employment of computer and information systems managers is expected to grow rapidly due to the increasing use of information technologies. In order to remain competitive, firms will continue to install sophisticated computer networks, set up Internet and intranet sites, and engage in electronic commerce. The fast-paced expansion of the computer and data processing services industry will contribute strongly to the increased demand for these managers. In addition, employment growth is expected across a variety of industries reflecting the widespread importance of information technology.

Opportunities for those who wish to become engineering, natural science, and computer and information systems managers should be closely related to the growth of the occupations they supervise and the industries in which they are found.

Earnings

Earnings for engineering, natural science, and computer and information systems managers vary by specialty and level of responsibility. Median annual earnings of these managers in 1998 were $75,330. The middle 50 percent earned between $57,610 and $94,450. The lowest 10 percent earned less than $44,580, and the highest 10 percent earned more than $119,900. Median annual earnings in the industries employing the largest numbers of these managers in 1997 were:

Computer and office equipment manufacturing	$87,500
Electronic components and accessories manufacturing	79,000
Research and testing services	77,700
Computer and data processing services	76,800
Engineering and architectural services	74,300
Federal government	73,200
State government, except education and hospitals	63,500

According to RHI Consulting, average starting salaries in 1999 for information technology managers ranged from $50,500 to well over $100,000, depending on the area of specialization. A survey of manufacturing firms, conducted by Abbot, Langer & Associates, reported that in 1998, the median annual income of engineering department managers and superintendents was $85,600; the corresponding figure for research and development managers was about $75,400.

In addition, engineering, natural science, and computer and information systems managers, especially those at higher levels, often receive more benefits—such as expense accounts, stock option plans, and bonuses—than non-managerial workers in their organizations.

Related Occupations

The work of engineering, natural science, and computer and information systems managers is closely related to that of engineers, life scientists, physical scientists, computer professionals, and mathematicians. It is also related to the work of other managers, especially general managers and top executives.

Sources of Additional Information

Information on obtaining these positions with the Federal Government is available from the Office of Personnel Management through a telephone-based system. Consult your telephone directory under U.S. Government for a local number or call (912) 757-3000; TDD (912) 744-2299. That number is not toll free, and charges may result. Information is also available from the Internet site: http://www.usajobs.opm.gov.

High school students interested in obtaining general information on a variety of engineering disciplines should contact the Junior Engineering Technical Society by sending a self-addressed business-size envelope with six first-class stamps affixed to it to:

- JETS-Guidance, 1420 King St., Suite 405, Alexandria, VA 22314-2794. Internet: http://www.jets.org

Non-high school students and those wanting more detailed information on engineering should contact societies representing the individual branches of engineering. Each can provide information about careers in the particular branch.

Aerospace Engineering

- Aerospace Industries Association, 1250 Eye St., NW., Washington, DC 20005. Internet: http://www.aia-aerospace.org
- American Institute of Aeronautics and Astronautics, Inc., Suite 500, 1801 Alexander Bell Dr., Reston, VA 20191-4344. (Enclose $2 to receive guidance materials and information.) Internet: http://www.aiaa.org

Chemical Engineering

- American Institute of Chemical Engineers, Three Park Ave., New York, NY 10016-5901. Internet: http://www.aiche.org
- American Chemical Society, Department of Career Services, 1155 16th St. NW., Washington, DC 20036. Internet: http://www.acs.org

Civil Engineering

- American Society of Civil Engineers, 1801 Alexander Bell Dr., Reston, VA 20191-4400. Internet: http://www.asce.org

Electrical and Electronics Engineering

- Institute of Electrical and Electronics Engineers—United States of America, 1828 L St. NW., Suite 1202, Washington, DC 20036. Internet: http://www.ieee-usa.org

Industrial Engineering

- Institute of Industrial Engineers, Inc., 25 Technology Park/Atlanta, Norcross, GA 30092. Internet: http://www.iienet.org

Materials Engineering

- The Minerals, Metals, & Materials Society, 184 Thorn Hill Rd., Warrendale, PA 15086. Internet: http://www.tms.org
- ASM International Foundation, Materials Park, OH 44073-0002. Internet: http://www.asm-intl.org

Mechanical Engineering

- The American Society of Mechanical Engineers, Three Park Ave., New York, NY 10016. Internet: http://www.asme.org
- American Society of Heating, Refrigerating, and Air-Conditioning Engineers, Inc., 1791 Tullie Circle NE, Atlanta, GA 30329. Internet: http://www.ashrae.org

Mining Engineering

- The Society for Mining, Metallurgy, and Exploration, Inc., P.O. Box 625002, Littleton, CO 80162-5002. Internet: http://www.smenet.org

Nuclear Engineering

- American Nuclear Society, 555 North Kensington Ave., LaGrange Park, IL 60525. Internet: http://www.ans.org

Petroleum Engineering

- Society of Petroleum Engineers, P.O. Box 833836, Richardson, TX 75083-3836. Internet: http://www.spe.org

For information on careers in natural science, contact the specific organizations listed here:

Agricultural Science

- American Society of Agronomy, Crop Science Society of America, Soil Science Society of America, 677 S. Segoe Rd., Madison, WI 53711-1086.
- Food and Agricultural Careers for Tomorrow, Purdue University, 1140 Agricultural Administration Bldg., West Lafayette, IN 47907-1140.

Biological Science

- American Institute of Biological Sciences, Suite 200, 1444 I St. NW., Washington, DC 20005. Internet: http://www.aibs.org

Forestry (include a self-addressed, stamped business envelope)

- Society of American Foresters, 5400 Grosvenor Ln., Bethesda, MD 20814. Internet: http://www.safnet.org

Meteorology

- American Meteorological Society, 45 Beacon St., Boston, MA 02108. Internet: http://www.ametsoc.org/AMS

Chemistry

- American Chemical Society, Education Division, 1155 16th St. NW., Washington, DC 20036. Internet: http://www.acs.org

Geology

- American Geological Institute, 4220 King St., Alexandria, VA 22302-1502. Internet: http://www.agiweb.org
- Geological Society of America, P.O. Box 9140, Boulder, CO 80301-9140. Internet: http://www.geosociety.org
- American Association of Petroleum Geologists, P.O. Box 979, Tulsa, OK 74101. Internet: http://www.aapg.org

Oceanography

- Marine Technology Society, 1828 L St. NW, Suite 906, Washington, DC 20036. Internet: http://www.mtsociety.org

Physics

- American Institute of Physics, Career Services Division and Education and Employment Division, One Physics Ellipse, College Park, MD 20740-3843. Internet: http://www.aip.org
- The American Physical Society, One Physics Ellipse, College Park, MD 20740-3844. Internet: http://www.aps.org

Astronomy

- American Astronomical Society, Education Office, University of Chicago, 5640 South Ellis Ave., Chicago IL 60637. Internet: http://www.aas.org

Further information about computer careers is available from:

- Association for Computing Machinery (ACM), 1515 Broadway, New York, NY 10036. Internet: http://www.acm.org
- Institute of Electrical and Electronics Engineers—United States of America, 1828 L Street, NW., Suite 1202, Washington, DC 20036. Internet: http://www.ieee.org

Farmers and Farm Managers

(O*NET 79999C, 79999D, 79999G, 79999J, 79999K, 79999L, and 79999M)

Significant Points

- Modern farming requires a combination of formal education and work experience, sometimes acquired through growing up on a farm or through internships now becoming available.

- Overall employment is projected to decline because of increasing productivity and consolidation.

- New developments in marketing and organic farming are making small-scale farming economically viable again.

Nature of the Work

American farmers and farm managers direct the activities of one of the world's largest and most productive agricultural sectors. They produce enough food and fiber to meet the needs of our Nation and for export.

Farmers may be owners or tenants who rent the use of land. The type of farm they operate determines their specific tasks. On crop farms—farms growing grain, cotton, and other fibers, fruit, and vegetables—farmers are responsible for planning, tilling, planting, fertilizing, cultivating, spraying, and harvesting. After the harvest, they make sure the crops are properly packaged, stored, or marketed. Livestock, dairy, and poultry farmers must feed, plan, and care for the animals and keep barns, pens, coops, and other farm buildings clean and in good condition. They also oversee breeding and marketing activities. Horticultural specialty farmers oversee the production of ornamental plants, nursery products—such as flowers, bulbs, shrubbery, and sod—and fruits and vegetables grown in greenhouses. Aquaculture farmers raise fish and shellfish in marine, brackish, or fresh water, usually in ponds, floating net pens, raceways, or recirculating systems. They stock, feed, protect, and otherwise manage aquatic life sold for consumption or used for recreational fishing.

Farmers make many managerial decisions. Their farm output is strongly influenced by the weather, disease, fluctuations in prices of domestic and foreign farm products, and Federal farm programs. In a crop operation, farmers usually determine the best time to plant seed, apply fertilizer and chemicals, harvest, and market. They use different strategies to protect themselves from unpredictable changes in the markets for agricultural products. Many farmers carefully plan the combination of crops they grow so if the price of one crop drops, they will have sufficient income from another to make up for the loss. Others, particularly operators of smaller farms, may choose to sell their goods directly through farmers' markets or use cooperatives to reduce their financial risk. For example, Community Supported Agriculture (CSA) is a cooperative where

consumers buy shares of a harvest prior to the planting season, thus freeing the farmer from having to bear all the financial risks.

Farmers who plan ahead may be able to store their crops or keep their livestock to take advantage of better prices later in the year. Those who participate in the futures market—where contracts and options on futures contracts on commodities are traded through stock brokers—try to anticipate or track changes in the supply of and demand for agricultural commodities, and thus changes in the prices of farm products. By buying or selling futures contracts, or by pricing their products in advance of future sales, they attempt to either limit their risk or reap greater profits than would normally be realized. They may have to secure loans from credit agencies to finance the purchase of machinery, fertilizer, livestock, and feed. Farming operations have become more complex in recent years, so many farmers use computers to keep financial and inventory records. They also use computer databases and spreadsheets to manage breeding, dairy, and other farm operations.

Farmers' tasks range from caring for livestock, to operating machinery, and to maintaining equipment and facilities. The size of the farm often determines which of these tasks farmers will handle themselves. Operators of small farms usually perform all tasks, physical and administrative. They keep records for tax purposes, service machinery, maintain buildings, and grow vegetables and raise animals. Operators of large farms have employees who help with the physical work that small-farm operators do themselves. Although employment on most farms is limited to the farmer and one or two family workers or hired employees, some large farms have 100 or more full-time and seasonal workers. Some of these employees are in nonfarm occupations, working as truckdrivers, sales representatives, bookkeepers, and computer specialists.

Farm managers guide and assist farmers and ranchers in maximizing the financial returns to their land by managing the day-to-day activities. Their duties and responsibilities vary widely. For example, the owner of a very large livestock farm may employ a farm manager to oversee a single activity, such as feeding livestock. On the other hand, when managing a small crop farm for an absentee owner, a farm manager may assume responsibility for all functions, from selecting the crops to participating in planting and harvesting. Farm management firms and corporations involved in agriculture employ highly trained professional farm managers who may manage farm operations or oversee tenant operators of several farms. In these cases, farm managers may establish output goals; determine financial constraints; monitor production and marketing; hire, assign, and supervise workers; determine crop transportation and storage requirements; and oversee maintenance of the property and equipment.

Working Conditions

The work of farmers and farm managers is often strenuous, their work hours are frequently long, and their days off during the planting, growing, and harvesting seasons are rare. Nevertheless, for those who enter farming, these disadvantages are outweighed by the opportunities for living in a rural area, working outdoors, being self-employed, and making a living working the land. Farmers and farm managers on crop farms usually work from sunrise to sunset during the planting and harvesting seasons. During the rest of the year they plan next season's crops, market their output, and repair machinery; some may earn additional income by working a second job off the farm.

On livestock producing farms, work goes on throughout the year. Unless they are grazing, animals must be fed and watered every day, and dairy cows must be milked two or three times a day. Many livestock and dairy farmers monitor and attend to the health of their herds, which may include assisting birthing animals. Such farmers rarely get the chance to get away unless they hire an assistant or arrange for a temporary substitute.

Farmers who grow produce and perishables have different demands on their time. For example, organic farmers must maintain cover crops during the cold months, which keeps them occupied with farming beyond the typical growing season.

Farm work also can be hazardous. Tractors and other farm machinery can cause serious injury, and workers must be constantly alert on the job. The proper operation of equipment and handling of chemicals is necessary to avoid accidents and protect the environment.

On very large farms, farmers spend substantial time meeting with farm managers or farm supervisors in charge of various activities. Professional farm managers overseeing several farms may divide their time between traveling to meet farmers or landowners and planning the farm operations in their offices. As farming practices and agricultural technology become more sophisticated, farmers and farm managers are spending more time in offices and at computers, where they electronically manage many aspects of their businesses. Some farmers also spend time at conferences, particularly during the winter months, trading information.

Employment

Farmers and farm managers held nearly 1.5 million jobs in 1998. About 88 percent were self-employed farmers. Most farmers manage crop production activities; others manage livestock and dairy production. A relatively small number were involved in agricultural services, such as contract harvesting and farm labor contracting.

The soil, topography of the land, and the climate of an area generally determine the type of farming done. For example, wheat, corn, and other grains are most efficiently grown on large farms on level land where large, complex machinery can be used. Thus, these crops are prevalent on the prairies and plains of Iowa, Illinois, Indiana, Nebraska, Ohio, Kansas, and southern Minnesota and Wisconsin. Crops requiring longer growing seasons, such as cotton, tobacco, and peanuts, are grown chiefly in the South. Most of the country's fruits and vegetables come from California, Texas, and Florida. Many dairy herds are found in the areas with good pasture land, such as Wisconsin, New York, and Minnesota. However, in recent years, dairy farming has expanded rapidly in California, Arizona, and Texas.

Training, Other Qualifications, and Advancement

Growing up on a family farm and participating in agricultural programs for young people (sponsored by the National Future Farmers of America Organization or the 4-H youth educational programs) are important sources of training for those interested in pursuing agriculture as a career. However, modern farming requires increasingly complex scientific, business, and financial decisions. Therefore, even people who were raised on farms must acquire the appropriate education.

Not all farm managers grew up on farms. For these people, a bachelor's degree in business with a concentration in agriculture is important. In addition to formal education, they need several years of work experience in the different aspects of farm operations in order to qualify for a farm manager position.

Students should select the college most appropriate to their specific interests and location. In the United States, all State university systems have one land-grant university with a school of agriculture. Common programs of study include agronomy, dairy science, agricultural economics and business, horticulture, crop and fruit science, and animal science. For students interested in aquaculture, formal programs are available, and include coursework in fisheries biology, fish culture, hatchery management and maintenance, and hydrology. Whatever one's interest, the college curriculum should include courses in agricultural production, marketing, and economics.

Professional status can be enhanced through voluntary certification as an Accredited Farm Manager (AFM) by the American Society of Farm Managers and Rural Appraisers. Certification requires several years of farm management experience, the appropriate academic background—a bachelor's degree or preferably a master's degree in a field of agricultural science—and passing courses and examinations relating to business, financial, and legal aspects of farm management.

Farmers and farm managers need to keep abreast of continuing advances in farming methods both in the United States and abroad. Besides print journals that inform the agricultural community, the spread of the Internet and the World Wide Web allows quick access to the latest developments in areas such as agricultural marketing, legal arrangements, or growing crops, vegetables and livestock. Electronic mail, on-line journals and newsletters from agricultural organizations also speed the exchange of information directly between farming associations and individual farmers.

Farmers must also have enough technical knowledge of crops, growing conditions, and plant diseases to make decisions ensuring the successful operation of their farms. A rudimentary knowledge of veterinary science, as well as animal husbandry, is important for livestock and dairy farmers. Knowledge of the relationship between farm operations—for example, the use of pesticides—and environmental conditions is essential. Mechanical aptitude and the ability to work with tools of all kinds are also valuable skills for the operator of a small farm, who often maintains and repairs machinery or farm structures.

Farmers and farm managers need the managerial skills necessary to organize and operate a business. A basic knowledge of accounting and bookkeeping is essential in keeping financial records, and a knowledge of credit sources is vital for buying seed, fertilizer, and other inputs necessary for planting. Farmers and farm managers must also be familiar with complex safety regulations and requirements of governmental agricultural support programs. Computer skills are increasingly important, especially on large farms, where computers are widely used for record keeping and business analysis. For example, some farmers use personal computers to access the Internet to get the latest information on prices of farm products and other agricultural news.

High school training should include courses in mathematics and biology and other life sciences. Completion of a two-year and preferably a four-year bachelor's degree program in a college of agriculture is becoming increasingly important. But even after obtaining formal education, novices may need to spend time working under an experienced farmer to learn how to put to practice the skills learned through academic training. A small number of farms offer, on a formal basis, apprenticeships to help young people acquire such practical skills.

Job Outlook

The expanding world population is increasing the demand for food and fiber. Demand for U.S. agricultural exports of beef, poultry, and feed grain is expected to grow in the long run as developing nations improve their economies and personal incomes. However, increasing productivity in the highly efficient U.S. agricultural production industry is expected to meet domestic consumption needs and export requirements with fewer workers. Employment of farmers and farm managers is expected to continue to decline through the year 2008. The overwhelming majority of job openings will result from the need to replace farmers who retire or leave the occupation for economic or other reasons.

Market pressures will continue the long-term trend toward consolidation into fewer and larger farms over the 1998-2008 period, further reducing the number of jobs for farmers and farm managers. Some farmers acquire farms by inheritance; however, purchasing a farm or additional land is expensive and requires substantial capital. In addition, sufficient funds are required to withstand the adverse effects of climate and price fluctuations upon farm output and income and to cover operating costs—livestock, feed, seed, and fuel. Also, the complexity of modern farming and keen competition among farmers leaves little room for the marginally successful farmer.

Despite the expected continued consolidation of farm land and the projected decline in overall employment of farmers and farm managers, an increasing number of small-scale farmers have developed successful market niches that involve personalized, direct contact with their customers. Many are finding opportunities in organic food production, as more consumers demand food grown without pesticides or chemicals. Others use farmers' markets that cater directly to urban and suburban consumers, allowing the farmers to capture a greater share of consumers' food dollar. Some small-scale farmers, such as some dairy farmers, belong to collectively owned marketing cooperatives that process and sell their product. Other farmers participate in Community Supported Agriculture cooperatives that allow consumers to directly buy a share of the farmer's harvest.

Aquaculture should also continue to provide some new employment opportunities over the 1998-2008 period. Overfishing has resulted in declining ocean catches, and the growing demand for certain seafood items—such as shrimp, salmon, and catfish—has spurred the growth of aquaculture farms. Aquaculture output increased strongly between 1983 and the mid-1990s. Efforts to pro-

duce more farm-raised fish and shellfish should continue to increase in response to demand growth.

Earnings

Farmers' incomes vary greatly from year to year because prices of farm products fluctuate depending upon weather conditions and other factors that influence the amount and quality of farm output and the demand for those products. A farm that shows a large profit in one year may show a loss in the following year. Under the 1996 Farm Act, Federal government subsidy payments, which have traditionally shielded some grain producers from the ups and downs of the market, were set at fixed levels regardless of yields or prices. Consequently, these farmers may experience more income variability from year to year than in the past. The Act also phases out price supports for dairy farmers and may result in lower incomes for dairy producers. Many farmers—primarily operators of small farms—have income from off-farm business activities, often greater than that of their farm income.

Full-time, salaried farm managers, with the exception of horticultural managers, had median weekly earnings of $447 in 1998. The middle half earned between $302 and $619. The highest paid 10 percent earned more than $852, and the lowest paid 10 percent earned less than $220. Horticultural specialty farm managers generally earn considerably more.

Farmers and self-employed farm managers make their own provisions for benefits. As members of farm organizations, they may derive benefits such as group discounts on health and life insurance premiums.

Related Occupations

Farmers and farm managers strive to improve the quality of agricultural products and the efficiency of farms. Workers with similar functions include agricultural engineers, animal breeders, animal scientists, county agricultural agents, dairy scientists, extension service specialists, feed and farm management advisors, horticulturists, plant breeders, and poultry scientists.

Sources of Additional Information

For general information about farming and agricultural occupations, contact:

- Center for Rural Affairs, P.O. Box 46, Walthill, NE 68067.

For information about certification as an accredited farm manager, contact:

- American Society of Farm Managers and Rural Appraisers, 950 Cherry St., Suite 508, Denver, CO 80222. Internet: http://www.agri-associations.org

For information on aquaculture, education, training, or Community Supported Agriculture, contact:

- Alternative Farming System Information Center (AFSIC), National Agricultural Library USDA, 10301 Baltimore Ave., Room 304, Beltsville, MD 20705-2351. Internet: http://www.nal.usda.gov/afsic
- Appropriate Technology Transfer for Rural Areas, P.O. Box 3657, Fayetteville, AR 72702. Internet: http://www.attra.org/attra-pub/atmatlst.html#resource

For general information about farm occupations, opportunities, and 4-H activities, contact your local county extension service office.

File Clerks

(O*NET 55321)

Significant Points

- Most jobs required only a high school diploma.

- Numerous job opportunities should arise due to high turnover in this occupation.

Nature of the Work

The amount of information generated by organizations continues to grow rapidly. File clerks classify, store, retrieve, and update this information. In many small offices, they often have additional responsibilities, such as data entry, word processing, sorting mail, and operating copying or fax machines. They are employed across the Nation by organizations of all types.

File clerks, also called records, information, or record center clerks, examine incoming material and code it numerically, alphabetically, or by subject matter. They then store forms, letters, receipts, or reports in paper form or enter necessary information into other storage devices. Some clerks operate mechanized files that rotate to bring the needed records to them; others convert documents to films that are then stored on microforms, such as microfilm or microfiche. A growing number of file clerks use imaging systems that scan paper files or film and store the material on optical disks.

In order for records to be useful, they must be up-to-date and accurate. File clerks ensure that new information is added to the files in a timely manner and may get rid of outdated file materials or transfer them to inactive storage. They also check files at regular intervals to make sure that all items are correctly sequenced and placed. Whenever records cannot be found, the file clerk attempts to locate the missing material. As an organization's needs for information change, file clerks also implement changes to the filing system established by supervisory personnel.

When records are requested, file clerks locate them and give them to the borrower. The record may be a sheet of paper stored in a file cabinet or an image on microform. In the first example, the clerk manually retrieves the document and hands or forwards it to the borrower. In the latter example, the clerk retrieves the microform and displays it on a microform reader. If necessary, file clerks make copies of records and distribute them. In addition, they keep track of materials removed from the files to ensure that borrowed files are returned.

Increasingly, file clerks use computerized filing and retrieval systems. These systems use a variety of storage devices, such as a mainframe computer, magnetic tape, CD-ROM, or floppy disk. To retrieve a document in these systems, the clerk enters the document's identification code, obtains the location, and pulls the document. Accessing files in a computer database is much quicker than locating and physically retrieving paper files. Even when files are stored electronically, however, backup paper or electronic copies usually are also kept.

Working Conditions

Most file clerks typically are employed in an office environment. Most work alongside other clerical workers, but some work in centralized units away from the front office.

Because the majority of clerks use computers on a daily basis, these workers may experience eye and muscle strain, backaches, headaches, and repetitive motion injuries. Also, clerks who review detailed data may have to sit for extended periods of time. Although the work does not require heavy lifting, file clerks spend a lot of time on their feet and frequently stoop, bend, and reach. Most clerks work regular business hours.

Employment

File clerks held about 272,000 jobs in 1998. Although file clerk jobs are found in nearly every sector of the economy, about 90 percent of these workers are employed in services, government, finance, insurance, and real estate. More than 1 out of every 4 is employed in temporary services firms, and about 1 out of 3 worked part time in 1998.

Training, Other Qualifications, and Advancement

Employers typically require applicants to have at least a high school diploma or its equivalent, although many employers prefer to hire clerks with a higher level of education. Most employers prefer workers who are computer-literate. Knowledge of word processing and spreadsheet software is especially valuable, as are experience working in an office and good interpersonal skills.

File clerks often learn the skills they need in high schools, business schools, and community colleges. Business education programs offered by these institutions typically include courses in typing, word processing, shorthand, business communications, records management, and office systems and procedures.

Some entrants are college graduates with degrees in business, finance, or liberal arts. Although a degree is rarely required, many graduates accept entry-level clerical positions to get into a particular company with the hope of being promoted to professional or managerial positions. Once hired, clerks usually receive on-the-job training. Under the guidance of a supervisor or other senior worker, new employees learn company procedures. Some formal classroom training may also be necessary, such as training in specific computer software.

Clerks must be careful, orderly, and detail-oriented in order to avoid making errors and to recognize errors made by others. These workers should also be discreet and trustworthy because they frequently come in contact with confidential material.

Clerks usually advance by taking on more duties in the same occupation for higher pay or transferring to a closely related occupation.

Most companies fill office and administrative support supervisory and managerial positions by promoting individuals from within their organizations, so clerks who acquire additional skills, experience, and training improve their advancement opportunities.

Job Outlook

Employment of file clerks is expected to grow about as fast as the average for all occupations through 2008. Projected job growth stems from rising demand for file clerks to record and retrieve information in organizations across the economy. This growth will be moderated, however, by productivity gains stemming from office automation and the consolidation of clerical jobs. Nonetheless, job opportunities for file clerks should be plentiful because a large number of workers will be needed to replace workers who leave the occupation each year. High turnover among file clerks reflects the lack of formal training requirements, limited advancement potential, and relatively low pay.

Jobseekers who have typing and other secretarial skills and are familiar with a wide range of office machines, especially personal computers, should have the best job opportunities. File clerks should find many opportunities for temporary or part-time work, especially during peak business periods.

Earnings

Salaries of file clerks vary. The region of the country, size of city, and type and size of establishment all influence salary levels. The level of industry or technical expertise required and the complexity and uniqueness of a clerk's responsibilities may also affect earnings. Median annual earnings of full-time file clerks in 1998 were $16,830.

Related Occupations

Other clerical workers who classify, update, and retrieve information include bank tellers, statistical clerks, receiving clerks, medical record clerks, hotel and motel clerks, credit clerks, and reservation and transportation ticket agents.

Sources of Additional Information

State employment service offices can provide information about job openings for records processing occupations.

Financial Managers

(O*NET 13002A and 13002B)

Significant Points

- A bachelor's degree in finance, accounting, or a related field is the minimum academic preparation, but many employers increasingly seek graduates with a master's degree and a strong analytical background.

- The continuing need for skilled financial managers will spur average employment growth.

Nature of the Work

Almost every firm, government agency, and organization has one or more financial managers who oversee the preparation of financial reports, direct investment activities, and implement cash management strategies. As computers are increasingly used to record and organize data, many financial managers are spending more time developing strategies and implementing the long-term goals of their organization.

The duties of financial managers vary with their specific titles, which include chief financial officer, vice president of finance, controller, treasurer, credit manager, and cash manager. *Chief financial officers* (CFOs), for example, are the top financial executives of an organization. They oversee all financial and accounting functions and formulate and administer the organization's overall financial plans and policies. In small firms, CFOs usually handle all financial management functions. In large firms, they direct these activities through other financial managers who head each financial department.

Controllers direct the preparation of financial reports that summarize and forecast the organization's financial position, such as income statements, balance sheets, and analysis of future earnings or expenses. Controllers are also in charge of preparing special reports required by regulatory authorities. Often, controllers oversee the accounting, audit, and budget departments. *Treasurers* and *finance officers* direct the organization's financial goals, objectives, and budgets. They oversee the investment of funds and manage associated risks, supervise cash management activities, execute capital-raising strategies to support a firm's expansion, and deal with mergers and acquisitions.

Cash managers monitor and control the flow of cash receipts and disbursements to meet the business and investment needs of the firm. For example, cash flow projections are needed to determine whether loans must be obtained to meet cash requirements or whether surplus cash should be invested in interest-bearing instruments. *Risk* and *insurance managers* oversee programs to minimize risks and losses that may arise from financial transactions and business operations undertaken by the institution. They also manage the organization's insurance budget. *Credit managers* oversee the firm's issuance of credit. They establish credit rating criteria, determine credit ceilings, and monitor the collections of past due accounts. Managers specializing in international finance develop financial and accounting systems for the banking transactions of multinational organizations.

Financial institutions, such as commercial banks, savings and loan associations, credit unions, and mortgage and finance companies, employ additional financial managers, often with the title Vice President. These executives oversee various functions, such as lending, trusts, mortgages, and investments, or programs, including sales, operations, or electronic financial services. They may be required to solicit business, authorize loans, and direct the investment of funds, always adhering to Federal and State laws and regulations.

Branch managers of financial institutions administer and manage all the functions of a branch office, which may include hiring personnel, approving loans and lines of credit, establishing a rapport with the community to attract business, and assisting customers with account problems. Financial managers who work for financial institutions must keep abreast of the rapidly growing array of financial services and products.

In addition to the general duties described above, all financial managers perform tasks unique to their organization or industry. For example, government financial managers must be experts on the government appropriations and budgeting processes, whereas health care financial managers must be knowledgeable about issues surrounding health care financing. Moreover, financial managers must be aware of special tax laws and regulations that affect their industry.

Areas in which financial managers are playing an increasingly important role involve mergers and consolidations and global expansion and financing. These developments require extensive specialized knowledge on the part of the financial manager to reduce risks and maximize profit. Financial managers are increasingly hired on a temporary basis to advise senior managers on these and other matters. In fact, some firms contract out all accounting and financial functions to companies that provide these services.

The role of financial manager, particularly in business, is changing in response to technological advances that have significantly reduced the amount of time it takes to produce financial reports. Financial managers now perform more data analysis and use it to offer ideas to senior managers on how to maximize profits. They often work on teams, acting as business advisors to top management. Financial managers need to keep abreast of the latest computer technology in order to increase the efficiency of their firm's financial operations.

Working Conditions

Financial managers work in comfortable offices, often close to top managers and to departments that develop the financial data these managers need. They typically have direct access to state-of-the-art computer systems and information services. Financial managers commonly work long hours, often up to 50 or 60 per week. They are generally required to attend meetings of financial and economic associations and may travel to visit subsidiary firms or meet customers.

Employment

Financial managers held about 693,000 jobs in 1998. Although these managers are found in virtually every industry, more than a third were employed by services industries, including business, health, social, and management services. Nearly 3 out of 10 were employed by financial institutions, such as banks, savings institutions, finance companies, credit unions, insurance companies, securities dealers, and real estate firms.

Training, Other Qualifications, and Advancement

A bachelor's degree in finance, accounting, economics, or business administration is the minimum academic preparation for financial managers. However, many employers increasingly seek graduates with a master's degree, preferably in business administration, economics, finance, or risk management. These academic programs develop analytical skills and provide knowledge of the latest financial analysis methods and technology.

Experience may be more important than formal education for some financial manager positions—notably branch managers in banks. Banks typically fill branch manager positions by promoting experienced loan officers and other professionals who excel at their jobs. Other financial managers may enter the profession through formal management trainee programs offered by the company.

Continuing education is vital for financial managers, reflecting the growing complexity of global trade, shifting Federal and State laws and regulations, and a proliferation of new, complex financial instruments. Firms often provide opportunities for workers to broaden their knowledge and skills by encouraging employees to take graduate courses at colleges and universities or attending conferences related to their specialty. Financial management, banking, and credit union associations, often in cooperation with colleges and universities, sponsor numerous national and local training programs. Persons enrolled prepare extensively at home and then attend sessions on subjects such as accounting management, budget management, corporate cash management, financial analysis, international banking, and information systems. Many firms pay all or part of the costs for those who successfully complete courses. Although experience, ability, and leadership are emphasized for promotion, advancement may be accelerated by this type of special study.

In some cases, financial managers may also broaden their skills and exhibit their competency in specialized fields by attaining professional certification. For example, the Association for Investment Management and Research confers the Chartered Financial Analyst designation on investment professionals who have a bachelor's degree, pass three test levels, and meet work experience requirements. The National Association of Credit Management administers a three-part certification program for business credit professionals. Through a combination of experience and examinations, these financial managers pass through the level of Credit Business Associate, to Credit Business Fellow, and finally to Certified Credit Executive. The Treasury Management Association confers the Certified Cash Manager credential on those who have two years of relevant experience and pass an exam, and the Association confers the Certified Treasury Executive designation on those who meet more extensive experience and continuing education requirements. More recently, the Association of Government Accountants has begun to offer the Certified Government Financial Manager certification to those who have the appropriate education and experience and who pass three examinations. Financial managers who specialize in accounting may earn the Certified Public Accountant (CPA) or Certified Management Accountant (CMA) designations.

Candidates for financial management positions need a broad range of skills. Interpersonal skills are increasingly important because these jobs involve managing people and working as part of a team to solve problems. Financial managers must have excellent communication skills to explain complex financial data. Because financial managers work extensively with various departments in their firm, a broad overview of the business is essential.

Financial managers should be creative thinkers and problem solvers, applying their analytical skills to business. They must be comfortable with computer technology. As financial operations are increasingly affected by the global economy, they must have knowledge of international finance; even a foreign language may be important.

Because financial management is critical for efficient business operations, well-trained, experienced financial managers who display a strong grasp of the operations of various departments within their organization are prime candidates for promotion to top management positions. Some financial managers transfer to closely related positions in other industries. Those with extensive experience and access to sufficient capital may start their own consulting firms.

Job Outlook

The outlook for financial managers is good for those with the right skills. Expertise in accounting and finance is fundamental, and a master's degree enhances one's job prospects. Strong computer skills and knowledge of international finance are important, as are excellent communication skills as the job increasingly involves working on strategic planning teams. Mergers, acquisitions, and corporate downsizing will continue to adversely affect employment of financial managers, but growth of the economy and the need for financial expertise will keep the profession growing about as fast as the average for all occupations through 2008.

The banking industry, which employs the most financial managers, is expected to continue to consolidate and reduce the number of financial managers. Employment of bank branch managers, in particular, will grow very little or not at all as banks open fewer branches and promote electronic and Internet banking to cut costs. In contrast, the securities and commodities industry will hire more financial managers to handle increasingly complex financial transactions and manage investments. Financial managers are being hired throughout industry to manage assets and investments, handle mergers and acquisitions, raise capital, and assess global financial transactions. Risk managers, who assess risks for insurance and investment purposes, are in especially great demand.

Some financial managers may be hired on a temporary basis to see a company through a short-term crisis or to offer suggestions for boosting profits. Other companies may contract out all accounting and financial operations. Even in these cases, however, financial managers may be needed to oversee the contracts.

Computer technology has reduced the time and staff required to produce financial reports. As a result, forecasting earnings, profits, and costs, and generating ideas and creative ways to increase profitability will become the major role of corporate financial managers over the next decade. Financial managers who are familiar with computer software and applications that can assist them in this role will be needed.

Earnings

Median annual earnings of financial managers were $55,070 in 1998. The middle 50 percent earned between $38,240 and $83,800. The lowest 10 percent had earnings of less than $27,680, while the top 10 percent earned over $118,950. Median annual earnings in

the industries employing the largest number of financial managers in 1997 are shown below.

Security brokers and dealers	$95,100
Computer and data processing	63,200
Management and public relations	62,800
Local government, excluding education and hospitals	48,700
Commercial banks	45,800
Savings institutions	41,800

According to a 1999 survey by Robert Half International, a staffing services firm specializing in accounting and finance, salaries of assistant controllers and treasurers varied from $42,700 in the smallest firms to $84,000 in the largest firms; corporate controllers earned between $47,500 and $141,000; and chief financial officers and treasurers earned from $65,000 to $319,200. Salaries are generally 10 percent higher for those with a graduate degree or Certified Public Accountant or Certified Management Accountant designation.

The results of the Treasury Management Association's 1999 compensation survey are presented in Table 1. The earnings listed in the table represent total compensation, including bonuses and deferred compensation.

TABLE 1

Average earnings for selected financial managers, 1999

Vice president of finance	$165,400
Chief financial officer	150,100
Treasurer	129,800
Controller	109,700
Assistant treasurer	96,500
Director treasury/finance	93,200
Assistant controller	75,900
Senior analyst	63,000
Cash manager	56,600
Analyst	45,500

SOURCE: Treasury Management Association

Large organizations often pay more than small ones, and salary levels can also vary by the type of industry and location. Many financial managers in private industry receive additional compensation in the form of bonuses, which also vary substantially by size of firm. Deferred compensation in the form of stock options is also becoming more common.

Related Occupations

Financial managers combine formal education with experience in one or more areas of finance, such as asset management, lending, credit operations, securities investment, or insurance risk and loss control. Workers in other occupations requiring similar training and skills include accountants and auditors, budget officers, credit analysts, loan officers, insurance consultants, portfolio managers, pension consultants, real estate advisors, securities analysts, and underwriters.

Sources of Additional Information

For information about financial management careers, contact:

- American Bankers Association, 1120 Connecticut Ave. NW., Washington, DC 20036. Internet: http://www.aba.com
- Financial Management Association International, College of Business Administration, University of South Florida, Tampa, FL 33620-5500. Internet: http://www.fma.org
- Financial Executives Institute, 10 Madison Ave., P.O. Box 1938, Morristown, NJ 07962-1938. Internet: http://www.fei.org

For information about financial careers in business credit management; the Credit Business Associate, Credit Business Fellow, and Certified Credit Executive programs; and institutions offering graduate courses in credit and financial management, contact:

- National Association of Credit Management, Credit Research Foundation, 8840 Columbia 100 Parkway, Columbia, MD 21045-2158. Internet: http://www.nacm.org

For information about careers in treasury and financial management and the Certified Cash Manager and Certified Treasury Executive programs, contact:

- Treasury Management Association, 7315 Wisconsin Ave., Suite 600 West, Bethesda, MD 20814. Internet: http://www.tma-net.org

For information about the Chartered Financial Analyst program, contact:

- Association for Investment Management and Research, P.O. Box 3668, Charlottesville, VA 22903. Internet: http://www.aimr.org

For information about the Certified Government Financial Manager designation, contact:

- Association for Government Accountants, 2208 Mount Vernon Ave., Alexandria, VA 22301-1314. Internet: http://www.agacgfm.org

Funeral Directors and Morticians

(O*NET 39011 and 39014)

Significant Points

- Job opportunities should be good, but mortuary science graduates may have to relocate to find jobs as funeral directors.
- Funeral directors must be licensed by their State.

Nature of the Work

Funeral practices and rites vary greatly among various cultures and religions. Among the many diverse groups in the United States, funeral practices usually share some common elements: removal of the deceased to a mortuary, preparation of the remains, performance of a ceremony that honors the deceased and addresses the spiritual needs of the family, and the burial or destruction of the remains. Funeral directors arrange and direct these tasks for grieving families.

Funeral directors also are called morticians or undertakers. This career may not appeal to everyone, but those who work as funeral directors take great pride in their ability to provide efficient and appropriate services. They also comfort the family and friends of the deceased.

Funeral directors arrange the details and handle the logistics of funerals. They interview the family to learn what they desire with regard to the nature of the funeral, the clergy members or other persons who will officiate, and the final disposition of the remains. Sometimes the deceased leaves detailed instructions for his or her own funeral. Together with the family, funeral directors establish the location, date, and time of the wake, memorial service, and burial. They arrange for a hearse to carry the body to the funeral home or mortuary.

Funeral directors also prepare obituary notices and have them placed in newspapers, arrange for pallbearers and clergy, schedule the opening and closing of a grave with the cemetery, decorate and prepare the sites of all services, and provide transportation for the remains, mourners, and flowers between sites. They also direct preparation and shipment of remains for out-of-State burial.

Most funeral directors also are trained, licensed, and practicing *embalmers*. Embalming is a sanitary, cosmetic, and preservative process through which the body is prepared for interment. If more than 24 hours elapse between death and interment, State laws usually require that the remains be refrigerated or embalmed.

The embalmer washes the body with germicidal soap and replaces the blood with embalming fluid to preserve the body. Embalmers may reshape and reconstruct disfigured or maimed bodies using materials such as clay, cotton, plaster of Paris, and wax. They also may apply cosmetics to provide a natural appearance, and then dress the body and place it in a casket. Embalmers maintain records such as embalming reports and itemized lists of clothing or valuables delivered with the body. In large funeral homes, an embalming staff of two or more embalmers, plus several apprentices, may be employed.

Funeral services may take place in a home, house of worship, funeral home, or at the gravesite or crematory. Services may be non-religious, but often they reflect the religion of the family, so funeral directors must be familiar with the funeral and burial customs of many faiths, ethnic groups, and fraternal organizations. For example, members of some religions seldom have the bodies of the deceased embalmed or cremated.

Burial in a casket is the most common method of disposing of remains in this country, although entombment also occurs. Cremation, which is the burning of the body in a special furnace, is increasingly selected because it can be more convenient and less costly. Cremations are appealing because the remains can be shipped easily, kept at home, buried, or scattered. Memorial services can be held anywhere, and at any time, sometimes months later when all relatives and friends can get together. Even when the remains are cremated, many people still want a funeral service.

A funeral service followed by cremation need not be any different from a funeral service followed by a burial. Usually cremated remains are placed in some type of permanent receptacle, or urn, before being committed to a final resting place. The urn may be buried, placed in an indoor or outdoor mausoleum or columbarium, or interred in a special urn garden that many cemeteries provide for cremated remains.

Funeral directors handle the paper work involved with the person's death, such as submitting papers to State authorities so that a formal certificate of death may be issued and copies distributed to the heirs. They may help family members apply for veterans' burial benefits and notify the Social Security Administration of the death. Also, funeral directors may apply for the transfer of any pensions, insurance policies, or annuities on behalf of survivors.

Funeral directors also prearrange funerals. Increasingly, they arrange funerals in advance of need to provide peace of mind by ensuring that the client's wishes will be taken care of in a way that is satisfying to the person and to those who will survive.

Most funeral homes are small, family-run businesses, and the funeral directors either are owner-operators or employees of the operation. Funeral directors, therefore, are responsible for the success and the profitability of their businesses. Directors keep records of expenses, purchases, and services rendered; prepare and send invoices for services; prepare and submit reports for unemployment insurance; prepare Federal, State, and local tax forms; and prepare itemized bills for customers. Funeral directors increasingly are using computers for billing, bookkeeping, and marketing. Some are beginning to use the Internet to communicate with clients who are pre-planning their funerals and to assist clients by developing electronic obituaries and guest books. Directors strive to foster a cooperative spirit and friendly attitude among employees and a compassionate demeanor towards the families. A growing number of funeral directors also are involved in helping individuals adapt to changes in their lives following a death through post-death support group activities.

Most funeral homes have a chapel, one or more viewing rooms, a casket-selection room, and a preparation room. An increasing number also have a crematory on the premises. Equipment may include a hearse, a flower car, limousines, and sometimes an ambulance. They usually stock a selection of caskets and urns for families to purchase or rent.

Working Conditions

Funeral directors often work long, irregular hours. Many work on an on-call basis, because they may be needed to remove remains in the middle of the night. Shift work sometimes is necessary because funeral home hours include evenings and weekends. In smaller funeral homes, working hours vary, but in larger homes, employees usually work eight hours a day, five or six days a week.

Funeral directors occasionally come into contact with the remains of persons who had contagious diseases, but the possibility of infection is remote if strict health regulations are followed.

To show proper respect and consideration for the families and the dead, funeral directors must dress appropriately. The profession usually requires short, neat haircuts and trim beards, if any, for men. Suits, ties, and dresses are customary for a conservative look.

Employment

Funeral directors held about 28,000 jobs in 1998. Almost 1 in 10 were self-employed. Nearly all worked in the funeral service and crematory industry.

Training, Other Qualifications, and Advancement

Funeral directors must be licensed in all but one State (Colorado). Licensing laws vary from State to State, but most require applicants to be 21 years old, have two years of formal education that includes studies in mortuary science, serve a one-year apprenticeship, and pass a qualifying examination. After becoming licensed, new funeral directors may join the staff of a funeral home. Embalmers must be licensed in all States, and some States issue a single license for both funeral directors and embalmers. In States that have separate licensing requirements for the two positions, most people in the field obtain both licenses. Persons interested in a career as a funeral director should contact their State licensing board for specific requirements.

College programs in mortuary science usually last from two to four years; the American Board of Funeral Service Education accredits 49 mortuary science programs. Two-year programs are offered by a small number of community and junior colleges, and a few colleges and universities offer both two- and four-year programs. Mortuary science programs include courses in anatomy, physiology, pathology, embalming techniques, restorative art, business management, accounting and use of computers in funeral home management, and client services. They also include courses in the social sciences and legal, ethical, and regulatory subjects, such as psychology, grief counseling, oral and written communication, funeral service law, business law, and ethics.

The Funeral Service Educational Foundation and many State associations offer continuing education programs designed for licensed funeral directors. These programs address issues in communications, counseling, and management. Thirty-two States require funeral directors to receive continuing education credits in order to maintain their licenses.

Apprenticeships must be completed under an experienced and licensed funeral director or embalmer. Depending on State regulations, apprenticeships last from one to three years and may be served before, during, or after mortuary school. Apprenticeships provide practical experience in all facets of the funeral service, from embalming to transporting remains.

State board licensing examinations vary, but they usually consist of written and oral parts and include a demonstration of practical skills. Persons who want to work in another State may have to pass the examination for that State; however, some States have reciprocity arrangements and will grant licenses to funeral directors from another State without further examination.

High school students can start preparing for a career as a funeral director by taking courses in biology and chemistry and participating in public speaking or debate clubs. Part-time or summer jobs in funeral homes consist mostly of maintenance and clean-up tasks, such as washing and polishing limousines and hearses, but these tasks can help students become familiar with the operation of funeral homes.

Important personal traits for funeral directors are composure, tact, and the ability to communicate easily with the public. They also should have the desire and ability to comfort people in their time of sorrow.

Advancement opportunities are best in larger funeral homes: Funeral directors may earn promotions to higher paying positions, such as branch manager or general manager. Some directors eventually acquire enough money and experience to establish their own funeral home businesses.

Job Outlook

Employment of funeral directors is expected to increase about as fast as the average for all occupations through 2008. Not only is the population expanding, but also the proportion of people over the age of 55 is projected to grow during the coming decade. Consequently, the number of deaths is expected to increase, spurring demand for funeral services.

The need to replace funeral directors and morticians who retire or leave the occupation for other reasons will account for even more job openings than employment growth. Typically, a number of mortuary science graduates leave the profession shortly after becoming licensed funeral directors to pursue other career interests, and this trend is expected to continue. Also, more funeral directors are 55 years old and over compared to workers in other occupations, and they will be retiring in greater numbers between 1998 and 2008. Although employment opportunities for funeral directors are expected to be good, mortuary science graduates may have to relocate to find jobs in funeral service.

Earnings

Median annual earnings for funeral directors were $35,040 in 1998. The middle 50 percent earned between $25,510 and $48,260. The lowest 10 percent earned less than $17,040, and the top 10 percent more than $78,550.

Salaries of funeral directors depend on the number of years of experience in funeral service, the number of services performed, the number of facilities operated, the area of the country, the size of the community, and the level of formal education. Funeral directors in large cities earned more than their counterparts in small towns and rural areas.

Related Occupations

The job of a funeral director requires tact, discretion, and compassion when dealing with grieving people. Others who need these qualities include members of the clergy, social workers, psychologists, psychiatrists, and other health care professionals.

Sources of Additional Information

For a list of accredited mortuary science programs and information on the funeral service profession, write to:

● The National Funeral Directors Association, 13625 Bishop's Drive, Brookfield, WI 53005.

For information about college programs in mortuary science, scholarships, and funeral service as a career, contact:

● The American Board of Funeral Service Education, 38 Florida Avenue, Portland, ME 04103.

For information on continuing education programs in funeral service, contact:

● The Funeral Service Educational Foundation, 13625 Bishop's Drive, Brookfield, WI 53005.

General Managers and Top Executives

(O*NET 19005B)

Significant Points

● General managers and top executives are among the highest paid workers; however, long hours and considerable travel are often required.

● Competition for top managerial jobs should remain intense due to the large number of qualified applicants and relatively low turnover.

Nature of the Work

All organizations have specific goals and objectives that they strive to meet. General managers and top executives devise strategies and formulate policies to ensure that these objectives are met. Although they have a wide range of titles—such as chief executive officer, president, executive vice president, owner, partner, brokerage office manager, school superintendent, and police chief—all formulate policies and direct the operations of businesses and corporations, nonprofit institutions, and other organizations.

A corporation's goals and policies are established by the chief executive officer in collaboration with other top executives, who are overseen by a board of directors. In a large corporation, the chief executive officer meets frequently with subordinate executives to ensure that operations are implemented in accordance with these policies. The chief executive officer of a corporation retains overall accountability; however, a chief operating officer may be delegated several responsibilities, including the authority to oversee executives who direct the activities of various departments and implement the organization's policies on a day-to-day basis. In publicly held and nonprofit corporations, the board of directors is ultimately accountable for the success or failure of the enterprise, and the chief executive officer reports to the board.

The nature of other high-level executives' responsibilities depends upon the size of the organization. In large organizations, their duties are highly specialized. Managers of cost and profit centers, for instance, are responsible for the overall performance of one aspect of the organization, such as manufacturing, marketing, sales, purchasing, finance, personnel, training, administrative services, electronic data processing, property management, transportation, or the legal services department.

In smaller organizations, such as independent retail stores or small manufacturers, a partner, owner, or general manager is often also responsible for purchasing, hiring, training, quality control, and day-to-day supervisory duties.

Working Conditions

Top executives are usually provided with spacious offices and support staff. General managers in large firms or nonprofit organizations usually have comfortable offices close to the top executives to whom they report. Long hours, including evenings and weekends, are standard for most top executives and general managers, though their schedules may be flexible.

Substantial travel between international, national, regional, and local offices to monitor operations and meet with customers, staff, and other executives often is required of managers and executives. Many managers and executives also attend meetings and conferences sponsored by various associations. The conferences provide an opportunity to meet with prospective donors, customers, contractors, or government officials and allow managers and executives to keep abreast of technological and managerial innovations.

In large organizations, frequent job transfers between local offices or subsidiaries are common. General managers and top executives are under intense pressure to earn higher profits, provide better service, or attain fundraising and charitable goals. Executives in charge of poorly performing organizations or departments usually find their jobs in jeopardy.

Employment

General managers and top executives held over 3.3 million jobs in 1998. They are found in every industry, but wholesale, retail, and services industries employ more than 6 out of 10.

Training, Other Qualifications, and Advancement

The educational background of managers and top executives varies as widely as the nature of their responsibilities. Many general managers and top executives have a bachelor's degree or higher in liberal arts or business administration. Their major often is related to the departments they direct; for example, a manager of finance may have a degree in accounting, and a manager of information systems might have a degree in computer science. Graduate and professional degrees are common. Many managers in administrative, marketing, financial, and manufacturing activities have a master's degree in business administration. Managers in highly technical manufacturing and research activities often have a master's degree in engineering or a doctoral degree in a scientific discipline. A law degree is mandatory for managers of legal departments; hospital administrators generally have a master's degree in health services administration or business administration.

In the public sector, many managers have liberal arts degrees in public administration or one of the social sciences. Park superintendents, for example, often have liberal arts degrees, whereas police chiefs are usually graduates of law enforcement academies and hold degrees in criminal justice or a related field. College presidents typically have a doctorate in the field they originally taught, and school superintendents often have a masters degree in education administration.

Since many general manager and top executive positions are filled by promoting experienced lower level managers when an opening occurs, many are promoted from within the organization. In industries such as retail trade or transportation, for instance, it is possible for individuals without a college degree to work their way up within the company and become managers. Many companies prefer, however, that their top executives have specialized backgrounds, and they hire individuals who are managers in other organizations.

General managers and top executives must have highly developed personal skills. An analytical mind able to quickly assess large amounts of information and data is very important, as is the ability to consider and evaluate the interrelationships of numerous factors. General managers and top executives must also be able to communicate clearly and persuasively. Other qualities critical for managerial success include leadership, self-confidence, motivation, decisiveness, flexibility, sound business judgment, and determination.

Advancement may be accelerated by participation in company training programs that impart a broader knowledge of company policy and operations. Managers can also help their careers by becoming familiar with the latest developments in management techniques at national or local training programs sponsored by various industry and trade associations. Senior managers who often have experience in a particular field, such as accounting or engineering, also attend executive development programs to facilitate their promotion to general managers. Participation in conferences and seminars can expand knowledge of national and international issues influencing the organization and can help develop a network of useful contacts.

General managers may advance to top executive positions (such as executive vice president) in their own firms, or they may take corresponding positions in other firms. They may even advance to peak corporate positions such as chief operating officer or chief executive officer. Chief executive officers often become members of the board of directors of one or more firms, typically as a director of their own firm and often as chair of its board of directors. Some general managers and top executives establish their own firms or become independent consultants.

Job Outlook

Employment of general managers and top executives is expected to grow about as fast as the average for all occupations through 2008. These high-level managers are essential employees because they plan, organize, direct, control, and coordinate the operations of an organization and its major departments or programs. Therefore, top managers should be more immune to automation and corporate restructuring—factors which are expected to adversely affect employment of lower level managers. Because this is a large occupation,

many openings will occur each year as executives transfer to other positions, start their own businesses, or retire. Because many executives who leave their jobs transfer to other executive or managerial positions, however, openings for new entrants are limited, and intense competition is expected for top managerial jobs.

Projected employment growth of general managers and top executives varies widely among industries, largely reflecting overall industry growth. Overall employment growth is expected to be faster than average in services industries, but only about as fast as average in finance, insurance, and real estate industries. Employment of general managers and top executives is projected to decline along with overall employment in most manufacturing industries.

Experienced managers whose accomplishments reflect strong leadership qualities and the ability to improve the efficiency or competitive position of an organization will have the best opportunities. In an increasingly global economy, experience in international economics, marketing, information systems, and knowledge of several languages may also be beneficial.

Earnings

General managers and top executives are among the highest paid workers. However, salary levels vary substantially depending upon the level of managerial responsibility, length of service, and type, size, and location of the firm. For example, a top manager in a very large corporation can earn significantly more than a counterpart in a small firm.

Median annual earnings of general managers and top executives in 1998 were $55,890. The middle 50 percent earned between $34,970 and $94,650. Because the specific responsibilities of general managers vary significantly within industries, earnings also tend to vary considerably. Median annual earnings in the industries employing the largest numbers of general managers and top executives in 1997 were:

Management and public relations	$91,400
Computer and data processing services	90,600
Wholesale trade machinery, equipment, and supplies	65,900
Gasoline service stations	36,800
Eating and drinking places	33,000

Salaries vary substantially by type and level of responsibilities and by industry. According to a salary survey done by Executive Compensation Reports (a division of Harcourt Brace & Company), the median salary for CEOs of public companies from the fiscal year 1998 *Fortune 500* list was approximately $800,000. Three quarters of CEOs in the nonprofit sector made under $100,000 in 1998, according to a survey by Abbott, Langer, & Associates.

In addition to salaries, total compensation often includes stock options, dividends, and other performance bonuses. The use of executive dining rooms and company cars, expense allowances, and company-paid insurance premiums and physical examinations also are among benefits commonly enjoyed by general managers and top executives in private industry. A number of CEOs also are provided with company-paid club memberships, a limousine with driver, and other amenities.

Related Occupations

General managers and top executives plan, organize, direct, control, and coordinate the operations of an organization and its major departments or programs. The members of the board of directors and lower level managers are also involved in these activities. Other managerial occupations have similar responsibilities; however, they are concentrated in specific industries or are responsible for a specific department within an organization. They include administrative services managers, education administrators, financial managers, and restaurant and food service managers. Government occupations with similar functions are President, governor, mayor, commissioner, and legislator.

Sources of Additional Information

For a variety of information on general managers and top executives, including educational programs and job listings, contact:

- American Management Association, 1601 Broadway, New York, NY 10019-7420. Internet: http://www.amanet.org
- National Management Association, 2210 Arbor Blvd., Dayton, OH 45439. Internet: http://www.nma1.org

Government Chief Executives and Legislators

(O*NET 19005A)

Significant Points

- More than 9 out of 10 government chief executives and legislators work in local government.

- Most government chief executives and legislators are elected; local government managers are appointed.

- Few long-term career opportunities are available.

- There is less competition for executive and legislative jobs in small communities that offer part-time positions with little or no compensation or staff support.

Nature of the Work

Chief executives and legislators at the Federal, State, and local levels direct government activities and pass laws that affect us daily. These officials consist of the President and Vice President of the United States, members of Congress, State governors and lieutenant governors, members of the State legislators, county chief executives and commissioners, city, town and township council members, mayors, and city, county, town, and township managers. (Many small communities have top government officials who are volunteers and receive no salary. These individuals are not included in the employment or salary numbers provided in this statement.)

Most chief executives are elected by their constituents, but many managers are hired by a local government executive, council, or commission, to whom they are directly responsible. These officials formulate and establish government policy and develop Federal, State, or local laws and regulations.

Government chief executives, like their counterparts in the private sector, have overall responsibility for the performance of their organizations. Working with legislators, they set goals and organize programs to attain them. These executives also appoint department heads, who oversee the civil servants who carry out programs enacted by legislative bodies. As in the private sector, government chief executives oversee budgets and ensure that resources are used properly and programs are carried out as planned.

Chief executives carry out a number of other important functions, such as meeting with legislators and constituents to determine the level of support for proposed programs. In addition, they often nominate citizens to boards and commissions, encourage business investment, and promote economic development in their communities. To do all of these varied tasks effectively, chief executives of large governments rely on a staff of highly skilled aides and assistants to research issues that concern the public. Executives that control small governmental bodies, however, often do this work by themselves.

Legislators are elected officials who enact or amend laws. They include U.S. Senators and Representatives, State senators and representatives, and county, city, and town commissioners and council members. Legislators introduce, examine, and vote on bills to pass official legislation. In preparing such legislation, they study staff reports and hear testimony from constituents, representatives of interest groups, board and commission members, and others with an interest in the issue under consideration. They usually must approve budgets and the appointments of nominees for leadership posts who are submitted by the chief executive. In some bodies, the legislative council appoints the city, town, or county manager.

Working Conditions

The working conditions of chief executives and legislators vary with the size and budget of the governmental unit. Time spent at work ranges from a few hours a week for some local leaders to stressful weeks of 60 or more hours for members of the U.S. Congress. Similarly, some jobs require only occasional out-of-town travel, while others involve long periods away from home, such as when attending sessions of the legislature.

U.S. Senators and Representatives, governors and lieutenant governors, and chief executives and legislators in municipalities work full time, year-round, as do most county and city managers. Many State legislators work full time on government business while the legislature is in session (usually for two to six months a year or every other year) and work only part time when the legislature is not in session. Some local elected officials work a schedule that is officially designated as part time, but actually is the equivalent of a full-time schedule when unpaid duties are taken into account. In addition to their regular schedules, most chief executives are on call to handle emergencies.

Employment

Chief executives and legislators held about 80,000 jobs in 1998. About 9 out of 10 worked in local government. Chief executives and legislators in the Federal government consist of the 100 Senators, 435 Representatives, and the President and Vice President. State governors, lieutenant governors, legislators, chief executives, professional managers, and council and commission members of local governments make up the remainder.

Government chief executives and legislators who do not hold full-time, year-round positions often continue to work in the occupation they held before being elected.

Training, Other Qualifications, and Advancement

Apart from meeting minimum age, residency, and citizenship requirements, candidates for public office have no established training or qualifications. Candidates come from a wide variety of occupations, but many do have some political experience as staffers or members of government bureaus, boards, or commissions. Successful candidates usually become well-known through their political campaigns and some have built voter name recognition through their work with community religious, fraternal, or social organizations.

Increasingly, candidates target information to voters through advertising paid for by their respective campaigns, so fund raising skills are essential for candidates. Management-level work experience and public service help develop the fund raising, budgeting, public speaking, and problem solving skills that are needed to run an effective political campaign. Candidates must make decisions quickly, sometimes on the basis of limited or contradictory information. They should also be able to inspire and motivate their constituents and staff. Additionally, they must know how to reach compromises and satisfy conflicting demands of constituents. National, State, and some local campaigns require massive amounts of energy and stamina, traits vital to successful candidates.

Virtually all town, city, and county managers have at least a bachelor's degree, and the majority hold a master's degree. A master's degree in public administration is recommended, including courses in public financial management and legal issues in public administration. Working in management support positions in government is a prime source of the experience and personal contacts required to eventually secure a manager position. For example, applicants often gain experience as management analysts or assistants in government departments working for committees, councils, or chief executives. In this capacity, they learn about planning, budgeting, civil engineering, and other aspects of running a government. With sufficient experience, they may be hired to manage a small government.

Generally, a town, city, or county manager is first hired by a smaller community. Advancement often takes the form of securing positions with progressively larger towns, cities, or counties. A broad knowledge of local issues, combined with communication skills and the ability to compromise, are essential for advancement in this field.

Advancement opportunities for elected officials are not clearly defined. Because elected positions normally require a period of residency and local public support is critical, officials usually advance to other offices only in the jurisdictions where they live. For example, council members may run for mayor or for a position in the State government, and State legislators may run for governor or for Congress. Many officials are not politically ambitious, however, and do not seek advancement. Others lose their bids for reelection or voluntarily leave the occupation. A lifetime career as a government chief executive or legislator is rare.

Job Outlook

Overall, little or no change in employment is expected among government chief executives and legislators through 2008. Few new governments at any level are likely to form, and the number of chief executives and legislators in existing governments rarely changes. However, some increase will occur at the local level as counties, cities, and towns take on professional managers or move from volunteer to paid, career executives to deal with population growth, Federal regulations, and long-range planning.

Elections give newcomers the chance to unseat incumbents or to fill vacated positions. The level of competition in elections varies from place to place. There tends to be less competition in small communities that offer part-time positions with low or no salaries and little or no staff compared to large municipalities with prestigious full-time positions offering high salaries, staff, and greater exposure.

Earnings

Median annual earnings of government chief executives and legislators were $19,130 in 1998. The middle 50 percent earned between $12,090 and $47,470. The lowest 10 percent earned less than $11,460, and the highest 10 percent earned more than $81,230.

Earnings of public administrators vary widely, depending on the size of the governmental unit and on whether the job is part time, full time and year round, or full time for only a few months a year. Salaries range from little or nothing for a small town council member to $200,000 a year for the President of the United States.

The International City/County Management Association reports the average annual salary of chief elected city officials was about $12,900, and the average salary for city managers was $70,500 in 1997. According to the International Personnel Management association, city managers earned an average of $101,800 and county managers $95,500 in 1999. Also, the National Conference of State Legislatures reports that the salary for legislators in the 40 States that paid an annual salary and the District of Columbia ranged from $3,700 in South Dakota on even years to $75,600 in California and $80,600 in the District of Columbia. In 8 States, legislators received a daily salary plus an additional allowance for living expenses while legislatures were in session. New Hampshire paid no expenses and $200 per two-year term, while New Mexico paid no salary at all but did pay a daily expense allowance.

The Council of State Governments reports in their *Book of the States, 1998-99* that gubernatorial annual salaries ranged from a low of $60,000 in Arkansas to a high of $130,000 in New York. In addition to a salary, most governors received benefits such as transportation and an official residence. The governor of Florida has the largest staff with 264, while the governor of Wyoming has the smallest with 14.

In 1999, U.S. Senators and Representatives earned $136,700, the Senate and House Majority and Minority leaders earned $151,800, and the Vice President was paid $175,400.

Related Occupations

Related occupations include managerial positions that require a broad range of skills and administrative expertise, such as corporate chief executives and board members, as well as high ranking officers in the military.

Sources of Additional Information

Information on appointed officials in local government can be obtained from:

- The Council of State Governments, P.O. Box 11910, Iron Works Pike, Lexington, KY 40578-1910. Internet: http://www.statesnews.org
- International City Management Association (ICMA), 777 North Capital NE., Suite 500, Washington, DC 20002. Internet: http://www.icma.org
- National Association of Counties, 440 First St. NW., Suite 800, Washington, DC 20001. Internet: http://www.naco.org
- National League of Cities, 1301 Pennsylvania Ave. NW., Washington, DC 20004. Internet: http://www.nlc.org

Health Services Managers

(O*NET 15008A and 15008B)

Significant Points

- Earnings of health services managers are high, but long work hours are common.

- Employment will grow fastest in home health agencies, residential care facilities, and practitioners' offices and clinics.

Nature of the Work

Health care is a business, and like every other business, it needs good management to keep it running smoothly, especially during times of change. The term "health services manager" encompasses individuals who plan, direct, coordinate, and supervise the delivery of health care. Health services managers include generalists and specialists. Generalists manage or help to manage an entire facility or system, while specialists are in charge of specific clinical departments or services.

The structure and financing of health care is changing rapidly. Future health services managers must be prepared to deal with evolving integrated health care delivery systems, restructuring of work,

technological innovations, and an increased focus on preventive care. They will be called upon to improve efficiency in health care facilities and the quality of the health care provided. Increasingly, health services managers work in organizations in which they must optimize efficiency of a variety of interrelated services, ranging from inpatient care to outpatient follow-up care, for example.

Large facilities usually have several assistant administrators to aid the top administrator and to handle daily decisions. They may direct activities in clinical areas (such as nursing, surgery, therapy, medical records or health information) or in nonhealth areas (such as finance, housekeeping, human resources, and information management). Because the nonhealth departments are not directly related to health care, these managers are not included in this job description.

In smaller facilities, top administrators handle more of the details of daily operations. For example, many nursing home administrators manage personnel, finance, facility operations, and admissions and have a larger role in resident care.

Clinical managers have more specific responsibilities than generalists do, and they have training and/or experience in a specific clinical area. For example, directors of physical therapy are experienced physical therapists, and most health information and medical record administrators have a bachelor's degree in health information or medical record administration. These managers establish and implement policies, objectives, and procedures for their departments; evaluate personnel and work; develop reports and budgets; and coordinate activities with other managers.

In group practices, managers work closely with physicians. Whereas an office manager may handle business affairs in small medical groups and leave policy decisions to the physicians themselves, larger groups usually employ a full-time administrator to advise on business strategies and coordinate day-to-day business.

A small group of 10 or 15 physicians might employ one administrator to oversee personnel matters, billing and collection, budgeting, planning, equipment outlays, and patient flow. A large practice of 40 or 50 physicians may have a chief administrator and several assistants, each of which is responsible for different areas.

Health services managers in health maintenance organizations (HMOs) and other managed care settings perform functions similar to those in large group practices, except their staffs may be larger. In addition, they may do more work in the areas of community outreach and preventive care than managers of a group practice. The size of the administrative staff in HMOs varies according to the size and type of HMO.

Some health services managers oversee the activities of a number of facilities in health systems. Such systems may contain both inpatient and outpatient facilities and offer a wide range of patient services.

Working Conditions

Most health services managers work long hours. Facilities such as nursing homes and hospitals operate around the clock, and administrators and managers may be called at all hours to deal with problems. They may also travel to attend meetings or inspect satellite facilities.

Employment

Health services managers held about 222,000 jobs in 1998. Almost one-half of all jobs were in hospitals. About 1 in 4 were in nursing and personal care facilities or offices and clinics of physicians. The remainder worked mostly in home health agencies, ambulatory facilities run by State and local governments, offices of dentists and other health practitioners, medical and dental laboratories, residential care facilities, and other social service agencies.

Training, Other Qualifications, and Advancement

Health services managers must be familiar with management principles and practices. A master's degree in health services administration, long-term care administration, health sciences, public health, public administration, or business administration is the standard credential for most generalist positions in this field. However, a bachelor's degree is adequate for some entry-level positions in smaller facilities and for some entry-level positions at the departmental level within health care organizations. Physicians' offices and some other facilities may substitute on-the-job experience for formal education.

For clinical department heads, a degree in the appropriate field and work experience may be sufficient for entry, but a master's degree in health services administration or a related field may be required to advance. For example, nursing service administrators are usually chosen from among supervisory registered nurses with administrative abilities and a graduate degree in nursing or health services administration.

Bachelor's, master's, and doctoral degree programs in health administration are offered by colleges, universities, and schools of public health, medicine, allied health, public administration, and business administration. In 1999, 67 schools had accredited programs leading to the master's degree in health services administration, according to the Accrediting Commission on Education for Health Services Administration.

Some graduate programs seek students with undergraduate degrees in business or health administration; however, many graduate programs prefer students with a liberal arts or health profession background. Candidates with previous work experience in health care may also have an advantage. Competition for entry to these programs is keen, and applicants need above-average grades to gain admission.

These programs usually last between two and three years. They may include up to one year of supervised administrative experience and course work in areas such as hospital organization and management, marketing, accounting and budgeting, human resources administration, strategic planning, health economics, and health information systems. Some programs allow students to specialize in one type of facility: hospitals, nursing homes, mental health facilities, HMOs, or medical groups. Other programs encourage a generalist approach to health administration education.

New graduates with master's degrees in health services administration may start as department managers or in staff positions. The level of the starting position varies with the experience of the applicant and size of the organization. Hospitals and other health facilities offer postgraduate residencies and fellowships, which usually are staff positions. Graduates from master's degree programs also take jobs in HMOs, large group medical practices, clinics, mental health facilities, multifacility nursing home corporations, and consulting firms.

Graduates with bachelor's degrees in health administration usually begin as administrative assistants or assistant department heads in larger hospitals or as department heads or assistant administrators in small hospitals or nursing homes.

All States and the District of Columbia require nursing home administrators to have a bachelor's degree, pass a licensing examination, complete a State-approved training program, and pursue continuing education. A license is not required in other areas of health services management.

Health services managers are often responsible for millions of dollars of facilities and equipment and hundreds of employees. To make effective decisions, they need to be open to different opinions and good at analyzing contradictory information. They must understand finance and information systems and be able to interpret data. Motivating others to implement their decisions requires strong leadership abilities. Tact, diplomacy, flexibility, and communication skills are essential because health services managers spend most of their time interacting with others.

Health services managers advance by moving into more responsible and higher paying positions, such as assistant or associate administrator, or by moving to larger facilities.

Job Outlook

Employment of health services managers is expected to grow faster than the average for all occupations through 2008 as health services continue to expand and diversify. Opportunities for health services managers should be closely related to growth in the industry in which they are employed. Opportunities will be especially good in home health care, long-term care, and nontraditional health organizations (such as managed care operations and consulting firms), particularly for health services managers with work experience in the health care field and strong business and management skills.

Hospitals will continue to employ the most managers, although the number of jobs will grow slowly compared to other areas. As hospitals continue to consolidate, centralize, and diversify functions, competition will increase at all job levels.

Employment will grow the fastest in home health agencies, residential care facilities, and practitioners' offices and clinics. Many services previously provided in hospitals will be shifted to these sectors, especially as medical technologies improve. Demand in medical group practice management will grow as medical group practices become larger and more complex. Health services managers will need to deal with the pressures of cost containment and financial accountability, as well as the increased focus on preventive care. They will also become more involved in trying to improve the health of their communities.

Health services managers will also be employed by health care management companies who provide management services to hospitals and other organizations, as well as specific departments such as emergency, information management systems, managed care contract negotiations, and physician recruiting.

Earnings

Median annual earnings of medical and health service managers were $48,870 in 1998. The middle 50 percent earned between $37,900 and $71,580 a year. The lowest 10 percent earned less than $28,600, and the highest 10 percent earned more than $88,730 a year. Median annual earnings in the industries employing the largest number of medical and health service managers in 1997 were as follows:

Hospitals $52,600

Home health care services 45,800

Health and allied services, not elsewhere classified 44,700

Nursing and personal care facilities 43,600

Offices and clinics of medical doctors 39,600

Earnings of health services managers vary by type and size of the facility, as well as by level of responsibility. For example, the Medical Group Management Association reported the following median salaries in 1998 for administrators by group practice size: fewer than 7 physicians, $60,000; 7 to 25 physicians, $76,700; and more than 26 physicians, $124,500.

A survey by *Modern Healthcare* magazine reported the following median annual compensations in 1998 for managers of specific clinical departments: Respiratory therapy, $57,700; home health care, $62,400; ambulatory and outpatient services, $66,200; radiology, $66,800; clinical laboratory, $66,900; physical therapy, $68,100; rehabilitation services, $73,400; and nursing services, $100,200. Salaries also varied according to size of facility and geographic region.

According to the Buck Survey conducted by the American Health Care Association in 1997, nursing home administrators' median annual earnings were $52,800. The middle 50 percent earned between $44,300 and $60,300 a year. Assistant administrators had median annual earnings of about $35,000, with the middle 50 percent earning between $28,700 and $41,200.

Related Occupations

Health services managers have training or experience in both health and management. Other occupations requiring knowledge of both fields are public health directors, social welfare administrators, directors of voluntary health agencies and health professional associations, and underwriters in health insurance companies.

Sources of Additional Information

General information about health administration is available from:

● American College of Healthcare Executives, One North Franklin St., Suite 1700, Chicago, IL 60606. Internet: http://www.ache.org

Information about undergraduate and graduate academic programs in this field is available from:

● Association of University Programs in Health Administration, 730 11th St., NW., Washington, DC 20001-4510. Internet: http://www.aupha.org

For a list of accredited graduate programs in health services administration, contact:

● Accrediting Commission on Education for Health Services Administration, 730 11th St., NW., Washington, DC 20001-4510.

For information about career opportunities in long-term care administration, contact:

● American College of Health Care Administrators, 325 S. Patrick St., Alexandria, VA 22314.

For information about career opportunities in medical group practices and ambulatory care management, contact:

● Medical Group Management Association, 104 Inverness Terrace East, Englewood, CO 80112.

For information about health care office managers, contact:

● Professional Association of Health Care Office Managers, 461 East Ten Mile Rd., Pensacola, FL 32534-9712. Internet: http://www.pahcom.com

Home Health and Personal Care Aides

(O*NET 66011 and 68035)

Significant Points

● Numerous job openings will result due to very fast employment growth and very high turnover.

● Education required for entry-level jobs is generally minimal, but earnings are low.

Nature of the Work

Home health and personal care aides help elderly, disabled, and ill persons live in their own homes instead of in a health facility. Most work with elderly or disabled clients who need more extensive care than family or friends can provide. Some home health and personal care aides work with families in which a parent is incapacitated and small children need care. Others help discharged hospital patients who have relatively short-term needs.

In general, *home health aides* provide health-related services, such as administering oral medications under physicians' orders or direction of a nurse. In contrast, *personal care* and *home care aides* provide mainly housekeeping and routine personal care services. However, there can be substantial variation in job titles and overlap of duties.

Most home health and personal care aides provide some housekeeping services, as well as personal care to their clients. They clean clients' houses, do laundry, and change bed linens. Some aides plan

meals (including special diets), shop for food, and cook. Home health and personal care aides may also help clients move from bed, bathe, dress, and groom. Some accompany clients outside the home, serving as guide, companion, and aide.

Home health and personal care aides also provide instruction and psychological support. For example, they may assist in toilet training a severely mentally handicapped child, or just listen to clients talk about their problems.

Home health aides may check pulse, temperature, and respiration; help with simple prescribed exercises; and assist with medication routines. Occasionally, they change nonsterile dressings, use special equipment such as a hydraulic lift, give massages and alcohol rubs, or assist with braces and artificial limbs.

In home care agencies, it is usually a registered nurse, a physical therapist, or a social worker who assigns specific duties and supervises home health and personal care aides. Aides keep records of services performed and of clients' condition and progress. They report changes in the client's condition to the supervisor or case manager. Home health and personal care aides also participate in case reviews, consulting with the team caring for the client, which might include registered nurses, therapists, and other health professionals.

Working Conditions

The home health and personal care aide's daily routine may vary. Aides may go to the same home every day for months or even years. However, most aides work with a number of different clients, each job lasting a few hours, days, or weeks. Aides often visit four or five clients on the same day.

Surroundings differ from case to case. Some homes are neat and pleasant, while others are untidy or depressing. Some clients are angry, abusive, depressed, or otherwise difficult; others are pleasant and cooperative.

Home health and personal care aides generally work on their own, with periodic visits by their supervisor. They receive detailed instructions explaining when to visit clients and what services to perform. Many aides work part time, and weekend hours are common.

Aides are individually responsible for getting to the client's home. They may spend a good portion of the work day traveling from one client to another; motor vehicle accidents are always a danger. They are particularly susceptible to injuries resulting from all types of overexertion when assisting patients and to falls inside and outside their patients' homes. Mechanical lifting devices that are available in institutional settings are seldom available in patients' homes.

Employment

Home health and personal care aides held about 746,000 jobs in 1998. Most aides are employed by home health and personal care agencies, visiting nurse associations, residential care facilities with home health departments, hospitals, public health and welfare departments, community volunteer agencies, nursing and personal care facilities, and temporary help firms. Self-employed aides have no agency affiliation or supervision; they accept clients, set fees, and arrange work schedules on their own.

Training, Other Qualifications, and Advancement

In some States, this occupation is open to individuals with no formal training. On-the-job training is generally provided. Other States may require formal training, depending on Federal or State law.

The Federal government has enacted guidelines for home health aides whose employers receive reimbursement from Medicare. Federal law requires home health aides to pass a competency test covering 12 areas: communication skills; observation, reporting, and documentation of patient status and the care or services furnished; reading and recording vital signs; basic infection control procedures; basic elements of body function and changes; maintenance of a clean, safe, and healthy environment; recognition of, and procedures for, emergencies; the physical, emotional, and developmental characteristics of the patients served; personal hygiene and grooming; safe transfer techniques; normal range of motion and positioning; and basic nutrition.

A home health aide may take training before taking the competency test. Federal law suggests at least 75 hours of classroom and practical training supervised by a registered nurse. Training and testing programs may be offered by the employing agency, but must meet the standards of the Health Care Financing Administration. Training programs vary depending upon State regulations.

The National Association for Home Care offers national certification for home health and personal care aides. The certification is a voluntary demonstration that the individual has met industry standards.

Successful home health and personal care aides like to help people and do not mind hard work. They should be responsible, compassionate, emotionally stable, and cheerful. Aides should also be tactful, honest, and discreet because they work in private homes.

Home health and personal care aides must be in good health. A physical examination including State regulated tests (such as those for tuberculosis) may be required.

Advancement is limited. In some agencies, workers start out performing homemaker duties, such as cleaning. With experience and training, they may take on personal care duties. The most experienced home health aides assist with medical equipment such as ventilators, which help patients breathe.

Job Outlook

A large number of job openings are expected for home health and personal care aides, due to substantial growth and very high turnover. Home health and personal care aides is expected to be one of the fastest growing occupations through the year 2008.

The number of people in their seventies and older is projected to rise substantially. This age group is characterized by mounting health problems requiring some assistance. Also, there will be an increasing reliance on home care for patients of all ages. This trend reflects several developments: efforts to contain costs by moving patients out of hospitals and nursing facilities as quickly as possible, the realization that treatment can be more effective in familiar surroundings than in clinical surroundings, and the development and improvement of medical technologies for in-home treatment.

In addition to jobs created by the increase in demand for these workers, replacement needs are expected to produce numerous openings. Turnover is high, a reflection of the relatively low skill requirements, low pay, and high emotional demands of the work. For these same reasons, many people are unwilling to perform this kind of work. Therefore, persons who are interested in this work and suited for it should have excellent job opportunities, particularly those with experience or training as home health, personal care, or nursing aides.

Earnings

Median hourly earnings of home health and personal care aides were $7.58 in 1998. The middle 50 percent earned between $6.41 and $8.81 an hour. The lowest 10 percent earned less than $5.73, and the highest 10 percent earned more than $10.51 an hour. Median hourly earnings in the industries employing the largest number of home health aides in 1997 were as follows:

Home health care services	$8.00
Hospitals	7.90
Personnel supply services	7.70
Residential care	7.20
Individual and family services	7.20

Median hourly earnings in the industries employing the largest number of personal and home care aides in 1997 are shown below:

Local government, except education and hospitals	$8.00
Job training and related services	7.30
Residential care	7.20
Individual and family services	7.00
Home health care services	6.00

Most employers give slight pay increases with experience and added responsibility. Aides are usually paid only for the time worked in the home. They normally are not paid for travel time between jobs. Most employers hire only "on-call" hourly workers and provide no benefits.

Related Occupations

Home health and personal care aide is a service occupation combining duties of health workers and social service workers. Workers in related occupations that involve personal contact to help or instruct others include attendants in children's institutions, child care attendants in schools, child monitors, companions, nursing aides, nursery school attendants, occupational therapy aides, nursing aides, physical therapy aides, playroom attendants, and psychiatric aides.

Sources of Additional Information

General information about training and referrals to State and local agencies about opportunities for home health and personal care aides, a list of relevant publications, and information on national

certification are available from:

● National Association for Home Care, 228 7th St. SE., Washington, DC 20003. Internet: http://www.nahc.org

For information about a career as a home health aide and schools offering training, contact:

● National Association of Health Career Schools, 2301 Academy Dr., Harrisburg, PA 17112.

Hotel Managers and Assistants

(O*NET 15026A)

Significant Points

● Long hours and the stress of dealing with hotel patrons result in high turnover among hotel managers.

● College graduates with degrees in hotel or restaurant management should have good job opportunities.

Nature of the Work

A comfortable room, good food, and a helpful hotel staff can make being away from home an enjoyable experience for both vacationing families and business travelers. Hotel managers and assistant managers help their guests have a pleasant stay by providing many of the comforts of home, including cable television, fitness equipment, and voice mail. Additionally, some hotels have health spas and other specialized services that the hotel manager and assistant help keep running smoothly. For business travelers, hotel managers often schedule available meeting rooms and electronic equipment, including slide projectors and fax machines.

Hotel managers are responsible for keeping the operation of their establishments efficient and profitable. In a small hotel, motel, or inn with a limited staff, the manager may oversee all aspects of operations. However, large hotels may employ hundreds of workers, and the general manager is usually aided by a number of assistant managers assigned to the various departments of the operation. In hotels of every size, managerial duties vary significantly by job title.

The *general manager*, for example, has overall responsibility for the operation of the hotel. Within guidelines established by the owners of the hotel or executives of the hotel chain, the general manager sets room rates, allocates funds to departments, approves expenditures, and establishes standards for guest services, decor, housekeeping, food quality, and banquet operations. Managers who work for chains may also organize and staff a newly built hotel, refurbish an older hotel, or reorganize a hotel or motel that is not operating successfully. In order to fill some low-paying service and clerical jobs in hotels, some general managers attend career fairs.

Resident managers live in hotels and are on call 24 hours a day to resolve problems or emergencies. In general, though, they typi-

cally work an 8-hour day and oversee the day-to-day operations of the hotel. In many hotels, the general manager is also the resident manager.

Executive housekeepers make sure that guest rooms, meeting and banquet rooms, and public areas are clean, orderly, and well maintained. They also train, schedule, and supervise the work of housekeepers, inspect rooms, and order cleaning supplies.

Front office managers coordinate reservations and room assignments and train and direct the hotel's front desk staff. They ensure that guests are treated courteously, complaints and problems are resolved, and requests for special services are carried out. Front office managers often have authorization to adjust charges posted on a customer's bill.

Food and beverage managers direct the food service operations of hotels. They oversee the hotels' restaurants, cocktail lounges, and banquet facilities. These managers also supervise food and beverage preparation and service workers, plan menus, set schedules, estimate costs, and deal with food suppliers.

Convention services managers coordinate the activities of large hotels' various departments for meetings, conventions, and special events. They meet with representatives of groups or organizations to plan the number of rooms to reserve, the desired configuration of hotel meeting space, and the banquet services. During the meeting or event, they resolve unexpected problems and monitor activities to ensure that hotel operations conform to the expectations of the group.

Assistant managers help run the day-to-day operations of the hotel. In large hotels they may be responsible for activities such as personnel, accounting, office administration, marketing and sales, purchasing, security, maintenance, and pool, spa, or recreational facilities. In smaller hotels, these duties may be combined into one position. Some hotels allow an assistant manager to make decisions regarding hotel guest charges when a manager is unavailable.

Computers are used extensively by hotel managers and their assistants to keep track of the guest's bill, reservations, room assignments, meetings, and special events. In addition, computers are used to order food, beverages, and supplies, as well as to prepare reports for hotel owners and top-level managers. Managers work with computer specialists to ensure that the hotel's computer system functions properly. Should the hotel's computer system fail, managers must continue to meet guests' needs.

Working Conditions

Because hotels are open around the clock, night and weekend work is common. Many hotel managers work more than 40 hours per week. Managers who live in the hotel usually have regular work schedules, but they may be called to work at any time. Some employees of resort hotels are managers during the busy season and have other duties during the rest of the year.

Hotel managers sometimes experience the pressures of coordinating a wide range of functions. Conventions and large groups of tourists may present unusual problems. Moreover, dealing with irate guests can be stressful. The job can be particularly hectic for front office managers during check-in and check-out time. Computer failures can further complicate an already busy time.

Employment

Hotel managers and assistant managers held about 76,000 jobs in 1998. Self-employed managers—primarily owners of small hotels and motels—held a significant number of these jobs. Companies that manage hotels and motels under contract employed some managers.

Training, Other Qualifications, and Advancement

Hotels increasingly emphasize specialized training. Post-secondary training in hotel or restaurant management is preferred for most hotel management positions, although a college liberal arts degree may be sufficient when coupled with related hotel experience. Internships or part-time or summer work is an asset to students seeking a career in hotel management. The experience gained and the contacts made with employers can greatly benefit them after graduation. Most bachelor's degree programs include work-study opportunities.

In the past, many managers were promoted from the ranks of front desk clerks, housekeepers, waiters and chefs, and hotel sales workers. Although some employees still advance to hotel management positions without education beyond high school, post-secondary education is preferred. Restaurant management training or experience is also a good background for entering hotel management because the success of a hotel's food service and beverage operations is often of great importance to the profitability of the entire establishment.

In 1998, nearly 200 community and junior colleges and some universities offered associate, bachelor's, and graduate degree programs in hotel or restaurant management. Combining that with technical institutes, vocational and trade schools, and other academic institutions, more than 800 educational facilities have programs leading to formal recognition in hotel or restaurant management. Hotel management programs include instruction in hotel administration, accounting, economics, marketing, housekeeping, food service management and catering, and hotel maintenance engineering. Computer training is also an integral part of hotel management training due to the widespread use of computers in reservations, billing, and housekeeping management.

Hotel managers must be able to get along with many different people, even in stressful situations. They must be able to solve problems and concentrate on details. Initiative, self-discipline, effective communication skills, and the ability to organize and direct the work of others are also essential for managers at all levels.

Most hotels promote employees who have proven their ability and completed formal education in hotel management. Graduates of hotel or restaurant management programs usually start as trainee assistant managers. Some large hotels sponsor specialized on-the-job management training programs allowing trainees to rotate among various departments and gain a thorough knowledge of the hotel's operation. Other hotels may help finance formal training in hotel management for outstanding employees. Newly built hotels, particularly those without well-established on-the-job training programs, often prefer experienced personnel for managerial positions.

Large hotel and motel chains may offer better opportunities for advancement than small, independently owned establishments, but relocation every several years often is necessary for advancement. The large chains have more extensive career ladder programs and offer managers the opportunity to transfer to another hotel or motel in the chain or to the central office. Career advancement can be accelerated by completion of certification programs offered by the associations listed below. These programs usually require a combination of course work, examinations, and experience.

Job Outlook

Employment of hotel managers and assistants is expected to grow more slowly than the average for all occupations through 2008. Long hours and stressful working conditions result in high turnover in this field, so additional job openings are expected to occur as experienced managers transfer to other occupations, retire, or stop working for other reasons. Job opportunities in hotel management are expected to be especially good for persons with college degrees in hotel or restaurant management.

Increasing business travel and domestic and foreign tourism will drive employment growth of hotel managers and assistants. Managerial jobs are not expected to grow as rapidly as the hotel industry overall, however. As the industry consolidates, many chains and franchises will acquire independently owned establishments and increase the number of economy-class rooms to accommodate bargain-conscious guests. Economy hotels offer clean, comfortable rooms and front desk services without costly extras like restaurants and room service. Because there are not as many departments in these hotels, fewer managers will be needed. In addition, front desk clerks are increasingly assuming some responsibilities previously reserved for managers, further limiting the growth of managers and their assistants.

Additional demand for managers, however, is expected in suite hotels as some guests, especially business customers, are willing to pay higher prices for rooms with kitchens and suites that provide the space needed to conduct meetings. In addition to job growth in suite hotels and economy-class hotels, large full-service hotels—offering restaurants, fitness centers, large meeting rooms, and play areas for children, among other amenities—will continue to offer many trainee and managerial opportunities.

Earnings

Median annual earnings of hotel managers and assistants were $26,700 in 1998. The middle 50 percent of these workers earned between $19,820 and $34,690. The lowest 10 percent had earnings of less than $14,430, while the top 10 percent earned more than $45,520. In 1997, median annual earnings in the hotel and other lodging places industry, where nearly all of these workers are employed, were $28,600.

Salaries of hotel managers and assistants vary greatly according to their responsibilities and the segment of the hotel industry in which they are employed. Managers may earn bonuses up to 25 percent of their basic salary in some hotels and may also be furnished with lodging, meals, parking, laundry, and other services. In addition to typical benefits, some hotels offer profit-sharing plans and educational assistance to their employees.

Related Occupations

Other occupations concerned with organizing and directing a business where customer service is the cornerstone of their success include restaurant managers, apartment building managers, retail store managers, and office managers.

Sources of Additional Information

For information on careers and scholarships in hotel management, contact:

- The American Hotel and Motel Association (AH&MA), Information Center, 1201 New York Ave. NW., Washington, DC 20005-3931.

Information on careers in the lodging industry and professional development and training programs may be obtained from:

- The Educational Institute of the American Hotel and Motel Association, P.O. Box 531126 Orlando, FL 32853-1126. Internet: http://www.ei-ahma.org

For information on educational programs, including correspondence courses, in hotel and restaurant management, write to:

- Council on Hotel, Restaurant, and Institutional Education, 1200 17th St. NW., Washington, DC 20036-3097.

Information on careers in housekeeping management may be obtained from:

- National Executive Housekeepers Association, Inc., 1001 Eastwind Dr., Suite 301, Westerville, OH 43081. Phone: (800) 200-6342.

Hotel, Motel, and Resort Desk Clerks

(O*NET 53808)

Significant Points

- A high school diploma or its equivalent is the most common educational requirement.

- Because these workers deal with the public, a professional appearance and pleasant personality are imperative.

Nature of the Work

Hotel, motel, and resort desk clerks perform a variety of services for guests of hotels, motels, and other lodging establishments. Regardless of the type of accommodation, most desk clerks have similar responsibilities. Primarily, they register arriving guests, assign rooms, and check guests out at the end of their stay. They also keep records of room assignments and other registration information on computers. When guests check out, they prepare and explain the charges, as well as process payments.

Front desk clerks are always in the public eye and, through their attitude and behavior, greatly influence the public's impressions

of the establishment. When answering questions about services, checkout times, the local community, or other matters of public interest, clerks must be courteous and helpful. Should guests report problems with their rooms, clerks contact members of the housekeeping or maintenance staff to correct them.

In some smaller hotels and motels, clerks may have a variety of additional responsibilities, usually performed by specialized employees in larger establishments. In these places, the desk clerk is often responsible for all front office operations, information, and services. These clerks, for example, may perform the work of a bookkeeper, advance reservation agent, cashier, laundry attendant, or telephone switchboard operator.

Working Conditions

Most clerks work in areas that are clean, well lit, and relatively quiet because they must greet customers and visitors. Although most clerks work a standard 40-hour week, many work part time. The job requires working evenings, late night shifts, weekends, and holidays. The work of hotel, motel, and resort desk clerks can be stressful when a worker is trying to serve the needs of difficult or angry customers. When guests are dissatisfied, these clerks must bear the brunt of the customers' anger. Hotel desk clerks may be on their feet most of the time.

Employment

Hotel, motel, and resort desk clerks held about 159,000 jobs in 1998. This occupation is well suited to flexible work schedules, as more than 1 in 4 desk clerks works part time. Because hotels and motels need to be staffed 24 hours a day, evening and weekend work is common.

Training, Other Qualifications, and Advancement

A high school diploma or its equivalent is the most common educational requirement. Increasingly, familiarity or experience with computers and good interpersonal skills are often equally important to employers.

Clerks deal directly with the public, so a professional appearance and pleasant personality are important. A clear speaking voice and fluency in the English language also are essential because these employees frequently use the telephone or public address systems. Good spelling and computer literacy are often needed, particularly because the work involves computer use. It also is increasingly helpful for those wishing to enter the lodging or travel industries to speak a foreign language fluently.

Orientation and training usually takes place on the job and usually includes an explanation of the job duties and information about the establishment, such as room locations and available services. New employees learn job tasks through on-the-job training under the guidance of a supervisor or an experienced clerk. They often need additional training in how to use the computerized reservation, room assignment, and billing systems and equipment. Most clerks continue to receive instruction on new procedures and company policies after their initial training ends.

Clerks can improve their chances for advancement by taking home or group study courses in lodging management, such as those sponsored by the Educational Institute of the American Hotel and Motel Association. Workers commonly are promoted through the ranks. A hotel and motel desk clerk position offers good opportunities for qualified workers to get started in the business. In a number of industries, a college degree may be required for advancement to management ranks.

Job Outlook

Employment of hotel, motel, and resort desk clerks is expected to grow about as fast as the average for all occupations through 2008 as more hotels, motels, and other lodging establishments are built and occupancy rates rise. Job opportunities for hotel and motel desk clerks will result from an unusually high turnover rate. These openings occur each year as thousands of workers transfer to other occupations that offer better pay and advancement opportunities or simply leave the work force altogether. Opportunities for part-time work should continue to be plentiful, as nearly all front desks are staffed 24 hours a day 7 days a week.

Employment of hotel and motel desk clerks should be favorably affected by an increase in business and leisure travel. Shifts in travel preference away from long vacations and toward long weekends and other, more frequent, shorter trips also should increase demand as this trend increases the total number of nights spent in hotels. The expansion of smaller budget hotels relative to larger luxury establishments reflects a change in the composition of the hotel and motel industry. As employment shifts from luxury hotels to more "no-frills" operations, the proportion of hotel desk clerks should increase in relation to staff such as waiters and waitresses and recreation workers.

However, the growing effort to cut labor costs while moving toward more efficient service is expected to slow the growth of desk clerk employment. The role of the front desk is changing as some of the more traditional duties are automated. New technologies automating check-in and check-out procedures now allow guests to bypass the front desk in many larger establishments, reducing staffing needs. The expansion of other technologies, such as interactive television and computer systems to dispense information, should further impact employment in the future as such services become more widespread.

Employment of desk clerks is sensitive to cyclical swings in the economy. During recessions, vacation and business travel declines, and hotels and motels need fewer clerks. Similarly, desk clerk employment is affected by seasonal fluctuations in travel during high and low tourist seasons.

Earnings

Median annual 1998 earnings for hotel, motel, and resort desk clerks were $15,160. Yet earnings vary considerably depending on the location, size, and type of establishment in which clerks work. For example, clerks at large luxury hotels and those located in metropolitan and resort areas generally pay clerks more than less-exclusive or "budget" establishments and those located in less-populated areas.

Related Occupations

A number of other workers deal with the public, receive and provide information, or direct people to others who can assist them. Among these are dispatchers, security guards, bank tellers, guides, telephone operators, records processing clerks, counter and rental clerks, survey workers, and ushers and lobby attendants.

Sources of Additional Information

Information on careers in the lodging industry, as well as information about professional development and training programs, may be obtained from:

- The Educational Institute of the American Hotel and Motel Association, P.O. Box 531126 Orlando, FL 32853-1126. Internet: http://www.ei-ahma.org

Human Resources Clerks, Except Payroll and Timekeeping

(O*NET 55314)

Significant Points

- Most jobs require only a high school diploma.
- Replacement needs will account for most job openings for human resources clerks.

Nature of the Work

Human resources clerks maintain the personnel records of an organization's employees. These records include information such as name, address, job title, and earnings, benefits such as health and life insurance, and tax withholding. On a daily basis, these clerks record and answer questions about employee absences and supervisory reports on job performance. When an employee receives a promotion or switches health insurance plans, the human resources clerk updates the appropriate form. Human resources clerks may also prepare reports for managers elsewhere within the organization. For example, they might compile a list of employees eligible for an award.

In smaller organizations, some human resources clerks perform a variety of other clerical duties. They answer telephone or letter inquiries from the public, send out announcements of job openings or job examinations, and issue application forms. When credit bureaus and finance companies request confirmation of a person's employment, the human resources clerk provides authorized information from the employee's personnel records. Payroll departments and insurance companies may also be contacted to verify changes to records.

Some human resources clerks are also involved in hiring. They screen job applicants to obtain information such as education and work experience; administer aptitude, personality, and interest tests; explain the organization's employment policies and refer qualified applicants to the employing official; and request references from present or past employers. Also, human resources clerks inform job applicants, by telephone or letter, of their acceptance or rejection for employment.

Other human resources clerks are known as assignment clerks. Their role is to notify a firm's existing employees of position vacancies and to identify and assign qualified applicants. They keep track of vacancies throughout the organization and complete and distribute vacancy advertisement forms. These clerks review applications in response to advertisements and verify information using personnel records. After a selection is made, they notify all the applicants of their acceptance or rejection.

In some job settings, human resources clerks have specific job titles. Identification clerks are responsible for security matters at defense installations. They compile and record personal data about vendors, contractors, and civilian and military personnel and their dependents. Job duties include interviewing applicants; corresponding with law enforcement authorities; and preparing badges, passes, and identification cards.

Working Conditions

Most clerks typically are employed in an office environment. Because the majority of clerks uses computers on a daily basis, these workers may experience eye and muscle strain, backaches, headaches, and repetitive motion injuries. Also, clerks who review detailed data may have to sit for extended periods of time. Most clerks work regular business hours.

Employment

Human resources clerks held about 142,000 jobs in 1998. Although these workers are found in most industries, about 1 in every 5 works for a government agency. Colleges and universities, hospitals, department stores, and banks also employ large numbers of human resources clerks.

Training, Other Qualifications, and Advancement

Employers typically require applicants to have at least a high school diploma or its equivalent, although many employers prefer to hire clerks with a higher level of education. Regardless of the type of work, most employers prefer workers who are computer-literate. Knowledge of word processing and spreadsheet software is especially valuable, as are experience working in an office and good interpersonal skills.

Clerks often learn the skills they need in high schools, business schools, and community colleges. Business education programs offered by these institutions typically include courses in typing, word processing, shorthand, business communications, records management, and office systems and procedures. Some entrants are college graduates. Although a degree is rarely required, many graduates accept entry-level positions to get into a particular company or to enter the field with the hope of being promoted to professional or managerial positions.

Once hired, clerks usually receive on-the-job training. Under the guidance of a supervisor or other senior worker, new employees learn company procedures. Some formal classroom training may also be necessary, such as training in specific computer software.

Clerks must be careful, orderly, and detail-oriented in order to avoid making errors and to recognize errors made by others. These workers should also be discreet and trustworthy because they frequently come in contact with confidential material.

Clerks usually advance by taking on more duties in the same occupation for higher pay or transferring to a closely related occupation. Most companies fill office and administrative support supervisory and managerial positions by promoting individuals from within their organizations, so clerks who acquire additional skills, experience, and training improve their advancement opportunities. With appropriate experience and education, some clerks may become personnel specialists.

Job Outlook

Replacement needs will account for most job openings for human resources clerks. Jobs will open up as clerks advance within the personnel department, take jobs unrelated to personnel administration, or leave the labor force. Little or no change is expected in employment of human resources clerks through the year 2008, largely due to the increased use of computers. The growing use of computers in personnel or human resource departments means that a lot of data entry done by human resources clerks can be eliminated, as employees themselves enter the data and send it to the personnel office. This is most feasible in large organizations with multiple personnel offices. The increasing use of computers and other automated office equipment by managers and professionals in personnel offices also could mean less work for human resources clerks.

Earnings

Salaries of human resources clerks vary. The region of the country, size of city, and type and size of establishment all influence salary levels. The level of industry or technical expertise required and the complexity and uniqueness of a clerk's responsibilities may also affect earnings. Median annual earnings of full-time human resources clerks in 1998 were $24,360. The average salary for all human resources clerks employed by the Federal government was $29,500 in 1999.

Related Occupations

Today, most clerks enter data into a computer system and perform basic analysis of the information. Other clerical workers who enter and manipulate data include bank tellers, statistical clerks, receiving clerks, medical record clerks, hotel and motel clerks, credit clerks, and reservation and transportation ticket agents.

Sources of Additional Information

State employment service offices can provide information about job openings for this occupation.

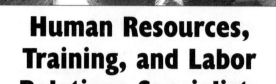

Human Resources, Training, and Labor Relations Specialists and Managers

(O*NET 13005A, 13005B, 13005C, 13005E, 21511A, 21511B, 21511C, 21511D, 21511E, and 21511F)

Significant Points

- Employers usually seek college graduates for entry-level jobs.

- Depending on the job duties, a strong background in human resources, business, technical, or liberal arts subjects may be preferred.

- The job market is likely to remain competitive because of the abundant supply of qualified college graduates and experienced workers.

Nature of the Work

Attracting the most qualified employees and matching them to the jobs for which they are best suited is important for the success of any organization. However, many enterprises are too large to permit close contact between top management and employees. Human resources, training, and labor relations specialists and managers provide this link. These individuals recruit and interview employees and advise on hiring decisions in accordance with policies and requirements that have been established in conjunction with top management. In an effort to improve morale and productivity and limit job turnover, they also help their firms effectively use employee skills, provide training opportunities to enhance those skills, and boost employee satisfaction with their jobs and working conditions. Although some jobs in the human resources field require only limited contact with people outside the office, dealing with people is an essential part of the job.

In a small organization, a *human resources generalist* may handle all aspects of human resources work, requiring a broad range of knowledge. The responsibilities of human resources generalists can vary widely, depending on their employer's needs. In a large corporation, the top human resources executive usually develops and coordinates personnel programs and policies. These policies are usually implemented by a director or manager of human resources and, in some cases, a director of industrial relations.

The *director of human resources* may oversee several departments, each headed by an experienced manager, who most likely specializes in one personnel activity such as employment, compensation, benefits, training and development, or employee relations.

Employment and placement managers oversee the hiring and separation of employees and supervise various workers, including equal employment opportunity specialists and recruitment specialists.

Recruiters maintain contacts within the community and may travel extensively, often to college campuses, to search for promising job applicants. Recruiters screen, interview, and in some cases, test applicants. They may also check references and extend job offers. These workers must be thoroughly familiar with the organization and its personnel policies to discuss wages, working conditions, and promotional opportunities with prospective employees. They must also keep informed about equal employment opportunity (EEO) and affirmative action guidelines and laws, such as the Americans With Disabilities Act.

EEO officers, representatives, or *affirmative action coordinators* handle this area in large organizations. They investigate and resolve EEO grievances, examine corporate practices for possible violations, and compile and submit EEO statistical reports.

Employer relations representatives, who usually work in government agencies, maintain working relationships with local employers and promote the use of public employment programs and services. Similarly, *employment interviewers*—whose many job titles include *personnel consultants, personnel development specialists,* and *human resources coordinators*—help match jobseekers with employers.

Job analysts, sometimes called *position classifiers,* perform very exacting work. They collect and examine detailed information about job duties to prepare job descriptions. These descriptions explain the duties, training, and skills each job requires. Whenever a large organization introduces a new job or reviews existing jobs, it calls upon the expert knowledge of the job analyst.

Occupational analysts conduct research, usually in large firms. They are concerned with occupational classification systems and study the effects of industry and occupational trends upon worker relationships. They may serve as technical liaisons between the firm and industry, government, and labor unions.

Establishing and maintaining a firm's pay system is the principal job of the *compensation manager.* Assisted by staff specialists, compensation managers devise ways to ensure fair and equitable pay rates. They may conduct surveys to see how their rates compare with others and to see that the firm's pay scale complies with changing laws and regulations. In addition, compensation managers often oversee their firm's performance evaluation system, and they may design reward systems such as pay-for-performance plans.

Employee benefits managers handle the company's employee benefits program, notably its health insurance and pension plans. Expertise in designing and administering benefits programs continues to gain importance as employer-provided benefits account for a growing proportion of overall compensation costs, and as benefit plans increase in number and complexity. For example, pension benefits might include savings and thrift, profit sharing, and stock ownership plans; health benefits may include long-term cata-

strophic illness insurance and dental insurance. Familiarity with health benefits is a top priority, as more firms struggle to cope with the rising cost of health care for employees and retirees. In addition to health insurance and pension coverage, some firms offer employees life and accidental death and dismemberment insurance, disability insurance, and relatively new benefits designed to meet the needs of a changing work force, such as parental leave, child and elder care, long-term nursing home care insurance, employee assistance and wellness programs, and flexible benefits plans. Benefits managers must keep abreast of changing Federal and State regulations and legislation that may affect employee benefits.

Employee assistance plan managers, also called *employee welfare managers,* are responsible for a wide array of programs covering occupational safety and health standards and practices; health promotion and physical fitness, medical examinations, and minor health treatment, such as first aid; plant security; publications; food service and recreation activities; car pooling and transportation programs, such as transit subsidies; employee suggestion systems; child and elder care; and counseling services. Child care and elder care are increasingly important due to growth in the number of dual-income households and the elderly population. Counseling may help employees deal with emotional disorders, alcoholism, and marital, family, consumer, legal, and financial problems. Some employers offer career counseling as well. In large firms, certain programs, such as security and safety, may be in separate departments headed by other managers.

Training and development managers supervise training. Increasingly, management recognizes that training offers a way of developing skills, enhancing productivity and quality of work, and building loyalty to the firm. Training is widely accepted as a method of improving employee morale, but this is only one of the reasons for its growing importance. Other factors include the complexity of the work environment, the rapid pace of organizational and technological change, and the growing number of jobs in fields that constantly generate new knowledge. In addition, advances in learning theory have provided insights into how adults learn, and how training can be organized most effectively for them.

Training specialists plan, organize, and direct a wide range of training activities. Trainers conduct orientation sessions and arrange on-the-job training for new employees. They help rank-and-file workers maintain and improve their job skills and possibly prepare for jobs requiring greater skill. They help supervisors improve their interpersonal skills in order to deal effectively with employees. They may set up individualized training plans to strengthen an employee's existing skills or teach new ones. Training specialists in some companies set up programs to develop executive potential among employees in lower-level positions. In government-supported training programs, training specialists function as case managers. They first assess the training needs of clients and then guide them through the most appropriate training method. After training, clients may either be referred to employer relations representatives or receive job placement assistance.

Planning and program development is an important part of the training specialist's job. In order to identify and assess training needs within the firm, trainers may confer with managers and supervisors or conduct surveys. They also periodically evaluate training effectiveness.

Depending on the size, goals, and nature of the organization, trainers may differ considerably in their responsibilities and in the methods they use. Training methods include on-the-job training; schools in which shop conditions are duplicated for trainees prior to putting them on the shop floor; apprenticeship training; classroom training; programmed instruction, which may involve interactive videos and other computer-aided instructional technologies; simulators; conferences; and workshops.

The *director of industrial relations* forms labor policy, oversees industrial labor relations, negotiates collective bargaining agreements, and coordinates grievance procedures to handle complaints resulting from disputes with unionized employees. The director of industrial relations also advises and collaborates with the director of human resources, other managers, and members of their staff, because all aspects of personnel policy—such as wages, benefits, pensions, and work practices—may be involved in drawing up a new or revised contract.

Labor relations managers and their staff implement industrial labor relations programs. When a collective bargaining agreement is up for negotiation, labor relations specialists prepare information for management to use during negotiation, which requires familiarity with economic and wage data as well as extensive knowledge of labor law and collective bargaining trends. The labor relations staff interprets and administers the contract with respect to grievances, wages and salaries, employee welfare, health care, pensions, union and management practices, and other contractual stipulations. As union membership continues to decline in most industries, industrial relations personnel work more with employees who are not members of a labor union.

Dispute resolution—attaining tacit or contractual agreements—has become increasingly important as parties to a dispute attempt to avoid costly litigation, strikes, or other disruptions. Dispute resolution also has become more complex, involving employees, management, unions, other firms, and government agencies. Specialists involved in dispute resolution must be highly knowledgeable and experienced and often report to the director of industrial relations. *Conciliators*, or *mediators*, advise and counsel labor and management to prevent and, when necessary, resolve disputes over labor agreements or other labor relations issues. *Arbitrators*, sometimes called umpires or referees, decide disputes that bind both labor and management to specific terms and conditions of labor contracts. Labor relations specialists who work for unions perform many of the same functions on behalf of the union and its members.

Other emerging specialists include *international human resources managers*, who handle human resources issues related to a company's foreign operations, and *human resources information system specialists*, who develop and apply computer programs to process personnel information, match jobseekers with job openings, and handle other personnel matters.

Working Conditions

Personnel work usually takes place in clean, pleasant, and comfortable office settings. Arbitrators and mediators may work out of their homes. Many human resources, training, and labor relations specialists and managers work a standard 35- to 40-hour week. However, longer hours might be necessary for some workers—for example, labor relations specialists and managers, arbitrators, and mediators—when contract agreements are being prepared and negotiated.

Although most human resources, training, and labor relations specialists and managers work in the office, some travel extensively. For example, recruiters regularly attend professional meetings and visit college campuses to interview prospective employees; arbitrators and mediators often must travel to the site chosen for negotiations.

Employment

Human resources, training, and labor relations specialists and managers held about 597,000 jobs in 1998. They were employed in virtually every industry. Specialists accounted for 3 out of 5 positions and managers for 2 out of 5. About 14,000 specialists were self-employed, working as consultants to public and private employers.

The private sector accounted for about 80 percent of salaried jobs. Among these salaried jobs, services industries—including business, health, social, management, and educational services—accounted for about 40 percent of jobs. Labor organizations, the largest employer among specific services industries, accounted for more than 20 percent of those. Manufacturing industries accounted for 17 percent of salaried jobs, while finance, insurance, and real estate firms accounted for about 11 percent of jobs.

Federal, State, and local governments employed about 14 percent of human resources specialists and managers. They handled the recruitment, interviewing, job classification, training, salary administration, benefits, employee relations, and related matters of the Nation's public employees.

Training, Other Qualifications, and Advancement

Because of the diversity of duties and level of responsibility, the educational backgrounds of human resources, training, and labor relations specialists and managers vary considerably. When filling entry-level jobs, employers usually seek college graduates. Many employers prefer applicants who have majored in human resources, personnel administration, or industrial and labor relations. Others look for college graduates with a technical or business background or a well-rounded liberal arts education.

Many colleges and universities have programs leading to a degree in personnel, human resources, or labor relations. Some offer degree programs in personnel administration or human resources management, training and development, or compensation and benefits. Depending on the school, courses leading to a career in human resources management may be found in departments of business administration, education, instructional technology, organizational development, human services, communication, or public administration or within a separate human resources institution or department.

Because an interdisciplinary background is appropriate in this field, a combination of courses in the social sciences, business, and behavioral sciences is useful. Some jobs may require a more technical or specialized background in engineering, science, finance, or law, for example. Most prospective human resources specialists should take courses in compensation, recruitment, training and development, and performance appraisal, as well as courses in principles of management, organizational structure, and industrial psychology. Other relevant courses include business administration, public administration, psychology, sociology, political science, economics, and statistics. Courses in labor law, collective bargaining, labor economics, labor history, and industrial psychology also provide a valuable background for the prospective labor relations specialist. As in many other fields, knowledge of computers and information systems is also useful.

An advanced degree is increasingly important for some jobs. Many labor relations jobs require graduate study in industrial or labor relations. A strong background in industrial relations and law is highly desirable for contract negotiators, mediators, and arbitrators; in fact, many people in these specialties are lawyers. A background in law is also desirable for employee benefits managers and others who must interpret the growing number of laws and regulations. A master's degree in human resources, labor relations, or in business administration with a concentration in human resources management is highly recommended for those seeking general and top management positions.

For many specialized jobs in the human resources field, previous experience is an asset; for more advanced positions (including managers, as well as arbitrators and mediators), it is essential. Many employers prefer entry-level workers who have gained some experience through an internship or work-study program while in school. Personnel administration and human resources development require the ability to work with individuals as well as a commitment to organizational goals. This field also demands other skills people may develop elsewhere—using computers, selling, teaching, supervising, and volunteering, among others. This field offers clerical workers opportunities for advancement to professional positions. Responsible positions are sometimes filled by experienced individuals from other fields, including business, government, education., social services administration, and the military.

The human resources field demands a range of personal qualities and skills. Human resources, training, and labor relations specialists and managers must speak and write effectively. The growing diversity of the workforce requires that they work with or supervise people with various cultural backgrounds, levels of education, and experience. They must be able to cope with conflicting points of view, function under pressure, and demonstrate discretion, integrity, fair-mindedness, and a persuasive, congenial personality.

The duties given to entry-level workers will vary depending on whether they have a degree in human resource management, have completed an internship, or have some other type of human resources-related experience. Entry-level employees commonly learn the profession by performing administrative duties, such as helping to enter data into computer systems, compiling employee handbooks, researching information for a supervisor, or answering the phone and handling routine questions. Entry-level workers often enter formal or on-the-job training programs in which they learn how to classify jobs, interview applicants, or administer employee benefits. They then are assigned to specific areas in the personnel department to gain experience. Later, they may advance to a managerial position, overseeing a major element of the personnel program—compensation or training, for example.

Exceptional human resources workers may be promoted to director of personnel or industrial relations, which can eventually lead to a top managerial or executive position. Others may join a consulting firm or open their own business. A Ph.D. is an asset for teaching, writing, or consulting work.

Most organizations specializing in human resources offer classes intended to enhance the marketable skills of their members. Some organizations offer certification programs, which are signs of competence and can enhance one's advancement opportunities. For example, the International Foundation of Employee Benefit Plans confers the Certified Employee Benefit Specialist designation to persons who complete a series of college-level courses and pass exams covering employee benefit plans. The Society for Human Resources Management has two levels of certification: Professional in Human Resources, and Senior Professional in Human Resources. Both require experience and a comprehensive exam.

Job Outlook

The job market for human resources, training, and labor relations specialists and managers is likely to remain competitive given the abundant supply of qualified college graduates and experienced workers. In addition to openings due to growth, many job openings will result from the need to replace workers who transfer to other occupations or leave the labor force.

Employment of human resources, training, and labor relations specialists and managers is expected to grow about as fast as the average for all occupations through 2008. New jobs will stem from increasing efforts throughout industry to recruit and retain quality employees. Employers are expected to devote greater resources to job-specific training programs in response to the increasing complexity of many jobs, the aging of the work force, and technological advances that can leave employees with obsolete skills. In addition, legislation and court rulings setting standards in various areas—occupational safety and health, equal employment opportunity, wages, health, pension, and family leave, among others—will increase demand for human resources, training, and labor relations experts. Rising health care costs, in particular, should spur demand for specialists to develop creative compensation and benefits packages that firms can offer prospective employees. Employment of labor relations staff, including arbitrators and mediators, should grow as firms become more involved in labor relations and attempt to resolve potentially costly labor-management disputes out of court. Additional job growth may stem from increasing demand for specialists in international human resources management and human resources information systems.

Employment demand should be strong among firms involved in management, consulting, and personnel supply, as businesses increasingly contract out personnel functions or hire personnel specialists on a temporary basis to meet the increasing cost and complexity of training and development programs. Demand should also increase in firms that develop and administer complex employee benefits and compensation packages for other organizations.

Demand for human resources, training, and labor relations specialists and managers is also governed by the staffing needs of the firms for which they work. A rapidly expanding business is likely to hire additional human resources workers either as permanent

employees or consultants, while a business that has experienced a merger or a reduction in its work force will require fewer human resources workers. Also, as human resources management becomes increasingly important to the success of an organization, some small and medium-size businesses that do not have a human resources department may assign employees various human resources duties together with other unrelated responsibilities. In any particular firm, the size and the job duties of the human resources staff are determined by the firm's organizational philosophy and goals, skills of its work force, pace of technological change, government regulations, collective bargaining agreements, standards of professional practice, and labor market conditions.

Job growth could be limited by the widespread use of computerized human resources information systems that make workers more productive. Similar to other workers, employment of human resources, training, and labor relations specialists and managers, particularly in larger firms, may be adversely affected by corporate downsizing and restructuring.

Earnings

Median annual earnings of human resources managers were $49,010 in 1998. The middle 50 percent earned between $35,400 and $73,830. The lowest 10 percent earned less than $25,750, and the highest 10 percent earned more than $91,040. Median annual earnings in the industries employing the largest numbers of human resources managers in 1997 were:

Local government, except education and hospitals	$50,800
Hospitals	48,200
Management and public relations	44,800
Labor organizations	36,700
Personnel supply services	35,900

Median annual earnings of human resources, training, and labor relations specialists were $37,710 in 1998. The middle 50 percent earned between $28,200 and $50,160. The lowest 10 percent earned less than $20,310, and the highest 10 percent earned more than $75,440. Median annual earnings in the industries employing the largest numbers of human resources, training, and labor relations specialists in 1997 were:

Federal government	$51,800
Local government, except education and hospitals	39,900
Hospitals	35,000
State government, except education and hospitals	34,100
Labor organizations	29,700

According to a 1999 salary survey conducted by the National Association of Colleges and Employers, bachelor's degree candidates majoring in human resources, including labor relations, received starting offers averaging $29,800 a year.

According to a November 1998 survey of compensation in the human resources field, conducted by Abbott, Langer, and Associates of Crete, Illinois, the median total cash compensation for selected personnel and labor relations occupations were:

Industrial and labor relations directors	$183,900
Compensation and benefits directors	88,000
Divisional human resources directors	84,100
Training directors	79,400
Recruitment and interviewing managers	75,100
Employee and community relations directors	73,500
Plant/location human resources managers	62,000
Compensation supervisors	53,300
Human resources information systems specialists	49,300
Employee assistance and employee counseling specialists	47,500
Employee services and employee recreation specialists	47,300
Employee and industrial plant nurses	46,000
EEO and affirmative action specialists	44,800
Safety specialists	43,700
Training material development specialists	43,500
Benefits specialists (managerial and professional jobs)	41,500
Training generalists (computer)	39,600
Classroom instructors	35,300
Employment interviewing specialists	35,100
Job evaluation specialists	34,100
Human resources records specialists	32,400

In the Federal government, persons with a bachelor's degree or three years' general experience in the personnel field generally started at $23,300 a year in 1999. Those with a superior academic record or an additional year of specialized experience started at $28,000 a year. Those with a master's degree may start at $33,400, and those with a doctorate in a personnel field may start at $44,500. Beginning salaries were slightly higher in areas where the prevailing local pay level was higher. There are no formal entry-level requirements for managerial positions. Applicants must possess a suitable combination of educational attainment, experience, and record of accomplishment.

Related Occupations

All human resources occupations are closely related. Other workers with skills and expertise in interpersonal relations include counselors, lawyers, psychologists, sociologists, social workers, public relations specialists, and teachers.

Sources of Additional Information

For information about careers in employee training and development, contact:

- American Society for Training and Development, 1640 King St., Box 1443, Alexandria, VA 22313. Internet: http://www.astd.org

For information about careers and certification in employee compensation and benefits, contact:

- American Compensation Association, 14040 Northsight Blvd., Scottsdale, AZ 85260. Internet: http://www.acaonline.org

Information about careers and certification in employee benefits is available from:

- International Foundation of Employee Benefit Plans, 18700 W. Bluemound Rd., P.O. Box 69, Brookfield, WI 53008-0069. Internet: http://www.ifebp.org

For information about academic programs in industrial relations, write to:

- Industrial Relations Research Association, University of Wisconsin, 7226 Social Science Bldg., 1180 Observatory Dr., Madison, WI 53706. Internet: http://www.irra.ssc.wisc.edu

Information about personnel careers in the health care industry is available from:

- American Society for Healthcare Human Resources Administration, One North Franklin, 31st Floor, Chicago, IL 60606. Internet: http://www.ashhra.org

Industrial Production Managers

(O*NET 15014)

Significant Points

- The projected decline in employment reflects increasing productivity and organizational restructuring.

- Applicants with college degrees in industrial engineering, management, or business administration, and particularly those with an undergraduate engineering degree and a master's degree in business administration, enjoy the best job prospects.

Nature of the Work

Industrial production managers coordinate the resources and activities required to produce millions of goods every year in the United States. Although their duties vary from plant to plant, industrial production managers share many of the same major responsibilities. These include production scheduling, staffing, equipment, quality control, inventory control, and the coordination of production activities with those of other departments.

The primary mission of industrial production managers is planning the production schedule within budgetary limitations and time constraints. This entails analyzing the plant's personnel and capital resources to select the best way of meeting the production quota. Industrial production managers determine which machines will be used, whether overtime or extra shifts are necessary, and the sequence of production. They also monitor the production run to make sure it stays on schedule, and they correct any problems that may arise.

Industrial production managers must also monitor product standards. When quality drops below the established standard, they must determine why standards are not being maintained and how to improve the product. If the problem is poor work, the manager may implement better training programs, reorganize the manufacturing process, or institute employee suggestion or involvement programs. If the cause is substandard materials, the manager works with the purchasing department to improve the quality of the product's components.

Because the work of many departments is interrelated, managers work closely with heads of other departments such as sales, purchasing, and traffic to plan and implement company goals, policies, and procedures. For example, the production manager works with the purchasing department to ensure that plant inventories are maintained at their optimal level. This is vital to a firm's operation because maintaining the inventory of materials necessary for production ties up the firm's financial resources, yet insufficient quantities cause delays in production. A breakdown in communications between the production manager and the purchasing department can cause slowdowns and a failure to meet production schedules. Computers are important in this coordination and also in providing up-to-date information on inventory, work-in-progress, and quality standards.

Production managers usually report to the plant manager or the vice president for manufacturing, and they may act as liaisons between executives and first-line supervisors. In many plants, one production manager is responsible for all aspects of production. In large plants with several operations—aircraft assembly, for example—there is a manager in charge of each operation, such as machining, assembly, or finishing.

Working Conditions

Most industrial production managers divide their time between the shop floor and their offices. While on the floor, they must follow established health and safety practices and wear the required protective clothing and equipment. The time in the office, which is often located on or near the production floor, is usually spent meeting with subordinates or other department managers, analyzing production data, and writing and reviewing reports.

Most industrial production managers work more than 40 hours a week, especially when production deadlines must be met. In facilities that operate around the clock, managers often work late shifts and may be called at any hour to deal with emergencies. This could mean going to the plant to resolve the problem, regardless of the hour, and staying until the situation is under control. Dealing with production workers as well as superiors when working under the pressure of production deadlines or emergency situations can be stressful. Restructuring has eliminated levels of management and support staff, which shifts more responsibilities to production managers and compounds this stress.

Employment

Industrial production managers held about 208,000 jobs in 1998. Although employed throughout the manufacturing sector, about one half are employed in firms that produce industrial machinery and equipment, transportation equipment, electronic and electrical equipment, fabricated metal products, instruments and related products, and food products. Production managers work in all parts

of the country, but jobs are most plentiful in areas where manufacturing is concentrated.

Training, Other Qualifications, and Advancement

Because of the diversity of manufacturing operations and job requirements, there is no standard preparation for this occupation. Many industrial production managers have a college degree in business administration, management, or industrial engineering. Others have a master's degree in business administration (MBA). Some are former production line supervisors who have been promoted. Although many employers prefer candidates with a business or engineering background, some companies hire well-rounded liberal arts graduates.

As production operations become more sophisticated, an increasing number of employers are looking for candidates with MBAs. Combined with an undergraduate degree in engineering, this is considered particularly good preparation. Companies also are placing greater importance on a candidate's personality. Because the job requires the ability to compromise, persuade, and negotiate, successful production managers must be well-rounded and have excellent communication skills.

Those who enter the field directly from college or graduate school often are unfamiliar with the firm's production process. As a result, they may spend their first few months on the job in the company's training program. These programs familiarize trainees with the production line, company policies, and the requirements of the job. In larger companies, they may also include assignments to other departments, such as purchasing and accounting. A number of companies hire college graduates as blue-collar worker supervisors and later promote them.

Some industrial production managers have worked their way up the ranks, perhaps after having worked as blue-collar worker supervisors. These workers already have an intimate knowledge of the production process and the firm's organization. To be selected for promotion, they must have demonstrated leadership qualities and usually have taken company-sponsored courses in management skills and communication techniques.

In addition to formal training, industrial production managers must keep informed of new production technologies and management practices. Many belong to professional organizations and attend trade shows where new equipment is displayed; they also attend industry conferences and conventions where changes in production methods and technological advances are discussed.

Industrial production managers with a proven record of superior performance may advance to plant manager or vice president for manufacturing. Others transfer to jobs at larger firms with more responsibilities. Opportunities also exist as consultants.

Job Outlook

Employment of industrial production managers is expected to decline slightly through 2008. However, a number of job openings will stem from the need to replace workers who transfer to other occupations or leave the labor force. Applicants with a college degree in industrial engineering, management, or business administration, and particularly those with an undergraduate engineering degree and a master's degree in business administration, enjoy the best job prospects. Employers also are likely to seek candidates who have excellent communication skills and who are personable, flexible, and eager to enhance their knowledge and skills through ongoing training.

Although manufacturing output is projected to rise, growing productivity among production managers and organizational restructuring will limit the demand for these workers. Productivity gains will result from the increasing use of computers for scheduling, planning, and coordination. Scheduling or planning has become less important as manufacturers have become more responsive to changing demand. In addition, a growing emphasis on quality in the production process has redistributed some of the production manager's oversight responsibilities to supervisors and workers on the production line. Because production managers are so essential to the efficient operation of a plant, they have not been greatly affected by recent efforts to flatten management structures. Nevertheless, this trend has led production managers to assume more responsibilities and has discouraged the creation of more employment opportunities.

Earnings

Median annual earnings for industrial production managers in 1998 were $56,320. The middle 50 percent earned between $41,300 and $79,830. The lowest 10 percent earned less than $31,790, and the highest 10 percent earned more than $97,310. Median annual earnings in the manufacturing industries employing the largest numbers of industrial production managers in 1997 were

Motor vehicles	$68,700
Electronic components and accessories	59,700
Miscellaneous plastics products, not elsewhere classified	48,500
Fabricated structural metal products	46,400
Commercial printing	45,800

Salaries of industrial production managers vary significantly by industry and plant size. According to Abbott, Langer, and Associates, the average salary for all production managers was $50,400 in 1998. In addition to salary, industrial production managers may receive bonuses based on job performance.

Related Occupations

Industrial production managers oversee production staff and equipment, ensure that production goals and quality standards are being met, and implement company policies. Individuals with similar functions include materials, operations, purchasing, and transportation managers. Other occupations requiring similar training and skills are sales engineer, manufacturer's sales representative, materials engineer, and industrial engineer.

Sources of Additional Information

Information on industrial production management can be obtained from:

- National Management Association, 2210 Arbor Blvd., Dayton, OH 45439. Internet: http://www.nma1.org

- American Management Association, 1601 Broadway, 10th Floor, New York, NY 10019. Internet: http://www.amanet.org

Information Clerks

Significant Points

- Numerous job openings should arise for most types of information clerks due to employment growth and high turnover.

- A high school diploma or its equivalent is the most common educational requirement.

- Because many information clerks deal directly with the public, a professional appearance and pleasant personality are imperative.

Nature of the Work

Information clerks are found in nearly every industry in the Nation, gathering data and providing information to the public. The specific duties of these clerks vary as widely as the job titles they hold. *Hotel, motel, and resort desk clerks,* for example, are a guest's first contact for check-in, check-out, and other services within hotels, motels, and resorts. *Interviewing and new account clerks,* found most often in medical facilities, research firms, and financial institutions, assist the public in completing forms, applications, or questionnaires. *Receptionists* are often a visitor's or caller's first contact within an organization, providing information and routing calls. *Reservation and transportation ticket agents and travel clerks* assist the public in making travel plans, making reservations, and purchasing tickets for a variety of transportation services.

Although their day-to-day duties vary widely, most information clerks greet customers, guests, or other visitors. Many also answer telephones and either obtain information from or provide information to the public. Most information clerks use multiline telephones, fax machines, and personal computers. This section, which contains an overall discussion of information clerks, is followed by separate sections providing additional information on the four types of clerks identified above.

Working Conditions

Working conditions vary for different types of information clerks, but most clerks work in areas that are clean, well lit, and relatively quiet. This is especially true for information clerks who greet customers and visitors and usually work in highly visible areas that are furnished to make a good impression. Reservation agents and interviewing clerks who spend much of their day talking on the telephone, however, commonly work away from the public, often in large centralized reservation or phone centers. Because a num-

ber of agents or clerks may share the same workspace, it may be crowded and noisy. Interviewing clerks may conduct surveys on the street, in shopping malls, or door to door.

Although most information clerks work a standard 40-hour week, about 3 out of 10 work part time. Some high school and college students work part time as information clerks, after school or during vacations. Some jobs (such as those in the transportation industry—hospitals and hotels in particular) may require working evenings, late night shifts, weekends, and holidays. This is also the case for a growing number of new accounts clerks who work for large banks with call centers that are staffed around the clock. Interviewing clerks conducting surveys or other research may mainly work evenings or weekends. In general, employees with the least seniority tend to be assigned the less desirable shifts.

The work performed by information clerks may be repetitious and stressful. For example, many receptionists spend all day answering telephones while performing additional clerical or secretarial tasks. Reservation agents and travel clerks work under stringent time constraints or have quotas on the number of calls answered or reservations made. Additional stress is caused by technology that enables management to electronically monitor use of computer systems, tape record telephone calls, or limit the time spent on each call.

The work of hotel, motel, and resort desk clerks and transportation ticket agents also can be stressful when a worker is trying to serve the needs of difficult or angry customers. When flights are canceled, reservations are mishandled, or guests are dissatisfied, these clerks must bear the brunt of the customers' anger. Hotel desk clerks and ticket agents may be on their feet most of the time, and ticket agents may have to lift heavy baggage. In addition, prolonged exposure to a video display terminal may lead to eyestrain for the many information clerks who work with computers.

Employment

Information clerks held more than 1.9 million jobs in 1998. The following table shows employment for the individual occupations.

Receptionists	1,293,000
Interviewing and new account clerks	239,000
Reservation and transportation ticket agents and travel clerks	218,000
Hotel, motel, and resort desk clerks	159,000

Although information clerks are found in a variety of industries, employment is concentrated in hotels and motels, health services, banks and savings institutions, transportation, and firms providing business or real estate services.

Training, Other Qualifications, and Advancement

Although hiring requirements for information clerk jobs vary from industry to industry, a high school diploma or its equivalent is the most common educational requirement. Increasingly, familiarity or experience with computers and good interpersonal skills are often equally important to employers. For new account clerk and

airline reservation and ticket agent jobs, some college education may be preferred.

Many information clerks deal directly with the public, so a professional appearance and pleasant personality are important. A clear speaking voice and fluency in the English language also are essential because these employees frequently use the telephone or public address systems. Good spelling and computer literacy are often needed, particularly because most work involves considerable computer use. It also is increasingly helpful for those wishing to enter the lodging or travel industries to speak a foreign language fluently.

With the exception of airline reservation and transportation ticket agents, orientation and training for information clerks usually takes place on the job. For example, orientation for hotel and motel desk clerks usually includes an explanation of the job duties and information about the establishment, such as room locations and available services. New employees learn job tasks through on-the-job training under the guidance of a supervisor or an experienced clerk. They often need additional training in how to use the computerized reservation, room assignment, and billing systems and equipment. Most information clerks continue to receive instruction on new procedures and company policies after their initial training ends.

Receptionists usually receive on-the-job training, which may include procedures for greeting visitors, operating telephone and computer systems, and distributing mail, fax, and parcel deliveries. Some employers look for applicants who already possess certain skills, such as prior computer and word processing experience or previous formal education.

Most airline reservation and ticket agents learn their skills through formal company training programs. In a classroom setting, they learn company and industry policies, computer systems, and ticketing procedures. They also learn to use the airline's computer system to obtain information on schedules, seat availability, and fares; to reserve space for passengers; and to plan passenger itineraries. They must also become familiar with airport and airline code designations, regulations, and safety procedures, and they may be tested on this knowledge. After completing classroom instruction, new agents work on the job with supervisors or experienced agents for a period of time. During this period, supervisors may monitor telephone conversations to improve the quality of customer service. Agents are expected to provide good service while limiting the time spent on each call without being discourteous to customers. In contrast to the airlines, automobile clubs, bus lines, and railroads tend to train their ticket agents or travel clerks on the job through short in-house classes that last several days.

Most banks prefer to hire college graduates for new account clerk positions. Nevertheless, many new accounts clerks without college degrees start out as bank tellers and are promoted by demonstrating excellent communication skills and motivation to learn new skills. If a new accounts clerk has not been a teller before, he or she will often receive such training and work for several months as a teller. In both cases, new accounts clerks undergo formal training regarding the bank's procedures, products, and services.

Advancement for information clerks usually comes about either by transfer to a position with more responsibilities or by promotion to a supervisory position. Most companies fill office and ad-

ministrative support supervisory and managerial positions by promoting individuals within their organization, so information clerks who acquire additional skills, experience, and training improve their advancement opportunities. Receptionists, interviewers, and new accounts clerks with word processing or other clerical skills may advance to a better paying job as a secretary or administrative assistant. Within the airline industry, a ticket agent may advance to lead worker on the shift.

Additional training is helpful in preparing information clerks for promotion. In the lodging industry, clerks can improve their chances for advancement by taking home or group study courses in lodging management, such as those sponsored by the Educational Institute of the American Hotel and Motel Association. In some industries—such as lodging, banking, or the airlines—workers commonly are promoted through the ranks. Positions such as airline reservation agent or hotel and motel desk clerk offer good opportunities for qualified workers to get started in the business. In a number of industries, a college degree may be required for advancement to management ranks.

Job Outlook

Overall employment of information clerks is expected to grow about as fast as average for all occupations through 2008. In addition to many openings occurring as businesses and organizations expand, numerous job openings for information clerks will result from the need to replace experienced workers who transfer to other occupations or leave the labor force. Replacement needs are expected to be especially large in this occupation due to high turnover because many young people work as information clerks for a few years before switching to other, higher paying jobs. The occupation is well suited to flexible work schedules, and many opportunities for part-time work will continue to be available, particularly as organizations attempt to cut labor costs by hiring more part-time or temporary workers.

The outlook for different types of information clerks is expected to vary in the coming decade. Economic growth and general business expansion are expected to stimulate faster than average growth among receptionists. Hotel, motel, and resort desk clerks are expected to grow faster than the average, as the composition of the lodging industry changes and services provided by these workers expand. Employment of interviewing clerks will also grow faster than average as these workers benefit from rapid growth in the health services industry, while average growth is expected among new accounts clerks as more of their functions are provided electronically. Much of this growth, however, will be due to an increase in part-time and temporary jobs. Reservation and transportation ticket agents and travel clerks are expected to grow more slowly than average due to productivity gains brought by technology and the increasing use of the Internet for travel services.

Earnings

Earnings vary widely by occupation and experience. Annual earnings ranged from less than $11,750 for the lowest paid 10 percent of hotel clerks to more than $39,540 for the top 10 percent of reservation agents in 1998. Salaries of reservation and transportation ticket agents and travel clerks tend to be significantly higher than for other information clerks, while hotel, motel, and resort desk clerks tend to earn quite a bit less, as the following table of median annual earnings shows.

Reservation and transportation ticket agents and
travel clerks $22,120

New accounts clerks 21,340

Receptionists 18,620

Interviewing clerks 18,540

Hotel, motel, and resort desk clerks 15,160

Earnings of hotel and motel desk clerks also vary considerably depending on the location, size, and type of establishment in which they work. For example, clerks at large luxury hotels and those located in metropolitan and resort areas generally pay clerks more than less-exclusive or "budget" establishments and those located in less-populated areas.

In early 1999, the Federal government typically paid salaries ranging from $16,400 to $18,100 a year to beginning receptionists with a high school diploma or six months of experience. The average annual salary for all receptionists employed by the Federal government was about $22,700 in 1999.

In addition to their hourly wage, full-time information clerks who work evenings, nights, weekends, or holidays may receive shift differential pay. Some employers offer educational assistance to their employees. Reservation and transportation ticket agents and travel clerks receive free or reduced rate travel on their company's carriers for themselves and their immediate family and, in some companies, for friends.

Related Occupations

A number of other workers deal with the public, receive and provide information, or direct people to others who can assist them. Among these are dispatchers, security guards, bank tellers, guides, telephone operators, records processing clerks, counter and rental clerks, survey workers, and ushers and lobby attendants.

Hotel, Motel, and Resort Desk Clerks

(O*NET 53808)

Nature of the Work

Hotel, motel, and resort desk clerks perform a variety of services for guests of hotels, motels, and other lodging establishments. Regardless of the type of accommodation, most desk clerks have similar responsibilities. Primarily, they register arriving guests, assign rooms, and check guests out at the end of their stay. They also keep records of room assignments and other registration information on computers. When guests check out, they prepare and explain the charges, as well as process payments.

Front desk clerks are always in the public eye and, through their attitude and behavior, greatly influence the public's impressions

of the establishment. When answering questions about services, checkout times, the local community, or other matters of public interest, clerks must be courteous and helpful. Should guests report problems with their rooms, clerks contact members of the housekeeping or maintenance staff to correct them.

In some smaller hotels and motels, clerks may have a variety of additional responsibilities, usually performed by specialized employees in larger establishments. In these places, the desk clerk is often responsible for all front office operations, information, and services. These clerks, for example, may perform the work of a bookkeeper, advance reservation agent, cashier, laundry attendant, or telephone switchboard operator.

Employment

Hotel, motel, and resort desk clerks held about 159,000 jobs in 1998. This occupation is well suited to flexible work schedules, as more than 1 in 4 desk clerks works part time. Because hotels and motels need to be staffed 24 hours a day, evening and weekend work is common.

Job Outlook

Employment of hotel, motel, and resort desk clerks is expected to grow about as fast as the average for all occupations through 2008 as more hotels, motels, and other lodging establishments are built and occupancy rates rise. Job opportunities for hotel and motel desk clerks will result from an unusually high turnover rate. These openings occur each year as thousands of workers transfer to other occupations that offer better pay and advancement opportunities or simply leave the work force altogether. Opportunities for part-time work should continue to be plentiful, as nearly all front desks are staffed 24 hours a day 7 days a week.

Employment of hotel and motel desk clerks should be favorably affected by an increase in business and leisure travel. Shifts in travel preference away from long vacations and toward long weekends and other, more frequent, shorter trips also should increase demand as this trend increases the total number of nights spent in hotels. The expansion of smaller budget hotels relative to larger luxury establishments reflects a change in the composition of the hotel and motel industry. As employment shifts from luxury hotels to more "no-frills" operations, the proportion of hotel desk clerks should increase in relation to staff such as waiters and waitresses and recreation workers.

However, the growing effort to cut labor costs while moving toward more efficient service is expected to slow the growth of desk clerk employment. The role of the front desk is changing as some of the more traditional duties are automated. New technologies automating check-in and check-out procedures now allow guests to bypass the front desk in many larger establishments, reducing staffing needs. The expansion of other technologies, such as interactive television and computer systems to dispense information, should further impact employment in the future as such services become more widespread.

Employment of desk clerks is sensitive to cyclical swings in the economy. During recessions, vacation and business travel declines, and hotels and motels need fewer clerks. Similarly, desk clerk em-

ployment is affected by seasonal fluctuations in travel during high and low tourist seasons.

Sources of Additional Information

Information on working conditions, training requirements, and earnings appears in the "Information Clerks" introduction to this section. Information on careers in the lodging industry, as well as information about professional development and training programs, may be obtained from:

- The Educational Institute of the American Hotel and Motel Association, P.O. Box 531126 Orlando, FL 32853-1126. Internet: http://www.ei-ahma.org

Interviewing and New Accounts Clerks

(O*NET 53105 and 55332)

Nature of the Work

Interviewing and new accounts clerks obtain information from individuals and business representatives who are opening bank accounts, gaining admission to medical facilities, participating in consumer surveys, and completing various other forms. By mail, telephone, or in person, these workers solicit and verify information, create files, and perform a number of other related tasks.

The specific duties and job titles of interviewing and new accounts clerks depend upon the type of employer. In doctors' offices and other health care facilities, for example, interviewing clerks are also known as admitting interviewers or patient representatives. These workers obtain all preliminary information required for admission, such as the patient's name, address, age, medical history, present medications, previous hospitalizations, religion, persons to notify in case of emergency, attending physician, and the party responsible for payment. In some cases, interviewing clerks may be required to verify benefits with the person's insurance provider or work out financing options for those who might need it.

Other duties of interviewers in health care include assigning patients to rooms and summoning escorts to take patients to their rooms; sometimes these workers may escort patients themselves. Using the facility's computer system, they schedule lab work, x-rays, and surgeries and prepare admitting and discharge records and route them to appropriate departments. They may also bill patients, receive payments, and answer the telephone. In an outpatient or office setting, they also schedule appointments, keep track of cancellations, and provide general information about care. In addition, the role of the admissions staff, particularly in hospitals, is expanding to include a wide range of patient services from assisting patients with financial and medical questions to helping family members find hotel rooms.

Interviewing clerks who conduct market research surveys and polls for research firms have somewhat different responsibilities. These interviewers ask a series of prepared questions, record the responses, and forward the results to management. They may ask individuals questions about their occupation and earnings, political preferences, buying habits, or customer satisfaction. Although most interviews are conducted over the telephone, some are conducted in focus groups or by randomly polling people at a shopping mall. More recently, the Internet is being used to elicit people's opinions. Almost all interviewers use computers or similar devices to enter the responses to questions.

New accounts clerks, more commonly referred to as customer service representatives, handle a wide variety of operations in banks, credit unions, and other financial institutions. Their principal tasks are to handle customer inquiries, explain the institution's products and services to people, and refer customers to the appropriate sales personnel. If a person wants to open a checking or savings account or an IRA, the customer service representative will interview the customer and enter the required information into a computer for processing. He or she will also assist people in applying for other services, such as ATM cards, direct deposit, and certificates of deposit. Some customer service representatives also sell traveler's checks, handle savings bonds, perform foreign currency transactions, and perform teller duties, as required. Although the majority of customer service representatives work in branch offices and deal directly with customers, a growing number are being hired by banks to work in central call centers, taking questions from customers 24 hours a day, entering appropriate information into customer records, and (if necessary) referring customers to other specialists in the financial institution.

Employment

Interviewing and new accounts clerks held about 239,000 jobs in 1998. More than half were employed by commercial banks and other depository institutions. The remainder worked mostly in hospitals and other health care facilities and for research and testing firms. Around 3 out of every 10 clerks worked part time.

Job Outlook

Overall employment of interviewing and new accounts clerks is expected to increase about as fast as the average for all occupations through 2008. Much of this growth will stem from an increase in part-time and temporary jobs. In addition to growth, a larger number of job openings is expected to arise from the need to replace the thousands of interviewing and new accounts clerks who leave the occupation or the work force each year. Job prospects to fill these openings will be best for applicants with a broad range of job skills, such as good customer service, math, and telephone skills.

The number of interviewing clerks is projected to grow faster than average, reflecting growth in the health services industry. This industry will hire more admissions interviewers as health care facilities consolidate staff and expand the role of the admissions staff, and as an aging and growing population requires more visits to health care practitioners. In addition, increasing use of market research will create more jobs for interviewers to collect data. In the future, though, more market research is expected to be conducted over the Internet, thus reducing the need for telephone interviewers to make individual calls.

Employment of new accounts clerks, on the other hand, is expected to grow only as fast as average as bank employment slows and more services are provided electronically. However, these changes will favor employment of new accounts clerks over other workers in banks, particularly tellers, because of their ability to provide a wide range of services. Also, new accounts clerks will be hired in increasing numbers by banks to handle customer inquiries at their call centers.

Sources of Additional Information

Information on working conditions, training requirements, and earnings appears in the "Information Clerks" introduction to this section. State employment service offices can provide information about employment opportunities.

Receptionists

(O*NET 55305)

Nature of the Work

Receptionists are charged with a responsibility that may have a lasting impact on the success of an organization—making a good first impression. These workers are often the first representatives of an organization that a visitor encounters, so they need to be courteous, professional, and helpful. Receptionists answer telephones, route calls, greet visitors, respond to inquiries from the public, and provide information about the organization. In addition, receptionists contribute to the security of an organization by helping to monitor the access of visitors.

Whereas some tasks are common to most receptionists, the specific responsibilities of receptionists vary depending upon the type of establishment in which they work. For example, receptionists in hospitals and doctors' offices may gather personal and financial information and direct patients to the proper waiting rooms. In beauty or hair salons, however, they arrange appointments, direct customers to the hairstylist, and may serve as cashier. In factories, large corporations, and government offices, they may provide identification cards and arrange for escorts to take visitors to the proper offices. Those working for bus and train companies respond to inquiries about departures, arrivals, stops, and other related matters.

Increasingly, receptionists use multiline telephone systems, personal computers, and fax machines. Despite the widespread use of automated answering systems or voice mail, many receptionists still take messages and inform other employees of visitors' arrivals or cancellation of an appointment. When they are not busy with callers, most receptionists are expected to perform a variety of office duties including opening and sorting mail, collecting and distributing parcels, making fax transmittals and deliveries, updating appointment calendars, preparing travel vouchers, and performing basic bookkeeping, word processing, and filing.

Employment

Receptionists held about 1.3 million jobs in 1998, accounting for more than two-thirds of all information clerk jobs. More than two-thirds of all receptionists worked in services industries, and almost half of these were employed in the health services industry in doctors' and dentists' offices, hospitals, nursing homes, urgent care centers, surgical centers, and clinics. Manufacturing, wholesale and retail trade, government, and real estate industries also employed large numbers of receptionists. About 3 of every 10 receptionists worked part time.

Job Outlook

Employment of receptionists is expected to grow faster than the average for all occupations through 2008. This increase will result from rapid growth in services industries—including physician's offices, law firms, temporary help agencies, and consulting firms—where most receptionists are employed. In addition, high turnover in this large occupation will create numerous openings as receptionists transfer to other occupations or leave the labor force altogether. Opportunities should be best for persons with a wide range of clerical skills and experience.

Technology should have conflicting effects on the demand for receptionists. The increasing use of voice mail and other telephone automation reduces the need for receptionists by allowing one receptionist to perform work that formerly required several receptionists. However, increasing use of technology also has caused a consolidation of clerical responsibilities and growing demand for workers with diverse clerical skills. Because receptionists may perform a wide variety of clerical tasks, they should continue to be in demand. Further, receptionists perform many tasks that are of an interpersonal nature and are not easily automated, ensuring continued demand for their services in a variety of establishments. Receptionists tend to be less subject to layoffs during recessions than other clerical workers because establishments need someone to perform their duties even during economic downturns.

Sources of Additional Information

Information on working conditions, training requirements, and earnings appears in the "Information Clerks" introduction to this section. State employment offices can provide information on job openings for receptionists.

Reservation and Transportation Ticket Agents and Travel Clerks

(O*NET 53802 and 53805)

Nature of the Work

Each year, millions of Americans travel by plane, train, ship, bus, and automobile. Many of these travelers rely on the services of reservation and transportation ticket agents and travel clerks. These ticket agents and clerks perform functions as varied as selling tickets, confirming reservations, checking baggage, and providing tourists with useful travel information.

Most reservation agents work for large hotel chains or airlines, helping people plan trips and make reservations. They usually work in large reservation centers answering telephone inquiries and offer-

ing suggestions on travel arrangements, such as routes, time schedules, rates, and types of accommodation. Reservation agents quote fares and room rates, provide travel information, and make and confirm transportation and hotel reservations. Most agents use proprietary networks to quickly obtain information needed to make, change, or cancel reservations for customers.

Transportation ticket agents are sometimes known as passenger service agents, passenger-booking clerks, reservation clerks, airport service agents, ticket clerks, or ticket sellers. They work in airports, train, and bus stations selling tickets, assigning seats to passengers, and checking baggage. In addition, they may answer inquiries and give directions, examine passports and visas, or check in pets. Other ticket agents, more commonly known as gate or station agents, work in airport terminals assisting passengers boarding airplanes. These workers direct passengers to the correct boarding area, check tickets and seat assignments, make boarding announcements, and provide special assistance to young, elderly, or disabled passengers when they board or disembark.

Most travel clerks are employed by membership organizations, such as automobile clubs. These workers, sometimes called member services counselors or travel counselors, plan trips, calculate mileage, and offer travel suggestions (such as the best route from the point of origin to the destination) for club members. Travel clerks also may prepare an itinerary indicating points of interest, restaurants, overnight accommodations, and availability of emergency services during the trip. In some cases, they make rental car, hotel, and restaurant reservations for club members.

Passenger rate clerks generally work for bus companies. They sell tickets for regular bus routes and arrange nonscheduled or chartered trips. They plan travel routes, compute rates, and keep customers informed of appropriate details. They also may arrange travel accommodations.

Employment

Reservation and transportation ticket agents and travel clerks held about 219,000 jobs in 1998. About 7 of every 10 are employed by airlines. Others work for membership organizations, such as automobile clubs; hotels and other lodging places; railroad companies; bus lines; and other companies that provide transportation services.

Although agents and clerks are found throughout the country, most work in large metropolitan airports, downtown ticket offices, large reservation centers, and train or bus stations. The remainder work in small communities served only by inter-city bus or railroad lines.

Job Outlook

Applicants for reservation and transportation ticket agent jobs are likely to encounter considerable competition, because the supply of qualified applicants exceeds the expected number of job openings. Entry requirements for these jobs are minimal, and many people seeking to get into the airline industry or travel business often start out in these types of positions. These jobs provide excellent travel benefits, and many people view airline and other travel-related jobs as glamorous.

Employment of reservation and transportation ticket agents and travel clerks is expected to grow more slowly than the average for all occupations through 2008. Although a growing population will demand additional travel services, employment of these workers will grow more slowly than this demand because of the significant impact of technology on productivity. Automated reservations and ticketing, as well as "ticketless" travel, for example, are reducing the need for some workers. Most train stations and airports now have satellite ticket printer locations, or "kiosks," that enable passengers to make reservations and purchase tickets themselves. Many passengers also are able to check flight times and fares, make reservations, and purchase tickets on the Internet. Nevertheless, all travel-related passenger services can never be fully automated, primarily for safety and security reasons. As a result, jobs will continue to become available as the occupation grows and as workers transfer to other occupations, retire, or leave the labor force altogether.

Employment of reservation and transportation ticket agents and travel clerks is sensitive to cyclical swings in the economy. During recessions, discretionary passenger travel declines, and transportation service companies are less likely to hire new workers and even may resort to layoffs.

Sources of Additional Information

Information on working conditions, training requirements, and earnings appears in the "Information Clerks" introduction to this section. For information about job opportunities as reservation and transportation ticket agents and travel clerks, write the personnel manager of individual transportation companies. Addresses of airlines are available from:

- Air Transport Association of America, 1301 Pennsylvania Ave. NW., Suite 1100, Washington, DC 20004-1707.

Inspectors and Compliance Officers, Except Construction

(O*NET 21911A, 21911B, 21911D, 21911E, 21911F, 21911H, 21911J, 21911L, 21911P, 21911R, and 21911T)

Significant Points

- About 4 out of 5 inspection and compliance jobs are in Federal, State, and local government agencies that enforce rules on health, safety, food quality, licensing, and finance.

- Because of the diversity of functions these workers perform, job qualifications vary widely.

Nature of the Work

Inspectors and compliance officers help to keep workplaces safe, food healthy, and the environment clean. They also ensure that workers' rights are recognized in a variety of settings. These workers enforce rules on matters as diverse as health, safety, food quality, licensing, and finance. As the following occupations demonstrate, their duties vary widely, depending on their area of responsibility and level of experience.

Aviation safety inspectors work for the Federal Aviation Administration (FAA) and oversee the avionics, maintenance, and operations of air carriers and similar establishments. They evaluate technicians, pilots, and other personnel; assess facilities and training programs; inspect aircraft and related equipment for airworthiness, and investigate and report on accidents and violations.

Bank examiners investigate financial institutions concerning compliance with Federal or State charters and regulations governing the institution's operations and solvency. Examiners schedule audits to protect the institution's shareholders and the interests of depositors. They recommend acceptance or rejection of applications for mergers and acquisitions, and they testify as to the viability of chartering new institutions. They interview officials in the firm or other persons with knowledge of the bank's operations, review financial reports, and identify deficiencies and deviations from Federal and State laws.

Consumer safety inspectors and *officers* inspect food, feeds, pesticides, weights and measures, biological products, cosmetics, drugs, medical equipment, and radiation emitting products. Working individually or in teams under a senior inspector, they check on firms that use, produce, handle, store, or market products they regulate. They ensure that standards are maintained and respond to consumer complaints by questioning employees, vendors, and others to obtain evidence. Inspectors look for inaccurate product labeling, inaccurate scales, and decomposition or chemical or bacteriological contamination that could cause a product to be harmful to health. After completing their inspection, inspectors discuss their observations with plant managers or business owners to point out areas where corrective measures are needed. They write reports of their findings and compile evidence for use in court if legal action must be taken.

Environmental health inspectors work primarily for governments. They analyze substances in order to determine contamination or the presence of disease, and they investigate sources of contamination to try to ensure that food, water, and air meet government standards. They certify the purity of food and beverages produced in dairies and processing plants or served in restaurants, hospitals, and other institutions. Inspectors may find pollution sources through collection and analysis of air, water, or waste samples. When they determine the nature and cause of pollution, they initiate action to stop it and force the firm or individual who caused the pollutants to pay to clean it up.

Equal opportunity specialists enforce laws and regulations that prohibit discrimination on the basis of race, color, national origin, religion, sex, disability, and age in employment and the provision of services. They conduct on-site compliance reviews in accordance with agency and Department of Justice policy and regulations, gather facts related to allegations of discrimination, and make recommendations for resolving complaints. They then prepare statistical analysis and reports relative to implementation of civil rights and equal opportunity programs and refer cases to the legal system for adjudication when necessary.

Food Inspectors ensure that the product is fit for human consumption in compliance with Federal laws governing the wholesome-

ness and purity of meat and poultry products. This is accomplished through inspection involving a visual examination of the live animal or poultry prior to slaughter, as well as post-mortem inspection to determine that the product is not contaminated and that sanitation procedures are maintained. Processing food inspectors specialize in processed meat and poultry products, and all other ingredients contained in the final product, including frozen dinners, canned goods, and cured and smoked products. They have the authority to shut the plant down if there is a problem that they are unable to resolve.

Mine safety and health inspectors carry out the major operational mission of the Department of Labor's Mine Safety and Health Administration (MSHA). They primarily conduct on-site inspections or investigations of underground and surface mines, mills, and quarries in search of conditions that are potentially hazardous to the safety and health of workers. They inspect to ensure that equipment is properly maintained and used and that mining practices are carried out in accordance with safety and health laws and regulations. They also investigate accidents and disasters and may help direct rescue and fire fighting operations when fires or explosions occur. MSHA's inspectors work to identify the causes of accidents to determine how they might be prevented in the future, and they investigate complaints to determine whether laws and regulations have been violated. Inspectors discuss findings directly with mine management and issue citations describing violations and hazards that must be corrected. They have the authority to close a mining operation if they encounter a work situation that presents an imminent danger to workers. They may also be called upon by mine personnel to provide technical advice and assistance.

Occupational Safety and Health Administration (OSHA) inspectors serve the Department of Labor as expert consultants on the application of safety principles, practices, and techniques in the workplace. They conduct fact-finding investigations of workplaces to determine the existence of specific safety hazards. They may be assigned to conduct safety inspections and investigations and use technical equipment and sampling and measuring devices and supplies required in the field. These inspectors attempt to prevent accidents by using their knowledge of engineering safety codes and standards, and they may order suspension of activities that pose threats to workers.

Park rangers enforce laws and regulations in State and national parks. They protect natural, cultural, and human resources, and enforce criminal laws of the United States including the apprehension of violators. Rangers also implement wilderness and backcountry management plans; monitor grazing, mining, and concessions activities; and work closely with resource management specialists and employees to identify and communicate resource threats, perform resource inventories, implement resource projects, and monitor researchers. Other rangers give natural resources talks, lead guided walks, and conduct community outreach and environmental education programs.

Securities compliance examiners implement regulations concerning securities and real estate transactions. They investigate applications for registration of securities sales and complaints of irregular securities transactions, and they recommend legal action when necessary.

Other inspectors and compliance officers include attendance officers, logging operations inspectors, travel accommodations raters, coroners, code inspectors, mortician investigators, and dealer-compliance representatives.

Working Conditions

Inspectors and compliance officers work with many different people and in a variety of environments. Their jobs often involve considerable field work, and some inspectors travel frequently. When traveling, they are generally furnished with an automobile or are reimbursed for travel expenses.

Inspectors may experience unpleasant, stressful, and dangerous working conditions. For example, mine safety and health inspectors are exposed to many of the same physically strenuous conditions and hazards as miners, and the work may be performed in unpleasant, stressful, and dangerous working conditions. Federal food inspectors work in highly mechanized plant environments near operating machinery with moving parts or with poultry or livestock in confined areas in extreme temperatures and on slippery floors. The duties often require working with sharp knives, moderate lifting, and walking or standing for long periods of time. Park rangers often work outdoors in rugged terrain and in very hot or bitterly cold weather for extended periods.

Many inspectors work long and often irregular hours. Inspectors may find themselves in adversarial roles when the organization or individual being inspected objects to the process or its consequences.

Employment

Inspectors and compliance officers held about 176,000 jobs in 1998. State governments employed 30 percent, the Federal government—chiefly the Departments of Defense, Labor, Treasury, and Agriculture—employed 31 percent, and local governments employed 19 percent. The remaining 20 percent were employed throughout the private sector in education, hospitals, insurance companies, and manufacturing firms.

Inspectors and compliance officers who work for the Federal government are employed by a wide range of agencies. Some consumer safety inspectors, for example, work for the U.S. Food and Drug Administration, but the majority of these inspectors work for State governments. Most food inspectors and agricultural commodity graders are employed by the U.S. Department of Agriculture. Many health inspectors work for State and local governments. Compliance inspectors are employed primarily by the Departments of Treasury and Labor on the Federal level, as well as by State and local governments. The Department of Defense employs the most quality assurance inspectors. Aviation safety inspectors work for the Federal Aviation Administration. The Environmental Protection Agency employs inspectors to verify compliance with pollution control and other laws. The U.S. Department of Labor and many State governments employ safety and health inspectors, equal opportunity officers, and mine safety and health inspectors. The U.S. Department of Interior employs park rangers.

Training, Other Qualifications, and Advancement

Because of the diversity of the functions they perform, qualifications for inspector and compliance officer jobs vary widely. Requirements include a combination of education, experience, and passing scores on written examinations. Many employers, including the Federal government, require college degrees for some positions. Experience in the area being investigated is also a prerequisite for many positions. Although not exhaustive, the following examples illustrate the range of qualifications for various inspector jobs.

Air carrier avionics inspector positions must possess aircraft electronics work experience involving the maintenance and repair of avionics systems in large aircraft, aircraft avionics experience in a repair station, air carrier repair facility, or military repair facility; three years of supervisory experience in aircraft avionics as a lead mechanic or repairer who supervises others; and aircraft avionics work experience within the last three years.

Air carrier maintenance inspectors must possess an FAA mechanic certificate with airframe and power plant ratings; aviation maintenance work experience involving the maintenance and repair of airframes, power plants, and systems of large aircraft under an airworthiness maintenance and inspection program; aircraft maintenance experience in a repair station, air carrier repair facility, or military repair facility; three years of supervisory experience in aviation maintenance as a lead mechanic or repairer who supervises others; and some aviation maintenance work experience within the last three years.

Air carrier operations inspectors must possess an airline transport pilot certificate or commercial pilot certificate with instrument airplane rating; pilot experience in large multiengine aircraft with a minimum of 1,500 total flight hours as a pilot or copilot; pilot-in-command experience in large aircraft within the last three years; a minimum of 100 flight hours within the last three years; 1,000 flight hours within the last five years; the successful completion of turbojet evaluation; and no more than two flying accidents in the last five years.

Applicants for positions as mine safety and health inspectors generally must have experience in mine safety, management, or supervision. Some may possess a skill such as that of an electrician (for mine electrical inspectors). Applicants must meet strict medical requirements and be physically able to perform arduous duties efficiently. Many mine safety inspectors are former miners.

Bank examiners need five or more years of experience in examining or auditing (internal or external) financial institutions. Candidates should have demonstrated a thorough understanding of a broad range of business risks as well as safety and soundness issues. Successful candidates typically have experience in evaluating computer risk management in financial institutions, including recovery planning, information security, and data integrity.

Environmental health inspectors, also called sanitarians in many States, may have completed a full four-year course of study that meets all the requirements for a bachelor's degree, and that included or was supplemented by at least 30 semester hours in a science or any combination of sciences directly related to environmental health—for example, sanitary science, public health, chemistry, microbiology, or any appropriate agricultural, biological, or physical science. Alternately, they may have four years of specialized experience in inspectional, investigational, technical support, or other work that provided a fundamental understanding of environmental health principles, methods, and techniques equivalent to that which would have been gained through a four-year college curriculum or some combination of education and experience as described above. In most States, they are licensed by examining boards.

All inspectors and compliance officers are trained in the applicable laws or inspection procedures through some combination of classroom and on-the-job training. In general, people who want to enter this occupation should be responsible and like detailed work. Inspectors and compliance officers should be able to communicate well.

Federal government inspectors and compliance officers whose job performance is satisfactory advance through their career ladder to a specified full-performance level. For positions above this level, usually supervisory positions, advancement is competitive and based on agency needs and individual merit. Advancement opportunities in State and local governments and the private sector are often similar to those in the Federal government.

Job Outlook

Average growth in employment of inspectors and compliance officers is expected through 2008, reflecting a balance of continuing public demand for a safe environment and quality products against the desire for smaller government and fewer regulations. Additional job openings will arise from the need to replace those who transfer to other occupations, retire, or leave the labor force for other reasons. In private industry, employment growth will reflect industry growth and the continuing self-enforcement of government and company regulations and policies, particularly among franchise operations in various industries.

Employment of inspectors and compliance officers is seldom affected by general economic fluctuations. Federal, State, and local governments, which employ four-fifths of all inspectors, provide considerable job security.

Earnings

The median annual salary of inspectors and compliance officers, except construction, was $36,820 in 1998. The middle half earned between $28,540 and $48,670. The lowest 10 percent earned less than $22,750, while the highest 10 percent earned more than $72,280. Inspectors and compliance officers employed by local governments had earnings of $31,800 in 1997; those who worked for State governments earned a median annual salary of $33,700; and those in the Federal government earned $39,900.

In the Federal government, the annual starting salaries for inspectors varied from $25,500 to $31,200 in 1999, depending on the nature of the inspection or compliance activity. Beginning salaries were slightly higher in selected areas where the prevailing local pay level was higher. The following presents average salaries for selected inspectors and compliance officers in the Federal government in nonsupervisory, supervisory, and managerial positions in early 1999.

Air safety investigators	$68,900
Highway safety inspectors	68,100
Aviation safety inspectors	65,100
Railroad safety inspectors	60,500
Mine safety and health inspectors	58,000

Environmental protection specialists	58,000
Equal employment opportunity officials	57,900
Safety and occupational health managers	54,000
Public health quarantine inspectors	52,500
Quality assurance inspectors	50,600
Securities compliance examiners	43,300
Park ranger	42,100
Agricultural commodity graders	41,600
Consumer safety inspectors	37,300
Food inspectors	35,200
Environmental protection assistants	31,600

Most inspectors and compliance officers work for Federal, State, and local governments or in large private firms, most of which generally offer more generous benefits than do smaller firms.

Related Occupations

Inspectors and compliance officers ensure that laws and regulations are obeyed. Others who enforce laws and regulations include construction and building inspectors; fire marshals; Federal, State, and local law enforcement professionals; correctional officers; and fish and game wardens.

Sources of Additional Information

Information on obtaining a job with the Federal government is available from the Office of Personnel Management through a telephone-based system. Consult a telephone directory under U.S. Government for a local number or call (912) 757-3000; TDD (912) 744-2299. The number is not toll free, and charges may result. Information also is available from their Internet site: http://www.usajobs.opm.gov.

Information about jobs in Federal, State, and local government as well as in private industry is available from the State Employment Service.

Insurance Sales Agents

(O*NET 43002)

Significant Points

- In spite of little or no employment growth, job opportunities should be good for people with the right skills.

- Employers prefer to hire college graduates and persons with proven sales ability or success in other occupations.

- Many beginners find it difficult to establish a sufficiently large clientele in this highly competitive business; consequently, some eventually leave for other jobs.

Nature of the Work

Most people have their first contact with an insurance company through an insurance sales agent or broker. These professionals help individuals, families, and businesses select insurance policies that provide the best protection for their lives, health, and property. *Insurance sales agents* may work exclusively for one insurance company or as "independent agents" selling for several companies. *Insurance brokers* represent several companies and place insurance policies for their clients with the company that offers the best rate and coverage. In either case, agents and brokers prepare reports, maintain records, seek out new clients, and, in the event of a loss, help policyholders settle insurance claims. Increasingly, some may also offer their clients financial analysis or advice on ways they can minimize risk.

Technology has greatly impacted the insurance agency, making it much more efficient and giving the agent the ability to take on more clients. Computers are now linked directly to the insurance companies, making the tasks of obtaining price quotes and processing applications and service requests much easier and faster. Computers also allow the agent to be better informed about new products the insurance carriers may be offering.

Insurance sales agents sell one or more types of insurance, such as life, property damage and liability, health, disability, and long-term care. Life insurance agents specialize in selling policies that pay beneficiaries when a policyholder dies. Depending on the policyholder's circumstances, a cash-value policy can be designed to provide retirement income, funds for the education of children, or other benefits. Life insurance agents also sell annuities that promise a retirement income. Health insurance agents sell health insurance policies that cover the costs of medical care and loss of income due to illness or injury. They may also sell dental insurance and short- and long-term disability insurance policies.

Property and casualty insurance agents and brokers sell policies that protect individuals and businesses from financial loss resulting from automobile accidents, fire, theft, storms, and other events that can damage property. For businesses, property and casualty insurance can also cover injured workers' compensation, product liability claims, or medical malpractice claims.

An increasing number of insurance agents and brokers offer comprehensive financial planning services to their clients, such as retirement planning, estate planning, or assistance in setting up pension plans for businesses. As a result, many insurance agents and brokers are involved in "cross-selling" or "total account development." Besides insurance, these agents may become licensed to sell mutual funds, variable annuities, and other securities.

Because insurance sales agents obtain many new accounts through referrals, it is important that agents maintain regular contact with their clients to ensure their financial needs are being met. Developing a satisfied clientele that will recommend an agent's services to other potential customers is a key to success in this field. It is also becoming increasingly necessary for agents to develop new ways of marketing to compete with the insurance companies who sell directly to clients. Therefore, familiarity with the Internet may become important for obtaining future sales.

Working Conditions

Most insurance agents and brokers are based in small offices, from which they contact clients and provide insurance policy information. However, most of their time may be spent outside their offices, traveling locally to meet with clients, close sales, or investigate claims. Agents usually determine their own hours of work and often schedule evening and weekend appointments for the convenience of clients. Although most agents and brokers work a 40-hour week, some work 60 hours a week or more. Commercial sales agents and brokers in particular may meet with clients during business hours and then spend evenings doing paperwork and preparing presentations to prospective clients.

Employment

Insurance agents and brokers held about 387,000 jobs in 1998. The following table shows the percent distribution of wage and salary jobs by industry:

Insurance agents, brokers, and services	48
Life insurance carriers	26
Property and casualty insurance carriers	13
Medical service and health insurance carriers	6
Pension funds and miscellaneous insurance carriers	2
Other industries	5

While most insurance agents employed in wage and salary positions work for insurance agencies, nearly an equal number work directly for insurance carriers. Most of these agents are employed by life insurance companies, and a smaller number work for property, casualty, and medical and health insurance companies. Although most insurance agents specialize in life and health or property and casualty insurance, a growing number of "multiline agents" sell all lines of insurance. Approximately 3 out of 10 agents and brokers are self-employed.

Agents and brokers are employed throughout the country, but most work in or near large urban centers. Some insurance agents and brokers are employed in the headquarters of insurance companies, but the majority work out of local offices or independent agencies.

Training, Other Qualifications, and Advancement

For insurance agency jobs, most companies and independent agencies prefer to hire college graduates—particularly those who have majored in business or economics. A few hire high school graduates with proven sales ability or who have been successful in other types of work. In fact, most entrants to agent and broker jobs transfer from other occupations. In selling commercial insurance, technical experience in a field can be very beneficial in helping to sell policies to those in the same profession. As a result, new agents and brokers tend to be older than entrants in many other occupations.

College training may help agents or brokers grasp the technical aspects of insurance policies and the fundamentals and procedures of selling insurance. Many colleges and universities offer courses in insurance, and a few schools offer a bachelor's degree in insurance. College courses in finance, mathematics, accounting, economics, business law, marketing, and business administration enable insurance agents or brokers to understand how social and economic conditions relate to the insurance industry. Courses in psychology, sociology, and public speaking can prove useful in improving sales techniques. In addition, familiarity with computers and popular software packages has become very important, as computers provide instantaneous information on a wide variety of financial products and greatly improve agents' and brokers' efficiency.

Insurance agents and brokers must obtain a license in the States where they plan to sell insurance. Separate licenses are required for agents to sell life and health insurance and property and casualty insurance. In most States, licenses are issued only to applicants who complete specified pre-licensing courses and pass State examinations covering insurance fundamentals and State insurance laws. Agents and brokers who plan to sell mutual funds and other securities must also obtain a separate securities license from the National Association of Securities Dealers.

A number of organizations offer professional designation programs, which certify expertise in specialties such as life, health, property and casualty insurance, or financial consulting. Although these are voluntary, such programs assure clients and employers that an agent has a thorough understanding of the relevant specialty. Many professional societies now require agents to commit to continuing education in order to retain their designation.

Indeed, as the diversity of financial products sold by insurance agents and brokers increases, employers are placing greater emphasis on continuing professional education. It is important for insurance agents and brokers to keep up to date with issues concerning clients. Changes in tax laws, government benefit programs, and other State and Federal regulations can affect the insurance needs of clients and how agents conduct business. Agents and brokers can enhance their selling skills and broaden their knowledge of insurance and other financial services by taking courses at colleges and universities and by attending institutes, conferences, and seminars sponsored by insurance organizations. Most States have mandatory continuing education requirements focusing on insurance laws, consumer protection, and the technical details of various insurance policies.

Insurance agents and brokers should be enthusiastic, confident, disciplined, hard working, willing to solve problems, and able to communicate effectively. They should be able to inspire customer confidence. Because they usually work without supervision, agents and brokers must be able to plan their time well and have the initiative to locate new clients.

An insurance agent who shows sales ability and leadership may become a sales manager in a local office. A few advance to agency superintendent or executive positions. However, many who have built up a good clientele prefer to remain in sales work. Some, particularly in the property/casualty field, establish their own independent agencies or brokerage firms.

Job Outlook

Although employment of insurance agents and brokers is expected to show little growth through 2008, opportunities for agents will be favorable for persons with the right skills. This includes ambitious people who enjoy competitive sales work, have excellent interpersonal skills, and have developed expertise in a wide range of insurance and financial services. Because many beginners find it difficult to establish a sufficiently large clientele in this commission-based occupation, some eventually leave for other jobs. Most job openings are likely to result from the need to replace agents who leave the occupation and the large number of agents expected to retire in the coming years.

Future demand for agents and brokers largely depends on the volume of sales of insurance and other financial products. While sales of life insurance are down, rising incomes and a concern for financial security during retirement are lifting sales of annuities, mutual funds, and other financial products sold by insurance agents. Sales of health and long-term care insurance are also expected to rise sharply as the population ages and as the law provides more people access to health insurance. In addition, a growing population will increase the demand for insurance for automobiles, homes, and high-priced valuables and equipment. As new businesses emerge and existing firms expand coverage, sales of commercial insurance should also increase, including coverage such as product liability, workers' compensation, employee benefits, and pollution liability insurance.

Employment of agents and brokers will not keep up with the rising level of insurance sales, however. One of the major reasons for this is rising productivity resulting from the growing application of computers to record keeping and cost calculations in insurance. Also, as competition grows and insurance companies attempt to find ways to reduce costs, many are seeking alternative, cheaper ways to distribute their products. For example, an increasing number of insurance companies are hiring their own sales staff to sell personal lines policies directly to the consumer over the phone and through the mail, thereby reducing the need for independent sales agents. In addition, sales of insurance products over the Internet are expected to increase.

A major source of growing competition over the next 10 years is the prospect of banks entering into this market. Currently, only a small number of banks sell insurance directly to consumers due to regulations that prohibit most banks from selling insurance and securities. These barriers are expected to fall in the near future, and banks are anticipated to enter the broader financial services market. This will hurt the demand for agents in the long run as bank employees sell more insurance policies. In the short run, however, it may open up new opportunities for agents as banks hire licensed, experienced agents to sell insurance for them.

In spite of these trends, insurance and investments are becoming more complex, and many people and businesses lack the time and expertise to buy insurance without the advice of an agent. Insurance agents who are knowledgeable about their products and sell multiple lines of insurance and other financial products will remain in demand. Additionally, agents who take advantage of direct mail and Internet resources to advertise and promote their products can reduce the time it takes to develop sales leads, allowing them to concentrate on following up on potential clients. Most individuals and businesses consider insurance a necessity, regardless of economic conditions. Therefore, agents are not likely to face unemployment because of a recession.

Earnings

The median annual earnings of wage and salary insurance sales workers were $34,370 in 1998. The middle 50 percent earned between $24,650 and $52,020. The lowest 10 percent had earnings of $17,870 or less, while the top 10 percent earned more than $91,890. Median annual earnings in the industries employing the largest number of insurance sales workers in 1997 were:

Fire, marine, and casualty insurance	$34,100
Insurance agents, brokers, and services	33,200
Medical service and health insurance	31,600
Life insurance	31,500

Many independent agents are paid by commission only, whereas sales workers who are employees of an agency or an insurance carrier may be paid in one of three ways: salary only, salary plus commission, or salary plus bonus. In general, commissions are the most common form of compensation, especially for experienced agents. The amount of commission depends on the type and amount of insurance sold and whether the transaction is a new policy or a renewal. Bonuses are usually awarded when agents meet their sales goals or when an agency's profit goals are met. Some agents involved with financial planning receive a fee for their services instead of a commission.

Company-paid benefits to sales agents usually include continuing education, paid licensing training, group insurance plans, and office space and clerical support services. Some may pay for automobile and transportation expenses, attendance at conventions and meetings, promotion and marketing expenses, and retirement plans. Independent agents working for insurance agencies receive fewer benefits, but their commissions may be higher to help them pay for marketing and other expenses.

Related Occupations

Other workers who sell financial products or services include real estate agents and brokers, securities and financial services sales representatives, financial advisors, estate planning specialists, and manufacturers' sales workers.

Sources of Additional Information

Occupational information about insurance agents and brokers is available from the home office of many life and casualty insurance companies. Information on State licensing requirements may be obtained from the department of insurance at any State capital.

For information about insurance sales careers and training, contact:

- Independent Insurance Agents of America, 127 S. Peyton St., Alexandria, VA 22314. Internet: http://www.iiaa.org
- Insurance Vocational Education Student Training (InVEST), 127 S. Peyton St., Alexandria, VA 22314. Internet: http://www.investprogram.org
- National Association of Professional Insurance Agents, 400 N. Washington St., Alexandria, VA 22314. Internet: http://www.pianet.com

For information about health insurance sales careers, contact:

- National Association of Health Underwriters, 2000 N. 14th St., Suite 450, Arlington, VA 22201. Internet: http://www.nahu.org

For information about insurance careers in the property and casualty field, contact:

- Insurance Information Institute, 110 William Street, New York, NY 10038.

For information regarding training for life insurance sales careers, contact:

- Life Underwriting Training Council, 7625 Wisconsin Ave., Bethesda, MD 20814.

For information about professional designation programs, contact:

- The American College, 270 Bryn Mawr Ave., Bryn Mawr, PA 19010-2195. Internet: http://www.amercoll.edu
- Society of Certified Insurance Counselors, 3630 North Hills Dr., Austin, TX 78731. Internet: http://www.scic.com/alliance
- The American Institute for Chartered Property and Casualty Underwriters, and the Insurance Institute of America, 720 Providence Rd., P.O. Box 3016, Malvern, PA 19355. Internet: http://www.aicpcu.org

Insurance Underwriters

(O*NET 21102)

Significant Points

- Employment is projected to grow more slowly than average as insurance companies increasingly use "smart" underwriting software systems that automatically analyze and rate insurance applications.

- Most large insurance companies prefer college graduates who have a degree in business administration, finance, or related fields and possess excellent communications and problem-solving skills.

Nature of the Work

Insurance companies protect individuals and organizations from financial loss by assuming billions of dollars in risks each year. Underwriters are needed to identify and calculate the risk of loss from policyholders, establish appropriate premium rates, and write policies that cover these risks. An insurance company may lose business to competitors if the underwriter appraises risks too conservatively, or it may have to pay more claims if the underwriting actions are too liberal.

With the aid of computers, underwriters analyze information in insurance applications to determine if a risk is acceptable and will not result in a loss. Applications are often supplemented with reports from loss-control consultants, medical reports, and actuarial studies. Underwriters then must decide whether to issue the policy and the appropriate premium to charge. In making this determination, underwriters serve as the main link between the insurance

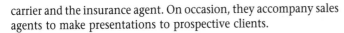

carrier and the insurance agent. On occasion, they accompany sales agents to make presentations to prospective clients.

Technology plays an important role in an underwriter's job. Underwriters use computer applications called "smart systems" to manage risks more efficiently and accurately. These systems automatically analyze and rate insurance applications, recommending acceptance or denial of the risk, and adjusting the premium rate in accordance with the risk. With these systems, underwriters are better equipped to make sound decisions and avoid excessive losses.

Most underwriters specialize in one of three major categories of insurance: life, health, or property and casualty. Life and health insurance underwriters may further specialize in group or individual policies. The increased complexity of insurance plans and attention to the "bottom line" is changing the nature of underwriting. In the past, insurance agents acting as underwriters, particularly in the life and health fields, could accept or reject applications. Now this underwriting role is done mostly by full-time underwriters in the home or field office of the insurance company.

Property and casualty underwriters usually specialize in commercial or personal lines and then often by type of risk insured, such as fire, homeowners, automobile, marine, liability, or workers' compensation. In cases where casualty companies provide insurance through a single "package" policy that covers various types of risks, the underwriter must be familiar with different lines of insurance. For business insurance, the underwriter often must be able to evaluate the firm's entire operation in appraising its application for insurance.

An increasing proportion of insurance sales, particularly in life and health insurance, is being made through group contracts. A standard group policy insures everyone in a specified group through a single contract at a standard premium rate. The group underwriter analyzes the overall composition of the group to assure that the total risk is not excessive. Another type of group policy provides members of a group—a labor union, for example—with individual policies reflecting their needs. These usually are casualty policies, such as those covering automobiles. The casualty underwriter analyzes the application of each group member and makes individual appraisals. Some group underwriters meet with union or employer representatives to discuss the types of policies available to their group.

Working Conditions

Underwriters have desk jobs that require no unusual physical activity. Their offices usually are comfortable and pleasant. Although underwriters typically work a standard 40-hour week, more are working longer hours due to the downsizing of many insurance companies. Most underwriters are based in a home office, but they occasionally attend meetings away from home for several days. Construction and marine underwriters frequently travel to inspect work sites and assess risks.

Employment

Insurance underwriters held about 97,000 jobs in 1998. The following table shows the percent distribution of employment by industry:

Property and casualty insurance carriers	34
Insurance agents, brokers, and services	31
Life insurance carriers	16
Medical service and health insurance carriers	6
Pension funds and miscellaneous insurance carriers	5
Other industries	8

The majority of underwriters work for insurance companies called "carriers." Of these underwriters, most work for property and casualty insurance carriers, and secondly for life insurance carriers. Most of the remaining underwriters work in insurance agencies or for organizations that offer insurance services to insurance companies and policyholders. A small number of underwriters work in agencies owned and operated by banks, mortgage companies, or real estate firms.

Most underwriters are based in the insurance company's home office, but some, mostly in the property and casualty area, work out of regional branch offices of the insurance company. These underwriters usually have the authority to underwrite risks and determine an appropriate rating without consulting the home office.

Training, Other Qualifications, and Advancement

For entry-level underwriting jobs, most large insurance companies prefer college graduates who have a degree in business administration or finance, with courses or experience in accounting. However, a bachelor's degree in almost any field—plus courses in business law and accounting—provides a good general background and may be sufficient to qualify. Computer knowledge is essential.

New employees usually start as underwriter trainees or assistant underwriters. They may help collect information on applicants and evaluate routine applications under the supervision of an experienced risk analyst. Property and casualty trainees study claim files to become familiar with factors associated with certain types of losses. Many larger insurers offer work-study training programs, lasting from a few months to a year. As trainees gain experience, they are assigned policy applications that are more complex and cover greater risks. These require the use of computers for more efficient analysis and processing.

Continuing education is necessary for advancement. Insurance companies usually pay tuition for underwriting courses that their trainees successfully complete; some also offer salary incentives. Independent study programs for experienced property and casualty underwriters are also available. The Insurance Institute of America offers a program called "Introduction to Underwriting" for beginning underwriters and the specialty designation, AU (or Associate in Underwriting), the second formal step in developing a career in underwriting. To earn the AU designation, underwriters complete a series of courses and examinations that generally last two years.

The American Institute for Chartered Property Casualty Underwriters awards the designation CPCU (or Chartered Property and Casualty Underwriter), the third and final stage of development for an

underwriter. Earning the more advanced CPCU designation takes about five years and requires passing ten examinations covering personal and commercial insurance, risk management, business and insurance law, accounting, finance, management, economics, and ethics. Although CPCUs may be underwriters, the CPCU is intended for everyone working in all aspects of property and casualty insurance. The American College offers the Chartered Life Underwriter (CLU) designation and the Registered Health Underwriter (RHU) designation for all professionals working in the fields of life and health insurance.

Underwriting can be a satisfying career for people who enjoy analyzing information and paying attention to detail. In addition, underwriters must possess good judgment in order to make sound decisions. Excellent communication and interpersonal skills are also essential, as much of their work involves dealing with agents and other insurance professionals.

Experienced underwriters who complete courses of study may advance to senior underwriter or underwriting manager positions. Some underwriting managers are promoted to senior managerial jobs. At some carriers, a master's degree is needed to achieve this level. Other underwriters are attracted to the earnings potential of sales and, therefore, obtain State licenses to sell insurance and insurance products as agents or brokers.

Job Outlook

Employment of underwriters is expected to increase more slowly than the average for all occupations through 2008. Computer-assisted software that helps underwriters analyze policy applications more quickly and accurately has made underwriters more productive and capable of taking on a greater workload. Mergers and acquisitions of insurance companies are also expected to continue to result in more downsizing of insurance carriers. Most job openings will result from the need to replace underwriters who transfer or leave the occupation, although several new job openings are being created for underwriters in the area of product development. These underwriters help set the premiums for new insurance products, such as in the growing field of long-term care insurance.

The best job prospects will be for underwriters with the right skills and credentials, such as excellent computer and communication skills, coupled with a background in finance. Job prospects may be better in health insurance than in property and casualty and life insurance. As Federal and State laws require health insurers to accept more applicants for insurance, the number of policies sold will increase. Also, as the population ages, there will be a greater need for health and long-term care insurance.

Because insurance is considered a necessity for people and businesses, there will always be a need for underwriters. It is a profession that is less subject to recession and layoffs than other fields. Underwriters who specialize, though, may have difficulty transferring to another underwriting specialty if downsizing occurs.

Earnings

Median annual earnings of insurance underwriters were $38,710 in 1998. The middle 50 percent earned between $29,790 and $51,460 a year. The lowest 10 percent earned less than $23,750,

while the top 10 percent earned more than $77,430. Median annual earnings in the industries employing the largest number of insurance underwriters in 1997 were:

Medical service and health insurance	$40,000
Life insurance	39,800
Fire, marine, and casualty insurance	39,100
Insurance agents, brokers, and service	32,200

Insurance companies usually provide better-than-average benefits, including employer-financed group life, health, and retirement plans.

Related Occupations

Underwriters make decisions on the basis of financial data. Other workers with the same type of responsibility include auditors, budget analysts, financial advisers, loan officers, credit managers, real estate appraisers, and risk managers.

Sources of Additional Information

Information about a career as an insurance underwriter is available from the home offices of many life insurance and property-liability insurance companies. Information about careers in the property-casualty insurance field can be obtained by contacting:

- The Insurance Information Institute, 110 William St., New York, NY 10038. Internet: http://www.iii.org

Information on the underwriting function in particular and the CPCU and AU designation can be obtained from:

- The American Institute for Chartered Property and Casualty Underwriters, and the Insurance Institute of America, 720 Providence Rd., P.O. Box 3016, Malvern, PA 19355-0716. Internet: http://www.aicpcu.org

Interviewing and New Accounts Clerks

(O*NET 53105 and 55332)

Significant Points

- Numerous job openings should arise for most types of information clerks due to employment growth and high turnover.

- A high school diploma or its equivalent is the most common educational requirement.

- Because many information clerks deal directly with the public, a professional appearance and pleasant personality are imperative.

Nature of the Work

Interviewing and new accounts clerks obtain information from individuals and business representatives who are opening bank accounts, gaining admission to medical facilities, participating in consumer surveys, and completing various other forms. By mail, telephone, or in person, these workers solicit and verify information, create files, and perform a number of other related tasks.

The specific duties and job titles of interviewing and new accounts clerks depend upon the type of employer. In doctors' offices and other health care facilities, for example, interviewing clerks are also known as admitting interviewers or patient representatives. These workers obtain all preliminary information required for admission, such as the patient's name, address, age, medical history, present medications, previous hospitalizations, religion, persons to notify in case of emergency, attending physician, and the party responsible for payment. In some cases, interviewing clerks may be required to verify benefits with the person's insurance provider or work out financing options for those who might need it.

Other duties of interviewers in health care include assigning patients to rooms and summoning escorts to take patients to their rooms; sometimes these workers may escort patients themselves. Using the facility's computer system, they schedule lab work, x-rays, and surgeries and prepare admitting and discharge records and route them to appropriate departments. They may also bill patients, receive payments, and answer the telephone. In an outpatient or office setting, they also schedule appointments, keep track of cancellations, and provide general information about care. In addition, the role of the admissions staff, particularly in hospitals, is expanding to include a wide range of patient services from assisting patients with financial and medical questions to helping family members find hotel rooms.

Interviewing clerks who conduct market research surveys and polls for research firms have somewhat different responsibilities. These interviewers ask a series of prepared questions, record the responses, and forward the results to management. They may ask individuals questions about their occupation and earnings, political preferences, buying habits, or customer satisfaction. Although most interviews are conducted over the telephone, some are conducted in focus groups or by randomly polling people at a shopping mall. More recently, the Internet is being used to elicit people's opinions. Almost all interviewers use computers or similar devices to enter the responses to questions.

New accounts clerks, more commonly referred to as customer service representatives, handle a wide variety of operations in banks, credit unions, and other financial institutions. Their principal tasks are to handle customer inquiries, explain the institution's products and services to people, and refer customers to the appropriate sales personnel. If a person wants to open a checking or savings account or an IRA, the customer service representative will interview the customer and enter the required information into a computer for processing. He or she will also assist people in applying for other services, such as ATM cards, direct deposit, and certificates of deposit. Some customer service representatives also sell traveler's checks, handle savings bonds, perform foreign currency transactions, and perform teller duties, as required. Although the majority of customer service representatives work in branch offices and deal directly with customers, a growing number are being hired by banks to work in central call centers, taking questions from customers 24 hours a day, entering appropriate information into customer records, and (if necessary) referring customers to other specialists in the financial institution.

Working Conditions

Working conditions vary, but most clerks work in areas that are clean, well lit, and relatively quiet. This is especially true for clerks who greet customers and visitors and usually work in highly visible areas that are furnished to make a good impression. Interviewing clerks who spend much of their day talking on the telephone, however, commonly work away from the public, often in large centralized reservation or phone centers. Because a number of agents or clerks may share the same workspace, it may be crowded and noisy. Interviewing clerks may conduct surveys on the street, in shopping malls, or door to door.

Although most clerks work a standard 40-hour week, about 3 out of 10 work part time. Some high school and college students work part time as information clerks, after school or during vacations. Some jobs may require working evenings, late night shifts, weekends, and holidays. This is also the case for a growing number of new accounts clerks who work for large banks with call centers that are staffed around the clock. Interviewing clerks conducting surveys or other research may mainly work evenings or weekends. In general, employees with the least seniority tend to be assigned the less desirable shifts.

The work performed by clerks may be repetitious and stressful. Additional stress is caused by technology that enables management to electronically monitor use of computer systems, tape record telephone calls, or limit the time spent on each call. In addition, prolonged exposure to a video display terminal may lead to eyestrain for the many clerks who work with computers.

Employment

Interviewing and new accounts clerks held about 239,000 jobs in 1998. More than half were employed by commercial banks and other depository institutions. The remainder worked mostly in hospitals and other health care facilities and for research and testing firms. Around 3 out of every 10 clerks worked part time.

Training, Other Qualifications, and Advancement

Although hiring requirements for clerk jobs vary from industry to industry, a high school diploma or its equivalent is the most common educational requirement. Increasingly, familiarity or experience with computers and good interpersonal skills are often equally important to employers. For new account clerk jobs, some college education may be preferred.

Many clerks deal directly with the public, so a professional appearance and pleasant personality are important. A clear speaking voice and fluency in the English language also are essential because these employees frequently use the telephone or public address systems. Good spelling and computer literacy are often needed, particularly because most work involves considerable computer use.

Orientation and training for clerks usually takes place on the job. New employees learn job tasks through on-the-job training under the guidance of a supervisor or an experienced clerk. They often need additional training in how to use the computerized systems and equipment. Most clerks continue to receive instruction on new procedures and company policies after their initial training ends.

Some employers look for applicants who already possess certain skills, such as prior computer and word processing experience or previous formal education.

Most banks prefer to hire college graduates for new account clerk positions. Nevertheless, many new accounts clerks without college degrees start out as bank tellers and are promoted by demonstrating excellent communication skills and motivation to learn new skills. If a new accounts clerk has not been a teller before, he or she will often receive such training and work for several months as a teller. In both cases, new accounts clerks undergo formal training regarding the bank's procedures, products, and services.

Advancement for clerks usually comes about either by transfer to a position with more responsibilities or by promotion to a supervisory position. Most companies fill office and administrative support supervisory and managerial positions by promoting individuals within their organization, so clerks who acquire additional skills, experience, and training improve their advancement opportunities. Interviewers and new accounts clerks with word processing or other clerical skills may advance to a better paying job as a secretary or administrative assistant.

Additional training is helpful in preparing clerks for promotion. In a number of industries, a college degree may be required for advancement to management ranks.

Job Outlook

Overall employment of interviewing and new accounts clerks is expected to increase about as fast as the average for all occupations through 2008. Much of this growth will stem from an increase in part-time and temporary jobs. In addition to growth, a larger number of job openings is expected to arise from the need to replace the thousands of interviewing and new accounts clerks who leave the occupation or the workforce each year. Job prospects to fill these openings will be best for applicants with a broad range of job skills, such as good customer service, math, and telephone skills.

The number of interviewing clerks is projected to grow faster than average, reflecting growth in the health services industry. This industry will hire more admissions interviewers as health care facilities consolidate staff and expand the role of the admissions staff, and as an aging and growing population requires more visits to health care practitioners. In addition, increasing use of market research will create more jobs for interviewers to collect data. In the future, though, more market research is expected to be conducted over the Internet, thus reducing the need for telephone interviewers to make individual calls.

Employment of new accounts clerks, on the other hand, is expected to grow only as fast as average as bank employment slows and more services are provided electronically. However, these changes will favor employment of new accounts clerks over other workers in banks, particularly tellers, because of their ability to provide a wide range of services. Also, new accounts clerks will be hired in in-creasing numbers by banks to handle customer inquiries at their call centers.

Earnings

Earnings vary widely by occupation and experience. The following table shows median annual earnings.

New accounts clerks $21,340
Interviewing clerks 18,540

In addition to their hourly wage, full-time clerks who work evenings, nights, weekends, or holidays may receive shift differential pay. Some employers offer educational assistance to their employees.

Related Occupations

A number of other workers deal with the public, receive and provide information, or direct people to others who can assist them. Among these are dispatchers, security guards, bank tellers, guides, telephone operators, records processing clerks, counter and rental clerks, survey workers, and ushers and lobby attendants.

Sources of Additional Information

State employment service offices can provide information about employment opportunities.

Landscape Architects

(O*NET 22308)

Significant Points

- More than 40 percent are self-employed; that's four times the proportion for all professionals.

- A bachelor's degree in landscape architecture is the minimum requirement for entry-level jobs; many employers prefer to hire landscape architects who have completed at least one internship.

- Because many landscape architects work for small firms or are self-employed, benefits tend to be less generous than those provided to workers in large organizations.

Nature of the Work

Everyone enjoys attractively designed residential areas, public parks and playgrounds, college campuses, shopping centers, golf courses, parkways, and industrial parks. Landscape architects design these areas so that they are not only functional, but beautiful and compatible with the natural environment as well. They plan the location of buildings, roads, and walkways and the arrangement of flowers, shrubs, and trees. Historic preservation and natural resource conservation and reclamation are other important objectives to which landscape architects may apply their knowledge of the environment as well as their design and artistic talents.

Many types of organizations—from real estate development firms starting new projects to municipalities constructing airports or parks—hire landscape architects, who are often involved with the development of a site from its conception. Working with architects, surveyors, and engineers, landscape architects help determine the best arrangement of roads and buildings. They also collaborate with environmental scientists, foresters, and other professionals to find the best way to conserve or restore natural resources. Once these decisions are made, landscape architects create detailed plans indicating new topography, vegetation, walkways, and other landscaping details, such as fountains and decorative features.

In planning a site, landscape architects first consider the nature and purpose of the project and the funds available. They analyze the natural elements of the site, such as the climate, soil, slope of the land, drainage, and vegetation; observe where sunlight falls on the site at different times of the day and examine the site from various angles; and assess the effect of existing buildings, roads, walkways, and utilities on the project.

After studying and analyzing the site, they prepare preliminary designs. To account for the needs of the client as well as the conditions at the site, they frequently make changes before a final design is approved. They also take into account any local, State, or Federal regulations such as those protecting wetlands and historic resources. Computer-aided design (CAD) has become an essential tool for most landscape architects in preparing designs. Many landscape architects also use video simulation to help clients envision the proposed ideas and plans. For larger scale site planning, landscape architects also use geographic information systems technology, a computer mapping system.

Throughout all phases of the planning and design, landscape architects consult with other professionals involved in the project. Once the design is complete, they prepare proposals for the clients. They produce detailed plans of the site, including written reports, sketches, models, photographs, land-use studies, and cost estimates, and submit them for approval by the client and by regulatory agencies. When the plans are approved, landscape architects prepare working drawings showing all existing and proposed features. They also outline in detail the methods of construction and draw up a list of necessary materials.

Although many landscape architects supervise the installation of their designs, some are involved in the construction of the site. However, the developer or landscape contractor usually does this.

Some landscape architects work on a variety of projects. Others specialize in a particular area, such as residential development, historic landscape restoration, waterfront improvement projects, parks and playgrounds, or shopping centers. Still others work in regional planning and resource management; feasibility, environmental impact, and cost studies; or site construction.

Most landscape architects do at least some residential work, but relatively few limit their practice to individual homeowners. Residential landscape design projects usually are too small to provide suitable income compared with larger commercial or multiunit residential projects. Some nurseries offer residential landscape design services, but these services often are performed by lesser qualified landscape designers or others with training and experience in related areas.

Landscape architects who work for government agencies do site and landscape design for government buildings, parks, and other public lands, as well as park and recreation planning in national parks and forests. In addition, they prepare environmental impact statements and studies on environmental issues such as public land-use planning. Some restore degraded land, such as mines or landfills.

Working Conditions

Landscape architects spend most of their time in offices creating plans and designs, preparing models and cost estimates, doing research, or attending meetings with clients and other professionals involved in a design or planning project. The remainder of their time is spent at the site. During the design and planning stage, landscape architects visit and analyze the site to verify that the design can be incorporated into the landscape. After the plans and specifications are completed, they may spend additional time at the site observing or supervising the construction. Those who work in large firms may spend considerably more time out of the office because of travel to sites outside the local area.

Salaried employees in both government and landscape architectural firms usually work regular hours; however, they may work overtime to meet a project deadline. Hours of self-employed landscape architects vary.

Employment

Landscape architects held about 22,000 jobs in 1998. About 1 out of 2 salaried workers were employed in firms that provide landscape architecture services. Architectural and engineering firms employed most of the rest. The Federal Government also employs these workers, primarily in the U.S. Departments of Agriculture, Defense, and Interior. About 2 of every 5 landscape architects were self-employed.

Employment of landscape architects is concentrated in urban and suburban areas throughout the country. Some landscape architects work in rural areas, particularly those in the Federal government who plan and design parks and recreation areas.

Training, Other Qualifications, and Advancement

A bachelor's or master's degree in landscape architecture is usually necessary for entry into the profession. The bachelor's degree in landscape architecture takes four or five years to complete. There are two types of accredited master's degree programs. The master's degree as a first professional degree is a three-year program designed for students with an undergraduate degree in another discipline; this is the most common type. The master's degree as the second professional degree is a two-year program for students who have a bachelor's degree in landscape architecture and wish to teach or specialize in some aspect of landscape architecture, such as regional planning or golf course design.

In 1999, 58 colleges and universities offered 75 undergraduate and graduate programs in landscape architecture that were accredited by the Landscape Architecture Accreditation Board of the American Society of Landscape Architects.

College courses required in this field usually include technical subjects such as surveying, landscape design and construction, landscape ecology, site design, and urban and regional planning. Other courses include history of landscape architecture, plant and soil science, geology, professional practice, and general management. Many landscape architecture programs are adding courses that address environmental issues. In addition, most students at the undergraduate level take a year of prerequisite courses such as English, mathematics, and social and physical science. The design studio is an important aspect of many landscape architecture curriculums. Whenever possible, students are assigned real projects, providing them with valuable hands-on experience. While working on these projects, students become more proficient in the use of computer-aided design, geographic information systems, and video simulation.

In 1999, 46 States required landscape architects to be licensed or registered. Licensing is based on the Landscape Architect Registration Examination (L.A.R.E.), sponsored by the Council of Landscape Architectural Registration Boards and administered over a three-day period. Admission to the exam usually requires a degree from an accredited school plus one to four years of work experience, although standards vary from State to State. Currently, 17 States require the passage of a State examination in addition to the L.A.R.E. to satisfy registration requirements. State examinations, which are usually one hour in length and are completed at the end of the L.A.R.E., focus on laws, environmental regulations, plants, soils, climate, and any other characteristics unique to the State.

Because State requirements for licensure are not uniform, landscape architects may not find it easy to transfer their registration from one State to another. However, those who meet the national standards of graduating from an accredited program, serving three years of internship under the supervision of a registered landscape architect, and passing the L.A.R.E. can satisfy requirements in most States. Through this means, a landscape architect can obtain certification from the Council of Landscape Architectural Registration Boards and so gain reciprocity (the right to work) in other States.

In the Federal government, candidates for entry positions should have a bachelor's or master's degree in landscape architecture. The Federal government does not require its landscape architects to be licensed.

Persons planning a career in landscape architecture should appreciate nature, enjoy working with their hands, and possess strong analytical skills. Creative vision and artistic talent are also desirable qualities. Good oral communication skills are essential; landscape architects must be able to convey their ideas to other professionals and clients and to make presentations before large groups. Strong writing skills are also valuable, as is knowledge of computer applications of all kinds, including word processing, desktop publishing, and spreadsheets. Landscape architects use these tools to develop presentations, proposals, reports, and land impact studies for clients, colleagues, and superiors. The ability to draft and design using CAD software is essential. Many employers recommend that prospective landscape architects complete at least one summer internship with a landscape architecture firm in order to gain an understanding of the day-to-day operations of a small business, including how to win clients, generate fees, and work within a budget.

In States where licensure is required, new hires may be called "apprentices" or "intern landscape architects" until they become licensed. Their duties vary depending on the type and size of employing firm. They may do project research or prepare working drawings, construction documents, or base maps of the area to be landscaped. Some are allowed to participate in the actual design of a project. However, interns must perform all work under the supervision of a licensed landscape architect. Additionally, all drawings and specifications must be signed and sealed by the licensed landscape architect, who takes legal responsibility for the work. After gaining experience and becoming licensed, landscape architects usually can carry a design through all stages of development. After several years, they may become project managers, taking on the responsibility for meeting schedules and budgets, in addition to overseeing the project design; and later, they might become associates or partners, with a proprietary interest in the business.

Many landscape architects are self-employed because start-up costs, after an initial investment in CAD software, are relatively low. Self-discipline, business acumen, and good marketing skills are important qualities for those who choose to open their own business. Even with these qualities, however, some may struggle while building a client base.

Those with landscape architecture training also qualify for jobs closely related to landscape architecture, and may, after gaining some experience, become construction supervisors, land or environmental planners, or landscape consultants.

Job Outlook

Employment of landscape architects is expected to increase as fast as the average for all occupations through the year 2008. The level of new construction plays an important role in determining demand for landscape architects. Overall, anticipated growth in construction is expected to increase demand for landscape architectural services over the long run.

Increased development of open space into recreation areas, wildlife refuges, and parks will also require the skills of landscape architects. The recent passage of the Transportation Equity Act for the Twenty-First Century is expected to spur employment for landscape architects, particularly in State and local governments. This Act, known as TEA-21, provides funds for surface transportation and transit programs, such as interstate highway maintenance and environment-friendly pedestrian and bicycle trails. However, opportunities will vary from year to year and by geographic region, depending on local economic conditions. During a recession, when real estate sales and construction slow down, landscape architects may face layoffs and greater competition for jobs. The need to replace landscape architects who retire or leave the labor force for other reasons is expected to produce nearly as many job openings as employment growth.

An increasing proportion of office and other commercial and industrial development will occur outside cities. These projects are typically located on larger sites with more surrounding land that needs to be designed by a landscape architect, in contrast to urban development, which often includes little or no surrounding land. Also, as the cost of land rises, the importance of good site planning and landscape design grows. Increasingly, new development is contingent upon compliance with environmental regulations and land use zoning, spurring demand for landscape architects to help plan sites and integrate man-made structures with the natural environment in the least disruptive way.

Budget tightening in the Federal government might restrict hiring in the Forest Service and the National Park Service, agencies that traditionally employ the most landscape architects in the Federal government. Instead, such agencies may increasingly contract out for landscape architecture services, providing additional employment opportunities in private landscape architecture firms.

In addition to the work related to new development and construction, landscape architects are expected to be involved in historic preservation, land reclamation, and refurbishment of existing sites. Because landscape architects can work on many different types of projects, they may have an easier time than other design professionals finding employment when traditional construction slows down.

New graduates can expect to face competition for jobs in the largest and most prestigious landscape architecture firms. The number of professional degrees awarded in landscape architecture has remained steady over the years, even during times of fluctuating demand due to economic conditions. Opportunities will be best for landscape architects who develop strong technical and communication skills and a knowledge of environmental codes and regulations. Those with additional training or experience in urban planning increase their opportunities for employment in landscape architecture firms that specialize in site planning as well as landscape design. Many employers prefer to hire entry-level landscape architects who have internship experience, which significantly reduces the amount of on-the-job training required.

Earnings

In 1998, median annual earnings for landscape architects were $37,930. The middle 50 percent earned between $28,820 and $50,550. The lowest 10 percent earned less than $22,800, and the highest 10 percent earned more than $78,920. Most landscape architects worked in the landscape and horticultural services industry, where their median annual earnings were $33,600 in 1997.

In 1999, the average annual salary for all landscape architects in the Federal government in nonsupervisory, supervisory, and managerial positions was about $57,500.

Because many landscape architects work for small firms or are self-employed, benefits tend to be less generous than those provided to workers in large organizations.

Related Occupations

Landscape architects use their knowledge of design, construction, land-use planning, and environmental issues to develop a landscape project. Others whose work requires similar skills are architects, surveyors, civil engineers, soil conservationists, and urban and regional planners. Landscape architects also know how to grow and use plants in the landscape. Botanists, who study plants in general, and horticulturists, who study ornamental plants as well as fruit, vegetable, greenhouse, and nursery crops, do similar work.

Sources of Additional Information

Additional information, including a list of colleges and universities offering accredited programs in landscape architecture, is available from:

● American Society of Landscape Architects, Career Information, 636 Eye Street, NW., Washington, DC 20001. Internet: http://www.asla.org

General information on registration or licensing requirements is available from:

● Council of Landscape Architectural Registration Boards, 12700 Fair Lakes Circle, Suite 110, Fairfax, VA 22033.

Lawyers and Judicial Workers

(O*NET 28102, 28105, and 28108)

Significant Points

● Formal educational requirements for lawyers include a four-year college degree, three years in law school, and successful completion of a written bar examination.

● Competition for admission to most law schools is intense.

● Aspiring lawyers and judges should encounter significant competition for jobs.

Nature of the Work

The legal system affects nearly every aspect of our society, from buying a home to crossing the street. Lawyers and judicial workers form the backbone of this vital system, linking the legal system and society in myriad ways. For this reason, they hold positions of great responsibility and are obligated to adhere to a strict code of ethics.

Lawyers, also called *attorneys*, act both as advocates and advisors in our society. As advocates, they represent one of the parties in criminal and civil trials by presenting evidence and arguing in court to support their client. As advisors, lawyers counsel their clients concerning their legal rights and obligations and suggest particular courses of action in business and personal matters. Whether acting as advocate or advisor, all attorneys research the intent of laws and judicial decisions and apply the law to the specific circumstances faced by their client.

The more detailed aspects of a lawyer's job depend upon his or her field of specialization and position. While all lawyers are licensed to represent parties in court, some appear in court more frequently than others. Trial lawyers, who specialize in trial work, must be able to think quickly and speak with ease and authority. In addition, familiarity with courtroom rules and strategy are particularly important in trial work. Still, trial lawyers spend the majority of their time outside the courtroom conducting research, interviewing clients and witnesses, and handling other details in preparation for trial.

Lawyers may specialize in a number of different areas, such as bankruptcy, probate, international, or elder law. Those specializing in environmental law, for example, may represent public interest groups, waste disposal companies, or construction firms in their dealings with the Environmental Protection Agency (EPA) and other State and Federal agencies. They help clients prepare and file for licenses and applications for approval before certain activities may occur. In addition, they represent clients' interests in administrative adjudications.

Some lawyers concentrate in the growing field of intellectual property. These lawyers help protect clients' claims to copyrights, art work under contract, product designs, and computer programs. Still other lawyers advise insurance companies about the legality of insurance transactions. They write insurance policies to conform with the law and to protect companies from unwarranted claims. When claims are filed against insurance companies, they review the claims and represent the companies in court.

The majority of lawyers are found in private practice, where they concentrate on criminal or civil law. In criminal law, lawyers represent individuals who have been charged with crimes and argue their cases in courts of law. Attorneys dealing with civil law assist clients with litigation, wills, trusts, contracts, mortgages, titles, and leases. Other lawyers handle only public interest cases—civil or criminal—which may have an impact extending well beyond the individual client.

Lawyers are sometimes employed full time by a single client. If the client is a corporation, the lawyer is known as "house counsel," and he or she usually advises the company concerning legal issues related to its business activities. These issues might involve patents, government regulations, contracts with other companies, property interests, or collective bargaining agreements with unions.

A significant number of attorneys are employed at the various levels of government. Lawyers who work for State attorneys general, prosecutors, public defenders, and courts play a key role in the criminal justice system. At the Federal level, attorneys investigate cases for the Department of Justice and other agencies. Government lawyers also help develop programs, draft and interpret laws and legislation, establish enforcement procedures, and argue civil and criminal cases on behalf of the government.

Other lawyers work for legal aid societies—private, nonprofit organizations established to serve disadvantaged people. These lawyers generally handle civil, rather than criminal cases. A relatively small number of trained attorneys work in law schools. Most are faculty members who specialize in one or more subjects; however, some serve as administrators. Others work full time in nonacademic settings and teach part time.

To perform the varied tasks described above more efficiently, lawyers increasingly utilize various forms of technology. While all lawyers continue to use law libraries to prepare cases, some supplement their search of conventional printed sources with computer sources,

such as the Internet and legal databases. Software is used to search this legal literature automatically and to identify legal texts relevant to a specific case. In litigation involving many supporting documents, lawyers may use computers to organize and index material. Lawyers also use electronic filing, videoconferencing, and voice-recognition technology to more effectively share information with other parties involved in a case.

Many attorneys advance to become *judges* and other *judicial workers*. Judges apply the law and oversee the legal process in courts according to local, State, and Federal statutes. They preside over cases concerning every aspect of society, from traffic offenses to disputes over management of professional sports, or from the rights of huge corporations to questions of disconnecting life support equipment for terminally ill persons. They must ensure that trials and hearings are conducted fairly and that the court administers justice in a manner that safeguards the legal rights of all parties involved.

The most visible responsibility of judges is presiding over trials or hearings and listening as attorneys represent the parties present. Judges rule on the admissibility of evidence and the methods of conducting testimony, and they may be called upon to settle disputes between opposing attorneys. They ensure that rules and procedures are followed, and if unusual circumstances arise for which standard procedures have not been established, judges determine the manner in which the trial will proceed based on their interpretation of the law.

Judges often hold pretrial hearings for cases. They listen to allegations and determine whether the evidence presented merits a trial. In criminal cases, judges may decide that persons charged with crimes should be held in jail pending their trial, or they may set conditions for release. In civil cases, judges occasionally impose restrictions upon the parties until a trial is held.

In many trials, juries are selected to decide guilt or innocence in criminal cases or liability and compensation in civil cases. Judges instruct juries on applicable laws, direct them to deduce the facts from the evidence presented, and hear their verdict. When the law does not require a jury trial or when the parties waive their right to a jury, judges decide the cases. In such cases, the judge determines guilt and imposes sentences in a criminal case; in civil cases, the judge rewards relief—such as compensation for damages—to the parties in the lawsuit (also called litigants).

Judges also work outside the courtroom "in chambers." In their private offices, judges read documents on pleadings and motions, research legal issues, write opinions, and oversee the court's operations. In some jurisdictions, judges also manage the courts' administrative and clerical staff.

Judges' duties vary according to the extent of their jurisdictions and powers. *General trial court judges* of the Federal and State court systems have jurisdiction over any case in their system. They usually try civil cases transcending the jurisdiction of lower courts and all cases involving felony offenses. Federal and State *appellate court judges*, although few in number, have the power to overrule decisions made by trial court or administrative law judges if they determine that legal errors were made in a case or if legal precedent does not support the judgment of the lower court. They rule on a small number of cases and rarely have direct contacts with litigants. Instead, they usually base their decisions on lower court records and lawyers' written and oral arguments.

Many State court judges preside in courts in which jurisdiction is limited by law to certain types of cases. A variety of titles are assigned to these judges, but among the most common are *municipal court judge, county court judge, magistrate,* or *justice of the peace.* Traffic violations, misdemeanors, small claims cases, and pretrial hearings constitute the bulk of the work of these judges, but some States allow them to handle cases involving domestic relations, probate, contracts, and other selected areas of the law.

Administrative law judges, sometimes called *hearing officers* or *adjudicators,* are employed by government agencies to make determinations for administrative agencies. They make decisions on a person's eligibility for various Social Security benefits or worker's compensation, protection of the environment, enforcement of health and safety regulations, employment discrimination, and compliance with economic regulatory requirements.

Working Conditions

Lawyers and judicial workers do most of their work in offices, law libraries, and courtrooms. Lawyers sometimes meet in clients' homes or places of business and, when necessary, in hospitals or prisons. They may travel to attend meetings, gather evidence, and appear before courts, legislative bodies, and other authorities.

Salaried lawyers usually have structured work schedules. Lawyers in private practice may work irregular hours while conducting research, conferring with clients, or preparing briefs during nonoffice hours. Lawyers often work long hours; about half regularly work 50 hours or more per week. They may face particularly heavy pressure, especially when a case is being tried. Preparation for court includes keeping abreast of the latest laws and judicial decisions.

Although work is not generally seasonal, the work of tax lawyers and other specialists may be an exception. Because lawyers in private practice can often determine their own workload and when they will retire, many stay in practice well beyond the usual retirement age.

Many judges work a standard 40-hour week, but a third of all judges work over 50 hours per week. Some judges with limited jurisdiction are employed part time and divide their time between their judicial responsibilities and other careers.

Employment

Lawyers held about 681,000 jobs in 1998; judges, magistrates and other judicial workers about 71,000. About 7 out of 10 lawyers practiced privately, either in law firms or in solo practices. Most of the remaining lawyers held positions in government, the greatest number at the local level. In the Federal Government, lawyers work for many different agencies but are concentrated in the Departments of Justice, Treasury, and Defense. A small number of lawyers are employed as house counsel by public utilities, banks, insurance companies, real estate agencies, manufacturing firms, welfare and religious organizations, and other business firms and nonprofit organizations. Some salaried lawyers also have part-time independent practices; others work as lawyers part time while working full time in another occupation.

All judges, magistrates, and other judicial workers were employed by Federal, State, or local governments; about 4 out of 10 held positions in the Federal government.

Training, Other Qualifications, and Advancement

To practice law in the courts of any State or other jurisdiction, a person must be licensed, or admitted to its bar, under rules established by the jurisdiction's highest court. All States require that applicants for admission to the bar pass a written bar examination; most jurisdictions also require applicants to pass a separate written ethics examination. Lawyers who have been admitted to the bar in one jurisdiction may occasionally be admitted to the bar in another without taking an examination if they meet that jurisdiction's standards of good moral character and have a specified period of legal experience. Federal courts and agencies set their own qualifications for those practicing before them.

To qualify for the bar examination in most States, an applicant must usually obtain a college degree and graduate from a law school accredited by the American Bar Association (ABA) or the proper State authorities. ABA accreditation signifies that the law school—particularly its library and faculty—meets certain standards developed to promote quality legal education. ABA currently accredits 183 law schools; others are approved by State authorities only. With certain exceptions, graduates of schools not approved by the ABA are restricted to taking the bar examination and practicing in the State or other jurisdiction in which the school is located; most of these schools are in California. In 1997, seven States accepted the study of law in a law office or in combination with study in a law school; only California accepts the study of law by correspondence as qualifying for taking the bar examination. Several States require registration and approval of students by the State Board of Law Examiners either before they enter law school or during the early years of legal study.

Although there is no nationwide bar examination, 47 States, the District of Columbia, Guam, the Northern Mariana Islands, Puerto Rico and the Virgin Islands require the six-hour Multistate Bar Examination (MBE) as part of the bar examination; the MBE is not required in Indiana, Louisiana, and Washington. The MBE covers issues of broad interest and is sometimes given in addition to a locally prepared State bar examination. The three-hour Multistate Essay Examination (MEE) is used as part of the State bar examination in several States. States vary in their use of MBE and MEE scores.

Many states have begun to require Multistate Performance Testing (MPT) to test the practical skills of beginning lawyers. This program has been well received, and many more States are expected to require performance testing in the future. Requirements vary by State, although the test usually is taken at the same time as the bar exam and is a one-time requirement.

The required college and law school education usually takes seven years of full-time study after high school: four years of undergraduate study followed by three years in law school. Although some law schools accept a very small number of students after three years of college, most require applicants to have a bachelor's degree. To meet the needs of students who can attend only part time, a number of law schools have night or part-time divisions that usually require four years of study; about 1 in 10 graduates from ABA approved schools attends part time.

Although there is no recommended "prelaw" major, prospective lawyers should develop proficiency in writing and speaking, read-

ing, researching, analyzing, and thinking logically—skills needed to succeed both in law school and in the profession. Regardless of major, a multidisciplinary background is recommended. Courses in English, foreign languages, public speaking, government, philosophy, history, economics, mathematics, and computer science, among others, are useful. Students interested in a particular aspect of law may find related courses helpful. For example, prospective patent lawyers need a strong background in engineering or science, and future tax lawyers must have extensive knowledge of accounting.

Acceptance by most law schools depends on the applicant's ability to demonstrate an aptitude for the study of law, usually through good undergraduate grades, the Law School Admission Test (LSAT), the quality of the applicant's undergraduate school, any prior work experience, and sometimes a personal interview. However, law schools vary in the weight they place on each of these and other factors.

All law schools approved by the ABA, except for those in Puerto Rico, require applicants to take the LSAT. Nearly all law schools require applicants to have certified transcripts sent to the Law School Data Assembly Service, which then sends applicants' LSAT scores and their standardized records of college grades to the law schools of their choice. Both this service and the LSAT are administered by the Law School Admission Council.

Competition for admission to many law schools is intense, especially for the most prestigious schools. Enrollments in these schools rose very rapidly during the 1970s, as applicants far outnumbered available seats. Although the number of applicants decreased markedly in the 1990s, the number of applicants to most law schools still greatly exceeds the number that can be admitted.

During the first year or year and a half of law school, students usually study core courses such as constitutional law, contracts, property law, torts, civil procedure, and legal writing. In the remaining time, they may elect specialized courses in fields such as tax, labor, or corporate law. Law students often acquire practical experience by participation in school-sponsored legal clinic activities, in the school's moot court competitions in which students conduct appellate arguments, in practice trials under the supervision of experienced lawyers and judges, and through research and writing on legal issues for the school's law journal.

A number of law schools have clinical programs in which students gain legal experience through practice trials and law school projects under the supervision of practicing lawyers and law school faculty. Law school clinical programs might include work in legal aid clinics, for example, or on the staff of legislative committees. Part-time or summer clerkships in law firms, government agencies, and corporate legal departments also provide valuable experience. Such training can lead directly to a job after graduation and help students decide what kind of practice best suits them. Clerkships may also be an important source of financial aid.

In 1997, law students in 52 jurisdictions were required to pass the Multistate Professional Responsibility Examination (MPRE), which tests their knowledge of the ABA codes on professional responsibility and judicial conduct. In some States, the MPRE may be taken during law school, usually after completing a course on legal ethics.

Law school graduates receive the degree of *juris doctor* (J.D.) as the first professional degree. Advanced law degrees may be desirable for those planning to specialize, research, or teach. Some law students pursue joint degree programs, which usually require an additional semester or year. Joint degree programs are offered in a number of areas, including law and business administration or public administration.

After graduation, lawyers must keep informed about legal and nonlegal developments that affect their practice. Currently, 39 States and jurisdictions mandate Continuing Legal Education (CLE). Many law schools and State and local bar associations provide continuing education courses that help lawyers stay abreast of recent developments. Some States allow CLE credits to be obtained through participation in seminars on the Internet.

The practice of law involves a great deal of responsibility. Individuals planning careers in law should like to work with people and be able to win the respect and confidence of their clients, associates, and the public. Perseverance, creativity, and reasoning ability are also essential to lawyers, who often analyze complex cases and handle new and unique legal problems.

Most beginning lawyers start in salaried positions. Newly hired, salaried attorneys usually start as associates and work with more experienced lawyers or judges. After several years of gaining more responsibilities, some lawyers are admitted to partnership in their firm or go into practice for themselves. Others become full-time law school faculty or administrators; a growing number of these lawyers have advanced degrees in other fields as well.

Some attorneys use their legal training in administrative or managerial positions in various departments of large corporations. A transfer from a corporation's legal department to another department often is viewed as a way to gain administrative experience and rise in the ranks of management.

A number of lawyers become judges, and most judges have first been lawyers. In fact, Federal and State judges are usually required to be lawyers. About 40 States allow nonlawyers to hold limited jurisdiction judgeships, but opportunities are better for those with law experience. Federal administrative law judges must be lawyers and pass a competitive examination administered by the U.S. Office of Personnel Management. Some State administrative law judges and other hearing officials are not required to be lawyers, but law degrees are preferred for most positions.

Federal judges are appointed for life by the President and are confirmed by the Senate. Federal administrative law judges are appointed by the various Federal agencies with virtually lifetime tenure. Some State judges are appointed, and the remainder are elected in partisan or nonpartisan State elections. Many State and local judges serve fixed renewable terms, which range from four or six years for some trial court judgeships to as long as 14 years or life for other trial or appellate court judges. Judicial nominating commissions, composed of members of the bar and the public, are used to screen candidates for judgeships in many States and for some Federal judgeships.

All States have some type of orientation for newly elected or appointed judges. The Federal Judicial Center, ABA, National Judicial College, and National Center for State Courts provide judicial education and training for judges and other judicial branch personnel. General and continuing education courses usually last from a couple of days to three weeks in length. Over half of all States and Puerto Rico require judges to enroll in continuing education courses while serving on the bench.

Job Outlook

Individuals interested in pursuing careers as lawyers or judicial workers should encounter stiff competition through 2008. The number of law school graduates is expected to continue to strain the economy's capacity to absorb them. As for judges, the prestige associated with serving on the bench should ensure continued, intense competition for openings.

Employment of lawyers grew very rapidly from the early 1970s through the early 1990s but has started to level off recently. Through 2008, employment is expected to grow about as fast as the average for all occupations. Continuing demand for lawyers will result primarily from growth in the population and the general level of business activities. Demand will also be spurred by growth of legal action in such areas as health care, intellectual property, international law, elder law, environmental law, and sexual harassment. In addition, the wider availability and affordability of legal clinics and prepaid legal service programs should result in increased use of legal services by middle-income people.

However, employment growth is expected to be slower than in the past. In an effort to reduce the money spent on legal fees, many businesses are increasingly utilizing large accounting firms and paralegals to perform some of the same functions as lawyers. For example, accounting firms may provide employee benefit counseling, process documents, or handle various other services previously performed by the law firm. Also, mediation and dispute resolution are increasingly used as alternatives to litigation.

Competition for job openings should continue to be keen because of the large numbers graduating from law school each year. During the 1970s, the annual number of law school graduates more than doubled, outpacing the rapid growth of jobs. Growth in the yearly number of law school graduates slowed during the early to mid-1980s, but increased again to current levels in the late 1980s to early 1990s. Although graduates with superior academic records from well-regarded law schools will have more job opportunities, most graduates should encounter stiff competition for jobs.

Perhaps as a result of this fierce competition, lawyers are increasingly finding work in nontraditional areas for which legal training is an asset but not normally a requirement—for example, administrative, managerial, and business positions in banks, insurance firms, real estate companies, government agencies, and other organizations. Employment opportunities are expected to continue to arise in these organizations at a growing rate.

As in the past, some graduates may have to accept positions in areas outside their field of interest or for which they feel overqualified. Some recent law school graduates who are unable to find permanent positions are turning to the growing number of temporary staffing firms that place attorneys in short-term jobs until they are able to secure full-time positions. This service allows companies to hire lawyers on an "as needed" basis and allows beginning lawyers to develop practical skills while looking for permanent positions.

Due to the competition for jobs, a law graduate's geographic mobility and work experience assume greater importance. The willingness to relocate may be an advantage in getting a job, but to be licensed in another State, a lawyer may have to take an additional State bar examination. In addition, employers increasingly seek graduates who have advanced law degrees and experience in a specialty such as tax, patent, or admiralty law.

Employment growth for lawyers will continue to be concentrated in salaried jobs, as businesses and all levels of government employ a growing number of staff attorneys, and as employment in the legal services industry grows in larger law firms. Most salaried positions are in urban areas where government agencies, law firms, and big corporations are concentrated. The number of self-employed lawyers is expected to increase slowly, reflecting the difficulty of establishing a profitable new practice in the face of competition from larger, established law firms. Moreover, the growing complexity of law, which encourages specialization, along with the cost of maintaining up-to-date legal research materials, favors larger firms.

For lawyers who wish to work independently, establishing a new practice will probably be easiest in small towns and expanding suburban areas. In such communities, competition from larger established law firms is likely to be less than in big cities, and new lawyers may find it easier to become known to potential clients.

Some lawyers are adversely affected by cyclical swings in the economy. During recessions, the demand declines for some discretionary legal services, such as planning estates, drafting wills, and handling real estate transactions. Also, corporations are less likely to litigate cases when declining sales and profits result in budgetary restrictions. Some corporations and law firms will not hire new attorneys until business improves or may cut staff to contain costs. Several factors, however, mitigate the overall impact of recessions on lawyers. During recessions, for example, individuals and corporations face other legal problems, such as bankruptcies, foreclosures, and divorces requiring legal action.

Employment of judges is expected to grow more slowly than the average for all occupations. Contradictory social forces affect the demand for judges. Growing public concerns about crime, safety, and efficient administration of justice should spur demand, while public budgetary pressures will limit job growth.

Competition for judgeships should remain intense. As in the past, most job openings will arise as judges retire. Although judges traditionally have held their positions until late in life, early retirement is becoming more common, a factor which should increase job openings. Nevertheless, becoming a judge will still be difficult; not only must judicial candidates compete with other qualified people, they often must also gain political support in order to be elected or appointed.

Earnings

In 1998, the median annual earnings of all lawyers was $78,170. The middle half of the occupation earned between $51,450 and $114,520. The bottom decile earned less than $37,310. Median annual earnings in the industries employing the largest numbers of lawyers in 1997 were as follows.

Legal services	$78,700
Federal government	78,200
Fire, marine, and casualty insurance	74,400
State government	59,400
Local government	49,200

Median salaries of lawyers six months after graduation from law school in 1998 varied by type of work, as indicated by Table 1.

TABLE 1

Median salaries of lawyers six months after graduation, 1998

All graduates	$45,000
Type of work	
Private practice	60,000
Business/industry	50,000
Academe	38,000
Judicial clerkship	37,500
Government	36,000
Public interest	31,000

SOURCE: National Association for Law Placement

Salaries of experienced attorneys vary widely according to the type, size, and location of their employer. Lawyers who own their own practices usually earn less than those who are partners in law firms. Lawyers starting their own practice may need to work part time in other occupations to supplement their income until their practice is well established.

Earnings among judicial workers also vary significantly. According to the Administrative Office of the U.S. Courts, the Chief Justice of the United States Supreme Court earned $175,400, and the Associate Justices earned $167,900. Federal district court judges had salaries of $136,700 in 1998, as did judges in the Court of Federal Claims and the Court of International Trade; circuit court judges earned $145,000 a year. Federal judges with limited jurisdiction, such as magistrates and bankruptcy court judges, had salaries of $125,800.

According to a survey by the National Center for State Courts, annual salaries of associate justices of States' highest courts averaged $105,100 in 1997, and ranged from about $77,100 to $137,300. Salaries of State intermediate appellate court judges averaged $103,700, and ranged from $79,400 to $124,200. Salaries of State judges of general jurisdiction trial courts averaged $94,000, and ranged from $72,000 to $115,300.

Most salaried lawyers and judges are provided health and life insurance, and contributions are made on their behalf to retirement plans. Lawyers who practice independently are covered only if they arrange and pay for such benefits themselves.

Related Occupations

Legal training is useful in many other occupations. Some of these are arbitrator, mediator, journalist, patent agent, title examiner, legislative assistant, lobbyist, FBI special agent, political office holder, and corporate executive.

Sources of Additional Information

Information on law schools and a career in law may be obtained from:

- American Bar Association, 750 North Lake Shore Dr., Chicago, IL 60611. Internet: http://www.abanet.org

Information on the LSAT, the Law School Data Assembly Service, applying to law school, and financial aid for law students may be obtained from:

- Law School Admission Council, P.O. Box 40, Newtown, PA 18940. Internet: http://www.lsac.org

Information on acquiring a job as a lawyer with the Federal government may be obtained from the Office of Personnel Management through a telephone-based system. Consult your telephone directory under U.S. Government for a local number or call (912) 757-3000; TDD (912) 744-2299. This number is not toll-free, and charges may result. Information also is available from their Internet site: http://www.usajobs.opm.gov.

The requirements for admission to the bar in a particular State or other jurisdiction may also be obtained at the State capital from the clerk of the Supreme Court or the administrator of the State Board of Bar Examiners.

Librarians

(O*NET 31502A and 31502B)

Significant Points

- A master's degree in library science is usually required; special librarians often need an additional graduate or professional degree.

- Applicants for librarian jobs in large cities or suburban areas will face competition, while those willing to work in rural areas should have better job prospects.

Nature of the Work

The traditional concept of a library is being redefined, from a place to access paper records or books, to one which also houses the most advanced mediums, including CD-ROM, the Internet, virtual libraries, and remote access to a wide range of resources. Consequently, librarians are increasingly combining traditional duties with tasks involving quickly changing technology. Librarians assist people in finding information and using it effectively in their personal and professional lives. They must have knowledge of a wide variety of scholarly and public information sources, and follow trends related to publishing, computers, and the media to effectively oversee the selection and organization of library materials. Librarians manage staff and develop and direct information programs and systems for the public to ensure information is organized to meet users' needs.

Most librarian positions incorporate three aspects of library work: user services, technical services, and administrative services. Even librarians specializing in one of these areas perform other responsibilities. Librarians in user services, such as reference and children's librarians, work with the public to help them find the information they need. This involves analyzing users' needs to determine what information is appropriate and searching for, acquiring, and providing information. It also includes an instructional role, such as showing users how to access information. For example, librarians commonly help users navigate the Internet, showing them how to most efficiently search for relevant information. Librarians in technical services, such as acquisitions and cataloguing, acquire and prepare materials for use and often do not deal directly with the public. Librarians in administrative services oversee the management and planning of libraries; negotiate contracts for services, materials, and equipment; supervise library employees; perform public relations and fundraising duties; prepare budgets; and direct activities to ensure that everything functions properly.

In small libraries or information centers, librarians usually handle all aspects of the work. They read book reviews, publishers' announcements, and catalogues to keep up with current literature and other available resources, and they select and purchase materials from publishers, wholesalers, and distributors. Librarians prepare new materials by classifying them by subject matter, and describe books and other library materials so they are easy to find. They supervise assistants who prepare cards, computer records, or other access tools that direct users to resources. In large libraries, librarians often specialize in a single area, such as acquisitions, cataloguing, bibliography, reference, special collections, or administration. Teamwork is increasingly important to ensure quality service to the public.

Librarians also compile lists of books, periodicals, articles, and audiovisual materials on particular subjects, analyze collections, and recommend materials. They collect and organize books, pamphlets, manuscripts, and other materials in a specific field, such as rare books, genealogy, or music. In addition, they coordinate programs such as storytelling for children and literacy skills and book talks for adults; conduct classes; publicize services; provide reference help; write grants; and oversee other administrative matters.

Librarians are classified according to the type of library in which they work—public libraries, school library media centers, academic libraries, and special libraries. Some librarians work with specific groups, such as children, young adults, adults, or the disadvantaged. In school library media centers, librarians help teachers develop curricula, acquire materials for classroom instruction, and sometimes team-teach.

Librarians also work in information centers or libraries maintained by government agencies, corporations, law firms, advertising agencies, museums, professional associations, medical centers, hospitals, religious organizations, and research laboratories. They build and arrange an organization's information resources, which are usually limited to subjects of special interest to the organization. These special librarians can provide vital information services by preparing abstracts and indexes of current periodicals, organizing bibliographies, or analyzing background information and preparing reports on areas of particular interest. For instance, a special librarian working for a corporation could provide the sales department with information on competitors or new developments affecting their field.

Many libraries have access to remote databases and maintain their own computerized databases. The widespread use of automation in libraries makes database searching skills important to librarians. Librarians develop and index databases and help train users to develop searching skills for the information they need. Some libraries are forming consortiums with other libraries through electronic mail. This allows patrons to simultaneously submit information requests to several libraries. The Internet is also expanding the amount of available reference information. Librarians must be aware of how to use these resources in order to locate information.

Librarians with computer and information systems skills can work as automated systems librarians, planning and operating computer systems, and information science librarians, designing information storage and retrieval systems and developing procedures for collecting, organizing, interpreting, and classifying information. These librarians analyze and plan for future information needs. The increased use of automated information systems enables librarians to focus on administrative and budgeting responsibilities, grant writing, and specialized research requests, while delegating more technical and user services responsibilities to technicians.

Increasingly, librarians apply their information management and research skills to arenas outside of libraries—for example, database development, reference tool development, information systems, publishing, Internet coordination, marketing, and training of database users. Entrepreneurial librarians sometimes start their own consulting practices, acting as freelance librarians or information brokers and providing services to other libraries, businesses, or government agencies.

Working Conditions

Librarians spend a significant portion of time at their desks or in front of computer terminals; extended work at video display terminals can cause eyestrain and headaches. Assisting users in obtaining information for their jobs, recreational purposes, and other uses can be challenging and satisfying; at the same time, working with users under deadlines can be demanding and stressful.

More than 2 out of 10 librarians work part time. Public and college librarians often work weekends and evenings and have to work some holidays. School librarians usually have the same workday schedule as classroom teachers and similar vacation schedules. Special librarians usually work normal business hours, but in fast-paced industries, such as advertising or legal services, they can work longer hours during peak times.

Employment

Librarians held about 152,000 jobs in 1998. Most were in school and academic libraries; others were in public and special libraries. A small number of librarians worked for hospitals and religious organizations. Others worked for governments.

Training, Other Qualifications, and Advancement

A master's degree in library science (MLS) is necessary for librarian positions in most public, academic, and special libraries, and in some school libraries. The Federal government requires an MLS or the equivalent in education and experience. Many colleges and universities offer MLS programs, but employers often prefer graduates of the approximately 50 schools accredited by the American Library Association. Most MLS programs require a bachelor's degree; any liberal arts major is appropriate.

Most MLS programs take one year to complete; others take two. A typical graduate program includes courses in the foundations of library and information science, including the history of books and printing, intellectual freedom and censorship, and the role of libraries and information in society. Other basic courses cover material selection and processing, the organization of information, reference tools and strategies, and user services. Courses are adapted to educate librarians to use new resources brought about by advancing technology such as on-line reference systems, Internet search methods, and automated circulation systems. Course options can include resources for children or young adults; classification, cataloguing, indexing, and abstracting; library administration; and library automation. Computer-related course work is an increasingly important part of an MLS degree.

An MLS provides general preparation for library work, but some individuals specialize in a particular area such as reference, technical services, or children's services. A Ph.D. degree in library and information science is advantageous for a college teaching position or a top administrative job in a college or university library or large library system.

In special libraries, an MLS is also usually required. In addition, most special librarians supplement their education with knowledge of the subject specialization, sometimes earning a master's, doctoral, or professional degree in the subject. Subject specializations include medicine, law, business, engineering, and the natural and social sciences. For example, a librarian working for a law firm may also be a licensed attorney, holding both library science and law degrees. In some jobs, knowledge of a foreign language is needed.

State certification requirements for public school librarians vary widely. Most States require school librarians, often called library media specialists, to be certified as teachers and have courses in library science. In some cases, an MLS, perhaps with a library media specialization, or a master's in education with a specialty in school library media or educational media, is needed. Some States require certification of public librarians employed in municipal, county, or regional library systems.

Librarians participate in continuing training once they are on the job to keep abreast of new information systems brought about by changing technology.

Experienced librarians can advance to administrative positions, such as department head, library director, or chief information officer.

Job Outlook

Slower than average employment growth, coupled with an increasing number of MLS graduates, will result in more applicants competing for fewer jobs. However, because MLS programs increasingly focus on computer skills, graduates will be qualified for other, computer-related occupations. Applicants for librarian jobs in large metropolitan areas, where most graduates prefer to work, will face competition; those willing to work in rural areas should have better job prospects.

Some job openings for librarians will stem from projected slower-than-average employment growth through 2008. Replacement needs will account for more job openings over the next decade, as some librarians reach retirement age.

The increasing use of computerized information storage and retrieval systems could contribute to slow growth in the demand for librarians. Computerized systems make cataloguing easier, which library technicians now handle. In addition, many libraries are equipped for users to access library computers directly from their homes or offices. These systems allow users to bypass librarians and conduct research on their own. However, librarians are needed to manage staff, help users develop database searching techniques, address complicated reference requests, and define users' needs.

Opportunities will be best for librarians outside traditional settings. Nontraditional library settings include information brokers, private corporations, and consulting firms. Many companies are turning to librarians because of their research and organizational skills and knowledge of computer databases and library automation systems. Librarians can review vast amounts of information and analyze, evaluate, and organize it according to a company's specific needs. Librarians are also hired by organizations to set up information on the Internet. Librarians working in these settings may be classified as systems analysts, database specialists and trainers, webmasters or web developers, or LAN (local area network) coordinators.

Earnings

Salaries of librarians vary according to the individual's qualifications and the type, size, and location of the library. Librarians with primarily administrative duties often have greater earnings. Median annual earnings of librarians in 1998 were $38,470. The middle 50 percent earned between $30,440 and $48,130. The lowest 10 percent earned less than $22,970, and the highest 10 percent earned more than $67,810. Median annual earnings in the industries employing the largest numbers of librarians in 1997 were as follows:

Elementary and secondary schools	$38,900
Colleges and universities	38,600
Local government, except education and hospitals	32,600

The average annual salary for all librarians in the Federal government in nonsupervisory, supervisory, and managerial positions was $56,400 in 1999.

Related Occupations

Librarians play an important role in the transfer of knowledge and ideas by providing people with access to the information they need and want. Jobs requiring similar analytical, organizational, and communicative skills include archivists, information scientists, museum curators, publishers' representatives, research analysts, information brokers, and records managers. The management aspect of a librarian's work is similar to the work of managers in a variety of business and government settings. School librarians have many duties similar to those of school teachers. Other jobs requiring the computer skills of some librarians include webmasters or web developers, database specialists, and systems analysts.

Sources of Additional Information

Information on librarianship, including information on scholarships or loans, is available from the American Library Association. For a listing of accredited library education programs, check their homepage:

- American Library Association, Office for Human Resource Development and Recruitment, 50 East Huron St., Chicago, IL 60611. Internet: http://www.ala.org

For information on a career as a special librarian, write to:

- Special Libraries Association, 1700 18th St. NW., Washington, DC 20009.

Information on graduate schools of library and information science can be obtained from:

- Association for Library and Information Science Education, P.O. Box 7640, Arlington, VA 22207. Internet: http://www.sils.umich.edu/ALISE

For information on a career as a law librarian, scholarship information, and a list of ALA-accredited schools offering programs in law librarianship, contact:

- American Association of Law Libraries, 53 West Jackson Blvd., Suite 940, Chicago, IL 60604. Internet: http://www.ala.org

For information on employment opportunities as a health sciences librarian, scholarship information, credentialing information, and a list of MLA-accredited schools offering programs in health sciences librarianship, contact:

- Medical Library Association, 6 N. Michigan Ave., Suite 300, Chicago, IL 60602. Internet: http://www.mlanet.org

Information on acquiring a job as a librarian with the Federal government may be obtained from the Office of Personnel Management through a telephone-based system. Consult your telephone directory under U.S. Government for a local number or call (912) 757-3000; TDD (912) 744-2299. That number is not toll free, and charges may result. Information also is available from their Internet site: http://www.usajobs.opm.gov.

Information concerning requirements and application procedures for positions in the Library of Congress can be obtained directly from:

- Human Resources Office, Library of Congress, 101 Independence Ave. SE., Washington, DC 20540-2231.

State library agencies can furnish information on scholarships available through their offices, requirements for certification, and general information about career prospects in the State. Several of these agencies maintain job hotlines reporting openings for librarians.

State departments of education can furnish information on certification requirements and job opportunities for school librarians.

Many library science schools offer career placement services to their alumni and current students. Some allow non-affiliated students and jobseekers to use their services.

Library Assistants and Bookmobile Drivers

(O*NET 53902)

Significant Points

- Most jobs require only a high school diploma.
- Numerous opportunities should arise due to high turnover.

Nature of the Work

Library assistants and bookmobile drivers organize library resources and make them available to users. They assist librarians and, in some cases, library technicians.

Library assistants—sometimes referred to as library media assistants, library aides, or circulation assistants—register patrons so they can borrow materials from the library. They record the borrower's name and address from an application and then issue a library card. Most library assistants enter and update patrons' records using computer databases.

At the circulation desk, assistants lend and collect books, periodicals, video tapes, and other materials. When an item is borrowed, assistants stamp the due date on the material and record the patron's identification from his or her library card. They inspect returned materials for damage, check due dates, and compute fines for overdue material. They review records to compile a list of overdue materials and send out notices. They also answer patrons' questions and refer those they cannot answer to a librarian.

Throughout the library, assistants sort returned books, periodicals, and other items and return them to their designated shelves, files, or storage areas. They locate materials to be loaned, either for a patron or another library. Many card catalogues are computerized, so library assistants must be familiar with the computer system. If any materials have been damaged, these workers try to repair them. For example, they use tape or paste to repair torn pages or book covers and other specialized processes to repair more valuable materials.

Some library assistants specialize in helping patrons who have vision problems. Sometimes referred to as library, talking-books, or Braille-and-talking-books clerks, they review the borrower's list of desired reading material. They locate those materials or closely related substitutes from the library collection of large type or Braille volumes, tape cassettes, and open-reel talking books. They complete the paperwork and give or mail the materials to the borrower.

To extend library services to more patrons, many libraries operate bookmobiles. Bookmobile drivers take trucks stocked with books to designated sites on a regular schedule. Bookmobiles serve community organizations such as shopping centers, apartment complexes, schools, and nursing homes. They may also be used to

extend library service to patrons living in remote areas. Depending on local conditions, drivers may operate a bookmobile alone or may be accompanied by a library technician.

When working alone, the drivers perform many of the same functions as a library assistant in a main or branch library. They answer patrons' questions, receive and check out books, collect fines, maintain the book collection, shelve materials, and occasionally operate audiovisual equipment to show slides or films. They participate and may assist in planning programs sponsored by the library such as reader advisory programs, used book sales, or outreach programs. Bookmobile drivers keep track of their mileage, the materials lent out, and the amount of fines collected. In some areas, they are responsible for maintenance of the vehicle and any photocopiers or other equipment in it. They record statistics on circulation and the number of people visiting the bookmobile. Drivers may also record requests for special items from the main library and arrange for the materials to be mailed or delivered to a patron during the next scheduled visit. Many bookmobiles are equipped with personal computers and CD-ROM systems linked to the main library system; this allows bookmobile drivers to reserve or locate books immediately. Some bookmobiles now offer Internet access to users.

Because bookmobile drivers may be the only link some people have to the library, much of their work is helping the public. They may assist handicapped or elderly patrons to the bookmobile, or shovel snow to assure their safety. They may enter hospitals or nursing homes to deliver books to patrons who are bedridden.

Working Conditions

Because most library assistants use computers on a daily basis, these workers may experience eye and muscle strain, backaches, headaches, and repetitive motion injuries. Also, assistants who review detailed data may have to sit for extended periods of time. Although the work does not require heavy lifting, library assistants spend a lot of time on their feet and frequently stoop, bend, and reach. Library assistants may work evenings and weekends, but those employed in school libraries usually work only during the school year.

Bookmobile drivers must maneuver large vehicles in all kinds of traffic and weather conditions and may also be responsible for the maintenance of the bookmobile. The schedules of bookmobile drivers depend on the size of the area being served. Some of these workers go out on their routes every day, while others go only on certain days. On these other days, they work at the library. Some also work evenings and weekends to give patrons as much access to the library as possible.

Employment

Library assistants and bookmobile drivers held about 127,000 jobs in 1998. Over one-half of these workers were employed by local government in public libraries; most of the remaining worked in school libraries. Opportunities for flexible schedules are abundant; over one-half of these workers were on part-time schedules.

Training, Other Qualifications, and Advancement

Employers typically require applicants to have at least a high school diploma or its equivalent. Most employers prefer workers who are computer-literate. Knowledge of word processing and spreadsheet software is especially valuable, as are experience working in an office and good interpersonal skills.

Library assistants often learn the skills they need in high schools, business schools, and community colleges. Business education programs offered by these institutions typically include courses in typing, word processing, shorthand, business communications, records management, and office systems and procedures.

Some entrants are college graduates with degrees in liberal arts. Although a degree is rarely required, many graduates accept entry-level positions with the hope of being promoted. Workers with college degrees are likely to start at higher salaries and advance more easily than those without degrees.

Once hired, library assistants and bookmobile drivers usually receive on-the-job training. Under the guidance of a supervisor or other senior worker, new employees learn procedures. Some formal classroom training may also be necessary, such as training in specific computer software. Library assistants and bookmobile drivers must be careful, orderly, and detail-oriented in order to avoid making errors and to recognize errors made by others. Many bookmobile drivers are now required to have a commercial driver's license.

These employees usually advance by taking on more duties in the same occupation for higher pay or transferring to a closely related occupation. Most companies fill supervisory and managerial positions by promoting individuals from within their organizations, so those who acquire additional skills, experience, and training improve their advancement opportunities. With appropriate experience and education, some may become librarians.

Job Outlook

Opportunities should be good for persons interested in jobs as library assistants or bookmobile drivers through 2008. Turnover of these workers is quite high, reflecting the limited investment in training and subsequent weak attachment to this occupation. This work is attractive to retirees, students, and others who want a part-time schedule, and there is a lot of movement into and out of the occupation. Many openings will become available each year to replace workers who transfer to other occupations or leave the labor force. Some positions become available as library assistants move within the organization. Library assistants can be promoted to library technicians and eventually supervisory positions in public service or technical service areas. Advancement opportunities are greater in larger libraries and may be more limited in smaller ones.

Employment is expected to grow about as fast as the average for all occupations through 2008. The vast majority of library assistants and bookmobile drivers work in public or school libraries. Efforts to contain costs in local governments and academic institutions of all types may result in more hiring of library support staff than librarians. Because most are employed by public institutions, library assistants and bookmobile drivers are not directly affected by the ups and downs of the business cycle. Some of these workers may lose their jobs, however, if there are cuts in government budgets.

Earnings

Salaries of library assistants and bookmobile drivers vary. The region of the country, size of city, and type and size of establishment all influence salary levels. Median annual earnings of full-time library assistants and bookmobile drivers in 1998 were $16,980.

Related Occupations

Other clerical workers who enter and manipulate data include bank tellers, statistical clerks, receiving clerks, medical record clerks, hotel and motel clerks, credit clerks, and reservation and transportation ticket agents.

Sources of Additional Information

Information about a career as a library assistant can be obtained from:

- Council on Library/Media Technology, P.O. Box 951, Oxon Hill, MD 20750. Internet: http://library.ucr.edu/COLT

Public libraries and libraries in academic institutions can provide information about job openings for library assistants and bookmobile drivers.

Library Technicians

(O*NET 31505)

Significant Points

- Training ranges from on-the-job to a bachelor's degree.
- Experienced library technicians can advance by obtaining a Master of Library Science degree.

Nature of the Work

Library technicians help librarians acquire, prepare, and organize material, and assist users in finding information. Technicians in small libraries handle a range of duties; those in large libraries usually specialize. As libraries increasingly use new technologies (such as CD-ROM, the Internet, virtual libraries, and automated databases) the duties of library technicians will expand and evolve accordingly. Library technicians are assuming greater responsibilities, in some cases taking on tasks previously performed by librarians.

Depending on the employer, library technicians can have other titles, such as library technical assistants. Library technicians direct library users to standard references, organize and maintain periodicals, prepare volumes for binding, handle interlibrary loan requests, prepare invoices, perform routine cataloguing and coding of library materials, retrieve information from computer data-

bases, and supervise support staff.

The widespread use of computerized information storage and retrieval systems has resulted in technicians handling more technical and user services (such as entering catalogue information into the library's computer) that were once performed by librarians. Technicians assist with customizing databases. In addition, technicians instruct patrons how to use computer systems to access data. The increased use of automation has reduced the amount of clerical work performed by library technicians. Many libraries now offer self-service registration and circulation with computers, decreasing the time library technicians spend manually recording and inputting records.

Some library technicians operate and maintain audiovisual equipment, such as projectors, tape recorders, and videocassette recorders, and assist users with microfilm or microfiche readers. They also design posters, bulletin boards, or displays.

Those in school libraries encourage and teach students to use the library and media center. They also help teachers obtain instructional materials and assist students with special assignments. Some work in special libraries maintained by government agencies, corporations, law firms, advertising agencies, museums, professional societies, medical centers, and research laboratories, where they conduct literature searches, compile bibliographies, and prepare abstracts, usually on subjects of particular interest to the organization.

Working Conditions

Technicians answer questions and provide assistance to library users. Those who prepare library materials sit at desks or computer terminals for long periods and can develop headaches or eyestrain from working with video display terminals. Some duties, like calculating circulation statistics, can be repetitive and boring. Others, such as performing computer searches using local and regional library networks and cooperatives, can be interesting and challenging.

Library technicians in school libraries work regular school hours. Those in public libraries and college and university (academic) libraries also work weekends, evenings, and some holidays. Library technicians in special libraries usually work normal business hours, although they often work overtime as well.

Library technicians usually work under the supervision of a librarian, although they work independently in certain situations.

Employment

Library technicians held about 72,000 jobs in 1998. Most worked in school, academic, or public libraries. Some worked in hospitals and religious organizations. The Federal government, primarily the Department of Defense and the Library of Congress, and State and local governments also employed library technicians.

Training, Other Qualifications, and Advancement

Training requirements for library technicians vary widely, ranging from a high school diploma to specialized post-secondary train-

ing. Some employers hire individuals with work experience or other training; others train inexperienced workers on the job. Other employers require that technicians have an associate or bachelor's degree. Given the rapid spread of automation in libraries, computer skills are needed for many jobs. Knowledge of databases, library automation systems, on-line library systems, on-line public access systems, and circulation systems is valuable.

Some two-year colleges offer an associate of arts degree in library technology. Programs include both liberal arts and library-related study. Students learn about library and media organization and operation and how to order, process, catalogue, locate, and circulate library materials and work with library automation. Libraries and associations offer continuing education courses to keep technicians abreast of new developments in the field.

Library technicians usually advance by assuming added responsibilities. For example, technicians often start at the circulation desk, checking books in and out. After gaining experience, they may become responsible for storing and verifying information. As they advance, they may become involved in budget and personnel matters in their department. Some library technicians advance to supervisory positions and are in charge of the day-to-day operation of their department.

Job Outlook

Employment of library technicians is expected to grow about as fast as the average for all occupations through 2008. Some job openings will result from the need to replace library technicians who transfer to other fields or leave the labor force. Similar to other fields, willingness to relocate enhances an aspiring library technician's job prospects.

The increasing use of library automation is expected to spur job growth among library technicians. Computerized information systems have simplified certain tasks, such as descriptive cataloguing, which can now be handled by technicians instead of librarians. For instance, technicians can now easily retrieve information from a central database and store it in the library's computer. Although budgetary constraints could dampen employment growth of library technicians in school, public, and college and university libraries, libraries sometimes use technicians to perform some librarian duties in an effort to stretch shrinking budgets. Growth in the number of professionals and other workers who use special libraries should result in relatively fast employment growth among library technicians in those settings.

Earnings

Median annual earnings of library technicians in 1998 were $21,730. The middle 50 percent earned between $16,500 and $27,340. The lowest 10 percent earned less than $12,610, and the highest 10 percent earned more than $33,370. Median annual earnings in the industries employing the largest numbers of library technicians in 1997 are shown below:

Local government, except education and hospitals $22,200

Colleges and universities 21,400

Elementary and secondary schools 18,300

Salaries of library technicians in the Federal government averaged $29,700 in 1999.

Related Occupations

Library technicians perform organizational and administrative duties. Workers in other occupations with similar duties include library assistants, information clerks, record clerks, medical record technicians, and title searchers.

Sources of Additional Information

Information about a career as a library technician can be obtained from:

- Council on Library/Media Technology, P.O. Box 951, Oxon Hill, MD 20750. Internet: http://library.ucr.edu/COLT

For information on training programs for library/media technical assistants, write to:

- American Library Association, Office for Human Resource Development and Recruitment, 50 East Huron St., Chicago, IL 60611. Internet: http://www.ala.org

Information on acquiring a job as a library technician with the Federal government may be obtained from the Office of Personnel Management through a telephone-based system. Consult your telephone directory under U.S. Government for a local number or call (912) 757-3000; TDD (912) 744-2299. That number is not toll free, and charges may result. Information also is available from their Internet site: http://www.usajobs.opm.gov.

Information concerning requirements and application procedures for positions in the Library of Congress can be obtained directly from:

- Human Resources Office, Library of Congress, 101 Independence Ave. SE., Washington, DC 20540-2231.

State library agencies can furnish information on requirements for technicians, as well as general information about career prospects in the State. Several of these agencies maintain job hotlines reporting openings for library technicians.

State departments of education can furnish information on requirements and job opportunities for school library technicians.

Loan Clerks and Credit Authorizers, Checkers, and Clerks

(O*NET 53114, 53117, and 53121)

Significant Points

- A high school education is the minimum requirement; telephone, typing, and computer skills are also helpful.

- Increasing automation will result in slower-than-average employment growth despite an increase in loans and credit applications.

Nature of the Work

Loan clerks and credit authorizers, checkers, and clerks review credit history and obtain the information needed to determine the creditworthiness of loan and credit card applicants. They spend much of their day on the phone obtaining credit information from credit bureaus, employers, banks, credit institutions, and other sources to determine the applicant's credit history and ability to pay back the loan or charge.

Loan clerks, also called *loan processing clerks*, *loan closers*, or *loan service clerks*, assemble loan documents, process the paperwork associated with the loan, and assure that all information is complete and verified. Mortgage loans are the primary type of loan handled by loan clerks, who may also have to order appraisals on the property, set up escrow accounts, and secure any additional information required to transfer the property.

The specific duties of loan clerks vary by specialty. *Loan closers*, for example, complete the loan process by gathering the proper documents for signature at the closing, including deeds of trust, property insurance papers, and title commitments. They set the time and place for the closing, make sure all parties are present, and ensure that all conditions for settlement have been met. After settlement, the loan closer records all documents and submits the final loan package to the owner of the loan. *Loan service clerks* maintain the payment records once the loan is issued. These clerical workers process the paperwork for payment of fees to insurance companies and tax authorities and may also record changes to client addresses and loan ownership. When necessary, they answer calls from customers with routine inquiries.

The duties of *loan interviewers* are similar to those of loan clerks. They interview potential borrowers and help them fill out loan applications. Interviewers may then investigate the applicant's background and references, verify information on the application, and forward any findings, reports, or documents to the appraisal department. Finally, interviewers inform the applicant whether the loan has been accepted or denied.

Credit authorizers, *checkers*, and *clerks* process and authorize applications for credit, including credit cards. Although the distinctions between the three are becoming less, some generalities can still be made. *Credit clerks* typically handle the processing of the credit applications by verifying the information on the application, calling applicants if they need additional data, contacting credit bureaus for a credit rating, and obtaining any other information necessary to determine the applicant's creditworthiness. If the clerk works in a department store or other establishment that offers instant credit, the clerk enters applicant information into a computer at the point-of-sale. A credit rating will then be transmitted from a central office within seconds to determine whether the application should be rejected or approved.

Some organizations have *credit checkers*, who investigate a person's or business's credit history and current credit standing prior to issuing a loan or line of credit. They may also telephone or write to credit departments of businesses and service companies to obtain information about an applicant's credit standing. Credit reporting agencies and bureaus hire a number of checkers to secure, update, and verify information for credit reports. These workers are often called credit investigators or reporters.

Credit authorizers approve charges against customers' existing accounts. Most charges are approved automatically by computer. When accounts are past due, overextended, invalid, or show a change of address, however, sales persons refer transactions to credit authorizers located in a central office. These authorizers evaluate the customers' computerized credit records and payment histories to quickly decide whether or not to approve new charges.

Working Conditions

Loan clerks and credit authorizers, checkers, and clerks usually work a standard 35- to 40-hour week. However, they may work overtime during particularly busy periods. Loan clerks handling residential real estate experience busy periods during spring and summer and at the end of each month. For credit authorizers, busy periods are during the holiday shopping seasons and store sales. In retail establishments, authorizers may work nights and weekends during store hours. Authorizers and checkers may also work in call centers if they are employed by companies that have centralized this function at one location. Part-time work is available for a number of these occupations.

Employment

Loan clerks and credit authorizers, checkers, and clerks held about 254,000 jobs in 1998. About 8 out of 10 were employed by commercial and savings banks, credit unions, mortgage banks, and personal and business credit institutions. Credit reporting and collection agencies, and wholesale and retail trade establishments also employ these clerks.

Training, Other Qualifications, and Advancement

A high school education or equivalent is usually the minimum requirement for these entry-level positions. Other requirements of the job include good telephone and organizational skills as well as the ability to pay close attention to details and meet tight deadlines. To enter and retrieve data quickly, computer skills are also important.

Most new employees are trained on the job, working under close supervision of more experienced employees. Some firms offer formal training that may include courses in telephone etiquette, computer use, and customer service skills. A number of credit workers also take courses in credit offered by banking and credit associations, public and private vocational schools, and colleges and universities. Workers in these positions can typically advance to loan or credit department supervisor, underwriter, loan officer, or team leader of a small group of clerks.

Job Outlook

Slower-than-average employment growth for loan clerks and credit authorizers, checkers, and clerks is expected through 2008. Despite a projected increase in the number of loans and credit applica-

tions, automation will allow fewer workers to process, check, and authorize applications than in the past. The effects of automation on employment will be moderated, however, by the many interpersonal aspects of the job. Mortgage loans, for example, require loan processors to personally verify financial data on the application, and loan closers are needed to assemble documents and prepare them for settlement.

Employment will also be adversely affected by changes in the financial services industry. For example, significant consolidation has occurred among mortgage loan servicing companies. As a result, fewer mortgage banking companies are involved in loan servicing, making the function more efficient and reducing the need for loan servicing clerks.

Credit scoring is another major development that has improved the productivity of these workers, further limiting employment growth. Companies and credit bureaus can now purchase software that quickly analyzes a person's creditworthiness and summarizes it into a "score." Credit issuers can then easily decide whether or not to accept or reject the application depending on the score, which speeds up the authorization of loans or credit. Obtaining credit ratings is also much easier for credit checkers and authorizers, as businesses now have computer terminals that are directly linked to credit bureaus that provide immediate access to a person's credit history.

The job outlook for loan clerks and credit authorizers, checkers, and clerks is sensitive to overall economic activity. A downturn in the economy and a rise in interest rates usually lead to a decline in demand for credit and loans, particularly mortgage loans, possibly causing layoffs. Even in slow economic times, however, job openings will arise from the need to replace those who leave the occupation for various reasons.

Earnings

Median annual earnings of loan and credit clerks, the largest occupation among loan clerks and credit authorizers, checkers, and clerks, were about $22,580 in 1998. The middle 50 percent earned between $18,620 and $27,740. The lowest 10 percent had earnings of less than $14,820, while the top 10 percent earned over $33,870. Median annual earnings in the industries employing the largest number of loan and credit clerks in 1997 were:

Mortgage bankers and brokers	$24,300
Savings institutions	22,100
Commercial banks	20,300
Credit unions	20,200
Personal credit institutions	19,300

Among other workers in this occupational grouping, median annual earnings of credit checkers were $21,550 in 1998; credit authorizers earned $22,990; and loan interviewers made $23,190. In addition to standard benefits, workers in retail establishments usually receive a discount on store purchases.

Related Occupations

Occupations with duties similar to those of loan clerks and credit authorizers, checkers, and clerks include claim clerks, customer complaint clerks, procurement clerks, probate clerks, and collection clerks.

Sources of Additional Information

General information about local job opportunities for loan clerks and credit authorizers, checkers, and clerks may be obtained from banks and credit institutions, retail stores, and credit reporting agencies.

For specific information on a career as a loan processor or loan closer, contact:

- Mortgage Bankers Association of America, 1125 15th St. NW., Washington, DC 20005. Internet: http://www.mbaa.org

Loan Officers and Counselors

(O*NET 21108)

Significant Points

- Loan officer positions generally require a bachelor's degree in finance, economics, or a related field; training or experience in banking, lending, or sales is advantageous.

- Low interest rates will keep demand for loans high, causing employment of loan officers to grow about as fast as average; growth will be tempered by technology that makes these employees more productive.

Nature of the Work

For many individuals, taking out a loan may be the only way to afford a house, car, or college education. Likewise for businesses, loans are essential to start many companies, purchase inventory, or invest in capital equipment. *Loan officers* facilitate this lending by seeking potential clients and assisting them in applying for loans. Loan officers also gather information about clients and businesses to ensure that an informed decision is made regarding the quality of the loan and the probability of repayment.

Loan officers usually specialize in commercial, consumer, or mortgage loans. Commercial or business loans help companies pay for new equipment or expand operations; consumer loans include home equity, automobile, and personal loans; and mortgage loans are made to purchase real estate or to refinance an existing mortgage. In addition, banks and other lenders are offering a growing variety of loans. Loan officers must keep abreast of new types of loans and other financial products and services, so they can meet their customers' needs.

In many instances, loan officers act as salespeople. Commercial loan officers, for example, contact firms to determine the firms' demand for loans. If the firm is seeking new funds, the loan officer will try to persuade the company to obtain the loan from their institution. Similarly, mortgage loan officers develop relationships with commercial and residential real estate agencies, so when an individual or firm buys a property, the real estate agent might recommend contacting that loan officer for financing.

Once this initial contact has been made, loan officers guide clients through the process of applying for a loan. This process begins with a formal meeting or telephone call with a prospective client, during which the loan officer obtains basic information about the purpose of the loan and explains the different types of loans and credit terms that are available to the applicant. Sometimes the loan officer assists the client in filling out the application and answers questions about the process.

After completing the forms, the loan officer begins the process of analyzing and verifying the application to determine the client's creditworthiness. The loan officer may request a copy of the client's credit history from one of the major credit reporting agencies, or in the case of commercial loans, she or he may request copies of the company's financial statements. Loan officers include this information and their written comments in a loan file, used to analyze the viability of the loan vis-à-vis the lending institution's requirements. At this point, the loan officer, in consultation with her or his manager, decides whether to grant the loan. If approved, a repayment schedule is then arranged with the client.

A loan that would otherwise be denied may be approved if the customer can provide the lender with appropriate collateral—property pledged as security for the payment of a loan. For example, when lending money for a college education, the bank may insist that the borrower offer her or his home as collateral. If the borrower were ever unable to repay the loan, the borrower would have to sell the home to raise the necessary money.

Once the loan has been granted, *loan counselors*, also called loan collection officers, may need to contact borrowers with delinquent accounts to help them find a method of repayment to avoid default on the loan. If a repayment plan cannot be developed, the loan counselor initiates collateral liquidation, in which case the collateral used to secure the loan—a home or car, for example—is seized by the lender and sold to repay the loan. A loan officer can also perform this function.

Working Conditions

Working as a loan officer usually involves considerable travel. For example, commercial and mortgage loan officers frequently work away from their offices and rely on laptop computers, cellular phones, and pagers to keep in contact with their offices and clients. Mortgage loan officers often work out of their home or car, visiting offices or homes of clients while completing loan applications. Commercial loan officers sometimes travel to other cities to prepare complex loan agreements. Consumer loan officers and loan counselors, however, are likely to spend most of their time in an office.

Most loan officers and counselors work a standard 40-hour week, but many work longer, depending on the number of clients and the demand for loans. Mortgage loan officers can work especially long hours, because they are free to take on as many customers as they choose. Loan officers usually carry a heavy caseload and some-times cannot accept new clients until they complete current cases. They are especially busy when interest rates are low, triggering a surge in loan applications.

Employment

Loan officers and counselors held about 227,000 jobs in 1998. Approximately half were employed by commercial banks, savings institutions, and credit unions. Others were employed by nonbank financial institutions, such as mortgage banking and brokerage firms and personal credit firms.

Loan officers are employed throughout the Nation, but most work in urban and suburban areas. In rural areas, the branch or assistant manager often handles the loan application process.

Training, Other Qualifications, and Advancement

Loan officer positions generally require a bachelor's degree in finance, economics, or a related field. Most employers prefer applicants who are familiar with computers and their applications in banking. For commercial or mortgage loan officer jobs, training or experience in sales is highly valued by potential employers. Loan officers without college degrees usually have reached their positions by advancing through the ranks of an organization and acquiring several years of work experience in various other occupations, such as teller or customer service representative.

The American Institute of Banking, which is affiliated with the American Bankers Association, offers correspondence courses and college and university classes for students interested in lending, as well as for experienced loan officers who want to keep their skills current. The Mortgage Bankers Association's School of Mortgage Banking also offers classes, both classroom and Internet-based, for people involved in real estate lending. Completion of these courses and programs enhances one's employment and advancement opportunities.

Persons planning a career as a loan officer or counselor should be capable of developing effective working relationships with others, confident in their abilities, and highly motivated. For public relations purposes, loan officers must be willing to attend community events as a representative of their employer.

Capable loan officers and counselors may advance to larger branches of the firm or to managerial positions, while less capable workers—and those having inadequate academic preparation—could be assigned to smaller branches and might find promotion difficult. Advancement beyond a loan officer position usually includes supervising other loan officers and clerical staff.

Job Outlook

Employment of loan officers and counselors is expected to grow faster than the average for all occupations through 2008. Job growth will be driven by an increasing population, expanding economy, and low interest rates, which will lead to more applications for commercial, consumer, and mortgage loans. Growth in the variety and complexity of loans, coupled with the importance of loan of-

ficers to the success of banks and other lending institutions, should also assure employment growth. Although increased demand will generate many new jobs, most openings will result from the need to replace workers who leave the occupation or retire.

Employment growth will be tempered by several factors. First, refinancing of mortgages, a major contributor to the recent growth in the number of loan officers, is expected to diminish, because people who needed to refinance have already done so. Also, computers, underwriting software, and communication technologies are making loan officers more productive. They can now spend more time in the field with prospective clients, while still keeping in touch with the office. Also, qualifying applicants for loans is being made easier with computers performing much of the analysis. The Internet is also expected to slightly dampen the demand for loan officers, as a growing number of people apply for loans online.

Employment of loan officers is subject to the upturns and downturns of the economy. When interest rates decline dramatically, there is a surge in real estate buying and refinancing that requires additional loan officers specializing in mortgage financing. When the real estate market returns to normal, loan officers can be subject to layoffs. The same applies to commercial loan officers whose workloads increase during good economic times, as companies seek to invest more in their businesses. In difficult economic conditions, loan counselors are likely to see an increase in the number of delinquent loans.

Even in economic downturns, however, loans remain the major source of revenue for banks, so the fundamental role of loan officers will contribute to job stability. Moreover, because loan officers are often paid by commission, the bank may retain them simply by paying less compensation. As in the past, college graduates and those with banking, lending, or sales experience should have the best job prospects.

Earnings

Median annual earnings of loan officers and counselors were $35,340 in 1998. The middle 50 percent earned between $26,380 and $50,240. The lowest 10 percent had earnings of less than $20,990, while the top 10 percent earned more than $82,270. Median annual earnings in the industries employing the largest number of loan officers and counselors in 1997 were:

Commercial banks	$36,400
Mortgage bankers and brokers	34,700
Savings institutions	34,700
Personal credit institutions	26,800
Credit unions	25,300

The form of compensation for loan officers varies. Most loan officers are paid a commission that is based on the number of loans they originate. In this way, commissions are used to motivate loan officers to bring in more loans. Some institutions pay only salaries, while others pay their loan officers a salary plus a commission or bonus based on the number of loans originated. Banks and other lenders sometimes offer their loan officers free checking privileges and somewhat lower interest rates on personal loans.

According to a salary survey conducted by Robert Half International, a staffing services firm specializing in accounting and finance, residential real estate mortgage loan officers earned between $31,600 and $47,000 in 1998; commercial real estate mortgage loan officers, between $46,000 and $74,000; consumer loan officers, between $30,000 and $49,000; and commercial loan officers, between $38,400 and $85,000. Smaller banks ordinarily paid 15 percent less than larger banks. Loan officers who are paid on a commission basis usually earn more than those on salary only.

Related Occupations

Loan officers help the public manage financial assets and secure loans. Occupations that involve similar functions include securities and financial services sales representatives, financial aid officers, real estate agents and brokers, and insurance agents and brokers.

Sources of Additional Information

Information about a career as a loan officer or counselor can be obtained from:

- American Bankers Association, 1120 Connecticut Ave. NW., Washington, DC 20036. Internet: http://www.aba.com
- Mortgage Bankers Association of America, 1125 15th St. NW., Washington, DC 20005. Internet: http://www.mbaa.org

State bankers' associations can furnish specific information about job opportunities in their State. Also, individual banks can supply information about job openings and the activities, responsibilities, and preferred qualifications of their loan officers.

Mail Clerks and Messengers

(O*NET 57302 and 57311A)

Significant Points

- This is a first job for many because there are no formal qualifications or training requirements.
- Automated mail systems and other computerized innovations are expected to limit employment growth; nevertheless, favorable job opportunities are expected due to the need to replace the large number of mail clerks and messengers who leave the occupation each year.

Nature of the Work

Mail clerks and messengers move and distribute information, documents, and small packages for businesses, institutions, and government agencies. *Mail clerks* handle the internal mail for most large organizations. Internal mail goes back and forth among people, offices, or departments within a firm or institution. It ranges from memos that are being sent to key personnel to bulletins regarding job issues that are being sent to all employees. Mail clerks sort internal mail and deliver it to their fellow employees, often using carts to carry the mail.

Mail clerks also handle external mail, serving as a link between the U.S. Postal Service and individual offices and workers. They sort incoming mail and deliver mail within large office buildings. They also prepare outgoing mail—which may range from advertising flyers, to customers' orders, to legal documents—for delivery to the post office. To facilitate delivery of outgoing mail, mail clerks often determine if the mail is to be sent registered, certified, special delivery, or first, second, third, or fourth class, and they may group mailings by ZIP code. When necessary, they contact delivery services to send important letters or parcels. In larger organizations, or organizations with a large volume of outgoing mail, mail clerks operate machines that collate, fold, and insert into envelopes certain material that is to be mailed. They also operate machines that affix postage. In addition, mail clerks increasingly use computers to keep records of incoming and outgoing items.

Messengers, also called couriers, pick up and deliver letters, important business documents, or packages, which need to be sent or received in a hurry from within a local area. By sending an item by messenger, the sender ensures that it reaches its destination the same day or even within the hour. Messengers also deliver items, which the sender is unwilling to entrust to other means of delivery, such as important legal or financial documents. Some messengers pick up and deliver important packages, such as medical samples to be tested.

Messengers receive their instructions either by reporting to their office in person, by telephone, or by two-way radio. They then pick up the item and carry it to its destination. After a delivery, they check with their office and receive instructions about the next delivery. Consequently, most messengers spend much of their time outdoors or in their vehicle. Messengers usually maintain records of deliveries and often obtain signatures from the persons receiving the items.

Most messengers deliver items within a limited geographic area, such as a city or metropolitan area. Items that need to go longer distances usually are sent by mail or by an overnight delivery service. Some messengers carry items only for their employer, which typically might be a law firm, bank, or financial institution. Other messengers may act as part of an organization's internal mail system and mainly carry items between an organization's buildings or entirely within one building. Many messengers work for messenger or courier services; for a fee they pick up items from anyone and deliver them to specified destinations within a local area.

Messengers reach their destination by several methods. Many drive vans or cars or ride motorcycles. A few travel by foot, especially in urban areas or when making deliveries nearby. In congested urban areas, messengers often use bicycles to make deliveries. Bicycle messengers usually are employed by messenger or courier services. Although fax machines and computerized electronic mail can deliver information faster than messengers, an electronic copy cannot substitute for the original document for many types of business transactions.

Working Conditions

Working conditions for mail clerks are much different from the working conditions for most messengers. Most mail clerks work regular hours, spending much of their time in mailrooms, which are usually located in office buildings. They spend the remaining time making mail deliveries throughout the office building. Although mailrooms are usually clean and well lighted, there may be noise from mail-handling machines. Mail clerks spend most of their time on their feet, which can be tiring and physically demanding. They are sometimes required to lift heavy objects or operate a motor vehicle to make deliveries and pick-ups.

Messengers work in a less structured environment than mail clerks because they spend most of their time alone making deliveries and usually are not closely supervised. Although many messengers work full time during regular business hours, some messengers work nights and weekends. Messengers who deliver by bicycle must be physically fit and are exposed to all weather conditions as well as the many hazards connected with heavy traffic. The pressure of making as many deliveries as possible to increase earnings can be stressful and may lead to unsafe driving or bicycling practices.

Employment

Mail clerks and messengers together held about 247,000 jobs in 1998; about 120,000 were messengers, and about 128,000 were mail clerks. About 14 percent of messengers worked for law firms, another 13 percent worked for hospitals and medical and dental laboratories, and 13 percent for local and long distance trucking establishments. Financial institutions, such as commercial banks, savings institutions, and credit unions, employed 7 percent. The rest were employed in a variety of other industries. Technically, many messengers are self-employed independent contractors because they provide their vehicles and, to a certain extent, set their own schedules; however, in many respects they are like employees because they usually work for one company. Almost 1 of every 3 worked part time. In 1998, about 12 percent of all mail clerks worked in Federal, State, and local governments, and both the insurance industry and personnel supply services industry employed 27 percent. Others were employed in a wide range of industries.

Training, Other Qualifications, and Advancement

There are no formal qualifications or training required to be a mail clerk or messenger, although some employers prefer high school graduates. This is a first job for many.

Mail clerks must be careful and dependable workers. They must be able to do routine work and work well with their hands. They are usually trained on the job. If they operate computers and mail-handling machinery to help prepare mailings, training may be provided by another employee or by a representative of the machinery manufacturer. Mail clerks are sometimes required to have a driver's license if they make deliveries to other buildings.

Messengers who work as independent contractors for a messenger or delivery service may be required to have a valid driver's license, a registered and inspected vehicle, a good driving record, and insurance coverage. Many messengers who are employees, rather than independent contractors, are also required to provide and maintain their own vehicle. A good knowledge of the geographic area in which they travel, as well as a good sense of direction, are also important.

Some mail clerks, depending on the size of the operation, advance to positions as clerical staff supervisors or office managers. Other mail clerks transfer to related jobs with the U.S. Postal Service if they pass the competitive entrance examination. Messengers, especially those who work for messenger or courier services, have limited advancement opportunities.

Job Outlook

Favorable employment opportunities are expected for mail clerks and messengers due to the need to replace the large number of workers who leave the occupation each year. Mail clerk and messenger jobs are attractive to many persons seeking their first job or a short-term source of income because the limited formal education and training requirements allow easy entry. This is especially true for messengers, many of whom work in this occupation a relatively short time.

Employment of mail clerks and messengers is expected to grow more slowly than average through 2008 despite an increasing volume of internal mail, parcels, business documents, promotional materials, and other written information that must be handled and delivered as the economy expands. Businesses' growing reliance on direct mail advertising and promotional materials to prospective customers will result in increasing amounts of mail to be handled. However, increasing automation of mail handling will enable mail clerks to handle a growing volume of mail.

Employment of messengers will continue to be adversely impacted by the more widespread use of electronic information-handling technology. For example, fax machines that allow copies of documents to be immediately sent across town or around the world have become standard office equipment. The transmission of information using electronic mail has also become commonplace and will continue to reduce the demand for messengers as more computers are networked or gain access to the Internet. However, messengers will still be needed to transport materials that cannot be sent electronically—such as legal documents, blueprints and other over-sized materials, large multipage documents, and securities. Also, messengers will still be required by medical and dental laboratories to pick up and deliver medical samples, specimens, and other materials.

Earnings

Median hourly earnings of mail clerks, except mail machine operators or postal service workers, were $8.49 in 1998. The middle 50 percent earned between $7.03 and $10.44. The lowest 10 percent earned less than $6.00, and the highest 10 percent earned more than $12.61. Median hourly earnings in the industries employing the largest numbers of mail clerks in 1997 were:

Federal government	$10.00
Colleges and universities	8.90
Newspapers	7.30
Personnel supply services	7.20
Mailing, reproduction, stenographic services	7.10

Median hourly earnings of couriers and messengers were $8.02 in 1998. The middle 50 percent of messengers earned between $6.43 and $10.04. The lowest 10 percent earned less than $5.73, and the highest 10 percent earned more than $12.54. Messengers occasionally receive tips from clients, but this is not a significant part of their earnings. Median hourly earnings in the industries employing the largest numbers of couriers and messengers in 1997 were:

Hospitals	$8.00
Medical and dental laboratories	7.90
Commercial banks	7.80
Legal services	7.40
Trucking and courier services, except air	6.80

Messengers are compensated by salary, commission, or a combination of both. The commission usually is based on the fee charged to the customer and is usually considerably higher for those who strictly work by commission than for those messengers whose earnings are based on a combination of salary and commission. Other factors like the number of deliveries made and the distance traveled may also be taken into consideration when determining earnings. The more deliveries they make and the faster they travel, the more they earn. Some messengers work as independent contractors and therefore seldom receive paid vacations, sick leave, health insurance, or other typical benefits from the messenger or delivery company. They must provide their own transportation and must pay fuel and maintenance costs. Messengers working for employers other than messenger and courier services usually are paid by the hour and receive the benefits offered to all employees.

Related Occupations

Messengers and mail clerks sort and deliver letters, parcels, and other items. They also keep accurate records of their work. Others who do similar work are postal clerks and mail carriers; route drivers; traffic, shipping, and receiving clerks; and parcel post clerks.

Sources of Additional Information

Information about job opportunities may be obtained from local employers and local offices of the State employment service. Persons interested in mail clerk and messenger jobs may also contact messenger and courier services, mail order firms, banks, printing and publishing firms, utility companies, retail stores, or other large firms. For information on training and certification programs in mail systems management, contact:

- Mail Systems Management Association, J.A.F. Building, P.O. Box 2155, New York, NY 10116-2155. Internet: http://www.msma.com

Management Analysts

(O*NET 21905)

Significant Points

- Almost 55 percent are self-employed; that's about four times the average for other executive, administrative, and managerial occupations.

- Most positions in the private sector require a master's degree and at least five years of specialized experience.

- Despite projected faster-than-average employment growth, intense competition is expected for jobs.

Nature of the Work

As the business environment becomes more complex, the Nation's firms are continually faced with new challenges. Firms increasingly rely on management analysts to help them remain competitive amidst these changes. Management analysts, often referred to as management consultants in the private sector, analyze and propose ways to improve an organization's structure, efficiency, or profits. For example, a small but rapidly growing company that needs help improving the system of control over inventories and expenses may decide to employ a consultant who is an expert in just-in-time inventory management. In another case, a large company that has recently acquired a new division may hire management analysts to help reorganize their corporate structure and eliminate duplicate or non-essential jobs.

Firms providing management analysis range in size from a single practitioner to large international organizations employing thousands of consultants. Some analysts and consultants specialize in a specific industry, while others specialize by type of business function, such as human resources or information systems. In government, management analysts tend to specialize by type of agency. The work of management analysts and consultants varies with each client or employer and from project to project. Some projects require a team of consultants, each specializing in one area. In other projects, consultants work independently with the organization's managers. In all cases, analysts and consultants collect, review, and analyze information in order to make recommendations to management.

Both public and private organizations use consultants for a variety of reasons. Some lack the internal resources needed to handle a project, while others need a consultant's expertise to determine what resources will be required and what problems may be encountered if they pursue a particular opportunity. To retain a consultant, a company first solicits proposals from a number of consulting firms specializing in the area in which it needs assistance. These proposals include the estimated cost and scope of the project, staffing requirements, references from a number of previous clients, and a completion deadline. The company then selects the proposal that best suits its needs.

After obtaining an assignment or contract, management analysts first define the nature and extent of the problem. During this phase, they analyze relevant data, which may include annual revenues, employment, or expenditures, and they interview managers and employees while observing their operations. The analyst or consultant then develops solutions to the problem. In the course of preparing their recommendations, they take into account the nature of the organization, the relationship it has with others in that industry, and its internal organization and culture. Insight into the problem is often gained by building and solving mathematical models.

Once they have decided on a course of action, consultants report their findings and recommendations to the client. These sugges-

tions are usually submitted in writing, but oral presentations regarding findings are also common. For some projects, management analysts are retained to help implement their suggestions.

Management analysts in government agencies use the same skills as their private-sector colleagues to advise managers on many types of issues, most of which are similar to the problems faced by private firms. For example, if an agency is planning to purchase personal computers, it must first determine which type to buy, given its budget and data processing needs. In this case, management analysts would assess the prices and characteristics of various machines and determine which best meets their department's needs.

Working Conditions

Management analysts usually divide their time between their offices and the client's site. In either situation, much of an analyst's time is spent indoors in clean, well-lit offices. Because they must spend a significant portion of their time with clients, analysts travel frequently.

Analysts and consultants generally work at least 40 hours a week. Uncompensated overtime is common, especially when approaching project deadlines. Analysts may experience a great deal of stress as a result of trying to meet a client's demands, often on a tight schedule.

Self-employed consultants can set their workload and hours and work at home. On the other hand, their livelihood depends on their ability to maintain and expand their client base. Salaried consultants also must impress potential clients to get and keep clients for their company.

Employment

Management analysts held about 344,000 jobs in 1998. They are found throughout the country, but employment is concentrated in large metropolitan areas. Almost 55 percent of these workers were self-employed. Most of the remainder worked in financial and management consulting firms and for Federal, State, and local governments. The majority of those working for the Federal government are in the Department of Defense.

Training, Other Qualifications, and Advancement

Educational requirements for entry-level jobs in this field vary widely between private industry and government. Employers in private industry generally seek individuals with a master's degree in business administration or a related discipline and at least five years of experience in the field in which they plan to consult. Most government agencies hire people with a bachelor's degree and no pertinent work experience for entry-level management analyst positions.

Many fields of study provide a suitable educational background for this occupation because of the wide range of areas addressed by management analysts. These include most academic programs in business and management, as well as computer and information sciences and engineering. In addition to the appropriate formal education, most entrants to this occupation have years of experience in management, human resources, inventory control, or other specialties. Analysts also routinely attend conferences to keep abreast of current developments in their field.

Management analysts often work with minimal supervision, so they should be self-motivated and disciplined. Analytical skills, the ability to get along with a wide range of people, strong oral and written communication skills, good judgment, time management skills, and creativity are other desirable qualities. The ability to work in teams is also becoming a more important attribute in the field as consulting teams become more common.

As consultants gain experience, they often become solely responsible for a specific project full time, taking on more responsibility and managing their own hours. At the senior level, consultants may supervise lower-level workers and become more involved in seeking out new business. Those with exceptional skills may eventually become a partner or principal in the firm. Others with entrepreneurial ambition may open their own firm.

A high percentage of management consultants are self-employed, partly because business start-up costs are low. Self-employed consultants also can share office space, administrative help, and other resources with other self-employed consultants or small consulting firms—thus reducing overhead costs. Because many small consulting firms fail each year for lack of managerial expertise and clients, those interested in opening their own firms must have good organizational and marketing skills and several years of consulting experience.

The Institute of Management Consultants, a division of the Council of Consulting Organizations, Inc., offers the Certified Management Consultant (CMC) designation to those who pass an examination and meet minimum levels of education and experience. Certification is not mandatory for management consultants, but it may give a jobseeker a competitive advantage.

Job Outlook

Despite projected rapid employment growth, keen competition is expected for jobs as management analysts. Because analysts can come from such diverse educational backgrounds, the pool of applicants from which employers can draw is quite large. Furthermore, the independent and challenging nature of the work, combined with high earnings potential, make this occupation attractive to many. Job opportunities are expected to be best for those with a graduate degree, industry expertise, and a talent for salesmanship and public relations.

Employment of management analysts is expected to grow faster than the average for all occupations through 2008, as industry and government increasingly rely on outside expertise to improve the performance of their organizations. Job growth is projected in very large consulting firms with international expertise and in smaller niche consulting firms that specialize in specific areas, such as biotechnology, health care, human resources, engineering, and telecommunications. Growth in the number of individual practitioners may be hindered, however, by clients' increasing demand for a team approach, which enables examination of a variety of different issues and problems within an organization.

Employment growth of management analysts and consultants has been driven by a number a changes in the business environment that have forced American firms to take a closer look at their operations. As international and domestic markets have become more competitive, firms have needed to use resources more efficiently. Management analysts are increasingly sought to help reduce costs, streamline operations, and develop marketing strategies. As this process continues and businesses downsize, even more opportunities will be created for analysts to perform duties that were previously handled internally.

In addition, many companies will rely on analysts to organize and evaluate their restructuring efforts. Businesses attempting to expand internationally will need the skills of management analysts to help with organizational, administrative, and other issues. Further, as businesses increasingly rely on technology, there will be more demand for analysts with a technical background, such as engineering or biotechnology, particularly when combined with a master's degree in business administration. Finally, management analysts will also be in greater demand in the public sector, as Federal, State, and local agencies are expected to seek ways to become more efficient.

Earnings

Salaries for management analysts vary widely by experience, education, and employer. Median annual earnings of management analysts in 1998 were $49,470. The middle 50 percent earned between $39,420 and $72,690. The lowest 10 percent earned less than $31,800, and the highest 10 percent earned more than $88,470. Median annual earnings in the industries employing the largest numbers of management analysts and consultants in 1997 were:

Management and public relations	$57,200
Federal government	56,400
Local government, except education and hospitals	47,500
Computer and data processing services	47,500
State government, except education and hospitals	39,600

According to a 1998 survey by the Association of Management Consulting Firms, earnings—including bonuses and/or profit sharing—for research associates in member firms averaged $38,900; for entry-level consultants, $50,500; for management consultants, $69,700; for senior consultants, $96,800; for junior partners, $151,100; and for senior partners, $266,700.

Salaried management analysts usually receive common benefits such as health and life insurance, a retirement plan, and vacation and sick leave, as well as less common benefits such as profit sharing and bonuses for outstanding work. In addition, all travel expenses usually are reimbursed by the employer. Self-employed consultants have to maintain their own office and provide their own benefits.

Related Occupations

Management analysts collect, review, and analyze data; make recommendations; and implement their ideas. Others who use similar skills include managers, computer systems analysts, operations research analysts, economists, and financial analysts. Researchers prepare data and reports for analysts to use in their recommendations.

Sources of Additional Information

Information about career opportunities in management consulting is available from:

- The Association of Management Consulting Firms, 3580 Lexington Ave., Suite 1700, New York, NY 10168. Internet: http://www.amcf.org

Information about the Certified Management Consultant designation can be obtained from:

- The Institute of Management Consultants, 1200 19th St. NW., Suite 300, Washington DC 20036. Internet: http://www.imcusa.org

For information about a career as a State or local government management analyst, contact your State or local employment service. Information on obtaining a management analyst position with the Federal government may be obtained from the Office of Personnel Management through a telephone based system. Consult your telephone directory under U.S. Government for a local number or call (912) 757-3000; TDD (912) 744-2299. That number is not toll free, and charges may result. Information also is available from their Internet site: http://www.usajobs.opm.gov.

Manufacturers' and Wholesale Sales Representatives

(O*NET 49002, 49005B, 49005C, 49005D, 49005F, 49005G, and 49008)

Significant Points

- Many are self-employed manufacturers' agents who work for a commission.

- Although employers place an emphasis on a strong educational background, many individuals with previous sales experience still enter the occupation without a college degree.

- Many jobs require a great deal of travel.

Nature of the Work

Sales representatives are an important part of manufacturers' and wholesalers' success. Regardless of the type of product they sell, their primary duties are to interest wholesale and retail buyers and purchasing agents in their merchandise and to address any of the client's questions or concerns. They also advise clients on methods to reduce costs, use their products, and increase sales. Sales representatives market their company's products to manufacturers, wholesale and retail establishments, government agencies, and other institutions.

Depending on where they work, sales representatives have different job titles. Those employed directly by a manufacturer or wholesaler usually are called *sales representatives*. *Manufacturers' agents* are self-employed sales workers who contract their services to all types of manufacturing companies. Those selling technical products, for both manufacturers and wholesalers, are usually called *industrial sales workers* or *sales engineers*. However, many of these titles are used interchangeably.

Manufacturers' and wholesale sales representatives spend much of their time traveling to and visiting with prospective buyers and current clients. During a sales call, they discuss the customers' needs and suggest how their merchandise or services can meet those needs. They may show samples or catalogs that describe items their company stocks and inform customers about prices, availability, and how their products can save money and improve productivity. A vast number of manufacturers and wholesalers sell similar products, thus sales representatives must emphasize any unique qualities of their products and services. As independent agents, they might sell several complementary products made by different manufacturers and thus take an overall systems approach to their customer's business. Sales representatives may help install new equipment and train employees. They also take orders and resolve any problems or complaints with the merchandise.

Sales engineers are among the most highly trained sales workers. They usually sell products whose installation and optimal use requires a great deal of technical expertise and support (products such as material handling equipment, numerical-control machinery, and computer systems). Additionally, they provide information on their firm's products, help prospective and current buyers with technical problems, recommend improved materials and machinery for a firm's manufacturing process, design plans of proposed machinery layouts, estimate cost savings, and suggest training schedules for employees. In a process that may take several months, they present this information and negotiate the sale. Aided by a laptop computer connected to the Internet, they can often answer technical and nontechnical questions immediately.

Frequently, sales representatives who lack technical expertise work as a team with a technical expert. In this arrangement, the technical expert will attend the sales presentation to explain the product and answer questions or concerns. The sales representative makes the preliminary contact with customers, introduces the company's product, and closes the sale. The representative is then able to spend more time maintaining and soliciting accounts and less time acquiring technical knowledge. After the sale, representatives may make follow-up visits to ensure the equipment is functioning properly and may even help train customers' employees to operate and maintain new equipment.

Those selling consumer goods often suggest how and where merchandise should be displayed. Working with retailers, they may help arrange promotional programs, store displays, and advertising.

Obtaining new accounts is an important part of the job. Sales representatives follow leads from other clients, track advertisements in trade journals, participate in trade shows and conferences, and may visit potential clients unannounced. In addition, they may spend time meeting with and entertaining prospective clients during evenings and weekends.

Sales representatives have several duties beyond selling products. They also analyze sales statistics; prepare reports; and handle administrative duties, such as filing their expense account reports, scheduling appointments, and making travel plans. They study literature about new and existing products and monitor the sales, prices, and products of their competitors.

Manufacturers' agents who operate a sales agency must also manage their business. This requires organizational skills, as well as knowledge of accounting, marketing, and administration.

Working Conditions

Some manufacturers' and wholesale sales representatives have large territories and travel considerably. A sales region may cover several States, and so they may be away from home for several days or weeks at a time. Others work near their "home base" and travel mostly by automobile. Due to the nature of the work and the amount of travel, sales representatives typically work more than 40 hours per week.

Although the hours are long and often irregular, most sales representatives have the freedom to determine their own schedule. Consequently, they can arrange their appointments so they can have time off when they want it.

Dealing with different types of people can be demanding but stimulating. Sales representatives often face competition from representatives of other companies as well as from fellow workers. Companies usually set goals or quotas that representatives are expected to meet. Because their earnings depend on commissions, manufacturers' agents are also under the added pressure to maintain and expand their clientele.

Employment

Manufacturers' and wholesale sales representatives held about 1.5 million jobs in 1998. Three of every four salaried representatives worked in wholesale trade—mostly for distributors of machinery and equipment, groceries and related products, and motor vehicles and parts. Others were employed in manufacturing and mining. Due to the diversity of products and services sold, employment opportunities are available in every part of the country in all kinds of industries.

In addition to those working directly for a firm, many sales representatives are self-employed manufacturers' agents. They often form small sales firms and work for a straight commission based on the value of their own sales. However, manufacturers' agents usually gain experience and recognition with a manufacturer or wholesaler before becoming self-employed.

Training, Other Qualifications, and Advancement

The background needed for sales jobs varies by product line and market. The number of college graduates has increased and the job requirements have become more technical and analytical. Most firms now emphasize a strong educational background. Nevertheless, many employers still hire individuals with previous sales experience who do not have a college degree. For some consumer products, other factors such as sales ability, personality, and familiarity with brands are as important as a degree. On the other hand, firms selling industrial products often require a degree in science or engineering in addition to some sales experience. In general, companies are looking for the best and brightest individuals who have the personality and desire to sell.

Many companies have formal training programs for beginning sales representatives lasting up to two years. However, most businesses are accelerating these programs to reduce costs and expedite the returns from training. In some programs, trainees rotate among jobs in plants and offices to learn all phases of production, installation, and distribution of the product. In others, trainees take formal classroom instruction at the plant, followed by on-the-job training under the supervision of a field sales manager. Some sales representatives complete certification courses to become Certified Professional Manufacturers' Representatives (CPMRs).

New workers may be trained by accompanying experienced workers on their sales calls. As they gain familiarity with the firm's products and clients, these workers are given increasing responsibility until they are eventually assigned their own territory. As businesses experience greater competition, increased pressure is placed upon sales representatives to produce faster.

These workers stay abreast of new merchandise and the changing needs of their customers in a variety of ways. They attend trade shows where new products and technologies are showcased. They also attend conferences and conventions to meet other sales representatives and clients and discuss new product developments. In addition, the entire sales force may participate in company-sponsored meetings to review sales performance, product development, sales goals, and profitability.

Those who want to become manufacturers' and wholesale sales representatives should be goal-oriented, persuasive, and work well both independently and as part of a team. A pleasant personality and appearance, the ability to communicate well with people, and problem-solving skills are highly valued. Furthermore, completing a sale can take several months and thus requires patience and perseverance. These workers are on their feet for long periods and may carry heavy sample cases, which necessitates some physical stamina. They should also enjoy traveling. Sales representatives spend much of their time visiting current and prospective clients.

Frequently, promotion takes the form of an assignment to a larger account or territory where commissions are likely to be greater. Experienced sales representatives may move into jobs as sales trainers, who instruct new employees on selling techniques and company policies and procedures. Those who have good sales records and leadership ability may advance to sales supervisor or district manager.

In addition to advancement opportunities within a firm, some manufacturers' agents go into business for themselves. Others find opportunities in purchasing, advertising, or marketing research.

Job Outlook

Overall, employment of manufacturers' and wholesale sales representatives is expected to grow more slowly than the average for all occupations through the year 2008. Continued growth due to the increasing variety and number of goods to be sold will be tempered by the increased effectiveness and efficiency of sales workers. Many job openings will result from the need to replace workers who transfer to other occupations or leave the labor force.

Prospective customers will still require sales workers to demonstrate or illustrate the particulars about the good or service. However, technology is expected to make them more effective and productive, for example, by providing accurate and current information to customers during sales presentations.

Within manufacturing, job opportunities for manufacturers' agents should be somewhat better than those for sales representatives. Manufacturers are expected to continue outsourcing sales duties to manufacturers' agents rather than using in-house or direct selling personnel. To their advantage, these agents are more likely to work in a sales area or territory longer than representatives, creating a better working relationship and understanding how customers operate their businesses. Also, by using agents who usually lend their services to more than one company, companies can share costs with the other companies involved with that agent.

Those interested in this occupation should keep in mind that direct selling opportunities in manufacturing are likely to be best for products with strong demand. Furthermore, jobs will be most plentiful in small wholesale and manufacturing firms because a growing number of these companies will rely on wholesalers' and manufacturers' agents to market their products as a way to control their costs and expand their customer base.

Employment opportunities and earnings may fluctuate from year to year because sales are affected by changing economic conditions, legislative issues, and consumer preferences. Prospects will be best for those with the appropriate knowledge or technical expertise as well as the personal traits necessary for successful selling.

Earnings

Compensation methods vary significantly by the type of firm and product sold. Most employers use a combination of salary and commission or salary plus bonus. Commissions are usually based on the amount of sales, whereas bonuses may depend on individual performance, on the performance of all sales workers in the group or district, or on the company's performance.

Median annual earnings of sales representatives, except retail, were $36,540, including commission, in 1998. The middle 50 percent earned between $26,350 and $51,580 a year. The lowest 10 percent earned less than $19,220, and the highest 10 percent earned more than $83,000 a year. Median annual earnings in the industries employing the largest number of sales representatives, except retail, in 1997 are shown here.

Electrical goods	$36,700
Paper and paper products	36,700
Machinery, equipment, and supplies	36,400
Professional and commercial equipment	35,300
Groceries and related products	31,900

Median annual earnings of sales engineers, including commission, in 1998 were $54,600. The middle 50 percent earned between $41,240 and $79,480 a year. The lowest 10 percent earned less than $30,560, and the highest 10 percent earned more than $97,700 a

year. Median annual earnings in the industries employing the largest number of sales engineers in 1997 are shown here.

Computer and data processing services	$62,800
Electrical goods	56,600
Professional and commercial equipment	51,700
Machinery, equipment, and supplies	48,900

In addition to their earnings, sales representatives and engineers are usually reimbursed for expenses such as transportation costs, meals, hotels, and entertaining customers. They often receive benefits such as health and life insurance, pension plan, vacation and sick leave, personal use of a company car, and frequent flyer mileage. Some companies offer incentives such as free vacation trips or gifts for outstanding sales workers.

Unlike those working directly for a manufacturer or wholesaler, manufacturers' agents are paid strictly on commission. Depending on the type of product or products they are selling, their experience in the field, and the number of clients, their earnings can be significantly higher or lower than those working in direct sales. In addition, self-employed manufacturers' agents must pay their own travel, entertainment, and benefit expenses.

Related Occupations

Manufacturers' and wholesale sales representatives must have sales ability and knowledge of the products they sell. Other occupations that require similar skills are advertising, marketing, and public relations managers; insurance sales agents; purchasing managers, buyers, and purchasing agents; real estate agents and brokers; securities, commodities, and financial services sales representatives; and services sales representatives.

Sources of Additional Information

Information on manufacturers' agents is available from:

- Manufacturers' Agents National Association, P.O. Box 3467, Laguna Hills, CA 92654-3467. Internet: http://www.manaonline.org

Career and certification information is available from:

- Sales and Marketing Executives International, 5500 Interstate North Pkwy., No. 545, Atlanta, GA 30328. Internet: http://www.smei.org
- Manufacturers' Representatives Educational Research Foundation, P.O. Box 247, Geneva, IL 60134. Internet: http://www.mrerf.org

Material Recording, Scheduling, Dispatching, and Distributing Occupations

Significant Points

- Slower-than-average job growth is expected as additional automation increases worker productivity.

- Many of these occupations are entry level and require no more than a high school diploma.

Nature of the Work

Workers in this group are responsible for a variety of communications, record keeping, and scheduling operations. Typically, they coordinate, expedite, and track orders for personnel, materials, and equipment.

Dispatchers receive requests for service and initiate action to provide that service. Duties vary, depending on the needs of the employer. Police, fire, and ambulance dispatchers, also called public safety dispatchers, handle calls from people reporting crimes, fires, and medical emergencies. Truck, bus, and train dispatchers schedule and coordinate the movement of these vehicles to ensure they arrive on schedule. Taxicab dispatchers relay requests for cabs to individual drivers, tow truck dispatchers take calls for emergency road service, and utility company dispatchers handle calls related to utility and telephone service.

Shipping, receiving, and traffic clerks track all incoming and outgoing shipments of goods transferred between businesses, suppliers, and customers. These clerks may be required to lift cartons of various sizes. Shipping clerks assemble, address, stamp, and ship merchandise or materials. Receiving clerks unpack, verify, and record incoming merchandise. In a small company, one clerk may perform all of these tasks. Traffic clerks record destination, weight, and charge of all incoming and outgoing shipments.

Stock clerks receive, unpack, and store materials and equipment, and maintain and distribute inventories. Inventories may be merchandise in wholesale and retail establishments, or equipment, supplies, or materials in other kinds of organizations. In small firms, stock clerks may perform all of the above tasks, as well as those usually handled by shipping and receiving clerks. In large establishments, they may be responsible only for one task.

(This introductory statement is followed by statements that provide more detail on dispatchers; shipping, receiving, and traffic clerks; and stock clerks.)

Other administrative support occupations in this group include *production, planning, and expediting clerks* (who coordinate and expedite the flow of work and material according to production schedules); *procurement clerks* (who draw up purchase orders to obtain merchandise or material); *weighers, measurers, checkers, and samplers* (who weigh, measure, and check materials); and *utility meter readers* (who read electric, gas, water, or steam meters and record the quantity used).

Working Conditions

Working conditions vary considerably by occupation and employment setting. Meter readers, for example, spend a good portion of their workday traveling around communities and neighborhoods taking readings either directly or with remote reading equipment. The work of dispatchers can be very hectic when many calls come in at the same time. The job of public safety dispatcher is particularly stressful, because slow or improper response to a call can result in serious injury or further harm. Also, callers who are anxious or afraid may become excited and be unable to provide necessary information; some may become abusive. Despite provocations, dispatchers must remain calm, objective, and in control of the situation.

Dispatchers sit for long periods, using telephones, computers, and two-way radios. Much of their time is spent at video display terminals, viewing monitors and observing traffic patterns. As a result of working for long stretches with computers and other electronic equipment, dispatchers can experience significant eyestrain and back discomfort. Generally, dispatchers work a 40-hour week; however, rotating shifts and compressed work schedules are common. Alternative work schedules are necessary to accommodate evening, weekend, and holiday work, as well as 24-hours-per-day, seven-days-per-week operations.

Shipping, receiving, traffic, and stock clerks work in a wide variety of businesses, institutions, and industries. Some work in warehouses, stock rooms, or shipping and receiving rooms that may not be temperature controlled. Others may spend time in cold storage rooms or outside on loading platforms, where they are exposed to the weather. Most jobs involve frequent standing, bending, walking, and stretching. Some lifting and carrying of smaller items may also be involved. Although automation, robotics, and pneumatic devices have lessened the physical demands in this occupation, their use remains somewhat limited. Work still can be strenuous, even though mechanical material handling equipment is employed to move heavy items. The typical workweek is Monday through Friday; however, evening and weekend hours are standard for some jobs (such as stock clerks who work in retail trade) and may be required in others when large shipments are involved or when inventory is taken.

Employment

In 1998, material recording, scheduling, dispatching, and distributing workers held about 4 million jobs. Employment was distributed among the detailed occupations as follows:

Stock clerks	2,300,000
Shipping, receiving, and traffic clerks	774,000
Production, planning, and expediting clerks	248,000
Dispatchers	248,000
Procurement clerks	58,000
Weighers, measurers, checkers, and samplers	51,000
Meter readers, utilities	50,000
All other material recording, scheduling, dispatching, and distributing workers	196,000

About 7 out of 10 material recording, scheduling, dispatching, and distributing jobs were in services or wholesale and retail trade. Although these workers are found throughout the country, most work near population centers where retail stores, warehouses, factories, and large communications centers are concentrated.

Training, Other Qualifications, and Advancement

Many material recording, scheduling, dispatching, and distributing occupations are entry level and require no more than a high school diploma. Increasingly however, employers prefer to hire those familiar with computers and other electronic office and business equipment. Those who have taken business courses or have previous business, dispatching, or specific job-related experience may be preferred. Because the nature of the work is to communicate effectively with other people, good oral and written communications skills are essential. Typing, filing, record keeping, and other clerical skills are also important.

State or local government civil service regulations usually govern police, fire, emergency medical, and ambulance dispatching jobs. Candidates for these positions may have to pass written, oral, and performance tests. Also, they may be asked to attend training classes and attain the proper certification in order to qualify for advancement.

Trainees usually develop the necessary skills on the job. This informal training lasts from several days to a few months, depending on the complexity of the job. Dispatchers usually require the most extensive training. Working with an experienced dispatcher, they monitor calls and learn how to operate a variety of communications equipment, including telephones, radios, and wireless appliances. As trainees gain confidence, they begin to handle calls themselves. Many public safety dispatchers also participate in structured training programs sponsored by their employer. Some employers offer a course designed by the Association of Public Safety Communications Officials. This course covers topics such as interpersonal communications; overview of the police, fire, and rescue functions; modern public safety telecommunications systems; basic radio broadcasting; local, State, and National crime information computer systems; and telephone complaint/report processing procedures. Other employers develop in-house programs based on their own needs. Emergency medical dispatchers often receive special training or have special skills. Increasingly, public safety dispatchers receive training in stress and crisis management, as well as family counseling. Employers are recognizing the toll this work has on daily living and the potential impact stress has on the job, on the work environment, and in the home.

Communications skills and the ability to work under pressure are important personal qualities for dispatchers. Residency in the city or county of employment frequently is required for public safety dispatchers. Dispatchers in transportation industries must be able to deal with sudden influxes of shipments and disruptions of shipping schedules caused by bad weather, road construction, or accidents.

Although there are no mandatory licensing or certification requirements, some States require that public safety dispatchers possess a certificate to work on a State network, such as the Police Information Network. The Association of Public Safety Communications Officials, the National Academy of Emergency Medical Dispatch, and the International Municipal Signal Association all offer certification programs. Many dispatchers participate in these programs in order to improve their prospects for career advancement.

Stock clerks and shipping, receiving, and traffic clerks usually learn the job by doing routine tasks under close supervision. They learn how to count and mark stock, and then start keeping records and taking inventory. Strength, stamina, good eyesight, and an ability to work at repetitive tasks, sometimes under pressure, are important characteristics. Stock clerks, whose sole responsibility is to bring merchandise to the sales floor, stock shelves and racks, need little

or no training. Shipping, receiving, and traffic clerks and stock clerks who handle jewelry, liquor, or drugs may be bonded.

Shipping, receiving, and traffic clerks start out by checking items to be shipped and then attaching labels and making sure the addresses are correct. Training in the use of automated equipment is usually done informally on the job. As these occupations become more automated, however, workers in these jobs may need longer training in order to master the use of the equipment.

Advancement opportunities for material recording, scheduling, dispatching, and distributing workers vary with the place of employment. Dispatchers who work for private firms, which are usually small, will find few opportunities for advancement. Public safety dispatchers, on the other hand, may become a shift or divisional supervisor or chief of communications or move to higher paying administrative jobs. Some go on to become police officers or firefighters. In large firms, stock clerks can advance to invoice clerk, stock control clerk, or procurement clerk. Shipping, receiving, and traffic clerks are promoted to head clerk, and those with a broad understanding of shipping and receiving may enter a related field such as industrial traffic management. With additional training, some stock clerks and shipping, receiving, and traffic clerks advance to jobs as warehouse managers or purchasing agents.

Job Outlook

Overall employment of material recording, scheduling, dispatching, and distributing workers is expected to grow more slowly than the average for all occupations through 2008. However, projected employment growth varies by detailed occupation. Employment of stock clerks, for example, will be affected by increased automation. New technologies will enable clerks to handle more stock, thus holding down employment growth. The effect of automation also will tend to restrict potential employment growth among shipping, receiving, and traffic clerks. Automation in warehouses and stockrooms plus other productivity improvements will enable these clerks to handle materials more efficiently and more accurately than before. Overall employment of dispatchers, on the other hand, is projected to grow about as fast as the average for all occupations. While employment of public safety dispatchers is expected to grow more slowly than average as governments endeavor to combine dispatching services across governmental units and across governmental jurisdictions, average growth is expected among dispatchers not involved in public safety.

Because employment in material recording, scheduling, dispatching, and distributing occupations is substantial, workers who leave the labor force or transfer to other occupations are expected to create many job openings each year.

Earnings

Earnings of material recording, scheduling, dispatching, and distributing occupations vary somewhat by occupation and industry. The range of median hourly earnings in 1998 are shown in the following table.

Production, planning, and expediting clerks $14.07

Dispatchers, except police, fire, and ambulance 12.68

Meter readers, utilities 12.20

Dispatchers, police, fire, and ambulance 11.38

Procurement clerks 10.88

Shipping, receiving, and traffic clerks 10.82

Weighers, measurers, checkers, and samplers,
   record keeping 10.72

Stock clerks and order fillers 7.94

All other material recording, scheduling,
   and distribution workers 10.13

Workers in material recording, scheduling, dispatching, and distributing occupations usually receive the same benefits as most other workers. If uniforms are required, employers usually provide either the uniforms or an allowance to purchase them.

Dispatchers

(O*NET 58002 and 58005)

Nature of the Work

The work of dispatchers varies greatly depending on the industry. Dispatchers keep records, logs, and schedules of the calls they receive, transportation vehicles they monitor and control, and actions they take. They maintain information on each call and then prepare a detailed report on all activities occurring during the shift. Many dispatchers employ computer-aided dispatch systems to accomplish these tasks.

Regardless of where they work, all dispatchers are assigned a specific territory and have responsibility for all communications within this area. Many work in teams, especially in large communications centers or companies. One person usually handles all dispatching calls to the response units or company's drivers, while the other members of the team usually receive the incoming calls and deal with the public.

Police, fire, and ambulance dispatchers, also called public safety dispatchers, monitor the location of emergency services personnel from any one or all of the jurisdiction's emergency services departments. They dispatch the appropriate type and number of units in response to calls for assistance. Dispatchers, or call takers, often are the first people the public contacts when they call for emergency assistance. If certified for emergency medical services, the dispatcher may provide medical instruction to those on the scene until the medical staff arrives.

Usually, dispatchers constitute the communications workforce on a shift. A dispatcher is responsible for communication within an assignment area, while the call takers receive calls and transfer information to the dispatchers. During the course of the shift, personnel will rotate such that the assignment responsibility of the dispatcher will be shared with those in the call taker role.

Police, fire, and ambulance dispatchers work in a variety of settings; they may work in a police station, a fire station, a hospital, or a centralized city communications center. In many cities, the police department serves as the communications center. In these situations, all 911 emergency calls go to the police department, where a dispatcher handles the police calls and screens the others before transferring them to the appropriate service.

When handling calls, dispatchers carefully question each caller to determine the type, seriousness, and location of the emergency. This information is posted either electronically by computer or, with decreasing frequency, by hand, and communicated immediately to uniformed or supervisory personnel. They quickly decide on the priority of the incident, the kind and number of units needed, and the location of the closest and most suitable units available. Typically, a team of call takers answer calls and relay the information to the dispatchers. Responsibility then shifts to the dispatchers, who send response units to the scene and monitor the activity of the public safety personnel answering the dispatch.

When appropriate, dispatchers stay in close contact with other service providers—for example, a police dispatcher would monitor the response of the fire department when there is a major fire. In a medical emergency, dispatchers not only keep in close touch with the dispatched units, but also with the caller. They may give extensive pre-arrival first aid instructions while the caller is waiting for the ambulance. They continuously give updates on the patient's condition to the ambulance personnel, and often serve as a link between the medical staff in a hospital and the emergency medical technicians in the ambulance.

Other dispatchers coordinate deliveries, service calls, and related activities for a variety of firms. Truck dispatchers, who work for local and long distance trucking companies, coordinate the movement of trucks and freight between cities. They direct the pickup and delivery activities of drivers. They receive customers' requests for pickup and delivery of freight; consolidate freight orders into truckloads for specific destinations; assign drivers and trucks; and draw up routes and pickup and delivery schedules. Bus dispatchers make sure local and long distance buses stay on schedule. They handle all problems that may disrupt service and dispatch other buses, or arrange for repairs to restore service and schedules. Train dispatchers ensure the timely and efficient movement of trains according to train orders and schedules. They must be aware of track switch positions, track maintenance areas, and the location of other trains running on the track. Taxicab dispatchers, or starters, dispatch taxis in response to requests for service and keep logs on all road service calls. Tow truck dispatchers take calls for emergency road service. They relay the problem to a nearby service station or a tow truck service and see to it that the emergency road service is completed. Gas and water service dispatchers monitor gas lines and water mains and send out service trucks and crews to take care of emergencies.

Employment

Dispatchers held 248,000 jobs in 1998. About one-third were police, fire, and ambulance dispatchers, almost all of whom worked for State and local governments—primarily for local police and fire departments. Most of the remaining dispatchers worked for local and long distance trucking companies and bus lines; telephone, electric, and gas utility companies; wholesale and retail establishments; railroads; and companies providing business services.

Although dispatching jobs are found throughout the country, most dispatchers work in urban areas where large communications centers and businesses are located.

Job Outlook

Overall employment of dispatchers is expected to grow about as fast as the average for all occupations through 2008. In addition to job growth, job openings will result from the need to replace those who transfer to other occupations or leave the labor force. Employment of police, fire, and ambulance dispatchers is expected to grow more slowly than the average for all occupations. Intense competition for available resources among governmental units should limit the ability of many growing communities to keep pace with rapidly growing emergency services needs. To balance the increased demand for emergency services, many districts are seeking to consolidate their communications centers into a shared, areawide facility, which will further restrict opportunities in this industry. Individuals with computer skills and experience will have a greater opportunity for employment as public safety dispatchers.

Population growth and economic expansion are expected to lead to average employment growth for dispatchers not involved in public safety. Although the overall increase will be about average, not all specialties will be affected in the same way. For example, employment of taxicab, train, and truck dispatchers is sensitive to economic conditions. When economic activity falls, demand for transportation services declines. They may experience layoffs or a shortened workweek, and jobseekers may have some difficulty finding entry-level jobs. Employment of tow truck dispatchers, on the other hand, is seldom affected by general economic conditions because of the emergency nature of their business.

Related Occupations

Other occupations that involve directing and controlling the movement of vehicles, freight, and personnel, as well as information and message distribution, are airline dispatchers, air traffic controllers, radio and television transmitter operators, telephone operators, customer service representatives, and transportation agents.

Sources of Additional Information

For further information on training and certification for police, fire, and emergency dispatchers, contact:

- National Academy of Emergency Medical Dispatch, 139 East South Temple, Suite 530, Salt Lake City, UT 84111. Internet: http://www.naemd.org

- Association of Public Safety Communications Officials, 2040 S. Ridgewood, South Daytona, FL 32119-2257. Internet: http://www.apcointl.org

- International Municipal Signal Association, 165 East Union St., P.O. Box 539, Newark, NY 14513-1526.Internet: http://www.imsafety.org

For general information on dispatchers, contact:

- Service Employees International Union, AFL-CIO, CLC, 1313 L St. NW., Washington, DC 20005-4100. Internet: http://www.seiu.org

- American Train Dispatchers Association, 1370 Ontario St., Cleveland, OH 44113. Internet: http://www.ble.org/atdd/dwv.html

Information on job opportunities for police, fire, and emergency dispatchers is available from personnel offices of State and local governments or police departments. Information about work opportunities for other types of dispatchers is available from local employers and State employment service offices.

Shipping, Receiving, and Traffic Clerks

(O*NET 58028)

Nature of the Work

Shipping, receiving, and traffic clerks keep records of all goods shipped and received. Their duties depend on the size of the establishment and the level of automation employed. Larger companies typically are better able to finance the purchase of computers and other equipment to handle some or all of a clerk's responsibilities. In smaller companies, a clerk maintains records, prepares shipments, and accepts deliveries. Working in both environments, shipping, receiving, and traffic clerks may lift cartons of various sizes.

Shipping clerks are record keepers responsible for all outgoing shipments. They prepare shipping documents and mailing labels, and make sure orders have been filled correctly. Also, they record items taken from inventory and note when orders were filled. Sometimes they fill the order themselves, obtaining merchandise from the stockroom, noting when inventories run low, and wrapping it or packing it in shipping containers. They also address and label packages, look up and compute freight or postal rates, and record the weight and cost of each shipment. Shipping clerks also may prepare invoices and furnish information about shipments to other parts of the company, such as the accounting department. Once a shipment is checked and ready to go, shipping clerks may move the goods from the plant—sometimes by forklift truck—to the shipping dock and direct its loading.

Receiving clerks perform tasks similar to those of shipping clerks. They determine whether orders have been filled correctly by verifying incoming shipments against the original order and the accompanying bill of lading or invoice. They make a record of the shipment and the condition of its contents. In many firms, receiving clerks use hand-held scanners to record bar codes on incoming products or by entering it into a computer. These data then can be transferred to the appropriate departments. The shipment is checked for any discrepancies in quantity, price, and discounts. Receiving clerks may route or move shipments to the proper department, warehouse section, or stockroom. They may also arrange for adjustments with shippers whenever merchandise is lost or damaged. Receiving clerks in small businesses also may perform duties similar to those of stock clerks. In larger establishments, receiving clerks may control all receiving-platform operations, such as truck scheduling, recording of shipments, and handling of damaged goods.

Traffic clerks maintain records on the destination, weight, and charges on all incoming and outgoing freight. They verify rate charges by comparing the classification of materials with rate charts. In many companies, this work may be automated. Information either is scanned or is manually entered into a computer for use by accounting or other departments within the company. Also, they keep a file of claims for overcharges and for damage to goods in transit.

Employment

Shipping, receiving, and traffic clerks held about 774,000 jobs in 1998. Nearly 2 out of 3 were employed in manufacturing or by wholesale and retail establishments. Although jobs for shipping, receiving, and traffic clerks are found throughout the country, most clerks work in urban areas, where shipping depots in factories and wholesale establishments usually are located.

Job Outlook

Employment of shipping, receiving, and traffic clerks is expected to grow more slowly than the average for all occupations through 2008. Employment growth will continue to be affected by automation, as all but the smallest firms move to hold down labor costs by using computers to store and retrieve shipping and receiving records.

Methods of material handling have changed significantly in recent years. Large warehouses are increasingly automated, using equipment such as computerized conveyor systems, robots, computer-directed trucks, and automatic data storage and retrieval systems. Automation, coupled with the growing use of hand-held scanners and personal computers in shipping and receiving departments, has increased the productivity of these workers.

Despite technology, job openings will continue to arise due to increasing economic and trade activity and because certain tasks cannot be automated. For example, someone needs to check shipments before they go out and when they arrive to ensure everything is in order. In addition to job growth, openings will occur because of the need to replace shipping, receiving, and traffic clerks who leave the occupation. Because this is an entry-level occupation, many vacancies are created by normal career progression.

Related Occupations

Shipping, receiving, and traffic clerks record, check, and often store materials that a company receives. They also process and pack goods for shipment. Other workers who perform similar duties are stock clerks, material clerks, distributing clerks, routing clerks, express clerks, expediters, and order fillers.

Sources of Additional Information

General information about shipping, receiving, and traffic clerks can be obtained from:

* National Retail Federation, 325 Seventh St. NW., Suite 1000, Washington, DC 20004. Internet: http://www.nrf.com/nri/

Stock Clerks

(O*NET 49021, 58023, and 58026)

Nature of the Work

Stock clerks receive, unpack, check, store, and track merchandise or materials. They keep records of items entering or leaving the stock room and inspect damaged or spoiled goods. They sort, organize, and mark items with identifying codes, such as prices or stock or inventory control codes, so that inventories can be located quickly and easily. In larger establishments, where they may be responsible for only one task, they are called inventory clerk, stock-control clerk, merchandise distributor, order filler, property custodian, or storekeeper. In smaller firms, they may also perform tasks usually handled by shipping and receiving clerks.

In many firms, stock clerks use hand-held scanners connected to computers to keep inventories up to date. In retail stores, stock clerks bring merchandise to the sales floor and stock shelves and racks. In stockrooms and warehouses, they store materials in bins, on floors, or on shelves. They may also be required to lift cartons of various sizes.

Employment

Stock clerks held about 2.3 million jobs in 1998, with about 80 percent working in wholesale and retail trade. The greatest numbers were employed in grocery and department stores, respectively. Jobs for stock clerks are found in all parts of the country, but most work in large urban areas that have many large suburban shopping centers, warehouses, and factories.

Job Outlook

Job prospects for stock clerks should be favorable even though employment is expected to grow more slowly than the average for all occupations through 2008. Because this occupation is very large and many jobs are entry level, numerous job openings will occur each year to replace those who transfer to other jobs or leave the labor force.

The growing use of computers for inventory control and the installation of new, automated equipment are expected to slow growth in demand for stock clerks. This is especially true in manufacturing and wholesale trade, industries whose operations are automated most easily. In addition to computerized inventory control systems, firms in these industries rely more on sophisticated conveyor belts and automatic high stackers to store and retrieve goods. Also, expanded use of battery-powered, driverless, automatically guided vehicles can be expected.

Employment of stock clerks who work in grocery, general merchandise, department, apparel, and accessories stores is expected to be somewhat less affected by automation because much of their work is done manually on the sales floor and is difficult to automate. In addition, the increasing role of large retail outlets and warehouses, as well as catalogue, mail, telephone, and Internet shopping services should bolster employment of stock clerks and order fillers in these sectors of retail trade.

Related Occupations

Workers who also handle, move, organize, and store materials include shipping and receiving clerks, distributing clerks, routing clerks, stock supervisors, and cargo checkers.

Sources of Additional Information

State employment service offices can provide information about job openings for stock clerks.

General information about stock clerks can be obtained from:

- National Retail Federation, 325 Seventh Street NW., Suite 1000, Washington, DC 20004. Internet: http://www.nrf.com/nri/

Office and Administrative Support Supervisors and Managers

(O*NET 51002A and 51002B)

Significant Points

- Most jobs are filled by promoting individuals from within the organization, very often from the ranks of clerks they subsequently supervise.

- Office automation will cause employment in some office and administrative support occupations to slow or even decline, but supervisors are more likely to retain their jobs because of their relatively higher skills and longer tenure.

- Applicants for office and administrative support supervisor or manager jobs are likely to encounter keen competition because their number should greatly exceed the number of job openings.

Nature of the Work

All organizations need timely and effective office and administrative support to operate efficiently. Office and administrative support supervisors and managers coordinate this support. These workers are employed in virtually every sector of the economy, working in positions as varied as customer services manager, chief telephone operator, and shipping-and-receiving supervisor.

Although specific functions of office and administrative support supervisors and managers vary considerably, they share many common duties. For example, supervisors perform administrative tasks to ensure that their staffs can work efficiently. Equipment and machinery used in their departments must be in good working order. If the computer system goes down or a fax machine malfunctions, they must try to correct the problem or alert repair personnel. They also request new equipment or supplies for their department when necessary.

Planning the work of their staff and supervising them is a key function of this job. To do this effectively, the supervisor must know the strengths and weaknesses of each member of the staff, as well as the required level of quality and time allotted to each job. They must make allowances for unexpected absences and other disruptions by adjusting assignments or performing the work themselves if the situation requires it.

After allocating work assignments and issuing deadlines, office and administrative support supervisors oversee the work to ensure that it is proceeding on schedule and meets established quality standards. This may involve reviewing each person's work on a computer, as in the case of accounting clerks, or in the case of customer services representatives, listening to how they deal with customers. When supervising long-term projects, the supervisor may meet regularly with staff members to discuss their progress.

Office and administrative support supervisors also evaluate each worker's performance. If a worker has done a good job, the supervisor records it in the employee's personnel file and may recommend a promotion or other award. Alternatively, if a worker is performing poorly, the supervisor discusses the problem with the employee to determine the cause and helps the worker improve his or her performance. This might require sending the employee to a training course or arranging personal counseling. If the situation does not improve, the supervisor may recommend a transfer, demotion, or dismissal.

Office and administrative support supervisors usually interview and evaluate prospective clerical employees. When new workers arrive on the job, supervisors greet them and provide orientation to acquaint them with the organization and its operating routines. Some supervisors may be actively involved in recruiting new workers, for example, by making presentations at high schools and business colleges. They may also serve as the primary liaisons between their offices and the general public through direct contact and by preparing promotional information.

Supervisors also help train new employees in organization and office procedures. They may teach new employees how to use the telephone system and operate office equipment. Because much clerical work is computerized, they must also teach new employees to use the organization's computer system. When new office equipment or updated computer software is introduced, supervisors retrain experienced employees in using it efficiently. If this is not possible, they may arrange for special outside training for their employees.

Office and administrative support supervisors often act as liaisons between the clerical staff and the professional, technical, and managerial staff. This may involve implementing new company policies or restructuring the workflow in their departments. They must also keep their superiors informed of their progress and abreast of any potential problems. Often this communication takes the form of research projects and progress reports. Because they have access to information such as their department's performance records, they may compile and present this data for use in planning or designing new policies.

Office and administrative support supervisors also may have to resolve interpersonal conflicts among the staff. In organizations covered by union contracts, supervisors must know the provisions of labor-management agreements and run their departments accordingly. They may meet with union representatives to discuss work problems or grievances.

Working Conditions

Office and administrative support supervisors and managers are employed in a wide variety of work settings, but most work in clean, well-lit, and usually comfortable offices.

Most work a standard 40-hour week. Because some organizations operate around the clock, office and administrative support supervisors may have to work nights, weekends, and holidays. Sometimes supervisors rotate among the three shifts; in other cases, shifts are assigned on the basis of seniority.

Employment

Office and administrative support supervisors and managers held more than 1.6 million jobs in 1998. Although jobs for office and administrative support supervisors are found in practically every industry, the largest number are found in organizations with a large clerical work force such as banks, wholesalers, government agencies, retail establishments, business service firms, and insurance companies. Due to the need in most organizations for continuity of supervision, few office and administrative support supervisors and managers work on a temporary or part-time basis.

Training, Other Qualifications, and Advancement

Most firms fill administrative and office support supervisory and managerial positions by promoting clerical or administrative support workers within their organization. To become eligible for promotion to a supervisory position, clerical or administrative support workers must prove they are capable of handling additional responsibilities. When evaluating candidates, superiors look for strong teamwork, problem solving, leadership, and communication skills, as well as determination, loyalty, poise, and confidence. They also look for more specific supervisory attributes, such as the ability to organize and coordinate work efficiently, set priorities, and motivate others. Increasingly, supervisors need a broad base of office skills coupled with personal flexibility to adapt to changes in organizational structure and move among departments when necessary.

In addition, supervisors must pay close attention to detail in order to identify and correct errors made by the staff they oversee. Good working knowledge of the organization's computer system is also an advantage. Many employers require post-secondary training, in some cases an associate's or even a bachelor's degree.

A clerk with potential supervisory abilities may be given occasional supervisory assignments. To prepare for full-time supervisory duties, he or she may attend in-house training or take courses in time management or interpersonal relations.

Some office and administrative support supervisor positions are filled with people from outside the organization. These positions may serve as entry-level training for potential higher-level managers. New college graduates may rotate through departments of an organization at this level to learn the work of the organization.

Job Outlook

Like other supervisory occupations, applicants for office and administrative support supervisor or manager jobs are likely to encounter keen competition because the number of applicants should greatly exceed the number of job openings. Employment of office and administrative support supervisors and managers is expected to grow about as fast as the average for all occupations through 2008. In addition to the job openings arising from growth, a larger number of openings will stem from the need to replace workers who transfer to other occupations or leave this large occupation for other reasons.

Employment of office and administrative support supervisors is primarily affected by the demand for clerical workers. Despite an increasing amount of clerical work, the spread of office automation should allow a wider variety of tasks to be performed by fewer office and administrative support workers. This will cause employment in some clerical occupations to slow or even decline, leading supervisors to have smaller staffs and perform more professional tasks. However, office and administrative support managers still will be needed to coordinate the increasing amount of clerical work and make sure the technology is applied and running properly. In addition, organizational restructuring continues to reduce some middle management positions, distributing more responsibility to office and administrative support supervisors. This added responsibility, combined with relatively higher skills and longer tenure, will place office and administrative support supervisors and managers among the clerical workers most likely to retain their jobs.

Earnings

Median annual earnings of full-time office and administrative support supervisors were $31,090 in 1998; the middle 50 percent earned between $23,950 and $40,250. The lowest paid 10 percent earned less than $19,060, while the highest paid 10 percent earned more than $52,570. In 1997, median earnings in the industries employing the largest numbers of office and administrative support supervisors were:

Federal government	$49,200
Local government, except education and hospitals	30,600
Hospitals	29,700
Offices and clinics of medical doctors	29,200
Commercial banks	27,400

In addition to typical benefits, some office and administrative support supervisors in the private sector may receive additional compensation in the form of bonuses and stock options.

Related Occupations

Office and administrative support supervisors and managers must understand and sometimes perform the work of the people whom they oversee, including accounting clerks, cashiers, bank tellers, and telephone operators. Their supervisory and administrative duties are similar to those of other supervisors and managers.

Sources of Additional Information

For a wide variety of information related to management occupations, including educational programs, contact:

- American Management Association, 1601 Broadway, New York, NY 10019-7420. Internet: http://www.amanet.org
- National Management Association, 2210 Arbor Blvd., Dayton, OH 45439. Internet: http://www.nma1.org

Office Clerks, General

(O*NET 55347)

Significant Points

- Although most jobs are entry level, previous office or business experience may be required for some positions.

- Plentiful job opportunities should stem from employment growth, the large size of the occupation, and turnover.

Nature of the Work

As opposed to a single specialized task, the daily responsibilities of a general office clerk change with the needs of the specific jobs and the employer. Whereas some clerks spend their days filing or typing, others enter data at a computer terminal. They can also be called upon to operate photocopiers, fax machines, and other office equipment; prepare mailings; proofread copies; and answer telephones and deliver messages.

The specific duties assigned to a clerk vary significantly depending upon the type of office in which a clerk works. An office clerk in a doctor's office, for example, would not perform the same tasks as a clerk in a large financial institution or in the office of an auto parts wholesaler. Although they may sort checks, keep payroll records, take inventory, and access information, clerks also perform duties unique to their employer, such as organizing medications, making transparencies for a presentation, or filling orders received by fax machine.

The specific duties assigned to a clerk also vary by level of experience. Whereas inexperienced employees make photocopies, stuff envelopes, or record inquiries, experienced clerks are usually given additional responsibilities. For example, they may maintain financial or other records, verify statistical reports for accuracy and completeness, handle and adjust customer complaints, make travel arrangements, take inventory of equipment and supplies, answer questions on departmental services and functions, or help prepare invoices or budgetary requests. Senior office clerks may be expected to monitor and direct the work of lower level clerks.

Working Conditions

For the most part, working conditions for office clerks are the same as those for other office employees within the same company. Those on a full-time schedule usually work a standard 40-hour week; however, some work shifts or overtime during busy periods. About 1 in 3 works part time, whereas many other office clerks work as temporary workers.

Employment

Office clerks held about 3,021,000 jobs in 1998. Most are employed in relatively small businesses. Although they work in every sector of the economy, almost 60 percent worked in the services or wholesale and retail trade industries.

Training, Other Qualifications, and Advancement

Although most office clerk jobs are entry-level administrative support positions, some previous office or business experience may be needed. Employers usually require a high school diploma, and some require typing, basic computer skills, and other general office skills. Familiarity with computer word processing software and applications is becoming increasingly important.

Training for this occupation is available through business education programs offered in high schools, community and junior colleges, and post-secondary vocational schools. Courses in word processing, other computer applications, and office practices are particularly helpful.

Because office clerks usually work with other office staff, they should be cooperative and able to work as part of a team. In addition, they should have good communication skills, be detail-oriented, and adaptable.

General office clerks who exhibit strong communication, interpersonal, and analytical skills may be promoted to supervisory positions. Others may move into different, more senior clerical or administrative jobs, such as receptionist, secretary, and administrative assistant. After gaining some work experience or specialized skills, many workers transfer to jobs with higher pay or greater advancement potential. Advancement to professional occupations within an establishment normally requires additional formal education, such as a college degree.

Job Outlook

Plentiful job opportunities are expected for general office clerks due to employment growth, the large size of the occupation, and turnover. Furthermore, growth in part-time and temporary clerical positions will lead to a large number of job openings. Prospects should be brightest for those who have knowledge of basic computer applications and office machinery, such as fax machines and copiers.

Employment of general office clerks is expected to grow about as fast as the average for all occupations through 2008. The employment outlook for office clerks will be affected by the increasing use of computers, expanding office automation, and the consolidation of clerical tasks. Automation has led to productivity gains, allowing a wide variety of duties to be performed by few office workers. However, automation also has led to a consolidation of clerical staffs and a diversification of job responsibilities. This consolidation increases the demand for general office clerks, because they perform a variety of clerical tasks. It will become increasingly common within small businesses to find a single general office clerk in charge of all clerical work.

Earnings

Median annual earnings of full-time office clerks were $19,580 in 1998; the middle 50 percent earned between $15,210 and $24,370 annually. Ten percent earned less than $12,570, and 10 percent earned more than $30,740. Median annual salaries in the industries employing the largest number of office clerks in 1997 were as follows:

Local government, except education and hospitals $20,300

State government, except education and hospitals 20,100

Hospitals 19,400

Colleges and universities 18,600

Personnel supply services 16,700

In early 1999, the Federal government paid office clerks a starting salary of between $13,400 and $18,400 a year, depending on education and experience. Office clerks employed by the Federal government earned an average annual salary of about $28,100 in 1999.

Related Occupations

The duties of office clerks can include a combination of bookkeeping, typing, office machine operation, and filing; other administrative support workers who perform similar duties include information clerks and records processing clerks. Nonclerical entry-level jobs include cashier, medical assistant, teacher aide, and food and beverage service worker.

Sources of Additional Information

State employment service offices and agencies can provide information about job openings for general office clerks.

Operations Research Analysts

(O*NET 25302)

Significant Points

- Individuals with a master's degree or Ph.D. in management science, operations research, or a closely related field should have good job prospects.

- Employment growth is projected to be slower than average.

Nature of the Work

Operations research (OR) and management science are terms that are used interchangeably to describe the discipline of applying quantitative techniques to make decisions and solve problems. Many methods used in operations research were developed during World War II to help take the guesswork out of missions such as deploying radar, searching for enemy submarines, and getting supplies where they were most needed. Following the war, numerous peacetime applications emerged, leading to the use of OR and management science in many industries and occupations.

The prevalence of operations research in the Nation's economy reflects the growing complexity of managing large organizations that require the efficient use of materials, equipment, and people.

OR analysts determine the optimal means of coordinating these elements to achieve specified goals by applying mathematical principles to organizational problems. They solve problems in different ways and propose alternative solutions to management, which then chooses the course of action that best meets their goals. In general, OR analysts are concerned with issues such as strategy, forecasting, resource allocation, facilities layout, inventory control, personnel schedules, and distribution systems.

The duties of the operations research analyst vary according to the structure and management philosophy of the employer or client. Some firms centralize operations research in one department; others use operations research in each division. Some organizations contract operations research services with a consulting firm. Economists, systems analysts, mathematicians, industrial engineers, and others may apply operations research techniques to address problems in their respective fields. Operations research analysts may also work closely with senior managers to identify and solve a variety of problems.

Regardless of the type or structure of the client organization, operations research in its classic role of carrying out analysis to support management's quest for performance improvement entails a similar set of procedures. Managers begin the process by describing the symptoms of a problem to the analyst, who then formally defines the problem. For example, an operations research analyst for an auto manufacturer may be asked to determine the best inventory level for each of the parts needed on a production line and to determine the number of windshields to be kept in inventory. Too many windshields would be wasteful and expensive, while too few could result in an unintended halt in production.

Operations research analysts study such problems and then break them into their component parts. Analysts then gather information about each of these parts from a variety of sources. To determine the most efficient amount of inventory to be kept on hand, for example, OR analysts might talk with engineers about production levels, discuss purchasing arrangements with buyers, and examine data on storage costs provided by the accounting department.

With this information in hand, the analyst is ready to select the most appropriate analytical technique. Analysts could use several techniques—including simulation, linear and non-linear optimization, networks, waiting lines, discrete and random variables methods, dynamic programming, queuing models and other stochastic-process models, Markov decision processes, econometric methods, data envelopment analysis, neural networks, genetic algorithms, decision analysis, and the analytic hierarchy process. All of these techniques, however, involve the construction of a mathematical model that attempts to describe the system in use. The use of models enables the analyst to assign values to the different components and determine the relationships between them. These values can be altered to examine what will happen to the system under different circumstances.

In most cases, the computer program used to solve the model must be modified repeatedly to reflect these different solutions. A model for airline flight scheduling, for example, might include variables for the cities to be connected, amount of fuel required to fly the routes, projected levels of passenger demand, varying ticket and fuel prices, pilot scheduling, and maintenance costs. By choosing different variables for the model, the analyst is able to produce the best flight schedule consistent with various sets of assumptions.

Upon concluding the analysis, the operations research analyst presents management with recommendations based on the results of the analysis. Additional computer programming based on different assumptions may be needed to help select the best recommendation offered by the OR analyst. When management reaches a decision, the analyst may work with others in the organization to ensure the plan's successful implementation.

Working Conditions

Operations research analysts generally work regular hours in an office environment. Because they work on projects that are of immediate interest to top management, OR analysts often are under pressure to meet deadlines and work more than a 40-hour week.

Employment

Operations research analysts held about 76,000 jobs in 1998. Major employers include telecommunication companies, air carriers, computer and data processing services, financial institutions, insurance carriers, engineering and management services firms, and the Federal government. Most operations research analysts in the Federal government work for the Armed Forces, and many OR analysts in private industry work directly or indirectly on national defense. About 1 out of 5 analysts work for management, research, public relations, and testing agencies that do operations research consulting.

Training, Other Qualifications, and Advancement

Employers generally prefer applicants with at least a master's degree in operations research, engineering, business, mathematics, information systems, or management science, coupled with a bachelor's degree in computer science or a quantitative discipline such as economics, mathematics, or statistics. Dual graduate degrees in operations research and computer science are especially attractive to employers. Operations research analysts also must be able to think logically and work well with people, and employers prefer workers with good oral and written communication skills.

In addition to formal education, employers often sponsor training for experienced workers, helping them keep up with new developments in OR techniques and computer science. Some analysts attend advanced university classes on these subjects at their employer's expense.

Because computers are the most important tools for quantitative analysis, training and experience in programming are required. Operations research analysts typically need to be proficient in database collection and management, programming, and in the development and use of sophisticated software programs.

Beginning analysts usually perform routine work under the supervision of more experienced analysts. As they gain knowledge and experience, they are assigned more complex tasks and given greater autonomy to design models and solve problems. Operations research analysts advance by assuming positions as technical specialists or supervisors. The skills acquired by operations research analysts are useful for higher-level management jobs, and experienced analysts may leave the field to assume nontechnical managerial or administrative positions.

Job Outlook

Individuals who hold a master's degree or Ph.D. in operations research, management science, or a closely related field should find good job opportunities through 2008, as the number of openings generated by employment growth and the need to replace those leaving the occupation is expected to exceed the number of persons graduating with these credentials. In addition, graduates with bachelor's degrees in operations research or management science from the limited number of schools offering these degree programs should find opportunities in a variety of related fields that allow them to use their quantitative abilities.

The slower-than-average employment growth expected for OR analysts will be driven by the continuing use of operations research and management science techniques to improve productivity, ensure quality, and reduce costs in private industry and government. This should result in a steady demand for workers knowledgeable in operations research techniques in the years ahead. Nevertheless, this growth will be relatively slow because few job openings in this field are expected to have the title operations research analyst.

Earnings

Median annual earnings of OR analysts were $49,070 in 1998. The middle 50 percent earned between $36,890 and $72,090. The lowest 10 percent had earnings of less than $29,780, while the top 10 percent earned more than $87,720. Median annual earnings in the industries employing the largest number of OR analysts in 1997 are shown below.

Research and testing services	$64,000
Computer and data processing services	45,400
Commercial banks	37,500

The average annual salary for operations research analysts in the Federal government in nonsupervisory, supervisory, and managerial positions was $72,000 in early 1999.

Related Occupations

Operations research analysts apply mathematical principles to large, complicated problems. Workers in other occupations that stress quantitative analysis include computer scientists, systems analysts, modeling specialists, logistics consultants, engineers, mathematicians, statisticians, and economists. Because its goal is improved organizational effectiveness, operations research also is closely allied to managerial occupations.

Sources of Additional Information

Information on career opportunities for operations research analysts is available from:

- The Institute for Operations Research and the Management Sciences, 901 Elkridge Landing Rd., Suite 400, Linthicum, MD 21090. Internet: http://www.informs.org

For information on OR careers in the Armed Forces and Department of Defense, contact:

- Military Operations Research Society, 101 South Whiting St., Suite 202, Alexandria, VA 22304. Internet: http://www.mors.org

Opticians, Dispensing

(O*NET 32514)

Significant Points

- Although training requirements vary by State, most dispensing opticians receive training on the job or through apprenticeships lasting two to four years.

- Employment of dispensing opticians is expected to increase as fast as the average for all occupations through 2008 as demand grows for corrective lenses.

Nature of Work

Dispensing opticians fit eyeglasses and contact lenses, following prescriptions written by ophthalmologists or optometrists.

Dispensing opticians examine written prescriptions to determine lens specifications. They recommend eyeglass frames, lenses, and lens coatings after considering the prescription and the customer's occupation, habits, and facial features. Dispensing opticians measure clients' eyes, including the distance between the centers of the pupils and the distance between the eye surface and the lens. For customers without prescriptions, dispensing opticians may use a lensometer to record the present eyeglass prescription. They also may obtain a customer's previous record or verify a prescription with the examining optometrist or ophthalmologist.

Dispensing opticians prepare work orders that give ophthalmic laboratory technicians information needed to grind and insert lenses into a frame. The work order includes lens prescriptions and information on lens size, material, color, and style. Some dispensing opticians grind and insert lenses themselves. After the glasses are made, dispensing opticians verify that the lenses have been ground to specifications. Then they may reshape or bend the frame, by hand or using pliers, so that the eyeglasses fit the customer properly and comfortably. Some also fix, adjust, and refit broken frames. They instruct clients about adapting to, wearing, or caring for eyeglasses.

Some dispensing opticians specialize in fitting contacts, artificial eyes, or cosmetic shells to cover blemished eyes. To fit contact lenses, dispensing opticians measure eye shape and size, select the type of contact lens material, and prepare work orders specifying the prescription and lens size. Fitting contact lenses requires considerable skill, care, and patience. Dispensing opticians observe customers' eyes, corneas, lids, and contact lenses with special instruments and microscopes. During several visits, opticians show customers how to insert, remove, and care for their contacts and ensure the fit is correct.

Dispensing opticians keep records on customer prescriptions, work orders, and payments; track inventory and sales; and perform other administrative duties.

Working Conditions

Dispensing opticians work indoors in attractive, well-lighted, and well-ventilated surroundings. They may work in medical offices or small stores where customers are served one at a time, or in large stores where several dispensing opticians serve a number of customers at once. Opticians spend a lot of time on their feet. If they prepare lenses, they need to take precautions against the hazards associated with glass cutting, chemicals, and machinery.

Most dispensing opticians work a 40-hour week, although some work longer hours. Those in retail stores may work evenings and weekends. Some work part time.

Employment

Dispensing opticians held about 71,000 jobs in 1998. About 50 percent worked for ophthalmologists or optometrists who sell glasses directly to patients. Many also work in retail optical stores that offer one-stop shopping. Customers may have their eyes examined, choose frames, and have glasses made on the spot. Some work in optical departments of drug and department stores.

Training, Other Qualifications, and Advancement

Employers usually hire individuals with no background in opticianry or those who have worked as ophthalmic laboratory technicians and then provide the required training. Training may be informal, on-the-job, or formal apprenticeship. Some employers, however, seek people with post-secondary training in opticianry.

Knowledge of physics, basic anatomy, algebra, geometry, and mechanical drawing is particularly valuable because training usually includes instruction in optical mathematics, optical physics, and the use of precision measuring instruments and other machinery and tools. Dispensing opticians deal directly with the public so they should be tactful, pleasant, and communicate well. Manual dexterity and the ability to do precision work are essential.

Large employers usually offer structured apprenticeship programs, and small employers provide more informal on-the-job training. In the 21 States that offer a license to dispensing opticians, individuals without post-secondary training work from two to four years as apprentices. Apprenticeship or formal training is offered in most States as well.

Apprentices receive technical training and learn office management and sales. Under the supervision of an experienced optician, optometrist, or ophthalmologist, apprentices work directly with patients, fitting eyeglasses and contact lenses. In the 21 States requiring licensure, information about apprenticeships and licensing procedures is available from the State board of occupational licensing.

Formal opticianry training is offered in community colleges and a few colleges and universities. In 1999, there were 25 programs accredited by the Commission on Opticianry Accreditation that awarded two-year associate degrees in ophthalmic dispensing or optometric technology. There are also shorter programs of one year or less. Some States that offer a license to dispensing opticians allow graduates to take the licensure exam immediately upon graduation; others require a few months to a year of experience.

Dispensing opticians may apply to the American Board of Opticianry and the National Contact Lens Examiners for certification of their skills. Certification must be renewed every three years through continuing education.

Many experienced dispensing opticians open their own optical stores. Others become managers of optical stores or sales representatives for wholesalers or manufacturers of eyeglasses or lenses.

Job Outlook

Employment in this occupation is expected to increase as fast as the average for all occupations through 2008 as demand grows for corrective lenses. The number of middle-aged and elderly persons is projected to increase rapidly. Middle age is a time when many individuals use corrective lenses for the first time, and elderly persons require more vision care, on the whole, than others.

Fashion, too, influences demand. Frames come in a growing variety of styles and colors—encouraging people to buy more than one pair. Demand is also expected to grow in response to the availability of new technologies that improve the quality and look of corrective lenses, such as anti-reflective coatings and bifocal lenses without the line that was visible in old-style bifocals. Improvements in bifocal, extended wear, and disposable contact lenses will also spur demand.

The need to replace those who leave the occupation will result in job openings. Nevertheless, the total number of job openings will be relatively small because the occupation is small. This occupation is vulnerable to changes in the business cycle because eyewear purchases can often be deferred for a time. Employment of opticians can fall somewhat during economic downturns.

Earnings

Median annual earnings of dispensing opticians were $22,440 in 1998. The middle 50 percent earned between $17,680 and $28,560 a year. The lowest 10 percent earned less than $14,240, and the highest 10 percent earned more than $37,080 a year. Median annual earnings in the industries employing the largest number of dispensing opticians in 1997 were as follows:

Offices and clinics of medical doctors $25,900

Retail stores, not elsewhere classified 21,500

Offices of other health care practitioners 20,100

Related Occupations

Other workers who deal with customers and perform delicate work include jewelers, locksmiths, ophthalmic laboratory technicians, orthodontic technicians, dental laboratory technicians, prosthetics technicians, camera repairers, and watch repairers.

Sources of Additional Information

For general information about a career as a dispensing optician, contact:

● Opticians Association of America, 10341 Democracy Lane, Fairfax, VA 22030-2521. Internet: http://www.opticians.org

For general information about a career as a dispensing optician and a list of accredited training programs, contact:

● Commission on Opticianry Accreditation, 10341 Democracy Lane, Fairfax, VA 22030-2521. Internet: http://www.coaccreditation.com

For general information on opticianry and a list of home-study programs, seminars, and review materials, contact:

● National Academy of Opticianry, 8401 Corporate Drive, Suite 605, Landover, MD 20785. Internet: http://www.nao.org

Optometrists

(O*NET 32108)

Significant Points

● All States and the District of Columbia require that optometrists be licensed, which requires a Doctor of Optometry degree from an accredited optometry school and passing both a written and a clinical State board examination.

● Employment growth will be fastest in retail optical stores and outpatient clinics.

● Optometrists usually remain in practice until they retire, so job openings arising from replacement needs are low.

Nature of the Work

Over half of the people in the United States wear glasses or contact lenses. Optometrists (doctors of optometry, also known as O.D.'s) provide most primary vision care.

Optometrists examine people's eyes to diagnose vision problems and eye diseases. They use instruments and observation to examine eye health and to test patients' visual acuity, depth and color perception, and their ability to focus and coordinate the eyes. They analyze test results and develop a treatment plan. Optometrists prescribe eyeglasses and contact lenses and provide vision therapy and low vision rehabilitation. They administer drugs to patients to aid in the diagnosis of eye vision problems and prescribe drugs to treat some eye diseases. Optometrists often provide pre- and postoperative care to cataract, laser vision correction, and other eye surgery patients. They also diagnose conditions due to systemic diseases such as diabetes and high blood pressure, and they refer patients to other health practitioners as needed.

Optometrists should not be confused with ophthalmologists or dispensing opticians. Ophthalmologists are physicians who perform eye surgery and who diagnose and treat eye diseases and in-

juries. Like optometrists, they also examine eyes and prescribe eyeglasses and contact lenses. Dispensing opticians fit and adjust eyeglasses and in some States may fit contact lenses according to prescriptions written by ophthalmologists or optometrists.

Most optometrists are in general practice. Some specialize in work with the elderly, children, or partially sighted persons who need specialized visual devices. Others develop and implement ways to protect workers' eyes from on-the-job strain or injury. Some specialize in contact lenses, sports vision, or vision therapy. A few teach optometry, perform research, or consult.

Most optometrists are private practitioners who also handle the business aspects of running an office, such as developing a patient base, hiring employees, keeping records, and ordering equipment and supplies. Optometrists who operate franchise optical stores may also have some of these duties.

Working Conditions

Optometrists work in places—usually their own offices—which are clean, well lighted, and comfortable. Most full-time optometrists work about 40 hours a week. Many work Saturdays and evenings to suit the needs of patients. Emergency calls, once uncommon, have increased with the passage of therapeutic drug laws expanding optometrists' ability to prescribe medications.

Employment

Optometrists held about 38,000 jobs in 1998. The number of jobs is greater than the number of practicing optometrists because some optometrists hold two or more jobs. For example, an optometrist may have a private practice but also work in another practice, clinic, or vision care center. According to the American Optometric Association, about two-thirds of practicing optometrists are in private practice.

Although many optometrists practice alone, a growing number are in a partnership or group practice. Some optometrists work as salaried employees of other optometrists or of ophthalmologists, hospitals, health maintenance organizations (HMOs), or retail optical stores. A small number of optometrists are consultants for industrial safety programs, insurance companies, manufacturers of ophthalmic products, HMOs, and others.

Training, Other Qualifications, and Advancement

All States and the District of Columbia require that optometrists be licensed. Applicants for a license must have a Doctor of Optometry degree from an accredited optometry school and pass both a written and a clinical State board examination. In many States, applicants can substitute the examinations of the National Board of Examiners in Optometry, usually taken during the student's academic career, for part or all of the written examination. Licenses are renewed every one to three years and in all States, continuing education credits are needed for renewal.

The Doctor of Optometry degree requires completion of a four-year program at an accredited optometry school preceded by at least three years of preoptometric study at an accredited college or university (most optometry students hold a bachelor's degree or higher). In 1999, 17 U.S. schools and colleges of optometry held an accredited status with the Council on Optometric Education of the American Optometric Association.

Requirements for admission to schools of optometry include courses in English, mathematics, physics, chemistry, and biology. A few schools require or recommend courses in psychology, history, sociology, speech, or business. Applicants must take the Optometry Admissions Test, which measures academic ability and scientific comprehension. Most applicants take the test after their sophomore or junior year. Competition for admission is keen.

Optometry programs include classroom and laboratory study of health and visual sciences, as well as clinical training in the diagnosis and treatment of eye disorders. Included are courses in pharmacology, optics, vision science, biochemistry, and systemic disease.

Business ability, self-discipline, and the ability to deal tactfully with patients are important for success. The work of optometrists requires attention to detail and good manual dexterity.

Optometrists wishing to teach or do research may study for a master's degree or Ph.D. in visual science, physiological optics, neurophysiology, public health, health administration, health information and communication, or health education. One-year postgraduate clinical residency programs are available for optometrists who wish to specialize in any of the following areas: family practice optometry, pediatric optometry, geriatric optometry, vision therapy, contact lenses, hospital based optometry, primary care optometry, or ocular disease.

Job Outlook

Employment of optometrists is expected to grow about as fast as the average for all occupations through 2008 in response to the vision care needs of a growing and aging population. As baby boomers age, they will be more likely to visit optometrists and ophthalmologists because of the onset of vision problems in middle age, including computer-related vision problems. The demand for optometric services will also increase because of growth in the oldest age group, with their increased likelihood of cataracts, glaucoma, diabetes, and hypertension. Employment of optometrists will also grow due to greater recognition of the importance of vision care, rising personal incomes, and growth in employee vision care plans. Employment growth will be fastest in retail optical stores and outpatient clinics.

Employment of optometrists would grow more rapidly were it not for anticipated productivity gains that will allow each optometrist to see more patients. These gains will result from greater use of optometric assistants and other support personnel and the introduction of new equipment and procedures. New surgical procedures using lasers are available that can correct some vision problems, but they remain expensive.

In addition to growth, the need to replace optometrists who leave the occupation will create employment opportunities. Relatively few opportunities from this source are expected, however, because most optometrists continue to practice until they retire; few transfer to other occupations.

Earnings

Median annual earnings of salaried optometrists were $68,500 in 1998. The middle 50 percent earned between $43,750 and $93,700 a year. The lowest 10 percent earned less than $24,820, and the highest 10 percent earned more than $123,770 a year. Salaried optometrists tend to earn more initially than optometrists who set up independent practices. In the long run, however, those in private practice usually earn more.

According to the American Optometric Association, new optometry graduates in their first year of practice earned median net incomes of $55,000 in 1998. Overall, optometrists earned median net incomes of $92,000.

Related Occupations

Workers in other occupations who apply scientific knowledge to prevent, diagnose, and treat disorders and injuries are chiropractors, dentists, physicians, podiatrists, veterinarians, speech-language pathologists, and audiologists.

Sources of Additional Information

For information on optometry as a career and a listing of accredited optometric educational institutions, as well as required preoptometry courses, contact:

- American Optometric Association, Educational Services, 243 North Lindbergh Blvd., St. Louis, MO 63141-7881. Internet: http://www.aoanet.org
- Association of Schools and Colleges of Optometry, 6110 Executive Blvd., Suite 510, Rockville, MD 20852. Internet: http://www.opted.org

The Board of Optometry in each State can supply information on licensing requirements.

For information on specific admission requirements and sources of financial aid, contact the admissions officer of individual optometry schools.

Order Clerks

(O*NET 55323)

Significant Points

- Most jobs require only a high school diploma.
- Numerous jobs will become available each year.

Nature of the Work

Order clerks receive and process incoming orders for a wide variety of goods or services, such as spare parts for machines, consumer appliances, gas and electric power connections, film rentals, and articles of clothing. They are sometimes called order-entry clerks, customer service representatives, sales representatives, order processors, or order takers.

Orders for materials, merchandise, or services can come from inside or from outside of an organization. In large companies with many work sites, such as automobile manufacturers, clerks order parts and equipment from the company's warehouses. *Inside order clerks* receive orders from other workers employed by the same company or from salespersons in the field.

Many other order clerks, however, receive orders from outside companies or individuals. Order clerks in wholesale businesses, for instance, receive orders for merchandise from retail establishments that the retailer, in turn, sells to the public. An increasing number of order clerks work for catalogue companies and online retailers, receiving orders from individual customers by either phone, fax, regular mail, or e-mail. Order clerks dealing primarily with the public sometimes are referred to as *outside order clerks*.

Computers provide order clerks with ready access to information such as stock numbers, prices, and inventory. Orders frequently depend on which products are in stock and which products are most appropriate for the customer's needs. Some order clerks, especially those in industrial settings, must be able to give price estimates for entire jobs, not just single parts. Others must be able to take special orders, give expected arrival dates, prepare contracts, and handle complaints.

Many order clerks receive orders directly by telephone, entering the required information as the customer places the order. However, a rapidly increasing number of orders are now received through computer systems, the Internet, faxes, and e-mail. In some cases, these orders are sent directly from the customer's terminal to the order clerk's terminal. Orders received by regular mail are sometimes scanned into a database that's instantly accessible to clerks.

Clerks review orders for completeness and clarity. They may complete missing information or contact the customer for the information. Similarly, clerks contact customers if customers need additional information, such as prices or shipping dates, or if delays in filling the order are anticipated. For orders received by regular mail, clerks extract checks or money orders, sort them, and send them for processing. After an order has been verified and entered, the customer's final cost is calculated. The clerk then routes the order to the proper department—such as the warehouse—that actually sends out or delivers the item in question.

In organizations with sophisticated computer systems, inventory records are adjusted automatically, as sales are made. In less automated organizations, order clerks may adjust inventory records. Clerks may also notify other departments when inventories are low or when orders would deplete supplies.

Some order clerks must establish priorities in filling orders. For example, an order clerk in a blood bank may receive a request from a hospital for a certain type of blood. The clerk must first find out if the request is routine or an emergency and then take appropriate action.

Working Conditions

Clerks typically are employed in an office environment. Most work alongside other clerical workers, but some work in centralized units away from the front office. Because most clerks use computers on a daily basis, these workers may experience eye and muscle strain, backaches, headaches, and repetitive motion injuries. Also, clerks

who review detailed data may have to sit for extended periods of time. Most clerks work regular business hours. Order clerks in retail establishments typically work overtime during busy seasons.

Employment

Order clerks held about 362,000 jobs in 1998. About one half were in wholesale and retail establishments and about one quarter in manufacturing firms. Most of the remaining jobs for order clerks were in business services.

Training, Other Qualifications, and Advancement

Employers typically require applicants to have at least a high school diploma or its equivalent, although many employers prefer to hire clerks with a higher level of education. Most employers prefer workers who are computer-literate. Knowledge of word processing and spreadsheet software is especially valuable, as are experience working in an office and good interpersonal skills.

Clerks often learn the skills they need in high schools, business schools, and community colleges. Business education programs offered by these institutions typically include courses in typing, word processing, shorthand, business communications, records management, and office systems and procedures. Specialized order clerks in technical positions obtain their training from technical institutes and two- and four-year colleges.

Some entrants are college graduates with degrees in business, finance, or liberal arts. Although a degree is rarely required, many graduates accept entry-level clerical positions to get into a particular company or to enter the finance or accounting field with the hope of being promoted to professional or managerial positions. Workers with college degrees are likely to start at higher salaries and advance more easily than those without degrees.

Once hired, clerks usually receive on-the-job training. Under the guidance of a supervisor or other senior worker, new employees learn company procedures. Some formal classroom training may also be necessary, such as training in specific computer software.

Clerks must be careful, orderly, and detail-oriented in order to avoid making errors and to recognize errors made by others. These workers should also be discreet and trustworthy because they frequently come in contact with confidential material.

Clerks usually advance by taking on more duties in the same occupation for higher pay or transferring to a closely related occupation. For example, some order clerks use their experience to move into sales positions. Most companies fill office and administrative support supervisory and managerial positions by promoting individuals from within their organizations, so clerks who acquire additional skills, experience, and training improve their advancement opportunities.

Job Outlook

Job openings for order clerks should be plentiful through the year 2008 due to sizable replacement needs. Numerous jobs will become available each year to replace order clerks who transfer to other occupations or leave the labor force completely. Many of these openings will be for seasonal work, especially in catalogue companies or online retailers catering to holiday gift buyers.

Employment of order clerks is expected to grow more slowly than the average through the year 2008, as office automation continues to increase worker productivity. As the economy grows, increasingly more orders for goods and services will be placed. Demand for outside order clerks who deal mainly with the public or other businesses should remain fairly strong. The increasing use of online retailing and toll-free numbers that make placing orders easy and convenient will stimulate demand for these workers. However, productivity gains from increased automation will offset some of the growth in demand for outside order clerks, as each clerk is able to handle an increasingly higher volume of orders. In addition, orders placed over the Internet and other computer systems are often entered directly into the computer by the customer; thus, the order clerk is not involved at all in placing the order.

Employment growth of inside clerks will also be constrained by productivity gains due to automation. The spread of electronic data interchange, a system enabling computers to communicate directly with one another, allows orders within establishments to be placed with little human intervention. Besides electronic data interchange, *extranets* and other systems allowing a firm's employees to place orders directly are increasingly common.

Other types of automation will also limit the demand for order clerks. Sophisticated inventory control and automatic billing systems allow companies to track inventory and accounts with much less help from order clerks than in the past. Some companies use automated phone menus accessible with a touch-tone phone to receive orders, and others use answering machines. Developments in voice recognition technology may also further reduce the demand for order clerks.

Earnings

Salaries of clerks vary. The region of the country, size of city, and type and size of establishment all influence salary levels. The level of industry or technical expertise required and the complexity and uniqueness of a clerk's responsibilities may also affect earnings. Median annual earnings of full-time order clerks in 1998 were $21,550.

Related Occupations

Today, most clerks enter data into a computer system and perform basic analysis of the data. Other clerical workers who enter and manipulate data include bank tellers, statistical clerks, receiving clerks, medical record clerks, hotel and motel clerks, credit clerks, and reservation and transportation ticket agents.

Sources of Additional Information

State employment service offices can provide information about job openings for records processing occupations.

Paralegals

(O*NET 28305)

Significant Points

- While some paralegals train on the job, employers increasingly prefer graduates of post-secondary paralegal training programs.

- Paralegals are projected to rank among the fastest growing occupations in the economy as they increasingly perform many legal tasks formerly carried out by lawyers.

- Stiff competition is expected as the number of graduates of paralegal training programs and others seeking to enter the profession outpaces job growth.

Nature of the Work

While lawyers assume ultimate responsibility for legal work, they often delegate many of their tasks to paralegals. In fact, paralegals continue to assume a growing range of tasks in the Nation's legal offices and perform many of the same tasks as lawyers. Nevertheless, they are still explicitly prohibited from carrying out duties that are considered to be the practice of law, such as setting legal fees, giving legal advice, and presenting cases in court.

One of a paralegal's most important tasks is helping lawyers prepare for closings, hearings, trials, and corporate meetings. Paralegals investigate the facts of cases and ensure all relevant information is considered. They also identify appropriate laws, judicial decisions, legal articles, and other materials that are relevant to assigned cases. After they analyze and organize the information, paralegals may prepare written reports that attorneys use in determining how cases should be handled. Should attorneys decide to file lawsuits on behalf of clients, paralegals may help prepare the legal arguments, draft pleadings and motions to be filed with the court, obtain affidavits, and assist attorneys during trials. Paralegals also organize and track files of all important case documents and make them available and easily accessible to attorneys.

In addition to this preparatory work, paralegals also perform a number of other vital functions. For example, they help draft contracts, mortgages, separation agreements, and trust instruments. They may also assist in preparing tax returns and planning estates. Some paralegals coordinate the activities of other law office employees and maintain financial records for the office. Various additional tasks may differ depending on the employer.

Paralegals are found in all types of organizations, but most are employed by law firms, corporate legal departments, and various levels of government. In these organizations, they may work in all areas of the law, including litigation, personal injury, corporate law, criminal law, employee benefits, intellectual property, labor law, and real estate. Within specialties, functions often are broken down further so paralegals may deal with a specific area. For example, paralegals specializing in labor law may deal exclusively with employee benefits.

The duties of paralegals also differ widely based on the type of organization in which they are employed. Paralegals who work for corporations often assist attorneys with employee contracts, shareholder agreements, stock option plans, and employee benefit plans. They may also help prepare and file annual financial reports, maintain corporate minute books and resolutions, and secure loans for the corporation. Paralegals also occasionally review government regulations to ensure the corporation operates within the law.

The duties of paralegals who work in the public sector usually vary in each agency. In general, they analyze legal material for internal use, maintain reference files, conduct research for attorneys, and collect and analyze evidence for agency hearings. They may then prepare informative or explanatory material on laws, agency regulations, and agency policy for general use by the agency and the public. Paralegals employed in community legal service projects help the poor, the aged, and others in need of legal assistance. They file forms, conduct research, and prepare documents, and when authorized by law, they may represent clients at administrative hearings.

Paralegals in small and medium-sized law firms usually perform a variety of duties that require a general knowledge of the law. For example, they may research judicial decisions on improper police arrests or help prepare a mortgage contract. Paralegals employed by large law firms, government agencies, and corporations, however, are more likely to specialize in one aspect of the law.

A growing number of paralegals use computers in their work. Computer software packages and the Internet are increasingly used to search legal literature stored in computer databases and on CD-ROM. In litigation involving many supporting documents, paralegals may use computer databases to retrieve, organize, and index various materials. Imaging software allows paralegals to scan documents directly into a database, while billing programs help them to track hours billed to clients. Computer software packages may also be used to perform tax computations and explore the consequences of possible tax strategies for clients.

Working Conditions

Paralegals employed by corporations and government usually work a standard 40-hour week. Although most paralegals work year round, some are temporarily employed during busy times of the year and then released when the workload diminishes. Paralegals who work for law firms sometimes work very long hours when they are under pressure to meet deadlines. Some law firms reward such loyalty with bonuses and additional time off.

These workers handle many routine assignments, particularly when they are inexperienced. As they gain experience, paralegals usually assume more varied tasks with additional responsibility. Paralegals do most of their work at desks in offices and law libraries. Occasionally, they travel to gather information and perform other duties.

Employment

Paralegals held about 136,000 jobs in 1998. Private law firms employed the vast majority; most of the remainder worked for corporate legal departments and the various levels of government. Within

the Federal government, the Department of Justice is the largest employer, followed by the Departments of Treasury and Defense and the Federal Deposit Insurance Corporation. Other employers include State and local governments, publicly funded legal service centers, banks, real estate development companies, and insurance companies. A small number of paralegals own their own businesses and work as freelance legal assistants, contracting their services to attorneys or corporate legal departments.

Training, Other Qualifications, and Advancement

There are several ways to become a paralegal. Employers usually require formal paralegal training obtained through associate or bachelor's degree programs or through a certification program. Increasingly, employers prefer graduates of four-year paralegal programs or college graduates who have completed paralegal certificate programs. Some employers prefer to train paralegals on the job, hiring college graduates with no legal experience or promoting experienced legal secretaries. Other entrants have experience in a technical field that is useful to law firms, such as a background in tax preparation for tax and estate practice or nursing or health administration for personal injury practice.

More than 800 formal paralegal training programs are offered by four-year colleges and universities, law schools, community and junior colleges, business schools, and proprietary schools. There are currently 232 programs approved by the American Bar Association (ABA). Although this approval is neither required nor sought by many programs, graduation from an ABA-approved program can enhance one's employment opportunities. The requirements for admission to these programs vary. Some require certain college courses or a bachelor's degree; others accept high school graduates or those with legal experience; and a few schools require standardized tests and personal interviews.

Paralegal programs include two-year associate's degree programs, four-year bachelor's degree programs, and certificate programs that take only a few months to complete. Many certificate programs require only a high school diploma or GED for admission. Programs typically include courses on law and legal research techniques, in addition to courses covering specialized areas of law, such as real estate, estate planning and probate, litigation, family law, contracts, and criminal law. Many employers prefer applicants with specialized training.

The quality of paralegal training programs varies; the better programs usually include job placement. Programs increasingly include courses introducing students to the legal applications of computers. Many paralegal training programs include an internship in which students gain practical experience by working for several months in a law office, corporate legal department, or government agency. Experience gained in internships is an asset when seeking a job after graduation. Prospective students should examine the experiences of recent graduates before enrolling in those programs.

Although most employers do not require certification, earning a voluntary certificate from a professional society may offer advantages in the labor market. The National Association of Legal Assistants, for example, has established standards for certification requiring various combinations of education and experience. Para-

legals who meet these standards are eligible to take a two-day examination, which is given three times each year at several regional testing centers. Those who pass this examination may use the designation Certified Legal Assistant (CLA). In addition, the Paralegal Advanced Competency Exam, established in 1996 and administered through the National Federation of Paralegal Associations, offers professional recognition to paralegals with a bachelor's degree and at least two years of experience. Those who pass this examination may use the designation Registered Paralegal (RP).

Paralegals must be able to document and present their findings and opinions to their supervising attorney. They need to understand legal terminology and have good research and investigative skills. Familiarity with the operation and applications of computers in legal research and litigation support is also increasingly important. Paralegals should stay informed of new developments in the laws that affect their area of practice. Participation in continuing legal education seminars allows paralegals to maintain and expand their legal knowledge.

Because paralegals frequently deal with the public, they should be courteous and uphold the ethical standards of the legal profession. The National Association of Legal Assistants, the National Federation of Paralegal Associations, and a few States have established ethical guidelines for paralegals to follow.

Paralegals are usually given more responsibilities and less supervision as they gain work experience. Experienced paralegals who work in large law firms, corporate legal departments, and government agencies may supervise and delegate assignments to other paralegals and clerical staff. Advancement opportunities also include promotion to managerial and other law-related positions within the firm or corporate legal department. However, some paralegals find it easier to move to another law firm when seeking increased responsibility or advancement.

Job Outlook

Paralegals are projected to rank among the fastest growing occupations in the economy through 2008. However, stiff competition for jobs should continue as the number of graduates of paralegal training programs and others seeking to enter the profession outpaces job growth. Employment growth stems from law firms and other employers with legal staffs increasingly hiring paralegals in order to lower the cost and increase the availability and efficiency of legal services. The majority of job openings for paralegals in the future will be new jobs created by rapid employment growth; other job openings will arise as people leave the occupation.

Private law firms will continue to be the largest employers of paralegals, but a growing array of other organizations, such as corporate legal departments, insurance companies, real estate and title insurance firms, and banks will also continue to hire paralegals. These organizations are expected to grow as an increasing population requires additional legal services, especially in areas such as intellectual property, health care, international, elder, sexual harassment, and environmental law. The growth of prepaid legal plans should also contribute to the demand for legal services. Paralegal employment in these organizations is expected to increase as paralegals are assigned a growing range of tasks and are increasingly employed in small and medium-sized establishments.

Job opportunities for paralegals will expand in the public sector as well. Community legal service programs, which provide assistance to poor, aged, minorities, and middle-income families, will employ additional paralegals to minimize expenses and serve the most people. Federal, State, and local government agencies, consumer organizations, and the courts should also continue to hire paralegals in increasing numbers.

To a limited extent, paralegal jobs are affected by the business cycle. During recessions, demand declines for some discretionary legal services, such as planning estates, drafting wills, and handling real estate transactions. Corporations are less inclined to initiate litigation when falling sales and profits lead to fiscal belt tightening. As a result, full-time paralegals employed in offices adversely affected by a recession may be laid off or have their work hours reduced. On the other hand, during recessions, corporations and individuals are more likely to face other problems that require legal assistance, such as bankruptcies, foreclosures, and divorces. Paralegals, who provide many of the same legal services as lawyers at a lower cost, tend to fare relatively better in difficult economic conditions.

Earnings

Earnings of paralegals vary greatly. Salaries depend on education, training, experience, type and size of employer, and the geographic location of the job. In general, paralegals who work for large law firms or in large metropolitan areas earn more than those who work for smaller firms or in less populated regions. In 1998, full-time, wage and salary paralegals had median annual earnings of $32,760. The middle 50 percent earned between $26,240 and 40,960. The top 10 percent earned more than $50,290, while the bottom 10 percent earned less than $21,770. Median annual earnings in the industries employing the largest numbers of paralegals in 1997 are shown below:

Federal government	$43,900
Local government	32,200
Legal services	30,300

According to the National Association of Legal Assistants, paralegals had an average salary of $34,000 in 1997. In addition to a salary, many paralegals received a bonus, which averaged about $2,100. According to the National Federation of Paralegal Associations, starting salaries of paralegals with one year or less experience averaged $30,700 in 1997.

Related Occupations

Several other occupations call for a specialized understanding of the law and the legal system but do not require the extensive training of a lawyer. These include abstractors, claim examiners, compliance and enforcement inspectors, occupational safety and health workers, patent agents, and title examiners.

Sources of Additional Information

General information on a career as a paralegal can be obtained from:

- Standing Committee on Legal Assistants, American Bar Association, 750 North Lake Shore Dr., Chicago, IL 60611. Internet: http://www.abanet.org/legalassts

For information on the Certified Legal Assistant exam, schools that offer training programs in a specific State, and standards and guidelines for paralegals, contact:

- National Association of Legal Assistants, Inc., 1516 South Boston St., Suite 200, Tulsa, OK 74119. Internet: http://www.nala.org

Information on a career as a paralegal, schools that offer training programs, job postings for paralegals, the Paralegal Advanced Competency Exam, and local paralegal associations can be obtained from:

- National Federation of Paralegal Associations, P.O. Box 33108, Kansas City, MO 64114. Internet: http://www.paralegals.org

Information on paralegal training programs, including the pamphlet "How to Choose a Paralegal Education Program," may be obtained from:

- American Association for Paralegal Education, P.O. Box 40244, Overland Park, KS 66204. Internet: http://www.aafpe.org

Information on acquiring a job as a paralegal specialist with the Federal government may be obtained from the Office of Personnel Management through a telephone-based system. Consult your telephone directory under U.S. Government for a local number or call (912) 757-3000; TDD (912) 744-2299. This call is not toll-free, and charges may result. Information also is available from their Internet site: http://www.usajobs.opm.gov.

Payroll and Timekeeping Clerks

(O*NET 55341)

Significant Points

- Most jobs require only a high school diploma.
- Most payroll clerks use this position as a steppingstone to higher-level accounting jobs.

Nature of the Work

Payroll and timekeeping clerks perform a vital function—ensuring that employees are paid on time and that their paychecks are accurate. If inaccuracies arise, such as monetary errors or incorrect amounts of vacation time, these workers research and correct the records. In addition, they may also perform various other clerical tasks.

The fundamental task of *timekeeping clerks* is distributing and collecting timecards each pay period. They review employee work charts, timesheets, and timecards to ensure that information is properly recorded and that records have the signatures of authorizing officials. In companies that bill for the time spent by staff

(such as law or accounting firms), timekeeping clerks make sure the hours recorded are charged to the correct job so clients can be properly billed. These clerks also review computer reports listing timecards that cannot be processed because of errors, and they contact the employee or the employee's supervisor to resolve the problem. In addition, timekeeping clerks are responsible for informing managers and other employees of procedural changes in payroll policies.

Payroll clerks, also called payroll technicians, screen timecards for calculating, coding, or other errors. They compute pay by subtracting allotments (including Federal and State taxes, retirement, insurance, and savings) from gross earnings. Increasingly, computers perform these calculations and alert payroll clerks to problems or errors in the data. In small organizations, or for new employees whose records are not yet entered into a computer system, clerks may perform the necessary calculations manually. In some small offices, clerks or other employees in the accounting department process payroll.

Payroll clerks also maintain paper backup files for research and reference. They record changes in employee addresses; close out files when workers retire, resign, or transfer; and advise employees on income tax withholding and other mandatory deductions. They also issue and record adjustments to pay because of previous errors or retroactive increases. Payroll clerks need to follow changes in tax and deduction laws so they are aware of the most recent revisions. Finally, they prepare and mail earnings and tax withholding statements for employees' use in preparing income tax returns.

In small offices, payroll and timekeeping duties are likely to be included in the duties of a general office clerk, secretary, or accounting clerk. However, large organizations employ specialized payroll and timekeeping clerks to perform these functions.

Working Conditions

Clerks typically are employed in an office environment. Most work alongside other clerical workers, but some clerks work in centralized units away from the front office. Because most clerks use computers on a daily basis, these workers may experience eye and muscle strain, backaches, headaches, and repetitive motion injuries. Also, clerks who review detailed data may have to sit for extended periods of time. Most clerks work regular business hours.

Employment

Payroll and timekeeping clerks held about 172,000 jobs in 1998. About 35 percent of all payroll and timekeeping clerks worked in business, health, education, and social services; another 25 percent worked in manufacturing; and more than 10 percent were in wholesale and retail trade or in government. About 11 percent of all payroll and timekeeping clerks worked part time in 1998.

Training, Other Qualifications, and Advancement

Employers typically require applicants to have at least a high school diploma or its equivalent, although many employers prefer to hire clerks with a higher level of education. Most employers prefer work-

ers who are computer-literate. Knowledge of word processing and spreadsheet software is especially valuable, as are experience working in an office and good interpersonal skills.

Clerks often learn the skills they need in high schools, business schools, and community colleges. Business education programs offered by these institutions typically include courses in typing, word processing, shorthand, business communications, records management, and office systems and procedures. Some entrants are college graduates with degrees in business, finance, or liberal arts. Although a degree is rarely required, many graduates accept entry-level clerical positions to get into a particular company or to enter the finance or accounting field with the hope of being promoted to professional or managerial positions. Workers with college degrees are likely to start at higher salaries and advance more easily than those without degrees.

Once hired, clerks usually receive on-the-job training. Under the guidance of a supervisor or other senior worker, new employees learn company procedures. Some formal classroom training may also be necessary, such as training in specific computer software.

Clerks must be careful, orderly, and detail-oriented in order to avoid making errors and to recognize errors made by others. These workers should also be discreet and trustworthy because they frequently come in contact with confidential material. Payroll clerks should have a strong aptitude for numbers.

Clerks usually advance by taking on more duties in the same occupation for higher pay or transferring to a closely related occupation. Most companies fill office and administrative support supervisory and managerial positions by promoting individuals from within their organizations, so clerks who acquire additional skills, experience, and training improve their advancement opportunities.

Job Outlook

Employment of payroll and timekeeping clerks is expected to decline through 2008 due to the continuing automation of payroll and timekeeping functions and the consolidation of clerical jobs. Nevertheless, a number of job openings should arise in coming years, as payroll and timekeeping clerks leave the labor force or transfer to other occupations. Many payroll clerks use this position as a stepping stone to higher-level accounting jobs.

As in many other clerical occupations, new technology will continue to allow many of the tasks formerly handled by payroll and timekeeping clerks to be partially or completely automated. For example, automated timeclocks, which calculate employee hours, allow large organizations to centralize their timekeeping duties in one location. At individual sites, employee hours are increasingly tracked by computer and verified by managers. This information is then compiled and sent to a central office to be processed by payroll clerks, eliminating the need to have payroll clerks at every site. In addition, the growing use of direct deposit eliminates the need to draft paychecks because these funds are automatically transferred each pay period. Furthermore, timekeeping duties are increasingly being distributed to secretaries, general office clerks, or accounting clerks or are being contracted out to organizations that specialize in these services.

Earnings

Salaries of clerks vary. The region of the country, size of city, and type and size of establishment all influence salary levels. Median annual earnings of full-time payroll and timekeeping clerks in 1998 were $24,560.

Related Occupations

Today, most clerks enter data into a computer system and perform basic analysis of the data. Other clerical workers who enter and manipulate data include bank tellers, statistical clerks, receiving clerks, medical record clerks, hotel and motel clerks, credit clerks, and reservation and transportation ticket agents.

Sources of Additional Information

State employment service offices can provide information about job openings for records processing occupations.

Pharmacists

(O*NET 32517)

Significant Points

- Pharmacists are becoming more involved in drug therapy decision-making and patient counseling.

- Earnings are very high, but some pharmacists work long hours, nights, weekends, and holidays.

Nature of the Work

Pharmacists dispense drugs prescribed by physicians and other health practitioners and provide information to patients about medications and their use. They advise physicians and other health practitioners on the selection, dosages, interactions, and side effects of medications. Pharmacists must understand the use, composition, and clinical effects of drugs. Compounding—the actual mixing of ingredients to form powders, tablets, capsules, ointments, and solutions—is only a small part of a pharmacist's practice, because most medicines are produced by pharmaceutical companies in a standard dosage and drug delivery form.

Pharmacists in community or retail pharmacies counsel patients, as well as answer questions about prescription drugs, such as possible adverse reactions or interactions. They provide information about over-the-counter drugs and make recommendations after asking a series of health questions, such as whether the customer is taking any other medications. They also give advice about durable medical equipment and home health care supplies. Those who own or manage community pharmacies may sell nonhealth-related merchandise, hire and supervise personnel, and oversee the general operation of the pharmacy. Some community pharmacists pro-

vide specialized services to help patients manage conditions such as diabetes, asthma, smoking cessation, or high blood pressure.

Pharmacists in hospitals and clinics dispense medications and advise the medical staff on the selection and effects of drugs. They may make sterile solutions and buy medical supplies. They also assess, plan, and monitor drug regimens. They counsel patients on the use of drugs while in the hospital and on their use at home when they are discharged. Pharmacists may also evaluate drug use patterns and outcomes for patients in hospitals or managed care organizations.

Pharmacists who work in home health care monitor drug therapy and prepare infusions—solutions that are injected into patients—and other medications for use in the home.

Most pharmacists keep confidential computerized records of patients' drug therapies to ensure that harmful drug interactions do not occur. They frequently teach pharmacy students serving as interns in preparation for graduation and licensure.

Some pharmacists specialize in specific drug therapy areas, such as psychiatric disorders, intravenous nutrition support, oncology, nuclear pharmacy, and pharmacotherapy.

Working Conditions

Pharmacists usually work in clean, well-lighted, and well-ventilated areas. Many pharmacists spend most of their workday on their feet. When working with sterile or potentially dangerous pharmaceutical products, pharmacists wear gloves and masks and work with other special protective equipment. Many community and hospital pharmacies are open for extended hours or around the clock, so pharmacists may work evenings, nights, weekends, and holidays. Consultant pharmacists may travel to nursing homes or other facilities to monitor people's drug therapy.

About 1 out of 7 pharmacists worked part time in 1998. Most full-time salaried pharmacists worked about 40 hours a week. Some, including most self-employed pharmacists, worked more than 50 hours a week.

Employment

Pharmacists held about 185,000 jobs in 1998. About 3 out of 5 worked in community pharmacies that were either independently owned or part of a drug store chain, grocery store, department store, or mass merchandiser. Most community pharmacists were salaried employees, but some were self–employed owners. About one-quarter of salaried pharmacists worked in hospitals, and others worked in clinics, mail-order pharmacies, pharmaceutical wholesalers, home health care agencies, or the Federal government.

Some pharmacists hold more than one job. They may work a standard week in their primary work setting and work part time elsewhere.

Training, Other Qualifications, and Advancement

A license to practice pharmacy is required in all States, the District of Columbia, and U.S. territories. To obtain a license, one must

serve an internship under a licensed pharmacist, graduate from an accredited college of pharmacy, and pass a State examination. Most States grant a license without extensive reexamination to qualified pharmacists already licensed by another State (check with State boards of pharmacy for details). Many pharmacists are licensed to practice in more than one State. States may require continuing education for license renewal.

In 1998, 81 colleges of pharmacy were accredited to confer degrees by the American Council on Pharmaceutical Education. Nearly all pharmacy programs grant the degree of Doctor of Pharmacy (Pharm.D.) which requires at least six years of post-secondary study. A small number of pharmacy schools continue to award the five-year Bachelor of Science (B.S.) in pharmacy degree. However, all accredited pharmacy schools are expected to graduate their last B.S. class by the year 2005. Either a Pharm.D. or B.S. degree currently fulfills the requirements to take the licensure examination of a state board of pharmacy.

Requirements for admission to colleges of pharmacy vary. A few colleges admit students directly from high school. However, most colleges of pharmacy, require one or two years of college-level prepharmacy education. Entry requirements usually include mathematics and basic sciences, such as chemistry, biology, and physics, as well as courses in the humanities and social sciences. Some colleges require the applicant to take the Pharmacy College Admissions Test.

All colleges of pharmacy offer courses in pharmacy practice, designed to teach students to dispense prescriptions, to communicate with patients and other health professionals, and to strengthen their understanding of professional ethics and practice management responsibilities. Pharmacists' training increasingly emphasizes direct patient care, as well as consultative services to other health professionals.

In the 1997-1998 academic year, 60 colleges of pharmacy awarded the Master of Science degree or the Ph.D. degree. Although a number of pharmacy graduates interested in further training pursue an advanced degree in pharmacy, there are other options. Some complete one- or two-year residency programs or fellowships. Pharmacy residencies are postgraduate training programs in pharmacy practice. Pharmacy fellowships are highly individualized programs designed to prepare participants to work in research laboratories.

Areas of graduate study include pharmaceutics and pharmaceutical chemistry (physical and chemical properties of drugs and dosage forms), pharmacology (effects of drugs on the body), and pharmacy administration, including pharmacoeconomics and social-behavioral aspects of patient care.

Prospective pharmacists should have scientific aptitude, good communication skills, and a desire to help others. They must also be conscientious and pay close attention to detail, because the decisions they make affect human lives.

In community pharmacies, pharmacists usually begin at the staff level. After they gain experience and secure the necessary capital, some become owners or part owners of pharmacies. Pharmacists in chain drug stores may be promoted to pharmacy supervisor or manager at the store level, then to the district or regional level, and later to an executive position within the chain's headquarters.

Hospital pharmacists may advance to supervisory or administrative positions. Pharmacists in the pharmaceutical industry may advance in marketing, sales, research, quality control, production, packaging, and other areas.

Job Outlook

Employment of pharmacists is expected to grow slower than the average for all occupations through the year 2008, despite the increased pharmaceutical needs of a larger and older population and greater use of medication.

Retail pharmacies are taking steps to increase their prescription volume to make up for declining dispensing fees. Automation of drug dispensing and greater use of pharmacy technicians will help them to dispense more prescriptions. The number of community pharmacists needed in the future will depend on the expansion rate of chain drug stores and the willingness of insurers to reimburse pharmacists for providing clinical services to patients taking prescription medications. With its emphasis on cost control, managed care encourages growth of lower-cost prescription drug distributors such as mail-order firms for certain medications. Slower employment growth is expected in traditional chain and independent pharmacies.

Employment in hospitals is also expected to grow slowly, as hospitals reduce inpatient stays, downsize, and consolidate departments. Pharmacy services are shifting to long-term, ambulatory, and home care settings, where opportunities for pharmacists will be best. New opportunities for pharmacists are emerging in managed care organizations, where pharmacists analyze trends and patterns in medication use for their populations of patients. Fast growth is also expected for pharmacists trained in research, disease management, and pharmacoeconomics—determining the costs and benefits of different drug therapies.

Cost-conscious insurers and health systems may continue to emphasize the role of pharmacists in primary and preventive health services. They realize that the expense of using medication to treat diseases and conditions is often considerably less than the potential costs for patients whose conditions go untreated. Pharmacists can also reduce the expenses resulting from unexpected complications due to allergic reactions or medication interactions.

The increased number of middle aged and elderly people will spur demand for pharmacists in all practice settings. The number of prescriptions influences the demand for pharmacists, and the middle aged and elderly populations use more prescription drugs, on average, than younger people.

Other factors likely to increase the demand for pharmacists through the year 2008 include the likelihood of scientific advances that will make more drug products available, new developments in administering medication, and increasingly sophisticated consumers seeking more information about drugs.

Earnings

Median annual earnings of pharmacists in 1998 were $66,220. The middle 50 percent earned between $52,310 and $80,250 a year. The lowest 10 percent earned less than $42,550, and the highest 10 percent earned more than $88,670 a year. Median annual earnings in the industries employing the largest numbers of pharmacists in 1997 were as follows:

Grocery stores	$67,000
Drug stores and proprietary stores	63,400
Hospitals	62,600
Federal government	61,700

According to a survey by *Drug Topics* magazine, published by Medical Economics Co., average base salaries of full-time, salaried pharmacists were about $59,700 a year in 1998. Pharmacists working in chain drug stores had an average base salary of about $62,300 a year, while pharmacists working in independent drug stores averaged about $56,300, and hospital pharmacists averaged about $59,500 a year. Overall, salaries for pharmacists were highest on the West coast. Many pharmacists also receive compensation in the form of bonuses, overtime, and profit-sharing.

Related Occupations

Persons in other professions who may work with pharmaceutical compounds are biological technicians, medical scientists, pharmaceutical chemists, and pharmacologists.

Sources of Additional Information

For information on pharmacy as a career, preprofessional and professional requirements, programs offered by all the colleges of pharmacy, and student financial aid, contact:

- American Association of Colleges of Pharmacy, 1426 Prince St., Alexandria, VA 22314. Internet: http://www.aacp.org

General information on careers in pharmacy is available from:

- American Society of Health-System Pharmacists, 7272 Wisconsin Ave., Bethesda, MD 20814. Internet: http://www.ashp.org
- American Pharmaceutical Association, 2215 Constitution Ave. NW., Washington, DC 20037-2985. Internet: http://www.aphanet.org
- National Association of Chain Drug Stores, 413 N. Lee St., P.O. Box 1417-D49, Alexandria, VA 22313-1480. Internet: www.nacds.org

State licensure requirements are available from each State's Board of Pharmacy.

Information on specific college entrance requirements, curriculums, and financial aid is available from any college of pharmacy.

Physicians

(O*NET 32102A, 32102B, 32102E, 32102F, 32102J, and 32102U)

Significant Points

- Physicians are much more likely to work as salaried employees of group medical practices, clinics, or health care networks than in the past.

- Formal education and training requirements are among the longest of any occupation, but earnings are among the highest.

Nature of the Work

Physicians serve a fundamental role in our society and have an effect upon all our lives. They diagnose illnesses and prescribe and administer treatment for people suffering from injury or disease. Physicians examine patients, obtain medical histories, and order, perform, and interpret diagnostic tests. They counsel patients on diet, hygiene, and preventive health care.

There are two types of physicians: The M.D.—Doctor of Medicine—and the D.O.—Doctor of Osteopathic Medicine. M.D.s are also known as allopathic physicians. While both M.D.s and D.O.s may use all accepted methods of treatment (including drugs and surgery), D.O.s place special emphasis on the body's musculoskeletal system, preventive medicine, and holistic patient care.

About a third of M.D.s—and more than half of D.O.s—are primary care physicians. They practice general and family medicine, general internal medicine, or general pediatrics and are usually the first health professionals patients consult. Primary care physicians tend to see the same patients on a regular basis for preventive care and to treat a variety of ailments. General and family practitioners emphasize comprehensive health care for patients of all ages and for the family as a group. Those in general internal medicine provide care mainly for adults who may have problems associated with the body's organs. General pediatricians focus on the whole range of children's health issues. When appropriate, primary care physicians refer patients to specialists, who are experts in medical fields such as obstetrics and gynecology, cardiology, psychiatry, or surgery (see Table 1).

TABLE 1

Percent distribution of M.D.s by specialty, 1997

	Percent
Total	100.0
Primary care	
Internal medicine	17.0
General and family practice	10.7
Pediatrics	7.3
Medical specialties	
Allergy	.5
Cardiovascular diseases	2.5
Dermatology	1.2
Gastroenterology	1.3
Obstetrics and gynecology	5.2
Pediatric cardiology	.2
Pulmonary diseases	.9

Surgical specialties

Colon and rectal surgery	.1
General surgery	5.4
Neurological surgery	.6
Ophthalmology	2.3
Orthopedic surgery	3.0
Otolaryngology	1.2
Plastic surgery	.8
Thoracic surgery	.3
Urological surgery	1.3

Other specialties

Aerospace medicine	.1
Anesthesiology	4.4
Child psychiatry	.7
Diagnostic radiology	2.6
Emergency medicine	2.7
Forensic pathology	.1
General preventive medicine	.2
Neurology	1.6
Nuclear medicine	.2
Occupational medicine	.4
Pathology	2.4
Physical medicine and rehabilitation	.8
Psychiatry	5.2
Public health	.2
Radiology	1.1
Radiation oncology	.5
Other specialty	.8
Unspecified/unknown/inactive	14.1

SOURCE: American Medical Association

D.O.s are more likely to be primary care providers than M.D.s, although they can be found in all specialties. Over half of D.O.s practice general or family medicine, general internal medicine, or general pediatrics. Common specialties for D.O.s include emergency medicine, anesthesiology, obstetrics and gynecology, psychiatry, and surgery.

Working Conditions

Many physicians work long, irregular hours. More than one-third of all full-time physicians worked 60 hours or more a week in 1998. They must travel frequently between office and hospital to care for their patients. Increasingly, physicians practice in groups or health care organizations that provide back-up coverage and allow for more time off. These physicians often work as part of a team coordinating care for a population of patients; they are less independent than solo practitioners of the past. Physicians who are on call deal with many patients' concerns over the phone and may make emergency visits to hospitals or nursing homes.

Employment

Physicians (M.D.s and D.O.s) held about 577,000 jobs in 1998. About 7 out of 10 were in office-based practice, including clinics and Health Maintenance Organizations (HMOs); about 2 out of 10 were employed by hospitals. Others practiced in the Federal government, most in Department of Veterans Affairs hospitals and clinics or in the Public Health Service of the Department of Health and Human Services.

A growing number of physicians are partners or salaried employees of group practices. Organized as clinics or as groups of physicians, medical groups can afford expensive medical equipment and realize other business advantages. Also, hospitals are integrating physician practices into health care networks that provide a continuum of care both inside and outside the hospital setting.

The New England and Middle Atlantic States have the highest ratio of physicians to population; the South Central States, the lowest. D.O.s are more likely than M.D.s to practice in small cities and towns and in rural areas. M.D.s tend to locate in urban areas, close to hospital and educational centers.

Training, Other Qualifications, and Advancement

It takes many years of education and training to become a physician: four years of undergraduate school, four years of medical school, and three to eight years of internship and residency, depending on the specialty selected. A few medical schools offer a combined undergraduate and medical school program that lasts six years instead of the customary eight years.

Premedical students must complete undergraduate work in physics, biology, mathematics, English, and inorganic and organic chemistry. Students also take courses in the humanities and the social sciences. Some students also volunteer at local hospitals or clinics to gain practical experience in the health professions.

The minimum educational requirement for entry to a medical or osteopathic school is three years of college; most applicants, however, have at least a bachelor's degree, and many have advanced degrees. There are 144 medical schools in the United States—125 teach allopathic medicine and award a Doctor of Medicine (M.D.) degree; 19 teach osteopathic medicine and award the Doctor of Osteopathic Medicine (D.O.) degree. Acceptance to medical school is very competitive. Applicants must submit transcripts, scores from the Medical College Admission Test, and letters of recommendation. Schools also consider character, personality, leadership qualities, and participation in extracurricular activities. Most schools require an interview with members of the admissions committee.

Students spend most of the first two years of medical school in laboratories and classrooms taking courses such as anatomy, biochemistry, physiology, pharmacology, psychology, microbiology, pathology, medical ethics, and laws governing medicine. They also learn to take medical histories, examine patients, and diagnose illness. During the last two years, students work with patients under the supervision of experienced physicians in hospitals and clinics to learn acute, chronic, preventive, and rehabilitative care. Through rotations in internal medicine, family practice, obstetrics and gynecology, pediatrics, psychiatry, and surgery, they gain experience in the diagnosis and treatment of illness.

Following medical school, almost all M.D.s enter a residency—graduate medical education in a specialty that takes the form of paid on-the-job training, usually in a hospital. Most D.O.s serve a 12-month rotating internship after graduation before entering a residency, which may last two to six years. Physicians may benefit from residencies in managed care settings by gaining experience with this increasingly common type of medical practice.

All States, the District of Columbia, and U.S. territories license physicians. To be licensed, physicians must graduate from an accredited medical school, pass a licensing examination, and complete one to seven years of graduate medical education. Although physicians licensed in one State can usually get a license to practice in another without further examination, some States limit reciprocity. Graduates of foreign medical schools can usually qualify for licensure after passing an examination and completing a U.S. residency.

M.D.s and D.O.s seeking board certification in a specialty may spend up to seven years—depending on the specialty—in residency training. A final examination immediately after residency, or after one or two years of practice, is also necessary for board certification by the American Board of Medical Specialists (ABMS) or the American Osteopathic Association (AOA). There are 24 specialty boards, ranging from allergy and immunology to urology. For certification in a subspecialty, physicians usually need another one to two years of residency.

A physician's training is costly, and whereas education costs have increased, student financial assistance has not. More than 80 percent of medical students borrow money to cover their expenses.

People who wish to become physicians must have a desire to serve patients, be self-motivated, and be able to survive the pressures and long hours of medical education and practice. Physicians must also have a good bedside manner, emotional stability, and the ability to make decisions in emergencies. Prospective physicians must be willing to study throughout their career to keep up with medical advances. They will also need to be flexible to respond to the changing demands of a rapidly evolving health care system.

Job Outlook

Employment of physicians will grow faster than the average for all occupations through the year 2008 due to continued expansion of the health care industries. The growing and aging population will drive overall growth in the demand for physician services. In addition, new technologies permit more intensive care: Physicians can do more tests, perform more procedures, and treat conditions previously regarded as untreatable.

Although job prospects may be better for primary care physicians such as general and family practitioners, general pediatricians, and general internists, a substantial number of jobs for specialists will also be created in response to patient demand for access to specialty care.

The number of physicians in training has leveled off and is likely to decrease over the next few years, alleviating the effects of any physician oversupply. However, future physicians may be more likely to work fewer hours, retire earlier, have lower earnings, or have to practice in underserved areas. Opportunities should be good in some rural and low income areas, because some physicians find these areas unattractive due to lower earnings potential, isolation from medical colleagues, or other reasons.

Unlike their predecessors, newly trained physicians face radically different choices of where and how to practice. New physicians are much less likely to enter solo practice and more likely to take salaried jobs in group medical practices, clinics, and health care networks.

Earnings

Physicians have among the highest earnings of any occupation. According to the American Medical Association, median income, after expenses, for allopathic physicians was about $164,000 in 1997. The middle 50 percent earned between $120,000 and $250,000 a year. Self-employed physicians—those who own or are part owners of their medical practice—had higher median incomes than salaried physicians. Earnings vary according to number of years in practice; geographic region; hours worked; and skill, personality, and professional reputation. As shown in Table 2, median income of allopathic physicians, after expenses, also varies by specialty.

TABLE 2

Median net income of M.D.s after expenses, 1997

All physicians	$164,000
Radiology	260,000
Anesthesiology	220,000
Surgery	217,000
Obstetrics/gynecology	200,000
Emergency medicine	195,000
Pathology	175,000
General internal medicine	147,000
General/Family practice	132,000
Psychiatry	130,000
Pediatrics	120,000

SOURCE: American Medical Association

Average salaries of medical residents ranged from about $34,100 in 1998-99 for those in their first year of residency to about $42,100 for those in their sixth year, according to the Association of American Medical Colleges.

Related Occupations

Physicians work to prevent, diagnose, and treat diseases, disorders, and injuries. Professionals in other occupations requiring similar skills and critical judgment include acupuncturists, audiologists, chiropractors, dentists, nurse practitioners, optometrists, physician assistants, podiatrists, speech pathologists, and veterinarians.

Sources of Additional Information

For a list of allopathic medical schools and residency programs, as well as general information on premedical education, financial aid, and medicine as a career, contact:

- Association of American Medical Colleges, Section for Student Services, 2450 N St. NW., Washington, DC 20037-1131. Internet: http://www.aamc.org

For a list of osteopathic medical schools, as well as general information on premedical education, financial aid, and medicine as a career, contact:

- American Association of Colleges of Osteopathic Medicine, 5550 Friendship Blvd., Suite 310, Chevy Chase, MD 20815-7321. Internet: http://www.aacom.org

For general information on physicians, contact:

- American Medical Association, Department of Communications and Public Relations, 515 N. State St., Chicago, IL 60610. Internet: http://www.ama-assn.org

- American Osteopathic Association, Department of Public Relations, 142 East Ontario St., Chicago, IL 60611. Internet: http://www.aoa-net.org

Information on Federal scholarships and loans is available from the directors of student financial aid at schools of allopathic and osteopathic medicine.

Information on licensing is available from State boards of examiners.

Podiatrists

(O*NET 32111)

Significant Points

- A limited number of job openings for podiatrists is expected because the occupation is small and most podiatrists remain in the occupation until they retire.

- Most podiatrists are solo practitioners, although more are entering partnerships and multi-specialty group practices.

- Podiatrists enjoy very high earnings.

Nature of the Work

Americans spend a great deal of time on their feet. As the Nation becomes more active across all age groups, the need for foot care will become increasingly important to maintaining a healthy lifestyle.

The human foot is a complex structure. It contains 26 bones—plus muscles, nerves, ligaments, and blood vessels—and is designed for balance and mobility. The 52 bones in your feet make up about one fourth of all the bones in your body. Podiatrists, also known as doctors of podiatric medicine (DPMs), diagnose and treat disorders, diseases, and injuries of the foot and lower leg to keep this part of the body working properly.

Podiatrists treat corns, calluses, ingrown toenails, bunions, heel spurs, and arch problems; ankle and foot injuries, deformities and infections; and foot complaints associated with diseases such as diabetes. To treat these problems, podiatrists prescribe drugs, order physical therapy, set fractures, and perform surgery. They also fit corrective inserts called orthotics, design plaster casts and strappings to correct deformities, and design custom-made shoes. Podiatrists may use a force plate to help design the orthotics. Patients walk across a plate connected to a computer that "reads" the patients' feet, picking up pressure points and weight distribution. From the computer readout, podiatrists order the correct design or recommend treatment.

To diagnose a foot problem, podiatrists also order x-rays and laboratory tests. The foot may be the first area to show signs of serious conditions such as arthritis, diabetes, and heart disease. For example, diabetics are prone to foot ulcers and infections due to poor circulation. Podiatrists consult with and refer patients to other health practitioners when they detect symptoms of these disorders.

Most podiatrists have a solo practice, although more are forming group practices with other podiatrists or health practitioners. Some specialize in surgery, orthopedics, primary care, or public health. Besides these board-certified specialties, podiatrists may practice a subspecialty such as sports medicine, pediatrics, dermatology, radiology, geriatrics, or diabetic foot care.

Podiatrists who are in private practice are responsible for running a small business. They may hire employees, order supplies, and keep records, among other tasks. In addition, some educate the community on the benefits of foot care through speaking engagements and advertising.

Working Conditions

Podiatrists usually work in their own offices. They may also spend time visiting patients in nursing homes or performing surgery at a hospital, but they usually have fewer after-hours emergencies than other doctors. Those with private practices set their own hours but may work evenings and weekends to meet the needs of their patients.

Employment

Podiatrists held about 14,000 jobs in 1998. Most podiatrists are solo practitioners, although more are entering partnerships and multi-specialty group practices. Others are employed in hospitals, nursing homes, the U.S. Public Health Service, and the Department of Veterans Affairs.

Training, Other Qualifications, and Advancement

All States and the District of Columbia require a license for the practice of podiatric medicine. Each defines its own licensing requirements. Generally, the applicant must be a graduate of an accredited college of podiatric medicine and pass written and oral examinations. Some States permit applicants to substitute the examination of the National Board of Podiatric Examiners, given in the second and fourth years of podiatric medical college, for part or all of the written State examination. Most States also require completion of a postdoctoral residency program. Many States grant reciprocity to podiatrists who are licensed in another State. Most States require continuing education for licensure renewal.

Prerequisites for admission to a college of podiatric medicine include the completion of at least 90 semester hours of undergraduate study, an acceptable grade point average, and suitable scores on the Medical College Admission Test (MCAT). All require eight semester hours each of biology, inorganic chemistry, organic chemistry, and physics, and six hours of English. The science courses should be those designed for premedical students. Potential podiatric medical students may also be evaluated on the basis of extracurricular and community activities, personal interviews, and letters of recommendation. More than 90 percent of podiatric students have at least a bachelor's degree.

Colleges of podiatric medicine offer a four-year program whose core curriculum is similar to that in other schools of medicine. During the first two years, students receive classroom instruction in basic sciences, including anatomy, chemistry, pathology, and pharmacology. Third- and fourth-year students have clinical rotations in private practices, hospitals, and clinics. During these rotations, they learn how to take general and podiatric histories, perform routine physical examinations, interpret tests and findings, make diagnoses, and perform therapeutic procedures. Graduates receive the doctor of podiatric medicine (DPM) degree.

Most graduates complete a hospital residency program after receiving a DPM. Residency programs last from one to three years. Residents receive advanced training in podiatric medicine and surgery and serve clinical rotations in anesthesiology, internal medicine, pathology, radiology, emergency medicine, and orthopedic and general surgery. Residencies lasting more than one year provide more extensive training in specialty areas.

There are a number of certifying boards for the podiatric specialties of orthopedics, primary medicine, or surgery. Certification means that the DPM meets higher standards than those required for licensure. Each board requires advanced training, completion of written and oral examinations, and experience as a practicing podiatrist. Most managed care organizations prefer board-certified podiatrists.

People planning a career in podiatry should have scientific aptitude, manual dexterity, interpersonal skills, and good business sense.

Podiatrists may advance to become professors at colleges of podiatric medicine, department chiefs of hospitals, or general health administrators.

Job Outlook

Employment of podiatrists is expected to grow about as fast as the average for all occupations through 2008. More people will turn to podiatrists for foot care as the elderly population grows. The elderly have more years of wear and tear on their feet and legs than most younger people, so they are more prone to foot ailments. Injuries sustained by an increasing number of men and women of all ages leading active lifestyles will also spur demand for podiatric care.

Medicare and most private health insurance programs cover acute medical and surgical foot services, as well as diagnostic x-rays and leg braces. Details of such coverage vary among plans. However, routine foot care—including the removal of corns and calluses—is ordinarily not covered unless the patient has a systemic condition that has resulted in severe circulatory problems or areas of desensitization in the legs or feet. Like dental services, podiatric care is more dependent on disposable income than other medical services.

Employment of podiatrists would grow even faster were it not for continued emphasis on controlling the costs of specialty health care. Insurers will balance the cost of sending patients to podiatrists against the cost and availability of substitute practitioners, such as physicians and physical therapists. Opportunities will be better for board-certified podiatrists, because many managed care organizations require board certification. Opportunities for newly trained podiatrists will be better in group medical practices, clinics, and health networks than in traditional solo practices. Establishing a practice will be most difficult in the areas surrounding colleges of podiatric medicine because podiatrists are concentrated in these locations.

Over the next 10 years, members of the "baby boom" generation will begin to retire, creating vacancies. Relatively few job openings from this source are expected, however, because the occupation is small.

Earnings

Median annual earnings of salaried podiatrists were $79,530 in 1998. However, only about one-half of podiatrists were salaried in 1998. Salaried podiatrists tend to earn less than self-employed podiatrists.

According to a survey by the American Podiatric Medical Association, average net income for podiatrists in private practice was about $116,000 in 1997. Those practicing for less than two years earned an average of about $61,000; those practicing 16 to 30 years earned an average of about $146,000.

Related Occupations

Workers in other occupations who apply scientific knowledge to prevent, diagnose, and treat disorders and injuries are chiropractors, dentists, optometrists, physicians, and veterinarians.

Sources of Additional Information

For information on podiatric medicine as a career, contact:

- American Podiatric Medical Association, 9312 Old Georgetown Rd., Bethesda, MD 20814-1621. Internet: http://www.apma.org

Information on colleges of podiatric medicine, entrance requirements, curriculums, and student financial aid is available from:

- American Association of Colleges of Podiatric Medicine, 1350 Piccard Dr., Suite 322, Rockville, MD 20850-4307. Internet: http://www.aacpm.org

Police and Detectives

(O*NET 21911C, 61005, 63011A, 63011B, 63014A, 63014B, 63021, 63023, 63026, 63028A, 63028B, 63032, 63038, and 63041)

Significant Points

- Police work can be dangerous and stressful.

- The number of qualified candidates exceeds the number of job openings in Federal and State law enforcement agencies but is inadequate to meet growth and replacement needs in many local and special police departments.

- The largest number of employment opportunities will arise in urban communities with relatively low salaries and high crime rates.

Nature of the Work

People depend on police officers and detectives to protect their lives and property. Law enforcement officers, some of whom are State or Federal special agents or inspectors, perform these duties in a variety of ways, depending on the size and type of their organization. In most jurisdictions, they are expected to exercise authority when necessary, whether on or off duty.

According to the Bureau of Justice Statistics, about 65 percent of State and local law enforcement officers are uniformed personnel, who regularly patrol and respond to calls for service. Police officers who work in small communities and rural areas have general law enforcement duties. They may direct traffic at the scene of a fire, investigate a burglary, or give first aid to an accident victim. In large police departments, officers usually are assigned to a specific type of duty. Many urban police agencies are becoming more involved in community policing—a practice in which an officer builds relationships with the citizens of local neighborhoods and mobilizes the public to help fight crime.

Police agencies are usually organized into geographic districts, with uniformed officers assigned to patrol a specific area, such as part of the business district or outlying residential neighborhoods. Officers may work alone, but in large agencies, they often patrol with a partner. While on patrol, officers attempt to become thoroughly familiar with their patrol area and remain alert for anything unusual. Suspicious circumstances and hazards to public safety are investigated or noted, and officers are dispatched to individual calls for assistance within their district. During their shift, they may identify, pursue, and arrest suspected criminals, resolve problems within the community, and enforce traffic laws.

Some police officers specialize in such diverse fields as chemical and microscopic analysis, training and firearms instruction, or handwriting and fingerprint identification. Others work with special units such as horseback, bicycle, motorcycle or harbor patrol, canine corps, or special weapons and tactics (SWAT) or emergency response teams. About 1 in 10 local and special law enforcement officers perform jail-related duties, and around 4 percent work in

courts. Regardless of job duties or location, police officers and detectives at all levels must write reports and maintain meticulous records that will be needed if they testify in court.

Detectives are plainclothes investigators who gather facts and collect evidence for criminal cases. Some are assigned to interagency task forces to combat specific types of crime. They conduct interviews, examine records, observe the activities of suspects, and participate in raids or arrests. Detectives and State and Federal agents and inspectors usually specialize in one of a wide variety of violations such as homicide or fraud. They are assigned cases on a rotating basis and work on them until an arrest and conviction occurs or until the case is dropped.

Sheriffs and deputy sheriffs enforce the law on the county level. Sheriffs are usually elected to their posts and perform duties similar to those of a local or county police chief. Sheriffs' departments tend to be relatively small, most having fewer than 25 sworn officers. A deputy sheriff in a large agency will have similar specialized law enforcement duties as an officer in an urban police department. Nationwide, about 40 percent of full-time sworn deputies are uniformed officers assigned to patrol and respond to calls, 12 percent are investigators, 30 percent are assigned to jail-related duties, and 11 percent perform court-related duties, with the balance in administration. Police and sheriffs' deputies who provide security in city and county courts are sometimes called bailiffs.

State police officers (sometimes called State troopers or highway patrol officers) arrest criminals statewide and patrol highways to enforce motor vehicle laws and regulations. Uniformed officers are best known for issuing traffic citations to motorists who violate the law. At the scene of accidents, they may direct traffic, give first aid, and call for emergency equipment. They also write reports used to determine the cause of the accident. State police officers are frequently called upon to render assistance to other law enforcement agencies.

State law enforcement agencies operate in every State except Hawaii. Seventy percent of the full-time sworn personnel in the 49 State police agencies are uniformed officers who regularly patrol and respond to calls for service. Fifteen percent are investigators; 2 percent are assigned to court-related duties; and the remaining 13 percent work in administrative or other assignments.

Public college and university police forces, public school district police, and agencies serving transportation systems and facilities are examples of special police agencies. There are more than 1,300 of these agencies with special geographic jurisdictions or enforcement responsibilities in the United States. More than three-fourths of the sworn personnel in special agencies are uniformed officers, and about 15 percent are investigators.

The Federal government maintains a high profile in many areas of law enforcement. The Department of Justice is the largest employer of sworn Federal officers. *Federal Bureau of Investigation (FBI)* agents are the government's principal investigators, responsible for investigating violations of more than 260 statutes and conducting sensitive National security investigations. Agents may conduct surveillance, monitor court-authorized wiretaps, examine business records, investigate white-collar crime, track the interstate movement of stolen property, collect evidence of espionage activities, or participate in sensitive undercover assignments. The FBI investigates organized crime, public corruption, financial crime, fraud against the government, bribery, copyright infringement, civil rights violations, bank robbery, extortion, kidnapping, air piracy, terrorism, foreign counterintelligence, interstate criminal activity, drug trafficking, and other violations of Federal statutes.

Drug Enforcement Administration (DEA) agents enforce laws and regulations relating to illegal drugs. Not only is the DEA the lead agency for domestic enforcement of Federal drug laws, but it also has sole responsibility for coordinating and pursuing U.S. drug investigations abroad. Agents may conduct complex criminal investigations, carry out surveillance of criminals, and infiltrate illicit drug organizations using undercover techniques.

U.S. marshals and deputy marshals protect the Federal courts and ensure the effective operation of the judicial system. They provide protection for the Federal judiciary, transport Federal prisoners, protect Federal witnesses, and manage assets seized from criminal enterprises. In addition, the Marshals Service pursues and arrests 55 percent of all Federal fugitives, more than all other Federal agencies combined.

Immigration and Naturalization Service (INS) agents and inspectors facilitate the entry of legal visitors and immigrants to the United States and detain and deport those arriving illegally. They consist of border patrol agents, immigration inspectors, criminal investigators and immigration agents, and detention and deportation officers. Nearly half of sworn INS officers are border patrol agents. *U.S. Border Patrol agents* protect more than 8,000 miles of international land and water boundaries. Their missions are to detect and prevent the smuggling and unlawful entry of undocumented aliens into the United States, apprehend those persons found in violation of the immigration laws, and interdict contraband, such as narcotics. *Immigration* inspectors interview and examine people seeking entrance to the United States and its territories. They inspect passports to determine whether people are legally eligible to enter the United States. Immigration inspectors also prepare reports, maintain records, and process applications and petitions for immigration or temporary residence in the United States.

Special agents and inspectors employed by the U.S. Department of the Treasury work for the Bureau of Alcohol, Tobacco, and Firearms, the Customs Service, and the Secret Service. *Bureau of Alcohol, Tobacco, and Firearms* (ATF) agents regulate and investigate violations of Federal firearms and explosives laws, as well as Federal alcohol and tobacco tax regulations. *Customs agents* investigate violations of narcotics smuggling, money laundering, child pornography, customs fraud, and enforcement of the Arms Export Control Act. Domestic and foreign investigations involve the development and use of informants, physical and electronic surveillance, and examination of records from importers/exporters, banks, couriers, and manufacturers. They conduct interviews, serve on joint task forces with other agencies, and get and execute search warrants.

Customs inspectors inspect cargo, baggage, and articles worn or carried by people and carriers including vessels, vehicles, trains and aircraft entering or leaving the U.S. to enforce laws governing imports and exports. These inspectors examine, count, weigh, gauge, measure, and sample commercial and noncommercial cargoes entering and leaving the United States. Customs inspectors seize prohibited or smuggled articles, intercept contraband, and apprehend, search, detain, and arrest violators of U.S. laws. *U.S. Secret Service* special agents protect the President, Vice President, and their immediate families, Presidential candidates, ex-Presidents, and foreign dignitaries visiting the United States. Secret Service agents also investigate counterfeiting, forgery of government checks or bonds, and fraudulent use of credit cards.

The U.S. Department of State *Bureau of Diplomatic Security* special agents are engaged in the battle against terrorism, and their numbers are expected to grow rapidly as the threat of terrorism increases. Overseas, they advise ambassadors on all security matters and manage a complex range of security programs designed to protect personnel, facilities, and information. In the United States, they investigate passport and visa fraud, conduct personnel security investigations, issue security clearances, and protect the Secretary of State and a number of foreign dignitaries. They also train foreign civilian police and administer counter-terrorism and counter-narcotics reward programs.

Other Federal agencies employ police and special agents with sworn arrest powers and the authority to carry firearms. These agencies include the U.S. Postal Service, the Bureau of Indian Affairs Office of Law Enforcement under the Department of the Interior, the U.S. Forest Service under the Department of Agriculture, the National Park Service under the Department of the Interior, and Federal Air Marshals under the Department of Transportation. Other police agencies have evolved from the need for security for the agency's property and personnel. The largest such agency is the General Services Administration's Federal Protective Service, which provides security for Federal workers, buildings, and property.

Working Conditions

Police work can be very dangerous and stressful. In addition to the obvious dangers of confrontations with criminals, officers need to be constantly alert and ready to deal appropriately with a number of other threatening situations. Many law enforcement officers witness death and suffering resulting from accidents and criminal behavior. A career in law enforcement may take a toll on officers' private lives.

Uniformed officers, detectives, agents, and inspectors are usually scheduled to work 40-hour weeks, but paid overtime is common. Shift work is necessary because protection must be provided around the clock. Junior officers frequently work weekends, holidays, and nights. Police officers and detectives are required to work at any time their services are needed and may work long hours during investigations. In most jurisdictions, whether on or off duty, officers are expected to be armed and to exercise their arrest authority whenever necessary.

The jobs of some Federal agents such as U.S. Secret Service and DEA special agents require extensive travel, often on very short notice. They may relocate a number of times over the course of their careers. Some special agents in agencies such as the U.S. Border Patrol work outdoors in rugged terrain for long periods and in all kinds of weather.

Employment

Police and detectives held about 764,000 jobs in 1998. About 64 percent of police detectives and investigators were employed by

local governments, primarily in cities with more than 25,000 inhabitants. Some cities have very large police forces, while hundreds of small communities employ fewer than 25 officers each. State police agencies employed about 11 percent of all police, detectives, and investigators; and various Federal agencies employed the other 25 percent. Seventy local, special, and State agencies employed 1,000 or more full-time sworn officers, including 41 local police agencies, 15 State police agencies, 12 sheriffs' departments, and two special police agencies—the New York City public school system and the Port Authority of New York/New Jersey.

Training, Other Qualifications, and Advancement

Civil service regulations govern the appointment of police and detectives in practically all States, large municipalities, and special police agencies, as well as in many smaller ones. Candidates must be U.S. citizens, usually at least 20 years of age, and must meet rigorous physical and personal qualifications. Physical examinations for entrance into law enforcement often include tests of vision, hearing, strength, and agility. Eligibility for appointment usually depends on performance in competitive written examinations and previous education and experience. In larger departments, where the majority of law enforcement jobs are found, applicants usually must have at least a high school education. Federal and State agencies typically require a college degree.

Because personal characteristics such as honesty, judgment, integrity, and a sense of responsibility are especially important in law enforcement, candidates are interviewed by senior officers, and their character traits and backgrounds are investigated. In some agencies, candidates are interviewed by a psychiatrist or a psychologist or given a personality test. Most applicants are subjected to lie detector examinations or drug testing. Some agencies subject sworn personnel to random drug testing as a condition of continuing employment. Candidates for these positions should enjoy working with people and meeting the public.

The FBI has the largest number of special agents. To be considered for appointment as an FBI agent, an applicant must be either a graduate of an accredited law school or a college graduate with a major in accounting, fluency in a foreign language, or three years of full-time work experience. All new agents undergo 16 weeks of training at the FBI academy on the U.S. Marine Corps base in Quantico, Virginia.

Applicants for special agent jobs with the U.S. Department of Treasury's Secret Service and the Bureau of Alcohol, Tobacco, and Firearms must have a bachelor's degree or a minimum of three years' work experience. Prospective special agents undergo 10 weeks of initial criminal investigation training at the Federal Law Enforcement Training Center in Glynco, Georgia and another 17 weeks of specialized training with their particular agencies.

Applicants for special agent jobs with the U.S. Drug Enforcement Administration (DEA) must have a college degree and either one year of experience conducting criminal investigations, one year of graduate school, or have achieved at least a 2.95 grade point average while in college. DEA special agents undergo 14 weeks of specialized training at the FBI Academy in Quantico, Virginia.

Postal inspectors must have a bachelor's degree and one year of work experience. It is desirable that they have one of several professional certifications, such as that of certified public accountant. They also must pass a background suitability investigation, meet certain health requirements, undergo a drug screening test, possess a valid State driver's license, and be a U.S. citizen between 21 and 36 years of age when hired.

Law enforcement agencies are encouraging applicants to take post-secondary school training in law enforcement-related subjects. Many entry-level applicants for police jobs have completed some formal post-secondary education, and a significant number are college graduates. Many junior colleges, colleges, and universities offer programs in law enforcement or administration of justice. Other courses helpful in preparing for a career in law enforcement include accounting, finance, electrical engineering, computer science, and foreign languages. Physical education and sports are helpful in developing the competitiveness, stamina, and agility needed for many law enforcement positions. Knowledge of a foreign language is an asset in many Federal agencies and urban departments.

Before their first assignments, officers usually go through a period of training. In State and large local departments, recruits get training in their agency's police academy, often for 12 to 14 weeks. In small agencies, recruits often attend a regional or State academy. Training includes classroom instruction in constitutional law and civil rights, State laws and local ordinances, and accident investigation. Recruits also receive training and supervised experience in patrol, traffic control, use of firearms, self-defense, first aid, and emergency response. Police departments in some large cities hire high school graduates who are still in their teens as police cadets or trainees. They do clerical work and attend classes for usually one to two years, at which point they reach the minimum age requirement and may be appointed to the regular force.

Police officers usually become eligible for promotion after a probationary period ranging from six months to three years. In a large department, promotion may enable an officer to become a detective or specialize in one type of police work, such as working with juveniles. Promotions to corporal, sergeant, lieutenant, and captain usually are made according to a candidate's position on a promotion list, as determined by scores on a written examination and on-the-job performance.

Continuing training helps police officers, detectives, and special agents improve their job performance. Through police department academies, regional centers for public safety employees established by the States, and Federal agency training centers, instructors provide annual training in self-defense tactics, firearms, use-of-force policies, sensitivity and communications skills, crowd-control techniques, relevant legal developments, and advances in law enforcement equipment. Many agencies pay all or part of the tuition for officers to work toward degrees in criminal justice, police science, administration of justice, or public administration, and pay higher salaries to those who earn such a degree.

Job Outlook

The opportunity for public service through law enforcement work is attractive to many because the job is challenging and involves much personal responsibility. Furthermore, law enforcement officers in many agencies may retire with a pension after 20 or 25 years of service, allowing them to pursue a second career while still in their 40s. Because of relatively attractive salaries and benefits, the number of qualified candidates exceeds the number of job openings in Federal law enforcement agencies and in most State, local, and special police departments—resulting in increased hiring standards and selectivity by employers. Competition is expected to remain keen for the higher paying jobs with State and Federal agencies and police departments in more affluent areas. Applicants with college training in police science, military police experience, or both should have the best opportunities. Opportunities will be best in urban communities whose departments offer relatively low salaries and where the crime rate is relatively high.

Employment of police officers and detectives is expected to increase faster than the average for all occupations through 2008. A more security-conscious society and concern about drug-related crimes should contribute to the increasing demand for police services. At the local and State levels, growth is likely to continue as long as crime remains a serious concern. However, employment growth at the Federal level will be tempered by continuing budgetary constraints faced by law enforcement agencies. Turnover in police and detective positions is among the lowest of all occupations. Even so, the need to replace workers who retire, transfer to other occupations, or stop working for other reasons will be the source of many job openings.

The level of government spending determines the level of employment for police officers, detectives, and special agents. The number of job opportunities, therefore, can vary from year to year and from place to place. Layoffs, on the other hand, are rare because retirements enable most staffing cuts to be handled through attrition. Trained law enforcement officers who lose their jobs because of budget cuts usually have little difficulty finding jobs with other agencies.

Earnings

In 1998, the median salary of police and detective supervisors was $48,700 a year. The middle 50 percent earned between $37,130 and $69,440; the lowest 10 percent were paid less than $28,780, while the highest 10 percent earned more than $84,710 a year.

In 1998, the median salary of detectives and criminal investigators was $46,180 a year. The middle 50 percent earned between $35,540 and $62,520; the lowest 10 percent were paid less than $27,950, and the highest 10 percent earned more than $80,120 a year.

Police patrol officers had a median salary of $37,710 in 1998. The middle 50 percent earned between $28,840 and $47,890; the lowest 10 percent were paid less than $22,270, while the highest 10 percent earned more than $63,530 annually.

Sheriffs and deputy sheriffs had a median annual salary of $28,270 in 1998. The middle 50 percent earned between $23,310 and $36,090; the lowest 10 percent were paid less than $19,070, and the highest 10 percent earned more than $44,420.

Federal law provides special salary rates to Federal employees who serve in law enforcement. Additionally, Federal special agents and inspectors receive law enforcement availability pay (LEAP) or administratively uncontrolled overtime (AUO)—equal to 25 percent

of the agent's grade and step—awarded because of the large amount of overtime that these agents are expected to work. For example, in 1999 FBI agents enter service as GS 10 employees on the government pay scale at a base salary of $34,400, yet they earned about $43,000 a year with availability pay. They can advance to the GS 13 grade level in field non-supervisory assignments at a base salary of $53,800, which is worth almost $67,300 with availability pay. Promotions to supervisory, management, and executive positions are available in grades GS 14 and GS 15, which pay a base salary of about $63,600 or $74,800 a year, respectively, and equaled $79,500 or $93,500 per year with availability pay. Salaries were slightly higher in selected areas where the prevailing local pay level was higher. Because Federal agents may be eligible for a special law enforcement benefits package, applicants should ask their recruiters for more information.

The International City-County Management Association's annual Police and Fire Personnel, Salaries, and Expenditures Survey revealed that 84 percent of the municipalities surveyed provided police services in 1997. The following pertains to sworn full-time positions in 1997.

Title	Minimum annual base salary	Maximum annual base salary
Police officer	$28,200	$38,500
Police Corporal	31,900	39,000
Police Sergeant	38,200	45,100
Police Lieutenant	42,900	51,200
Police Captain	46,500	56,600
Deputy Chief	48,400	59,800
Police Chief	56,300	69,600

Total earnings for local, State, and special police and detectives frequently exceed the stated salary because of payments for overtime, which can be significant. In addition to the common benefits—paid vacation, sick leave, and medical and life insurance—most police and sheriffs' departments provide officers with special allowances for uniforms. Because police officers usually are covered by liberal pension plans, many retire at half-pay after 20 or 25 years of service.

Related Occupations

Police and detectives maintain law and order. Workers in related occupations include correctional officers, guards, and fire marshals.

Sources of Additional Information

Information about entrance requirements may be obtained from Federal, State, and local law enforcement agencies.

Further information about qualifications for employment as an FBI Special Agent is available from the nearest State FBI office. The address and phone number are listed in the local telephone directory. Internet: http://www.fbi.gov

Information about qualifications for employment as a DEA Special Agent is available from the nearest DEA office, or call (800) DEA-4288. Internet: http://www.usdoj.gov/dea

Information about career opportunities, qualifications, and training to become a deputy marshal is available from:

- United States Marshals Service, Employment and Compensation Division, Field Staffing Branch, 600 Army Navy Dr., Arlington, VA 22202. Internet: http://www.usdoj.gov/marshals

Career opportunities, qualifications, and training for U.S. Secret Service Special Agents is available from:

- U.S. Secret Service, Personnel Division, Room 912, 1800 G St. NW., Washington, DC 20223. Internet: http://www.ustreas.gov/usss

Information on career opportunities and Bureau of Alcohol, Tobacco and Firearms operations by writing to:

- U.S. Bureau of Alcohol, Tobacco and Firearms, Personnel Division, 650 Massachusetts Avenue NW., Room 4170, Washington, DC 20226. Internet: http://www.atf.treas.gov

Information about careers in the United States Border Patrol is available from:

- U.S. Border Patrol, Chester A. Arthur Building, 425 I St. NW, Washington DC 20536. Internet: http://www.ins.usdoj.gov/bpmain/index.htm

Postal Clerks and Mail Carriers

(O*NET 57305, 57308, and 58028)

Significant Points

- Relatively few people become postal clerks or mail carriers as their first jobs.

- Qualification is based on an examination.

- Because of the large number of qualified applicants, keen competition is expected.

Nature of the Work

Each week, the U.S. Postal Service delivers billions of pieces of mail, including letters, bills, advertisements, and packages. To do this in an efficient and timely manner, the Postal Service employs about 900,000 individuals, almost two-thirds of whom are postal clerks or mail carriers. Postal clerks wait on customers and ensure that mail is properly collected, sorted, and paid for; mail carriers deliver mail to urban and rural residences and businesses throughout the United States.

Postal clerks, who are typically classified by job duties, perform a variety of functions in the Nation's post offices. Those who work as *window or counter clerks*, for example, sell stamps, money orders, postal stationery, and mailing envelopes and boxes. They also weigh packages to determine postage and check that packages are in satisfactory condition for mailing. These clerks register, certify, and insure mail and answer questions about postage rates, post office boxes, mailing restrictions, and other postal matters. Window and counter clerks also help customers file claims for damaged packages.

Postal clerks known as *distribution clerks* sort local mail for delivery to individual customers. A growing proportion of distribution clerks are known as mail processors and operate optical character readers (OCRs) and bar code sorters to arrange mail according to destination. OCRs "read" the ZIP code and spray a bar code onto the mail. Bar code sorters then scan the code and sort the mail. Because this is significantly faster than older sorting methods, it is becoming the standard sorting technology in mail processing centers.

Nevertheless, a number of distribution clerks still operate old electronic letter-sorting machines in some locations. These clerks push keys corresponding to the ZIP code of the local post office to which each letter will be delivered. The machine then drops the letter into the proper slot. Still other clerks sort odd-sized letters, magazines, and newspapers by hand. In small post offices, some clerks perform all the functions listed above.

Once clerks have processed and sorted the mail, it is ready to be delivered by mail carriers. Although carriers are classified by their type of route—either city or rural—duties of city and rural carriers are similar. Most travel established routes, delivering and collecting mail. Mail carriers start work at the post office early in the morning, where they arrange the mail in delivery sequence. Recently, automated equipment has reduced the time carriers need to sort the mail, allowing them to spend more time delivering mail.

Mail carriers cover their routes on foot, by vehicle, or a combination of both. On foot, they carry a heavy load of mail in a satchel or push it on a cart. In some urban and most rural areas, they use a car or small truck. Although the Postal Service provides vehicles to city carriers, most rural carriers have to use their own automobiles. Deliveries are made house-to-house, to roadside mailboxes, and to large buildings such as offices or apartments, which generally have all the mailboxes at one location.

Besides delivering and collecting mail, carriers collect money for postage-due and COD (cash on delivery) fees and obtain signed receipts for registered, certified, and insured mail. If a customer is not home, the carrier leaves a notice that tells where special mail is being held. After completing their routes, carriers return to the post office with mail gathered from street collection boxes, homes, and businesses and turn in the mail, receipts, and money collected during the day.

The duties of some city carriers can be specialized. Some deliver only parcel post, whereas others pick up mail from mail collection boxes. In contrast to city carriers, rural carriers provide a wider range of postal services in addition to delivering and picking up mail. For example, rural carriers may sell stamps and money orders and register, certify, and insure parcels and letters. All carriers, however, must be able to answer customers' questions about postal regulations and services and provide change-of-address cards and other postal forms when requested.

Working Conditions

Window clerks usually work in the public portion of clean, well-ventilated, and well-lit buildings. They have a variety of duties and frequent contact with the public, but they rarely work at night. However, they may have to deal with upset customers or stand for long periods, and they are held accountable for an assigned stock of stamps and funds. Depending on the size of the post office in which they work, they may be required to perform sorting duties as well.

The working conditions of other postal clerks can vary. In small post offices, clerks may sort mail by hand. In large post offices and mail processing centers, chutes and conveyors move the mail, and machines do much of the sorting. Despite the use of automated equipment, the work of postal clerks can be physically demanding. These workers are usually on their feet, reaching for sacks and trays of mail or placing packages and bundles into sacks and trays.

Mail distribution clerks can become tired and bored with the endless routine of moving and sorting mail. Many work at night or on weekends because most large post offices process mail around the clock, and the largest volume of mail is sorted during the evening and night shifts. Workers can experience stress as they process ever-larger quantities of mail under tight production deadlines and quotas.

Most carriers begin work early in the morning—those with routes in a business district can start as early as 4 a.m. Overtime hours are frequently required for urban carriers during peak delivery times, such as before the winter holidays. A carrier's schedule has its advantages, however. Carriers who begin work early in the morning are through by early afternoon and spend most of the day on their own, relatively free from direct supervision. Carriers spend most of their time outdoors, delivering mail in all kinds of weather. Even those who drive often must walk periodically when making deliveries and must lift heavy sacks of parcel post items when loading their vehicles. In addition, carriers must be cautious of potential hazards on their routes. Wet and icy roads and sidewalks can be treacherous, and each year numerous carriers are attacked by dogs.

Employment

The U.S. Postal Service employed 299,000 clerks and 332,000 mail carriers in 1998. About 95 percent of them worked full time. Most postal clerks provided window service and sorted mail at major metropolitan post offices, whereas some postal clerks worked at mail processing centers in mail distribution. Although the majority of mail carriers worked in cities and suburbs, about 53,000 were career rural carriers.

Postal clerks and mail carriers are classified as casual, part-time flexible, part-time regular, or full time. Casuals are hired for 90 days at a time to help process and deliver mail during peak mailing or vacation periods. Part-time flexible workers do not have a regular work schedule or weekly guarantee of hours but are called in as the need arises. Part-time regulars have a set work schedule of fewer than 40 hours per week, often replacing regular full-time workers on their scheduled day off. Full-time postal employees work a 40-hour week over a 5-day period.

Training, Other Qualifications, and Advancement

Postal clerks and mail carriers must be at least 18 years old and U.S. citizens or have been granted permanent resident-alien status in the United States. Qualification is based on a written examination that measures speed and accuracy at checking names and numbers and the ability to memorize mail distribution procedures. Applicants must pass a physical examination and drug test, as well, and may be asked to show that they can lift and handle mail sacks weighing 70 pounds. Applicants for mail carrier positions must have a driver's license, a good driving record, and receive a passing grade on a road test.

Jobseekers should contact the post office or mail processing center where they wish to work to determine when an exam will be given. Applicants' names are listed in order of their examination scores. Five points are added to the score of an honorably discharged veteran and 10 points to the score of a veteran who was wounded in combat or is disabled. When a vacancy occurs, the appointing officer chooses one of the top three applicants; the rest of the names remain on the list to be considered for future openings until their eligibility expires—usually two years after the examination date.

Relatively few people become postal clerks or mail carriers as their first job because of keen competition and the customary waiting period of one-two years or more after passing the examination. It is not surprising, therefore, that most entrants transfer from other occupations.

New postal clerks are trained on the job by experienced workers. Many post offices offer classroom instruction on safety and defensive driving. Workers receive additional instruction when new equipment or procedures are introduced. In these cases, workers usually are trained by another postal employee or a training specialist.

Window clerks and mail carriers should be courteous and tactful when dealing with the public, especially when answering questions or receiving complaints. A good memory and the ability to read rapidly and accurately are important. Good interpersonal skills are also vital, because mail distribution clerks work closely with other clerks, frequently under the tension and strain of meeting dispatch or transportation deadlines and quotas.

Postal clerks and mail carriers often begin on a part-time, flexible basis and become regular or full time, in order of seniority as vacancies occur. Full-time clerks may bid for preferred assignments, such as the day shift or a high level nonsupervisory position. Carriers can look forward to obtaining preferred routes as their seniority increases or to getting high level jobs, such as carrier technician. Both clerks and carriers can advance to supervisory positions on a competitive basis.

Job Outlook

Those seeking jobs as postal clerks and mail carriers can expect to encounter keen competition because the number of applicants will continue to exceed the number of openings. Employment of postal clerks and mail carriers is expected to increase more slowly than the average for all occupations through 2008. However, some jobs will become available because of the need to replace those who retire or stop working for other reasons.

Although efforts by the U.S. Postal Service to provide better service will increase the number of window clerks, the demand for window clerks will be offset by the use of electronic communications technologies and private delivery companies. Employment growth among distribution clerks will be slowed by the increasing use of automated materials handling equipment and optical character readers, bar code sorters, and other automated sorting equipment. However, despite greater use of productivity-increasing machinery, the expected increase in mail volume will require additional clerks.

Other conflicting factors are expected to influence demand for mail carriers. The competition from alternative delivery systems and new forms of electronic communication will not affect the volume of mail handled by the U.S. Postal Service. In fact, mail volume is expected to continue to increase, as population growth and partnerships with express delivery companies stimulate demand for mail delivery. However, increased use of the "delivery point sequencing" system, which allows machines to sort mail directly to the order of delivery, should decrease the amount of time carriers spend sorting their mail, allowing them more time to handle long routes. In addition, the Postal Service is moving toward more centralized mail delivery, such as the increased use of cluster boxes, to cut down on the number of door-to-door deliveries. These trends are expected to increase carrier productivity and lead to slower-than-average growth for these workers.

Employment and schedules in the Postal Service fluctuate with the demand for its services. When mail volume is high, full-time clerks and carriers work overtime, part-time clerks and carriers work additional hours, and casual clerks and carriers may be hired. When mail volume is low, overtime is curtailed, part-timers work fewer hours, and casual workers are discharged.

Earnings

Median annual earnings of postal mail carriers were $34,840 in 1998. The middle 50 percent earned between $30,430 and $37,950. The lowest 10 percent had earnings of less than $26,040, while the top 10 percent earned more than $39,820. Median annual earnings of postal service clerks were $35,100 in 1998. The middle 50 percent earned between $32,140 and $37,580. The lowest 10 percent had earnings of less than $25,350, while the top 10 percent earned more than $39,070.

Postal workers enjoy a variety of employer-provided benefits similar to those enjoyed by Federal government workers. The American Postal Workers Union or the National Association of Letter Carriers, both of which are affiliated with the AFL-CIO, represent most of these workers.

Related Occupations

Other workers whose duties are related to those of postal clerks include mail handlers, who unload the sacks of incoming mail and separate letters, parcel post, magazines, and newspapers. In addition, file clerks, routing clerks, sorters, material moving equipment operators, clerk typists, cashiers, and data entry operators do similar work. Others with duties related to those of mail carriers include messengers, merchandise deliverers, and delivery-route truckdrivers.

Sources of Additional Information

Local post offices and State employment service offices can supply details about entrance examinations and specific employment opportunities for postal clerks and mail carriers.

Private Detectives and Investigators

(O*NET 63035)

Significant Points

- Work hours are often irregular for beginning detectives and investigators, many of whom work part time.

- Most applicants have related experience in other areas, such as law enforcement, insurance, or the military.

- Stiff competition is expected for better paying jobs because of the large number of qualified people who are attracted to this occupation.

Nature of the Work

Private detectives and investigators use many means to determine the facts in a variety of matters. To carry out investigations, they may use various types of surveillance or searches. To verify facts, such as an individual's place of employment or income, they may make phone calls or visit a subject's workplace. In other cases, especially those involving missing persons and background checks, investigators often interview people to gather as much information as possible about an individual. In all cases, private detectives and investigators assist attorneys, businesses, and the public with a variety of legal, financial, and personal problems.

Private detectives and investigators offer many services, including executive, corporate, and celebrity protection; pre-employment verification; and individual background profiles. They also provide assistance in civil liability and personal injury cases, insurance claims and fraud, child custody and protection cases, and pre-marital screening. Increasingly, they are hired to investigate individuals to prove or disprove infidelity.

Most detectives and investigators are trained to perform physical surveillance, often for long periods of time, in a car or van. They may observe a site, such as the home of a subject, from an inconspicuous location. The surveillance continues using still and video cameras, binoculars, and a cell or car phone until the desired evidence is obtained. They also perform computer database searches or work with someone who does. Computers allow detectives and investigators to quickly obtain massive amounts of information on probate records, telephone numbers, motor vehicle registrations, association membership lists, registered sex offenders, and other matters.

The duties of private detectives and investigators depend on the needs of their client. In a case involving fraudulent workers' compensation claims for an employer, for instance, investigators carry out long-term covert observation of the subject. If the investigator observes the subject performing an activity that contradicts injuries stated in a workers' compensation claim, the investigator would take video or still photographs to document the activity and report it to the client.

Private detectives and investigators often specialize. Those who focus on intellectual property theft, for example, investigate and document acts of piracy, help clients stop the illegal activity, and provide intelligence for prosecution and civil action. Other investigators specialize in financial profiles and asset searches. Their reports reflect information gathered through interviews, investigation and surveillance, and research, including review of public documents.

Legal investigators specialize in cases involving the courts and are normally employed by law firms or lawyers. They frequently assist in preparing criminal defenses, locate witnesses, serve legal documents, interview police and prospective witnesses, and gather and review evidence. Legal investigators may also collect information on the parties to the litigation, take photographs, testify in court, and assemble evidence and reports for trials.

Corporate investigators work for corporations other than investigative firms, in which they conduct internal and external investigations. In internal investigations, they may investigate drug use in the workplace, ensure that expense accounts are not abused, or determine if employees are stealing merchandise or information. External investigations typically prevent criminal schemes originating outside the corporation, such as theft of company assets through fraudulent billing of products by suppliers.

Detectives and investigators who specialize in finance may be hired to develop confidential financial profiles of individuals or companies who are prospective parties to large financial transactions. These individuals are often Certified Public Accountants (CPAs) and work closely with investment bankers and accountants. They search for assets in order to recover damages awarded by a court in fraud or theft cases.

Detectives who work for retail stores or hotels are responsible for loss control and asset protection. Store detectives, also known as loss prevention agents, safeguard the assets of retail stores by apprehending anyone attempting to steal merchandise or destroy store property. They prevent theft by shoplifters, vendor representatives, delivery personnel, and even store employees. Store detectives also conduct periodic inspections of stock areas, dressing rooms, and restrooms, and sometimes assist in opening and closing the store. They may prepare loss prevention and security reports for management and testify in court against persons they apprehend. Hotel detectives protect guests of the establishment from theft of their belongings and preserve order in the restaurants and bars in the building. They also may keep undesirable individuals such as known thieves off the premises.

Working Conditions

Private detectives and investigators often work irregular hours because of the need to conduct surveillance and contact people who are not available during normal working hours. Early morning, evening, weekend, and holiday work is common.

Many detectives and investigators spend time away from their offices conducting interviews or doing surveillance, but some work in their office most of the day conducting computer searches and making phone calls. Those who have their own agencies and employ other investigators may work primarily in an office and have normal business hours.

When working on a case away from the office, the environment might range from plush boardrooms to seedy bars. Store and hotel detectives work in the businesses that they protect. Investigators generally work alone, but they sometimes work with others during surveillance or when following a subject in order to avoid detection by the subject.

Some of the work involves confrontation, so the job can be stressful and dangerous. Detectives and investigators who carry handguns must be licensed by the appropriate authority. Some situations call for the investigator to be armed, such as certain bodyguard assignments for corporate or celebrity clients. In most cases, however, a weapon is not necessary because the purpose of their work is gathering information and not law enforcement or criminal apprehension. Owners of investigative agencies have the added stress of having to deal with demanding and sometimes distraught clients.

Employment

Private detectives and investigators held about 61,000 jobs in 1998. About 1 out of 4 was self-employed. Approximately a third of salaried private detectives and investigators worked for detective agencies, while another third were employed as store detectives in department or clothing and accessories stores. The remainder worked for hotels and other lodging places, legal services firms, and in other industries.

Training, Other Qualifications, and Advancement

There are no formal education requirements for most private detective and investigator jobs, although many private detectives have college degrees. Almost all private detectives and investigators have previous experience in other occupations. Some work initially for insurance or collections companies or in the private security industry. Many investigators enter the field after serving in military, government intelligence, or law enforcement jobs.

Former law enforcement officers, military investigators, and government agents often become private detectives or investigators as a second career because they are frequently able to retire after 20 years of service. Others enter from such diverse fields as finance, accounting, commercial credit, investigative reporting, insurance, and law. These individuals often can apply their prior work experience in a related investigative specialty. A few enter the occupation directly after graduation from college, generally with associate or bachelor of criminal justice or police science degrees.

The majority of the States and the District of Colombia require private detectives and investigators to be licensed by the State or local authorities. Licensing requirements vary widely. Some States have few requirements, and five States—Alaska, Colorado, Idaho, Mississippi, and South Dakota—have no Statewide licensing requirements, while others have stringent regulations. For example, the California Department of Consumer Affairs, Bureau of Security and Investigative Services, requires private investigators to be 18 years of age or older; have a combination of education in police science, criminal law, or justice, and experience equaling three years (6,000 hours) of investigative experience; pass an evaluation by the Department of Justice and a criminal history background check; and receive a qualifying score on a two-hour written examination covering laws and regulations. There are additional requirements for a firearms permit. A growing number of States are enacting mandatory training programs for private detectives and investigators. In most States, convicted felons cannot receive a license.

For private detective and investigator jobs, most employers look for individuals with ingenuity who are persistent and assertive. A candidate must not be afraid of confrontation, should communicate well, and should be able to think on his or her feet. Good interviewing and interrogation skills also are important and are usually acquired in earlier careers in law enforcement or other fields. Because the courts are often the ultimate judge of a properly conducted investigation, the investigator must be able to present the facts in a manner a jury will believe.

Training in subjects such as criminal justice are helpful to aspiring private detectives and investigators. Most corporate investigators must have a bachelor's degree, preferably in a business-related field. Some corporate investigators have master's degrees in business administration or law, while others are certified public accountants. Corporate investigators hired by large companies may receive formal training from their employers on business practices, management structure, and various finance-related topics. The screening process for potential employees typically includes a background check of a candidate's criminal history.

Some investigators receive certification from a professional organization to demonstrate competency in a field. For example, the National Association of Legal Investigators (NALI) confers the designation Certified Legal Investigator on licensed investigators who devote a majority of their practice to negligence or criminal defense investigations. To receive the designation, applicants must satisfy experience, educational, and continuing training requirements and must pass written and oral exams administered by the NALI.

Most private detective agencies are small, with little room for advancement. Usually there are no defined ranks or steps, so advancement takes the form of increases in salary and assignment status. Many detectives and investigators work for detective agencies at the beginning of their careers and after a few years start their own firms. Corporate and legal investigators may rise to supervisor or manager of the security or investigations department.

Job Outlook

Stiff competition is expected because private detective and investigator careers attract many qualified people, including relatively young retirees from law enforcement and military careers. Oppor-

tunities will be best for entry-level jobs with detective agencies or as store detectives on a part-time basis. Those seeking store detective jobs have the best prospects with large chains and discount stores.

Employment of private detectives and investigators is expected to grow faster than the average for all occupations through 2008. In addition to growth, replacement of those who retire or leave the occupation for other reasons should create many additional job openings, particularly among salaried workers. Increased demand for private detectives and investigators will result from fear of crime, increased litigation, and the need to protect confidential information and property of all kinds. More private investigators also will be needed to assist attorneys working on criminal defense and civil litigation. Growing financial activity worldwide will increase the demand for investigators to control internal and external financial losses and to monitor competitors and prevent industrial spying.

Earnings

Median annual earnings of private detectives and investigators were $21,020 in 1998. The middle 50 percent earned between $16,340 and $31,520. The lowest 10 percent had earnings of less than $14,050, while the top 10 percent earned more than $42,560. Department stores, where store detectives work, paid an average of $17,600 per year, while miscellaneous business services, where private investigators firms are found, paid an average of about $29,200 annually in 1997.

Earnings of private detectives and investigators vary greatly depending on their employer, specialty, and the geographic area in which they work. According to a study by Abbott, Langer & Associates, security/loss prevention directors and vice presidents averaged $65,500 a year in 1998; investigators, $49,300; and store detectives, $17,700. In addition to typical benefits, most corporate investigators received profit-sharing plans.

Related Occupations

Private detectives and investigators often collect information and protect the property and other assets of companies. Others with related duties include security guards, insurance claims examiners, inspectors, bill collectors, and law enforcement officers. Investigators who specialize in conducting financial profiles and asset searches perform work closely related to that of accountants and financial analysts.

Sources of Additional Information

For information on local licensing requirements, contact your State Department of Public Safety, State Division of Licensing, or your local or State police headquarters.

For information on a career as a legal investigator, contact:

- The National Association of Legal Investigators, P.O. Box 905, Grand Blanc, MI 48439. Internet: http://www.nali.com/index.htm

Property, Real Estate, and Community Association Managers

(O*NET 15011B)

Significant Points

- Most enter the occupation as on-site managers of apartment complexes, condominiums, or community associations, or as assistant managers at large property management firms.

- Opportunities should be best for those with college degrees in business administration or related fields.

- Almost one half were self-employed; that's three times the average for all executive, administrative, and managerial occupations.

Nature of the Work

Many people own some type of real estate, such as a house. To businesses and investors, however, properly managed real estate is a potential source of income and profits rather than a place of shelter. Property, real estate, and community association managers maintain and increase the value of real estate investments for investors. *Property and real estate managers* oversee the performance of income-producing commercial or residential properties; *community association managers* manage the communal property and services of condominium or community associations.

When owners of apartments, office buildings, retail, or industrial properties lack the time or expertise needed for day-to-day management of their real estate investments, they often hire a property or real estate manager. The manager is either directly employed by the owner or indirectly employed through a contract with a property management firm.

Property managers handle the financial operations of the property, ensuring that mortgages, taxes, insurance premiums, payroll, and maintenance bills are paid on time. Some property managers, called *asset property managers*, supervise the preparation of financial statements and periodically report to the owners on the status of the property, occupancy rates, dates of lease expirations, and other matters.

If necessary, property managers negotiate contracts for janitorial, security, groundskeeping, trash removal, and other services. When contracts are awarded competitively, managers solicit bids from several contractors and recommend to the owners which bid to accept. They monitor the performance of contractors and investigate and resolve complaints from residents and tenants when services are not properly provided. Managers also purchase supplies and equipment for the property and make arrangements with specialists for repairs that cannot be handled by regular property maintenance staff.

In addition to these duties, property managers must understand and comply with provisions of legislation, such as the Americans with Disabilities Act and the Federal Fair Housing Amendment Act, as well as local fair housing laws. They must ensure that their renting and advertising practices are not discriminatory and that the property itself complies with State and Federal regulations.

On-site property managers are responsible for day-to-day operations for one piece of property, such as an office building, shopping center, or apartment complex. To ensure the property is safe and being maintained properly, on-site managers routinely inspect the grounds, facilities, and equipment to determine if repairs or maintenance are needed. They meet not only with current residents when handling requests for repairs or trying to resolve complaints, but also with prospective residents or tenants to show vacant apartments or office space. On-site managers are also responsible for enforcing the terms of rental or lease agreements, such as rent collection, parking and pet restrictions, and termination-of-lease procedures. Other important duties of on-site managers include keeping accurate, up-to-date records of income and expenditures from property operations and the submission of regular expense reports to the asset property manager or owners.

Property managers who do not work on-site act as a liaison between the on-site manager and the owner. They also market vacant space to prospective tenants through the use of a leasing agent, advertising, or by other means and establish rental rates in accordance with prevailing local conditions.

Some property managers, often called *real estate asset managers*, act as the property owners' agent and adviser for the property. They plan and direct the purchase, development, and disposition of real estate on behalf of the business and investors. These managers focus on long-term strategic financial planning rather than day-to-day operations of the property.

When deciding to acquire property, real estate asset managers take several factors into consideration, such as property values, taxes, zoning, population growth, and traffic volume and patterns. Once a site is selected, they negotiate contracts for the purchase or lease of the property, securing the most beneficial terms. Real estate asset managers periodically review their company's real estate holdings and identify properties that are no longer financially attractive. They then negotiate the sale or termination of the lease of properties selected for disposal.

The work of community association managers differs from that of other residential property managers. Instead of renters, they interact on a daily basis with homeowners—members of the community association employing the manager. Hired by the volunteer board of directors of the association, the community association manager administers the daily affairs and oversees the maintenance of property and facilities that the homeowners own and use jointly through the association. Smaller community associations usually cannot afford professional management, but managers of larger condominiums or homeowner associations have many of the same responsibilities as the managers of large apartment complexes. Some homeowner associations encompass thousands of homes, and, in addition to administering the associations' financial records and budget, their managers are responsible for the operation of community pools, golf courses, community centers, and the maintenance of landscaping and parking areas. Community association managers may also meet with the elected boards of directors to discuss and resolve legal and environmental issues or disputes between neighbors.

Property managers who work for land development companies acquire land and plan construction of shopping centers, houses, apartments, office buildings, or industrial parks. They negotiate with representatives of local governments, other businesses, community and public interest groups, and public utilities to eliminate obstacles to the development of land and gain support for a planned project. It sometimes takes years to win approval for a project, and in the process, managers may have to modify plans for the project many times. Once they are free to proceed with a project, managers negotiate short-term loans to finance the construction of the project, and later they negotiate long-term permanent mortgage loans. They then contract with architectural firms to draw up detailed plans and with construction companies to build the project.

Working Conditions

Offices of most property managers are clean, modern, and well-lighted. However, many spend a major portion of their time away from their desks. On-site managers in particular may spend a large portion of their workday away from their office visiting the building engineer, showing apartments, checking on the janitorial and maintenance staff, or investigating problems reported by tenants. Property managers frequently visit the properties they oversee, sometimes on a daily basis when contractors are doing major repair or renovation work. Real estate asset managers may spend time away from home while traveling to company real estate holdings or searching for properties that might be acquired.

Property managers often must attend meetings in the evening with residents, property owners, community association boards of directors, or civic groups. Not surprisingly, many property managers put in long work weeks, especially before financial and tax reports are due. Some apartment managers are required to live in apartment complexes where they work so they are available to handle any emergency that occurs when they are off duty. They usually receive compensatory time off for working nights or weekends. Many apartment managers receive time off during the week so that they are available on weekends to show apartments to prospective residents.

Employment

Property managers held about 315,000 jobs in 1998. Most worked for real estate operators and lessors or for property management firms. Others worked for real estate development companies, government agencies that manage public buildings, and corporations with extensive holdings of commercial properties. Almost one half of property managers were self-employed.

Training, Other Qualifications, and Advancement

Most employers prefer to hire college graduates for property management positions. Entrants with degrees in business administration, accounting, finance, real estate, public administration, or

related fields are preferred, but those with degrees in the liberal arts may also qualify. Good speaking, writing, computer, and financial skills, as well as an ability to deal tactfully with people, are essential in all areas of property management.

Most people enter property management as an on-site manager of an apartment complex, condominium, or community association or as an assistant manager at a large property management firm. As they acquire experience working under the direction of a property manager, they may advance to positions with greater responsibility at larger properties. Those who excel as on-site managers often transfer to assistant property manager positions where they can acquire experience handling a broad range of property management responsibilities.

Previous employment as a real estate agent may be an asset to on-site managers because it provides experience useful in showing apartments or office space. In the past, those with backgrounds in building maintenance have advanced to on-site manager positions on the strength of their knowledge of building mechanical systems, but this is becoming less common as employers are placing greater emphasis on administrative, financial, and communication abilities for managerial jobs.

Although most people entering jobs such as assistant property manager do so on the strength of on-site management experience, employers are increasingly hiring inexperienced college graduates with bachelor's or master's degrees in business administration, accounting, finance, or real estate for these positions. Assistants work closely with a property manager and learn how to prepare budgets, analyze insurance coverage and risk options, market property to prospective tenants, and collect overdue rent payments. In time, many assistants advance to property manager positions.

The responsibilities and compensation of property managers increase as they manage more and larger properties. Most property managers are responsible for several properties at a time, and as their careers advance, they are gradually entrusted with larger properties whose management is more complex. Many specialize in the management of one type of property, such as apartments, office buildings, condominiums, cooperatives, homeowner associations, or retail properties. Managers who excel at marketing properties to tenants may specialize in managing new properties, while those who are particularly knowledgeable about buildings and their mechanical systems might specialize in the management of older properties requiring renovation or more frequent repairs. Some experienced property managers open their own property management firms.

Persons most commonly enter real estate asset manager jobs by transferring from positions as property managers or real estate brokers. Real estate asset managers must be good negotiators, adept at persuading and handling people, and good at analyzing data to assess the fair market value of property or its development potential. Resourcefulness and creativity in arranging financing are essential for managers who specialize in land development.

Many employers encourage attendance at short-term formal training programs conducted by various professional and trade associations active in the real estate field. Employers send managers to these programs to improve their management skills and expand their knowledge of specialized subjects, such as the operation and maintenance of building mechanical systems, enhancing property values, insurance and risk management, personnel management, business and real estate law, tenant relations, communications, and accounting and financial concepts. Managers also participate in these programs to prepare themselves for positions of greater responsibility in property management. Completion of these programs, together with related job experience and a satisfactory score on a written examination, leads to certification, or the formal award of a professional designation, by the sponsoring association. In addition to these qualifications, some associations require their members to adhere to a specific code of ethics. Some of the organizations offering such programs are listed at the end of this job description.

Managers of public housing subsidized by the Federal government are required to be certified, but many property managers, who work with all types of property, choose to earn a professional designation voluntarily because it represents formal industry recognition of their achievements and status in the occupation. Real estate asset managers who buy or sell property are required to be licensed by the State in which they practice.

Job Outlook

Employment of property, real estate, and community association managers is projected to increase as fast as the average for all occupations through the year 2008. Many job openings are expected to occur as property managers transfer to other occupations or leave the labor force. Opportunities should be best for those with a college degree in business administration, real estate, or a related field or for those who attain a professional designation.

Growth in the demand for on-site property managers will be greatest in several areas. In commercial real estate, the demand for managers is expected to accompany the projected expansion in wholesale and retail trade; finance, insurance, and real estate; and services. Some additional employment growth will come from expansion of existing buildings.

An increase in the Nation's stock of apartments and houses also should require more property managers. Developments of new homes are increasingly being organized with community or homeowner associations that provide community services and oversee jointly owned common areas that require professional management. To help properties become more profitable, more commercial and multi-unit residential property owners are expected to place their investments in the hands of professional managers.

Growth in demand should also arise as a result of the changing demographic composition of the population. The number of older people will increase during the projection period, creating a need for various types of suitable housing, such as assisted living arrangements and retirement communities. Accordingly, there will be a need for property managers to operate these facilities, especially those who have a background in the operation and administrative aspects of running a health unit.

Earnings

Median annual earnings of salaried property, real estate, and community association managers were $29,930 in 1998. The middle 50 percent earned between $21,020 and $43,080 a year. The lowest 10 percent earned less than $14,570, and the highest 10 percent earned more than $74,500 a year. Median annual earnings of salaried property, real estate, and community association managers in 1997 were $29,700 in the real estate agents and managers industry and $26,900 in the real estate operators and lessors industry.

Many resident apartment managers receive the use of an apartment as part of their compensation package. Property managers often are given the use of a company automobile, and managers employed in land development often receive a small percentage of ownership in projects they develop.

Related Occupations

Property managers plan, organize, staff, and manage the real estate operations of businesses. Workers who perform similar functions in other fields include city managers, education administrators, facilities managers, health services managers, hotel managers and assistants, real estate agents and brokers, and restaurant and food service managers.

Sources of Additional Information

General information about education and careers in property management is available from:

- Institute of Real Estate Management, 430 N. Michigan Ave., Chicago, IL 60611. Internet: http://www.irem.org
- International Council of Shopping Centers, 665 5th Ave., New York, NY 10022. Internet: http://www.icsc.org

For information on careers and certification programs in commercial property management, contact:

- Building Owners and Managers Association International, 1201 New York Ave. NW., Suite 300, Washington, DC 20005. Internet: http://www.boma.org
- Building Owners and Managers Institute, 1521 Ritchie Hwy., Arnold, MD 21012. Internet: http://www.bomi-edu.org

For information on careers and certification programs in residential property management, contact:

- Community Associations Institute, 1630 Duke St., Alexandria, VA 22314. Internet: http://www.caionline.org
- National Apartment Association, 201 N. Union St., Suite 200, Alexandria, VA 22314. Internet: http://www.naahq.org
- National Association of Residential Property Managers, 6300 Dutchmans Pkwy., Louisville, KY 40205. Internet: http://www.narpm.org

Psychologists

(O*NET 27108A, 27108C, 27108D, 27108E, 27108G, 27108H, and 27108J)

Significant Points

- One half of psychologists are self-employed—about 5 times the average for professional workers.

- A doctoral degree is usually required for employment as a licensed clinical or counseling psychologist.

- Opportunities for employment in psychology for those with only a bachelor's degree are severely limited.

Nature of the Work

Psychologists study the human mind and human behavior. Research psychologists investigate the physical, cognitive, emotional, or social aspects of human behavior. Psychologists in applied fields provide mental health care in hospitals, clinics, schools, or private settings.

Like other social scientists, psychologists formulate hypotheses and collect data to test their validity. Research methods may vary depending on the topic under study. Psychologists sometimes gather information through controlled laboratory experiments or by administering personality, performance, aptitude, and intelligence tests. Other methods include observation, interviews, questionnaires, clinical studies, and surveys.

Psychologists apply their knowledge to a wide range of endeavors, including health and human services, management, education, law, and sports. In addition to a variety of work settings, psychologists usually specialize in one of a number of different areas. *Clinical psychologists*—who constitute the largest specialty—usually work in counseling centers, independent or group practices, hospitals, or clinics. They help mentally and emotionally disturbed clients adjust to life and may help medical and surgical patients deal with illnesses or injuries. Some work in physical rehabilitation settings, treating patients with spinal cord injuries, chronic pain or illness, stroke, arthritis, and neurologic conditions. Others help people deal with times of personal crisis, such as divorce or the death of a loved one.

Clinical psychologists often interview patients and give diagnostic tests. They may provide individual, family, or group psychotherapy, and design and implement behavior modification programs. Some clinical psychologists collaborate with physicians and other specialists to develop and implement treatment and intervention programs that patients can understand and comply with. Other clinical psychologists work in universities and medical schools, where they train graduate students in the delivery of mental health and behavioral medicine services. Some administer community mental health programs.

Areas of specialization within clinical psychology include health psychology, neuropsychology, and geropsychology. *Health psychologists* promote good health through health maintenance counseling programs designed to help people achieve goals such as to stop smoking or lose weight. *Neuropsychologists* study the relation between the brain and behavior. They often work in stroke and head injury programs. *Geropsychologists* deal with the special problems faced by the elderly. The emergence and growth of these specialties reflects the increasing participation of psychologists in providing direct services to special patient populations.

Counseling psychologists use various techniques, including interviewing and testing, to advise people on how to deal with problems of everyday living. They work in settings such as university counseling centers, hospitals, and individual or group practices.

School psychologists work in elementary and secondary schools or school district offices to resolve students' learning and behavior problems. They collaborate with teachers, parents, and school personnel to improve classroom management strategies or parenting skills, counter substance abuse, work with students with disabilities or gifted and talented students, and improve teaching and learning strategies. They may evaluate the effectiveness of academic programs, behavior management procedures, and other services provided in the school setting.

Industrial-organizational (I/O) psychologists apply psychological principles and research methods to the workplace in the interest of improving productivity and the quality of work life. They also are involved in research on management and marketing problems. They conduct applicant screening, training and development, counseling, and organizational development and analysis. An industrial psychologist might work with management to reorganize the work setting to improve productivity or quality of life in the workplace. They frequently act as consultants, brought in by management in order to solve a particular problem.

Developmental psychologists study the physiological, cognitive, and social development that takes place throughout life. Some specialize in behavior during infancy, childhood, and adolescence, or changes that occur during maturity or old age. They may also study developmental disabilities and their effects. Increasingly, research is developing ways to help elderly people stay as independent as possible.

Social psychologists examine people's interactions with others and with the social environment. They work in organizational consultation, marketing research, systems design, or other applied psychology fields. Prominent areas of study include group behavior, leadership, attitudes, and perception.

Experimental or *research psychologists* work in university and private research centers and in business, nonprofit, and governmental organizations. They study behavior processes with human beings and animals such as rats, monkeys, and pigeons. Prominent areas of study in experimental research include motivation, thinking, attention, learning and memory, sensory and perceptual processes, effects of substance abuse, and genetic and neurological factors affecting behavior.

Working Conditions

A psychologist's specialty and place of employment determine working conditions. Clinical, school, and counseling psychologists in private practice have their own offices and set their own hours. However, they often offer evening and weekend hours to accommodate their clients. Those employed in hospitals, nursing homes, and other health facilities may work shifts including evenings and weekends, while those who work in schools and clinics generally work regular hours.

Psychologists employed as faculty by colleges and universities divide their time between teaching and research and may also have administrative responsibilities. Many have part-time consulting practices. Most psychologists in government and industry have structured schedules.

Increasingly, many work as part of a team and consult with other psychologists and professionals. Many psychologists experience pressures due to deadlines, tight schedules, and overtime work. Their routines may be interrupted frequently. Travel is required to attend conferences or conduct research.

Employment

Psychologists held about 166,000 jobs in 1998. Educational institutions employed about 4 out of 10 salaried psychologists in positions other than teaching, such as counseling, testing, research, and administration. Three out of 10 were employed in health services, primarily in hospitals, mental health clinics, rehabilitation centers, nursing homes, and other health facilities. Government agencies at the Federal, State, and local levels employed about 17 percent. Governments employ psychologists in hospitals, clinics, correctional facilities, and other settings. The Department of Veterans Affairs and the Department of Defense employ a majority of the psychologists working for Federal agencies. Some psychologists work in social service organizations, research organizations, management consulting firms, marketing research firms, and other businesses.

After several years of experience, some psychologists—usually those with doctoral degrees—enter private practice or set up private research or consulting firms. About one half of psychologists are self-employed.

In addition to the jobs described above, many held positions as psychology faculty at colleges and universities and as high school psychology teachers.

Training, Other Qualifications, and Advancement

A doctoral degree is usually required for employment as a licensed clinical or counseling psychologist. Psychologists with a Ph.D. qualify for a wide range of teaching, research, clinical, and counseling positions in universities, elementary and secondary schools, private industry, and government. Psychologists with a Doctor of Psychology (Psy.D.) degree usually work in clinical positions. An Educational Specialist (Ed.S.) degree will qualify an individual to work as a school psychologist. Persons with a master's degree in psychology may work as industrial-organizational psychologists. Others work as psychological assistants under the supervision of doctoral-level psychologists and conduct research or psychological evaluations.

A bachelor's degree in psychology qualifies a person to assist psychologists and other professionals in community mental health centers, vocational rehabilitation offices, and correctional programs. They may work as research or administrative assistants or become sales or management trainees in business. Some work as technicians in related fields such as marketing research. However, without additional academic training, their opportunities in psychology are severely limited.

In the Federal government, candidates having at least 24 semester hours in psychology and one course in statistics qualify for entry-level positions. Because this is one of the few areas in which one can work as a psychologist without an advanced degree, competition for these jobs is keen.

Clinical psychologists usually must have completed the Ph.D. or Psy.D. requirements and served an internship. Vocational and guidance counselors usually need two years of graduate study in counseling and one year of counseling experience. School psychology requires a master's degree followed by a one-year internship.

Most students need at least two years of full-time graduate study to earn a master's degree in psychology. Requirements usually include practical experience in an applied setting and a master's thesis based on an original research project.

A doctoral degree usually requires five to seven years of graduate study. The Ph.D. degree culminates in a dissertation based on original research. Courses in quantitative research methods, which include the use of computer-based analysis, are an integral part of graduate study and are necessary to complete the dissertation. The Psy.D. may be based on practical work and examinations rather than a dissertation. In clinical or counseling psychology, the requirements for the doctoral degree usually include at least a one-year internship.

Competition for admission into graduate programs is keen. Some universities require an undergraduate major in psychology. Others prefer only course work in basic psychology with courses in the biological, physical, and social sciences, statistics, and mathematics.

The American Psychological Association (APA) presently accredits doctoral training programs in clinical, counseling, and school psychology. The National Council for Accreditation of Teacher Education, with the assistance of the National Association of School Psychologists, also is involved in the accreditation of advanced degree programs in school psychology. The APA also accredits institutions that provide internships for doctoral students in school, clinical, and counseling psychology.

Psychologists in independent practice or those who offer any type of patient care (including clinical, counseling, and school psychologists) must meet certification or licensing requirements in all States and the District of Columbia. Licensing laws vary by State and by type of position. Clinical and counseling psychologists usually require a doctorate in psychology, completion of an approved internship, and one to two years of professional experience. In addition, all States require that applicants pass an examination. Most State boards administer a standardized test and many supplement that with additional oral or essay questions. Most States certify those with a master's degree as school psychologists after completion of an internship. Some States require continuing education for license renewal.

Most States require that licensed or certified psychologists limit their practice to areas in which they have developed professional competence through training and experience.

The American Board of Professional Psychology (ABPP) recognizes professional achievement by awarding certification, primarily in clinical psychology, clinical neuropsychology, counseling, forensic, industrial-organizational, and school psychology. Candidates for ABPP certification need a doctorate in psychology, five years of experience, professional endorsements, and a passing grade on an examination.

Aspiring psychologists who are interested in direct patient care must be emotionally stable, mature, and able to deal effectively with

people. Sensitivity, compassion, and the ability to lead and inspire others are particularly important qualities for clinical work and counseling. Research psychologists should be able to do detailed work independently and as part of a team. Excellent communications skills are necessary to succeed in research. Patience and perseverance are vital qualities because results from psychological treatment of patients or from research usually take a long time.

Job Outlook

Employment of psychologists is expected to grow about as fast as the average for all occupations through 2008. Employment in health care will grow fastest in outpatient mental health and substance abuse treatment clinics. Numerous job opportunities will also arise in schools, public and private social service agencies, and management consulting services. Companies will use psychologists' expertise in survey design, analysis, and research to provide marketing evaluation and statistical analysis. The increase in employee assistance programs, which offer employees help with personal problems, should also spur job growth.

Opportunities for people holding doctorates from leading universities in areas with an applied emphasis, such as clinical, counseling, health, and educational psychology, should have particularly good prospects. Psychologists with extensive training in quantitative research methods and computer science may have a competitive edge over applicants without this background.

Graduates with a master's degree in psychology qualify for positions in school and industrial-organizational psychology. Graduates of master's degree programs in school psychology should have the best job prospects, as schools are expected to increase student counseling and mental health services. Masters' degree holders with several years of industrial experience can obtain jobs in consulting and marketing research. Other master's degree holders may find jobs as psychological assistants in the community mental health field, which often requires direct supervision by a licensed psychologist. Still others may find jobs involving research and data collection and analysis in universities, government, or private companies.

Very few opportunities directly related to psychology will exist for bachelor's degree holders. Some may find jobs as assistants in rehabilitation centers or in other jobs involving data collection and analysis. Those who meet State certification requirements may become high school psychology teachers.

Earnings

Median annual earnings of salaried psychologists were $48,050 in 1998. The middle 50 percent earned between $36,570 and $70,870 a year. The lowest 10 percent earned less than $27,960, and the highest 10 percent earned more than $88,280 a year. Median annual earnings in the industries employing the largest number of psychologists in 1997 were as follows:

Offices of other health care practitioners	$54,000
Hospitals	49,300
Elementary and secondary schools	47,400
State government, except education and hospitals	41,600
Health and allied services, not elsewhere classified	38,900

The Federal government recognizes education and experience in certifying applicants for entry-level positions. In general, the starting salary for psychologists having a bachelor's degree was about $20,600 in 1999; those with superior academic records could begin at $25,500. Psychologists with a master's degree and one year of experience could start at $31,200. Psychologists having a Ph.D. or Psy.D. degree and one year of internship could start at $37,800, and some individuals with experience could start at $45,200. Beginning salaries were slightly higher in selected areas of the country where the prevailing local pay level was higher. The average annual salary for psychologists in the Federal government was $66,800 in early 1999.

Related Occupations

Psychologists are trained to conduct research and teach, evaluate, counsel, and advise individuals and groups with special needs. Others who do this kind of work include marketing research analysts, advertising and public relations managers, clinical social workers, physicians, sociologists, clergy, special education teachers, and counselors.

Sources of Additional Information

For information on careers, educational requirements, financial assistance, and licensing in all fields of psychology, contact:

- American Psychological Association, Research Office and Education in Psychology and Accreditation Offices, 750 1st St. NE., Washington, DC 20002. Internet: http://www.apa.org

For information on careers, educational requirements, certification, and licensing of school psychologists, contact:

- National Association of School Psychologists, 4030 East West Hwy., Suite 402, Bethesda, MD 20814. Internet: http://www.naspweb.org

Information about State licensing requirements is available from:

- Association of State and Provincial Psychology Boards, P.O. Box 4389, Montgomery, AL 36103-4389. Internet: http://www.asppb.org

Information on obtaining a job with the Federal government may be obtained from the Office of Personnel Management through a telephone-based system. Consult your telephone directory under U.S. Government for a local number or call (912) 757-3000 (TDD 912 744-2299). This number is not toll free, and charges may result. Information also is available from their Internet site: http://www.usajobs.opm.gov.

Public Relations Specialists

(O*NET 34008)

Significant Points

- Employment of public relations specialists is expected to increase faster than average, but keen competition is expected for entry-level jobs.

- Opportunities should be best for college graduates who combine a degree in journalism, public relations, advertising, or other communications-related fields with public relations work experience.

Nature of the Work

An organization's reputation, profitability, and even its continued existence can depend on the degree to which its targeted "publics" support its goals and policies. Public relations specialists serve as advocates for businesses, governments, universities, hospitals, schools, and other organizations, and they build and maintain positive relationships with the public. As managers recognize the growing importance of good public relations to the success of their organizations, they increasingly rely on public relations specialists for advice on strategy and policy of such programs.

Public relations specialists handle organizational functions such as media, community, consumer, and governmental relations; political campaigns; interest-group representation; conflict mediation; or employee and investor relations. However, public relations is not only "telling the organization's story." Understanding the attitudes and concerns of consumers, employees, and various other groups is also a vital part of the job. To improve communications, public relations specialists establish and maintain cooperative relationships with representatives of community, consumer, employee, and public interest groups and those in print and broadcast journalism.

Informing the general public, interest groups, and stockholders of an organization's policies, activities, and accomplishments is an important part of a public relations specialist's job. Their work keeps management aware of public attitudes and concerns of the many groups and organizations with which they must deal.

Public relations specialists prepare press releases and contact people in the media who might print or broadcast their material. Many radio or television special reports, newspaper stories, and magazine articles start at the desks of public relations specialists. Sometimes the subject is an organization and its policies towards its employees or its role in the community. Often the subject is a public issue, such as health, nutrition, energy, or the environment.

Public relations specialists also arrange and conduct programs for contact between organization representatives and the public. For example, they set up speaking engagements and often prepare speeches for company officials. These specialists represent employers at community projects; make film, slide, or other visual presentations at meetings and school assemblies; and plan conventions. In addition, they are responsible for preparing annual reports and writing proposals for various projects.

In government, public relations specialists—who may be called press secretaries, information officers, public affairs specialists, or communications specialists—keep the public informed about the activities of government agencies and officials. For example, public affairs specialists in the Department of Energy keep the public informed about the proposed lease of offshore land for oil exploration. A press secretary for a member of Congress keeps constituents aware of their elected representative's accomplishments.

In large organizations, the key public relations executive, who is often a vice president, may develop overall plans and policies with other executives. In addition, public relations departments employ public relations specialists to write, do research, prepare materials, maintain contacts, and respond to inquiries.

People who handle publicity for an individual or who direct public relations for a small organization may deal with all aspects of the job. They contact people, plan and do research, and prepare material for distribution. They may also handle advertising or sales promotion work to support marketing.

Working Conditions

Some public relations specialists work a standard 35- to 40-hour week, but unpaid overtime is common. Occasionally they have to be at the job or on call around the clock, especially if there is an emergency or crisis. Public relations offices are busy places; work schedules can be irregular and frequently interrupted. Schedules often have to be rearranged to meet deadlines, deliver speeches, attend meetings and community activities, and travel out of town.

Employment

Public relations specialists held about 122,000 jobs in 1998. Almost two-thirds of salaried public relations specialists worked in services industries—management and public relations firms, educational institutions, membership organizations, health care organizations, social service agencies, and advertising agencies, for example. Others worked for manufacturing firms, financial institutions, and government agencies. About 13,000 public relations specialists were self-employed.

Public relations specialists are concentrated in large cities where press services and other communications facilities are readily available, and many businesses and trade associations have their headquarters. Many public relations consulting firms, for example, are in New York, Los Angeles, Chicago, and Washington, DC. There is a trend, however, for public relations jobs to be dispersed throughout the Nation.

Training, Other Qualifications, and Advancement

Although there are no defined standards for entry into a public relations career, a college degree combined with public relations experience, usually gained through an internship, is considered excellent preparation for public relations work. The ability to write and speak well is essential. Many entry-level public relations specialists have a college major in public relations, journalism, advertising, or communications. Some firms seek college graduates who have worked in electronic or print journalism. Other employers seek applicants with demonstrated communications skills and training or experience in a field related to the firm's business—science, engineering, sales, or finance, for example.

In 1998, well over 200 colleges and about 100 graduate schools offered degree programs or special curricula in public relations, usually in a journalism or communications department. In addition, many other colleges offered at least one course in this field. The Accrediting Council on Education in Journalism and Mass Communications is the only agency authorized to accredit schools or departments of public relations. A common public relations sequence includes courses in public relations principles and techniques; public relations management and administration, including organizational development; writing, emphasizing news releases, proposals, annual reports, scripts, speeches, and related items; preparing visual communications, including desktop publishing and computer graphics; and research, emphasizing social science research and survey design and implementation. Courses in advertising, journalism, business administration, political science, psychology, sociology, and creative writing also are helpful, as is familiarity with word processing and other computer applications. Specialties are offered in public relations for business, government, and nonprofit organizations.

Many colleges help students gain part-time internships in public relations that provide valuable experience and training. The Armed Forces can also be an excellent place to gain training and experience. Membership in local chapters of the Public Relations Student Society of America or the International Association of Business Communicators provides an opportunity for students to exchange views with public relations specialists and to make professional contacts that may help them find a job in the field. A portfolio of published articles, television or radio programs, slide presentations, and other work is an asset in finding a job. Writing for a school publication or television or radio station provides valuable experience and material for one's portfolio.

Creativity, initiative, good judgment, and the ability to express thoughts clearly and simply are essential. Decision making, problem solving, and research skills are also important.

People who choose public relations as a career need an outgoing personality, self-confidence, an understanding of human psychology, and an enthusiasm for motivating people. They should be competitive yet flexible, and able to function as part of a team.

Some organizations, particularly those with large public relations staffs, have formal training programs for new employees. In smaller organizations, new employees work under the guidance of experienced staff members. Beginners often maintain files of material about company activities, scan newspapers and magazines for appropriate articles to clip, and assemble information for speeches and pamphlets. They may also answer calls from the press and public, work on invitation lists and details for press conferences, or escort visitors and clients. After gaining experience, they write news releases, speeches, and articles for publication or design and carry out public relations programs. Public relations specialists in smaller firms usually get all-around experience, whereas those in larger firms tend to be more specialized.

The Public Relations Society of America accredits public relations specialists who have at least five years of experience in the field and have passed a comprehensive six-hour examination (five hours written, one hour oral). The International Association of Business Communicators also has an accreditation program for professionals in the communications field, including public relations specialists. Those who meet all the requirements of the program earn the Accredited Business Communicator designation. Candidates must have at least five years of experience in a communication field and pass a written and oral examination. They also must submit a portfolio of work samples demonstrating involvement in a range of communication projects and a thorough understanding of communication planning. Employers consider professional recognition through accreditation a sign of competence in this field, and it may be especially helpful in a competitive job market.

Promotion to supervisory jobs may come as public relations specialists show they can handle more demanding assignments. In public relations firms, a beginner may be hired as a research assistant or account assistant and be promoted to account executive, account supervisor, vice president, and eventually senior vice president. A similar career path is followed in corporate public relations, although the titles may differ. Some experienced public relations specialists start their own consulting firms.

Job Outlook

Keen competition will likely continue for entry-level public relations jobs as the number of qualified applicants is expected to exceed the number of job openings. Opportunities should be best for individuals who combine a college degree in journalism, public relations, advertising, or another communications-related field with relevant work experience. Public relations work experience as an intern is an asset in competing for entry-level jobs. Applicants without the appropriate educational background or work experience will face the toughest obstacles.

Employment of public relations specialists is expected to increase faster than the average for all occupations through 2008. The need for good public relations in an increasingly competitive business environment should spur demand for public relations specialists in organizations of all sizes. Employment in public relations firms should grow as firms hire contractors to provide public relations services rather than support full-time staff. In addition to growth, numerous job opportunities should result from the need to replace public relations specialists who take other jobs or who leave the occupation altogether.

Earnings

Median annual earnings for salaried public relations specialists were $34,550 in 1998. The middle 50 percent earned between $26,430 and $46,330; the lowest 10 percent earned less than $21,050, and the top 10 percent earned more than $71,360. Median annual earnings in the industries employing the largest numbers of public relations specialists in 1997 were:

Management and public relations $35,100

State government, except education and hospitals 32,100

Colleges and universities 30,600

According to a salary survey conducted for the Public Relations Society of America, the overall median salary in public relations was about $49,100. Salaries in public relations ranged from less than $22,800 to more than $141,400. There was little difference between the median salaries for account executives in public relations firms, corporations, government, health care, and nonprofit organizations; all ranged from over $32,000 to nearly $34,000.

Public relations specialists in the Federal government in nonsupervisory, supervisory, and managerial positions averaged about $56,700 a year in 1999.

Related Occupations

Public relations specialists create favorable attitudes among various organizations, special interest groups, and the public through effective communication. Other workers with similar jobs include fund raisers; lobbyists; advertising, marketing, and promotion managers; and police officers involved in community relations.

Sources of Additional Information

A comprehensive directory of schools offering degree programs or a sequence of study in public relations, a brochure on careers in public relations, and a $5 brochure entitled *Where Shall I go to Study Advertising and Public Relations* are available from:

- Public Relations Society of America, Inc., 33 Irving Place, New York, NY 10003-2376. Internet: http://www.prsa.org

Career information on public relations in hospitals and other health care settings is available from:

- The Society for Health Care Strategy and Market Development, One North Franklin St., 27th Floor, Chicago, IL 60606. Internet: http://www.shsmd.org

For a list of schools with accredited programs in public relations in their journalism departments, send a stamped self-addressed envelope to:

- The Accrediting Council on Education in Journalism and Mass Communications, University of Kansas School of Journalism, Stauffer Flint Hall, Lawrence, KS 66045. Internet: http://www.ukans.edu/~acejmc

For information on accreditation for public relations specialists, contact:

- International Association of Business Communicators, One Hallidie Plaza, Suite 600, San Francisco, CA 94102. Internet: http://www.iabc.com

Purchasing Managers, Buyers, and Purchasing Agents

(O*NET 13008, 21302, 21305A, and 21308A)

Significant Points

- Computerization has reduced the demand for lower-level buyers.
- About one-half were employed in wholesale trade or manufacturing establishments.

Nature of the Work

Purchasing managers, buyers, and purchasing agents seek to obtain the highest quality merchandise at the lowest possible purchase cost for their employers. In general, *purchasers* buy goods and services for their company or organization, whereas some *buyers* buy items for resale. They determine which commodities or services are best, choose the suppliers of the product or service, negotiate the lowest price, and award contracts that ensure the correct amount of the product or service is received at the appropriate time. In order to accomplish these tasks successfully, purchasing managers, buyers, and purchasing agents study sales records and inventory levels of current stock, identify foreign and domestic suppliers, and keep abreast of changes affecting both the supply of and demand for products and materials for which they are responsible.

Purchasing managers, buyers, and purchasing agents evaluate suppliers based upon price, quality, service support, availability, reliability, and selection. To assist them in their search, they review catalogs, industry periodicals, directories, trade journals, and Internet sites. They research the reputation and history of the suppliers and may advertise anticipated purchase actions in order to solicit bids. At meetings, trade shows, conferences, and visits to suppliers' plants and distribution centers, they examine products and services, assess a supplier's production and distribution capabilities, and discuss other technical and business considerations that influence the purchasing decision. When all the necessary information on suppliers is gathered, orders are placed and contracts are awarded to those suppliers who meet the purchasers' needs. Other specific job duties and responsibilities vary by employer and by the type of commodities or services to be purchased.

Purchasing professionals employed by government agencies or manufacturing firms are usually called purchasing directors, managers, or agents; buyers or industrial buyers; or contract specialists. These workers acquire product materials, intermediate goods, machines, supplies, services, and other materials used in the production of a final product. Some purchasing managers specialize in negotiating and supervising supply contracts and are called contract or supply managers. Purchasing agents and managers obtain items ranging from raw materials, fabricated parts, machinery, and office supplies to construction services and airline tickets. The flow of work—or even the entire production process—can be slowed or halted if the right materials, supplies, or equipment are not on hand when needed. To be effective, purchasing professionals must have a working technical knowledge of the goods or services to be purchased.

In large industrial organizations, a distinction often is drawn between the work of a buyer or purchasing agent and that of a purchasing manager. Purchasing agents and buyers commonly focus on routine purchasing tasks, often specializing in a commodity or group of related commodities (for example, steel, lumber, cotton, grains, fabricated metal products, or petroleum products). The purchaser usually tracks things such as market conditions, price trends, or futures markets. Purchasing managers usually handle the more complex or critical purchases and may supervise a group of purchasing agents handling other goods and services. Whether a person is titled purchasing manager, buyer, or purchasing agent depends more on industry and employer practices than on specific job duties.

Changing business practices have altered the traditional roles of purchasing professionals in many industries. For example, manufacturing companies increasingly involve purchasing professionals at most stages of product development because of their ability to forecast a part's or material's cost, availability, and suitability for its intended purpose. Furthermore, potential problems with the supply of materials may be avoided by consulting the purchasing department in the early stages of product design.

Businesses might also enter into integrated supply contracts. These contracts increase the importance of supplier selection because agreements are larger in scope and longer in duration. Integrated supply incorporates all members of the supply chain including the supplier, transportation companies, and the retailer. A major responsibility of most purchasers is to work out problems that may occur with a supplier because the success of the relationship affects the buying firm's performance.

Purchasing professionals often work closely with other employees in their own organization when deciding on purchases, an arrangement sometimes called team buying. For example, they may discuss the design of custom-made products with company design engineers, quality problems in purchased goods with quality assurance engineers and production supervisors, or shipment problems with managers in the receiving department before submitting an order.

Contract specialists and managers in various levels of government award contracts for an array of items, including office and building supplies, services for the public, and construction projects. They may use sealed bids, but usually they use negotiated agreements for complex items. Increasingly, purchasing professionals in government are placing solicitations for and accepting bids and offers through the Internet. Government purchasing agents and managers must follow strict laws and regulations in their work. These legal requirements occasionally are changed, so agents and contract specialists must stay informed about the latest regulations.

Other professionals, who buy finished goods for resale, are employed by wholesale and retail establishments, where they commonly are referred to as "buyers" or "merchandise managers." Wholesale and retail buyers are an integral part of a complex system of distribution and merchandising that caters to the vast array of consumer needs and desires. Wholesale buyers purchase goods directly from manufacturers or from other wholesale firms for resale to retail firms, commercial establishments, institutions, and other organizations. In retail firms, buyers purchase goods from wholesale firms or directly from manufacturers for resale to the public. Buyers largely determine which products their establishment will sell. Therefore, it is essential that they have the ability to accurately predict what will appeal to consumers. They must constantly stay informed of the latest trends because failure to do so could jeopardize profits and the reputation of their company. Buyers also follow ads in newspapers and other media to check competitors' sales activities and watch general economic conditions to anticipate consumer buying patterns. Buyers working for large and medium-sized firms usually specialize in acquiring one or two lines of merchandise, whereas buyers working for small stores may purchase their complete inventory.

The use of private-label merchandise and the consolidation of buying departments have increased the responsibilities of retail buyers. Private-label merchandise, produced for a particular retailer, requires buyers to work closely with vendors to develop and obtain the desired product. The downsizing and consolidation of

buying departments is also increasing the demands placed on buyers because, although the amount of work remains unchanged, there are fewer people to accomplish it. The result is an increase in the workloads and levels of responsibility.

Many merchandise managers assist in the planning and implementation of sales promotion programs. Working with merchandising executives, they determine the nature of the sale and purchase accordingly. They also work with advertising personnel to create the ad campaign. For example, they may determine the media in which the advertisement will be placed—newspapers, direct mail, television, or some combination of these. In addition, merchandising managers often visit the selling floor to ensure that the goods are properly displayed. Often, assistant buyers are responsible for placing orders and checking shipments.

Computers have a major effect on the jobs of purchasing managers, buyers, and purchasing agents. In manufacturing and service industries, computers handle most of the more routine tasks, enabling purchasing professionals to concentrate mainly on the analytical aspects of the job. Computers are used to obtain instant and accurate product and price listings, track inventory levels, process routine orders, and help determine when to make purchases. Computers also maintain lists of bidders and offers, record the history of supplier performance, and issue purchase orders.

Computerized systems have dramatically simplified many of the routine acquisition functions and improved the efficiency of determining which products are selling. For example, cash registers connected to computers, known as point-of-sale terminals, allow organizations to maintain centralized, up-to-date sales and inventory records. This information can then be used to produce weekly sales reports that reflect the types of products in demand. Buyers also use computers to gain instant access to the specifications for thousands of commodities, inventory records, and their customers' purchase records. Some firms are linked with manufacturers or wholesalers by electronic purchasing systems, the Internet, or extranets. These systems improve the speed for selection and ordering and provide information on availability and shipment, allowing buyers to better concentrate on the selection of goods and suppliers.

Working Conditions

Most purchasing managers, buyers, and purchasing agents work in comfortable, well-lighted offices. They frequently work more than the standard 40-hour week because of special sales, conferences, or production deadlines. Evening and weekend work is also common. For those working in retail trade, this is especially true prior to holiday seasons. Consequently, many retail firms discourage the use of vacation time from late November until early January.

Buyers and merchandise managers often work under great pressure because wholesale and retail stores are so competitive; buyers need physical stamina to keep up with the fast-paced nature of their work.

Many purchasing managers, buyers, and purchasing agents travel at least several days a month. Purchasers for worldwide manufacturing companies and large retailers, and buyers of high fashion may travel outside the United States.

Employment

Purchasing managers, buyers, and purchasing agents held about 547,000 jobs in 1998. About one-half worked in wholesale trade or manufacturing establishments such as distribution centers or factories, and another one-fifth worked in retail trade establishments such as grocery or department stores. The remainder worked mostly in service establishments or different levels of government. A small number were self-employed.

Training, Other Qualifications, and Advancement

Qualified persons usually begin as trainees, purchasing clerks, expediters, junior buyers, or assistant buyers. Retail and wholesale firms prefer to hire applicants who are familiar with the merchandise they sell as well as with wholesaling and retailing practices. Some retail firms promote qualified employees to assistant buyer positions; others recruit and train college graduates as assistant buyers. Most employers use a combination of methods.

Educational requirements tend to vary with the size of the organization. Large stores and distributors, especially those in wholesale and retail trade, prefer applicants who have completed a bachelor's degree program with a business emphasis. Many manufacturing firms tend to put a greater emphasis on formal training. They prefer applicants with a bachelor's or master's degree in business, economics, or technical training such as engineering or one of the applied sciences.

Regardless of academic preparation, new employees must learn the specifics of their employers' businesses. Training periods vary in length, but most last one to five years. In wholesale and retail establishments, most trainees begin by selling merchandise, supervising sales workers, checking invoices on material received, and keeping track of stock on hand (although widespread use of computers has simplified many of these tasks). As they progress, retail trainees are given increased buying-related responsibilities.

In manufacturing, new purchasing employees often are enrolled in company training programs and spend a considerable amount of time learning about company operations and purchasing practices. They work with experienced purchasers to learn about commodities, prices, suppliers, and markets. In addition, they may be assigned to the production planning department to learn about the material requirements system and the inventory system the company uses to keep production and replenishment functions working smoothly.

Purchasing managers, buyers, and purchasing agents must be computer literate, including knowing how to use word processing and spreadsheet software. Other important qualities include the ability to analyze technical data in suppliers' proposals; good communication, negotiation, and math skills; knowledge of supply chain management; and the ability to perform financial analyses.

Persons who wish to become wholesale or retail buyers should be good at planning and decision making and have an interest in merchandising. Anticipating consumer preferences and ensuring that goods are in stock when they are needed require resourcefulness, good judgment, and self-confidence. Buyers must be able to make decisions quickly and take risks. Marketing skills and the ability to identify products that will sell are also very important. Employers often look for leadership ability because buyers spend a large portion of their time supervising assistant buyers and dealing with manufacturers' representatives and store executives.

Experienced buyers may advance by moving to a department that manages a larger volume or by becoming a merchandise manager. Others may go to work in sales for a manufacturer or wholesaler.

An experienced purchasing agent or buyer may become an assistant purchasing manager in charge of a group of purchasing professionals before advancing to purchasing manager, supply manager, or director of materials management. At the top levels, duties may overlap with other management functions such as production, planning, or marketing.

Regardless of industry, continuing education is essential for advancement. Many purchasers participate in seminars offered by professional societies and take college courses in purchasing. Although no national standard exists, professional certification is becoming increasingly important.

In private industry, recognized marks of experience and professional competence are the designations Accredited Purchasing Practitioner (A.P.P.) and Certified Purchasing Manager (C.P.M.), conferred by the National Association of Purchasing Management, and Certified Purchasing Professional (C.P.P.), conferred by the American Purchasing Society. In Federal, State, and local government, the indications of professional competence are Certified Professional Public Buyer (C.P.P.B.) and Certified Public Purchasing Officer (C.P.P.O.), which are conferred by the National Institute of Governmental Purchasing.

Most of these are awarded only after work-related experience and education requirements are met and written or oral exams have been successfully completed.

Job Outlook

Employment of purchasing managers, buyers, and purchasing agents is expected to grow more slowly than average through the year 2008. Demand for these workers will not keep up with the rising level of economic activity because the increasing use of computers has allowed much of the paperwork typically involved in ordering and procuring supplies to be eliminated, reducing the demand for lower level buyers who perform these duties. Also, limited sourcing and long-term contracting have allowed companies to negotiate with fewer suppliers less frequently. Consequently, most job openings will result from the need to replace workers who transfer to other occupations or leave the labor force.

In retail trade, mergers and acquisitions have forced the consolidation of buying departments, eliminating jobs. In addition, larger retail stores are removing their buying departments from geographic markets and centralizing them at their headquarters, eliminating more jobs.

The increased use of credit cards by some employees to purchase supplies without using the services of the procurement or purchasing office, combined with the growing number of buys being made electronically, will restrict demand for purchasing agents within governments and many manufacturing firms.

Persons who have a bachelor's degree in business should have the best chance of obtaining a buying job in wholesale or retail trade or within government. A bachelor's degree combined with industry experience and knowledge of a technical field will be an advantage for those interested in working for a manufacturing or industrial company. Government agencies and larger companies usually require a master's degree in business or public administration for top-level purchasing positions.

Earnings

Median annual earnings of purchasing managers were $41,830 in 1998. The middle 50 percent earned between $29,930 and $63,520 a year. The lowest 10 percent earned less than $22,290, and the highest 10 percent earned more than $86,740 a year. Median annual earnings in the industries employing the largest number of purchasing managers in 1997 were as follows:

Electrical goods	$39,300
Professional and commercial equipment	37,700
Machinery, equipment, and supplies	36,400
Department stores	35,500
Grocery stores	25,900

Median annual earnings for purchasing agents (except wholesale, retail, and farm products) were $38,040 in 1998. The middle 50 percent earned between $29,660 and $49,660 a year. The lowest 10 percent earned less than $23,960, and the highest 10 percent earned more than $74,050 a year. Median annual earnings in the industries employing the largest number of purchasing agents (except wholesale, retail, and farm products) in 1997 were as follows:

Federal government	$47,200
Aircraft and parts	41,100
Electronic components and accessories	36,600
Local government, except education and hospitals	35,300
Hospitals	29,300

Median annual earnings for wholesale and retail buyers (except farm products) were $31,560 in 1998. The middle 50 percent earned between $23,490 and $42,920 a year. The lowest 10 percent earned less than $17,730, and the highest 10 percent earned more than $66,480 a year. Median annual earnings in the industries employing the largest number of wholesale and retail buyers (except farm products) in 1997 were as follows:

Groceries and related products	$36,200
Machinery, equipment, and supplies	29,300
Professional and commercial equipment	28,800
Grocery stores	25,100
Miscellaneous shopping goods stores	24,700

Purchasing managers, buyers, and purchasing agents receive the same benefits package as their coworkers, including vacations, sick leave, life and health insurance, and pension plans. In addition to standard benefits, retail buyers often earn cash bonuses based on their performance and may receive discounts on merchandise they buy from the employer.

Related Occupations

Workers in other occupations who need a knowledge of marketing and the ability to assess demand are advertising, marketing, and public relations managers; insurance sales agents; manufacturers' and wholesale sales representatives; material recording, scheduling, dispatching, and distributing occupations; retail salespersons; sales engineers; and sales managers.

Sources of Additional Information

Further information about education, training, and/or certification for purchasing careers is available from:

- American Purchasing Society, 430 W. Downer Pl., Aurora, IL 60506. Internet: http://www.american-purchasing.com

- National Association of Purchasing Management, P.O. Box 22160, Tempe, AZ 85285-2169. Internet: http://www.napm.org

- National Institute of Governmental Purchasing, Inc., 151 Spring St., Herndon, VA 20170. Internet: http://www.nigp.org

- Federal Acquisition Institute (MVI), Office of Acquisition Policy, General Services Administration, 1800 F St. NW., Room 4017, Washington, DC 20405. Internet: http://www.gsa.gov/staff/v/training.htm

Real Estate Agents and Brokers

(O*NET 43008)

Significant Points

- Real estate sales positions should continue to be relatively easy to obtain due to the large number of people who leave this occupation each year.

- Real estate agents and brokers must be licensed in every State and in the District of Columbia.

Nature of the Work

The purchase or sale of a home or investment property is not only one of the most important financial events in peoples' lives, but also one of the most complex transactions. As a result, people usually seek the help of real estate agents and brokers when buying or selling real estate.

Real estate agents and brokers have a thorough knowledge of the real estate market in their community. They know which neighborhoods will best fit clients' needs and budgets. They are familiar with local zoning and tax laws and know where to obtain financing. Agents and brokers also act as an intermediary in price negotiations between buyers and sellers. Real estate agents are usually independent sales workers who provide their services to a licensed broker on a contract basis. In return, the broker pays the agent a portion of the commission earned from the agent's sale of the property.

Brokers are independent business people who, for a fee, sell real estate owned by others; they also may rent and manage properties for a fee. When selling real estate, brokers arrange for title searches and for meetings between buyers and sellers where details of the transactions are agreed upon and the new owners take possession. A broker's knowledge, resourcefulness, and creativity in arranging favorable financing for the prospective buyer often mean the difference between success and failure in closing a sale. In some cases, brokers and agents assume primary responsibility for closing sales; in others, lawyers or lenders do this. Brokers supervise agents who may have many of the same job duties. Brokers also manage their own offices, advertise properties, and handle other business matters. Some combine other types of work, such as selling insurance or practicing law, with their real estate business.

There is more to an agent or broker's job than just making sales. They must have properties to sell. Consequently, they spend a significant amount of time obtaining listings—owner agreements to place properties for sale with the firm. When listing a property for sale, agents and brokers compare the listed property with similar properties that have recently sold to determine its competitive market price. Once the property is sold, the agent who sold the property and the agent who obtained the listing both receive a portion of the commission. Thus, agents who sell a property they also listed can increase their commission.

Most real estate agents and brokers sell residential property. A small number, usually employed in large or specialized firms, sell commercial, industrial, agricultural, or other types of real estate. Every specialty requires knowledge of that particular type of property and clientele. Selling or leasing business property requires an understanding of leasing practices, business trends, and location needs. Agents who sell or lease industrial properties must know about the region's transportation, utilities, and labor supply. Whatever the type of property, the agent or broker must know how to meet the client's particular requirements.

Before showing residential properties to potential buyers, agents meet with buyers to get a feeling for the type of home the buyers would like. In this prequalifying phase, the agent determines how much buyers can afford to spend. In addition, they usually sign a loyalty contract that states the agent will be the only one to show them houses. An agent or broker uses a computer to generate lists of properties for sale, their locations and descriptions, and available sources of financing. In some cases, agents and brokers use computers to give buyers a virtual tour of properties in which they are interested. Buyers can view interior and exterior images or floor plans without leaving the real estate office.

Agents may meet several times with prospective buyers to discuss and visit available properties. Agents identify and emphasize the most pertinent selling points. To a young family looking for a house, they may emphasize the convenient floor plan, the area's low crime rate, and the proximity to schools and shopping centers. To a potential investor, they may point out the tax advantages of owning a rental property and the ease of finding a renter. If bargaining over price becomes necessary, agents must carefully follow their client's instructions and may have to present counteroffers in order to get the best possible price.

When both parties have signed the contract, the real estate broker or agent must see to it that all special terms of the contract are met before the closing date. For example, if the seller agrees to a home inspection or a termite and radon inspection, the agent must make sure this is done. Also, if the seller agrees to any repairs, the broker or agent must see that they are made. Increasingly, brokers and agents handle environmental problems by making sure the properties they sell meet environmental regulations. For example, they may be responsible for dealing with problems such as lead paint on the walls. While loan officers, attorneys, or other persons handle many details, the agent must check to make sure that they are completed.

Working Conditions

Increasingly, real estate agents and brokers work out of their homes instead of real estate offices because of advances in telecommunications and the ability to retrieve data on properties over the Internet. Even with this convenience, much of their time is spent away from their desk—showing properties to customers, analyzing properties for sale, meeting with prospective clients, or researching the state of the market.

Agents and brokers often work more than a standard 40-hour week; nearly 1 out of every 4 worked 50 hours or more a week in 1998. They often work evenings and weekends and are always on call to suit the needs of clients. Business is usually slower during the winter season. Although the hours are long and often irregular, most agents and brokers also have the freedom to determine their own schedule. Consequently, they can arrange their work so they can have time off when they want it.

Employment

Real estate agents and brokers held about 347,000 jobs in 1998. Many worked part time, combining their real estate activities with other careers. More than two-thirds of real estate agents and brokers were self-employed. Real estate is sold in all areas, but employment is concentrated in large urban areas and in smaller, rapidly growing communities.

Most real estate firms are relatively small; indeed, some are a one-person business. Some large real estate firms have several hundred agents operating out of many branch offices. Many brokers have franchise agreements with national or regional real estate organizations. Under this type of arrangement, the broker pays a fee in exchange for the privilege of using the more widely known name of the parent organization. Although franchised brokers often receive help training salespeople and running their offices, they bear the ultimate responsibility for the success or failure of their firm.

Real estate agents and brokers are older, on average, than most other workers. Historically, many homemakers and retired persons were attracted to real estate sales by the flexible and part time work schedules characteristic of this field. They could enter, leave, and later reenter the occupation, depending on the strength of the real estate market, family responsibilities, or other personal circumstances. Recently, however, the attractiveness of part-time work has

declined, as increasingly complex legal and technological requirements raise startup costs associated with becoming an agent.

Training, Other Qualifications, and Advancement

In every State and in the District of Columbia, real estate agents and brokers must be licensed. Prospective agents must be a high school graduate, at least 18 years old, and pass a written test. The examination—more comprehensive for brokers than for agents—includes questions on basic real estate transactions and laws affecting the sale of property. Most States require candidates for the general sales license to complete between 30 and 90 hours of classroom instruction. Those seeking a broker's license need between 60 and 90 hours of formal training and a specific amount of experience selling real estate, usually one to three years. Some States waive the experience requirements for the broker's license for applicants who have a bachelor's degree in real estate.

State licenses typically must be renewed every one or two years, usually without reexamination. However, many States require continuing education for license renewal. Prospective agents and brokers should contact the real estate licensing commission of the State in which they wish to work to verify exact licensing requirements.

As real estate transactions have become more legally complex, many firms have turned to college graduates to fill positions. A large number of agents and brokers have some college training. College courses in real estate, finance, business administration, statistics, economics, law, and English are helpful. For those who intend to start their own company, business courses such as marketing and accounting are as important as those in real estate or finance.

Personality traits are equally as important as academic background. Brokers look for applicants who possess a pleasant personality, honesty, and a neat appearance. Maturity, tact, trust-worthiness, and enthusiasm for the job are required in order to motivate prospective customers in this highly competitive field. Agents should also be well organized, detail oriented, and have a good memory for names, faces, and business details.

Those interested in jobs as real estate agents often begin in their own communities. Their knowledge of local neighborhoods is a clear advantage. Under the direction of an experienced agent, beginners learn the practical aspects of the job, including the use of computers to locate or list available properties and identify sources of financing.

Many firms offer formal training programs for both beginners and experienced agents. Larger firms usually offer more extensive programs for both beginners and experienced agents. Larger firms usually offer more extensive programs than smaller firms do. More than 1,000 universities, colleges, and junior colleges offer courses in real estate. At some, a student can earn an associate or bachelor's degree with a major in real estate; several offer advanced degrees. Many local real estate associations that are members of the National Association of Realtors sponsor courses covering the fundamentals and legal aspects of the field. Advanced courses in mortgage financing, property development and management, and other subjects are also available through various affiliates of the National Association of Realtors.

Advancement opportunities for agents may take the form of higher commission rates. As agents gain knowledge and expertise, they become more efficient in closing a greater number of transactions and increase their earnings. Experienced agents can advance in many large firms to sales or general manager. Persons who have received their broker's license may open their own offices. Others with experience and training in estimating property value may become real estate appraisers, and people familiar with operating and maintaining rental properties may become property managers. Experienced agents and brokers with a thorough knowledge of business conditions and property values in their localities may enter mortgage financing or real estate investment counseling.

Job Outlook

Employment of real estate agents and brokers is expected to grow about as fast as the average for all occupations through the year 2008. However, a large number of job openings will arise due to replacement needs. Each year, thousands of jobs will become available as workers transfer to other occupations or leave the labor force. Not everyone is successful in this highly competitive field; many beginners become discouraged by their inability to get listings and to close a sufficient number of sales. Well-trained, ambitious people who enjoy selling should have the best chance for success.

Increasing use of electronic information technology will increase the productivity of agents and brokers as computers, faxes, modems, and databases become commonplace. Some real estate companies use computer-generated images to show houses to customers without leaving the office. Internet sites contain information on vast numbers of homes for sale, available to anyone. These devices enable an agent to serve a greater number of customers. Use of this technology may eliminate some marginal agents such as those practicing real estate part time or between jobs. These workers will not be able to compete as easily with full-time agents who have invested in this technology. Changing legal requirements, like disclosure laws, may also dissuade some that are not serious about practicing full time from continuing to work part time.

Another factor expected to impact the need for agents and brokers is the ability of prospective customers to conduct their own searches for properties that meet their criteria by accessing real estate information on the Internet. While they won't be able to conduct the entire real estate transaction on-line, it does allow the prospective buyer the convenience of making a more informed choice of properties to visit, as well as the ability to find out about financing, inspections, and appraisals.

Employment growth in this field will stem primarily from increased demand for home purchases and rental units. Shifts in the age distribution of the population over the next decade will result in a growing number of persons in the prime working ages with careers and family responsibilities. This is the most geographically mobile group in our society, and the one that traditionally makes most of the home purchases. As their incomes rise, they also may be expected to invest in additional real estate.

Employment of real estate agents and brokers is very sensitive to swings in the economy. During periods of declining economic activity and tight credit, the volume of sales and the resulting demand for sales workers falls. During these periods, the earnings of agents and brokers decline, and many work fewer hours or leave the occupation altogether.

Earnings

The median annual earnings of salaried real estate agents, including commission, in 1998 were $28,020. The middle 50 percent earned between $19,060 and $46,360 a year. The lowest 10 percent earned less than $13,800, and the highest 10 percent earned more than $83,330 a year. Median annual earnings in the industries employing the largest number of salaried real estate agents in 1997 were as follows:

Residential building construction	$32,300
Real estate agents and managers	25,500
Real estate operators and lessors	19,100

Median annual earnings of salaried real estate brokers, including commission, in 1998 were $45,640. The middle 50 percent earned between $28,680 and $80,070 a year.

Commissions on sales are the main source of earnings of real estate agents and brokers. The rate of commission varies according to agent and broker agreement, the type of property, and its value. The percentage paid on the sale of farm and commercial properties or unimproved land is usually higher than the percentage paid for selling a home.

Commissions may be divided among several agents and brokers. The broker and the agent in the firm who obtained the listing usually share their commission when the property is sold; the broker and the agent in the firm who made the sale also usually share their part of the commission. Although an agent's share varies greatly from one firm to another, often it is about half of the total amount received by the firm. Agents who both list and sell a property maximize their commission.

Income usually increases as an agent gains experience, but individual ability, economic conditions, and the type and location of the property also affect earnings. Sales workers who are active in community organizations and local real estate associations can broaden their contacts and increase their earnings. A beginner's earnings are often irregular because a few weeks or even months may go by without a sale. Although some brokers allow an agent a drawing account against future earnings, this practice is not usual with new employees. The beginner, therefore, should have enough money to live on for about six months or until commissions increase.

Related Occupations

Selling expensive items such as homes requires maturity, tact, and a sense of responsibility. Other sales workers who find these character traits important in their work include motor vehicle sales workers; securities, commodities, and financial services sales representatives; insurance sales agents; and manufacturers' and wholesale sales representatives.

Sources of Additional Information

Information on license requirements for real estate agents and brokers is available from most local real estate organizations or from the State real estate commission or board.

For more information about opportunities in real estate, contact:

- National Association of Realtors, Realtor Information Center, 430 North Michigan Ave., Chicago, IL 60611.

Receptionists

(O*NET 55305)

Significant Points

- Numerous job openings should arise due to employment growth and high turnover.

- A high school diploma or its equivalent is the most common educational requirement.

- Because receptionists deal directly with the public, a professional appearance and pleasant personality are imperative.

Nature of the Work

Receptionists are charged with a responsibility that may have a lasting impact on the success of an organization—making a good first impression. These workers are often the first representatives of an organization a visitor encounters, so they need to be courteous, professional, and helpful. Receptionists answer telephones, route calls, greet visitors, respond to inquiries from the public and provide information about the organization. In addition, receptionists contribute to the security of an organization by helping to monitor the access of visitors.

Whereas some tasks are common to most receptionists, the specific responsibilities of receptionists vary depending upon the type of establishment in which they work. For example, receptionists in hospitals and doctors' offices may gather personal and financial information and direct patients to the proper waiting rooms. In beauty or hair salons, however, they arrange appointments, direct customers to the hairstylist, and may serve as cashier. In factories, large corporations, and government offices, they may provide identification cards and arrange for escorts to take visitors to the proper office. Those working for bus and train companies respond to inquiries about departures, arrivals, stops, and other related matters.

Increasingly, receptionists use multiline telephone systems, personal computers, and fax machines. Despite the widespread use of automated answering systems or voice mail, many receptionists still take messages and inform other employees of visitors' arrivals or cancellation of an appointment. When they are not busy with callers, most receptionists are expected to perform a variety of office duties including opening and sorting mail, collecting and dis-

tributing parcels, making fax transmittals and deliveries, updating appointment calendars, preparing travel vouchers, and performing basic bookkeeping, word processing, and filing.

Working Conditions

Most receptionists work in areas that are clean, well lit, and relatively quiet. Most greet customers and visitors and usually work in highly visible areas that are furnished to make a good impression.

Although most receptionists work a standard 40-hour week, some work part time. The work performed by these employees may be repetitious and stressful. For example, many receptionists spend all day answering telephones while performing additional clerical or secretarial tasks. Additional stress is caused by technology that enables management to electronically monitor use of computer systems, tape record telephone calls, or limit the time spent on each call. Prolonged exposure to a video display terminal may lead to eyestrain for the many receptionists who work with computers.

Employment

Receptionists held about 1.3 million jobs in 1998, accounting for more than two-thirds of all information clerk jobs. More than two-thirds of all receptionists worked in services industries, and almost half of these were employed in the health services industry in doctors' and dentists' offices, hospitals, nursing homes, urgent care centers, surgical centers, and clinics. Manufacturing, wholesale and retail trade, government, and real estate industries also employed large numbers of receptionists. About 3 of every 10 receptionists worked part time.

Training, Other Qualifications, and Advancement

Although hiring requirements for receptionists vary from industry to industry, a high school diploma or its equivalent is the most common educational requirement. Increasingly, familiarity or experience with computers and good interpersonal skills is often equally important to employers.

Receptionists deal directly with the public, so a professional appearance and pleasant personality are important. A clear speaking voice and fluency in the English language also are essential because these employees frequently use the telephone or public address systems. Good spelling and computer literacy are often needed, particularly because most work involves considerable computer use.

Receptionists usually receive on-the-job training, which may include procedures for greeting visitors, operating telephone and computer systems, and distributing mail, fax, and parcel deliveries. Some employers look for applicants who already possess certain skills, such as prior computer and word processing experience or previous formal education. Most receptionists continue to receive instruction on new procedures and company policies after their initial training ends.

Advancement for receptionists usually comes about either by transfer to a position with more responsibilities or by promotion to a supervisory position. Most companies fill office and administrative support supervisory and managerial positions by promoting individuals within their organization, so those who acquire additional skills, experience, and training improve their advancement opportunities. A receptionist may advance to a better paying job as a secretary or administrative assistant.

Job Outlook

Employment of receptionists is expected to grow faster than the average for all occupations through 2008. This increase will result from rapid growth in services industries—including physician's offices, law firms, temporary help agencies, and consulting firms—where most receptionists are employed. In addition, high turnover in this large occupation will create numerous openings as receptionists transfer to other occupations or leave the labor force altogether. Opportunities should be best for persons with a wide range of clerical skills and experience.

Technology should have conflicting effects on the demand for receptionists. The increasing use of voice mail and other telephone automation reduces the need for receptionists by allowing one receptionist to perform work that formerly required several receptionists. However, increasing use of technology also has caused a consolidation of clerical responsibilities and growing demand for workers with diverse clerical skills. Because receptionists may perform a wide variety of clerical tasks, they should continue to be in demand. Further, receptionists perform many tasks that are of an interpersonal nature and are not easily automated, ensuring continued demand for their services in a variety of establishments. Receptionists tend to be less subject to layoffs during recessions than other clerical workers because establishments need someone to perform their duties even during economic downturns.

Earnings

Earnings vary widely, but the median annual earnings of receptionists in 1998 were $18,620. In early 1999, the Federal government typically paid salaries ranging from $16,400 to $18,100 a year to beginning receptionists with a high school diploma or six months of experience. The average annual salary for all receptionists employed by the Federal government was about $22,700 in 1999.

Related Occupations

A number of other workers deal with the public, receive and provide information, or direct people to others who can assist them. Among these are dispatchers, security guards, bank tellers, guides, telephone operators, records processing clerks, counter and rental clerks, survey workers, and ushers and lobby attendants.

Sources of Additional Information

State employment offices can provide information on job openings for receptionists.

Records Processing Occupations

Significant Points

- Most jobs require only a high school diploma.

- Numerous job opportunities should arise due to high turnover in this occupation.

- Little or no change is expected in overall employment, reflecting the spread of computers and other office automation as well as organizational restructuring.

Nature of the Work

Without the assistance of workers in records processing occupations, many organizations would be lost. These workers maintain, update, and process a variety of records, ranging from payrolls to information on the shipment of goods or bank statements. They ensure that other workers get paid on time, customers' questions are answered, and records are kept of all transactions. (Additional information about specific records processing occupations appears in separate statements that follow this introductory statement.)

Depending on their specific titles, these workers perform a wide variety of record keeping duties. *Billing clerks and billing machine operators*, for example, prepare bills and invoices. *Bookkeeping, accounting, and auditing clerks* maintain financial data in computer and paper files. *Brokerage clerks* prepare and maintain the records generated when stocks, bonds, and other types of investments are traded. *File clerks* store and retrieve various kinds of office information for use by staff members. *Human resources clerks* maintain employee records. *Library assistants and bookmobile drivers* assist library patrons. *Order clerks* process incoming orders for goods and services. *Payroll and timekeeping clerks* compute wages for payroll records and review employee timecards. *Statement clerks* prepare monthly statements for bank customers. Other records processing clerks include *advertising clerks* (who receive orders for classified advertising for newspapers or magazines, prepare copy according to customer specifications, and verify conformance of published ads to specifications for billing purposes) and *correspondence clerks* (who reply to customers regarding damage claims, delinquent accounts, incorrect billings, complaints of unsatisfactory service, and requests for merchandise exchanges or returns).

The duties of records processing clerks vary with the size of the firm. In a small business, a bookkeeping clerk may handle all financial records and transactions, as well as payroll and personnel duties. A large firm, on the other hand, may employ specialized accounting, payroll, and human resources clerks. In general, however, clerical staffs in firms of all sizes increasingly perform a broader variety of tasks than in the past. This is especially true for clerical occupations involving accounting work. As the growing use of computers enables bookkeeping, accounting, and auditing clerks to

become more productive, these workers may assume billing, payroll, and timekeeping duties.

Another change in these occupations is the growing use of financial software to enter and manipulate data. Computer programs automatically perform calculations on data that were previously calculated manually. Computers also enable clerks to access data within files more quickly than the former method of reviewing stacks of paper. Nevertheless, most workers still keep backup paper records for research, auditing, and reference purposes.

Despite the growing use of automation, interaction with the public and coworkers remains a basic part of the job for many records processing clerks. Payroll clerks, for example, answer questions concerning employee benefits; bookmobile drivers help patients in nursing homes and hospitals select books; and order clerks call customers to verify special mailing instructions.

Working Conditions

With the exception of library assistants and bookmobile drivers, records processing clerks typically are employed in an office environment. Most work alongside other clerical workers, but some records processing clerks work in centralized units away from the front office.

Because the majority of records processing clerks use computers on a daily basis, these workers may experience eye and muscle strain, backaches, headaches, and repetitive motion injuries. Also, clerks who review detailed data may have to sit for extended periods of time. Although the work does not require heavy lifting, file clerks and library assistants spend a lot of time on their feet and frequently stoop, bend, and reach. Finally, bookmobile drivers must maneuver large vehicles in all kinds of traffic and weather conditions and may also be responsible for the maintenance of the bookmobile.

Most records processing clerks work regular business hours. Library assistants may work evenings and weekends, but those employed in school libraries usually work only during the school year. Accounting clerks may work longer hours to meet deadlines at the end of the fiscal year, during tax time, or when monthly and yearly accounting audits are performed. Billing, bookkeeping, and accounting clerks in hotels, restaurants, and stores may work overtime during peak holiday and vacation seasons. Similarly, order clerks in retail establishments typically work overtime during these seasons. Brokerage clerks may also have to work overtime if there is a high volume of activity in the stock or bond market.

Employment

Records processing clerks held more than 3.7 million jobs in 1998. The following table shows employment in individual clerical occupations:

Bookkeeping, accounting, and auditing clerks 2,078,000

Billing clerks and billing machine operators 449,000

Order clerks 362,000

File clerks 272,000

Payroll and timekeeping clerks 172,000

Library assistants and bookmobile drivers 127,000

Human resources clerks 142,000

Brokerage and statement clerks 92,000

Correspondence clerks 25,000

Advertising clerks 14,000

These workers are employed in virtually every industry. The largest number of records processing clerks work for firms providing health, business, and other types of services. Many also work in trade; finance, insurance, and real estate; manufacturing; and government.

Training, Other Qualifications, and Advancement

Employers typically require applicants to have at least a high school diploma or its equivalent. Although many employers prefer to hire records clerks with a higher level of education, it is only required in a few records processing occupations. For example, brokerage firms usually seek college graduates for brokerage clerk jobs, and order clerks in high-technology firms often need to understand scientific and mechanical processes, which may require some college education. Regardless of the type of work, most employers prefer workers who are computer-literate. Knowledge of word processing and spreadsheet software is especially valuable, as are experience working in an office and good interpersonal skills.

Records processing clerks often learn the skills they need in high schools, business schools, and community colleges. Business education programs offered by these institutions typically include courses in typing, word processing, shorthand, business communications, records management, and office systems and procedures. Specialized order clerks in technical positions obtain their training from technical institutes and two- and four-year colleges.

Some entrants into records processing occupations are college graduates with degrees in business, finance, or liberal arts. Although a degree is rarely required, many graduates accept entry-level clerical positions to get into a particular company or to enter the finance or accounting field with the hope of being promoted to professional or managerial positions. Some companies, such as brokerage and accounting firms, have a set plan of advancement that tracks college graduates from entry-level clerical jobs into managerial positions. Workers with college degrees are likely to start at higher salaries and advance more easily than those without degrees.

Once hired, records processing clerks usually receive on-the-job training. Under the guidance of a supervisor or other senior worker, new employees learn company procedures. Some formal classroom training may also be necessary, such as training in specific computer software.

Records processing clerks must be careful, orderly, and detail-oriented in order to avoid making errors and to recognize errors made by others. These workers should also be discreet and trustworthy because they frequently come in contact with confidential material. Additionally, payroll clerks, billing clerks, and bookkeeping, accounting, and auditing clerks should have a strong aptitude for

numbers. Because statement clerks have access to confidential financial information, these workers must be bonded. Many bookmobile drivers are now required to have a commercial driver's license.

Records processing clerks usually advance by taking on more duties in the same occupation for higher pay or transferring to a closely related occupation. For example, some order clerks use their experience to move into sales positions. Most companies fill office and administrative support supervisory and managerial positions by promoting individuals from within their organizations, so information clerks who acquire additional skills, experience, and training improve their advancement opportunities. With appropriate experience and education, some clerks may become accountants; personnel specialists; securities, commodities, and financial services sales representatives; or librarians.

Job Outlook

Little or no change is expected in employment of records processing clerks through 2008. Despite continued growth in the volume of business transactions, rising productivity stemming from the spread of office automation, as well as organizational restructuring, will adversely affect demand for records processing clerks. Turnover in this very large occupation, however, places it among those occupations providing the most job openings. As a result, opportunities should be plentiful for full-time, part-time, and seasonal employment, as records processing clerks transfer to other occupations or leave the labor force.

Many record clerk jobs have already become heavily automated. Productivity has increased significantly, as workers use personal computers instead of more time-consuming equipment such as typewriters, adding machines, and calculators. The growing use of bar code readers, point-of-sale terminals, and optical scanners also reduces much of the data entry handled by records processing clerks. Additionally, managers and professionals now do much of their own clerical work, using computers to access, create, and store data directly in their computer systems. The growing use of local area networks is also facilitating electronic data interchange—the sending of data from computer to computer—abolishing the need for clerks to reenter the data. To further eliminate duplicate functions, many large companies are consolidating their clerical operations in a central office where accounting, billing, personnel, and payroll functions are performed for all offices—main and satellite—within the organization.

Despite the spread of automation and organizational restructuring, average or faster-than-average job growth is projected for some records processing clerks, including billing clerks, brokerage clerks, library assistants, and bookmobile drivers.

Earnings

Salaries of records processing clerks vary considerably. The region of the country, size of city, and type and size of establishment all influence salary levels. The level of industry or technical expertise required and the complexity and uniqueness of a clerk's responsibilities may also affect earnings. Median annual earnings of full-time records processing clerks in 1998 are shown in the following table:

Brokerage clerks $27,920

Payroll and timekeeping clerks 24,560

Human resources clerks 24,360

Bookkeeping, accounting, and auditing clerks 23,190

Billing clerks 22,670

Correspondence clerks 22,270

Order clerks 21,550

Billing machine operators 20,560

Advertising clerks 20,550

Statement clerks 18,640

Library assistants and bookmobile drivers 16,980

File clerks 16,830

In the Federal government, records processing clerks with a high school diploma or clerical experience typically started at $18,400 a year in 1999. Beginning salaries were slightly higher in areas where the prevailing local pay level was higher. The average salary for all human resources clerks employed by the Federal Government was $29,500 in 1999.

Related Occupations

Today, most records processing clerks enter data into a computer system and perform basic analysis of the data. Other clerical workers who enter and manipulate data include bank tellers, statistical clerks, receiving clerks, medical record clerks, hotel and motel clerks, credit clerks, and reservation and transportation ticket agents.

Sources of Additional Information

State employment service offices can provide information about job openings for records processing occupations.

Billing Clerks and Billing Machine Operators

(O*NET 55344 and 56002)

Significant Points

- Most jobs require only a high school diploma.
- Numerous job opportunities should arise due to high turnover in this occupation.

Nature of the Work

Billing clerks keep records, calculate charges, and maintain files of payments made for goods or services. Billing machine operators run machines that generate bills, statements, and invoices.

Billing clerks review purchase orders, bills of lading, sales tickets, hospital records, or charge slips to calculate the total amount due from a customer. Calculating the charges for an individual's hospital stay may require a letter to an insurance company; a clerk com-

puting trucking rates for machine parts may consult a rate book. In accounting, law, consulting, and similar firms, billing clerks calculate client fees based on the actual time required to perform the task. They keep track of the accumulated hours and dollar amounts to charge to each job, the type of job performed for a customer, and the percentage of work completed.

After billing clerks review all necessary information, they compute the charges using calculators or computers. They then prepare itemized statements, bills, or invoices used for billing and record keeping purposes, depending on the organization's needs. In one organization, the clerk might prepare a bill containing the amount due and date and type of service; in another, the clerk would produce a detailed invoice with codes for all goods and services provided. This latter form might list items sold, credit terms, date of shipment or dates services were provided, a salesperson's or doctor's identification if necessary, and the sales total.

After entering all information, *billing machine operators* run off the bill to send to the customer. Computers and specialized billing software allow many clerks to calculate charges and prepare bills in one step. Computer packages prompt clerks to enter data from handwritten forms and manipulate the necessary entries of quantities, labor, and rates to be charged. Billing clerks verify the entry of information and check for errors before the computer prints the bill. After the bills are printed, billing clerks check them again for accuracy.

Working Conditions

Billing clerks and billing machine operators typically are employed in an office environment. Most work alongside other clerical workers, but some work in centralized units away from the front office. Because the majority of billing clerks and billing machine operators use computers on a daily basis, these workers may experience eye and muscle strain, backaches, headaches, and repetitive motion injuries. Also, clerks who review detailed data may have to sit for extended periods of time. Most billing clerks and billing machine operators work regular business hours. Billing clerks in hotels, restaurants, and stores may work overtime during peak holiday and vacation seasons.

Employment

In 1998, billing clerks held about 342,000 jobs, and billing machine operators held about 107,000 jobs. One-third of the billing clerks' jobs were in health services, mostly in physicians' offices. Transportation and wholesale trade industries each accounted for 1 out of 10 jobs. Most of the remaining jobs were found in manufacturing or retail trade.

Wholesale and retail trade establishments provided about one-third of all billing machine operator jobs; service establishments, including health services, provided another third. Of the remaining jobs, most were found in banks and other financial institutions.

Training, Other Qualifications, and Advancement

Employers typically require applicants to have at least a high school diploma or its equivalent. Most employers prefer workers who are computer-literate. Knowledge of word processing and spreadsheet

software is especially valuable, as are experience working in an office and good interpersonal skills.

Billing clerks and billing machine operators often learn the skills they need in high schools, business schools, and community colleges. Business education programs offered by these institutions typically include courses in typing, word processing, shorthand, business communications, records management, and office systems and procedures.

Some entrants are college graduates with degrees in business, finance, or liberal arts. Although a degree is rarely required, many graduates accept entry-level clerical positions to get into a particular company or to enter the finance or accounting field with the hope of being promoted to professional or managerial positions. Workers with college degrees are likely to start at higher salaries and advance more easily than those without degrees.

Once hired, billing clerks and billing machine operators usually receive on-the-job training. Under the guidance of a supervisor or other senior worker, new employees learn company procedures. Some formal classroom training may also be necessary, such as training in specific computer software.

Billing clerks and billing machine operators must be careful, orderly, and detail-oriented in order to avoid making errors and to recognize errors made by others. These workers should also be discreet and trustworthy because they frequently come in contact with confidential material. Additionally, clerks should have a strong aptitude for numbers.

Billing clerks and billing machine operators usually advance by taking on more duties in the same occupation for higher pay or transferring to a closely related occupation. Most companies fill office and administrative support supervisory and managerial positions by promoting individuals from within their organizations, so those who acquire additional skills, experience, and training improve their advancement opportunities.

Job Outlook

Job openings for those seeking work as billing clerks or billing machine operators are expected to be numerous through the year 2008. Despite the lack of rapid employment growth, many job openings will occur as workers transfer to other occupations or leave the labor force. Turnover in this occupation is relatively high, which is characteristic of an entry-level occupation requiring only a high school diploma.

Employment of billing clerks is expected to grow about as fast as the average for all occupations through the year 2008. A growing economy and increased demand for billing services will result in more business transactions. Rising worker productivity as computers manage more account information will not keep employment from rising. More complex billing applications will increasingly require workers with greater technical expertise.

Employment of billing machine operators, on the other hand, is expected to decline through the year 2008. More advanced machines and computers will continue to replace billing machines, enabling billing clerks to perform the jobs formerly done by billing machine operators. In some organizations, productivity gains from billing software will increasingly allow accounting clerks to take over the responsibilities of billing clerks and billing machine operators.

Earnings

Salaries of billing clerks and billing machine operators vary considerably. The region of the country, size of city, and type and size of establishment all influence salary levels. The level of industry or technical expertise required and the complexity and uniqueness of responsibilities may also affect earnings. Median annual earnings for those working full time in 1998 were as follows:

Billing clerks $22,670

Billing machine operators 20,560

Related Occupations

Today, most clerks enter data into a computer system and perform basic analysis of the data. Other clerical workers who enter and manipulate data include bank tellers, statistical clerks, receiving clerks, medical records clerks, hotel and motel clerks, credit clerks, and reservation and transportation ticket agents.

Sources of Additional Information

State employment service offices can provide information about job openings for the occupation.

Bookkeeping, Accounting, and Auditing Clerks

(O*NET 49023B, 55338A, and 55338B)

Nature of the Work

Bookkeeping, accounting, and auditing clerks are an organization's financial record keepers. They compute, classify, record, and verify numerical data to develop and maintain financial records.

In small establishments, *bookkeeping clerks* handle all aspects of financial transactions. They record debits and credits, compare current and past balance sheets, summarize details of separate ledgers, and prepare reports for supervisors and managers. They may also prepare bank deposits by compiling data from cashiers, verifying and balancing receipts, and sending cash, checks, or other forms of payment to the bank.

In large offices and accounting departments, *accounting clerks* have more specialized tasks. Their titles often reflect the type of accounting they do, such as accounts payable clerk or accounts receivable clerk. In addition, responsibilities vary by level of experience. Entry-level accounting clerks post details of transactions, total accounts, and compute interest charges. They may also monitor loans and accounts to ensure that payments are up to date.

More advanced accounting clerks may total, balance, and reconcile billing vouchers; ensure completeness and accuracy of data on accounts; and code documents according to company procedures. They post transactions in journals and on computer files and update these files when needed. Senior clerks also review computer printouts against manually maintained journals and make necessary corrections. They may also review invoices and statements to ensure that all information is accurate and complete, and reconcile computer reports with operating reports.

Auditing clerks verify records of transactions posted by other workers. They check figures, postings, and documents for correct entry, mathematical accuracy, and proper codes. They also correct or note errors for accountants or other workers to adjust.

As organizations continue to computerize their financial records, many bookkeeping, accounting, and auditing clerks use specialized accounting software on personal computers. They increasingly post charges to accounts on computer spreadsheets and databases, as manual posting to general ledgers is becoming obsolete. These workers now enter information from receipts or bills into computers, which is then stored either electronically, as computer printouts, or both. Widespread use of computers has also enabled bookkeeping, accounting, and auditing clerks to take on additional responsibilities, such as payroll, timekeeping, and billing.

Employment

Bookkeeping, accounting, and auditing clerks held about 2.1 million jobs in 1998. About 25 percent worked in wholesale and retail trade, and 16 percent were in organizations providing business, health, and social services. Approximately 1 out of 3 of bookkeeping, accounting, and auditing clerks worked part time in 1998.

Job Outlook

Virtually all job openings for bookkeeping, accounting, and auditing clerks through 2008 will stem from replacement needs. Each year, numerous jobs will become available, as these clerks transfer to other occupations or leave the labor force. Although turnover is lower than among other record clerks, the large size of the occupation ensures plentiful job openings, including many opportunities for temporary and part-time work.

Employment of bookkeeping, accounting, and auditing clerks is expected to decline through 2008. Although a growing economy will result in more financial transactions and other activities that require these clerical workers, the continuing spread of office automation will lift worker productivity and contribute to employment decline. In addition, organizations of all sizes will continue to consolidate various record keeping functions, thus reducing the demand for these clerks.

Brokerage Clerks and Statement Clerks

(O*NET 53126 and 53128)

Significant Points

- Some of these jobs require only a high school diploma, while others are considered entry-level positions for which a bachelor's degree is needed.

- Employment of brokerage clerks is expected to increase faster than the average for all occupations.

Nature of the Work

Brokerage clerks perform a number of different jobs with wide ranging responsibilities, but all involve computing and recording data on securities transactions. Brokerage clerks may also contact customers, take orders, and inform clients of changes to their accounts. Some of these jobs are more clerical and require only a high school diploma, while others are considered entry-level positions for which a bachelor's degree is needed. Brokerage clerks, who work in the operations departments of securities firms, on trading floors, and in branch offices, are also called margin clerks, dividend clerks, transfer clerks, and broker's assistants.

The broker's assistant, also called sales assistant, is the most common type of brokerage clerk. These workers typically assist two brokers, for whom they take calls from clients, write up order tickets, process the paperwork for opening and closing accounts, record a client's purchases and sales, and inform clients of changes in their accounts. All brokers' assistants must be knowledgeable about investment products so they can clearly communicate with clients. Those with a "Series 7" license can make recommendations to clients at the instruction of the broker. The Series 7 license is issued to securities and commodities sales representatives by the National Association of Securities Dealers and allows them to provide advice on securities to the public.

Brokerage clerks in the operations areas of securities firms perform many duties to facilitate the sale and purchase of stocks, bonds, commodities, and other kinds of investments. These clerks produce the necessary records of all transactions that occur in their area of the business. Job titles for many of these clerks depend upon the type of work they perform. Purchase-and-sale clerks, for example, match orders to buy with orders to sell. They balance and verify stock trades by comparing the records of the selling firm to those of the buying firm. Dividend clerks ensure timely payments of stock or cash dividends to clients of a particular brokerage firm. Transfer clerks execute customer requests for changes to security registration and examine stock certificates for adherence to banking regulations. Receive-and-deliver clerks facilitate the receipt and delivery of securities among firms and institutions. Margin clerks post accounts and monitor activity in customers' accounts to ensure that clients make payments and stay within legal boundaries concerning stock purchases.

Technology is changing the nature of many of these workers' jobs. A significant and growing number of brokerage clerks use custom-designed software programs to process transactions more quickly. Only a few customized accounts are still handled manually.

Statement clerks assemble, verify, and send bank statements every month. In many banks, statement clerks are called statement operators because they spend much of their workday running sophisticated, high-speed machines. These machines fold computer-printed statements, collate those longer than one page, insert statements and canceled checks into envelopes, and seal and weigh them for postage. Statement clerks load the machine with statements, canceled checks, and envelopes. They then monitor the equipment and correct minor problems. For more serious problems, they call repair personnel.

In banks that do not have such machines, statement clerks perform all operations manually. They may also be responsible for verifying signatures and checking for missing information on checks, placing canceled checks into trays, and retrieving them to send with the statements. In a growing number of banks, only the statement is printed and sent to the account holder. The canceled checks are not returned; this is known as check truncation.

Statement clerks are employed primarily by large banks. In smaller banks, a teller or bookkeeping clerk, who performs other duties during the rest of the month, usually handles the statement clerk's function. Some small banks send their statement information to larger banks for processing, printing, and mailing.

Working Conditions

Brokerage and statement clerks typically are employed in an office environment. Most work alongside other clerical workers, but some records processing clerks work in centralized units away from the front office. Because the majority of clerks use computers on a daily basis, these workers may experience eye and muscle strain, backaches, headaches, and repetitive motion injuries. Also, clerks who review detailed data may have to sit for extended periods of time. Most clerks work regular business hours. Brokerage clerks may have to work overtime if there is a high volume of activity in the stock or bond market.

Employment

Brokerage clerks held about 77,000 jobs in 1998, and statement clerks held about 16,000 jobs. Brokerage clerks work in firms that sell securities and commodities. Banking institutions employed almost all statement clerks.

Training, Other Qualifications, and Advancement

Employers typically require applicants to have at least a high school diploma or its equivalent, and brokerage firms usually seek college graduates for brokerage clerk jobs. Most employers prefer workers who are computer-literate. Knowledge of word processing and spreadsheet software is especially valuable, as are experience working in an office and good interpersonal skills.

Clerks often learn the skills they need in high schools, business schools, and community colleges. Business education programs offered by these institutions typically include courses in typing, word processing, shorthand, business communications, records management, and office systems and procedures.

Some entrants are college graduates with degrees in business, finance, or liberal arts. Many graduates accept entry-level clerical positions to get into a particular company or to enter the finance or accounting field with the hope of being promoted to professional or managerial positions. Some companies, such as brokerage firms, have a set plan of advancement that tracks college graduates from entry-level clerical jobs into managerial positions. Workers with college degrees are likely to start at higher salaries and advance more easily than those without degrees.

Once hired, clerks usually receive on-the-job training. Under the guidance of a supervisor or other senior worker, new employees learn company procedures. Some formal classroom training may also be necessary, such as training in specific computer software.

Clerks must be careful, orderly, and detail-oriented in order to avoid making errors and to recognize errors made by others. These workers should also be discreet and trustworthy because they frequently come in contact with confidential material. Additionally, clerks should have a strong aptitude for numbers. Because statement clerks have access to confidential financial information, these workers must be bonded.

Clerks usually advance by taking on more duties in the same occupation for higher pay or transferring to a closely related occupation. Most companies fill office and administrative support supervisory and managerial positions by promoting individuals from within their organizations, so clerks who acquire additional skills, experience, and training improve their advancement opportunities. With appropriate experience and education, some clerks may become securities, commodities, and financial services sales representatives.

Job Outlook

Employment of brokerage clerks is expected to increase faster than the average for all occupations, while employment of statement clerks should decline. With people increasingly investing in securities, demand for brokerage clerks will climb to meet the needs of processing larger volumes of transactions. Because most back office operations are now computerized, employment growth among brokerage clerks is not expected to keep pace with overall employment growth in the securities and commodities industry; however, brokerage clerks will still be needed to update records, enter changes to customer's accounts, and verify securities transfers.

Broker's assistants will also increase in number along with the number of full-service brokers. Because these clerks spend much of their day answering telephone calls, placing orders, and often running the office, their jobs are not readily subject to automation.

The number of statement clerks is declining rapidly due to increasing technology in the Nation's banks. With the job of producing statements almost completely automated, the mailing of checks and statements is now done mostly by machine. In addition, the further spread of check truncation and the increased use of automated teller machines and other electronic money transfers should result in significantly fewer checks being written and processed.

Earnings

Salaries of clerks vary considerably. The region of the country, size of city, and type and size of establishment all influence salary levels. The level of industry or technical expertise required and the complexity and uniqueness of a clerk's responsibilities may also affect earnings. Median annual earnings of full-time workers in 1998 were as follows:

Brokerage clerks $27,920

Statement clerks 18,640

Related Occupations

Today, most clerks enter data into a computer system and perform basic analysis of the data. Other clerical workers who enter and manipulate data include bank tellers, statistical clerks, receiving clerks, medical records clerks, hotel and motel clerks, credit clerks, and reservation and transportation ticket agents.

Sources of Additional Information

State employment service offices can provide information about job openings for the occupation.

File Clerks

(O*NET 55321)

Nature of the Work

The amount of information generated by organizations continues to grow rapidly. File clerks classify, store, retrieve, and update this information. In many small offices, they often have additional responsibilities, such as data entry, word processing, sorting mail, and operating copying or fax machines. They are employed across the Nation by organizations of all types.

File clerks, also called records, information, or record center clerks, examine incoming material and code it numerically, alphabetically, or by subject matter. They then store forms, letters, receipts, or reports in paper form or enter necessary information into other storage devices. Some clerks operate mechanized files that rotate to bring the needed records to them; others convert documents to films that are then stored on microforms, such as microfilm or microfiche. A growing number of file clerks use imaging systems that scan paper files or film and store the material on optical disks.

In order for records to be useful, they must be up-to-date and accurate. File clerks ensure that new information is added to the files in a timely manner and may get rid of outdated file materials or transfer them to inactive storage. They also check files at regular intervals to make sure that all items are correctly sequenced and placed. Whenever records cannot be found, the file clerk attempts to locate the missing material. As an organization's needs for information change, file clerks also implement changes to the filing system established by supervisory personnel.

When records are requested, file clerks locate them and give them to the borrower. The record may be a sheet of paper stored in a file cabinet or an image on microform. In the first example, the clerk manually retrieves the document and hands or forwards it to the borrower. In the latter example, the clerk retrieves the microform and displays it on a microform reader. If necessary, file clerks make copies of records and distribute them. In addition, they keep track of materials removed from the files to ensure that borrowed files are returned.

Increasingly, file clerks use computerized filing and retrieval systems. These systems use a variety of storage devices, such as a mainframe computer, magnetic tape, CD-ROM, or floppy disk. To retrieve a document in these systems, the clerk enters the document's iden-

tification code, obtains the location, and pulls the document. Accessing files in a computer database is much quicker than locating and physically retrieving paper files. Even when files are stored electronically, however, backup paper or electronic copies usually are also kept.

Employment

File clerks held about 272,000 jobs in 1998. Although file clerk jobs are found in nearly every sector of the economy, about 90 percent of these workers are employed in services, government, finance, insurance, and real estate. More than 1 out of every 4 is employed in temporary services firms, and about 1 out of 3 worked part time in 1998.

Job Outlook

Employment of file clerks is expected to grow about as fast as the average for all occupations through 2008. Projected job growth stems from rising demand for file clerks to record and retrieve information in organizations across the economy. This growth will be moderated, however, by productivity gains stemming from office automation and the consolidation of clerical jobs. Nonetheless, job opportunities for file clerks should be plentiful because a large number of workers will be needed to replace workers who leave the occupation each year. High turnover among file clerks reflects the lack of formal training requirements, limited advancement potential, and relatively low pay.

Jobseekers who have typing and other secretarial skills and are familiar with a wide range of office machines, especially personal computers, should have the best job opportunities. File clerks should find many opportunities for temporary or part-time work, especially during peak business periods.

Human Resources Clerks, Except Payroll and Timekeeping

(O*NET 55314)

Nature of the Work

Human resources clerks maintain the personnel records of an organization's employees. These records include information such as name, address, job title, and earnings, benefits such as health and life insurance, and tax withholding. On a daily basis, these clerks record and answer questions about employee absences and supervisory reports on job performance. When an employee receives a promotion or switches health insurance plans, the human resources clerk updates the appropriate form. Human resources clerks may also prepare reports for managers elsewhere within the organization. For example, they might compile a list of employees eligible for an award.

In smaller organizations, some human resources clerks perform a variety of other clerical duties. They answer telephone or letter

inquiries from the public, send out announcements of job openings or job examinations, and issue application forms. When credit bureaus and finance companies request confirmation of a person's employment, the human resources clerk provides authorized information from the employee's personnel records. Payroll departments and insurance companies may also be contacted to verify changes to records.

Some human resources clerks are also involved in hiring. They screen job applicants to obtain information such as education and work experience; administer aptitude, personality, and interest tests; explain the organization's employment policies and refer qualified applicants to the employing official; and request references from present or past employers. Also, human resources clerks inform job applicants, by telephone or letter, of their acceptance or rejection for employment.

Other human resources clerks are known as assignment clerks. Their role is to notify a firm's existing employees of position vacancies and to identify and assign qualified applicants. They keep track of vacancies throughout the organization and complete and distribute vacancy advertisement forms. These clerks review applications in response to advertisements and verify information using personnel records. After a selection is made, they notify all the applicants of their acceptance or rejection.

In some job settings, human resources clerks have specific job titles. Identification clerks are responsible for security matters at defense installations. They compile and record personal data about vendors, contractors, and civilian and military personnel and their dependents. Job duties include interviewing applicants; corresponding with law enforcement authorities; and preparing badges, passes, and identification cards.

Employment

Human resources clerks held about 142,000 jobs in 1998. Although these workers are found in most industries, about 1 in every 5 works for a government agency. Colleges and universities, hospitals, department stores, and banks also employ large numbers of human resources clerks.

Job Outlook

Replacement needs will account for most job openings for human resources clerks. Jobs will open up as clerks advance within the personnel department, take jobs unrelated to personnel administration, or leave the labor force.

Little or no change is expected in employment of human resources clerks through the year 2008, largely due to the increased use of computers. The growing use of computers in personnel or human resource departments means that a lot of data entry done by human resources clerks can be eliminated, as employees themselves enter the data and send it to the personnel office. This is most feasible in large organizations with multiple personnel offices. The increasing use of computers and other automated office equipment by managers and professionals in personnel offices also could mean less work for human resources clerks.

Library Assistants and Bookmobile Drivers

(O*NET 53902)

Significant Points

- Most jobs require only a high school diploma.
- Numerous opportunities should arise due to high turnover.

Nature of the Work

Library assistants and bookmobile drivers organize library resources and make them available to users. They assist librarians and, in some cases, library technicians.

Library assistants—sometimes referred to as library media assistants, library aides, or circulation assistants—register patrons so they can borrow materials from the library. They record the borrower's name and address from an application and then issue a library card. Most library assistants enter and update patrons' records using computer databases. At the circulation desk, assistants lend and collect books, periodicals, video tapes, and other materials. When an item is borrowed, assistants stamp the due date on the material and record the patron's identification from his or her library card. They inspect returned materials for damage, check due dates, and compute fines for overdue material. They review records to compile a list of overdue materials and send out notices. They also answer patrons' questions and refer those they cannot answer to a librarian.

Throughout the library, assistants sort returned books, periodicals, and other items and return them to their designated shelves, files, or storage areas. They locate materials to be loaned, either for a patron or another library. Many card catalogues are computerized, so library assistants must be familiar with the computer system. If any materials have been damaged, these workers try to repair them. For example, they use tape or paste to repair torn pages or book covers and other specialized processes to repair more valuable materials.

Some library assistants specialize in helping patrons who have vision problems. Sometimes referred to as library, talking-books, or Braille-and-talking-books clerks, they review the borrower's list of desired reading material. They locate those materials or closely related substitutes from the library collection of large type or Braille volumes, tape cassettes, and open-reel talking books. They complete the paperwork and give or mail the materials to the borrower.

To extend library services to more patrons, many libraries operate bookmobiles. *Bookmobile drivers* take trucks stocked with books to designated sites on a regular schedule. Bookmobiles serve community organizations such as shopping centers, apartment complexes, schools, and nursing homes. They may also be used to extend library service to patrons living in remote areas. Depending on local conditions, drivers may operate a bookmobile alone or may be accompanied by a library technician.

When working alone, the drivers perform many of the same functions as a library assistant in a main or branch library. They answer patrons' questions, receive and check out books, collect fines, maintain the book collection, shelve materials, and occasionally operate audiovisual equipment to show slides or films. They participate and may assist in planning programs sponsored by the library such as reader advisory programs, used book sales, or outreach programs. Bookmobile drivers keep track of their mileage, the materials lent out, and the amount of fines collected. In some areas, they are responsible for maintenance of the vehicle and any photocopiers or other equipment in it. They record statistics on circulation and the number of people visiting the bookmobile. Drivers may also record requests for special items from the main library and arrange for the materials to be mailed or delivered to a patron during the next scheduled visit. Many bookmobiles are equipped with personal computers and CD-ROM systems linked to the main library system; this allows bookmobile drivers to reserve or locate books immediately. Some bookmobiles now offer Internet access to users.

Because bookmobile drivers may be the only link some people have to the library, much of their work is helping the public. They may assist handicapped or elderly patrons to the bookmobile, or shovel snow to assure their safety. They may enter hospitals or nursing homes to deliver books to patrons who are bedridden.

Working Conditions

Because most library assistants use computers on a daily basis, these workers may experience eye and muscle strain, backaches, headaches, and repetitive motion injuries. Also, assistants who review detailed data may have to sit for extended periods of time. Although the work does not require heavy lifting, library assistants spend a lot of time on their feet and frequently stoop, bend, and reach. Library assistants may work evenings and weekends, but those employed in school libraries usually work only during the school year.

Bookmobile drivers must maneuver large vehicles in all kinds of traffic and weather conditions and may also be responsible for the maintenance of the bookmobile. The schedules of bookmobile drivers depend on the size of the area being served. Some of these workers go out on their routes every day, while others go only on certain days. On these other days, they work at the library. Some also work evenings and weekends to give patrons as much access to the library as possible.

Employment

Library assistants and bookmobile drivers held about 127,000 jobs in 1998. Over one-half of these workers were employed by local government in public libraries; most of the remaining worked in school libraries. Opportunities for flexible schedules are abundant; over one-half of these workers were on part-time schedules.

Training, Other Qualifications, and Advancement

Employers typically require applicants to have at least a high school diploma or its equivalent. Most employers prefer workers who are computer-literate. Knowledge of word processing and spreadsheet software is especially valuable, as are experience working in an office and good interpersonal skills.

Library assistants often learn the skills they need in high schools, business schools, and community colleges. Business education programs offered by these institutions typically include courses in typing, word processing, shorthand, business communications, records management, and office systems and procedures.

Some entrants are college graduates with degrees in liberal arts. Although a degree is rarely required, many graduates accept entry-level positions with the hope of being promoted. Workers with college degrees are likely to start at higher salaries and advance more easily than those without degrees.

Once hired, library assistants and bookmobile drivers usually receive on-the-job training. Under the guidance of a supervisor or other senior worker, new employees learn procedures. Some formal classroom training may also be necessary, such as training in specific computer software. Library assistants and bookmobile drivers must be careful, orderly, and detail-oriented in order to avoid making errors and to recognize errors made by others. Many bookmobile drivers are now required to have a commercial driver's license.

These employees usually advance by taking on more duties in the same occupation for higher pay or transferring to a closely related occupation. Most companies fill supervisory and managerial positions by promoting individuals from within their organizations, so those who acquire additional skills, experience, and training improve their advancement opportunities. With appropriate experience and education, some may become librarians.

Job Outlook

Opportunities should be good for persons interested in jobs as library assistants or bookmobile drivers through 2008. Turnover of these workers is quite high, reflecting the limited investment in training and subsequent weak attachment to this occupation. This work is attractive to retirees, students, and others who want a part-time schedule, and there is a lot of movement into and out of the occupation. Many openings will become available each year to replace workers who transfer to other occupations or leave the labor force. Some positions become available as library assistants move within the organization. Library assistants can be promoted to library technicians and eventually supervisory positions in public service or technical service areas. Advancement opportunities are greater in larger libraries and may be more limited in smaller ones.

Employment is expected to grow about as fast as the average for all occupations through 2008. The vast majority of library assistants and bookmobile drivers work in public or school libraries. Efforts to contain costs in local governments and academic institutions of all types may result in more hiring of library support staff than librarians. Because most are employed by public institutions, library assistants and bookmobile drivers are not directly affected by the ups and downs of the business cycle. Some of these workers may lose their jobs, however, if there are cuts in government budgets.

Earnings

Salaries of library assistants and bookmobile drivers vary. The region of the country, size of city, and type and size of establishment

all influence salary levels. Median annual earnings of full-time library assistants and bookmobile drivers in 1998 were $16,980.

Related Occupations

Other clerical workers who enter and manipulate data include bank tellers, statistical clerks, receiving clerks, medical record clerks, hotel and motel clerks, credit clerks, and reservation and transportation ticket agents.

Sources of Additional Information

Information about a career as a library assistant can be obtained from:

- Council on Library/Media Technology, P.O. Box 951, Oxon Hill, MD 20750. Internet: http://library.ucr.edu/COLT

Public libraries and libraries in academic institutions can provide information about job openings for library assistants and bookmobile drivers.

Order Clerks

(O*NET 55323)

Nature of the Work

Order clerks receive and process incoming orders for a wide variety of goods or services, such as spare parts for machines, consumer appliances, gas and electric power connections, film rentals, and articles of clothing. They are sometimes called order-entry clerks, customer service representatives, sales representatives, order processors, or order takers.

Orders for materials, merchandise, or services can come from inside or from outside of an organization. In large companies with many work sites, such as automobile manufacturers, clerks order parts and equipment from the company's warehouses. *Inside order clerks* receive orders from other workers employed by the same company or from salespersons in the field.

Many other order clerks, however, receive orders from outside companies or individuals. Order clerks in wholesale businesses, for instance, receive orders for merchandise from retail establishments that the retailer, in turn, sells to the public. An increasing number of order clerks work for catalogue companies and online retailers, receiving orders from individual customers by either phone, fax, regular mail, or e-mail. Order clerks dealing primarily with the public sometimes are referred to as *outside order clerks*.

Computers provide order clerks with ready access to information such as stock numbers, prices, and inventory. Orders frequently depend on which products are in stock and which products are most appropriate for the customer's needs. Some order clerks, especially those in industrial settings, must be able to give price estimates for entire jobs, not just single parts. Others must be able to take special orders, give expected arrival dates, prepare contracts, and handle complaints.

Many order clerks receive orders directly by telephone, entering the required information as the customer places the order. How-

ever, a rapidly increasing number of orders are now received through computer systems, the Internet, faxes, and e-mail. In some cases, these orders are sent directly from the customer's terminal to the order clerk's terminal. Orders received by regular mail are sometimes scanned into a database that's instantly accessible to clerks.

Clerks review orders for completeness and clarity. They may complete missing information or contact the customer for the information. Similarly, clerks contact customers if customers need additional information, such as prices or shipping dates, or if delays in filling the order are anticipated. For orders received by regular mail, clerks extract checks or money orders, sort them, and send them for processing.

After an order has been verified and entered, the customer's final cost is calculated. The clerk then routes the order to the proper department—such as the warehouse—that actually sends out or delivers the item in question.

In organizations with sophisticated computer systems, inventory records are adjusted automatically, as sales are made. In less automated organizations, order clerks may adjust inventory records. Clerks may also notify other departments when inventories are low or when orders would deplete supplies.

Some order clerks must establish priorities in filling orders. For example, an order clerk in a blood bank may receive a request from a hospital for a certain type of blood. The clerk must first find out if the request is routine or an emergency and then take appropriate action.

Employment

Order clerks held about 362,000 jobs in 1998. About one half were in wholesale and retail establishments and about one quarter in manufacturing firms. Most of the remaining jobs for order clerks were in business services.

Job Outlook

Job openings for order clerks should be plentiful through the year 2008 due to sizable replacement needs. Numerous jobs will become available each year to replace order clerks who transfer to other occupations or leave the labor force completely. Many of these openings will be for seasonal work, especially in catalogue companies or online retailers catering to holiday gift buyers.

Employment of order clerks is expected to grow more slowly than the average through the year 2008, as office automation continues to increase worker productivity. As the economy grows, increasingly more orders for goods and services will be placed. Demand for outside order clerks who deal mainly with the public or other businesses should remain fairly strong. The increasing use of online retailing and toll-free numbers that make placing orders easy and convenient will stimulate demand for these workers. However, productivity gains from increased automation will offset some of the growth in demand for outside order clerks, as each clerk is able to handle an increasingly higher volume of orders. In addition, orders placed over the Internet and other computer systems are often entered directly into the computer by the customer; thus, the order clerk is not involved at all in placing the order.

Employment growth of inside clerks will also be constrained by productivity gains due to automation. The spread of electronic data interchange, a system enabling computers to communicate directly with one another, allows orders within establishments to be placed with little human intervention. Besides electronic data interchange, *extranets* and other systems allowing a firm's employees to place orders directly are increasingly common.

Other types of automation will also limit the demand for order clerks. Sophisticated inventory control and automatic billing systems allow companies to track inventory and accounts with much less help from order clerks than in the past. Some companies use automated phone menus accessible with a touch-tone phone to receive orders, and others use answering machines. Developments in voice recognition technology may also further reduce the demand for order clerks.

Payroll and Timekeeping Clerks

(O*NET 55341)

Nature of the Work

Payroll and timekeeping clerks perform a vital function—ensuring that employees are paid on time and that their paychecks are accurate. If inaccuracies arise, such as monetary errors or incorrect amounts of vacation time, these workers research and correct the records. In addition, they may also perform various other clerical tasks.

The fundamental task of *timekeeping clerks* is distributing and collecting timecards each pay period. They review employee work charts, timesheets, and timecards to ensure that information is properly recorded and that records have the signatures of authorizing officials. In companies that bill for the time spent by staff (such as law or accounting firms), timekeeping clerks make sure the hours recorded are charged to the correct job so clients can be properly billed. These clerks also review computer reports listing timecards that cannot be processed because of errors, and they contact the employee or the employee's supervisor to resolve the problem. In addition, timekeeping clerks are responsible for informing managers and other employees of procedural changes in payroll policies.

Payroll clerks, also called payroll technicians, screen timecards for calculating, coding, or other errors. They compute pay by subtracting allotments (including Federal and State taxes, retirement, insurance, and savings) from gross earnings. Increasingly, computers perform these calculations and alert payroll clerks to problems or errors in the data. In small organizations, or for new employees whose records are not yet entered into a computer system, clerks may perform the necessary calculations manually. In some small offices, clerks or other employees in the accounting department process payroll.

Payroll clerks also maintain paper backup files for research and reference. They record changes in employee addresses; close out files when workers retire, resign, or transfer; and advise employees on income tax withholding and other mandatory deductions. They also issue and record adjustments to pay because of previous errors or retroactive increases. Payroll clerks need to follow changes in tax and deduction laws so they are aware of the most recent revisions. Finally, they prepare and mail earnings and tax withholding statements for employees' use in preparing income tax returns.

In small offices, payroll and timekeeping duties are likely to be included in the duties of a general office clerk, secretary, or accounting clerk. However, large organizations employ specialized payroll and timekeeping clerks to perform these functions.

Employment

Payroll and timekeeping clerks held about 172,000 jobs in 1998. About 35 percent of all payroll and timekeeping clerks worked in business, health, education, and social services; another 25 percent worked in manufacturing; and more than 10 percent were in wholesale and retail trade or in government. About 11 percent of all payroll and timekeeping clerks worked part time in 1998.

Job Outlook

Employment of payroll and timekeeping clerks is expected to decline through 2008 due to the continuing automation of payroll and timekeeping functions and the consolidation of clerical jobs. Nevertheless, a number of job openings should arise in coming years, as payroll and timekeeping clerks leave the labor force or transfer to other occupations. Many payroll clerks use this position as a stepping stone to higher-level accounting jobs.

As in many other clerical occupations, new technology will continue to allow many of the tasks formerly handled by payroll and timekeeping clerks to be partially or completely automated. For example, automated timeclocks, which calculate employee hours, allow large organizations to centralize their timekeeping duties in one location. At individual sites, employee hours are increasingly tracked by computer and verified by managers. This information is then compiled and sent to a central office to be processed by payroll clerks, eliminating the need to have payroll clerks at every site. In addition, the growing use of direct deposit eliminates the need to draft paychecks because these funds are automatically transferred each pay period. Furthermore, timekeeping duties are increasingly being distributed to secretaries, general office clerks, or accounting clerks or are being contracted out to organizations that specialize in these services.

Reservation and Transportation Ticket Agents and Travel Clerks

(O*NET 53802 and 53805)

Significant Points

- A high school diploma or its equivalent is the most common educational requirement.

- These jobs provide excellent travel benefits.

Nature of the Work

Each year, millions of Americans travel by plane, train, ship, bus, and automobile. Many of these travelers rely on the services of reservation and transportation ticket agents and travel clerks. These ticket agents and clerks perform functions as varied as selling tickets, confirming reservations, checking baggage, and providing tourists with useful travel information.

Most reservation agents work for large hotel chains or airlines, helping people plan trips and make reservations. They usually work in large reservation centers answering telephone inquiries and offering suggestions on travel arrangements, such as routes, time schedules, rates, and types of accommodation. Reservation agents quote fares and room rates, provide travel information, and make and confirm transportation and hotel reservations. Most agents use proprietary networks to quickly obtain information needed to make, change, or cancel reservations for customers.

Transportation ticket agents are sometimes known as passenger service agents, passenger-booking clerks, reservation clerks, airport service agents, ticket clerks, or ticket sellers. They work in airports, train, and bus stations selling tickets, assigning seats to passengers, and checking baggage. In addition, they may answer inquiries and give directions, examine passports and visas, or check in pets. Other ticket agents, more commonly known as gate or station agents, work in airport terminals assisting passengers boarding airplanes. These workers direct passengers to the correct boarding area, check tickets and seat assignments, make boarding announcements, and provide special assistance to young, elderly, or disabled passengers when they board or disembark.

Most travel clerks are employed by membership organizations, such as automobile clubs. These workers, sometimes called member services counselors or travel counselors, plan trips, calculate mileage, and offer travel suggestions (such as the best route from the point of origin to the destination) for club members. Travel clerks also may prepare an itinerary indicating points of interest, restaurants, overnight accommodations, and availability of emergency services during the trip. In some cases, they make rental car, hotel, and restaurant reservations for club members.

Passenger rate clerks generally work for bus companies. They sell tickets for regular bus routes and arrange nonscheduled or chartered trips. They plan travel routes, compute rates, and keep customers informed of appropriate details. They also may arrange travel accommodations.

Working Conditions

Most clerks work in areas that are clean, well lit, and relatively quiet. This is especially true for clerks who greet customers and visitors and usually work in highly visible areas. Reservation agents who spend much of their day talking on the telephone, however, commonly work away from the public, often in large centralized reservation or phone centers. Because a number of agents or clerks may share the same workspace, it may be crowded and noisy. Although most clerks work a standard 40-hour week, about 3 out of 10 work part time. Some jobs may require working evenings, late night shifts, weekends, and holidays.

The work performed by clerks may be repetitious and stressful. Reservation agents and travel clerks work under stringent time constraints or have quotas on the number of calls answered or reservations made. Additional stress is caused by technology that enables management to electronically monitor use of computer systems, tape record telephone calls, or limit the time spent on each call.

The work of transportation ticket agents also can be stressful when a worker is trying to serve the needs of difficult or angry customers. When flights are canceled, reservations are mishandled, or guests are dissatisfied, these clerks must bear the brunt of the customers' anger. Ticket agents may have to lift heavy baggage. In addition, prolonged exposure to a video display terminal may lead to eyestrain for the many information clerks who work with computers.

Employment

Reservation and transportation ticket agents and travel clerks held about 219,000 jobs in 1998. About 7 of every 10 are employed by airlines. Others work for membership organizations, such as automobile clubs; hotels and other lodging places; railroad companies; bus lines; and other companies that provide transportation services.

Although agents and clerks are found throughout the country, most work in large metropolitan airports, downtown ticket offices, large reservation centers, and train or bus stations. The remainder work in small communities served only by inter-city bus or railroad lines.

Training, Other Qualifications, and Advancement

Although hiring requirements for vary, a high school diploma or its equivalent is the most common educational requirement. Increasingly, familiarity or experience with computers and good interpersonal skills are often equally important to employers. For ticket agent jobs, some college education may be preferred.

A professional appearance and pleasant personality are important. A clear speaking voice and fluency in the English language also are essential because these employees frequently use the telephone or public address systems. Good spelling and computer literacy are often needed, particularly because most work involves considerable computer use. It also is increasingly helpful for those wishing to enter the lodging or travel industries to speak a foreign language fluently.

Most airline reservation and ticket agents learn their skills through formal company training programs. In a classroom setting, they learn company and industry policies, computer systems, and ticketing procedures. They also learn to use the airline's computer system to obtain information on schedules, seat availability, and fares; to reserve space for passengers; and to plan passenger itineraries. They must also become familiar with airport and airline code designations, regulations, and safety procedures, and they may be tested on this knowledge. After completing classroom instruction, new agents work on the job with supervisors or experienced agents for a period of time. During this period, supervisors may monitor telephone conversations to improve the quality of customer service. Agents are expected to provide good service while limiting the time spent on each call without being discourteous to customers. In contrast to the airlines, automobile clubs, bus lines, and railroads tend to train their ticket agents or travel clerks on the job through short in-house classes that last several days.

Advancement usually comes about either by transfer to a position with more responsibilities or by promotion to a supervisory position. Most companies fill office and administrative support supervisory and managerial positions by promoting individuals within their organization, so clerks who acquire additional skills, experience, and training improve their advancement opportunities. Within the airline industry, a ticket agent may advance to lead worker on the shift.

Additional training is helpful in preparing clerks for promotion. In the airline industry, workers commonly are promoted through the ranks. Positions such as airline reservation agent offer good opportunities for qualified workers to get started in the business.

Job Outlook

Applicants for reservation and transportation ticket agent jobs are likely to encounter considerable competition, because the supply of qualified applicants exceeds the expected number of job openings. Entry requirements for these jobs are minimal, and many people seeking to get into the airline industry or travel business often start out in these types of positions. These jobs provide excellent travel benefits, and many people view airline and other travel-related jobs as glamorous.

Employment of reservation and transportation ticket agents and travel clerks is expected to grow more slowly than the average for all occupations through 2008. Although a growing population will demand additional travel services, employment of these workers will grow more slowly than this demand because of the significant impact of technology on productivity. Automated reservations and ticketing, as well as "ticketless" travel, for example, are reducing the need for some workers. Most train stations and airports now have satellite ticket printer locations, or "kiosks," that enable passengers to make reservations and purchase tickets themselves. Many passengers also are able to check flight times and fares, make reservations, and purchase tickets on the Internet. Nevertheless, all travel-related passenger services can never be fully automated, primarily for safety and security reasons. As a result, jobs will continue to become available as the occupation grows and as workers transfer to other occupations, retire, or leave the labor force altogether.

Employment of reservation and transportation ticket agents and travel clerks is sensitive to cyclical swings in the economy. During recessions, discretionary passenger travel declines, and transportation service companies are less likely to hire new workers and even may resort to layoffs.

Earnings

Median annual earnings for reservation and transportation ticket agents and travel clerks were $22,120 in 1998. Reservation and transportation ticket agents and travel clerks receive free or reduced rate travel on their company's carriers for themselves and their immediate family and, in some companies, for friends.

Related Occupations

A number of other workers deal with the public, receive and provide information, or direct people to others who can assist them. Among these are dispatchers, security guards, bank tellers, guides, telephone operators, records processing clerks, counter and rental clerks, survey workers, and ushers and lobby attendants.

Sources of Additional Information

For information about job opportunities as reservation and transportation ticket agents and travel clerks, write the personnel manager of individual transportation companies. Addresses of airlines are available from:

● Air Transport Association of America, 1301 Pennsylvania Ave. NW., Suite 1100, Washington, DC 20004-1707.

Restaurant and Food Service Managers

(O*NET 15026B)

Significant Points

● Although many experienced food and beverage preparation and service workers are promoted to fill jobs, job opportunities are expected to be best for those with bachelor's or associate degrees in restaurant and institutional food service management.

● Job opportunities should be better for salaried managers than for self-employed managers, as restaurants increasingly affiliate with national chains instead of being independently owned.

Nature of the Work

The daily responsibilities of many restaurant and food service managers can be as complicated as some meals prepared by a fine chef. In addition to the traditional duties of selecting and pricing menu items, using food and other supplies efficiently, and achieving quality in food preparation and service, managers are now responsible for a growing number of administrative and human resource tasks. For example, managers must carefully find and evaluate new ways of recruiting new employees in a tight job market. Once hired, managers must also find creative ways to retain experienced workers.

In most restaurants and institutional food service facilities, the manager is assisted in these duties by one or more assistant managers, depending on the size and operating hours of the establishment. In most large establishments, as well as in many smaller ones, the management team consists of a *general manager*, one or more *assistant managers*, and an *executive chef*. The executive chef is responsible for the operation of the kitchen, while the assistant managers oversee service in the dining room and other areas. In smaller restaurants, the executive chef also may be the general manager, and sometimes an owner. In fast-food restaurants and other food service facilities open for long hours, often 7 days a week, the manager is aided by several assistant managers, each of whom supervises a shift of workers.

One of the most important tasks of restaurant and food service managers is selecting successful menu items. This task varies by establishment because although many restaurants rarely change their menu, others make frequent alterations. Managers or executive chefs select menu items, taking into account the likely number of customers and the past popularity of dishes. Other issues taken into consideration when planning a menu include unserved food left over from prior meals that should not be wasted, the need for variety, and the availability of foods due to changing seasons. Managers or executive chefs analyze the recipes of the dishes to determine food, labor, overhead costs and to assign prices to various dishes. Menus must be developed far enough in advance that supplies can be ordered and received in time.

On a daily basis, managers estimate food consumption, place orders with suppliers, and schedule the delivery of fresh food and beverages. They receive and check the content of deliveries, evaluating the quality of meats, poultry, fish, fruits, vegetables, and baked goods. To ensure good service, managers meet with sales representatives from restaurant suppliers to place orders replenishing stocks of tableware, linens, paper, cleaning supplies, cooking utensils, and furniture and fixtures. They also arrange for equipment maintenance and repairs and coordinate a variety of services such as waste removal and pest control.

The quality of food and services in restaurants depends largely on a manager's ability to interview, hire, and, when necessary, fire employees. This is especially true in tight labor markets, when many managers report difficulty in hiring experienced food and beverage preparation and service workers. Managers may attend career fairs or arrange for newspaper advertising to expand their pool of applicants. Once a new employee is hired, managers explain the establishment's policies and practices and oversee any necessary training. Managers also schedule the work hours of employees, making sure there are enough workers present to cover peak dining periods. If employees are unable to work, managers may have to fill in for them. Some managers regularly help with cooking, clearing of tables, or other tasks.

Another fundamental responsibility of restaurant and food service managers is supervising the kitchen and dining room. For example, managers often oversee all food preparation and cooking, examining the quality and portion sizes to ensure that dishes are prepared and garnished correctly and in a timely manner. They also investigate and resolve customers' complaints about food quality or service. To maintain company and government sanitation standards, they direct the cleaning of the kitchen and dining areas and washing of tableware, kitchen utensils, and equipment. Managers also monitor the actions of their employees and patrons on a continual basis to ensure that health and safety standards and local liquor regulations are obeyed.

In addition to their regular duties, restaurant and food service managers have a variety of administrative responsibilities. Although much of this work is delegated to a bookkeeper in a larger establishment, managers in most smaller establishments, such as fast-food restaurants, must keep records of the hours and wages of employees, prepare the payroll, and fill out paperwork in compliance with licensing laws and reporting requirements of tax, wage and hour, unemployment compensation, and Social Security laws. Managers also maintain records of supply and equipment purchases and ensure that accounts with suppliers are paid on a regular basis. In addition, managers in full-service restaurants record the number, type, and cost of items sold to evaluate and discontinue dishes that may be unpopular or less profitable.

Many managers are able to ease the burden of record keeping and paperwork through the use of computers. Point-of-service (POS) systems are used in many restaurants to increase employee productivity and allow managers to track the sales of specific menu items. Using a POS system, a server keys in the customer's order and the computer immediately sends the order to the kitchen so preparation can begin. The same system totals checks, acts as a cash register and credit card authorizer, and tracks daily sales. To minimize food costs and spoilage, many managers use inventory tracking software to compare the record of daily sales from the POS with a record of present inventory. In some establishments, when supplies needed for the preparation of popular menu items run low, additional inventory can be ordered directly from the supplier using the computer. Computers also allow restaurant and food service managers to more efficiently keep track of employee schedules and pay.

Managers are among the first to arrive in the morning and the last to leave. At the conclusion of each day, or sometimes each shift, managers tally the cash and charge receipts received and balance them against the record of sales. In most cases, they are responsible for depositing the day's receipts at the bank or securing them in a safe place. Finally, managers are responsible for locking up, checking that ovens, grills, and lights are off, and switching on alarm systems.

Working Conditions

Evenings and weekends are popular dining periods, making night and weekend work common among managers. Many managers of institutional food service facilities work more conventional hours because factory and office cafeterias are usually open only on weekdays for breakfast and lunch. Hours for many managers are unpredictable, however, as managers may have to fill in for absent workers on short notice. It is common for restaurant and food service managers to work 50 to 60 hours or more per week.

Managers often experience the pressure of simultaneously coordinating a wide range of activities. When problems occur, it is the responsibility of the manager to resolve them with minimal disruption to customers. The job can be hectic during peak dining hours, and dealing with irate customers or uncooperative employees can be stressful.

Employment

Restaurant and food service managers held about 518,000 jobs in 1998. Most managers are salaried, but about 1 in 6 is self-employed. Most work in restaurants or for contract institutional food service companies, while a smaller number are employed by educational institutions, hospitals, nursing and personal care facilities, and civic, social, and fraternal organizations. Jobs are located throughout the country, with large cities and tourist areas providing more opportunities for full-service dining positions.

Training, Other Qualifications, and Advancement

Most food service management companies and national or regional restaurant chains recruit management trainees from two- and four-year college hospitality management programs. Food service and restaurant chains prefer to hire people with degrees in restaurant and institutional food service management, but they often hire graduates with degrees in other fields who have demonstrated interest and aptitude. Some restaurant and food service manager positions, particularly self-service and fast-food, are filled by promoting experienced food and beverage preparation and service workers. Waiters, waitresses, chefs, and fast-food workers demonstrating potential for handling increased responsibility sometimes advance to assistant manager or management trainee jobs. Executive chefs need extensive experience working as chefs, and general managers need experience as assistant managers.

A bachelor's degree in restaurant and food service management provides a particularly strong preparation for a career in this occupation. In 1998, more than 150 colleges and universities offered four-year programs in restaurant and hotel management or institutional food service management. For those not interested in pursuing a four-year degree, more than 800 community and junior colleges, technical institutes, and other institutions offer programs in these fields leading to an associate degree or other formal certification. Both two- and four-year programs provide instruction in subjects such as nutrition and food planning and preparation, as well as accounting, business law and management, and computer science. Some programs combine classroom and laboratory study with internships that provide on-the-job experience. In addition, many educational institutions offer culinary programs that provide food preparation training. This training can lead to a career as a cook or chef and provide a foundation for advancement to an executive chef position.

Most employers emphasize personal qualities when hiring managers. For example, self-discipline, initiative, and leadership ability are essential. Managers must be able to solve problems and concentrate on details. They need good communication skills to deal with customers and suppliers, as well as to motivate and direct their staff. A neat and clean appearance is a must because they often are in close personal contact with the public. Restaurant and food service management can be demanding, so good health and stamina also are important.

Most restaurant chains and food service management companies have rigorous training programs for management positions. Through a combination of classroom and on-the-job training, trainees receive instruction and gain work experience in all aspects of the operations of a restaurant or institutional food service facility. Topics include food preparation, nutrition, sanitation, security, company policies and procedures, personnel management, record keeping, and preparation of reports. Training on use of the restaurant's computer system is increasingly important as well. Usually after six months or a year, a trainee receives his or her first permanent assignment as an assistant manager.

A measure of professional achievement for restaurant and food service managers is the designation of certified Foodservice Management Professional (FMP). Although not a requirement for employment or advancement in the occupation, voluntary certification provides recognition of professional competence, particularly for managers who acquired their skills largely on the job. The Educational Foundation of the National Restaurant Association awards the FMP designation to managers who achieve a qualifying score on a written examination, complete a series of courses that cover a range of food service management topics, and meet standards of work experience in the field.

Willingness to relocate often is essential for advancement to positions with greater responsibility. Managers typically advance to larger establishments or regional management positions within restaurant chains. Some eventually open their own eating and drinking establishments. Others transfer to hotel management positions because their restaurant management experience provides a good background for food and beverage manager jobs in hotels and resorts.

Job Outlook

Employment of restaurant and food service managers is expected to increase about as fast as the average for all occupations through 2008. In addition to employment growth, the need to replace managers who transfer to other occupations or stop working will create many job openings. Opportunities to fill these openings are expected to be best for those with a bachelor's or associate degree in restaurant and institutional food service management.

Projected employment growth varies by industry. Eating and drinking places will provide the most new jobs as the number of eating and drinking establishments increases along with the population, personal incomes, and leisure time. In addition, manager jobs will increase in eating and drinking places as schools, hospitals, and other businesses contract out more of their food services to institutional food service companies within the eating and drinking industry.

Food service manager jobs still are expected to increase in many of these other industries, but growth will be slowed as contracting out becomes more common. Growth in the elderly population should result in more food service manager jobs in nursing homes and other health-care institutions and in residential-care and assisted-living facilities.

Job opportunities should be better for salaried managers than for self-employed managers. New restaurants are increasingly affiliated with national chains rather than being independently owned and operated. As this trend continues, fewer owners will manage restaurants themselves, and more restaurant managers will be employed by larger companies to run establishments.

Employment in eating and drinking establishments is not very sensitive to changes in economic conditions, so restaurant and food service managers are rarely laid off during hard times. However, competition among restaurants is always intense, and many restaurants do not survive.

Earnings

Median earnings of food service and lodging managers were $26,700 in 1998. The middle 50 percent earned between $19,820 and $34,690. The lowest paid 10 percent earned $14,430 or less, while the highest paid 10 percent earned more than $45,520. Median annual earnings in the industries employing the largest number of food service and lodging managers in 1997 are shown below.

Hotels and motels $28,600

Eating and drinking places 25,000

Elementary and secondary schools 21,300

In addition to typical benefits, most salaried restaurant and food service managers receive free meals and the opportunity for additional training depending on their length of service.

Related Occupations

Restaurant and food service managers direct the activities of businesses, which provide a service to customers. Other managers in service-oriented businesses include hotel managers and assistants, health services administrators, retail store managers, and bank managers.

Sources of Additional Information

Information about a career as a restaurant and food service manager, two- and four-year college programs in restaurant and food service management and certification as a Foodservice Management Professional is available from:

 • The Educational Foundation of the National Restaurant Association, Suite 1400, 250 South Wacker Dr., Chicago, IL 60606.

General information on hospitality careers may be obtained from:

 • Council on Hotel, Restaurant, and Institutional Education, 1200 17th St. NW., Washington, DC 20036-3097.

Additional information about job opportunities in the field may be obtained from local employers and local offices of the State employment service.

Retail Salespersons

(O*NET 49011 and 49999C)

Significant Points

 • Good employment opportunities are expected due to the need to replace the large number of workers who leave the occupation each year.

 • Most salespersons work evening and weekend hours and long hours during Christmas and other peak retail periods.

 • Opportunities for part-time work are plentiful.

Nature of the Work

Whether selling shoes, computer equipment, or automobiles, retail salespersons assist customers in finding what they are looking for and try to interest them in buying the merchandise. They describe a product's features, demonstrate its use, or show various models and colors. For some sales jobs, particularly those selling expensive and complex items, retail salespersons need special knowledge or skills. For example, salespersons who sell automobiles must be able to explain to customers the features of various models, the meaning of manufacturers' specifications, and the types of options and financing available.

Consumers spend millions of dollars every day on merchandise and often form their impressions of a store by evaluating its sales force. Therefore, retailers are increasingly stressing the importance of providing courteous and efficient service in order to remain competitive. When a customer wants an item that is not on the sales floor, for example, the salesperson may check the stockroom, place a special order, or call another store to locate the item.

In addition to selling, most retail salespersons, especially those who work in department and apparel stores, make out sales checks; receive cash, check, and charge payments; bag or package purchases; and give change and receipts. Depending on the hours they work, retail salespersons may have to open or close cash registers. This may include counting the money; separating charge slips, coupons, and exchange vouchers; and making deposits at the cash office. Salespersons are often held responsible for the contents of their registers, and repeated shortages are cause for dismissal in many organizations.

Salespersons may also handle returns and exchanges of merchandise, wrap gifts, and keep their work areas neat. In addition, they may help stock shelves or racks, arrange for mailing or delivery of purchases, mark price tags, take inventory, and prepare displays.

Frequently, salespersons must be aware of special sales and promotions. They must also recognize possible security risks and thefts and know how to handle or prevent such situations.

Working Conditions

Most salespersons in retail trade work in clean, comfortable, well-lighted stores. However, they often stand for long periods and may need supervisory approval to leave the sales floor.

The Monday through Friday 9 to 5 work week is the exception, rather than the rule, in retail trade. Most salespersons work some evening and weekend hours, and long hours during Christmas and other peak retail periods. In addition, most retailers restrict the use of vacation time from Thanksgiving until early January.

This job can be rewarding for those who enjoy working with people. Patience and courtesy are required, especially when the work is repetitious and the customers demanding.

Employment

Retail salespersons held about 4.6 million jobs in 1998. They worked in stores ranging from small specialty shops employing a few workers, to giant department stores with hundreds of salespersons. In addition, some were self-employed representatives of direct sales companies and mail-order houses. The largest employers of retail salespersons are department stores, clothing and accessories stores, furniture and home furnishing stores, and motor vehicle dealers.

This occupation offers many opportunities for part-time work and is especially appealing to students, retirees, and others looking to supplement their income. However, most of those selling "big ticket" items, such as cars, furniture, and electronic equipment, work full time and have substantial experience.

Because retail stores are found in every city and town, employment is distributed geographically in much the same way as the population.

Training, Other Qualifications, and Advancement

There usually are no formal education requirements for this type of work, although a high school diploma or equivalent is increasingly preferred. Employers look for people who enjoy working with others and have the tact and patience to deal with difficult customers. Among other desirable characteristics are an interest in sales work, a neat appearance, and the ability to communicate clearly and effectively. The ability to speak more than one language may be helpful for employment in stores in communities where people from various cultures tend to live and shop. Before hiring a salesperson, some employers may conduct a background check, especially for a job selling high-priced items.

In most small stores, an experienced employee or the proprietor instructs newly hired sales personnel in making out sales checks and operating cash registers. In large stores, training programs are more formal and usually conducted over several days. Topics usually discussed are customer service, security, the store's policies and procedures, and how to work a cash register. Depending on the type of product they are selling, they may be given additional specialized training by manufacturers' representatives. For example, those working in cosmetics receive instruction on the types of products available and for whom the cosmetics would be most beneficial. Likewise, salespersons employed by motor vehicle dealers may be required to participate in training programs designed to provide information on the technical details of standard and optional equipment available on new models. Because providing the best service to customers is a high priority for many employers, employees are often given periodic training to update and refine their skills.

As salespersons gain experience and seniority, they usually move to positions of greater responsibility and may be given their choice of departments. This often means moving to areas with potentially higher earnings and commissions. The highest earnings potential is usually found in selling big-ticket items. This type of position often requires the most knowledge of the product and the greatest talent for persuasion.

Opportunities for advancement vary in small stores. In some establishments, advancement is limited because one person (often the owner) does most of the managerial work. In others, however, some salespersons are promoted to assistant managers.

Traditionally, capable salespersons without college degrees could advance to management positions. However today, large retail businesses usually prefer to hire college graduates as management trainees, making a college education increasingly important. Despite this trend, motivated and capable employees without college degrees should still be able to advance to administrative or supervisory positions in large establishments.

Retail selling experience may be an asset when applying for sales positions with larger retailers or in other industries, such as financial services, wholesale trade, or manufacturing.

Job Outlook

As in the past, employment opportunities for retail salespersons are expected to continue to be good because of the many job openings created each year due to the need to replace the large number of workers who transfer to other occupations or leave the labor force. Additional openings will be created by growth in employment of retail salespersons. Employment is expected to increase about as fast as the average for all occupations through the year 2008 due to anticipated growth in retail sales created by a growing population. There will continue to be many opportunities for part-time workers, and demand will be strong for temporary workers during peak selling periods, such as the Christmas season.

During economic downturns, sales volumes and the resulting demand for sales workers usually decline. Purchases of costly items, such as cars, appliances, and furniture, tend to be postponed during difficult economic times. In areas of high unemployment, sales of many types of goods decline. However, because turnover of sales workers is usually very high, employers often can adjust employment levels simply by not replacing all those who leave.

Earnings

The starting wage for many retail sales positions is the Federal minimum wage, which was $5.15 an hour in 1999. In areas where employers have difficulty attracting and retaining workers, wages tend to be higher than the established minimum.

Median hourly earnings of retail salespersons, including commission, in 1998 were $7.61. The middle 50 percent earned between $6.18 and $9.84 an hour. The lowest 10 percent earned less than $5.76, and the highest 10 percent earned more than $14.53 an hour. Median hourly earnings in the industries employing the largest number of retail salespersons in 1997 were as follows:

New and used car dealers	$15.10
Department stores	6.90
Miscellaneous shopping goods stores	6.70
Family clothing stores	6.40
Women's clothing stores	6.20

Compensation systems vary by type of establishment and merchandise sold. Salespersons receive hourly wages, commissions, or a combination of wages and commissions. Under a commission system, salespersons receive a percentage of the sales that they make. This system offers sales workers the opportunity to significantly increase their earnings, but they may find their earnings strongly depend on their ability to sell their product and the ups and downs

of the economy. Employers may use incentive programs such as awards, banquets, bonuses, and profit-sharing plans to promote teamwork among the sales staff.

Benefits may be limited in smaller stores, but in large establishments, benefits are usually comparable to those offered by other employers. In addition, nearly all salespersons are able to buy their store's merchandise at a discount, with the savings depending upon on the type of merchandise.

Related Occupations

Salespersons use sales techniques coupled with their knowledge of merchandise to assist customers and encourage purchases. Workers in a number of other occupations use these skills, including manufacturers' and wholesale sales representatives; services sales representatives; securities, commodities, and financial services sales representatives; counter and rental clerks; real estate agents and brokers; purchasing managers, buyers, and purchasing agents; insurance sales agents; and cashiers.

Sources of Additional Information

Information on careers in retail sales may be obtained from the personnel offices of local stores or from State merchants' associations.

General information about retailing is available from:

* National Retail Federation, 325 7th St. NW., Suite 1100, Washington, DC 20004. Internet: http://www.nrf.com

Information about retail sales employment opportunities is available from:

* United Food and Commercial Workers International Union, Education Office, 1775 K St. NW., Washington, DC 20006-1502.

* Retail, Wholesale, and Department Store Union, 30 East 29th St., 4th Floor, New York, NY 10016.

Information about training for a career in automobile sales is available from:

* National Automobile Dealers Association, Public Relations Dept., 8400 Westpark Dr., McLean, VA 22102-3591.

Retail Sales Worker Supervisors and Managers

(O*NET 41002)

Significant Points

* Opportunities will be best for candidates with experience as a retail salesperson, cashier, or customer service worker.

* Work schedules may be irregular and often include evenings and weekends.

* Increasingly, a post-secondary degree is needed for advancement into upper management.

Nature of the Work

In every one of the thousands of retail stores across the country, there is at least one retail sales worker supervisor or manager. Because the retail trade industry provides goods and services directly to customers, the retail supervisor or manager is responsible for ensuring that customers receive satisfactory service and quality goods. They also answer customers' inquiries and handle complaints.

Retail supervisors and managers oversee the work of retail salespersons, cashiers, customer service representatives, stock clerks, and grocery clerks. They are responsible for interviewing, hiring, and training employees, as well as preparing work schedules and assigning workers to specific duties.

The responsibilities of retail sales worker supervisors and managers vary depending on the size and type of establishment, as well as the level of management. As the size of retail stores and the types of goods and services increase, these workers increasingly specialize in one department or one aspect of merchandising. Larger organizations tend to have many layers of management. As in other industries, supervisory-level retail managers usually report to their mid-level counterparts who, in turn, report to top-level managers. Small stores, and stores that carry specialized merchandise, usually have fewer levels of management.

Supervisory-level retail managers (often referred to as department managers) provide day-to-day oversight of individual departments, such as shoes, cosmetics, or housewares in large department stores; produce and meat in grocery stores; and sales in automotive dealerships. Department managers commonly are found in large retail stores. These managers establish and implement policies, goals, objectives, and procedures for their specific departments; coordinate activities with other department heads; and strive for smooth operations within their departments. They supervise employees who price and ticket goods and place them on display; clean and organize shelves, displays, and inventory in stockrooms; and inspect merchandise to ensure that none is outdated. Department managers also review inventory and sales records, develop merchandising techniques, coordinate sales promotions, and may greet and assist customers and promote sales and good public relations.

In small or independent retail stores, retail sales worker supervisors and managers not only directly supervise sales associates, but are also responsible for the operation of the entire store. In these instances, they may be called store managers. Some are also self-employed store owners.

Working Conditions

Most retail sales worker supervisors and managers have offices within the stores. Although some time is spent in the office completing merchandise orders or arranging work schedules, a large portion of their workday is spent on the sales floor.

Work hours of supervisors and managers vary greatly among retail establishments, because work schedules usually depend on customers' needs. Most managers and supervisors work 40 hours or more a week; long hours are not uncommon. This is particularly true during sales, holidays, busy shopping hours, and when inventory is taken. They are expected to work evenings and weekends but usually are compensated by getting a weekday off. Hours can change weekly, and managers sometimes must report to work on short notice, especially when employees are absent. Independent owners can often set their own schedules, but hours must be convenient to customers.

Employment

Retail sales worker supervisors and managers held about 1.7 million jobs in 1998. About 2 out of 5 were self-employed retail sales managers, mainly store owners. Although managers work throughout the retail trade industry, most are found in grocery and department stores, motor vehicle dealers, and clothing and accessory stores.

Training, Other Qualifications, and Advancement

Retail sales worker supervisors and managers usually acquire knowledge of management principles and practices—an essential requirement for a management position in retail trade—through work experience. Many supervisors and managers begin their careers on the sales floor as salespersons, cashiers, or customer service workers. In these positions, they learn merchandising, customer service, and the basic policies and procedures of the store.

The educational background of retail sales worker supervisors and managers varies widely. Regardless of the education received, business courses (including accounting), administration, marketing, management, and sales, as well as courses in psychology, sociology, and communication, are helpful. Supervisors and managers must be computer literate because almost all cash registers and inventory control systems are now computerized.

Most supervisors and managers who have post-secondary education hold associate or bachelor's degrees in liberal arts, social science, business, or management. To gain experience, many post-secondary students participate in internship programs that are usually developed jointly by individual schools and retail firms.

Once on the job, the type and amount of training available for supervisors and managers varies from store to store. Many national chains have formal training programs for management trainees that include both classroom and in-store training. Training may last from one week to one year or more, because many retail organizations require their trainees to gain experience during all shopping seasons. Other retail organizations may not have formal training programs.

Ordinarily, classroom training includes such topics as interviewing and customer service skills, employee and inventory management, and scheduling. Management trainees may work in one specific department while training on the job, or they may rotate through several departments to gain a well-rounded knowledge of the store's operation. Training programs for franchises are generally extensive, covering all functions of the company's operation, including promotion, marketing, management, finance, purchasing, product preparation, human resource management, and compensation. College graduates can usually enter management training programs directly.

Retail sales worker supervisors and managers must get along with all types of people. They need initiative, self-discipline, good judgment, and decisiveness. Patience and a mild temperament are necessary when dealing with demanding customers. They must also be able to motivate, organize, and direct the work of subordinates and communicate clearly and persuasively with customers and other managers.

Individuals who display leadership and team building skills, self-confidence, motivation, and decisiveness become candidates for promotion to assistant store manager or store manager. A post-secondary degree may speed advancement, because it is viewed by employers as a sign of motivation and maturity—qualities deemed important for promotion to more responsible positions. In many retail establishments, managers are promoted from within the company. In small retail establishments, where the number of positions is limited, advancement to a higher management position may come slowly. Large establishments most often have extensive career ladder programs and may offer managers the opportunity to transfer to another store in the chain or to the central office if an opening occurs. Although promotions may occur more quickly in large establishments, some managers must relocate every several years in order to advance. Within a central office, retail sales supervisors and managers can become advertising, marketing, and public relations managers. These managers coordinate marketing plans, monitor sales, and propose advertisements and promotions. Supervisors and managers can also become purchasing managers, buyers, and purchasing agents who purchase goods and supplies for their organization or for resale.

Some supervisors and managers who have worked in the retail industry for a long time open their own stores. However, retail trade is highly competitive, and although many independent retail owners succeed, some fail to cover expenses and eventually go out of business. To prosper, retail owners usually need good business sense and strong customer service and public relations skills.

Job Outlook

Because most jobs for retail sales worker supervisors and managers do not require post-secondary education, competition is expected for jobs with the most attractive earnings and working conditions. Candidates who have retail experience will have the best opportunities.

Employment of retail sales worker supervisors and managers is expected to grow more slowly than average for all occupations through the year 2008. Growth in this occupation will be restrained somewhat as retail companies place more emphasis on sales staff employment levels and increase the number of responsibilities their retail sales worker supervisors and managers have. Some companies may require their sales staff to report directly to upper management personnel, bypassing the department-level manager. However, many job openings are expected to occur as experienced supervisors and managers move into higher levels of management, transfer to other occupations, or leave the labor force.

Projected employment growth of retail managers will mirror, in part, the patterns of employment growth in the industries in which they are concentrated. For example, average growth is expected in grocery stores as they expand their selection of merchandise to accommodate customers' desires for one-stop shopping. The num-

ber of self-employed retail sales worker supervisors and managers is expected to decline as independent retailers face increasing competition from national chains.

Unlike middle- and upper-level management positions, store-level retail supervisors and managers generally will not be affected by the restructuring and consolidation taking place at the corporate and headquarters level of many retail chain companies.

Earnings

Salaries of retail managers vary substantially, depending upon the level of responsibility; length of service; and type, size, and location of the firm.

Median annual earnings of salaried marketing and sales worker supervisors, including commission, in 1998 were $29,570. The middle 50 percent earned between $21,850 and $42,640 a year. The lowest 10 percent earned less than $16,700, and the highest 10 percent earned more than $71,910 a year. Median annual earnings in the industries employing the largest number of salaried marketing and sales worker supervisors in 1997 were as follows:

New and used car dealers $50,100
Grocery stores 24,900
Miscellaneous shopping goods stores 22,400
Department stores 21,900
Gasoline service stations 21,000

Compensation systems vary by type of establishment and merchandise sold. Many managers receive either a commission or a combination of salary and commission. Under a commission system, retail managers receive a percentage of department or store sales. These systems offer managers the opportunity to significantly increase their earnings, but they may find that their earnings depend on their ability to sell their product and the condition of the economy. Managers who sell large amounts of merchandise often receive bonuses or other awards.

Retail managers receive typical benefits and, in some cases, stock options. In addition, retail managers generally are able to buy their store's merchandise at a discount.

Related Occupations

Retail supervisors and managers serve customers, supervise workers, and direct and coordinate the operations of an establishment. Others with similar responsibilities include managers in restaurants, wholesale trade, hotels, banks, and hospitals.

Sources of Additional Information

Information on employment opportunities for retail managers may be obtained from the employment offices of various retail establishments or State employment service offices.

General information on management careers in retail establishments is available from:

● National Retail Federation, 325 7th St. NW., Suite 1100, Washington, DC 20004. Internet: http://www.nrf.com

Information on management careers in grocery stores, and schools offering related programs, is available from:

● Food Marketing Institute, 800 Connecticut Ave. NW., Publications Dept., Washington, DC 20006-2701.

Information about management careers and training programs in the motor vehicle dealers industry is available from:

● National Automobile Dealers Association, Public Relations Dept., 8400 Westpark Dr., McLean, VA 22102-3591.

Information about management careers in convenience stores is available from:

● National Association of Convenience Stores, 1605 King St., Alexandria, VA 22314-2792.

School Teachers— Kindergarten, Elementary, and Secondary

(O*NET 31304, 31305, and 31308)

Significant Points

● Public school teachers must have at least a bachelor's degree, have completed an approved teacher education program, and be licensed.

● Many States offer alternative licensing programs to attract people into teaching, especially for hard-to-fill positions.

● Employment growth for secondary school teachers will be more rapid than for kindergarten and elementary school teachers due to student enrollments, but job outlook will vary by geographic area and subject specialty.

Nature of the Work

Teachers act as facilitators or coaches, using interactive discussions and "hands-on" learning to help students learn and apply concepts in subjects such as science, mathematics, or English. As teachers move away from the traditional repetitive drill approaches and rote memorization, they are using more "props" or "manipulatives" to help children understand abstract concepts, solve problems, and develop critical thought processes. For example, they teach the concepts of numbers or adding and subtracting by playing board games. As children get older, they use more sophisticated materials such as science apparatus, cameras, or computers.

Many classes are becoming less structured, with students working in groups to discuss and solve problems together. Preparing students for the future workforce is the major stimulus generating the changes in education. To be prepared, students must be able to interact with others, adapt to new technology, and logically think through problems. Teachers provide the tools and environment for their students to develop these skills.

Kindergarten and elementary school teachers play a vital role in the development of children. What children learn and experience during their early years can shape their views of themselves and the world and affect later success or failure in school, work, and their personal lives. Kindergarten and elementary school teachers introduce children to numbers, language, science, and social studies. They use games, music, artwork, films, slides, computers, and other tools to teach basic skills.

Most elementary school teachers instruct one class of children in several subjects. In some schools, two or more teachers work as a team and are jointly responsible for a group of students in at least one subject. In other schools, a teacher may teach one special subject—usually music, art, reading, science, arithmetic, or physical education—to a number of classes. A small but growing number of teachers instruct multilevel classrooms, with students at several different learning levels.

Secondary school teachers help students delve more deeply into subjects introduced in elementary school and expose them to more information about the world. Secondary school teachers specialize in a specific subject, such as English, Spanish, mathematics, history, or biology. They teach a variety of related courses—for example, American history, contemporary American problems, and world geography.

Teachers may use films, slides, overhead projectors, and the latest technology in teaching, including computers, telecommunication systems, and video discs. Use of computer resources, such as educational software and the Internet, exposes students to a vast range of experiences and promotes interactive learning. Through the Internet, American students can communicate with students in other countries. Students also use the Internet for individual research projects and information gathering. Computers are used in other classroom activities as well, from helping students solve math problems to learning English as a second language. Teachers may also use computers to record grades and perform other administrative and clerical duties. They must continually update their skills so they can instruct and use the latest technology in the classroom.

Teachers often work with students from varied ethnic, racial, and religious backgrounds. With growing minority populations in many parts of the country, it is important for teachers to establish rapport with a diverse student population. Accordingly, some schools offer training to help teachers enhance their awareness and understanding of different cultures. Teachers may also include multicultural programming in their lesson plans to address the needs of all students, regardless of their cultural backgrounds.

Teachers design classroom presentations to meet student needs and abilities. They also work with students individually. Teachers plan, evaluate, and assign lessons; prepare, administer, and grade tests; listen to oral presentations; and maintain classroom discipline. They observe and evaluate a student's performance and potential, and increasingly are asked to use new assessment methods. For example, teachers may examine a portfolio of a student's artwork or writing to judge the student's overall progress. They then can provide additional assistance in areas where a student needs help. Teachers also grade papers, prepare report cards, and meet with parents and school staff to discuss a student's academic progress or personal problems.

In addition to classroom activities, teachers oversee study halls and homerooms and supervise extracurricular activities. They identify physical or mental problems and refer students to the proper resource or agency for diagnosis and treatment. Secondary school teachers occasionally assist students in choosing courses, colleges, and careers. Teachers also participate in education conferences and workshops.

In recent years, site-based management, which allows teachers and parents to participate actively in management decisions, has gained popularity. In many schools, teachers are increasingly involved in making decisions regarding the budget, personnel, textbook choices, curriculum design, and teaching methods.

Working Conditions

Seeing students develop new skills and gain an appreciation of knowledge and learning can be very rewarding. However, teaching may be frustrating when dealing with unmotivated and disrespectful students. Occasionally, teachers must cope with unruly behavior and violence in the schools. Teachers may experience stress when dealing with large classes, students from disadvantaged or multicultural backgrounds, and heavy workloads.

Teachers are sometimes isolated from their colleagues because they work alone in a classroom of students. However, some schools are allowing teachers to work in teams and with mentors to enhance their professional development.

Including school duties performed outside the classroom, many teachers work more than 40 hours a week. Most teachers work the traditional 10-month school year with a 2-month vacation during the summer. Those on the 10-month schedule may teach in summer sessions, take other jobs, travel, or pursue other personal interests. Many enroll in college courses or workshops to continue their education. Teachers in districts with a year-round schedule typically work 8 weeks, are on vacation for 1 week, and have a 5-week midwinter break.

Most States have tenure laws that prevent teachers from being fired without just cause and due process. Teachers may obtain tenure after they have satisfactorily completed a probationary period of teaching, normally three years. Tenure does not absolutely guarantee a job, but it does provide some security.

Employment

Teachers held about 3.4 million jobs in 1998. Of those, about 1.9 million were kindergarten and elementary school teachers, and 1.4 million were secondary school teachers. Employment is distributed geographically, much the same as the population.

Training, Other Qualifications, and Advancement

All 50 States and the District of Columbia require public school teachers to be licensed. Licensure is not required for teachers in private schools. Usually licensure is granted by the State board of education or a licensure advisory committee. Teachers may be licensed to teach the early childhood grades (usually nursery school through grade 3); the elementary grades (grades 1 through 6 or 8); the middle grades (grades 5 through 8); a secondary education sub-

ject area (usually grades 7 through 12); or a special subject, such as reading or music (usually grades K through 12).

Requirements for regular licenses vary by State. However, all States require a bachelor's degree and completion of an approved teacher training program with a prescribed number of subject and education credits as well as supervised practice teaching. About one-third of the States also require technology training as part of the teacher certification process. A number of States require specific minimum grade point averages for teacher licensure. Other States require teachers to obtain a master's degree in education, which involves at least one year of additional coursework beyond the bachelor's degree with a specialization in a particular subject.

Almost all States require applicants for teacher licensure to be tested for competency in basic skills such as reading, writing, teaching, and subject matter proficiency. Most States require continuing education for renewal of the teacher's license. Many States have reciprocity agreements that make it easier for teachers licensed in one State to become licensed in another.

Increasingly, many States are moving towards implementing performance-based standards for licensure, which require passing a rigorous comprehensive teaching examination to obtain a provisional license. Teachers must then demonstrate satisfactory teaching performance over an extended period of time to obtain a full license.

Many States offer alternative teacher licensure programs for people who have bachelor's degrees in the subject they will teach, but lack the necessary education courses required for a regular license. Alternative licensure programs were originally designed to ease teacher shortages in certain subjects, such as mathematics and science. The programs have expanded to attract other people into teaching, including recent college graduates and mid-career changers. In some programs, individuals begin teaching quickly under provisional licensure. After working under the close supervision of experienced educators for one or two years while taking education courses outside school hours, they receive regular licensure if they have progressed satisfactorily. Under other programs, college graduates who do not meet licensure requirements take only those courses that they lack, and then they become licensed. This may take one or two semesters of full-time study. States may issue emergency licenses to individuals who do not meet requirements for a regular license when schools cannot attract enough qualified teachers to fill positions. Teachers who need licensure may enter programs that grant a master's degree in education, as well as a license.

For several years, the National Board for Professional Teaching Standards has offered voluntary national certification for teachers. To become nationally certified, teachers must prove their aptitude by compiling a portfolio showing their work in the classroom, and by passing a written assessment and evaluation of their teaching knowledge. Currently, teachers may become certified in one of seven areas. These areas are based on the age of the students and, in some cases, subject area. For example, teachers may obtain a certificate for teaching English Language Arts to early adolescents (ages 11-15), or they may become certified as early childhood generalists. All States recognize national certification, and many States and school districts provide special benefits to teachers holding national certification. Benefits typically include higher salaries and reimbursement for continuing education and certification fees.

Additionally, many States allow nationally certified teachers to carry a license from one State to another.

The National Council for Accreditation of Teacher Education currently accredits more than 500 teacher education programs across the United States. Generally, four-year colleges require students to wait until their sophomore year before applying for admission to teacher education programs. Traditional education programs for kindergarten and elementary school teachers include courses—designed specifically for those preparing to teach—in mathematics, physical science, social science, music, art, and literature, as well as prescribed professional education courses such as philosophy of education, psychology of learning, and teaching methods. Aspiring secondary school teachers either major in the subject they plan to teach while also taking education courses, or they major in education and take subject courses. Teacher education programs are now required to include classes in the use of computers and other technologies to maintain accreditation. Most programs require students to perform a student teaching internship.

Many States now offer professional development schools, which are partnerships between universities and elementary or secondary schools. Students enter these 1-year programs after completion of their bachelor's degree. Professional development schools merge theory with practice and allow the student to experience a year of teaching first-hand, with professional guidance.

In addition to being knowledgeable in their subject, the ability to communicate, inspire trust and confidence, and motivate students, as well as to understand their educational and emotional needs, is essential for teachers. Teachers must be able to recognize and respond to individual differences in students and employ different teaching methods that will result in higher student achievement. They also should be organized, dependable, patient, and creative. Teachers must also be able to work cooperatively and communicate effectively with other teaching staff, support staff, parents, and other members of the community.

With additional preparation, teachers may move into positions as school librarians, reading specialists, curriculum specialists, or guidance counselors. Teachers may become administrators or supervisors, although the number of these positions is limited and competition can be intense. In some systems, highly qualified, experienced teachers can become senior or mentor teachers, who receive higher pay and additional responsibilities. They guide and assist less experienced teachers while keeping most of their own teaching responsibilities.

Job Outlook

The job market for teachers varies widely by geographic area and by subject specialty. Many inner cities (often characterized by overcrowded conditions and higher-than-average crime and poverty rates) and rural areas (characterized by their remote location and relatively low salaries) have difficulty attracting enough teachers, so job prospects should continue to be better in these areas than in suburban districts. Currently, many school districts have difficulty hiring qualified teachers in some subjects—mathematics, science (especially chemistry and physics), bilingual education, and computer science. Specialties that currently have an abundance of qualified teachers include general elementary education, physical education, and social studies. Teachers who are geographically mobile and who obtain licensure in more than one subject should have a distinct advantage in finding a job. With enrollments of minorities increasing, coupled with a shortage of minority teachers, efforts to recruit minority teachers should intensify. Also, the number of non-English speaking students has grown dramatically, especially in California and Florida, which have large Spanish-speaking student populations, creating demand for bilingual teachers and those who teach English as a second language.

Overall employment of kindergarten, elementary, and secondary school teachers is expected to increase about as fast as the average for all occupations through the year 2008. The expected retirement of a large number of teachers currently in their 40s and 50s should open up many additional jobs. However, projected employment growth varies among individual teaching occupations.

Employment of secondary school teachers is expected to grow faster than the average for all occupations through the year 2008, while average employment growth is projected for kindergarten and elementary school teachers. Assuming relatively little change in average class size, employment growth of teachers depends on population growth rates and corresponding student enrollments. Enrollments of secondary school students are expected to grow throughout most of the projection period. On the other hand, elementary school enrollment is projected to increase until the year 2001 and then decline.

The number of teachers employed is also dependent on State and local expenditures for education. Pressures from taxpayers to limit spending could result in fewer teachers than projected; pressures to spend more to improve the quality of education could increase the teacher workforce.

In anticipation of growing student enrollments at the secondary school level, many States are implementing policies that will encourage more students to become teachers. Some are giving large signing bonuses that are distributed over the teacher's first few years of teaching. Some are expanding State scholarships; issuing loans for moving expenses; and implementing loan-forgiveness programs, allowing education majors with at least a B average to receive State-paid tuition as long as they agree to teach in the State for four years.

The supply of teachers also is expected to increase in response to reports of improved job prospects, more teacher involvement in school policy, and greater public interest in education. In recent years, the total number of bachelor's and master's degrees granted in education has steadily increased. In addition, more teachers will be drawn from a reserve pool of career changers, substitute teachers, and teachers completing alternative certification programs, relocating to different schools, and reentering the workforce.

Earnings

Median annual earnings of kindergarten, elementary, and secondary school teachers ranged from $33,590 to $37,890 in 1998. The lowest 10 percent earned $19,710 to $24,390; the top 10 percent earned $53,720 to $70,030.

According to the American Federation of Teachers, beginning teachers with a bachelor's degree earned an average of $25,700 in the

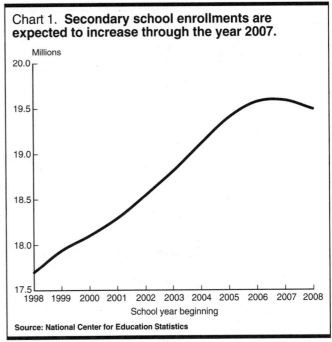

Chart 1. Secondary school enrollments are expected to increase through the year 2007.

Source: National Center for Education Statistics

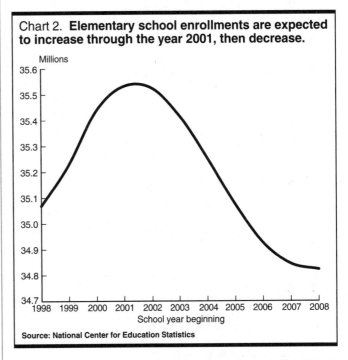

Chart 2. Elementary school enrollments are expected to increase through the year 2001, then decrease.

Source: National Center for Education Statistics

1997-98 school year. The estimated average salary of all public elementary and secondary school teachers in the 1997-98 school year was $39,300. Private school teachers generally earn less than public school teachers.

In 1998, over half of all public school teachers belonged to unions—mainly the American Federation of Teachers and the National Education Association—that bargain with school systems over wages, hours, and the terms and conditions of employment.

In some schools, teachers receive extra pay for coaching sports and working with students in extracurricular activities. Some teachers

earn extra income during the summer working in the school system or in other jobs.

Related Occupations

Kindergarten, elementary, and secondary school teaching requires a variety of skills and aptitudes, including a talent for working with children; organizational, administrative, and record keeping abilities; research and communication skills; the power to influence, motivate, and train others; patience; and creativity. Workers in other occupations requiring some of these aptitudes include college and university faculty, counselors, education administrators, employment interviewers, librarians, preschool teachers and child-care workers, public relations specialists, sales representatives, social workers, and trainers and employee development specialists.

Sources of Additional Information

Information on licensure or certification requirements and approved teacher training institutions is available from local school systems and State departments of education.

Information on teachers' unions and education-related issues may be obtained from:

- American Federation of Teachers, 555 New Jersey Ave. NW, Washington, DC 20001.
- National Education Association, 1201 16th St. NW, Washington, DC 20036.

A list of institutions with accredited teacher education programs can be obtained from:

- National Council for Accreditation of Teacher Education, 2010 Massachusetts Ave. NW., Suite 500, Washington, DC 20036. Internet: http://www.ncate.org

For information on national teacher certification, contact:

- National Board for Professional Teaching Standards, 26555 Evergreen Rd., Suite 400, Southfield, MI 48076. Internet: http://www.nbpts.org

For information on alternative certification programs, contact:

- ERIC Clearinghouse on Teacher Education, 1307 New York Ave. NW., Washington, DC 20005-4701.

Secretaries

(O*NET 21999C, 55102, 55105, and 55108)

Significant Points

- Increasing office automation and organizational restructuring will lead to little or no change in overall employment of secretaries.

- Employers increasingly require knowledge of software applications, such as word processing, spreadsheets, and database management.

- Job openings should be plentiful, especially for well-qualified and experienced secretaries, primarily due to the need to replace workers who leave this very large occupation.

Nature of the Work

As technology continues to expand in offices across the Nation, the role of the secretary has greatly evolved. Office automation and organizational restructuring have led secretaries to assume a wide range of new responsibilities once reserved for managerial and professional staff. Many secretaries now provide training and orientation to new staff, conduct research on the Internet, and learn to operate new office technologies. In the midst of these changes, however, their core responsibilities have remained much the same—performing and coordinating an office's administrative activities and ensuring that information is disseminated to staff and clients.

Secretaries are responsible for a variety of administrative and clerical duties necessary to run an organization efficiently. They serve as an information clearinghouse for an office, schedule appointments, provide information to callers, organize and maintain paper and electronic files, manage projects, and produce correspondence. They may also prepare correspondence, handle travel arrangements, and contact clients.

Secretaries are aided in these tasks by a variety of office equipment, such as fax machines, photocopiers, and telephone systems. In addition, secretaries increasingly use personal computers to run spreadsheet, word processing, database management, desktop publishing, and graphics programs—tasks previously handled by managers and other professionals. At the same time, these other workers have assumed many tasks traditionally assigned to secretaries, such as word processing and answering the telephone. Because secretaries are often relieved from dictation and typing, they can support several members of the professional staff. In a number of organizations, secretaries work in teams in order to work flexibly and share their expertise.

Specific job duties vary with experience and titles. Executive secretaries and administrative assistants, for example, perform fewer clerical tasks than lower level secretaries. In addition to greeting visitors, arranging conference calls, and scheduling meetings, they may handle more complex responsibilities such as conducting research, preparing statistical reports, training employees, and supervising other clerical staff.

Some secretaries, such as legal and medical secretaries, perform highly specialized work requiring knowledge of technical terminology and procedures. For instance, legal secretaries prepare correspondence and legal papers such as summonses, complaints, motions, responses, and subpoenas under the supervision of an attorney. They also may review legal journals and assist in other ways with legal research, such as verifying quotes and citations in legal briefs. Medical secretaries transcribe dictation, prepare correspondence, and assist physicians or medical scientists with reports, speeches, articles, and conference proceedings. They also record simple medical histories, arrange for patients to be hospitalized, and order supplies. Most medical secretaries need to be familiar with insurance rules, billing practices, and hospital or laboratory procedures. Other technical secretaries who assist engineers or scientists may prepare correspondence, maintain the technical library, and gather and edit materials for scientific papers.

Working Conditions

Secretaries usually work in offices with other professionals in schools, hospitals, or in legal and medical offices. Their jobs often involve sitting for long periods. If they spend a lot of time typing, particularly at a video display terminal, they may encounter problems of eyestrain, stress, and repetitive motion, such as carpal tunnel syndrome.

Office work can lend itself to alternative or flexible working arrangements, such as part time work. In fact, 1 secretary in 5 works part time, and many others work in temporary positions. A few participate in job sharing arrangements in which two people divide responsibility for a single job. The majority of secretaries, however, are full-time employees who work a standard 40-hour week.

Employment

Secretaries held about 3.2 million jobs in 1998, ranking among the largest occupations in the U.S. economy. The following table shows the distribution of employment by secretarial specialty.

Secretaries, total	3,195,000
Legal secretaries	285,000
Medical secretaries	219,000
Secretaries, except legal and medical	2,691,000

Secretaries are employed in organizations of every type. About 6 out of 10 secretaries are employed in firms providing services, ranging from education and health to legal and business services. Others work for firms engaged in manufacturing, construction, wholesale and retail trade, transportation, and communications. Banks, insurance companies, investment firms, and real estate firms are also important employers, as are Federal, State, and local government agencies.

Training, Other Qualifications, and Advancement

High school graduates who have basic office skills may qualify for entry-level secretarial positions. However, employers increasingly require knowledge of software applications, such as word processing, spreadsheets, and database management. Secretaries should be proficient in keyboarding and good at spelling, punctuation, grammar, and oral communication. Shorthand is necessary for some positions. Because secretaries must be tactful in their dealings with people, employers also look for good interpersonal skills. Discretion, good judgment, organizational ability, and initiative are especially important for higher level secretarial positions.

As office automation continues to evolve, retraining and continuing education will remain an integral part of secretarial jobs. Changes in the office environment have increased the demand for secretaries who are adaptable and versatile. Secretaries may have to attend classes to learn how to operate new office technologies, such as information storage systems, scanners, the Internet, or new or updated software packages.

Secretaries acquire skills in various ways. Training ranges from high school vocational education programs that teach office skills and keyboarding to one- to two-year programs in office administration offered by business schools, vocational-technical institutes, and community colleges. Many temporary help agencies also provide formal training in computer and office skills. These skills are most often acquired, however, through on-the-job instruction by other employees or by equipment and software vendors. Specialized training programs are available for students planning to become medical or legal secretaries or administrative technology specialists.

Testing and certification for entry-level office skills is available through the Office Proficiency Assessment and Certification program offered by the International Association of Administrative Professionals. As secretaries gain experience, they can earn the Certified Professional Secretary (CPS) designation by meeting certain experience requirements and passing an examination. Similarly, those without experience who want to be certified as a legal support professional may be certified as an Accredited Legal Secretary (ALS) by the Certifying Board of the National Association of Legal Secretaries. This organization also administers an examination to certify a legal secretary with three years of experience as a Professional Legal Secretary (PLS). Legal Secretaries International confers the designation Board Certified Civil Trial Legal Secretary in specialized areas such as litigation, real estate, probate, and corporate law, to those who have five years of law-related experience and pass an examination.

Secretaries generally advance by being promoted to other secretarial positions with more responsibilities. Qualified secretaries who broaden their knowledge of a company's operations and enhance their skills may be promoted to other positions such as senior or executive secretary, clerical supervisor, or office manager. Secretaries with word processing experience can advance to jobs as word processing trainers, supervisors, or managers within their own firms or in a secretarial or word processing service bureau. Secretarial experience can also lead to jobs such as instructor or sales representative with manufacturers of software or computer equipment. With additional training, many legal secretaries become paralegals.

Job Outlook

Job openings should be plentiful, particularly for well-qualified and experienced secretaries, stemming from the need to replace workers who transfer to other occupations or leave this very large occupation for other reasons each year. Overall, however, little or no change is expected in employment of secretaries over the 1998-2008 period.

Projected employment of secretaries will vary by occupational specialty. Rapid growth in the health and legal services industries should lead to average growth for medical and legal secretaries. However, employment of secretaries who do not specialize in legal or medical work (about 7 out of 8) is expected to remain flat. Rapidly growing industries—such as personnel supply, computer and data processing, and management and public relations—will generate new job opportunities.

Growing levels of office automation and organizational restructuring will continue to make secretaries more productive in coming years. Personal computers, electronic mail, scanners, fax machines, and voice message systems will allow secretaries to accomplish more in the same amount of time. The use of automated equipment is also changing the distribution of work in many offices. In some cases, such traditional secretarial duties as typing or keyboarding, filing, copying, and bookkeeping are being assigned to workers in other units or departments. Professionals and managers increasingly do their own word processing and much of their own correspondence rather than submit the work to secretaries and other support staff. Also, in some law offices and physicians' offices, paralegals and medical assistants are assuming some tasks formerly done by secretaries. As other workers assume more of these duties, there is a trend in many offices for professionals and managers to "share" secretaries. The traditional arrangement of one secretary per manager is becoming less prevalent; instead, secretaries increasingly support systems or units. This approach often means secretaries assume added responsibilities and are seen as valuable members of a team, but it also contributes to the decline in employment projected for most secretaries.

Developments in office technology are certain to continue, and they will bring about further changes in the secretary's work environment. However, many secretarial duties are of a personal, interactive nature and, therefore, are not easily automated. Responsibilities such as planning conferences, working with clients, and transmitting staff instructions require tact and communication skills. Because technology cannot substitute for these personal skills, secretaries will continue to play a key role in most organizations.

Earnings

Median annual earnings of secretaries, excluding legal and medical secretaries, were $23,560 in 1998. The middle 50 percent earned between $18,770 and $29,400. The lowest 10 percent earned less than $14,410, and the highest 10 percent earned more than $36,050. Secretaries earn slightly more in urban areas. In 1997, median annual earnings in the industries employing the largest numbers of secretaries, excluding legal and medical secretaries, were:

Local government	$23,900
Hospitals	23,000
Colleges and universities	22,600
Elementary and secondary schools	22,300
Personnel supply services	21,500

In 1998, median annual earnings of legal secretaries were $30,050. Median annual earnings of medical secretaries were $22,390 in 1998; in offices and clinics of medical doctors they earned approximately $22,000 in 1997, and in hospitals, $21,400.

According to the International Association of Administrative Professionals, secretaries averaged $25,500 a year in 1998. Salaries vary a great deal, however, reflecting differences in skill, experience, and level of responsibility. Salaries also vary in different parts of the country; earnings are usually lowest in southern cities, and highest in northern and western cities. In addition, salaries vary by industry; salaries of secretaries tend to be highest in transportation, legal services, and public utilities and lowest in retail trade and finance, insurance, and real estate. Certification in this field usually is rewarded by a higher salary.

The starting salary for inexperienced secretaries in the Federal government was $18,400 a year in 1999. Beginning salaries were slightly higher in selected areas where the prevailing local pay level was higher. All secretaries employed by the Federal government averaged about $30,200 a year in 1999.

Related Occupations

A number of other workers type, record information, and process paperwork. Among them are bookkeepers, receptionists, stenographers, personnel clerks, typists and word processors, paralegals, medical assistants, and medical record technicians. A growing number of secretaries share in managerial and human resource responsibilities. Occupations requiring these skills include office and administrative support supervisor, systems manager, office manager, and human resource specialist.

Sources of Additional Information

For information on the Certified Professional Secretary designation, contact:

- International Association of Administrative Professionals, 10502 NW Ambassador Dr., P.O. Box 20404, Kansas City, MO 64195-0404. Internet: http://www.iaap-hq.org

Information on the Board Certified Civil Trial Legal Secretary designation can be obtained from:

- Legal Secretaries International Inc., 8902 Sunnywood Dr., Houston, TX 77088-3729. Internet: http://www.compassnet.com/legalsec

Information on the Accredited Legal Secretary and Certified Professional Legal Secretary designations is available from:

- National Association of Legal Secretaries, 2448 East 81st St., Suite 3400, Tulsa, OK 74137-4238. Internet: http://www.nals.org

State employment offices provide information about job openings for secretaries.

Securities, Commodities, and Financial Services Sales Representatives

(O*NET 43014A and 43014B)

Significant Points

- A college degree and good sales ability are among the most important qualifications for this profession.

- Employment is expected to grow much faster than average due to increasing investment in securities and other financial products.

- Many beginning securities and commodities sales representatives leave the occupation because they are unable to establish a sufficient clientele; once established, however, these workers have a very strong attachment to their occupation because of high earnings and the considerable investment in training.

Nature of the Work

Most investors, whether they are individuals with a few hundred dollars to invest or large institutions with millions, use *securities, commodities, and financial services sales representatives* when buying or selling stocks, bonds, shares in mutual funds, insurance annuities, or other financial products. In addition, many clients use them for advice on investments and other financial matters.

Securities and commodities sales representatives, also called brokers, stockbrokers, registered representatives, account executives, or financial consultants, perform a variety of tasks depending on their specific job duties. When an investor wishes to buy or sell a security, for example, sales representatives may relay the order through their firms' computers to the floor of a securities exchange, such as the New York Stock Exchange. There, securities and commodities sales representatives known as *floor brokers* negotiate the price with other floor brokers, make the sale, and forward the purchase price to the sales representatives. If a security is not traded on an exchange, such as in the case of bonds and over-the-counter stocks, the broker sends the order to the firm's trading department. There, other securities and commodities sales representatives, known as *dealers*, buy and sell securities directly from other dealers using their own funds or those of the firm, with the intention of reselling the security to customers at a profit. After the transaction has been completed, the broker notifies the customer of the final price.

Securities and commodities sales representatives also provide many related services for their customers. They may explain stock market terms and trading practices; offer financial counseling or advice on the purchase or sale of particular securities; and devise an individual client financial portfolio, which could include securities, life insurance, corporate and municipal bonds, mutual funds, certificates of deposit, annuities, and other investments.

Not all customers have the same investment goals. Some individuals prefer long-term investments for capital growth or to provide income over a number of years; others might want to invest in speculative securities that they hope will rise in price quickly. Securities and commodities sales representatives furnish information about advantages and disadvantages of an investment based on each person's objectives. They also supply the latest price quotes on any security, as well as information on the activities and financial positions of the corporations issuing these securities.

Most securities and commodities sales representatives serve individual investors, but others specialize in institutional investors. In institutional investing, sales representatives usually concentrate on a specific financial product, such as stocks, bonds, options, annuities, or commodity futures. At other times, they may also handle the sale of new issues, such as corporate securities issued to finance plant expansion.

The most important part of a sales representative's job is finding clients and building a customer base. Thus, beginning securities and commodities sales representatives spend much of their time searching for customers—relying heavily on telephone solicitation. They may also meet clients through business and social contacts. Many sales representatives find it useful to contact potential clients by teaching adult education investment courses or by giving lectures at libraries or social clubs. Brokerage firms may give sales representatives lists of people with whom the firm has done business in the past. Some brokers inherit the clients of representatives who have retired.

Financial services sales representatives sell banking and related services. They contact potential customers to explain their services and to ascertain customers' banking and other financial needs. In doing so, they discuss services such as deposit accounts, lines of credit, sales or inventory financing, certificates of deposit, cash management, or investment services. They may also solicit businesses to participate in consumer credit card programs. As banks offer more and increasingly complex financial services—for example, securities brokerage and financial planning—financial services sales representatives assume greater importance.

Also included in this occupation are *financial planners*, who use their knowledge of tax and investment strategies, securities, insurance, pension plans, and real estate to develop and implement financial plans for individuals and businesses. Planners interview clients to determine their assets, liabilities, cash flow, insurance coverage, tax status, and financial objectives. They then analyze this information and develop a financial plan tailored to each client's needs. Planners may also sell financial products, such as stocks, bonds, mutual funds, and insurance, or refer clients to other resources.

Working Conditions

Most securities and commodities sales representatives work in offices under fairly stressful conditions. They have access to "quote boards" or computer terminals that continually provide information on the prices of securities. When sales activity increases, due perhaps to unanticipated changes in the economy, the pace can become very hectic.

Established securities and commodities sales representatives usually work a standard 40-hour week. Beginners who are seeking customers may work longer hours. New brokers spend a great deal of time learning the firm's products and services and studying for exams to qualify them to sell other products, such as insurance and commodities. Most securities and commodities sales representatives accommodate customers by meeting with them in the evenings or on weekends.

A growing number of securities and commodities sales representatives, employed mostly by discount brokerage firms, work in call center environments. In these centers, hundreds of representatives spend much of the day on the telephone taking orders from clients or offering advice and information on different securities. Often these call centers operate 24 hours a day, requiring representatives to work in shifts.

Financial services sales representatives normally work 40 hours a week in a comfortable, less stressful office environment. They may spend considerable time outside the office meeting with present and prospective clients, attending civic functions, and participat-

ing in trade association meetings. Some financial services sales representatives work exclusively inside banks, providing service to "walk-in" customers.

Financial planners work in offices or out of their homes. They usually work standard business hours, but they often have to visit clients in the evenings or on weekends. Many teach evening classes or put on seminars in order to bring in more clients.

Employment

Securities, commodities, and financial services sales representatives held 303,000 jobs in 1998; securities and commodities sales representatives accounted for 8 out of 10. Although securities and commodities sales representatives are employed by brokerage and investment firms in all parts of the country, most sales representatives work for a small number of large firms with main offices in cities, especially New York.

Financial services sales representatives are employed by banks, savings and loan associations, and other credit institutions. Financial planners can work for credit unions, credit counseling firms, banks, and companies that specialize in offering financial advice. Other planners are self-employed workers, many of whom contract out their services with these firms.

Training, Other Qualifications, and Advancement

Because securities and commodities sales representatives must be knowledgeable about economic conditions and trends, a college education is important, especially in larger securities firms. In fact, the overwhelming majority of workers in this occupation are college graduates. Although employers seldom require specialized academic training, courses in business administration, economics, and finance are helpful.

Many employers consider personal qualities and skills more important than academic training. Employers seek applicants who have considerable sales ability, good interpersonal and communication skills, and a strong desire to succeed. Some employers also make sure that applicants have a good credit history and a clean record. Self-confidence and an ability to handle frequent rejections are also important ingredients for success.

Because maturity and the ability to work independently are important, many employers prefer to hire those who have achieved success in other jobs. Some firms prefer candidates with sales experience, particularly those who have worked on commission in areas such as real estate or insurance. Therefore, most entrants to this occupation transfer from other jobs. Some begin working as securities and commodities sales representatives following retirement from other fields.

Securities and commodities sales representatives must meet State licensing requirements, which usually include passing an examination and, in some cases, furnishing a personal bond. In addition, sales representatives must register as representatives of their firm with the National Association of Securities Dealers, Inc. (NASD). Before beginners can qualify as registered representatives, they must pass the General Securities Registered Representative Examination

(Series 7 exam), administered by the NASD, and be an employee of a registered firm for at least four months. Most States require a second examination—the Uniform Securities Agents State Law Examination. These tests measure the prospective representative's knowledge of the securities business, customer protection requirements, and record keeping procedures. Many take correspondence courses in preparation for the securities examinations. Within two years, brokers are encouraged to take additional licensing exams in order to sell insurance and commodities.

Most employers provide on-the-job training to help securities and commodities sales representatives meet the registration requirements for certification. In most firms, this training period takes about four months. Trainees in large firms may receive classroom instruction in securities analysis, effective speaking, and the finer points of selling; take courses offered by business schools and associations; and undergo a period of on-the-job training lasting up to two years. Many firms like to rotate their trainees among various departments in the firm to give trainees a broad perspective of the securities business. In small firms, sales representatives often receive training in outside institutions and on the job.

Securities and commodities sales representatives must understand the basic characteristics of the wide variety of financial products offered by brokerage firms. Brokers periodically take training through their firms or outside institutions to keep abreast of new financial products and improve their sales techniques. Computer training is also important, as the securities sales business is highly automated. Since 1995, it has also become mandatory for all registered securities and commodities sales representatives to attend periodic continuing education classes to maintain their licenses. Courses consist of computer-based training in regulatory matters and company training on new products and services.

The primary form of advancement for securities and commodities sales representatives is an increase in the number and size of the accounts they handle. Although beginners usually service the accounts of individual investors, they may eventually handle very large institutional accounts, such as those of banks and pension funds. After taking a series of tests, some brokers become portfolio managers and have greater authority to make investment decisions over an account. Some experienced sales representatives become branch office managers and supervise other sales representatives while continuing to provide services for their own customers. A few representatives advance to top management positions or become partners in their firms.

Banks and other credit institutions prefer to hire college graduates for financial services sales jobs. A business administration degree with a specialization in finance or a liberal arts degree including courses in accounting, economics, and marketing serves as excellent preparation for this job.

In contrast to securities brokers, financial services sales representatives primarily learn their jobs through on-the-job training under the supervision of bank officers. Outstanding performance can lead to promotion to managerial positions.

There are no formal educational or licensure requirements for becoming a financial planner, but a license is required to offer advice or sell specific securities, mutual funds, or insurance products. And although a college education is not necessary to become a financial planner, the vast majority of planners have a bachelor's or master's degree. Courses in accounting, business administration, economics, and finance are particularly helpful.

Many planners also find it worthwhile to obtain a Certified Financial Planner (CFP) or Chartered Financial Consultant (ChFC) designation. These designations demonstrate to potential customers that a planner has extensive training and competency in the area of financial planning. The CFP designation is issued by the CFP Board of Standards in Denver, Colorado and requires relevant experience, completion of education requirements, passing an extensive examination, and adherence to an enforceable Code of Ethics. The ChFC designation is issued by the American College in Bryn Mawr, Pennsylvania, and requires experience and completion of a ten-course study program. Both programs have a continuing education requirement.

Job Outlook

Barring a significant decline in the stock market, the number of securities, commodities, and financial services sales representatives should grow much faster than the average for all occupations through 2008. As people's incomes continue to climb and they seek better returns on their investments, they will increasingly need the advice and services of a securities and commodities sales representative to realize their financial goals. Growth in the buying and selling of stocks over the Internet will reduce the need for brokers for many transactions. Nevertheless, the rapid overall increase in investment is expected to spur rapid employment growth among these workers, as a majority of transactions will still require the advice and services of securities, commodities, and financial services sales representatives.

Baby boomers in their peak savings years will fuel much of the investment boom. Saving for retirement is being made much easier by the government, which continues to offer a number of tax-favorable pension plans, such as the 401(k) and the Roth IRA. More women in the workforce also means higher incomes and more women qualifying for pensions. And many of these pensions are self-directed, meaning that the recipient has the responsibility for investing the money. With such large amounts of money to invest, brokers and financial planners will be in demand to provide investment advice.

Other factors that will impact the demand for brokers are the increasing number and complexity of investment products as well as the effects of globalization. As the public and businesses become more sophisticated about investing, they are venturing into the options and futures markets. Brokers are needed to buy or sell these products, which are not available for trading online. Also, markets for investment are expanding with the increase in global trading of stocks and bonds. Further, the New York Stock Exchange has announced its intention to extend its trading hours to accommodate trading in foreign stocks and compete with foreign exchanges. If this takes place, it will vastly increase the demand for brokers, both on the floor of the exchange and in brokerage firms to handle the larger volume of trades.

Employment of brokers, however, will be adversely affected if the stock market or the economy suddenly declines. Even in good times, turnover is relatively high for beginning brokers who are unable to establish a sizable clientele. Once established, though, securities

and commodities sales representatives have a very strong attachment to their occupation because of high earnings and the considerable investment in training. Competition is usually intense, especially in larger companies, with more applicants than jobs. Opportunities for beginning brokers should be better in smaller firms.

The number of financial services sales representatives in banks will increase faster than average as banks attempt to become a "one-stop-shop" for investing. Deregulation will allow banks to offer an increasing array of services, such as stocks and insurance, that they have been prevented from offering in the past. Financial planners can also be expected to grow faster than average as an increasingly wealthy population seeks advice on tax and estate planning, retirement planning, and investing.

Earnings

Median annual earnings of securities, commodities, and financial services sales representatives were $48,090 in 1998. The middle half earned between $31,400 and $103,040. The lowest 10 percent earned less than $22,660; the top 10 percent earned more than $124,800.

Median annual earnings in the industries employing the largest number of securities and financial services sales representatives in 1997 were:

Securities brokers and dealers	$53,700
Security and commodity services	46,900
Mortgage bankers and brokers	36,300
Commercial banks	33,000

Stockbrokers, who provide personalized service and more guidance over a client's investments, usually are paid a commission based on the amount of stocks, bonds, mutual funds, insurance, and other products they sell. Commission earnings are likely to be high when there is much buying and selling and low when there is a slump in market activity. Most firms provide sales representatives with a steady income by paying a "draw against commission"—a minimum salary based on commissions they can be expected to earn. Securities and commodities sales representatives who can provide their clients with the most complete financial services should enjoy the greatest income stability. Trainee brokers are usually paid a salary until they develop a client base. The salary gradually decreases in favor of commissions as the broker gains clients. A small but increasing number of full-service brokers are paid a percentage of the assets they oversee. This fee often includes a certain number of trades done for free.

Brokers who work for discount brokerage firms that promote the use of telephone and online trading services are usually paid a salary. Sometimes this salary is boosted by bonuses that reflect the profitability of the office.

Financial services sales representatives usually are paid a salary; some receive a bonus if they meet certain established goals. Earnings of financial planners can be wholly fee-based, which means they do not receive any commissions for selling a product they recommend. They simply charge by the hour or by the complexity

of the financial plan. The majority of financial planners, though, receive commissions on the sale of insurance products or securities, in addition to charging a fee.

Related Occupations

Similar sales jobs requiring specialized knowledge include insurance sales agents and real estate agents.

Sources of Additional Information

For general information on the securities industry, contact:

- The Securities Industry Association, 120 Broadway, New York, NY 10271. Internet: http://www.sia.com

For information about the Certified Financial Planner designation, contact:

- The Certified Financial Planner Board of Standards, 1700 Broadway, Suite 2100, Denver, CO 80290-2101. Internet: http://www.cfp-board.org

For information about job opportunities for financial services sales representatives in various States, contact State bankers' associations or write directly to a particular bank.

Services Sales Representatives

(O*NET 43017, 43023A, 43023B, 43099A, 43099B, and 49026)

Significant Points

- A significant part of earnings may be in the form of commissions, which can vary considerably depending on performance.

- Considerable travel may be required.

Nature of the Work

Services sales representatives, unlike sales representatives who sell manufactured products, sell an intangible product, a service. For example, services sales representatives for computer and data processing firms sell complex services such as inventory control, payroll processing, sales analysis, and financial reporting systems. Hotel services sales representatives contact associations, businesses, and social groups to solicit convention and conference business. Services sales representatives for personnel supply services firms locate clients and persuade them to hire their firm's employees. Those in the motion picture industry sell the rights for movie theaters to show their films. Other representatives sell automotive leasing, burial, shipping, protective, and management consulting services. Service sales representatives are also commonly known as "sales reps."

Services sales representatives act as industry experts, consultants, and problem solvers. In some cases, they create demand for the firm's services. To do so, they must thoroughly understand a client's specific needs and objectives. Successful representatives relate their knowledge and understanding of the client's business to the services they offer to meet their objectives. For example, they might persuade a business to start advertising its products in ways it had not considered before.

There are several different categories of services sales jobs. *Outside services sales representatives* call on clients and prospects at their homes or offices. They may have an appointment, or they may practice "cold calling," arriving without an appointment. *Inside services sales representatives* work on their employer's premises, assisting individuals interested in the company's services. *Telemarketing sales representatives* sell over the telephone. They make large numbers of calls to prospects, attempting to sell the company's service themselves, or to arrange an appointment between the prospect and an outside sales representative. Some services sales representatives deal exclusively with one, or just a few, major clients.

Despite the diversity of services sold, the jobs of all services sales representatives have much in common. All sales representatives follow similar procedures to acquire new clients and must fully understand and be able to discuss the services their company offers. Many sales representatives develop lists of prospective clients through telephone and business directories, asking business associates and customers for leads and calling on new businesses as they cover their assigned territory. Some services sales representatives acquire clients through inquiries about their company's services. The Internet now allows all sales reps to better target their clients, display information, research industry trends, and track competitors' offers.

Services sales representatives obtain many of their new accounts through referrals. Thus, their success hinges on developing a satisfied clientele who will continue to use their services and recommend them to other potential customers. Like other types of sales jobs, a respected reputation is crucial to success.

Regardless of how they first meet the client, all services sales representatives must explain how the offered service meet the client's needs. While demonstrating the company's service, they may answer questions about the nature and cost of the service. In addition, they might have to overcome objections in order to persuade potential customers to purchase the service. If they fail to make a sale on the first visit, they may follow up with more visits, letters, or phone calls. After closing a sale, services sales representatives generally follow up to see that the purchase meets the customer's needs and to determine if additional services can be sold. Good customer service is an important factor in developing a satisfied clientele and can give a company an advantage in competing for future business.

Services sales work varies with the kind of service sold. Selling highly technical services, such as communications systems or computer consulting services, involves complex and lengthy sales negotiations. In addition, sales of such complex services may require extensive after-sale support. In these situations, sales reps may operate as part of a team of sales representatives and experts from other departments. Sales representatives can receive valuable technical assistance from their other team members. For example, those who sell computer and data processing services might work with a systems engineer. Teams enhance customer service and build strong long-term relationships with customers, resulting in increased sales.

The entire sales process can be lengthy. Sometimes a sales rep may periodically contact a potential customer for years before he or she makes a sale. Because of the amount of time between the initial contact with a customer and the actual sale, representatives are in contact with numerous existing and potential clients at the same time. Sales representatives must be well organized and efficient in managing their work. When customers express an interest in the service, sales reps who sell complex technical services may have to develop detailed proposals for presentation to the customer outlining the detailed services to be provided and their cost. Sometimes proposals must be revised several times before a client is willing to accept it. Selling less complex services, such as linen supply, cleaning, or pest control services, generally involves simpler and shorter sales negotiations.

Sales representative jobs may also vary with the size of the employer. Those working for large companies may be assigned a specific territory, a specific line of services, or specific types of clients. In smaller companies, sales representatives may have broader responsibilities—administrative, marketing, or public relations, for example—in addition to their sales duties.

Sales representatives often service a specific territory. Representatives of companies offering services widely used by the public, such as Internet service providers, generally have numerous clients in a relatively small territory. On the other hand, sales representatives for firms that offer more specialized services, such as interpretation and translation, might need to service several States to acquire an adequate customer base.

Working Conditions

Many services sales workers frequently work more than 40 hours per week. Selling can be stressful work because their income and job security directly depends on their success in winning business for their employers. Companies generally set sales quotas and have contests with prizes for those with the most sales. Considerable pressure is placed on the sales representative to meet monthly sales quotas.

Working conditions for sales representatives vary. Outside sales representatives responsible for a large territory might spend a great deal of time traveling, sometimes for weeks at a time. Representatives with smaller territories might never travel overnight. Outside sales representatives usually spend part of their time in an office keeping records, setting up appointments with customers, and searching for new customers. Increasingly, outside sales representatives work out of home offices or share office space with others rather than have their own permanently assigned space. Inside sales representatives and telemarketers spend all their time in their offices, which can range from bright and cheerful customer showrooms to cramped and noisy rooms.

Representatives often have the flexibility to set their own schedules as long as they meet their company's goals. The Internet allows representatives to do more work from home or while on the road, enabling them to send messages and documents to clients and co-workers, keep up with industry news, and access databases that help them to better target potential customers. Although they may accomplish more in less time, many work more hours than in the past, spending additional time on follow up and service calls.

Employment

Services sales representatives held over 841,000 jobs in 1998. Firms providing business services such as computer and data processing, contract telemarketing, personnel supply, and advertising provided two-thirds of all wage and salary jobs. The remainder of services sales representatives' jobs were in other service industries, including hotels and motels, motion pictures, education, and engineering and management services.

Training, Other Qualifications, and Advancement

Some employers require services sales representatives to have a college degree, but requirements vary depending on the industry a company represents. Employers who market advertising services seek individuals with a college degree in advertising, marketing, or business administration. Companies marketing educational services prefer individuals with a degree in education, marketing, or a related field. Many hotels seek graduates of hotel or tourism administration programs. Companies selling computer, engineering, health or other highly technical services generally require a bachelor's degree appropriate to their field. Certification and licensing is also becoming more common for sales and marketing representatives.

Employers may hire sales reps with only a high school diploma if they have a proven sales record. This is particularly true for those who sell non-technical services, such as amusement and recreation services, cleaning services, Employers may hire sales reps with only a high school diploma if they have a proven sales record. This is particularly true for those who sell non-technical services, such as amusement and recreation services, cleaning services, or photographic studios. Applicants enhance their chances of being hired into these positions if they have taken some relevant college courses. In general, smaller companies are more willing to hire unproven individuals.

Many firms conduct intensive training programs to acquaint new services sales representatives with the services and products of the firm, the history of the business, effective selling techniques, and administrative duties and policies. Sales representatives also attend seminars on a wide range of subjects given by outside or in-house trainers. These sessions acquaint them with new services and products or update their sales techniques or procedures and might include training to make them more effective in dealing with prospective customers.

To succeed, sales representatives should be persuasive and have a pleasant, outgoing, and enthusiastic disposition. Sales representatives must be highly motivated, energetic, well organized, and efficient. Good grooming and a neat appearance are essential, as are self-confidence, reliability, and the ability to communicate effectively. Sales representatives should be self-starters who have the ability to thrive under pressure to meet sales goals. They must also develop a thorough knowledge of the service they are selling and

anticipate and respond to their clients' questions and objections in a professional manner. In addition, they must be flexible to adjust to delays, problems, and the schedules of others.

Sales representatives with leadership ability and good sales records may advance to supervisory and managerial positions. Frequent contact with people in other firms provides sales reps with leads about job openings, enhancing advancement opportunities.

Job Outlook

Employment of services sales representatives, as a group, is expected to grow much faster than the average for all occupations through the year 2008 in response to growth of the services industries employing them. However, projected employment growth of services sales representatives varies by industry. For example, continued growth in factory and office automation should lead to much faster-than-average employment growth for computer and data processing services sales representatives. Employment in personnel supply services will grow as companies continue to outsource and use temporary employees. Growth will be tempered in some industries by the expanded use of various technologies, such as voice and electronic mail, portable phones, and laptop computers that all increase sales workers' productivity—especially while out of the office.

In addition to the job openings generated by employment growth, openings will occur each year because of the need to replace sales workers who transfer to other occupations or leave the labor force. Each year, many sales representatives discover they are unable to earn enough money, and they leave the occupation. Turnover is generally higher among representatives who sell non-technical services. As a result of this turnover, job opportunities should be good, especially for those with a college degree or a proven sales record.

With improved technology, some companies are cutting back on the expense of travel and on-site presentations and putting more emphasis on in-house sales via the Internet, direct calling, and teleconferencing. In addition, temporary or contract sales people may be used more frequently for outside sales.

Earnings

Median annual earnings of services sales representatives in selected business services were $34,910, including commission, in 1998. The middle 50 percent earned between $24,700 and $49,030 a year. The lowest 10 percent earned less than $17,640, and the highest 10 percent earned more than $79,790 a year. Median annual earnings in the service industries employing the largest numbers of sales agents in selected business services in 1997 were as follows:

Computer and data processing services	$41,200
Management and public relations	34,000
Mailing, reproduction, and stenographic services	33,100
Miscellaneous business services	29,500
Personnel supply services	28,500

Median annual earnings of advertising sales agents, including commission, were $31,850 in 1998. The middle 50 percent earned between $22,600 and $47,660 a year. The lowest 10 percent earned less than $16,210, and the highest 10 percent earned more than $83,080 a year.

Median annual earnings of telemarketers and other related workers, including commission, were $17,090 in 1998. The middle 50 percent earned between $14,080 and $21,830 a year. The lowest 10 percent earned less than $12,350, and the highest 10 percent earned more than $30,290 a year.

Services sales representatives are paid under various systems. Some receive a straight salary; others are paid solely on a commission basis—a percentage of the dollar value of their sales. Most firms use a combination of salary and commission. Some services sales representatives receive a base salary, plus incentive pay that can add from 25 to 75 percent to their base salary. Many employers offer bonuses, including vacation trips and prizes for sales that exceed company quotas. Sales are affected by changing economic conditions and consumer and business expectations, so earnings may vary greatly from year to year. In addition to the same benefits package provided to other employees of the firm, employers may provide outside sales representatives expense accounts to cover meals and travel, computer and office equipment for use while traveling or at home, and sometimes a company car.

Related Occupations

Services sales representatives must have sales ability and knowledge of the service they sell. Workers in other occupations requiring these skills include advertising, marketing, and public relations managers; insurance sales agents; manufacturers' and wholesale sales representatives; purchasing managers, buyers, and purchasing agents; real estate agents and brokers; sales engineers; securities, commodities, and financial services sales representatives; and travel agents.

Sources of Additional Information

For details about career and certification information for services sales and marketing representatives, contact:

● Sales and Marketing Executives International, 5500 Interstate North Pkwy., Suite 545, Atlanta, GA 30328-4662. Internet: http://www.smei.org

Shipping, Receiving, and Traffic Clerks

(O*NET 58028)

Significant Points

● Job openings will continue to arise due to increasing economic activity and employee turnover.

● The occupation does not require more than a high school diploma.

Nature of the Work

Shipping, receiving, and traffic clerks keep records of all goods shipped and received. Their duties depend on the size of the establishment and the level of automation employed. Larger companies typically are better able to finance the purchase of computers and other equipment to handle some or all of a clerk's responsibilities. In smaller companies, a clerk maintains records, prepares shipments, and accepts deliveries. Working in both environments, shipping, receiving, and traffic clerks may lift cartons of various sizes.

Shipping clerks are record keepers responsible for all outgoing shipments. They prepare shipping documents and mailing labels, and make sure orders have been filled correctly. Also, they record items taken from inventory and note when orders were filled. Sometimes they fill the order themselves, obtaining merchandise from the stockroom, noting when inventories run low, and wrapping it or packing it in shipping containers. They also address and label packages, look up and compute freight or postal rates, and record the weight and cost of each shipment. Shipping clerks also may prepare invoices and furnish information about shipments to other parts of the company, such as the accounting department. Once a shipment is checked and ready to go, shipping clerks may move the goods from the plant—sometimes by forklift truck—to the shipping dock and direct its loading.

Receiving clerks perform tasks similar to those of shipping clerks. They determine whether orders have been filled correctly by verifying incoming shipments against the original order and the accompanying bill of lading or invoice. They make a record of the shipment and the condition of its contents. In many firms, receiving clerks use hand-held scanners to record bar codes on incoming products or by entering it into a computer. This data then can be transferred to the appropriate departments. The shipment is checked for any discrepancies in quantity, price, and discounts. Receiving clerks may route or move shipments to the proper department, warehouse section, or stockroom. They may also arrange for adjustments with shippers whenever merchandise is lost or damaged. Receiving clerks in small businesses also may perform duties similar to those of stock clerks. In larger establishments, receiving clerks may control all receiving-platform operations, such as truck scheduling, recording of shipments, and handling of damaged goods.

Traffic clerks maintain records on the destination, weight, and charges on all incoming and outgoing freight. They verify rate charges by comparing the classification of materials with rate charts. In many companies, this work may be automated. Information either is scanned or is hand-entered into a computer for use by accounting or other departments within the company. Also, they keep a file of claims for overcharges and for damage to goods in transit.

Working Conditions

Shipping, receiving, and traffic clerks work in a wide variety of businesses, institutions, and industries. Some work in warehouses, stock rooms, or shipping and receiving rooms that may not be temperature controlled. Others may spend time in cold storage rooms or outside on loading platforms, where they are exposed to the weather. Most jobs involve frequent standing, bending, walking, and stretching. Some lifting and carrying of smaller items may also be involved. Although automation, robotics, and pneumatic devices have lessened the physical demands in this occupation, their use remains somewhat limited. Work still can be strenuous, even though mechanical material handling equipment is employed to move heavy items. The typical workweek is Monday through Friday; however, evening and weekend hours are standard for some jobs and may be required in others when large shipments are involved or when inventory is taken.

Employment

Shipping, receiving, and traffic clerks held about 774,000 jobs in 1998. Nearly 2 out of 3 were employed in manufacturing or by wholesale and retail establishments. Although jobs for shipping, receiving, and traffic clerks are found throughout the country, most clerks work in urban areas, where shipping depots in factories and wholesale establishments usually are located.

Training, Other Qualifications, and Advancement

These jobs are entry level and require no more than a high school diploma. Increasingly however, employers prefer to hire those familiar with computers and other electronic office and business equipment. Those who have taken business courses or have previous related experience may be preferred. Because the nature of the work is to communicate effectively with other people, good oral and written communications skills are essential. Typing, filing, record keeping, and other clerical skills are also important.

Trainees usually develop the necessary skills on the job. This informal training lasts from several days to a few months, depending on the complexity of the job. Shipping, receiving, and traffic clerks usually learn the job by doing routine tasks under close supervision. They learn how to count and mark stock, and then start keeping records and taking inventory. Strength, stamina, good eyesight, and an ability to work at repetitive tasks, sometimes under pressure, are important characteristics. Clerks who handle jewelry, liquor, or drugs may be bonded.

Shipping, receiving, and traffic clerks start out by checking items to be shipped and then attaching labels and making sure the addresses are correct. Training in the use of automated equipment is usually done informally on the job. As these occupations become more automated, however, workers in these jobs may need longer training in order to master the use of the equipment.

Advancement opportunities for these workers vary with the place of employment. Shipping, receiving, and traffic clerks are promoted to head clerk, and those with a broad understanding of shipping and receiving may enter a related field such as industrial traffic management. With additional training, some clerks advance to jobs as warehouse managers or purchasing agents.

Job Outlook

Employment of shipping, receiving, and traffic clerks is expected to grow more slowly than the average for all occupations through 2008.

Employment growth will continue to be affected by automation, as all but the smallest firms move to hold down labor costs by using computers to store and retrieve shipping and receiving records.

Methods of material handling have changed significantly in recent years. Large warehouses are increasingly automated, using equipment such as computerized conveyor systems, robots, computer-directed trucks, and automatic data storage and retrieval systems. Automation, coupled with the growing use of hand-held scanners and personal computers in shipping and receiving departments, has increased the productivity of these workers.

Despite technology, job openings will continue to arise due to increasing economic and trade activity and because certain tasks cannot be automated. For example, someone needs to check shipments before they go out and when they arrive to ensure everything is in order. In addition to job growth, openings will occur because of the need to replace shipping, receiving, and traffic clerks who leave the occupation. Because this is an entry-level occupation, many vacancies are created by normal career progression.

Earnings

Shipping, receiving, and traffic clerks had median hourly earnings of $10.82 in 1998.

Related Occupations

Shipping, receiving, and traffic clerks record, check, and often store materials that a company receives. They also process and pack goods for shipment. Other workers who perform similar duties are stock clerks, material clerks, distributing clerks, routing clerks, express clerks, expediters, and order fillers.

Sources of Additional Information

General information about shipping, receiving, and traffic clerks can be obtained from:

- National Retail Federation, 325 Seventh St. NW., Suite 1000, Washington, DC 20004. Internet: http://www.nrf.com/nri/

Social Workers

(O*NET 27305A, 27305B, 27305C, and 27302)

Significant Points

- A bachelor's degree is the minimum requirement for many entry-level jobs, but a master's degree in social work (MSW) or a related field is required for clinical practice and is becoming the norm for many positions.

- Employment is projected to grow much faster than average.

- Competition for jobs is expected to be keen in cities, but opportunities should be good in rural areas.

Nature of the Work

Social work is a profession for those with a strong desire to help people, to make things better, and to make a difference. Social workers help people function the best way they can in their environment, deal with their relationships with others, and solve personal and family problems.

Social workers often see clients who face a life-threatening disease or a social problem. These problems may include inadequate housing, unemployment, lack of job skills, financial distress, serious illness or disability, substance abuse, unwanted pregnancy, or anti-social behavior. Social workers also assist families that have serious domestic conflicts, including those involving child or spousal abuse.

Through direct counseling, social workers help clients identify their concerns, consider effective solutions, and find reliable resources. Social workers typically consult and counsel clients and arrange for services that can help them. Often, they refer clients to specialists in services such as debt counseling, child care or elder care, public assistance, or alcohol or drug rehabilitation. Social workers then follow through with the client to assure that services are helpful and that clients make proper use of the services offered. Social workers may review eligibility requirements, help fill out forms and applications, visit clients on a regular basis, and provide support during crises.

Social workers practice in a variety of settings. In hospitals and psychiatric hospitals, they provide or arrange for a range of support services. In mental health and community centers, social workers provide counseling services on marriage, family, and adoption matters, and they help people through personal or community emergencies, such as dealing with loss or grief or arranging for disaster assistance. In schools, they help children, parents, and teachers cope with problems. In social service agencies, they help people locate basic benefits, such as income assistance, housing, and job training. Social workers also offer counseling to those receiving therapy for addictive or physical disorders in rehabilitation facilities and to people in nursing homes in need of routine living care. In employment settings, they counsel people with personal, family, professional, or financial problems affecting their work performance. Social workers who work in courts and correction facilities evaluate and counsel individuals in the criminal justice system to cope better in society. In private practice, they provide clinical or diagnostic testing services covering a wide range of personal disorders.

Social workers often provide social services in health-related settings that now are governed by managed care organizations. To contain costs, these organizations are emphasizing short-term intervention, ambulatory and community-based care, and greater decentralization of services.

Most social workers specialize in an area of practice. Although some conduct research or are involved in planning or policy development, most social workers prefer an area of practice in which they interact with clients.

Clinical social workers offer psychotherapy or counseling and a range of diagnostic services in public agencies, clinics, and private practice.

Child welfare or family services social workers may counsel children and youths who have difficulty adjusting socially, advise parents on how to care for disabled children, or arrange for homemaker services during a parent's illness. If children have serious problems in school, child welfare workers may consult with parents, teachers, and counselors to identify underlying causes and develop plans for treatment. Some social workers assist single parents, arrange adoptions, and help find foster homes for neglected, abandoned, or abused children. Child welfare workers also work in residential institutions for children and adolescents.

Child or adult protective services social workers investigate reports of abuse and neglect and intervene if necessary. They may initiate legal action to remove children from homes and place them temporarily in an emergency shelter or with a foster family.

Mental health social workers provide services for persons with mental or emotional problems. Such services include individual and group therapy, outreach, crisis intervention, social rehabilitation, and training in skills of everyday living. They may also help plan for supportive services to ease patients' return to the community.

Health care social workers help patients and their families cope with chronic, acute, or terminal illnesses and handle problems that may stand in the way of recovery or rehabilitation. They may organize support groups for families of patients suffering from cancer, AIDS, Alzheimer's disease, or other illnesses. They also advise family caregivers, counsel patients, and help plan for their needs after discharge by arranging for at-home services, ranging from meals-on-wheels to oxygen equipment. Some work on interdisciplinary teams that evaluate certain kinds of patients, geriatric or organ transplant patients, for example.

School social workers diagnose students' problems and arrange needed services, counsel children in trouble, and help integrate disabled students into the general school population. School social workers deal with problems such as student pregnancy, misbehavior in class, and excessive absences. They also advise teachers on how to cope with problem students.

Criminal justice social workers make recommendations to courts, prepare pre-sentencing assessments, and provide services to prison inmates and their families. Probation and parole officers provide similar services to individuals sentenced by a court to parole or probation.

Occupational social workers usually work in a corporation's personnel department or health unit. Through employee assistance programs, they help workers cope with job-related pressures or personal problems that affect the quality of their work. They often offer direct counseling to employees whose performance is hindered by emotional or family problems or substance abuse. They also develop education programs and refer workers to specialized community programs.

Gerontology social workers specialize in services to the aged. They run support groups for family caregivers or for the adult children of aging parents. Also, they advise elderly people or family members about the choices in such areas as housing, transportation, and long-term care; they also coordinate and monitor services.

Social work administrators perform overall management tasks in a hospital, clinic, or other setting that offers social worker services.

Social work planners and policy-makers develop programs to address such issues as child abuse, homelessness, substance abuse, poverty, and violence. These workers research and analyze policies, programs, and regulations. They identify social problems and suggest legislative and other solutions. They may help raise funds or write grants to support these programs.

Working Conditions

Full-time social workers usually work a standard 40-hour week; however, some occasionally work evenings and weekends to meet with clients, attend community meetings, and handle emergencies. Some, particularly in voluntary nonprofit agencies, work part time. Most social workers work in pleasant, clean offices that are well lit and well ventilated. Social workers usually spend most of their time in an office or residential facility, but also may travel locally to visit clients, to meet with service providers, or to attend meetings. Some may use one of several offices within a local area in which to meet with clients. The work, while satisfying, can be emotionally draining. Understaffing and large caseloads add to the pressure in some agencies.

Employment

Social workers held about 604,000 jobs in 1998. About 4 out of 10 jobs were in State, county, or municipal government agencies, primarily in departments of health and human services, mental health, social services, child welfare, housing, education, and corrections. Most private sector jobs were in social service agencies, hospitals, nursing homes, home health agencies, and other health centers or clinics.

Although most social workers are employed in cities or suburbs, some work in rural areas.

Training, Other Qualifications, and Advancement

A bachelor's in social work (BSW) degree is the most common minimum requirement to qualify for a job as a social worker; however, majors in psychology, sociology, and related fields may be sufficient to qualify for some entry-level jobs, especially in small community agencies. Although a bachelor's degree is required for entry into the field, an advanced degree has become the standard for many positions. A master's in social work (MSW) is necessary for positions in health and mental health settings and typically is required for certification for clinical work. Jobs in public agencies also may require an advanced degree, such as a master's in social service policy or administration. Supervisory, administrative, and staff training positions usually require at least an advanced degree. College and university teaching positions and most research appointments normally require a doctorate in social work (DSW or Ph.D).

As of 1999, the Council on Social Work Education accredited more than 400 BSW programs and more than 125 MSW programs. The Group for Advancement of Doctoral Education in Social Work listed 63 doctoral programs for Ph.D.s in social work or DSWs (Doctor of Social Work). BSW programs prepare graduates for direct service positions such as case worker or group worker. They include courses in social work practice, social welfare policies, human behavior and the social environment, social research methods, social work values and ethics, dealing with a culturally diverse clientele, promotion of social and economic justice, and populations-at-risk.

Accredited BSW programs require at least 400 hours of supervised field experience.

Master's degree programs prepare graduates for work in their chosen field of concentration and continue to develop their skills to perform clinical assessments, to manage large caseloads, and to explore new ways of drawing upon social services to meet the needs of clients. Master's programs last two years and include 900 hours of supervised field instruction, or internship. A part-time program may take four years. Entry into a master's program does not require a bachelor's in social work, but courses in psychology, biology, sociology, economics, political science, history, social anthropology, urban studies, and social work are recommended. In addition, a second language can be very helpful. Most master's programs offer advanced standing for those with a bachelor's degree from an accredited social work program.

All States and the District of Columbia have licensing, certification, or registration requirements regarding social work practice and the use of professional titles. Although standards for licensing vary by State, a growing number of States are placing greater emphasis on communications skills, professional ethics, and sensitivity for cultural diversity issues. Additionally, the National Association of Social Workers (NASW) offers voluntary credentials. The Academy of Certified Social Workers (ACSW) is granted to all social workers who have met established eligibility criteria. Social workers practicing in school settings may qualify for the School Social Work Specialist (SSWS) credential. Clinical social workers may earn either the Qualified Clinical Social Worker (QCSW) or the advanced credential—Diplomate in Clinical Social Work (DCSW). Social workers holding clinical credentials also may list themselves in the biannual publication of the *NASW Register of Clinical Social Workers*. Credentials are particularly important for those in private practice; some health insurance providers require them for reimbursement.

Social workers should be emotionally mature, objective, and sensitive to people and their problems. They must be able to handle responsibility, work independently, and maintain good working relationships with clients and coworkers. Volunteer or paid jobs as a social work aide offer ways of testing one's interest in this field.

Advancement to supervisor, program manager, assistant director, or executive director of a social service agency or department is possible, but usually requires an advanced degree and related work experience. Other career options for social workers include teaching, research, and consulting. Some also help formulate government policies by analyzing and advocating policy positions in government agencies, in research institutions, and on legislators' staffs.

Some social workers go into private practice. Most private practitioners are clinical social workers who provide psychotherapy, usually paid through health insurance. Private practitioners usually have at least a master's degree and a period of supervised work experience. A network of contacts for referrals also is essential.

Job Outlook

Employment of social workers is expected to increase much faster than the average for all occupations through 2008. The aged population is increasing rapidly, creating greater demand for health and other social services. Social workers also will be needed to help the sizable baby boom generation deal with depression and mental health concerns stemming from mid-life, career, or other personal and professional difficulties. In addition, continuing concern about crime, juvenile delinquency, and services for the mentally ill, the mentally retarded, AIDS patients, and individuals and families in crisis will spur demand for social workers in several areas of specialization. Many job openings will also stem from the need to replace social workers who leave the occupation.

The number of social workers in hospitals and many larger, long-term care facilities will increase in response to the need to ensure that the necessary medical and social services are in place when individuals leave the facility. However, this service need will be shared across several occupations. In an effort to control costs, these facilities increasingly emphasize discharging patients early, applying an interdisciplinary approach to patient care, and employing a broader mix of occupations—including clinical specialists, registered nurses, and health aides—to tend to patient care or client need.

Social worker employment in home health care services is growing, in part because hospitals are releasing patients earlier than in the past. However, the expanding senior population is an even larger factor. Social workers with backgrounds in gerontology are finding work in the growing numbers of assisted living and senior living communities.

Employment of social workers in private social service agencies will grow, but not as rapidly as demand for their services. Agencies increasingly will restructure services and hire more lower-paid human service workers and assistants instead of social workers. Employment in state and local government may grow somewhat in response to increasing needs for public welfare and family services; however, many of these services will be contracted out to private agencies. Additionally, employment levels may fluctuate depending on need and government funding for various social service programs.

Employment of school social workers is expected to grow, due to expanded efforts to respond to rising rates of teen pregnancy and to the adjustment problems of immigrants and children from single-parent families. Moreover, continued emphasis on integrating disabled children into the general school population will lead to more jobs. However, availability of State and local funding will dictate the actual job growth in schools.

Opportunities for social workers in private practice will expand because of the anticipated availability of funding from health insurance and public-sector contracts. Also, with increasing affluence, people will be better able to pay for professional help to deal with personal problems. The growing popularity of employee assistance programs also is expected to spur demand for private practitioners, some of whom provide social work services to corporations on a contractual basis.

Competition for social worker jobs is stronger in cities where demand for services often is highest, training programs for social workers are prevalent, and interest in available positions is strongest. However, opportunities should be good in rural areas, which often find it difficult to attract and retain qualified staff.

Earnings

Median annual earnings of social workers were $30,590 in 1998. The middle 50 percent earned between $24,160 and $39,240. The lowest 10 percent earned less than $19,250, and the top 10 percent earned more than $49,080. Median annual earnings in the industries employing the largest numbers of medical social workers in 1997 were:

Home health care services	$35,800
Offices and clinics of medical doctors	33,700
Offices of other health care practitioners	32,900
State government, except education and hospitals	31,800
Hospitals	31,500

Median annual earnings in the industries employing the largest numbers of social workers, except medical, in 1997 were:

Federal government	$45,300
Elementary and secondary schools	34,100
Local government, except education and hospitals	32,100
Hospitals	31,300
State government, except education and hospitals	30,800

Related Occupations

Through direct counseling or referral to other services, social workers help people solve a range of personal problems. Workers in occupations with similar duties include the clergy, mental health counselors, counseling psychologists, and human services workers and assistants.

Sources of Additional Information

For information about career opportunities in social work, contact:

- National Association of Social Workers, Career Information, 750 First St. NE., Suite 700, Washington, DC 20002-4241.

An annual *Directory of Accredited BSW and MSW Programs* is available for a nominal charge from:

- Council on Social Work Education, 1600 Duke St., Alexandria, VA 22314-3421. Internet: http://www.cswe.org

Information on licensing requirements and testing procedures for each State may be obtained from State licensing authorities or from:

- American Association of State Social Work Boards, 400 South Ridge Parkway, Suite B, Culpeper, VA 22701. Internet: http://www.aasswb.org

Special Education Teachers

(O*NET 31311A, 31311B, and 31311C)

Significant Points

- A bachelor's degree, completion of an approved teacher preparation program, and a license are required to qualify; many States require a master's degree.

- Many States offer alternative licensure programs to attract people into these jobs.

- Job openings arising from rapid employment growth and some job turnover mean excellent job prospects; many school districts report shortages of qualified teachers.

Nature of the Work

Special education teachers work with children and youths who have a variety of disabilities. Most special education teachers instruct students at the elementary, middle, and secondary school level, although some teachers work with infants and toddlers. Special education teachers design and modify instruction to meet a student's special needs. Teachers also work with students who have other special instructional needs, including the gifted and talented.

The various types of disabilities delineated in Federal legislation concerning special education programs include specific learning disabilities, speech or language impairments, mental retardation, emotional disturbance, multiple disabilities, hearing impairments, orthopedic impairments, other health impairments, visual impairments, autism, deaf-blindness, and traumatic brain injury. Students are classified under one of the categories, and special education teachers are prepared to work with specific groups.

Special education teachers use various techniques to promote learning. Depending on the disability, teaching methods can include individualized instruction, problem-solving assignments, and group or individual work. Special education teachers are legally required to help develop an Individualized Education Program (IEP) for each special education student. The IEP sets personalized goals for each student and is tailored to a student's individual learning style and ability. This program includes a transition plan outlining specific steps to prepare special education students for middle school or high school, or in the case of older students, a job or post-secondary study. Teachers review the IEP with the student's parents, school administrators, and often the student's general education teacher. Teachers work closely with parents to inform them of their child's progress and suggest techniques to promote learning at home.

Teachers design curricula, assign work geared toward each student's ability, and grade papers and homework assignments. Special education teachers are involved in a student's behavioral as well as academic development. They help special education students develop emotionally, be comfortable in social situations, and be aware of socially acceptable behavior. Preparing special education students for daily life after graduation is an important aspect of the job. Teachers help students learn routine skills, such as balancing a checkbook, or provide them with career counseling.

As schools become more inclusive, special education teachers and general education teachers increasingly work together in general education classrooms. Special education teachers help general educators adapt curriculum materials and teaching techniques to meet the needs of disabled students. They coordinate the work of teachers, teacher assistants, and themselves to meet the requirements of

inclusive special education programs, in addition to teaching special education students. A large part of a special education teacher's job involves interacting with others. They communicate frequently with parents, social workers, school psychologists, occupational and physical therapists, school administrators, and other teachers.

Special education teachers work in a variety of settings. Some have their own classrooms and teach only special education students; others work as special education resource teachers and offer individualized help to students in general education classrooms; and others teach with general education teachers in classes composed of both general and special education students. Some teachers work in a resource room, where special education students work several hours a day, separate from their general education classroom. A significantly smaller proportion of special education teachers works in residential facilities or tutor students in homebound or hospital environments.

Early identification of a child with special needs is another important part of a special education teacher's job. Early intervention is essential in educating these children. Special education teachers who work with infants usually travel to the child's home to work with the child and his or her parents.

Technology is playing an increasingly important role in special education. Special education teachers use specialized equipment such as computers with synthesized speech, interactive educational software programs, and audio tapes.

Working Conditions

Special education teachers enjoy the challenge of working with these students and the opportunity to establish meaningful relationships. Although helping students with disabilities can be highly rewarding, the work can also be emotionally and physically draining. Special education teachers are under considerable stress due to heavy workloads and tedious administrative tasks. They must produce a substantial amount of paperwork documenting each student's progress. Exacerbating this stress is the threat of litigation by students' parents if correct procedures are not followed, or if the parent feels their child is not receiving an adequate education. The physical and emotional demands of the job cause some special education teachers to leave the occupation.

Many schools offer year-round education for special education students, but most special education teachers work the traditional 10-month school year.

Employment

Special education teachers held about 406,000 jobs in 1998. The majority of special education teachers were employed in elementary, middle, and secondary public schools. The rest worked in separate educational facilities—public or private—residential facilities, or in homebound or hospital environments.

Training, Other Qualifications, and Advancement

All 50 States and the District of Columbia require special education teachers to be licensed. Special education licensure varies by State.

In many States, special education teachers receive a general education credential to teach kindergarten through grade 12. These teachers train in a specialty, such as learning disabilities or behavioral disorders. Some States offer general special education licenses, others license several different specialties within special education, while others require teachers to first obtain a general education license and then an additional license in special education. State boards of education or a licensure advisory committee usually grant licenses.

All States require a bachelor's degree and completion of an approved teacher preparation program with a prescribed number of subject and education credits and supervised practice teaching. Many States require special education teachers to obtain a master's degree in special education, involving at least one year of additional coursework, including a specialization, beyond the bachelor's degree.

Some States have reciprocity agreements allowing special education teachers to transfer their license from one State to another, but many still require special education teachers to pass licensing requirements for that State. In the future, employers may recognize certification or standards offered by national organization.

Many colleges and universities across the United States offer programs in special education, including undergraduate, master's, and doctoral programs. Special education teachers usually undergo longer periods of training than general education teachers. Most bachelor's degree programs are four-year programs including general and specialized courses in special education. However, an increasing number of institutions require a fifth year or other post-baccalaureate preparation. Courses include educational psychology, legal issues of special education, child growth and development, and knowledge and skills needed for teaching students with disabilities. Some programs require specialization. Others offer generalized special education degrees or study in several specialized areas. The last year of the program is usually spent student teaching in a classroom supervised by a certified teacher.

Alternative and emergency licenses are available in many States, due to the need to fill special education teaching positions. Alternative licenses are designed to bring college graduates and those changing careers into teaching more quickly. Requirements for an alternative license may be less stringent than for a regular license and vary by State. In some programs, individuals begin teaching quickly under a provisional license. They can obtain a regular license by teaching under the supervision of licensed teachers for a period of 1 to 2 years while taking education courses. Emergency licenses are granted when States have difficulty finding licensed special education teachers to fill positions.

Special education teachers must be patient, able to motivate students, understanding of their students' special needs, and accepting of differences in others. Teachers must be creative and apply different types of teaching methods to reach students who are having difficulty. Communication and cooperation are essential traits because special education teachers spend a great deal of time interacting with others, including students, parents, and school faculty and administrators.

Special education teachers can advance to become supervisors or administrators. They may also earn advanced degrees and become instructors in colleges that prepare others for special education teaching. In some school systems, highly experienced teachers can become mentor teachers to less experienced ones; they provide guidance to these teachers while maintaining a light teaching load.

Job Outlook

Employment of special education teachers is expected to increase faster than the average for all occupations through 2008, spurred by continued growth in the number of special education students needing services, legislation emphasizing training and employment for individuals with disabilities, and educational reform. Turnover will lead to additional job openings as special education teachers switch to general education or change careers altogether. Rapid employment growth and job turnover should result in a very favorable job market.

Special education teachers have excellent job prospects, as many school districts report shortages of qualified teachers. Job outlook varies by geographic area and specialty. Positions in rural areas and inner cities are more plentiful than job openings in suburban or wealthy urban areas. In addition, job opportunities may be better in certain specialties—such as speech or language impairments, and learning disabilities—because of large enrollment increases of special education students classified under these disability categories. Legislation encouraging early intervention and special education for infants, toddlers, and preschoolers has created a need for early childhood special education teachers. Special education teachers who are bilingual or have multicultural experience are also needed to work with an increasingly diverse student population.

The number of students requiring special education services has been steadily increasing. This trend is expected to continue because of legislation which expanded the age range of children receiving special education services to include those from birth to age 21; medical advances resulting in more survivors of accidents and illness; the postponement of childbirth by more women, resulting in a greater number of premature births and children born with birth defects; and growth in the general population.

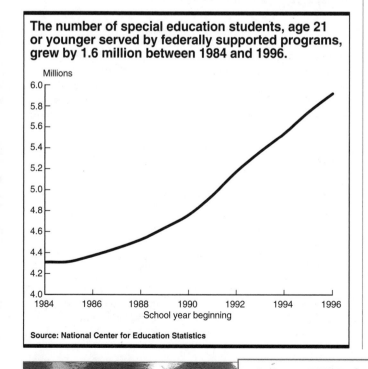

The number of special education students, age 21 or younger served by federally supported programs, grew by 1.6 million between 1984 and 1996.

Source: National Center for Education Statistics

Earnings

Median annual earnings of special education teachers in 1998 were $37,850. The middle 50 percent earned between $30,410 and $48,390. The lowest 10 percent earned less than $25,450; the highest 10 percent earned more than $78,030.

In 1998, about 58 percent of special education teachers belonged to unions—mainly the American Federation of Teachers and the National Education Association—that bargain with school systems over wages, hours, and the terms and conditions of employment.

In some schools, teachers receive extra pay for coaching sports and working with students in extracurricular activities. Some teachers earn extra income during the summer by working in the school system or in other jobs.

Related Occupations

Special education teachers work with students who have disabilities and special needs. Other occupations involved with the identification, evaluation, and development of students with disabilities include school psychologists, social workers, speech pathologists, rehabilitation counselors, adapted physical education teachers, special education technology specialists, and occupational, physical, creative arts, and recreational therapists.

Sources of Additional Information

For information on professions related to early intervention and education for children with disabilities, a list of accredited schools, teacher certification, financial aid information, and general information on related personnel issues—including recruitment, retention, and supply of and demand for special education professionals—contact:

● National Clearinghouse for Professions in Special Education, Council for Exceptional Children, 1920 Association Dr., Reston, VA 20191-1589. Internet: http://www.special-ed-careers.org

To learn more about the special education teacher certification and licensing requirements in your State, contact your State's department of education.

Speech-Language Pathologists and Audiologists

(O*NET 32314)

Significant Points

● About half work in schools, and most others are employed by health care facilities.

- A master's degree in speech-language pathology or audiology is the standard credential.

Nature of the Work

Speech-language pathologists assess, treat, and help to prevent speech, language, cognitive, communication, voice, swallowing, fluency, and other related disorders; audiologists identify, assess, and manage auditory, balance, and other neural systems.

Speech-language pathologists work with people who cannot make speech sounds or cannot make them clearly; those with speech rhythm and fluency problems, such as stuttering; people with voice quality problems, such as inappropriate pitch or harsh voice; those with problems understanding and producing language; and those with cognitive communication impairments, such as attention, memory, and problem solving disorders. They may also work with people who have oral motor problems that cause eating and swallowing difficulties.

Speech and language problems can result from hearing loss, brain injury or deterioration, cerebral palsy, stroke, cleft palate, voice pathology, mental retardation, or emotional problems. Problems can be congenital, developmental, or acquired. Speech-language pathologists use written and oral tests, as well as special instruments, to diagnose the nature and extent of impairment and to record and analyze speech, language, and swallowing irregularities. Speech-language pathologists develop an individualized plan of care, tailored to each patient's needs. For individuals with little or no speech capability, speech-language pathologists select augmentative alternative communication methods, including automated devices and sign language, and teach their use. They teach these individuals how to make sounds, improve their voices, or increase their language skills to communicate more effectively. Speech-language pathologists help patients develop, or recover, reliable communication skills so patients can fulfill their educational, vocational, and social roles.

Most speech-language pathologists provide direct clinical services to individuals with communication disorders. In speech and language clinics, they may independently develop and carry out treatment programs. In medical facilities, they may work with physicians, social workers, psychologists, and other therapists to develop and execute treatment plans. Speech-language pathologists in schools develop individual or group programs, counsel parents, and may assist teachers with classroom activities.

Speech-language pathologists keep records on the initial evaluation, progress, and discharge of clients. This helps pinpoint problems, tracks client progress, and justifies the cost of treatment when applying for reimbursement. They counsel individuals and their families concerning communication disorders and how to cope with the stress and misunderstanding that often accompany them. They also work with family members to recognize and change behavior patterns that impede communication and treatment, and they show the family communication-enhancing techniques to use at home.

Some speech-language pathologists conduct research on how people communicate. Others design and develop equipment or techniques for diagnosing and treating speech problems.

Audiologists work with people who have hearing, balance, and related problems. They use audiometers, computers, and other testing devices to measure the loudness at which a person begins to hear sounds, the ability to distinguish between sounds, and the nature and extent of hearing loss. Audiologists interpret these results and may coordinate them with medical, educational, and psychological information to make a diagnosis and determine a course of treatment.

Hearing disorders can result from a variety of causes including trauma at birth, viral infections, genetic disorders, exposure to loud noise, or aging. Treatment may include examining and cleaning the ear canal, fitting and dispensing hearing aids or other assistive devices, and audiologic rehabilitation (including auditory training or instruction in speech or lip reading). Audiologists may recommend, fit, and dispense personal or large area amplification systems, such as hearing aids and alerting devices. Audiologists provide fitting and tuning of cochlear implants and provide the necessary rehabilitation for adjustment to listening with implant amplification systems. They also measure noise levels in workplaces and conduct hearing protection programs in industry, as well as in schools and communities.

Audiologists provide direct clinical services to individuals with hearing or balance disorders. In audiology (hearing) clinics, they may independently develop and carry out treatment programs. Audiologists, in a variety of settings, work as members of interdisciplinary professional teams in planning and implementing service delivery for children and adults, from birth to old age. Similar to speech-language pathologists, audiologists keep records on the initial evaluation, progress, and discharge of clients. These records help pinpoint problems, track client progress, and justify the cost of treatment, when applying for reimbursement.

Audiologists may conduct research on types of and treatment for hearing, balance, and related disorders. Others design and develop equipment or techniques for diagnosing and treating these disorders.

Working Conditions

Speech-language pathologists and audiologists usually work at a desk or table in clean comfortable surroundings. The job is not physically demanding but does require attention to detail and intense concentration. The emotional needs of clients and their families may be demanding. Most full-time speech-language pathologists and audiologists work about 40 hours per week; some work part-time. Those who work on a contract basis may spend a substantial amount of time traveling between facilities.

Employment

Speech-language pathologists and audiologists held about 105,000 jobs in 1998. About one-half provided services in preschools, elementary and secondary schools, or colleges and universities. Others were in offices of speech-language pathologists and audiologists; hospitals; offices of physicians; speech, language, and hearing centers; home health agencies; or other facilities.

Some speech-language pathologists and audiologists are self-employed in private practice. They contract to provide services in schools, physician's offices, hospitals, or nursing homes, or work as consultants to industry. Audiologists are more likely to be employed in independent healthcare offices, while speech-language pathologists are more likely to work in school settings.

Training, Other Qualifications, and Advancement

Of the States that regulate licensing (44 for speech-language pathologists and 49 for audiologists), almost all require a master's degree or equivalent. Other requirements are 300 to 375 hours of supervised clinical experience, a passing score on a national examination, and nine months of postgraduate professional clinical experience. Thirty-six States have continuing education requirements for license renewal. Medicaid, Medicare, and private health insurers generally require a practitioner to be licensed to qualify for reimbursement.

About 235 colleges and universities offer graduate programs in speech-language pathology. Courses cover anatomy and physiology of the areas of the body involved in speech, language, and hearing; the development of normal speech, language, and hearing; the nature of disorders; acoustics; and psychological aspects of communication. Graduate students also learn to evaluate and treat speech, language, and hearing disorders and receive supervised clinical training in communication disorders.

About 115 colleges and universities offer graduate programs in audiology in the United States. Course work includes anatomy; physiology; basic science; math; physics; genetics; normal and abnormal communication development; auditory, balance and neural systems assessment and treatment; audiologic rehabilitation; and ethics.

Speech-language pathologists can acquire the Certificate of Clinical Competence in Speech-Language Pathology (CCC-SLP) offered by the American Speech-Language-Hearing Association, and audiologists can earn the Certificate of Clinical Competence in Audiology (CCC-A). To earn a CCC, a person must have a graduate degree and 375 hours of supervised clinical experience, complete a 36-week postgraduate clinical fellowship, and pass a written examination. According to the American Speech-Language Hearing Association, as of 2007, audiologists will need to have a bachelor's degree and complete 75 hours of credit toward a doctoral degree in order to seek certification. As of 2012, audiologists will have to earn doctoral degrees in order to be certified.

Speech-language pathologists and audiologists should be able to effectively communicate diagnostic test results, diagnoses, and proposed treatment in a manner easily understood by their clients. They must be able to approach problems objectively and provide support to clients and their families. Because a client's progress may be slow, patience, compassion, and good listening skills are necessary.

Job Outlook

Employment of speech-language pathologists and audiologists is expected to grow much faster than the average for all occupations through the year 2008. Because hearing loss is strongly associated with aging, rapid growth in the population age 55 and over will cause the number of persons with hearing impairment to increase markedly. In addition, baby boomers are now entering middle age,

when the possibility of neurological disorders and associated speech, language, and hearing impairments increases. Medical advances are also improving the survival rate of premature infants and trauma and stroke victims, who then need assessment and possible treatment.

Employment growth in health services would be even faster except for Federal legislation imposing limits on reimbursement for therapy services that may continue to adversely affect the job market for therapy providers over the near term. Because of the effects of these provisions, the majority of expected employment growth in health services will occur in the second half of the projection period.

Employment in schools will increase along with growth in elementary and secondary school enrollments, including enrollment of special education students. Federal law guarantees special education and related services to all eligible children with disabilities. Greater awareness of the importance of early identification and diagnosis of speech, language, and hearing disorders will also increase employment.

The number of speech-language pathologists and audiologists in private practice will rise due to the increasing use of contract services by hospitals, schools, and nursing homes. In addition to job openings stemming from employment growth, some openings for speech-language pathologists and audiologists will arise from the need to replace those who leave the occupation.

Earnings

Median annual earnings of speech-language pathologists and audiologists were $43,080 in 1998. The middle 50 percent earned between $34,580 and $55,260 a year. The lowest 10 percent earned less than $27,460 and the highest 10 percent earned more than $80,720 a year. Median annual earnings in the industries employing the largest number of speech-language pathologists and audiologists in 1997 were as follows:

Hospitals $44,800

Offices of other health care practitioners 44,500

Elementary and secondary schools 38,400

According to a 1999 survey by the American Speech-Language-Hearing Association, the median annual salary for full-time certified speech-language pathologists or audiologists who worked 11 or 12 months annually was $44,000. For those who worked 9 or 10 months annually, median annual salaries for speech-language pathologists were $40,000; for audiologists, $42,000.

Related Occupations

Speech-language pathologists specialize in the prevention, diagnosis, and treatment of speech and language problems. Workers in related occupations include occupational therapists, optometrists, physical therapists, psychologists, recreational therapists, and rehabilitation counselors.

Audiologists specialize in the prevention, diagnosis, and treatment of hearing problems. Workers in related occupations include neurologists, neonatologists, acoustical engineers, industrial hygienists, and other rehabilitation professionals.

Sources of Additional Information

State licensing boards can provide information on licensure requirements. State departments of education can supply information on certification requirements for those who wish to work in public schools.

General information on careers in speech-language pathology and audiology is available from:

- American Speech-Language-Hearing Association, 10801 Rockville Pike, Rockville, MD 20852. Internet: http://www.asha.org

Information on a career in audiology is also available from:

- American Academy of Audiology, 8201 Greensboro Dr., Suite 300, McLean, VA 22102.

Statisticians

(O*NET 25312)

Significant Points

- Many individuals with degrees in statistics enter jobs that do not have the title statistician.

- Job prospects as a statistician in private industry and academia will be best for those with a graduate degree and some work experience in statistics.

Nature of the Work

Statistics is the scientific application of mathematical principles to the collection, analysis and presentation of numerical data. Statisticians contribute to scientific inquiry by applying their mathematical knowledge to the design of surveys and experiments; collection, processing, and analysis of data; and interpretation of the results. Statisticians often apply their knowledge of statistical methods to a variety of subject areas, such as biology, economics, engineering, medicine, public health, psychology, marketing, and education. Many applications cannot occur without use of statistical techniques, such as designing experiments to gain Federal approval of a newly manufactured drug.

One especially useful technique used by statisticians is sampling—obtaining information about a population of people or group of things by surveying a small portion of the total. For example, to determine the size of the audience for particular programs, television-rating services survey only a few thousand families instead of all viewers. Statisticians decide where and how to gather the data, determine the type and size of the sample group, and develop the survey questionnaire or reporting form. They also prepare instructions for workers who will collect and tabulate the data. Finally, statisticians analyze, interpret, and summarize the data using computer software.

In manufacturing industries, statisticians play an important role in quality control and product improvement. In an automobile company, for example, statisticians might design experiments to determine the failure time of engines exposed to extreme weather conditions by running individual engines until failure and breakdown. Such destructive tests are conducted on a representative sample of the engines, and the results enable the company to identify changes that can improve engine performance.

Because statistical specialists are used in so many work areas, specialists who use statistics often have different professional designations. For example, a person using statistical methods on economic data may have the title econometrician, while statisticians in public health and medicine may hold titles of biostatistician, biometrician, or epidemiologist.

Working Conditions

Statisticians usually work regular hours in comfortable offices. Some statisticians travel to provide advice on research projects, supervise and set up surveys, or gather statistical data. Some may have duties that vary widely, such as designing experiments or performing fieldwork in various communities. Statisticians who work in academia generally have a mix of teaching and research responsibilities.

Employment

Persons holding the title of statistician held about 17,000 jobs in 1998. Over one-fourth of these jobs were in the Federal government, where statisticians were concentrated in the Departments of Commerce, Agriculture, and Health and Human Services. Most of the remaining jobs were in private industry, especially in the biopharmaceutical industry. In addition, many professionals with a background in statistics were among the 20,000 mathematics faculty in colleges and universities in 1998, according to the American Mathematical Society.

Training, Other Qualifications, and Advancement

Although more employment opportunities are becoming available to well-qualified statisticians with bachelor's degrees, a master's degree in statistics or mathematics is the minimum educational requirement for most jobs with job title statistician. Research positions in institutions of higher education, for example, require a graduate degree, usually a doctorate, in statistics. Beginning positions in industrial research often require a master's degree combined with several years of experience.

The training required for employment as an entry-level statistician in the Federal government, however, is a bachelor's degree, including at least 15 semester hours of statistics or a combination of 15 hours of mathematics and statistics, if at least 6 semester hours are in statistics. Qualifying as a mathematical statistician in the Federal government requires 24 semester hours of mathematics and statistics with a minimum of 6 semester hours in statistics and 12 semester hours in an area of advanced mathematics, such as calculus, differential equations, or vector analysis.

About 80 colleges and universities offered bachelor's degrees in statistics in 1998. Many other schools also offered degrees in mathematics, operations research, and other fields, which included a sufficient number of courses in statistics to qualify graduates for some beginning positions in the Federal government. Required subjects for statistics majors include differential and integral calculus, statistical methods, mathematical modeling, and probability theory. Additional courses that undergraduates should take include linear algebra, design and analysis of experiments, applied multivariate analysis, and mathematical statistics.

In 1998, approximately 110 universities offered a master's degree program in statistics, and about 60 offered a doctoral degree program. Many other schools also offered graduate-level courses in applied statistics for students majoring in biology, business, economics, education, engineering, psychology, and other fields. Acceptance into graduate statistics programs does not require an undergraduate degree in statistics, although good training in mathematics is essential.

Because computers are used extensively for statistical applications, a strong background in computer science is highly recommended. For positions involving quality and productivity improvement, training in engineering or physical science is useful. A background in biological, chemical, or health science is important for positions involving the preparation and testing of pharmaceutical or agricultural products. Courses in economics and business administration are helpful for many jobs in market research, business analysis, and forecasting.

Good communications skills are important for prospective statisticians, in order to qualify for many positions in industry, where the need to explain technical matters to laymen is common. A solid understanding of business and the economy is important for those who plan to work in private industry.

Beginning statisticians are assigned work supervised by an experienced statistician. With experience, they may advance to positions with ample technical and supervisory responsibility. However, opportunities for promotion increase with advanced degrees. master's and Ph.D. degree holders usually enjoy independence in their work and become qualified to engage in research, develop statistical methods, or (after a number of years of experience in a particular area) become statistical consultants.

Job Outlook

Job opportunities should remain favorable for individuals with statistical degrees, although many of these positions will not carry an explicit job title of statistician. Employment of those with the title statistician is expected to grow little through the year 2008. Many individuals will find positions in which they do not have the title statistician. This is especially true for those involved in analyzing and interpreting data from other disciplines such as economics, biological science, psychology, or engineering. In addition to the limited number of jobs resulting from growth, a number of openings will become available as statisticians retire, transfer to other occupations, or leave the work force for other reasons.

Among graduates with a bachelor's degree in statistics, those with a strong background in an allied field, such as finance, engineering, or computer science, should have the best prospects of finding jobs related to their field of study. Federal agencies will hire statisticians in many fields, including demography, agriculture,

consumer and producer surveys, Social Security, health care, and environmental quality. Competition for entry-level positions in the Federal government is expected to be strong for those just meeting the minimum qualification standards for statisticians, because this is one of the few employers that considers a bachelor's degree to be an adequate entry-level qualification. Those who meet state certification requirements may become high school statistics teachers.

Manufacturing firms will hire statisticians at the master's and doctoral degree levels for quality control of various products, including pharmaceuticals, motor vehicles, chemicals, and food. For example, pharmaceutical firms employ statisticians to assess the safety and effectiveness of new drugs. To address global product competition, motor vehicle manufacturers will need statisticians to improve the quality of automobiles, trucks, and their components by developing and testing new designs. Statisticians with knowledge of engineering and the physical sciences will find jobs in research and development, working with teams of scientists and engineers to help improve design and production processes to ensure consistent quality of newly developed products. Business firms will rely heavily on workers with a background in statistics, to forecast sales, analyze business conditions, and help solve management problems in order to maximize profits. In addition, sophisticated statistical services will increasingly be offered to other businesses by consulting firms.

Earnings

Median annual earnings of statisticians were $48,540 in 1998. The middle 50 percent earned between $35,800 and $71,030. The lowest 10 percent had earnings of less than $28,240, while the top 10 percent earned more than $87,180. The average annual salary for statisticians in the Federal government in nonsupervisory, supervisory, and managerial positions was $62,800 in early 1999, while mathematical statisticians averaged $69,000. According to a 1999 survey by the National Association of Colleges and Employers, starting salary offers for mathematics/statistics graduates with a bachelor's degree averaged about $37,300 a year.

Related Occupations

People in numerous occupations work with statistics. Among these are actuaries; mathematicians; operations research analysts; computer systems analysts and programmers; engineers; economists; financial analysts; and information, life, physical, and social scientists.

Sources of Additional Information

For information about career opportunities in statistics, contact:

- American Statistical Association, 1429 Duke St., Alexandria, VA 22314. Internet: http://amstat.org/index.html

For more information on careers and training in mathematics (a field closely related to statistics), especially for doctoral-level employment, contact:

- American Mathematical Society, Department of Professional Programs and Services, P.O. Box 6248, Providence, RI 02940-6248. Internet: http://www.ams.org

Information on obtaining a job as a statistician with the Federal government may be obtained from the Office of Personnel Management through a telephone-based system. Consult your telephone directory under U.S. Government for a local number, or call (912) 757-3000; TDD (912) 744-2299. This number is not toll free, and charges may result. Information may also be obtained through the Internet site: http://www.usajobs.opm.gov.

Stock Clerks

(O*NET 49021, 58023, and 58026)

Significant Points

- Job openings will continue to arise due to employee turnover.

- The occupation does not require more than a high school diploma.

Nature of the Work

Stock clerks receive, unpack, check, store, and track merchandise or materials. They keep records of items entering or leaving the stock room and inspect damaged or spoiled goods. They sort, organize, and mark items with identifying codes, such as prices or stock or inventory control codes, so that inventories can be located quickly and easily. In larger establishments, where they may be responsible for only one task, they are called *inventory clerk, stock-control clerk, merchandise distributor, order filler, property custodian,* or *storekeeper*. In smaller firms, they may also perform tasks usually handled by shipping and receiving clerks.

In many firms, stock clerks use hand-held scanners connected to computers to keep inventories up to date. In retail stores, stock clerks bring merchandise to the sales floor and stock shelves and racks. In stockrooms and warehouses, they store materials in bins, on floors, or on shelves. They may also be required to lift cartons of various sizes.

Working Conditions

Stock clerks work in a wide variety of businesses, institutions, and industries. Some work in warehouses, stock rooms, or shipping and receiving rooms that may not be temperature controlled. Others may spend time in cold storage rooms or outside on loading platforms, where they are exposed to the weather. Most jobs involve frequent standing, bending, walking, and stretching. Some lifting and carrying of smaller items may also be involved. Although automation, robotics, and pneumatic devices have lessened the physical demands in this occupation, their use remains somewhat limited. Work still can be strenuous, even though mechanical material handling equipment is employed to move heavy items.

The typical workweek is Monday through Friday; however, evening and weekend hours are standard for some jobs (such as stock clerks who work in retail trade) and may be required in others when large shipments are involved or when inventory is taken.

Employment

Stock clerks held about 2.3 million jobs in 1998, with about 80 percent working in wholesale and retail trade. The greatest numbers were employed in grocery and department stores, respectively. Jobs for stock clerks are found in all parts of the country, but most work in large urban areas that have many large suburban shopping centers, warehouses, and factories.

Training, Other Qualifications, and Advancement

Stock clerk positions are entry level and require no more than a high school diploma. Increasingly however, employers prefer to hire those familiar with computers and other electronic office and business equipment. Those who have taken business courses or have previous job-related experience may be preferred. Because the nature of the work is to communicate effectively with other people, good oral and written communications skills are essential. Typing, filing, record keeping, and other clerical skills are also important.

Stock clerks usually learn the job by doing routine tasks under close supervision. They learn how to count and mark stock, and then start keeping records and taking inventory. Strength, stamina, good eyesight, and an ability to work at repetitive tasks, sometimes under pressure, are important characteristics. Stock clerks whose sole responsibility is to bring merchandise to the sales floor and to stock shelves and racks need little or no training. Stock clerks who handle jewelry, liquor, or drugs may be bonded.

Advancement opportunities vary with the place of employment. In large firms, stock clerks can advance to invoice clerk, stock control clerk, or procurement clerk. With additional training, some stock clerks advance to jobs as warehouse managers or purchasing agents.

Job Outlook

Job prospects for stock clerks should be favorable even though employment is expected to grow more slowly than the average for all occupations through 2008. Because this occupation is very large and many jobs are entry level, numerous job openings will occur each year to replace those who transfer to other jobs or leave the labor force.

The growing use of computers for inventory control and the installation of new, automated equipment are expected to slow growth in demand for stock clerks. This is especially true in manufacturing and wholesale trade, industries whose operations are automated most easily. In addition to computerized inventory control systems, firms in these industries rely more on sophisticated conveyor belts and automatic high stackers to store and retrieve goods. Also, expanded use of battery-powered, driverless, automatically guided vehicles can be expected.

Employment of stock clerks who work in grocery, general merchandise, department, apparel, and accessories stores is expected to be somewhat less affected by automation because much of their work is done manually on the sales floor and is difficult to automate. In addition, the increasing role of large retail outlets and warehouses, as well as catalogue, mail, telephone, and Internet shopping services should bolster employment of stock clerks and order fillers in these sectors of retail trade.

Earnings

In 1998, median hourly earnings of stock clerks were $7.94.

Related Occupations

Workers who also handle, move, organize, and store materials include shipping and receiving clerks, distributing clerks, routing clerks, stock supervisors, and cargo checkers.

Sources of Additional Information

State employment service offices can provide information about job openings for stock clerks.

General information about stock clerks can be obtained from:

- National Retail Federation, 325 Seventh Street NW., Suite 1000, Washington, DC 20004. Internet: http://www.nrf.com/nri/

Surveyors, Cartographers, Photogrammetrists, and Surveying Technicians

(O*NET 22311A, 22311B, 22521A, 22521B, and 25103B)

Significant Points

- More than 8 out of 10 are employed in engineering services and government.
- Computer skills enhance employment opportunities.

Nature of the Work

Measuring and mapping the earth's surface is the responsibility of several different types of workers. Traditional *land surveyors* establish official land, air space, and water boundaries. They write descriptions of land for deeds, leases, and other legal documents; define air space for airports; and measure construction and mineral sites. Other surveyors provide data relevant to the shape, contour, location, elevation, or dimension of land or land features. *Surveying technicians* assist land surveyors by operating survey instruments and collecting information. *Cartographers* compile geographic, political, and cultural information and prepare maps of large areas.

Land surveyors manage survey parties that measure distances, directions, and angles between points and elevations of points, lines, and contours on the earth's surface. They plan the fieldwork, select known survey reference points, and determine the precise location of important features in the survey area. Surveyors research legal records and look for evidence of previous boundaries. They record the results of the survey, verify the accuracy of data, and prepare plots, maps, and reports. Surveyors who establish boundaries must be licensed by the State in which they work.

A survey party gathers the information needed by the land surveyor. A typical survey party consists of a party chief and several surveying technicians and helpers. The party chief, who may be either a land surveyor or a senior surveying technician, leads day-to-day work activities. Surveying technicians assist the party chief by adjusting and operating surveying instruments, such as the theodolite (used to measure horizontal and vertical angles) and electronic distance-measuring equipment. Surveying technicians or assistants position and hold the vertical rods, or targets, that the theodolite operator sights on to measure angles, distances, or elevations. They may also hold measuring tapes, if electronic distance-measuring equipment is not used. Surveying technicians compile notes, make sketches, and enter the data obtained from these instruments into computers. Survey parties may include laborers or helpers who perform less skilled duties, such as clearing brush from sight lines, driving stakes, or carrying equipment.

New technology is changing the nature of the work of surveyors and surveying technicians. For larger projects, surveyors are increasingly using the Global Positioning System (GPS), a satellite system that precisely locates points on the earth by using radio signals transmitted via satellites. To use this system, a surveyor places a satellite signal receiver—a small instrument mounted on a tripod—on a desired point. The receiver simultaneously collects information from several satellites to locate a precise position. The receiver can also be placed in a vehicle for tracing out road systems. Since receivers now come in different sizes and shapes and the cost of the receivers has fallen, much more surveying work is being done using GPS. Surveyors then must interpret and check the results produced by the new technology.

Cartographers measure, map, and chart the earth's surface, which involves everything from geographical research and data compilation to actual map production. They collect, analyze, and interpret both spatial data—such as latitude, longitude, elevation, and distance—and nonspatial data—such as population density, land use patterns, annual precipitation levels, and demographic characteristics. Cartographers prepare maps in either digital or graphic form, using information provided by geodetic surveys, aerial photographs, and satellite data. *Photogrammetrists* prepare detailed maps and drawings from aerial photographs, usually of areas that are inaccessible or difficult to survey by other methods. *Map editors* develop and verify map contents from aerial photographs and other reference sources.

Some surveyors perform specialized functions that are closer to those of a cartographer than to those of a traditional surveyor. For example, *geodetic surveyors* use high-accuracy techniques including satellite observations to measure large areas of the earth's surface. *Geophysical prospecting surveyors* mark sites for subsurface exploration, usually petroleum related. *Marine surveyors* survey harbors, rivers, and other bodies of water to determine shorelines, topography of the bottom, water depth, and other features.

The work of surveyors and cartographers is changing because of advancements in technology. These advancements include not only the GPS, but also new earth resources data satellites, improved aerial photography, and geographic information systems (GIS)—which are computerized data banks of spatial data. From the older specialties of photogrammetrist and cartographer, a new type of mapping scientist is emerging. The *geographic information specialist* combines the functions of mapping science and surveying into a broader field concerned with the collection and analysis of geographic information.

Working Conditions

Surveyors usually work 8 hours a day 5 days a week and may spend a lot of time outdoors. Sometimes they work longer hours during the summer, when weather and light conditions are most suitable for fieldwork.

Land surveyors and technicians engage in active, and sometimes strenuous, work. They often stand for long periods, walk considerable distances, and climb hills with heavy packs of instruments and other equipment. They can also be exposed to all types of weather. Traveling is often part of the job; they may commute long distances, stay overnight, or temporarily relocate near a survey site.

While surveyors can spend considerable time inside planning surveys, analyzing data, and preparing reports and maps, cartographers spend virtually all their time in offices and seldom visit the sites they are mapping.

Employment

Surveyors, cartographers, photogrammetrists, and surveying technicians held about 110,000 jobs in 1998. Engineering and architectural services firms employed about 64 percent of these workers. Federal, State, and local governmental agencies employed an additional 17 percent. Major Federal governmental employers are the U.S. Geological Survey, the Bureau of Land Management, the Army Corps of Engineers, the Forest Service, the National Oceanic and Atmospheric Administration, and the National Imagery and Mapping Agency (NIMA). Most surveyors in State and local government work for highway departments and urban planning and redevelopment agencies. Construction firms, mining and oil and gas extraction companies, and public utilities also employ surveyors, cartographers, photogrammetrists, and surveying technicians. About 6,800 were self-employed in 1998.

Training, Other Qualifications, and Advancement

Most people prepare for a career as a licensed surveyor by combining post-secondary school courses in surveying with extensive on-the-job training. However, as technology advances, a four-year degree is becoming more of a prerequisite. About 25 universities now offer four-year programs leading to a B.S. degree in surveying. Junior and community colleges, technical institutes, and vocational schools offer one-, two-, and three-year programs in both surveying and surveying technology.

All 50 States license land surveyors. For licensure, most State licensing boards require that individuals pass two written examinations, one prepared by the State and one given by the National Council of Examiners for Engineering and Surveying. In addition, they must meet varying standards of formal education and work experience in the field. In the past, many individuals started as members of survey crews and worked their way up to become licensed surveyors with little formal training in surveying. However, because of advancing technology and an increase in licensing standards, formal education requirements are increasing. At present, most States require some formal post-high school education coursework and 10 to 12 years of surveying experience to gain licensure. However, requirements vary among States. Generally, the quickest route to licensure is a combination of four years of college, two to four years of experience (a few States do not require any), and passing the licensing examinations. An increasing number of States require a bachelor's degree in surveying or a closely related field, such as civil engineering or forestry (with courses in surveying), regardless of the number of years of experience.

High school students interested in surveying should take courses in algebra, geometry, trigonometry, drafting, mechanical drawing, and computer science. High school graduates with no formal training in surveying usually start as an apprentice. Beginners with post-secondary school training in surveying can usually start as technicians or assistants. With on-the-job experience and formal training in surveying (either in an institutional program or from a correspondence school) workers may advance to senior survey technician, then to party chief, and in some cases, to licensed surveyor (depending on State licensing requirements).

The American Congress on Surveying and Mapping has a voluntary certification program for surveying technicians. Technicians are certified at four levels requiring progressive amounts of experience, in addition to passing written examinations. Although not required for State licensure, many employers require certification for promotion to positions with greater responsibilities.

Surveyors should have the ability to visualize objects, distances, sizes, and abstract forms. They must work with precision and accuracy because mistakes can be costly. Members of a survey party must be in good physical condition, because they work outdoors and often carry equipment over difficult terrain. They need good eyesight, coordination, and hearing to communicate verbally and manually (using hand signals). Surveying is a cooperative process, so good interpersonal skills and the ability to work as part of a team are important. Leadership qualities are important for party chief and other supervisory positions.

Cartographers and photogrammetrists usually have a bachelor's degree in a field such as engineering, forestry, geography, or a physical science. Although it is possible to enter these positions through previous experience as a photogrammetric or cartographic technician, most cartographic and photogrammetric technicians now have had some specialized post-secondary school training. With the development of Geographic Information Systems, cartographers and photogrammetrists need additional education and stronger technical skills—including more experience with computers—than in the past.

The American Society for Photogrammetry and Remote Sensing has a voluntary certification program for photogrammetrists. To qualify for this professional distinction, individuals must meet work experience standards and pass an oral or written examination.

Job Outlook

Overall employment of surveyors, cartographers, photogrammetrists, and surveying technicians is expected to grow about as fast as the average through the year 2008. The widespread availability and use of advanced technologies, such as the Global Positioning System, Geographic Information Systems, and remote sensing, are increasing both the accuracy and productivity of survey and mapping work. Job openings, however, will continue to result from the need to replace workers who transfer to other occupations or leave the labor force altogether.

Prospects will be best for surveying technicians, whose growth is expected to be slightly faster than the average for all occupations through 2008. The short training period needed to learn to operate the equipment, the current lack of any formal testing or licensing, and the relatively lower wages all make for a healthy demand for these technicians, as well as for a readily available supply.

As technologies become more complex, opportunities will be best for surveyors, cartographers, and photogrammetrists who have at least a bachelor's degree and strong technical skills. Increasing demand for geographic data, as opposed to traditional surveying services, will mean better opportunities for cartographers and photogrammetrists involved in the development and use of geographic and land information systems. New technologies, such as GPS and GIS may also enhance employment opportunities for surveyors and surveying technicians who have the educational background enabling them to use these systems, but upgraded licensing requirements will continue to limit opportunities for those with less education.

Even as demand increases in nontraditional areas such as urban planning and natural resource exploration and mapping, opportunities for surveyors, cartographers, and photogrammetrists should remain concentrated in engineering, architectural, and surveying services firms. Growth in construction through 2008 should require surveyors to lay out streets, shopping centers, housing developments, factories, office buildings, and recreation areas. However, employment may fluctuate from year to year along with construction activity.

Earnings

Median annual earnings of surveyors, cartographers, and photogrammetrists were $37,640 in 1998. The middle 50 percent earned between $27,580 and $50,380. The lowest 10 percent earned less than $21,510, and the highest 10 percent earned more than $76,880.

Median hourly earnings of surveying technicians were $11.20 in 1997 for those employed in engineering and architectural services, while those employed by local governments received median hourly earnings of $13.50. The middle 50 percent of all surveying technicians earned between $9.86 and $16.54 in 1998. The lowest 10 percent earned less than $7.61, and the highest 10 percent earned more than $21.14.

In 1999, land surveyors in nonsupervisory, supervisory, and managerial positions in the Federal government earned an average salary of $52,400; cartographers earned an average salary of $56,300. The average Federal salary for geodetic technicians is $48,800; for surveying technicians, about $31,300; and for cartographic technicians, about $37,200.

Related Occupations

Surveying is related to the work of civil engineers and architects, since an accurate survey is the first step in land development and construction projects. Cartography and geodetic surveying are related to the work of geologists and geophysicists, who study the earth's internal composition, surface, and atmosphere. Cartography is also related to the work of geographers and urban planners, who study and decide how the earth's surface is used.

Sources of Additional Information

Information about career opportunities, licensure requirements, and the surveying technician certification program is available from:

- American Congress on Surveying and Mapping, 5410 Grosvenor Lane, Suite 100, Bethesda, MD 20814-2122.

General information on careers in photogrammetry is available from:

- ASPRS: The Imaging and Geospacial Information Society, 5410 Grosvenor Lane, Suite 210, Bethesda, MD 20814.

General information on careers in cartography is available from:

- North American Cartographic Information Society, P.O. Box 399, Milwaukee, WI 53201-0399.

Travel Agents

(O*NET 43021)

Significant Points

- Training at a post-secondary vocational school or college or university is increasingly important for getting a job.

- Travel benefits, such as reduced rates for transportation and accommodations, attract many people to this occupation.

- Projected average employment growth reflects increases in spending on pleasure and business travel.

Nature of the Work

Constantly changing air fares and schedules, thousands of available vacation packages, and a vast amount of travel information on the Internet can make travel planning frustrating and time-consuming. To sort out the many travel options, tourists and businesspeople often turn to travel agents, who assess their needs and help them make the best possible travel arrangements. Also, many major cruise lines, resorts, and specialty travel groups use travel agents to promote travel packages to the millions of people who travel every year.

In general, travel agents give advice on destinations and make arrangements for transportation, hotel accommodations, car rentals, tours, and recreation. They may also advise on weather conditions, restaurants, and tourist attractions, and recreation. For international travel, agents also provide information on customs regulations, required papers (passports, visas, and certificates of vaccination), and currency exchange rates.

Travel agents consult a variety of published and computer-based sources for information on departure and arrival times, fares, and hotel ratings and accommodations. They may visit hotels, resorts, and restaurants to evaluate their comfort, cleanliness, and the quality of food and service so they can base recommendations on their own travel experiences or those of colleagues or clients.

Travel agents also promote their services by using telemarketing, direct mail, and the Internet. They make presentations to social and special interest groups, arrange advertising displays, and suggest company-sponsored trips to business managers. Depending on the size of the travel agency, an agent may specialize by type of travel, such as leisure or business, or destination, such as Europe or Africa.

Working Conditions

Travel agents spend most of their time behind a desk conferring with clients, completing paperwork, contacting airlines and hotels for travel arrangements, and promoting group tours. During vacation seasons and holiday periods they may be under a great deal of pressure. Many agents, especially those who are self-employed, frequently work long hours. With advanced computer systems and telecommunication networks, some travel agents are able to work at home.

Employment

Travel agents held about 138,000 jobs in 1998 and are found in every part of the country. More than 9 out of 10 salaried agents worked for travel agencies. Many of the remainder worked for membership organizations.

Training, Other Qualifications, and Advancement

The minimum requirement for those interested in becoming a travel agent is a high school diploma or equivalent. The minimum requirement for those interested in becoming a travel agent is a high school diploma or equivalent. Technology and computerization are having a profound effect on the work of travel agents, however, and formal or specialized training is becoming increasingly important. Many vocational schools offer 6- to 12-week full-time travel agent programs, as well as evening and weekend programs. Travel agent courses are also offered in public adult education programs and in community and four-year colleges. A few colleges offer bachelor's or master's degrees in travel and tourism. Although few college courses relate directly to the travel industry, a college education is sometimes desired by employers to establish a background in fields such as computer science, geography, communication, foreign languages, and world history. Courses in accounting and business management also are important, especially for those who expect to manage or start their own travel agencies.

The American Society of Travel Agents (ASTA) offers a correspondence course that provides a basic understanding of the travel industry. Travel agencies also provide on-the-job training for their employees, a significant part of which consists of computer instruction. Computer skills are required by all employers to operate airline and centralized reservation systems.

Experienced travel agents can take advanced self or group study courses from the Institute of Certified Travel Agents (ICTA) that lead to the designation of Certified Travel Counselor (CTC). The ICTA also offers marketing and sales skills development programs and destination specialist programs, which provide a detailed knowledge of regions such as North America, Western Europe, the Caribbean, and the Pacific Rim.

Travel experience (and experience as an airline reservation agent) is an asset because personal knowledge about a city or foreign country often helps to influence clients' travel plans. Patience and the ability to gain the confidence of clients are also useful qualities. Travel agents must be well-organized, accurate, and meticulous to compile information from various sources and plan and organize their clients' travel itineraries. Other desirable qualifications include good writing, computer, and sales skills.

Some employees start as reservation clerks or receptionists in travel agencies. With experience and some formal training, they can take on greater responsibilities and eventually assume travel agent duties. In agencies with many offices, travel agents may advance to office manager or to other managerial positions.

Those who start their own agencies generally have had experience in an established agency. Before they can receive commissions, these agents usually must gain formal approval from suppliers or corporations, such as airlines, ship lines, or rail lines. The Airlines Reporting Corporation and the International Airlines Travel Agency Network, for example, are the approving bodies for airlines. To gain approval, an agency must be financially sound and employ at least one experienced manager or travel agent.

There are no Federal licensing requirements for travel agents. However, nine States—California, Florida, Hawaii, Illinois, Iowa, Ohio, Oregon, Rhode Island, and Washington—require some form of registration or certification of retail sellers of travel services. More information may be obtained by contacting the Office of the Attorney General or Department of Commerce for each State.

Job Outlook

Employment of travel agents is expected to grow about as fast as the average for all occupations through 2008. Many job openings will arise as new agencies open and existing agencies expand, but most openings will occur as experienced agents transfer to other occupations or leave the labor force.

Projected employment growth stems from increased spending on tourism and business travel over the next decade. With rising household incomes, smaller families, and an increasing number of older people who are more likely to travel, more people are expected to travel on vacation—and to do so more frequently—than in the past. Business travel should also grow as business activity expands. Further, managerial, professional, and sales occupations are projected to be among the fastest growing, and people in these occupations do the most business travel.

A variety of other factors will also lead to greater business for travel agents. For example, charter flights and larger, more efficient planes have brought air transportation within the budgets of more people, and the easing of Federal regulation of air fares and routes has fostered greater competition among airlines, resulting in more affordable service. In addition, American travel agents now organize more tours for the growing number of foreign visitors. Also, travel agents are often able to offer various travel packages at a substantial discount. Although most travel agencies now have automated reservation systems, this has not weakened demand for travel agents.

Some developments, however, may reduce job opportunities for travel agents in the future. The Internet increasingly will allow people to access travel information from their personal computers and make their own travel arrangements. Further, suppliers of travel services are increasingly able to make their services available through other means, such as electronic ticketing machines and remote ticket printers. Also, airline companies have put a cap on the amount of commissions they will pay to travel agencies. The full effect of these practices, though, have yet to be determined, and many consumers will still prefer to use a professional travel agent to ensure reliability and to save time and, in some cases, money.

The travel industry is sensitive to economic downturns and international political crises, when travel plans are likely to be deferred. Therefore, the number of job opportunities fluctuates.

Earnings

Experience, sales ability, and the size and location of the agency determine the salary of a travel agent. Median annual earnings of travel agents overall and in the passenger transportation arrangement industry, where most worked, were $23,010 in 1998. Most travel agents earned between $17,960 and $28,430. The bottom 10 percent of travel agents earned less than $13,770, while the top 10 percent earned more than 34,670.

Salaried agents usually enjoy standard benefits that self-employed agents must provide for themselves. Among agencies, those focusing on corporate sales pay higher salaries and provide more extensive benefits, on average, than those who focus on leisure sales. When they travel for personal reasons, agents usually get reduced rates for transportation and accommodations. In addition, agents sometimes take "familiarization" trips, at no cost to themselves, to learn about various vacation sites. These benefits attract many people to this occupation.

Earnings of travel agents who own their agencies depend mainly on commissions from airlines and other carriers, cruise lines, tour operators, and lodging places. Commissions for domestic travel arrangements, cruises, hotels, sightseeing tours, and car rentals are about 7-10 percent of the total sale, and for international travel, about 10 percent. Travel agents may also charge clients a service fee for the time and expense involved in planning a trip.

During the first year of business or while awaiting corporation approval, self-employed travel agents often have low earnings. Their income usually is limited to commissions from hotels, cruises, and tour operators and to nominal fees for making complicated arrangements. Established agents may have lower earnings during economic downturns.

Related Occupations

Travel agents organize and schedule business, educational, or recreational travel or activities. Other workers with similar responsibilities include tour guides, meeting planners, airline reservation agents, rental car agents, and travel counselors.

Sources of Additional Information

For further information on training opportunities, contact:

- American Society of Travel Agents, Education Department, 1101 King St., Alexandria, VA 22314. Internet: http://www.astanet.com/www/asta/pub/car/becomingagent.htmlx

For information on certification qualifications, contact:

- The Institute of Certified Travel Agents, 148 Linden St., P.O. Box 812059, Wellesley, MA 02181-0012.

Urban and Regional Planners

(O*NET 27105)

Significant Points

- Most entry-level jobs require a master's degree, although a bachelor's degree and related work experience is sufficient for some positions.

- Most new jobs will arise in more affluent, rapidly growing urban and suburban communities.

Nature of the Work

Planners develop long- and short-term land use plans to provide for growth and revitalization of urban, suburban, and rural communities, while helping local officials make decisions concerning social, economic, and environmental problems. Because local governments employ the majority of urban and regional planners, they are often referred to as community, regional, or city planners.

Planners promote the best use of a community's land and resources for residential, commercial, institutional, and recreational purposes. Planners may be involved in various other activities, including decisions on alternative public transportation system plans, resource development, and protection of ecologically sensitive regions. They address issues such as traffic congestion, air pollution, and the effect of growth and change on a community. They may formulate plans relating to the construction of new school buildings, public housing, or other infrastructure. Some planners are involved in environmental issues ranging from pollution control to wetland preservation, forest conservation, or the location of new landfills. Planners also may be involved with drafting legislation on environmental, social, and economic issues, such as sheltering the homeless, planning a new park, or meeting the demand for new correctional facilities.

Planners examine proposed community facilities such as schools to be sure these facilities will meet the changing demands placed upon them over time. They keep abreast of economic and legal issues involved in zoning codes, building codes, and environmental regulations. They ensure that builders and developers follow these codes and regulations. Planners also deal with land use issues created by population movements. For example, as suburban growth and economic development create more new jobs outside cities, the need for public transportation that enables workers to get to these jobs increases. In response, planners develop transportation models for possible implementation and explain their details to planning boards and the general public.

Before preparing plans for community development, planners report on the current use of land for residential, business, and community purposes. These reports include information on the location and capacity of streets, highways, water and sewer lines, schools, libraries, and cultural and recreational sites. They also provide data on the types of industries in the community, characteristics of the population, and employment and economic trends. With this information, along with input from citizens' advisory committees, planners design the layout of land uses for buildings and other facilities such as subway lines and stations, and prepare reports showing how their programs can be carried out and what they will cost.

Planners use computers to record and analyze information, and to prepare reports and recommendations for government executives and others. Computer databases, spreadsheets, and analytical techniques are widely used to project program costs and forecast future trends in employment, housing, transportation, or population. Computerized geographic information systems enable planners to map land areas and overlay maps with geographic variables, such as population density, as well as to combine and manipulate geographic information to produce alternative plans for land use or development.

Urban and regional planners often confer with land developers, civic leaders, and public officials. They may function as mediators in community disputes and present alternatives acceptable to opposing parties. Planners may prepare material for community relations programs, speak at civic meetings, and appear before legislative committees and elected officials to explain and defend their proposals.

In large organizations, planners usually specialize in a single area such as transportation, demography, housing, historic preservation, urban design, environmental and regulatory issues, or economic development. In small organizations, planners must be able to do various kinds of planning.

Working Conditions

Urban and regional planners are often required to travel to inspect the features of land under consideration for development or regulation, including its current use and the types of structures on it. Some local government planners involved in site development inspections spend most of their time in the field. Although most planners have a scheduled 40-hour workweek, they frequently attend evening or weekend meetings or public hearings with citizens' groups. Planners may experience the pressure of deadlines and tight work schedules, as well as political pressure generated by interest groups affected by land use proposals.

Employment

Urban and regional planners held about 35,000 jobs in 1998, and about 6 out of 10 were employed by local governments. An increasing proportion of planners is employed in the private sector for companies involved with research and testing or management and public relations. Others are employed in State agencies dealing with housing, transportation, or environmental protection, and a small number work for the Federal government.

Training, Other Qualifications, and Advancement

Employers prefer workers who have advanced training. Most entry-level jobs in Federal, State, and local government agencies require a master's degree in urban or regional planning, urban design, geography, or a similar course of study. For some positions, a bachelor's degree and related work experience is sufficient. A bachelor's degree from an accredited planning program, coupled with a master's degree in architecture, landscape architecture, or civil engineering is good preparation for entry-level planning jobs in areas such as urban design, transportation, or the environment. A master's degree from an accredited planning program provides the best training for a number of planning fields. Although graduates from one of the limited number of accredited bachelor's degree programs qualify for many entry-level positions, their advancement opportunities are often limited unless they acquire an advanced degree.

Courses in related disciplines such as architecture, law, earth sciences, demography, economics, finance, health administration, geographic information systems, and management are highly recommended. In addition, familiarity with computer models and statistical techniques is necessary.

In 1999, about 80 colleges and universities offered an accredited master's degree program, and about 10 offered an accredited bachelor's degree program in urban or regional planning. These programs are accredited by the Planning Accreditation Board, which consists of representatives of the American Institute of Certified Planners, the American Planning Association, and the Association of Collegiate Schools of Planning. Most graduate programs in planning require a minimum of two years.

Specializations most commonly offered by planning schools are environmental planning, land use and comprehensive planning, economic development, housing, historic preservation, and social planning. Other popular offerings include community development, transportation, and urban design. Graduate students spend considerable time in studios, workshops, and laboratory courses learning to analyze and solve planning problems. They are often required to work in a planning office part time or during the summer. Local government planning offices frequently offer students internships, providing experience that proves invaluable in obtaining a full-time planning position after graduation.

The American Institute of Certified Planners (AICP), a professional institute within the American Planning Association (APA), grants certification to individuals who have the appropriate combination of education and professional experience and who pass an examination. Certification may be helpful for promotion.

Planners must be able to think in terms of spatial relationships and visualize the effects of their plans and designs. Planners should be flexible and able to reconcile different viewpoints and make constructive policy recommendations. The ability to communicate effectively, both orally and in writing, is necessary for anyone interested in this field.

After a few years of experience, planners may advance to assignments requiring a high degree of independent judgment, such as designing the physical layout of a large development or recommending policy and budget options. Some public sector planners are promoted to community planning director and spend a great deal of time meeting with officials, speaking to civic groups, and supervising a staff. Further advancement occurs through a transfer to a larger jurisdiction with more complex problems and greater responsibilities, or into related occupations, such as director of community or economic development.

Job Outlook

Employment of urban and regional planners is expected to grow about as fast as the average for all occupations through 2008, due to the need for State and local governments to provide public services such as regulation of commercial development, the environment, transportation, housing, and land use and development. Non-governmental initiatives dealing with historic preservation and redevelopment will provide additional openings. Some job openings will also arise from the need to replace experienced planners who transfer to other occupations, retire, or leave the labor force for other reasons.

Most planners work for local governments with limited resources and many demands for services. When communities need to cut expenditures, planning services may be cut before more basic services such as police or education. As a result, the number of openings in private industry for consulting positions is expected to grow more rapidly than the number of openings in government.

Most new jobs for urban and regional planners will arise in more affluent, rapidly expanding communities. Local governments need planners to address an array of problems associated with population growth. For example, new housing developments require roads, sewer systems, fire stations, schools, libraries, and recreation facilities that must be planned while considering budgetary constraints. Small town chambers of commerce, economic development authorities and tourism bureaus may hire planners, preferring candidates with some background in marketing and public relations.

Earnings

Median annual earnings of urban and regional planners were $42,860 in 1998. The middle 50 percent earned between $32,920 and $56,150 a year. The lowest 10 percent earned less than $26,020, and the highest 10 percent earned more than $80,090 a year. Median annual earnings for urban and regional planners in 1997 were $40,700 in local government and $38,900 in State government.

Related Occupations

Urban and regional planners develop plans for the growth of urban, suburban, and rural communities. Others whose work is simi-lar include architects, landscape architects, city managers, civil engineers, environmental engineers, directors of community or economic development, and geographers.

Sources of Additional Information

Information on careers, salaries, and certification in urban and regional planning is available from:

- American Planning Association, Education Division, 122 South Michigan Ave., Suite 1600, Chicago, IL 60603. Internet: http://www.planning.org

Veterinarians

(O*NET 32114A, 32114B, and 32114C)

Significant Points

- Graduation from an accredited college of veterinary medicine and a license to practice are required.

- Competition for admission to veterinary school is keen.

Nature of the Work

Veterinarians play a major role in the health care of pets, livestock, and zoo, sporting, and laboratory animals. Some veterinarians use their skills to protect humans against diseases carried by animals and conduct clinical research on human and animal health problems. Others work in basic research, broadening the scope of fundamental theoretical knowledge, and in applied research, developing new ways to use knowledge.

Most veterinarians perform clinical work in private practices. More than one-half of these veterinarians predominately, or exclusively, treat small animals. Small animal practitioners usually care for companion animals, such as dogs and cats, but also treat birds, reptiles, rabbits, and other animals that can be kept as pets. Some veterinarians work in mixed animal practices where they see pigs, goats, sheep, and some nondomestic animals in addition to companion animals. Veterinarians in clinical practice diagnose animal health problems; vaccinate against diseases, such as distemper and rabies; medicate animals suffering from infections or illnesses; treat and dress wounds; set fractures; perform surgery; and advise owners about animal feeding, behavior, and breeding.

A small number of private practice veterinarians work exclusively with large animals, focusing mostly on horses or cows, but may also care for various kinds of food animals. These veterinarians usually drive to farms or ranches to provide veterinary services for herds or individual animals. Much of this work involves preventive care to maintain the health of the food animals. These veterinarians test for and vaccinate against diseases and consult with farm or ranch owners and managers on animal production, feeding, and housing issues. They also treat and dress wounds, set fractures, and perform surgery—including cesarean sections on birthing animals. Veterinarians also euthanize animals when necessary. Other veterinarians care for zoo, aquarium, or laboratory animals.

Veterinarians who treat animals use medical equipment, such as stethoscopes; surgical instruments; and diagnostic equipment, such as radiographic and ultrasound equipment. Veterinarians working in research use a full range of sophisticated laboratory equipment.

Veterinarians can contribute to human as well as animal health. A number of veterinarians work with physicians and scientists as they research ways to prevent and treat human health problems, such as cancer, AIDS, and alcohol and drug abuse. Some determine the effects of drug therapies, antibiotics, or new surgical techniques by testing them on animals.

Some veterinarians are involved in food safety at various levels. Veterinarians who are livestock inspectors check animals for transmissible diseases, advise owners on treatment, and may quarantine animals. Veterinarians who are meat, poultry, or egg product inspectors examine slaughtering and processing plants, check live animals and carcasses for disease, and enforce government regulations regarding food purity and sanitation.

Working Conditions

Veterinarians often work long hours, with one-third of full-time workers spending 50 or more hours on the job. Those in group practices may take turns being on call for evening, night, or weekend work; and solo practitioners can work extended and weekend hours, responding to emergencies or squeezing in unexpected appointments.

Veterinarians in large animal practice also spend time driving between their office and farms or ranches. They work outdoors in all kinds of weather and have to treat animals or perform surgery under less-than-sanitary conditions. When working with animals that are frightened or in pain, veterinarians risk being bitten, kicked, or scratched.

Veterinarians working in non-clinical areas, such as public health and research, have working conditions similar to those of other professionals in those lines of work. In these cases, veterinarians enjoy clean, well-lit offices or laboratories and spend much of their time dealing with people rather than animals.

Employment

Veterinarians held about 57,000 jobs in 1998. About 30 percent were self-employed in solo or group practices. Most others were employees of another veterinary practice. The Federal government employed about 1,900 civilian veterinarians, chiefly in the U.S. Department of Agriculture, and about 400 military veterinarians in the U.S. Army and U.S. Air Force. Other employers of veterinarians are State and local governments, colleges of veterinary medicine, medical schools, research laboratories, animal food companies, and pharmaceutical companies. A few veterinarians work for zoos; but most veterinarians caring for zoo animals are private practitioners who contract with zoos to provide services, usually on a part-time basis.

Training, Other Qualifications, and Advancement

Prospective veterinarians must graduate from a four-year program at an accredited college of veterinary medicine with a Doctor of Veterinary Medicine (D.V.M. or V.M.D.) degree and obtain a license to practice. There are 27 colleges in 26 States that meet accreditation standards set by the Council on Education of the American Veterinary Medical Association. The prerequisites for admission vary by veterinary medical college. Many of these colleges do not require a bachelor's degree for entrance; but all require a significant number of credit hours—ranging from 45 to 90 semester hours—at the undergraduate level. However, most of the students admitted have completed an undergraduate program.

Preveterinary courses emphasize the sciences; and veterinary medical colleges typically require classes in organic and inorganic chemistry, physics, biochemistry, general biology, animal biology, animal nutrition, genetics, vertebrate embryology, cellular biology, microbiology, zoology, and systemic physiology. Some programs require calculus; some require only statistics, college algebra and trigonometry, or precalculus; and others require no math at all. Most veterinary medical colleges also require core courses, including some in English or literature, the social sciences, and the humanities.

Most veterinary medical colleges will only consider applicants who have a minimum grade point average (GPA). The required GPA varies by school, from a low of 2.5 to a high of 3.2, based on a maximum GPA of 4.0. However, the average GPA of candidates at most schools is higher than these minimums. Those who receive offers of admission usually have a GPA of 3.0 or better.

In addition to satisfying preveterinary course requirements, applicants must also submit test scores from the Graduate Record Examination (GRE), the Veterinary College Admission Test (VCAT), or the Medical College Admission Test (MCAT), depending on the preference of each college.

Additionally, in the admissions process, veterinary medical colleges weigh heavily a candidate's veterinary and animal experience. Formal experience, such as work with veterinarians or scientists in clinics, agribusiness, research, or in some area of health science, is particularly advantageous. Less formal experience, such as working with animals on a farm or ranch or at a stable or animal shelter, is also helpful. Students must demonstrate ambition and an eagerness to work with animals.

Competition for admission to veterinary school is keen. The number of accredited veterinary colleges has remained at 27 since 1983, whereas the number of applicants has risen. About 1 in 3 applicants was accepted in 1998. Most veterinary medical colleges are public, State-supported institutions and reserve the majority of their openings for in-state residents. Twenty-one States that do not have a veterinary medical college agree to pay a fee or subsidy to help cover the cost of veterinary education for a limited number of their residents at one or more out-of-state colleges. Nonresident students who are admitted under such a contract may have to pay out-of-state tuition, or they may have to repay their State of residency all, or part, of the subsidy provided to the contracting college. Residents of the remaining three States (Connecticut, Maine, and Vermont) and the District of Columbia may apply to any of the 27 veterinary medical colleges as an *at-large* applicant. The number of positions available to at-large applicants is very limited at most schools, making admission difficult.

While in veterinary medical college, students receive additional academic instruction in the basic sciences for the first two years. Later in the program, students are exposed to clinical procedures, such as diagnosing and treating animal diseases and performing surgery. They also do laboratory work in anatomy, biochemistry, medicine, and other scientific subjects. At most veterinary medical colleges, students who plan a career in research can earn both a D.V.M degree and a Doctor of Philosophy (Ph.D.) degree at the same time.

Veterinary graduates who plan to work with specific types of animals or specialize in a clinical area, such as pathology, surgery, radiology, or laboratory animal medicine, usually complete a one-year internship. Interns receive a small salary but usually find that their internship experience leads to a higher beginning salary relative to other starting veterinarians. Veterinarians who seek board certification in a specialty must also complete a two- to three-year residency program that provides intensive training in specialties, such as internal medicine, oncology, radiology, surgery, dermatology, anesthesiology, neurology, cardiology, ophthalmology, and exotic small animal medicine.

All States and the District of Columbia require that veterinarians be licensed before they can practice. The only exemptions are for veterinarians working for some Federal agencies and some State governments. Licensing is controlled by the States and is not strictly uniform, although all States require successful completion of the D.V.M. degree—or equivalent education—and passage of a national board examination. The Educational Commission for Foreign Veterinary Graduates (ECFVG) grants certification to individuals trained outside the U.S. who demonstrate that they meet specified requirements for the English language and clinical proficiency. ECFVG certification fulfills the educational requirement for licensure in all States except Nebraska. Applicants for licensure satisfy the examination requirement by passing the North American Veterinary Licensing Exam (NAVLE), which replaces the National Board Examination (NBE) and the Clinical Competency Test (CCT) as of April 2000. The new NAVLE, administered on computer, takes one day to complete and consists of 360 multiple-choice questions, covering all aspects of veterinary medicine. The NAVLE also includes visual materials designed to test diagnostic skills.

The majority of States also require candidates to pass a State jurisprudence examination covering State laws and regulations. Some States also do additional testing on clinical competency. There are few reciprocal agreements between States, making it difficult for a veterinarian to practice in a different State without first taking another State examination.

Thirty-nine States have continuing education requirements for licensed veterinarians. Requirements differ by State and may involve attending a class or otherwise demonstrating knowledge of recent medical and veterinary advances.

Most veterinarians begin as employees or partners in established practices. Despite the substantial financial investment in equipment, office space, and staff, many veterinarians with experience set up their own practices or purchase established ones.

Newly trained veterinarians can become U.S. government meat and poultry inspectors, disease-control workers, epidemiologists, research assistants, or commissioned officers in the U.S. Public Health Service, U.S. Army, or U.S. Air Force. A State license may be required.

Prospective veterinarians must have good manual dexterity. They should have an affinity for animals and the ability to get along with animal owners. Additionally, they should be able to quickly make decisions in emergencies.

Job Outlook

Employment of veterinarians is expected to grow faster than the average for all occupations through the year 2008. Job openings stemming from the need to replace veterinarians who retire or otherwise leave the labor force will be almost as numerous as new jobs resulting from employment growth over the 1998-2008 period.

Most veterinarians practice in animal hospitals or clinics and care primarily for companion animals. The number of pets is expected to increase more slowly during the projection period than in the previous decade and may moderate growth in the demand for veterinarians who specialize in small animals. One reason for this is that the large baby-boom generation is aging and will probably acquire fewer dogs and cats than earlier. However, as non-necessity income generally increases with age, those who own pets may be more inclined to seek veterinary services. In addition, pet owners are becoming more aware of the availability of advanced care and may increasingly take advantage of nontraditional veterinary services, such as preventive dental care, and may more willingly pay for intensive care than in the past. Finally, new technologies and medical advancements should permit veterinarians to offer better care to animals. Veterinarians who enter small animal practice will probably face competition. Large numbers of new graduates continue to be attracted to small animal medicine because they prefer to deal with pets and to live and work near highly populated areas. However, an oversupply does not necessarily limit the ability of veterinarians to find employment or to set up and maintain a practice in a particular area. Such an oversupply could result in veterinarians taking positions requiring much evening or weekend work to accommodate the extended hours of operation that many practices are offering. Others could take salaried positions in retail stores offering limited veterinary services. Most self-employed veterinarians will probably have to work hard and long to build a sufficient clientele.

The number of jobs for large animal veterinarians is expected to grow slowly, because productivity gains in the agricultural production industry mean demand for fewer veterinarians than before to treat food animals. Nevertheless, job prospects may be better for veterinarians who specialize in farm animals than for small animal practitioners, because most veterinary medical college graduates do not have the desire to work in rural or isolated areas.

Continued support for public health and food safety, disease control programs, and biomedical research on human health problems will contribute to the demand for veterinarians, although such positions are few in number. Also, anticipated budget tightening in the Federal government may lead to low funding levels for some programs, limiting job growth. Veterinarians with training in public health and epidemiology should have the best opportunities for a career in the Federal government.

Earnings

Median annual earnings of veterinarians were $50,950 in 1998. The middle 50 percent earned between $39,580 and $78,670. The lowest 10 percent earned less than $31,320, and the highest 10 percent earned more than $106,370.

Average starting salaries of 1998 veterinary medical college graduates varied by type of practice, as indicated by table 1.

TABLE 1

Average starting salaries of veterinary medical college graduates, 1998

Type of practice	
Large animal, exclusive	$37,200
Large animal, predominant	37,500
Mixed animal	35,900
Small animal, exclusive	37,600
Small animal, predominant	36,300
Equine	29,200

SOURCE: American Veterinary Medical Association

New veterinary medical college graduates who enter the Federal government usually start at $37,700. Beginning salaries were slightly higher in selected areas where the prevailing local pay level was higher. The average annual salary for veterinarians in the Federal government in nonsupervisory, supervisory, and managerial positions was $61,600 in 1999.

Related Occupations

Veterinarians prevent, diagnose, and treat diseases, disorders, and injuries in animals. Those who do similar work for humans include chiropractors, dentists, optometrists, physicians, and podiatrists. Veterinarians have extensive training in physical and life sciences, and some do scientific and medical research, closely paralleling occupations such as biological, medical, and animal scientists.

Animal trainers, animal breeders, and veterinary technicians work extensively with animals. Like veterinarians, they must have patience and feel comfortable with animals. However, the level of training required for these occupations is substantially less than that needed by veterinarians.

Sources of Additional Information

For more information on careers in veterinary medicine and a list of U.S. schools and colleges of veterinary medicine, send a letter-size, self-addressed, stamped envelope to:

- American Veterinary Medical Association, 1931 N. Meacham Rd., Suite 100, Schaumburg, IL 60173-4360.

For information on scholarships, grants, and loans, contact the financial aid officer at the veterinary schools to which you wish to apply.

For information on veterinary education, write to:

- Association of American Veterinary Medical Colleges, 1101 Vermont Ave. NW., Suite 710, Washington, DC 20005.

For information on the Federal agencies that employ veterinarians and a list of addresses for each agency, write to:

- National Association of Federal Veterinarians, 1101 Vermont Ave. NW., Suite 710, Washington, DC 20005.

Word Processors, Typists, and Data Entry Keyers

(O*NET 55307, 56017, and 56021)

Significant Points

- Workers can acquire their skills through high schools, community colleges, business schools, or self-teaching aids such as books or tapes.

- Overall employment is projected to decline due to the proliferation of personal computers and other technologies; however, the occupation's large size and high turnover should produce many job openings each year.

- Those with expertise in appropriate computer software applications should have the best job prospects.

Nature of the Work

Organizations need to process a rapidly growing amount of information. Word processors, typists, and data entry keyers help ensure this work is handled smoothly and efficiently. By typing texts, entering data into a computer, operating a variety of office machines, and performing other clerical duties, these workers help organizations keep up with the rapid changes of the "Information Age."

Word processors and typists usually set up and prepare reports, letters, mailing labels, and other text material. *Typists* make neat, typed copies of materials written by other clerical, professional, or managerial workers. They may begin as entry-level workers by typing headings on form letters, addressing envelopes, or preparing standard forms on typewriters or computers. As they gain experience, they are often assigned tasks requiring a higher degree of accuracy and independent judgment. Senior typists may work with highly technical material, plan and type complicated statistical tables, combine and rearrange materials from different sources, or prepare master copies.

Most keyboarding is now done on word processing equipment—usually a personal computer or part of a larger computer system—which normally includes a keyboard, video display terminal, and printer and may have "add-on" capabilities such as optical character recognition readers. *Word processors* use this equipment to record, edit, store, and revise letters, memos, reports, statistical tables, forms, and other printed materials. Although it is becoming less common, some word processing workers are employed in centralized word processing teams that handle the transcription and typing for several departments.

In addition to the duties mentioned above, word processors and typists often perform other office tasks, such as answering telephones, filing, and operating copiers or other office machines. Job titles of these workers often vary to reflect these duties. Clerk typists, for example, combine typing with filing, sorting mail, answering telephones, and other general office work. Note readers transcribe stenotyped notes of court proceedings into standard formats.

Data entry keyers usually input lists of items, numbers, or other data into computers or complete forms that appear on a computer screen. They may also manipulate existing data, edit current information, or proofread new entries to a database for accuracy. Some examples of data sources include customers' personal information, medical records, and membership lists. Usually this information is used internally by a company and may be reformatted before use by other departments or by customers.

Keyers use various types of equipment to enter data. Many keyers use a machine that converts the information they type to magnetic impulses on tapes or disks for entry into a computer system. Others prepare materials for printing or publication by using data entry composing machines. Some keyers operate on-line terminals or personal computers. Data entry keyers increasingly also work with non-keyboard forms of data entry such as scanners and electronically transmitted files. When using these new character recognition systems, data entry keyers often enter only those data which cannot be recognized by machines. In some offices, keyers also operate computer peripheral equipment such as printers and tape readers, act as tape librarians, and perform other clerical duties.

Working Conditions

Word processors, typists, and data entry keyers usually work a standard 40-hour week in clean offices. They sit for long periods and sometimes must contend with high noise levels caused by various office machines. These workers are susceptible to repetitive strain injuries, such as carpal tunnel syndrome and neck, back, and eye strain. To help prevent these from occurring, many offices have scheduled exercise breaks, ergonomically designed keyboards, and workstations that allow workers to stand or sit as they wish.

Employment

Word processors, typists, and data entry keyers held about 894,000 in 1998 and were employed in every sector of the economy. Some workers telecommute by working from their homes on personal computers linked by telephone lines to those in the main office. This enables them to type material at home while still being able to produce printed copy in their offices. About 3 out of 10 word processors, typists, and data entry keyers held jobs in firms providing business services, including temporary help, word processing, and computer and data processing. Nearly 2 out of 10 worked in Federal, State, and local government agencies.

Training, Other Qualifications, and Advancement

Employers generally hire high school graduates who meet their requirements for keyboarding speed. Increasingly, employers also expect applicants to have word processing or data entry training or experience. Spelling, punctuation, and grammar skills are important, as is familiarity with standard office equipment and procedures.

Students acquire skills in keyboarding and in the use of word processing, spreadsheet, and database management computer software packages through high schools, community colleges, business schools, temporary help agencies, or self-teaching aids such as books or tapes.

For many people, a job as a word processor, typist, or data entry keyer is their first job after graduating from high school or after a period of full-time family responsibilities. This work frequently serves as a stepping stone to higher paying jobs with increased responsibilities. Large companies and government agencies usually have training programs to help clerical employees upgrade their skills and advance to other positions. It is common for word processors, typists, and data entry keyers to transfer to other clerical jobs, such as secretary or statistical clerk, or to be promoted to a supervisory job in a word processing or data entry center.

Job Outlook

Despite the projected decline in employment of word processors and typists and relatively slow growth of data entry keyers, the need to replace those who transfer to other occupations or leave this large occupation for other reasons will produce numerous job openings each year. Job prospects will be most favorable for those with the best technical skills—in particular, expertise in appropriate computer software applications. Word processors, typists, and data entry keyers must be willing to continuously upgrade their skills with new technologies.

In spite of rapid increases in the volume of information and business transactions, overall employment of word processors, typists, and data entry keyers is projected to decline through 2008. Although word processors, typists, and data entry keyers are all affected by productivity gains stemming from organizational restructuring and the implementation of new technologies, projected growth differs among these workers. Employment of word processors and typists is expected to decline due to the proliferation of personal computers, which allow other workers to perform duties formerly assigned to word processors and typists. Most professionals and managers, for example, now use desktop personal computers to do their own word processing. Because technologies affecting data entry keyers tend to be costlier to implement, however, these workers will be less affected by technology and should experience slower-than-average growth.

Employment growth of data entry keyers still will be dampened by productivity gains, as various data capturing technologies, such as bar code scanners, voice recognition technologies and sophisticated character recognition readers, become more prevalent. These technologies can be applied to a variety of business transactions, such as inventory tracking, invoicing, and order placement. Moreover, as telecommunications technology improves, many organizations will increasingly take advantage of computer networks that allow data to be transmitted electronically, thereby avoiding the reentry of data. These technologies will allow more data to be entered automatically into computers, reducing the demand for data entry keyers.

In addition to technology, employment of word processors, typists, and data entry keyers will be adversely affected by domestic and international outsourcing. Many organizations have reduced or even eliminated permanent in-house staff, for example, in favor of temporary help and staffing services firms. Some large data entry and processing firms increasingly employ workers in nations with low wages to enter data. As international trade barriers continue to fall and telecommunications technology improves, this

transfer will mean reduced demand for data entry keyers in the United States.

Earnings

Median annual earnings of word processors and typists in 1998 were $22,590. The middle 50 percent earned between $18,490 and $27,320. The lowest 10 percent earned less than $14,480, while the highest 10 percent earned more than $32,550. The salaries of these workers vary by industry and by region. In 1997, median annual earnings in the industries employing the largest numbers of word processors and typists were:

Elementary and secondary schools	$23,200
State government, except education and hospitals	22,500
Local government, except education and hospitals	22,400
Offices and clinics of medical doctors	21,800
Personnel supply services	20,200

Median annual earnings of data entry keyers in 1998 were $19,190. The middle 50 percent earned between $15,810 and $22,910. The lowest 10 percent earned less than $13,660, and the highest 10 percent earned more than $27,840. In 1997, median annual earnings in the industries employing the largest numbers of data entry keyers were:

State government, except education and hospitals	$21,300
Accounting, auditing, and bookkeeping	19,600
Computer and data processing services	17,500
Commercial banks	17,400
Personnel supply services	16,900

In the Federal government, clerk-typists and data entry keyers without work experience started at about $16,400 a year in 1999. Beginning salaries were slightly higher in selected areas where the prevailing local pay level was higher. The average annual salary for all clerk-typists in the Federal government was about $22,900 in 1999.

Related Occupations

Word processors, typists, and data entry keyers must transcribe information quickly. Other workers who deliver information in a timely manner are stenographers, dispatchers, and telephone operators. Word processors, typists, and data entry keyers also must be comfortable working with office automation, and in this regard they are similar to court reporters, medical transcriptionists, secretaries, and computer and peripheral equipment operators.

Sources of Additional Information

For information about job opportunities for word processors, typists, and data entry keyers, contact the nearest office of the State employment service.

Writers and Editors, Including Technical Writers

(O*NET 34002B, 34002C, 34002D, 34002E, 34002F, 34002G, 34002J, 34002L, 34002M, and 34005)

Significant Points

- Most jobs require a college degree in the liberal arts—communications, journalism, and English are preferred—or a technical subject for technical writing positions.

- Competition is expected to be less for lower paying, entry-level jobs at small daily and weekly newspapers, trade publications, and radio and television broadcasting stations in small markets.

- Persons who fail to gain better paying jobs or earn enough as independent writers usually are able to transfer readily to communications-related jobs in other occupations.

Nature of the Work

Writers and editors communicate through the written word. *Writers* develop original fiction and nonfiction for books, magazines and trade journals, newspapers, technical reports, online distribution, company newsletters, radio and television broadcasts, movies, and advertisements. *Editors* select and prepare material for publication or broadcast and review and edit a writer's work.

Writers either select a topic or are assigned one by an editor. Then they gather information through personal observation, library and Internet research, and interviews. Writers select the material they want to use, organize it into a meaningful format, and use the written word to express ideas and convey information to readers. Often, writers revise or rewrite sections, searching for the best organization or the right phrasing.

Newswriters prepare news items for newspapers or news broadcasts, based on information supplied by reporters or wire services. Columnists analyze and interpret the news and write commentaries based on reliable sources, personal knowledge, and experience. Editorial writers express opinions in accordance with their publication's viewpoint to stimulate public debate on current affairs. Columnists and editorial writers are able to take sides on issues and express their opinions, while other newswriters must be objective and neutral in their coverage.

Technical writers put scientific and technical information into easily understandable language. They prepare operating and maintenance manuals, catalogs, parts lists, assembly instructions, sales promotion materials, and project proposals. They also plan and edit technical reports and oversee preparation of illustrations, photographs, diagrams, and charts.

Copywriters prepare advertising copy for use by publication or broadcast media, to promote the sale of goods and services.

Established writers may work on a freelance basis. They sell their work to publishers, publication enterprises, manufacturing firms, public relations departments, or advertising agencies. Sometimes, they contract with publishers to write a book or article or to complete specific assignments such as writing about a new product or technique.

Editors frequently write and almost always review, rewrite, and edit the work of writers. An editor's responsibilities vary depending on the employer and editorial position held. In the publishing industry, an editor's primary duties are to plan the contents of books, technical journals, trade magazines, and other general interest publications. Editors decide what material will appeal to readers, review and edit drafts of books and articles, offer comments to improve the work, and suggest possible titles. Additionally, they oversee the production of the publications.

Major newspapers and newsmagazines usually employ several types of editors. The *executive editor* oversees *assistant editors* who have responsibility for particular subjects, such as local news, international news, feature stories, or sports. Executive editors generally have the final say about what stories get published and how they should be covered. The *managing editor* usually is responsible for the daily operation of the news department. *Assignment editors* determine which reporters will cover a given story. *Copy editors* mostly review and edit a reporter's copy for accuracy, content, grammar, and style.

In smaller organizations, like small daily or weekly newspapers or membership newsletter departments, a single editor may do everything or share responsibility with only a few other people. Executive and managing editors typically hire writers, reporters, or other employees. They also plan budgets and negotiate contracts with freelance writers, sometimes called "stringers" in the news industry. In broadcasting companies, *program directors* have similar responsibilities.

Editors and program directors often have assistants. Many assistants, such as copy editors or *production assistants*, hold entry-level jobs. They review copy for errors in grammar, punctuation, and spelling, and check copy for readability, style, and agreement with editorial policy. They add and rearrange sentences to improve clarity or delete incorrect and unnecessary material. They also do research for writers and verify facts, dates, and statistics. Production assistants arrange page layouts of articles, photographs, and advertising; compose headlines; and prepare copy for printing. *Publication assistants* who work for publishing houses may read and evaluate manuscripts submitted by freelance writers, proofread printers' galleys, or answer letters about published material. Production assistants on small papers or in radio stations clip stories that come over the wire services' printers, answer phones, and make photocopies.

Most writers and editors use personal computers or word processors. Many use desktop or electronic publishing systems, scanners, and other electronic communications equipment.

Working Conditions

Some writers and editors work in comfortable, private offices; others work in noisy rooms filled with the sound of keyboards and computer printers as well as the voices of other writers tracking down information over the telephone. The search for information sometimes requires travel and visits to diverse workplaces, such as factories, offices, laboratories, the ballpark, or the theater, but many have to be content with telephone interviews and the library.

The workweek usually runs 35 to 40 hours. Those who prepare morning or weekend publications and broadcasts work some nights and weekends. Writers, especially newswriters, occasionally work overtime to meet deadlines or to cover late-developing stories. Deadlines and erratic work hours, often part of the daily routine for these jobs, may cause stress, fatigue, or burnout.

Employment

Writers and editors held about 341,000 jobs in 1998. Nearly one-third of salaried writers and editors works for newspapers, magazines, and book publishers. Substantial numbers, mostly technical writers, work for computer software firms. Other writers and editors work in educational facilities, in advertising agencies, in radio and television broadcasting, in public relations firms, and on journals and newsletters published by business and nonprofit organizations, such as professional associations, labor unions, and religious organizations. Some develop publications and technical materials for government agencies or write for motion picture companies.

Jobs with major book publishers, magazines, broadcasting companies, advertising agencies and public relations firms, and the Federal government are concentrated in New York, Chicago, Los Angeles, Boston, Philadelphia, San Francisco, and Washington, DC. Jobs with newspapers, business and professional journals, and technical and trade magazines are more widely dispersed throughout the country. Technical writers are employed throughout the country, but the largest concentrations are in the Northeast, Texas, and California.

Thousands of other individuals work as freelance writers, earning some income from their articles, books, and less commonly, television and movie scripts. Most support themselves with income derived from other sources.

Training, Other Qualifications, and Advancement

A college degree generally is required for a position as a writer or editor. Although some employers look for a broad liberal arts background, most prefer to hire people with degrees in communications, journalism, or English. For those who specialize in a particular area, such as science, fashion, or legal issues, additional background in the chosen field is helpful.

Technical writing requires a degree in, or some knowledge about, a specialized field—engineering, business, or one of the sciences, for example. In many cases, people with good writing skills can learn specialized knowledge on the job. Some transfer from jobs as technicians, scientists, or engineers. Others begin as research assistants or trainees in a technical information department, develop technical communication skills, and then assume writing duties.

Writers and editors must be able to express ideas clearly and logically and should love to write. Creativity, curiosity, a broad range of knowledge, self-motivation, and perseverance also are valuable.

Writers and editors must demonstrate good judgment and a strong sense of ethics in deciding what material to publish. Editors also need tact and the ability to guide and encourage others in their work.

For some jobs, the ability to concentrate amid confusion and to work under pressure is essential. Familiarity with electronic publishing, graphics, and video production equipment increasingly is needed. Online newspapers and magazines require knowledge of computer software used to combine online text with graphics, audio, video, and 3-D animation.

High school and college newspapers, literary magazines, community newspapers, and radio and television stations all provide valuable, but sometimes unpaid, practical writing experience. Many magazines, newspapers, and broadcast stations have internships for students. Interns write short pieces, conduct research and interviews, and learn about the publishing or broadcasting business.

In small firms, beginning writers and editors hired as assistants may actually begin writing or editing material right away. Opportunities for advancement can be limited, however. In larger businesses, jobs usually are more formally structured. Beginners generally do research, fact checking, or copy editing. They take on full-scale writing or editing duties less rapidly than do the employees of small companies. Advancement often is more predictable, though, coming with the assignment of more important articles.

Job Outlook

Employment of writers and editors is expected to increase faster than the average for all occupations through the year 2008. Employment of salaried writers and editors for newspapers, periodicals, book publishers, and nonprofit organizations is expected to increase as demand grows for their publications. Magazines and other periodicals increasingly are developing market niches, appealing to readers with special interests. Also, online publications and services are growing in number and sophistication, spurring the demand for writers and editors. Businesses and organizations are developing Internet websites, and more companies are experimenting with publishing materials directly for the Internet. Advertising and public relations agencies, which also are growing, should be another source of new jobs.

Demand for technical writers is expected to increase because of the continuing expansion of scientific and technical information and the need to communicate it to others. In addition to job openings created by employment growth, many openings will occur as experienced workers transfer to other occupations or leave the labor force. Turnover is relatively high in this occupation; many freelancers leave because they cannot earn enough money.

Despite projections of fast employment growth and high turnover, the outlook for most writing and editing jobs is expected to be competitive. Many people with writing or journalism training are attracted to the occupation. Opportunities should be best for technical writers because of the growth in the high technology and electronics industries and the resulting need for people to write users' guides, instruction manuals, and training materials. This work requires people who are not only technically skilled as writers but are able to keep pace with changing technology. Also, individuals with the technical skills for working on the Internet may have an advantage finding a job as a writer or editor.

Opportunities for newswriting and editing positions on small daily and weekly newspapers and in small radio and television stations, where the pay is low, should be better than those in larger media markets. Some small publications hire freelance copy editors as backup for staff editors or as additional help with special projects. Persons preparing to be writers and editors benefit from academic preparation in another discipline as well, either to qualify them as writers specializing in that discipline or as a career alternative if they are unable to get a job in writing.

Earnings

Median annual earnings for writers and editors, including technical writers, were $36,480 in 1998. The middle 50 percent earned between $27,030 and $49,380 a year. The lowest 10 percent earned less than $20,920, and the highest 10 percent earned over $76,660. Median annual earnings in the industries employing the largest numbers of writers and editors of nontechnical material in 1997 were as follows:

Advertising	$38,100
Periodicals	35,900
Books	35,200
Newspapers	28,500
Radio and television broadcasting	26,300

Median annual earnings of technical writers and editors in computer data and processing services were $39,200 in 1997.

Related Occupations

Writers and editors communicate ideas and information. Other communications occupations include news analysts, reporters, and correspondents; radio and television announcers; advertising and public relations workers; and teachers.

Sources of Additional Information

For information on careers in technical writing, contact:

- Society for Technical Communication, Inc., 901 N. Stuart St., Suite 904, Arlington, VA 22203. Internet: http://www.stc-va.org

For information on union wage rates for newspaper and magazine editors, contact:

- The Newspaper Guild, Research and Information Department, 501 Third Street NW., Suite 250, Washington, DC 20001.

SECTION TWO

THE QUICK JOB SEARCH

Advice on Planning Your Career and Getting a Good Job in Less Time

Features the Complete Text of a Results-Oriented Minibook

While *The Quick Job Search* is short, it covers **all** the major topics needed to explore career options and to conduct an effective job search. The techniques it presents have been proven to reduce the time it takes to find a job and are widely used by job search programs throughout North America.

Major topics include the following:

❖ **Skills identification.** Includes checklists and activities to help you identify your key skills–essential for career planning, interviewing, and writing resumes.

❖ **Career planning.** Provides activities to help define and research your ideal job.

❖ **Results-oriented job seeking skills.** Research-based advice on traditional and nontraditional job search methods, with an emphasis on the two most effective techniques: networking and cold contacts.

❖ **Interview skills, resumes, time management, and more.** Specific techniques on answering problem interview questions, writing a superior resume, setting a daily schedule, getting two interviews a day, and many other innovative and useful techniques.

❖ **Dealing with job loss.** Practical and upbeat advice on coping with the stress and discouragement of being unemployed.

❖ **Handling your finances while out of work.** Brief but helpful tips on conserving cash and stretching your resources.

Beginning on page 328, I've added sample resumes for some of America's top white-collar jobs. These resumes were written and designed by professional resume writers.

Introduction

I've spent much of the past 20 years of my professional life learning about career planning and job search methods. My original interest was in helping people find jobs in less time, and in helping them find better jobs. While there is a lot of complexity to these tasks, I have also found some elements of simplicity:

1. If you are going to work, you might as well define what it is you really want to do and are good at.
2. If you are looking for a job, you might as well use techniques that will reduce the time it takes to find one—and that help you get a better job than otherwise.

This section covers these topics, along with a few others. While I have written much more detailed works on career planning and job seeking, I present the basics of career planning and job seeking in this minibook. I think that there is enough information here to make a difference for most people, and I hope that it gives you some things to think about, as well as some techniques you have not considered.

About 10 years ago, I decided to write something very short that would cover the most important elements of effective career planning and job seeking. Writing short things is harder for me than writing longer things, since every word has to count. I began by asking myself, "If I only had 30 or so pages, what are the most important things to tell someone?"

The Quick Job Search was the result. While it is a section in this book, it has also been published, in an expanded form, as a book titled *How to Get a Job Now!* It has sold about 300,000 copies in its various forms. I hope you can make good use of this material.

Avoid the Temptation; Do the Activities

I already know that you will resist doing the activities included in *The Quick Job Search*. But trust me, doing them is worthwhile. Those who do them will have a better sense of what they are good at, what they want to do, and how to go about doing it. They are more likely to get more interviews and to present themselves better in those interviews. Is this worth giving up a night of TV? Yes, I think so.

Interestingly enough, you will—after reading *The Quick Job Search* and doing its activities—have spent more time on planning your career than most people. And you will know far more than the average job seeker about how to go about finding a job. While you may want to know more, I hope that this is enough to get you started.

> *While this minibook will teach you techniques to find a better job in less time, job seeking requires you to act, not just learn. So, in going through this minibook, consider what you can do to put the techniques to work for you. Do the activities. Create a daily plan. Get more interviews. Today, not tomorrow. You see, the sooner and harder you get to work on your job search, the shorter it is likely to be.*

Changing Jobs and Careers Is Often Healthy

Most of us were told from an early age that each career move must be up—involving more money, responsibility, and prestige. Yet research indicates people change careers for many other reasons as well.

In a survey conducted by the Gallup Organization for the National Occupational Information Coordinating Committee, 44 percent of the working adults surveyed expected to be in a different job within three years. This is a very high turnover rate.

Logical, ordered careers are found more often with increasing levels of education. For example, while 25 percent of high school dropouts took the only job available, this was true for only 8 percent of those with at least some college.

Many adult developmental psychologists believe occupational change is not only normal but may even be necessary for sound adult growth and development. It is common, even normal, to reconsider occupational roles during your twenties, thirties, and forties—even in the absence of economic pressure to do so.

One viewpoint is that a healthy occupational change allows some previously undeveloped aspect of yourself to emerge. The change may be as natural as from clerk to supervisor, or as drastic as from professional musician to airline pilot. Although risk is always a factor when change is involved, reasonable risks are healthy and can raise self-esteem.

But Not Just Any Job Should Do—Nor Any Job Search

Whether you are seeking similar work in another setting or changing careers, you need a workable plan to find the right job. This section will give you the information you need to help you find a good job quickly.

While the techniques are presented here briefly, they are based on my years of experience in helping people find good jobs (not just any job) and to find jobs in less time. The career decision-making section will help you consider several major issues. The job-seeking skills information has been proven to reduce the time required to find a good job.

Of course, more thorough books have been written on job-seeking techniques, and you may want to look into buying one or more of the better ones to obtain additional information. But, short as this section is, it *does* present the basic skills to find a good job in less time. The techniques work.

The Six Steps for a Quick and Successful Job Search

You can't just read about getting a job. The best way to get a job is to go out and get interviews! And the best way to get interviews is to make a job out of getting a job.

After many years of experience, I have identified just six basic things you need to do that make a big difference in your job search. Each will be covered in this minibook.

The Six Steps for a Quick Job Search

1. Know your skills.
2. Have a clear job objective.
3. Know where and how to look for job leads.
4. Spend at least 25 hours a week looking.
5. Get two interviews a day.
6. Follow up on all contacts.

Identify Your Key Skills

One survey of employers found that 90 percent of the people they interviewed did not present the skills they had to do the job they sought. They could not answer the basic question, "Why should I hire you?"

Knowing your skills is essential to doing well in an interview. This same knowledge is important in deciding what type of job you will enjoy and do well. For these reasons, I consider identifying your skills an essential part of a successful career plan or job search.

The Three Types of Skills

Most people think of "skills" as job-related skills such as using a computer. But we all have other types of skills that are important for success on a job—and that are very important to employers. The triangle below presents skills in three groups, and I think that this is a very useful way to consider skills for our purposes.

The Skills Triad

Let's review these three types of skills and identify those that are most important to you.

Self-Management Skills

Write down three things about yourself that you think make you a good worker.

Your "Good Worker" Traits

1. _____
2. _____
3. _____

The things you just wrote down are among the most important things for an employer to know about you! They have to do with your basic personality—your ability to adapt to a new environment. They are some of the most important things to emphasize in an interview, yet most job seekers don't realize their importance—and don't mention them.

Review the Self-Management Skills Checklist and put a check mark beside any skills you have. The Key Self-Management Skills are skills that employers find particularly important. If one or more of the Key Self-Management Skills apply to you, mentioning them in an interview can help you greatly.

Self-Management Skills Checklist

Key Self-Management Skills

____ accept supervision	____ hard worker
____ get along with coworkers	____ honest
____ get things done on time	____ productive
____ good attendance	____ punctual

Other Self-Management Skills

____ able to coordinate	____ friendly
____ ambitious	____ good-natured
____ assertive	____ helpful
____ capable	____ humble
____ cheerful	____ imaginative
____ competent	____ independent
____ complete assignments	____ industrious
____ conscientious	____ informal
____ creative	____ intelligent
____ dependable	____ intuitive
____ discreet	____ learn quickly
____ eager	____ loyal
____ efficient	____ mature
____ energetic	____ methodical
____ enthusiastic	____ modest
____ expressive	____ motivated
____ flexible	____ natural
____ formal	____ sense of humor

(continued)

(continued)

___ open-minded
___ optimistic
___ original
___ patient
___ persistent
___ physically strong
___ practice new skills
___ reliable
___ resourceful
___ responsible
___ self-confident

___ sincere
___ solve problems
___ spontaneous
___ steady
___ tactful
___ take pride in work
___ tenacious
___ thrifty
___ trustworthy
___ versatile
___ well-organized

Other Self-Management Skills You Have:

_____

_____

_____

After you are done with the list, circle the five skills you feel are most important and list them in the box that follows.

Note: Some people find it helpful to now complete the Essential Job Search Data Worksheet provided later in this section. It organizes skills and accomplishments from previous jobs and other life experiences.

Your Top Five Self-Management Skills ✓

1. _____

2. _____

3. _____

4. _____

5. _____

Transferable Skills

We all have skills that can transfer from one job or career to another. For example, the ability to organize events could be used in a variety of jobs and may be essential for success in certain occupations. Your mission should be to find a job that requires the skills you have and enjoy using.

In the following list, put a check mark beside the skills you have. You may have used them in a previous job or in some nonwork setting.

Transferable Skills Checklist ✓

Key Transferable Skills

___ instruct others
___ manage money, budget
___ manage people
___ meet deadlines
___ meet the public

___ negotiate
___ organize/manage projects
___ public speaking
___ written communication skills

Skills Working with Things

___ assemble things
___ build things
___ construct/repair things
___ drive, operate vehicles
___ good with hands
___ observe/inspect things

___ operate tools, machines
___ repair things
___ use complex equipment
___ use computers

Skills Working with Data

___ analyze data
___ audit records
___ budget
___ calculate/compute
___ check for accuracy
___ classify things
___ compare
___ compile
___ count
___ detail-oriented

___ evaluate
___ investigate
___ keep financial records
___ locate information
___ manage money
___ observe/inspect
___ record facts
___ research
___ synthesize
___ take inventory

Skills Working with People

___ administer
___ advise
___ care for
___ coach
___ confront others
___ counsel people
___ demonstrate
___ diplomatic
___ help others
___ instruct
___ interview people
___ kind
___ listen
___ negotiate

___ outgoing
___ patient
___ perceptive
___ persuade
___ pleasant
___ sensitive
___ sociable
___ supervise
___ tactful
___ tolerant
___ tough
___ trusting
___ understanding

Skills Working with Words, Ideas

___ articulate
___ communicate verbally
___ correspond with others
___ create new ideas
___ design
___ edit
___ ingenious

___ inventive
___ library research
___ logical
___ public speaking
___ remember information
___ write clearly

Leadership Skills

___ arrange social functions	___ mediate problems
___ competitive	___ motivate people
___ decisive	___ negotiate agreements
___ delegate	___ plan events
___ direct others	___ results-oriented
___ explain things to others	___ risk-taker
___ influence others	___ run meetings
___ initiate new tasks	___ self-confident
___ make decisions	___ self-motivate
___ manage or direct others	___ solve problems

Creative/Artistic Skills

___ artistic	___ expressive
___ dance, body movement	___ perform, act
___ drawing, art	___ present artistic ideas

Other Similar Skills You Have:

_____

_____

_____

_____

_____

_____

When you are finished, identify the five transferable skills you feel are most important for you to use in your next job and list them in the box below.

✓

Your Top Five Transferable Skills

1. _____

2. _____

3. _____

4. _____

5. _____

Job-Related Skills

Job content or job-related skills are those you need to do a particular job. A carpenter, for example, needs to know how to use various tools and be familiar with a variety of tasks related to that job.

You may already have a good idea of the type of job that you want. If so, it may be fairly simple for you to identify your job-related skills to emphasize in an interview. But I recommend that you complete at least two other things in this minibook first:

1. Complete the material that helps you define your job objective more clearly. Doing so will help you clarify just what sort of a job you want and allow you to better select those skills that best support it.

2. Complete the Essential Job Search Data Worksheet that appears later (pages 318–320). It will give you lots of specific skills and accomplishments to consider.

Once you have done these two things, come back and complete the box below. Include the job-related skills you have that you would most like to use in your next job.

✓

Your Top 5 Job-Related Skills

1. _____

2. _____

3. _____

4. _____

5. _____

Begin by Defining Your Ideal Job (You Can Compromise Later)

Too many people look for a job without having a good idea of exactly what they are looking for. Before you go out looking for "a" job, I suggest that you first define exactly what it is you really want—"the" job. Most people think a job objective is the same as a job title, but it isn't. You need to consider other elements of what makes a job satisfying for you. Then, later, you can decide what that job is called and what industry it might be in.

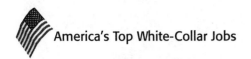
The Eight Factors to Consider in Defining the Ideal Job for You

Following are eight factors to consider when you define your ideal job. Once you know what you want, your task then becomes finding a job that is as close to your ideal job as you can find.

1. What skills do you want to use?

From the previous skills lists, select the top five skills that you enjoy using and most want to use in your next job.

1. _____

2. _____

3. _____

4. _____

5. _____

2. What type of special knowledge do you have?

Perhaps you know how to fix radios, keep accounting records, or cook food. Write down the things you know about from schooling, training, hobbies, family experiences, and other sources. One or more of them could make you a very special applicant in the right setting.

_____

_____

_____

_____

_____

3. With what types of people do you prefer to work?

Do you like to work with aggressive, hardworking folks, creative personalities, or some other types?

_____

_____

_____

_____

_____

4. What type of work environment do you prefer?

Do you want to work inside, outside, in a quiet place, a busy place, a clean place, or have a window with a nice view? List those things that are important to you.

_____

_____

_____

_____

_____

5. Where do you want your next job to be located— in what city or region?

Near a bus line? Close to a childcare center? If you are open to living and working anywhere, what would your ideal community be like?

_____

_____

_____

_____

_____

6. How much money do you hope to make in your next job?

Many people will take less money if the job is great in other ways—or if they quickly need a job to survive. Think about the minimum you would take as well as what you would eventually like to earn. Your next job will probably pay somewhere in between.

_____

_____

_____

_____

©2001 • JIST Works • Indianapolis, IN

7. How much responsibility are you willing to accept?

Usually, the more money you want to make, the more responsibility you must accept. Do you want to work by yourself, be part of a group, or be in charge? If so, at what level?

_____

_____

_____

_____

_____

_____

_____

8. What things are important or have meaning to you?

Do you have values that you would prefer to include as a basis of the work you do? For example, some people want to work to help others, clean up our environment, build things, make machines work, gain power or prestige, or care for animals or plants. Think about what is important to you and how you might include this in your next job.

_____

_____

_____

_____

_____

_____

Your Ideal Job

Use the points at left and on previous pages to help you define your ideal job. Think about each one and select the points that are most important to you. Don't worry about a job title yet; just focus on the most important things to include from the previous questions to define your ideal job.

My Ideal Job Objective:

_____

_____

_____

_____

_____

_____

_____

_____

_____

Setting a Specific Job Objective

Whether or not you have a good idea of the type of job you want, it is important to know more about various job options.

A very simple but effective way for exploring job alternatives is to go through the table of contents and check those about which you want to learn more. Then read the descriptions to learn more about the jobs that interest you.

If you need help figuring out what type of job to look for, remember that most areas have free or low-cost career counseling and testing services. Contact local government agencies and schools for referrals.

Job Search Methods That Help You Get a Better Job in Less Time

One survey found that 85 percent of all employers don't advertise at all. They hire people they already know, people who find out about the jobs through word of mouth, or people who simply happen to be in the right place at the right time. This is sometimes just luck, but this minibook will teach you ways to increase your "luck" in finding job openings.

Traditional Job Search Methods Are Not Very Effective

Most job seekers don't know how ineffective some traditional job hunting techniques tend to be.

How People Find Jobs

- Heard about opening from someone 35%
- Contacted employer directly 30%
- Answered want ad 14%
- Referred by private employment agency 6%
- Referred by state employment agency 5%
- Took civil service (government) tests 2%
- Other methods (referred by school, union referral, placed ads in journals, through the Internet, etc.) 8%

The chart above shows that fewer than 15 percent of all job seekers get jobs from reading the want ads. Let's take a quick look at want ads and other traditional job search methods.

Help wanted ads. As you should remember, only about 15 percent of all people get their jobs through the want ads. Everyone who reads the paper knows about these job openings, so competition for advertised jobs is fierce. The Internet also lists many job openings. But like want ads, these lists are viewed by many people. Still, some people do get jobs this way, so go ahead and apply. Just be sure to spend most of your time using more effective methods.

The state employment service. Each state has a network of local offices to administer unemployment compensation and provide job leads and other services. These services are provided without charge to you or employers. Names vary by state, so it may be called "Job

Service," "Department of Labor," "Unemployment Office," or another name.

Nationally, only about 5 percent of all job seekers get their jobs here, and these organizations typically know of only one-tenth (or fewer) of the actual job openings in a region. Still, it is worth a weekly visit. If you ask for the same counselor, you might impress the person enough to remember you and refer you for the better openings.

You should also realize that some of the state employment services provide substantial help in the form of job search workshops and other resources. Look into it; the price is right.

Private employment agencies. Studies have found that private agencies work reasonably well for those who use them. But there are cautions to consider. For one thing, these agencies work best for entry-level positions or for those with specialized skills that are in demand.

Private agencies also charge a fee either to you (as high as 20 percent of your annual salary!) or to the employer. Most of them call employers asking if they have any openings, something you could do yourself. Unless you have skills that are in high demand, you may do better on your own—and save money. At the least, you should rely on a private agency as only one of the techniques you use and not depend on them too heavily.

Temporary agencies. These can be a source of quick but temporary jobs to bring in some income as well as give you experience in a variety of settings—something that can help you land full-time jobs later. More and more employers are also using them as a way to evaluate workers for permanent jobs. So consider using these agencies if it makes sense to do so, but make certain that you continue an active search for a full-time job.

Sending out resumes. *One survey found that you would have to mail more than 500 unsolicited resumes to get one interview!* A much better approach is to contact the person who might hire you by phone to set up an interview directly; then send a resume. If you insist on sending out unsolicited resumes, do this on weekends—save your "prime time" for more effective job search techniques.

Filling out applications. Most applications are used to screen you out. Larger organizations may require them, but remember that your task is to get an interview, not fill out an application. If you do complete them, make them neat and error-free, and do not include anything that could get you screened out. If necessary, leave a problematic section blank. It can always be explained after you get an interview.

Personnel departments. Hardly anyone gets hired by interviewers in a personnel department. Their job is to screen you and refer the "best" applicants to the person who would actually supervise you. You may need to cooperate with them, but it is often better to go directly to the person who is most likely to supervise you—even if no job opening exists at the moment. And remember that most organizations don't even have a personnel office; only the larger ones do!

The Two Job Search Methods That Work Best

Two-thirds of all people get their jobs using informal methods. These jobs are often not advertised and are part of the "hidden" job market. How do *you* find them?

There are two basic informal job search methods: networking with people you know (which I call warm contacts), and making direct contacts with an employer (which I call cold contacts). They are both based on the most important job search rule of all.

The Most Important Job Search Rule:
Don't wait until the job is open
before contacting the employer!

Most jobs are filled by someone the employer meets before the job is formally "open." So the trick is to meet people who can hire you before a job is available! Instead of saying, "Do you have any jobs open?" say, "I realize you may not have any openings now, but I would still like to talk to you about the possibility of future openings."

Develop a Network of Contacts in Five Easy Steps

One study found that 40 percent of all people found their jobs through a lead provided by a friend, a relative, or an acquaintance. Developing new contacts is called "networking," and here's how it works:

1. **Make lists of people you know.** Develop a list of anyone with whom you are friendly; then make a separate list of all your relatives. These two lists alone often add up to 25–100 people or more. Next, think of other groups of people with whom you have something in common, such as former co-workers or classmates; members of your social or sports groups; members of your professional association; former employers; and members of your religious group. You may not know many of these people personally, but most will help you if you ask them.

2. **Contact them in a systematic way.** Each of these people is a contact for you. Obviously, some lists and some people on those lists will be more helpful than others, but almost any one of them could help you find a job lead.

3. **Present yourself well.** Begin with your friends and relatives. Call them and tell them you are looking for a job and need their help. Be as clear as possible about what you are looking for and what skills and qualifications you have. Look

at the sample JIST Card and phone script later in this minibook for presentation ideas.

4. **Ask them for leads.** It is possible that they will know of a job opening just right for you. If so, get the details and get right on it! More likely, however, they will not, so here are three questions you should ask.

The Three Magic Networking Questions

1. *Do you know of any openings for a person with my skills?* If the answer is no (which it usually is), then ask:

2. *Do you know of someone else who might know of such an opening?* If your contact does, get that name and ask for another one. If he or she doesn't, ask:

3. *Do you know of anyone who might know of someone else who might?* Another good way to ask this is, "Do you know someone who knows lots of people?" If all else fails, this will usually get you a name.

---

5. **Contact these referrals and ask them the same questions.** For each original contact, you can extend your network of acquaintances by hundreds of people. Eventually, one of these people will hire you or refer you to someone who will! This process is called networking, and it does work if you are persistent.

Contact Employers Directly

It takes more courage, but contacting an employer directly is a very effective job search technique. I call these cold contacts because you don't have an existing connection with these contacts. Following are two basic techniques for making cold contacts.

Use the Yellow Pages to Find Potential Employers

One effective cold contact technique uses the yellow pages. You can begin by looking at the index and asking for each entry, "Would an organization of this kind need a person with my skills?" If the answer is "yes," then that type of organization or business is a possible target. You can also rate "yes" entries based on your interest, giving an A to those that seem very interesting, a B to those you are not sure of, and a C to those that don't seem interesting at all.

Next, select a type of organization that got a "yes" response (such as "hotels") and turn to the section of the yellow pages where they are listed. Then call the organizations listed and ask to speak to the person who is most likely to hire or supervise you. A sample telephone script is included later in this section to give you ideas about what to say.

Drop In Without an Appointment

You can also simply walk in to many potential employers' organizations and ask to speak to the person in charge. This is particularly effective in small businesses, but it works surprisingly

well in larger ones too. Remember, you want an interview even if there are no openings now. If your timing is inconvenient, ask for a better time to come back for an interview.

Most Jobs Are with Small Employers

About 70 percent of all people now work in small businesses—those with 250 or fewer employees. While the largest corporations have reduced the number of employees, small businesses have been creating as many as 80 percent of the new jobs. There are many opportunities to obtain training and promotions in smaller organizations, too. Many do not even have a personnel department, so nontraditional job search techniques are particularly effective with them.

JIST Cards—an Effective "Mini Resume"

JIST Cards are a job search tool that gets results. Typed, printed, or even neatly written on a 3-by-5-inch card, a JIST Card contains the essential information most employers want to know. Look at the sample cards below.

JIST Cards are an effective job search tool! Give them to friends and to each of your network contacts. Attach one to your resume. Enclose one in your thank-you notes after an interview. Leave one with employers as a "business card." Use them in many creative ways. Even though they can be typed or even handwritten, it is best to have 100 or more printed so you can put lots of them in circulation. Thousands of job seekers have used them, and they get results!

Sandy Zaremba

Home: (219) 232-7608   **E-Mail:** szaremba@connect.com

Position: General Office/Clerical

Over two years of work experience, plus one year of training in office practices. Type 55 wpm, trained in word processing operations, post general ledger, handle payables, receivables, and most accounting tasks. Responsible for daily deposits averaging $5,000. Good interpersonal skills. Can meet strict deadlines and handle pressure well.

Willing to work any hours.

Organized, honest, reliable, and hardworking.

Chris Vorhees

Home: (602) 253-9678

Leave Message: (602) 257-6643

OBJECTIVE: Electronics—installation, maintenance, and sales

SKILLS: Four years of work experience, plus two years of ad-vanced training in electronics. A.S. degree in Electronics Engineering Technology. Managed a $300,000/yr. business while going to school full time, with grades in the top 25%. Familiar with all major electronic diagnostic and repair equipment. Hands-on experience with medical, consumer, communications, and industrial electronics equipment and applications. Good problem-solving and communication skills. Customer service oriented.

Willing to do what it takes to get the job done.

Use the Phone to Get Job Leads

Once you have created your JIST Card, it is easy to create a telephone contact "script" based on it. Adapt the basic script to call people you know or your yellow pages leads. Select yellow pages index categories that might use a person with your skills and get the numbers of specific organizations in that category. Then ask for the person who is most likely to supervise you and present your phone script.

While it doesn't work every time, most people, with practice, can get one or more interviews in an hour by making these "cold" calls. Here is a phone script based on a JIST Card:

"Hello, my name is Pam Nykanen. I am interested in a position in hotel management. I have four years' experience in sales, catering, and accounting with a 300-room hotel. I also have an associate degree in hotel management plus one year of experience with the Bradey Culinary Institute. During my employment, I helped double revenues from meetings and conferences and increased bar revenues by 46 percent. I have good problem-solving skills and am good with people. I am also well-organized, hardworking, and detail-oriented. When may I come in for an interview?"

While this example assumes you are calling someone you don't know, the script can be easily modified for presentation to warm contacts, including referrals. Using the script for making cold calls takes courage, but it does work for most people.

Make Your Job Search a Full-Time Job

On the average, job seekers spend fewer than 15 hours a week actually looking for work. The average length of unemployment is three or more months, with some people being out of work far longer (older workers and higher earners are two groups who take longer).

Based on many years of experience, I can say that the more time you spend on your job search each week, the less time you are likely to remain unemployed. Of course, using more effective job search methods also helps. Those who follow my advice have proven, over and over, that they get jobs in less than half the average time and they often get better jobs, too. Time management is the key.

Spend at Least 25 Hours a Week Looking for a Job

If you are unemployed and looking for a full-time job, you should look for a job on a full-time basis. It just makes sense to do so, although many do not because of discouragement, lack of good techniques, and lack of structure. Most job seekers have no idea what they are going to do next Thursday–they don't have a plan. The most important thing is to decide how many hours you can commit to your job search, and stay with it. You should spend a minimum of 25 hours a week on hard-core job search activities with no goofing around. Let me walk you through a simple but effective process to help you organize your job search schedule.

Write here how many hours you are willing to spend each week looking for a job: _____

Decide Which Days You Will Look for Work

Answering the questions below requires you to have a schedule and a plan, just as you had when you were working, right?

Which days of the week will you spend looking for a job?

_____

_____

How many hours will you look each day? _____

At what time will you begin and end your job search on each of these days? _____

Create a Specific Daily Schedule

Having a specific daily job search schedule is very important because most job seekers find it hard to stay productive each day. You already know which job search methods are most effective, and you should plan on spending most of your time using those methods. The sample daily schedule that follows has been very effective for people who have used it, and it will give you ideas for your own. Although you are welcome to create your own daily schedule, I urge you to consider one similar to this one. Why? Because it works.

A Daily Schedule That Works

7:00 - 8:00 a.m.	Get up, shower, dress, eat breakfast.
8:00 - 8:15 a.m.	Organize work space; review schedule for interviews or follow-ups; update schedule.
8:15 - 9:00 a.m.	Review old leads for follow-up; develop new leads (want ads, yellow pages, networking lists, etc.).
9:00 - 10:00 a.m.	Make phone calls, set up interviews.
10:00 - 10:15 a.m.	Take a break!
10:15 - 11:00 a.m.	Make more calls.
11:00 - 12:00 p.m.	Make follow-up calls as needed.
12:00 - 1:00 p.m.	Lunch break.
1:00 - 5:00 p.m.	Go on interviews; call cold contacts in the field; research for upcoming interviews at the library and on the Internet.

Do It Now: Get a Planner and Write Down Your Job Search Schedule

This is important: If you are not accustomed to using a daily schedule book or planner, promise yourself that you will get a good one tomorrow. Choose one that allows plenty of space for each day's plan on an hourly basis, plus room for daily "to do" listings. Write in your daily schedule in advance; then add interviews as they come. Get used to carrying it with you and use it!

Redefine What "Counts" As an Interview; Then Get Two a Day

The average job seeker gets about five interviews a month–fewer than two interviews a week. Yet many job seekers using the techniques I suggest routinely get two interviews a day. But to accomplish this, you must redefine what an interview is.

The New Definition of an Interview

An interview is any face-to-face contact with someone who has the authority to hire or supervise a person with your skills—even if the person doesn't have an opening at the time you interview.

With this definition, it is *much* easier to get interviews. You can now interview with all kinds of potential employers, not only those who have job openings. Many job seekers use the yellow pages to get two interviews with just one hour of calls by using the telephone contact script discussed earlier. Others simply drop in on potential employers and get an unscheduled interview. And getting names of others to contact from those you know–networking–is quite effective if you persist.

Getting two interviews a day equals 10 a week and 40 a month. That's 800 percent more interviews than the average job seeker gets. Who do you think will get a job offer quicker? So set out each day to get at least two interviews. It's quite possible to do, now that you know how.

How to Answer Tough Interview Questions

Interviews are where the job search action happens. You have to get them; then you have to do well in them. If you have done your homework, you are getting interviews for jobs that will maximize your skills. That is a good start, but your ability to communicate your skills in the interview makes an enormous difference. This is where, according to employer surveys, most job seekers have problems. They don't effectively communicate the skills they have to do the job, and they answer one or more problem questions poorly.

While thousands of problem interview questions are possible, I have listed just 10 that, if you can answer them well, will prepare you for most interviews.

The Top 10 Problem Questions

1. Why don't you tell me about yourself?

2. Why should I hire you?

3. What are your major strengths?

4. What are your major weaknesses?

5. What sort of pay do you expect to receive?

6. How does your previous experience relate to the jobs we have here?

7. What are your plans for the future?

8. What will your former employer (or references) say about you?

9. Why are you looking for this type of position, and why here?

10. Why don't you tell me about your personal situation?

I don't have the space here to give thorough answers to all of these questions. Instead, let me suggest several techniques that I have developed which you can use to answer almost any interview question.

A Traditional Interview Is Not a Friendly Exchange

Before I present the techniques for answering interview questions, it is important to understand what is going on. In a traditional interview situation, there is a job opening, and you are one of several (or one of a hundred) applicants. In this setting, the employer's task is to eliminate all but one applicant.

Assuming that you got as far as an interview, the interviewer's questions are designed to elicit information that can be used to screen you out. If you are wise, you know that your task is to avoid getting screened out. It's not an open and honest interaction, is it?

This illustrates yet another advantage of nontraditional job search techniques: the ability to talk to an employer before an opening exists. This eliminates the stress of a traditional interview. Employers are not trying to screen you out, and you are not trying to keep them from finding out stuff about you.

Having said that, knowing a technique for answering questions that might be asked in a traditional interview is good preparation for whatever you might run into during your job search.

The Three-Step Process for Answering Interview Questions

I know this might seem too simple, but the Three-Step Process is easy to remember. Its simplicity allows you to evaluate a question and create a good answer. The technique is based on sound principles and has worked for thousands of people, so consider trying it.

Step 1. Understand what is really being asked.

Most questions are really designed to find out about your self-management skills and personality. While they are rarely this blunt, the employer's *real* question is often:

✓ Can I depend on you?

✓ Are you easy to get along with?

✓ Are you a good worker?

✓ Do you have the experience and training to do the job if we hire you?

✓ Are you likely to stay on the job for a reasonable period of time and be productive?

Ultimately, if the employer is not convinced that you will stay and be a good worker, it won't matter if you have the best credentials–he or she won't hire you.

Step 2. Answer the question briefly.

Acknowledge the facts, but...

✓ Present them as an advantage, not a disadvantage.

There are lots of examples in which a specific interview question will encourage you to provide negative information. The classic is the "What are your major weaknesses?" question that I included in my top 10 problem questions list. Obviously, this is a trick question, and many people are just not prepared for it. A good response might be to mention something that is not all that damaging, such as "I have been told that I am a perfectionist, sometimes not delegating as effectively as I might." But your answer is not complete until you continue.

Step 3. Answer the real concern by presenting your related skills.

✓ Base your answer on the key skills that you have identified and that are needed in this job.

✓ Give examples to support your skills statements.

For example, an employer might say to a recent graduate, "We were looking for someone with more experience in this field. Why should we consider you?" Here is one possible answer: "I'm sure there are people who have more experience, but I *do* have more than six years of work experience including three years of advanced training and hands-on experience using the latest methods and techniques. Because my training is recent, I am open to new ideas and am used to working hard and learning quickly."

In the example I presented in Step 2 (about your need to delegate), a good skills statement might be, "I have been working on this problem and have learned to be more willing to let my staff do things, making sure that they have good training and supervision. I've found that their performance improves, and it frees me up to do other things."

Whatever your situation, learn to use it to your advantage. It is essential to communicate your skills during an interview, and the Three-Step Process gives you a technique that can dramatically improve your responses. It works!

Interview Dress and Grooming Rule

If you make a negative first impression, you won't get a second chance to make a good one. So do everything possible to make a good impression.

▼

A Good Rule for Dressing for an Interview
Dress as you think
the boss will dress—*only neater.*

Dress for success! If necessary, get help selecting an interview outfit from someone who dresses well. Pay close attention to your grooming too. Written things like correspondence and resumes must be neat and errorless because they create an impression as well.

Follow Up on All Contacts

People who follow up with potential employers and with others in their network get jobs faster than those who do not.

▼

Four Rules for Effective Follow-Up

1. Send a thank-you note to every person who helps you in your job search.

2. Send the thank-you note within 24 hours after you speak with the person.

3. Enclose JIST Cards with thank-you notes and all other correspondence.

4. Develop a system to keep following up with "good" contacts.

Thank-You Notes Make a Difference

Thank-you notes can be handwritten or typed on quality paper and matching envelopes. Keep them simple, neat, and errorless. Following is a sample:

April 16, 20XX

2234 Riverwood Ave.
Philadelphia, PA 17963

Ms. Sandra Kijek
Henderson & Associates, Inc.
1801 Washington Blvd., Suite 1201
Philadelphia, PA 17963

Dear Ms. Kijek:

Thank you for sharing your time with me so generously today. I really appreciated seeing your state-of-the-art computer equipment.

Your advice has already proved helpful. I have an appointment to meet with Mr. Robert Hopper on Friday as you anticipated.

Please consider referring me to others if you think of someone else who might need a person with my skills.

Sincerely,

William Richardson

William Richardson

Use Job Lead Cards to Organize Your Contacts

Use a simple 3-by-5-inch card to keep essential information on each person in your network. Buy a 3-by-5-inch card file box and tabs for each day of the month. File the cards under the date you want to contact the person, and the rest is easy. I've found that staying in touch with a good contact every other week can pay off big. Here's a sample card to give you ideas to create your own:

ORGANIZATION: _Mutual Health Insurance_

CONTACT PERSON: _Anna Tomey_   PHONE: _317-355-0216_

SOURCE OF LEAD: _Aunt Ruth_

NOTES: _4/10 Called. Anna on vacation. Call back 4/15. 4/15 Interview set 4/20 at 1:30. 4/20 Anna showed me around. They use the same computers we used in school! (Friendly people) Sent thank-you note and JIST Card, call back 5/1. 5/1 Second interview 5/8 at 9 a.m.!_

Resumes: Write a Simple One Now and a "Better" One Later

You have already learned that sending out resumes and waiting for responses is not an effective job-seeking technique. However, many employers *will* ask you for them, and they are a useful tool in your job search. If you feel that you need a resume, I suggest that you begin with a simple one that you can complete quickly. I've seen too many people spend weeks working on their resume while they could have been out getting interviews instead. If you want a "better" resume, you can work on it on weekends and evenings. So let's begin with the basics.

Basic Tips to Create a Superior Resume

The following tips make sense for any resume format.

Write it yourself. It's okay to look at other resumes for ideas, but write yours yourself. It will force you to organize your thoughts and background.

Make it errorless. One spelling or grammar error will create a negative impressionist (see what I mean?). Get someone else to review your final draft for any errors. Then review it again because these rascals have a way of slipping in.

Make it look good. Poor copy quality, cheap paper, bad type quality, or anything else that creates a poor physical appearance will turn off employers to even the best resume content. Get professional help with design and printing if necessary. Many resume writers and print shops have desktop publishing services and can do it all for you.

Be brief, be relevant. Many good resumes fit on one page and few justify more than two. Include only the most important points. Use short sentences and action words. If it doesn't relate to and support the job objective, cut it!

Be honest. Don't overstate your qualifications. If you end up getting a job you can't handle, it will not be to your advantage. Most employers will see right through it and not hire you.

Be positive. Emphasize your accomplishments and results. This is no place to be too humble or to display your faults.

Be specific. Instead of saying "I am good with people," say "I supervised four people in the warehouse and increased productivity by 30 percent." Use numbers whenever possible, such as the number of people served, percent of sales increase, or dollars saved.

You should also know that everyone feels he or she is a resume expert. Whatever you do, someone will tell you it is wrong. For this reason, it is important to understand that a resume is a job search tool. You should never delay or slow down your job search because your resume is not "good enough." The best approach is to create a simple and acceptable resume as soon as possible, then use it. As time permits, create a better one if you feel you must.

Chronological Resumes

Most resumes use the chronological format. It is a simple format where the most recent experience is listed first, followed by each previous job. This arrangement works fine for someone with work experience in several similar jobs, but not as well for those with limited experience or for career changers.

Look at the two Judith Jones resumes. Both use the chronological approach, but notice that the second one includes some improvements over her first. The improved resume is clearly better, but either would be acceptable to most employers.

Tips for Writing a Simple Chronological Resume

Here are some tips for writing a basic chronological resume.

Name. Use your formal name rather than a nickname if the formal name sounds more professional.

Address. Be complete. Include your zip code and avoid abbreviations. If moving is a possibility, use the address of a friend or relative or be certain to include a forwarding address.

Telephone number. Employers are most likely to try to reach you by phone, so having a reliable way to be reached is very important. Always include your area code because you never know where your resume might travel. If you don't have an answering machine, get one and make sure you leave it on whenever you are not home. Listen to your message to be sure it presents you in a professional way. Also available are a variety of communication systems: voice

Sample of a simple chronological resume.

Judith J. Jones

115 South Hawthorne Avenue
Chicago, Illinois 46204
(312) 653-9217 (home)
(312) 272-7608 (message)
E-Mail: jjones@pc.net

JOB OBJECTIVE

Desire a position in the office management or administrative assistant area. Prefer a position requiring responsibility and a variety of tasks.

EDUCATION AND TRAINING

Acme Business College, Chicago, Illinois
Graduate of a one-year business program, 2000

John Adams High School, South Bend, Indiana
Diploma: Business Education

Other: Continuing education classes and workshops in business communication, scheduling systems, and customer relations.

EXPERIENCE

1999-2000 — Returned to school to complete and update my business skills. Learned word processing and new office techniques.

1996-1999 — Claims Processor, Blue Spear Insurance Co., Chicago, Illinois. Handled customer medical claims, filed, miscellaneous clerical duties.

1994-1996 — Sales Clerk, Judy's Boutique, Chicago, Illinois. Responsible for counter sales, display design, and selected tasks.

1992-1994 — Specialist, U.S. Army. Assigned to various stations as a specialist in finance operations. Promoted prior to honorable discharge.

Previous Jobs — Held part-time and summer jobs throughout high school.

PERSONAL

I am reliable, hard working, and good with people.

finish a formal degree or program, list what you did complete. Include any special accomplishments.

Previous experience. The standard approach is to list employer, job title, dates employed, and responsibilities. But there are better ways of presenting your experience. Look over the improved chronological resume for ideas. The improved version emphasizes results, accomplishments, and performance.

Personal data. Neither of the sample resumes has the standard height, weight, or marital status information included on so many resumes. That information is simply not relevant! If you do include some personal data, put it at the bottom and keep it related to the job you want.

References. There is no need to list references. If employers want them, they will ask. If your references are particularly good, it's okay to say so.

Tips for an Improved Chronological Resume

Once you have a simple, errorless, and eye-pleasing resume, get on with your job search. There is no reason to delay! But you may want to create a better one in your spare time (evenings or weekends). If you do, here are some additional tips.

Job objective. Job objectives often limit the types of jobs for which you will be considered. Instead, think of the type of work you want to do and can do well and describe it in more general terms. Instead of writing "Restaurant Manager," write "Managing a small to mid-sized business" if that is what you are qualified to do.

mail, professional answering services, beepers, cell phones, e-mail, etc. If you do provide an alternative phone number or another way to reach you, just make it clear to the caller what to expect.

Job objective. This is optional for a very basic resume but is still important to include. Notice that Judy is keeping her options open with her objective. Writing "Secretary" or "Clerical" might limit her to lower-paying jobs or even prevent her from being considered for jobs she might take.

Education and training. Include any formal training you've had, plus any training that supports the job you seek. If you did not

Education and training. New graduates should emphasize their recent training and education more than those with five years or so of recent and related work experience. Think about any special accomplishments from school and include these if they relate to the job. Did you work full time while in school? Did you do particularly well in work-related classes, get an award, or participate in sports?

Skills and accomplishments. Employers are interested in what you accomplished and did well. Include those things that relate to doing well in the job you seek now. Even "small" things

Sample of an improved chronological resume.

Judith J. Jones

115 South Hawthorne Avenue
Chicago, Illinois 46204
(312) 653-9217 (home)
(312) 272-7608 (message)
E-Mail: jjones@pc.net

JOB OBJECTIVE

Seeking position requiring excellent management and administrative assistant skills in an office environment. Position should require a variety of tasks including typing, word processing, accounting/bookkeeping functions, and customer contact.

EDUCATION AND TRAINING

Acme Business College, Chicago, Illinois.
Completed one-year program in Business and Office Management. Grades in top 30 percent of my class. Courses: word processing, accounting theory and systems, time management, basic supervision, and others.

John Adams High School, South Bend, Indiana.
Graduated with emphasis on business courses.

Other: Continuing education at my own expense (business communications, customer relations, computer applications, other courses).

EXPERIENCE

1999-2000 — Returned to business school to update skills. Advanced course work in accounting and office management. Learned word processing and accounting and spreadsheet software. Gained operating knowledge of computers.

1996-1999 — Claims Processor, Blue Spear Insurance Company, Chicago, Illinois. Handled 50 complex medical insurance claims per day—18 percent above department average. Received two merit raises for performance.

1994-1996 — Assistant Manager, Judy's Boutique, Chicago, Illinois. Managed sales, financial records, inventory, purchasing, correspondence, and related tasks during owner's absence. Supervised four employees. Sales increased 15 percent during my tenure.

1992-1994 — Finance Specialist (E4), U.S. Army. Responsible for the systematic processing of 500 invoices per day from commercial vendors. Trained and supervised eight employees. Devised internal system allowing 15 percent increase in invoices processed with a decrease in personnel.

1988-1992 — Various part-time and summer jobs through high school. Learned to deal with customers, meet deadlines, work hard, and other skills.

SPECIAL SKILLS AND ABILITIES

Type 80 words per minute and can operate most office equipment. Good communication and math skills. Accept supervision, able to supervise others. Excellent attendance record.

Promotions. If you were promoted or got good evaluations, say so. A promotion to a more responsible job can be handled as a separate job if this makes sense.

Problem areas. Employers look for any sign of instability or lack of reliability. It is very expensive to hire and train someone who won't stay or who won't work out. Gaps in employment, jobs held for short periods of time, or a lack of direction in the jobs you've held are all things that employers are concerned about. If you have any legitimate explanation, use it. For example:

"1998–Continued my education at..."

"1999–Traveled extensively throughout the United States."

"1998 to present–Self-employed barn painter and widget maker."

"1997–Had first child, took year off before returning to work."

Use entire years or even seasons of years to avoid displaying a shorter gap you can't explain easily: "Spring 1998–Fall 1999" will not show you as unemployed from October to November, 1998, for example.

Remember that a resume can get you screened out, but it is up to you to get the interview and the job. So, cut out *anything* that is negative in your resume!

count. Maybe your attendance was perfect, you met a tight deadline, did the work of others during vacations, etc. Be specific and include numbers–even if you have to estimate them.

Job titles. Many job titles don't accurately reflect the job you did. For example, your job title may have been "Cashier" but you also opened the store, trained new staff, and covered for the boss on vacations. Perhaps "Head Cashier and Assistant Manager" would be more accurate. Check with your previous employer if you are not sure.

Sample of a simple skills resume.

ALAN ATWOOD
3231 East Harbor Road
Woodland Hills, California 91367
Home: (818) 447-2111   Message: (818) 547-8201

Objective: A responsible position in retail sales

Areas of Accomplishment:

Customer Service
- Communicate well with all age groups.
- Able to interpret customer concerns to help them find the items they want.
- Received 6 Employee of the Month awards in 3 years.

Merchandise Display
- Developed display skills via in-house training and experience.
- Received Outstanding Trainee Award for Christmas toy display.
- Dress mannequins, arrange table displays, and organize sale merchandise.

Stock Control and Marketing
- Maintained and marked stock during department manager's 6-week illness.
- Developed more efficient record-keeping procedures.

Additional Skills
- Operate cash register, IBM-compatible hardware, and calculators.
- Punctual, honest, reliable, and a hard-working self-starter.

Experience:
Harper's Department Store
Woodland Hills, California
1999 to Present

Education:
Central High School
Woodland Hills, California
3.6/4.0 Grade Point Average
Honor Graduate in Distributive Education

Two years of retail sales training in Distributive Education. Also courses in Business Writing, Accounting, and Word Processing.

Skills and Combination Resumes

The functional or "skills" resume emphasizes your most important *skills*, supported by specific examples of how you have used them. This approach allows you to use any part of your life history to support your ability to do the job you seek.

While the skills resume can be very effective, it does require more work to create. And some employers don't like them because they can hide a job seeker's faults (such as job gaps, lack of formal education, or no related work experience) better than a chronological resume.

Still, a skills resume may make sense for you. Look over the sample resumes for ideas. Notice that one resume includes elements of a skills *and* a chronological resume. This is called a "combination" resume—an approach that makes sense if your previous job history or education and training are positive.

> *Sample skills resume for someone with substantial experience—but using only one page. Note that no dates are included.*

Ann McLaughlin

Career Objective
Challenging position in programming or related areas that would best utilize expertise in the business environment. This position should have many opportunities for an aggressive, dedicated individual with leadership abilities to advance.

Programming Skills
Functional program design relating to business issues including payroll, inventory and database management, sales, marketing, accounting, and loan amortization reports. In conjunction with design would be coding, implementation, debugging, and file maintenance. Familiar with distributed network systems including PCs and Macs.

Areas of Expertise
Interpersonal communication strengths, public relations capabilities, plus innovative problem-solving and analytical talents.

Sales
A total of nine years of experience in sales and sales management. Sold security products to distributors and burglar alarm dealers. Increased company's sales from $16,000 to over $70,000 per month. Creatively organized sales programs and marketing concepts. Trained sales personnel in prospecting techniques while also training service personnel in proper installation of burglar alarms. Result: 90 percent of all new business was generated through referrals from existing customers.

Management
Managed burglar alarm company for four years while increasing profits yearly. Supervised office, sales, and installation personnel. Supervised and delegated work to assistants in accounting functions and inventory control. Worked as assistant credit manager, responsible for over $2 million per month in sales. Handled semiannual inventory of five branch stores totaling millions of dollars and supervised 120 people.

Accounting
Balanced all books and prepared tax forms for burglar alarm company. Eight years of experience in credit and collections, with emphasis on collections. Collection rates were over 98% each year; was able to collect a bad debt in excess of $250,000 deemed "uncollectible" by company.

Education
School of Computer Technology, Pittsburgh, PA
Business Applications Programming/TECH EXEC- 3.97 GPA

Robert Morris College, Pittsburgh, PA
Associate degree in Accounting, Minor in Management

2306 Cincinnati Street, Kingsford, PA 15171
(412) 437-6217
Cell Phone: (412) 464-1273
E-Mail: amclaughlin@enet.com

Sample combination resume emphasizing skills and accomplishments within jobs. Note that each position within a company is listed.

THOMAS P. MARRIN
80 Harrison Avenue
Baldwin L.I., New York 11563
Answering Service: (716) 223-4705
E-Mail: tmarrin@connect.com

OBJECTIVE:

A middle/upper-level management position with responsibilities including problem solving, planning, organizing, and budget management.

EDUCATION:

University of Notre Dame, B.S. in Business Administration. Course emphasis on accounting, supervision, and marketing. Upper 25% of class. Additional training: Advanced training in time management, organizational behavior, and cost control.

MILITARY:

U.S. Army — 2nd Infantry Division, 1990 to 1994, 1st Lieutenant and platoon leader — stationed in Korea and Ft. Knox, Kentucky. Supervised an annual budget of nearly $4 million and equipment valued at over $40 million. Responsible for training, scheduling, and activities of as many as 40 people. Received several commendations. Honorable discharge.

BUSINESS EXPERIENCE:

Wills Express Transit Co., Inc., Mineola, New York

Promoted to Vice President, Corporate Equipment — 1999 to Present
Controlled purchase, maintenance, and disposal of 1100 trailers and 65 company cars with $6.7 million operating and $8.0 million capital expense responsibilities.

- Scheduled trailer purchases, six divisions.
- Operated 2.3% under planned maintenance budget in company's second best profit year while operating revenues declined 2.5%.
- Originated schedule to correlate drivers' needs with available trailers.
- Developed systematic Purchase and Disposal Plan for company car fleet.
- Restructured Company Car Policy, saving 15% on per car cost.

Promoted to Asst. Vice President, Corporate Operations — 1998 to 1999
Coordinated activities of six sections of Corporate Operations with an operating budget over $10 million.

- Directed implementation of zero-base budgeting.
- Developed and prepared Executive Officer Analyses detailing achievable cost-reduction measures. Resulted in cost reduction of over $600,000 in first two years.
- Designed policy and procedure for special equipment leasing program during peak seasons. Cut capital purchases by over $1 million.

Manager of Communications — 1996 to 1998
Directed and managed $1.4 million communication network involving 650 phones, 150 WATS lines, 3 switchboards, 5 employees.

- Installed computerized WATS Control System. Optimized utilization of WATS lines and pinpointed personal abuse. Achieved payback earlier than originally projected.
- Devised procedures that allowed simultaneous 20% increase in WATS calls and a $75,000/year savings.

Hayfield Publishing Company, Hempstead, New York

Communications Administrator — 1994 to 1996

Managed daily operations of a large Communications Center. Reduced costs and improved services.

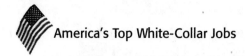

The Quick Job Search Review

There are a few thoughts I want to emphasize in closing my brief review of job-seeking skills:

1. Approach your job search as if it were a job itself.

2. Get organized and spend at least 25 hours per week actively looking.

3. Follow up on all the leads you generate and send out lots of thank-you notes and JIST Cards.

4. If you want to get a good job quickly, you must get lots of interviews!

5. Pay attention to all the details; then be yourself in the interview. Remember that employers are people, too. They will hire someone who they feel will do the job well, be reliable, and fit easily into the work environment.

6. When you want the job, tell the employer that you want the job and why. You need to have a good answer to the question "Why should I hire you?" It's that simple.

Essential Job Search Data Worksheet

Completing this worksheet will help you create your resume, fill out applications, and answer interview questions. Take it with you as a reference as you look for a job. Use an erasable pen or pencil so you can make changes. In all sections, emphasize skills and accomplishments that best support your ability to do the job you want. Use extra sheets as needed.

Key Accomplishments

List three accomplishments that best prove your ability to do well in the kind of job you want.

1. _____

   _____

2. _____

   _____

3. _____

   _____

Education/Training

Name of high school(s); years attended: _____

_____

_____

_____

Subjects related to job objective: _____

_____

_____

_____

Extracurricular activities/Hobbies/Leisure activities:

_____

_____

_____

_____

Accomplishments/Things you did well: _____

_____

_____

_____

Schools you attended after high school; years attended; degrees/certificates earned: _____

_____

_____

_____

_____

Courses related to job objective: _____

_____

_____

_____

Extracurricular activities/Hobbies/Leisure activities:

_____

_____

_____

_____

Accomplishments/Things you did well: _____

_____

_____

_____

_____

Military training, on-the-job, or informal training, such as from a hobby; dates of training; type of certificate earned: _____

_____

_____

_____

_____

Specific things you can do as a result: _____

_____

_____

_____

Work and Volunteer History

List your most recent job first, followed by each previous job. Include military experience and unpaid work here too, if it makes sense to do so. Use additional sheets to cover *all* your significant jobs or unpaid experiences.

Whenever possible, provide numbers to support what you did: number of people served over one or more years, number of transactions processed, percentage of sales increased, total inventory value you were responsible for, payroll of the staff you supervised, total budget you were responsible for, etc. As much as possible, mention results using numbers because they can be impressive in an interview or on a resume.

Job #1 _____

Name of organization: _____

_____

_____

Address: _____

_____

_____

Phone number: _____

_____

Dates employed: _____

Job title(s): _____

_____

_____

Supervisor's name: _____

_____

Details of any raises or promotions: _____

_____

_____

_____

Machinery or equipment you handled: _____

_____

_____

_____

Special skills this job required: _____

_____

_____

_____

_____

List what you accomplished or did well: _____

_____

_____

_____

Job #2 _____

Name of organization: _____

_____

_____

Address: _____

_____

_____

Phone number: _____

_____

Dates employed: _____

Job title(s): _____

_____

_____

Supervisor's name: _____

_____

Details of any raises or promotions: _____

_____

_____

_____

Machinery or equipment you handled: _____

_____

_____

_____

Special skills this job required: _____

_____

_____

_____

List what you accomplished or did well: _____

_____

_____

_____

Job #3 _____

Name of organization: _____

_____

_____

Address: _____

_____

_____

Phone number: _____

_____

Dates employed: _____

Job title(s): _____

_____

_____

Supervisor's name: _____

_____

Details of any raises or promotions: _____

_____

_____

_____

Machinery or equipment you handled: _____

_____

_____

_____

Special skills this job required: _____

_____

_____

_____

List what you accomplished or did well: _____

_____

_____

_____

References

Contact your references and let them know what type of job you want and why you are qualified. Be sure to review what they will say about you. Because some employers will not give out references by phone or in person, have previous employers write a letter of reference for you in advance. If you worry about a bad reference from a previous employer, negotiate what the employer will say about you or get written references from other people you worked with there. When creating your list of references, be sure to include your reference's name and job title, where he or she works, a business address and phone number, and how that person knows you.

The following material is based on content from a book titled Job Strategies for Professionals *written by a team of authors from the U.S. Employment Service.*

Some Tips for Coping with Job Loss

Being out of work is not fun for most people and is devastating to some. It may help you to know that you are not alone in this experience, and I've included some information here on what to expect and some suggestions for getting through it.

Some Problems You May Experience

Here are some feelings and experiences that you may have after losing your job.

✓ **Loss of professional identity.** Most of us identify strongly with our careers, and unemployment can often lead to a loss of self-esteem. Being employed garners respect in the community and in the family. When a job is lost, part of your sense of self may be lost as well.

✓ **Loss of a network.** The loss may be worse when your social life has been strongly linked to the job. Many ongoing "work friendships" are suddenly halted. Old friends and colleagues often don't call because they feel awkward or don't know what to say. Many don't want to be reminded of what could happen to them.

✓ **Emotional unpreparedness.** If you have never before been unemployed, you may not be emotionally prepared for it and devastated when it happens. It is natural and appropriate to feel this way. You might notice that some people you know don't take their job loss as hard as you have taken it. Studies show that those who change jobs frequently, or who are in occupations prone to cyclic unemployment, suffer far less emotional impact after job loss than those who have been steadily employed and who are unprepared for cutbacks.

Adjusting

You can often adjust to job loss by understanding its psychology. There have been a lot of studies done on how to deal with loss. Psychologists have found that people often have an easier time dealing with loss if they know what feelings they might experience during the "grieving process." Grief doesn't usually overwhelm us all at once; it usually is experienced in stages. The stages of loss or grief may include the following:

Shock—you may not be fully aware of what has happened.

Denial—usually comes next; you cannot believe that the loss is true.

Relief—you may feel a burden has lifted and opportunity awaits.

Anger—often follows; you blame (often without cause) those you think might be responsible, including yourself.

Depression—may set in some time later, when you realize the reality of the loss.

Acceptance—the final stage of the process; you come to terms with the loss and get the energy and desire to move beyond

it. The "acceptance" stage is the best place to be when starting a job search, but you might not have the luxury of waiting until this point to begin your search.

Knowing that a normal person will experience some predictable "grieving" reactions can help you deal with your loss in a constructive way. The faster you can begin an active search for a new job, the better off you will be.

Keeping Healthy

Unemployment is a stressful time for most people, and it is important to keep healthy and fit. Try to do the following:

✓ **Eat properly.** How you look and your sense of self-esteem can be affected by your eating habits. It is very easy to snack on junk food when you're home all day. Take time to plan your meals and snacks so they are well-balanced and nutritious. Eating properly will help you maintain the good attitude you need during your job search.

✓ **Exercise.** Include some form of exercise as part of your daily activities. Regular exercise reduces stress and depression and can help you get through those tough days.

✓ **Allow time for fun.** When you're planning your time, be sure to build fun and relaxation into your plans. You are allowed to enjoy life even if you are unemployed. Keep a list of activities or tasks that you want to accomplish such as volunteer work, repairs around the house, or hobbies. When free time occurs, you can refer to the list and have lots of things to do.

Family Issues

Unemployment is a stressful time for the entire family. For them, your unemployment means the loss of income and the fear of an uncertain future, and they are also worried about your happiness. Here are some ways you can interact with your family to get through this tough time.

✓ **Do not attempt to "shoulder" your problems alone.** Be open with family members even though it may be hard. Discussions about your job search and the feelings you have allow your family to work as a group and support one another.

✓ **Talk to your family.** Let them know your plans and activities. Share with them how you will be spending your time.

✓ **Listen to your family.** Find out their concerns and suggestions. Maybe there are ways they can assist you.

✓ **Build family spirit.** You will need a great deal of support from your family in the months ahead, but they will also need yours.

✓ **Seek outside help.** Join a family support group. Many community centers, mental health agencies, and colleges have support groups for the unemployed and their families. These groups can provide a place to let off steam and share frustrations. They can also be a place to get ideas on how to survive this difficult period.

Helping Children

If you have children, realize that they can be deeply affected by a parent's unemployment. It is important for them to know what has happened and how it will affect the family. However, try not to overburden them with the responsibility of too many emotional or financial details.

✓ **Keep an open dialogue with your children.** Letting them know what is really going on is vital. Children have a way of imagining the worst, so the facts can actually be far less devastating than what they envision.

✓ **Make sure your children know it's not anyone's fault.** Children may not understand about job loss and may think that *you* did something wrong to cause it. Or they may feel that somehow *they* are responsible or financially burdensome. They need reassurance in these matters, regardless of their age.

✓ **Children need to feel they are helping.** They want to help, and having them do something like taking a cut in allowance, deferring expensive purchases, or getting an after-school job can make them feel as if they are part of the team.

Some experts suggest that it can be useful to alert school counselors to your unemployment so that they can watch the children for problems at school before they become serious.

Coping with Stress

Here are some coping mechanisms that can help you deal with the stress of being unemployed.

✓ **Write down what seems to be causing the stress.** Identify the "stressors"; then think of possible ways to handle each one. Can some demands be altered, lessened, or postponed? Can you live with any of them just as they are? Are there some that you might be able to deal with more effectively?

✓ **Set priorities.** Deal with the most pressing needs or changes first. You cannot handle everything at once.

✓ **Establish a workable schedule.** When you set a schedule for yourself, make sure it is one that can be achieved. As you perform your tasks, you will feel a sense of control and accomplishment.

✓ **Reduce stress.** Learn relaxation techniques or other stress-reduction techniques. This can be as simple as sitting in a chair, closing your eyes, taking a deep breath and breathing out slowly while imagining all the tension going out with your breath. There are a number of other methods, including listening to relaxation tapes, that may help you cope with stress more effectively.

✓ **Avoid isolation.** Keep in touch with your friends, even former coworkers, if you can do that comfortably. Unemployed people often feel a sense of isolation and loneliness. See your friends, talk with them, socialize with them. You are the same person you were before unemployment. The same goes for the activities that you have enjoyed in the past. Evaluate them. Which can you afford to continue? If you find that your old hobbies or activities can't be part of your new budget, maybe you can substitute new activities that are less costly.

✓ **Join a support group.** No matter how understanding or caring your family or friends might be, they may not be able to understand all that you're going through, and you might be able to find help and understanding at a job-seeking support group.

These groups consist of people who are going through the same experiences and emotions as you. Many groups also share tips on job opportunities, as well as feedback on ways to deal more effectively in the job search process. *The National Business Employment Weekly,* available at major newsstands, lists support groups throughout the country. Local churches, YMCAs, YWCAs, and libraries often list or facilitate support groups.

Forty Plus is a national nonprofit organization and an excellent source of information about clubs around the country and on issues concerning older employees and the job search process. The address is 15 Park Row, New York, NY 10038. The telephone number is (212) 233-6086.

Keeping Your Spirits Up

Here are some ways you can build your self-esteem and avoid depression.

✓ **List your positives.** Make a list of your positive qualities and your successes. This list is always easier to make when you are feeling good about yourself. Perhaps you can enlist the assistance of a close friend or caring relative, or wait for a sunnier moment.

✓ **Replay your positives.** Once you have made this list, replay the positives in your mind frequently. Associate the replay with an activity you do often; for example, you might review the list in your mind every time you go to the refrigerator!

✓ **Use the list before performing difficult tasks.** Review the list when you are feeling down or to give you energy before you attempt some difficult task.

✓ **Recall successes.** Take time every day to recall a success.

✓ **Use realistic standards.** Avoid the trap of evaluating yourself using impossible standards that come from others. You are in a particular phase of your life; don't dwell on what you think society regards as success. Remind yourself that success will again be yours.

✓ **Know your strengths and weaknesses.** What things do you do well? What skills do you have? Do you need to learn new skills? Everyone has limitations. What are yours? Are there certain job duties that are just not right for you and that you might want to avoid? Balance your limitations against your strong skills so that you don't let the negatives eat at your self-esteem. Incorporate this knowledge into your planning.

✓ **Picture success.** Practice visualizing positive results or outcomes and view them in your mind before the event. Play out the scene in your imagination and picture yourself as successful in whatever you're about to attempt.

✓ **Build success.** Make a "to do" list. Include small, achievable tasks. Divide the tasks on your list and make a list for every day so you will have some "successes" daily.

✓ **Surround yourself with positive people.** Socialize with family and friends who are supportive. You want to be around people who will "pick you up," not "knock you down." You know who your fans are. Try to find time to be around them. It can really make you feel good.

✓ **Volunteer.** Give something of yourself to others through volunteer work. Volunteering will help you feel more worthwhile and may actually give you new skills.

Overcoming Depression

Are you depressed? As hard as it is to be out of work, it also can be a new beginning. A new direction may emerge that will change your life in positive ways. This may be a good time to reevaluate your attitudes and outlook.

✓ **Live in the present.** The past is over and you cannot change it. Learn from your mistakes and use that knowledge to plan for the future; then let the past go. Don't dwell on it or relive it over and over. Don't be overpowered by guilt.

✓ **Take responsibility for yourself.** Try not to complain or blame others. Save your energy for activities that result in positive experiences.

✓ **Learn to accept what you cannot change.** However, realize that in most situations, you do have some control. Your reactions and your behavior are in your control and will often influence the outcome of events.

✓ **Keep the job search under your own command.** This will give you a sense of control and prevent you from giving up and waiting for something to happen. Enlist everyone's aid in your job search, but make sure you do most of the work.

✓ **Talk things out with people you trust.** Admit how you feel. For example, if you realize you're angry, find a positive way to vent it, perhaps through exercise.

✓ **Face your fears.** Try to pinpoint them. "Naming the enemy" is the best strategy for relieving the vague feeling of anxiety. By facing what you actually fear, you can see if your fears are realistic or not.

✓ **Think creatively.** Stay flexible, take risks, and don't be afraid of failure. Try not to take rejection personally. Think of it as information that will help you later in your search. Take criticism as a way to learn more about yourself. Keep plugging away at the job search despite those inevitable setbacks. Most importantly, forget magic. What lies ahead is hard work!

Sources of Professional Help

If your depression won't go away or leads you to self-destructive behaviors such as abuse of alcohol or drugs, you may consider asking a professional for help. Many people who have never sought professional assistance before find that in a time of crisis, it really helps to have someone listen and give needed aid. Consult your local mental health clinics, social services agencies, religious organizations, or professional counselors for help for yourself and family members who are affected by your unemployment. Your health insurance may cover some assistance, or, if you do not have insurance, counseling is often available on a "sliding scale" fee, based on income.

Managing Your Finances While Out of Work

As you already know, being unemployed has financial consequences. While the best solution to this is to get a good job in as short a time as possible, you do need to manage your money differently during the time between jobs. Following are some things to think about.

Apply for Benefits Without Delay

Don't be embarrassed to apply for unemployment benefits as soon as possible, even if you're not sure you are eligible. This program is to help you make a transition between jobs, and you helped pay for it by your previous employment. Depending on how long you have worked, you can collect benefits for up to 26 weeks and sometimes even longer. Contact your state labor department or employment security agency for further information. Their addresses and telephone numbers are listed in your phone book.

Prepare Now to Stretch Your Money

Being out of work means lower income and the need to control your expenses. Don't avoid doing this, because the more you plan, the better you can control your finances.

Examine Your Income and Expenses

Create a budget and look for ways to cut expenses. The Monthly Income and Expense Worksheet can help you isolate income and expense categories, but your own budget may be considerably more detailed. I've included two columns for each expense category. Enter in the "Normal" column what you have been spending in that category during the time you were employed. Enter in the "Could Reduce To" column a lower number that you will spend by cutting expenses in that category.

Tips on Conserving Your Cash

While you are unemployed, it is likely that your expenses will exceed your income, and it is essential that you be aggressive in managing your money. Your objective here is very clear: you want to conserve as much cash as possible early on so you can have some for essentials later. Here are some suggestions.

✓ **Begin cutting all nonessential expenses right away.** Don't put this off! There is no way to know how long you will be out of work, and the faster you deal with the financial issues, the better.

✓ **Discuss the situation with other family members.** Ask them to get involved by helping you identify expenses they can cut.

✓ **Look for sources of additional income.** Can you paint houses on weekends? Pick up a temporary job or consulting assignment? Deliver newspapers in the early morning? Can a family member get a job to help out? Any new income will help, and the sooner the better.

✓ **Contact your creditors.** Even if you can make full payments for a while, work out interest-only or reduced-amount payments as soon as possible. When I was unemployed, I went to my creditors right away and asked them to help. They were very cooperative, and most are if you are reasonable with them.

✓ **Register with your local consumer credit counseling organization.** Many areas have free consumer credit counseling organizations that can help you get a handle on your finances and encourage your creditors to cooperate.

✓ **Review your assets.** Make a list of all your assets and their current value. Money in checking, savings, and other accounts is the most available, but you may have additional assets in pension programs, life insurance, and stocks that could be converted to cash if needed. You may also have an extra car that could be sold, equity in your home that could be borrowed against, and other assets that could be sold or used if needed.

✓ **Reduce credit card purchases.** Try to pay for things in cash to save on interest charges and prevent overspending. Be disciplined; you can always use your credit cards later if you are getting desperate for food and other basics.

✓ **Consider cashing in some "luxury" assets.** For example, sell a car or boat you rarely use to generate cash and to save on insurance and maintenance costs.

✓ **Comparison shop** for home/auto/life insurance and other expenses to lower costs.

✓ **Deduct job hunting expenses from your taxes.** Some job hunting expenses may be tax deductible as a "miscellaneous deduction" on your federal income tax return. Keep receipts for employment agency fees, resume expenses, and transportation expenses. If you find work in another city and you must relocate, some moving expenses are tax deductible. Contact an accountant or the IRS for more information.

Monthly Income and Expense Worksheet

Income

Unemployment benefits	_____	Interest/Dividends	_____
Spouse's income	_____	Other income	_____
Severance pay	_____	**TOTALS**	_____

Expenses

	NORMAL	COULD REDUCE TO		NORMAL	COULD REDUCE TO
Mortgage/rent:	____	____	**Health insurance:**	____	____
maintenance/repairs	____	____	medical expenses	____	____
Utilities:			dental expenses	____	____
electric	____	____	**Tuition:**	____	____
gas/oil heat	____	____	other school costs	____	____
water/sewer	____	____	**Clothing:**	____	____
telephone	____	____	**Entertainment:**	____	____
Food:	____	____	**Taxes:**	____	____
restaurants	____	____	**Job-hunting costs:**	____	____
Car payment:	____	____	**Other expenses:**	____	____
fuel	____	____		____	____
maintenance/repairs	____	____		____	____
insurance	____	____		____	____
Other loan payments:				____	____
____	____	____		____	____
____	____	____		____	____
____	____	____	**TOTALS**	____	____

Review Your Health Coverage

You know that it is dangerous to go without health insurance, but here are some tips.

✓ **You can probably maintain coverage at your own expense.** Under the COBRA law, if you worked for an employer that provided medical coverage and had 20 or more employees, you may continue your health coverage. However, you must tell your former employer within 60 days of leaving the job.

✓ **Contact professional organizations to which you belong.** They may provide group coverage for their members at low rates.

✓ **Speak to an insurance broker.** If necessary, arrange for health coverage on your own or join a local health maintenance organization (HMO).

✓ **Practice preventive medicine.** The best way to save money on medical bills is to stay healthy. Try not to ignore minor ills. If they persist, phone or visit your doctor.

✓ **Investigate local clinics.** Many local clinics provide services based on a sliding scale. These clinics often provide quality health care at affordable prices. In an emergency, most hospitals will provide you with services on a sliding scale, and most areas usually have one or more hospitals funded locally to provide services to those who can't afford them.

Using the Internet for Career Planning and Job Seeking

This brief review assumes you know how to use the Internet, so I won't get into how it works here. If the Internet and World Wide Web are new to you, I recommend a book titled *Cyberspace Job Search Kit* by Mary Nemnich and Fred Jandt. This book covers the basics about how the Internet works, how to get connected, plus a great deal of information on using it for career planning and job seeking.

Some Cautionary Comments

Let me begin by saying that the Internet has its problems as a tool for collecting information or for getting job leads. While the Internet has worked for many in finding job leads, far more users have been disappointed in the results they obtained. The problem is that many users assume that they can simply put their resume in resume databases and that employers will line up to hire them. It sometimes happens, but not often. That is the very same negative experience of people sending out lots of unsolicited resumes to personnel offices, a hopeful approach that has been around since long before computers.

There are two points that I made earlier about job-seeking methods which also apply to using the Internet:

1. It is unwise to rely on just one or two job search methods in conducting your job search.
2. It is essential that you conduct an active rather than a passive approach in your job search.

Just as with sending out lots of unsolicited resumes, simply listing your resume on the Internet is a passive approach that is unlikely to work well for you. Use the Internet in your job search, but plan to use other techniques, including direct contacts with employers.

A Success Story

Now that I have cautioned you regarding its limitations, you should know that the Internet does work very well for some people. To illustrate this, let me share with you a real situation I recently uncovered.

I was doing a series of interviews on jobs for a TV station in a rural area and asked the staff how they got their jobs there. They were all young, and the news anchor had told me that she had only been on the job a few months. It turned out that many of the previous employees had left the station about six months earlier to go to larger markets. That left a remaining recent graduate and new hire in charge but with few staff—and something of an emergency. He had obtained his job by responding to a job posting on a Web site used by broadcasters, so he went ahead and listed on that site all the jobs that were open at his station.

In a few days, new broadcasting graduates from all over the country saw the Internet postings and responded. E-mail went back and forth, and the relatively few willing to come to the station at their expense were invited to interview. Within a few weeks, most of the open positions were filled by young people who had responded on the Internet.

The crises for the TV station ended, and many of those hired told me that they were getting a great opportunity that they did not expect to obtain in any other way. I have to agree. More traditional recruiting methods would have created long delays for the employer and the job seekers. Traditional recruiting would also probably have screened out those with less experience and credentials. These job seekers got these jobs because of their using the Internet. While there were surely people with better credentials, they did not know about or get these jobs.

But note that the ones who got the jobs were those willing to take the chance and travel to the employer at their own expense. They had to be active and take some chances. And they had to be able to make a quick decision to move—something that a young person can more easily do. And they did not simply post their resumes in a resume database somewhere. The winning applicants were proactive in using the Internet to make direct contact with this employer, and then they followed up agressively.

Specific Tips to Increase Your Internet Effectiveness

Here are some things you can do to increase the effectiveness of using the Internet in your job search.

1. **Be as specific as possible in the job you seek.** This is important in using any job search method and even more so in using the Internet. I say this because the Internet is so enor-

mous in its reach that looking for a nonspecific job is simply not an appropriate task. So do your career planning homework and be specific in what you are looking for.

2. **Keep your expectations reasonable.** The people who have the most success on the Internet are those who best understand its limitations. For example, those with technical skills that are in short supply—such as network engineers—will have more employers looking for these skills and more success on the Internet. Keep in mind that many of the advertised jobs are already filled by the time you see them and that thousands of people may apply to those that sound particularly attractive. People do get job leads on the Internet, but be reasonable in your expectations and use a variety of job search methods in addition to the Internet.

3. **Consider your willingness to move.** If you don't want to move, or are willing only to move to certain locations, you should restrict your job search to geographic areas that meet your criteria. Many of the Internet databases allow you to view only those jobs that meet your criteria.

4. **Create a resume that is appropriate for use on the Internet.** With some exceptions, most of the resumes submitted on the Internet end up as simple text files with no graphic elements. Employers can then search a database of resumes for key words or use other searchable criteria. This is why your Internet resume should include a list of key words likely to be used by an employer as search criteria.

5. **Get your resume into the major resume databases used by employers.** Many of the major resume databases allow job seekers to list their resumes for free. Employers are typically charged for advertising their openings or sorting the database for candidates that meet their criteria. Most of these sites are easy to understand and use, and they often provide all sorts of useful information for job seekers.

6. **Seek out relevant sites.** Simply getting your resume listed on several Internet sites is often not enough. Many employers do not use these sites, or they use one but not another. Remember the example that I used earlier—those people found out about TV-related jobs from an Internet site that was run by a trade publication for broadcasters. Many professional associations post job openings on their sites or list other sites that would be of interest to that profession. Check out the resources that are available to people in the industries or occupations that interest you, since many of these resources also have Internet sites.

7. **Find specific employer sites.** Some employers have their own Internet sites that list job openings, allow you to apply online, and even provide access to staff who can answer your questions. While this is mostly used by larger technology-oriented companies, many smaller employers and government agencies have set up their own sites to attract candidates.

8. **Use informal chat rooms or request help.** Many Internet sites have interactive chat rooms or allow you to post a message for others to respond to. If you are not familiar with a chat room, it is a way for you to type responses to what someone else types as you are both online. Many sites also have a place for you to leave a message for others to respond to by sending you e-mail messages. Both of these methods allow you to meet potential employers or others in your field who can provide you with the advice or leads you seek.

9. **Use the listings of large Internet browsers or service providers.** While there are thousands of career-related Internet sites, some are better than others. Many sites provide links to other sites they recommend. Large service providers such as America Online (www.aol.com) and the Microsoft Network (www.msn.com) provide career-related information and job listings on their sites as well as links to other sites. Most of the larger portals provide links to recommended career-related sites and can be quite useful. Some of the larger such sites include Alta Vista (www.altavista.com), Lycos (www.lycos.com), and Yahoo (www.yahoo.com).

10. **Don't get ripped off.** Since the Internet has few regulations, many crooks use it as a way to take money from trusting souls. Remember that anyone can set up a site, even if the person does not provide a legitimate service, so be careful before you pay money for anything on the Internet. A general rule is that if it sounds too good to be true, it probably is. For example, if a site "guarantees" that it will find you a job or charges high fees, I recommend you look elsewhere.

Some Useful Internet Sites

There are hundreds and even thousands of Internet sites that provide information on careers or education, list job openings, or provide other career-related information.

Here are a few sites to get you started:

✓ The Riley Guide at www.rileyguide.com

✓ America's Job Bank at www.ajb.dni.us

✓ CareerPath.com at www.careerpath.com

✓ Monster.com at www.monster.com

✓ JIST at www.jist.com

In Closing

Few people will get a job offer because someone knocks on their door and offers one. The craft of job seeking does involve some luck, but you are far more likely to get lucky if you are out getting interviews. Structure your job search as if it were a full-time job and try not to get discouraged. There are lots of jobs out there, and someone needs what you can do—your job is to find that someone.

I hope this section helps, though you should consider learning more. Career planning and job seeking skills are, I believe, adult survival skills for our new economy. Good luck!

Mike Farr

Sample Resumes for Some of America's Top White-Collar Jobs

I've written many career and job search books, and several resume books are among them. If you've read the preceding *Quick Job Search* content, you know that I believe resumes are an overrated job search tool. Even so, you will probably need one, and you should have a good one.

Unlike some career authors, I do not preach that there is one right way to do a resume. I encourage you to be an individual and to do what you think will work well for you.

But I also know that some resumes are clearly better than others. To help you see examples of particularly good resumes, my editor has selected some from my book *The Quick Resume & Cover Letter Book.*

These resumes present real (but fictionalized) people and have these points in common:

- Each is for an occupation described in this book, although the job title may be a bit different. The resumes are organized alphabetically by occupation.

- Each was written by a professional resume writer who is a member of one or more professional associations, including the Professional Association of Résumé Writers or the National Résumé Writers' Association.

- Each is particularly good in some way. These resumes were selected from among many submitted for my books.

Notes on the resumes point out their features. Beneath each resume is the name of the professional resume writer who wrote it. Many of these folks provide help (for a fee) and welcome your contacting them (though this is not a personal endorsement). Their contact information appears at the end of this section.

I thank the professional resume writers whose resumes are included here. Their efforts bring a richness and diversity of style and design that can't be matched in any other way.

Here are the Web site addresses of the two professional associations. These sites list all association members along with contact information.

- Professional Association of Résumé Writers: www.parw.com

- National Résumé Writers' Association: www.nrwa.com

Advertising, Marketing, and Public Relations Managers

Writer's comments: Sasha chose a jungle-theme paper to apply for a marketing position with a zoo. Her old resume, intended for seeking education jobs, was completely revised to emphasize marketing abilities.

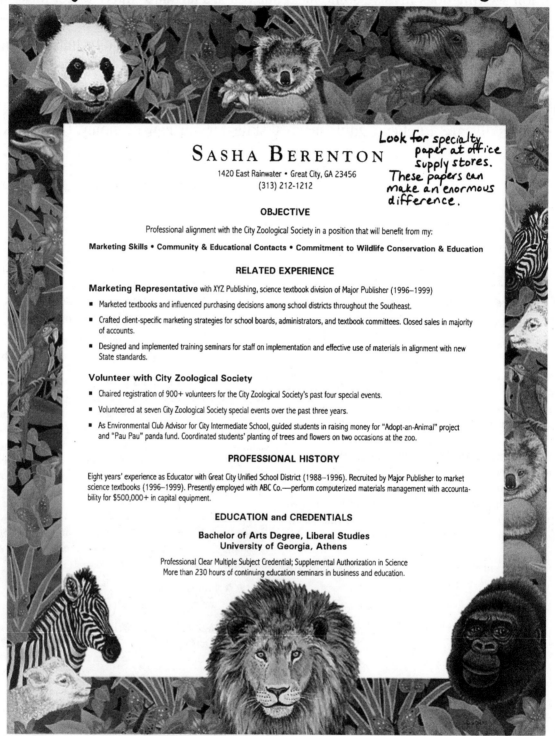

Look for specialty paper at office supply stores. These papers can make an enormous difference.

SASHA BERENTON

1420 East Rainwater • Great City, GA 23456
(313) 212-1212

OBJECTIVE

Professional alignment with the City Zoological Society in a position that will benefit from my:

Marketing Skills • Community & Educational Contacts • Commitment to Wildlife Conservation & Education

RELATED EXPERIENCE

Marketing Representative with XYZ Publishing, science textbook division of Major Publisher (1996–1999)

- Marketed textbooks and influenced purchasing decisions among school districts throughout the Southeast.

- Crafted client-specific marketing strategies for school boards, administrators, and textbook committees. Closed sales in majority of accounts.

- Designed and implemented training seminars for staff on implementation and effective use of materials in alignment with new State standards.

Volunteer with City Zoological Society

- Chaired registration of 900+ volunteers for the City Zoological Society's past four special events.

- Volunteered at seven City Zoological Society special events over the past three years.

- As Environmental Club Advisor for City Intermediate School, guided students in raising money for "Adopt-an-Animal" project and "Pau Pau" panda fund. Coordinated students' planting of trees and flowers on two occasions at the zoo.

PROFESSIONAL HISTORY

Eight years' experience as Educator with Great City Unified School District (1988–1996). Recruited by Major Publisher to market science textbooks (1996–1999). Presently employed with ABC Co.—perform computerized materials management with accountability for $500,000+ in capital equipment.

EDUCATION and CREDENTIALS

Bachelor of Arts Degree, Liberal Studies
University of Georgia, Athens

Professional Clear Multiple Subject Credential; Supplemental Authorization in Science
More than 230 hours of continuing education seminars in business and education.

Submitted by Susan Britton Whitcomb
Résumé Magic

Bookkeeping, Accounting, and Auditing Clerks

Jane Doe

80 Smith Road   (555) 555-5555   Teeney Town, Minnesota 55555

Writer's comments: This resume helped Jane get her "dream job" after being downsized.

Bookkeeper • Administrative Assistant • Secretary

Meticulous, accurate and detail-oriented professional with exceptional customer service skills ... Dependable and responsible ... Handle confidential information with discretion ... Function independently with efficiency ... Interact and contribute effectively in team setting ... Cultural and diversity sensitivity – grew up in bi-cultural family.

Presents key transferable and adaptive skills here

Skills and Experience

- typing 70 WPM, 3% error rate
- 10-key at 6,866 KPH, 6% error rate
- appointments and scheduling
- customer service
- payroll
- inventory and purchasing
- insurance claims
- work orders
- word processing
- filing, faxing, phones and mail

- accounts payable/receivable
- deposits and banking
- bank reconciliations
- accounts coding
- check writing
- financial statements
- billing and invoicing
- MN fuel tax refunds
- account collection calls
- petty cash and wire transfers

- IBM System 36
- IBM PC
- Windows 95 / 98, DOS
- Lotus 1-2-3
- Red Wing Systems
- Platinum Software
- WordPerfect
- Internet and Explorer
- Apple IIe
- AppleWorks

A spare, efficient presentation of her skills

Work History

Icey Systems, Inc., Teeney Town MN **Bookkeeper**	19XX to present
Albert's Ford, Teeney Town MN **Bookkeeper**	19XX to 19XX
Foodkeeper, Teeney Town MN **Secretary / Bookkeeper**	19XX to 19XX
Council for Minnesota, Teeney Town MN **Secretary for Farmstead Project**	19XX
Somat Lines, Teeney Town MN **Bookkeeper**	19XX to 19XX

A simple chronological list of jobs is all that is needed to present a good work history

Education

Riverland Technical and Community College, Albert Lea MN
Graduate – Secretarial Program

Continuing Education: Management Skills for Secretaries ... Phone Management Skills ... Computerized Payroll Training ... Tax Compliance

A nice touch that reinforces her work ethic

"Demand the best from yourself, because others will demand the best of you. Successful people don't simply give a project hard work. They give it their best work."

—Win Borden (as quoted in Commitment to Excellence)

Submitted by Beverley Drake

Computer Programmers

Writer's comments: This client was finishing computer programming school and had no work experience in the field. After listing the topics covered in the course, I summarized her employment experience, specifying that she earned promotions quickly. This **Mary Beth Kurzak** *would be attractive to any employer.*

2188 Huron River Drive • Ann Arbor, MI 48104 • 734-555-4912

Profile
➤ Strong educational preparation with practical applications in computer/internet programming.
➤ Highly motivated to excel in new career.
➤ A fast learner, as evidenced by success in accelerated training program.
➤ Self-directed, independent worker with proven ability to meet deadlines and work under pressure.
➤ Maintain team perspective with ability to build positive working relationships and foster open communication.

Education/Training
ADVANCED TECHNOLOGY CENTER • Dearborn, MI   xxxx-Present
Pursuing Certification in **Internet/Information Technology**   *Anticipated completion: Aug. xxxx*
An accelerated program focusing on computer and internet programming.
Highlights of Training:

Important to include specific things learned

- Networking Concepts	- Client Server	- UNIX
- Programming Concepts	- Visual Basic	- IIS
- Programming in Java/Java Script	- C/C++	- VB/ASP
- Web Authoring Using HTML	- Oracle	- CGI
- Photoshop	- DHTML, XML	- Perl

Highlights of Experience and Abilities

Experiences selected to support job objective

Customer Service
➤ Determined member eligibility and verified policy benefits.
➤ Responded to customer questions; interpreted and explained complex insurance concepts.
➤ Collaborated with health care providers regarding billing and claim procedures.

Leadership
➤ Creatively supervised 30 employees, many of whom were significantly older.
➤ Motivated employees and improved working conditions, resulting in greater camaraderie.
➤ Trained coworkers in various technical and nontechnical processes.

Analytical/Troubleshooting
➤ Investigated and resolved computer system errors.
➤ Researched discrepancies in claims and identified appropriate actions.
➤ Compiled and analyzed claims statistics.

Administrative Support and Accounting
➤ Managed and processed medical, mental health and substance abuse claims.
➤ Oversaw accounts receivable; reconciled receipts and prepared bank deposits.
➤ Coordinated 50+ line switchboard; routed calls as appropriate.

Employment History

MEDICAL SERVICES PLUS [Contracted by Health Solutions - Southfield, MI]   xxxx-xxxx
Promoted within eight months of hire.
Claims Supervisor / Claims Adjudicator

HANSEN AGENCY OF MICHIGAN • Ann Arbor, MI   xxxx-xxxx
Earned two promotions in one year.
Claims Adjudicator / Accounting Clerk / Receptionist

FORD WILLOW RUN TRANSMISSION PLANT • Ypsilanti, MI   Summer xxxx
Temporary Production Worker

PEARL HARBOR MEMORIAL MUSEUM • Pearl Harbor, HI   xxxx-xxxx
Assistant Crew Manager

References available on request

Submitted by Janet L. Beckstrom

Construction Managers

Writer's comment: Client had wonderful work history with one employer, but no formal education beyond high school. He knew he had marketable skills but needed help expressing them. We focused on his wide-ranging experience as well as demonstrating how he had worked his way up.

James P. Miller *I got a note from him within a month that he*
1254 Crestview Drive • Swartz Creek, MI 48473 • 810-555-1299 *had "gotten a good job."*

Highlights of Experience

— 14+ years in land development and construction management —

(1) RESIDENTIAL CONSTRUCTION MANAGEMENT

Organizes experience into three categories of importance to employers

- ➤ Supervised all aspects of construction: land development and groundbreaking through occupancy (total 150+ homes, average 15 simultaneously in progress).
- ➤ Utilized strong organizational skills and experience to perform critical path scheduling.
- ➤ Hired and directed subcontractors; monitored work for quality and safety issues.
- ➤ Ordered lumber and construction supplies; negotiated with vendors for lowest costs and just-in-time delivery service; approved accounts payable.
- ➤ Monitored costs and progress to ensure project completion within budget and deadlines.
- ➤ Facilitated communication between subcontractors, employees and management.
- ➤ Collaborated with home owners and architects regarding requests for deviations to plans.
- ➤ Represented company in interaction with building inspectors.

(2) LAND DEVELOPMENT

- ➤ Oversaw and participated in comprehensive land development and landscaping; hired and supervised direct-employ crews.
- ➤ Readied land above and below ground for electrical, water and sanitary/storm sewer services; prepared surfaces for concrete flat work and asphalt for roads.
- ➤ Operated back hoe, excavator, dozer, scraper, loader and dump truck.

(3) PROPERTY MANAGEMENT

- ➤ Managed 100+ lots/units.
- ➤ Acted as liaison with residents/owners regarding lot maintenance issues.
- ➤ Performed landscaping, lawn and street maintenance.

Employment History

JOHNSON DEVELOPMENT - MAPLE VILLAGE COURT - MILL CREEK CENTER -
BAY VIEW ESTATES • Bay City, MI   xxxx-xxxx

His experience is above, so he only needs the facts here

Condominium and mobile home developments under single ownership; two-time recipient of Bay City Parade of Homes awards
Superintendent - Bay View Estates (xxxx-xxxx)
Assistant Superintendent - Bay View Estates (xxxx-xxxx)
Manager - Mill Creek Center (xxxx-xxxx)
Heavy Equipment Operator - Maple Village Court (xxxx-xxxx & xxxx-xxxx)
Co-op Student & Lawn Maintenance Worker - Johnson Development (xxxx-xxxx)

Shows his promotions

Training & Education

DELTA COLLEGE • University Center, MI
Builders License course leading to earning
State of Michigan Builders License   xxxx

SWARTZ CREEK HIGH SCHOOL • Swartz Creek, MI
Diploma   xxxx

References available on request

Submitted by Janet L. Beckstrom

This resume was winner of the 1998 PARW Convention Best Résumé Contest—Finance Category.

Writer's comments: Unemployed for nearly a year, my client had a resume that presented a sketchy employment history. He had mailed over 1,000 resumes with no response. This format showcased his achievements in three areas. He immediately began interviewing and is now happily employed as CFO for a large company.

RAYMOND MONROE

12 Main Street
New York, New York 00000
(555) 555-5555

SENIOR FINANCE EXECUTIVE

**Finance & Accounting Management ... Banking & Cash Management ... Budgeting
Insurance & Risk Management ... Tax & Regulatory Compliance ... Information Systems**

Senior-level executive with extensive finance, administration and public accounting experience in diverse industries including retail/wholesale distribution, financial services and manufacturing. Proven ability to improve operations, impact business growth and maximize profits through achievements in finance management, cost reductions, internal controls, and productivity/efficiency improvements. Strong qualifications in general management, business planning, systems technology design and implementation, and staff development/leadership.

PROFESSIONAL EXPERIENCE

SOUTHINGTON COMPANY • New York, New York • 1991-XXXX
Treasurer/Senior Controller • 1993-XXXX
Corporate Controller • 1991-1993

Chief financial officer appointed to treasurer and Executive Committee member directing $500M international consumer products company. Accountable for strategic planning, development and leadership of entire finance function as well as day-to-day operations management of company's largest domestic division. Recruited, developed and managed team of finance professionals, managers and support staff.

(1) *Operations Achievements*

Uses numbers to reinforce his results

- **Instrumental in improving operating profits from less than $400K to over $4M, equity from $8.6M to $13.6M and assets from $29.7M to $44.4M.**
- **Boosted market penetration by 27% which increased gross sales 32% through acquisition of 25 operating units as key member of due diligence team.**
- **Initiated strategies to redeploy company resources, resulting in 54% increase in gross margin by partial withdrawal from high-risk/low-margin product lines.**
- **Directed annual plan review process and strengthened accountability by partnering with senior-level department and district managers in all business units.**

Organizes results into three major groups *(2)* *Financial Achievements*

- **Cut receivable write-offs $440K by developing credit policies, instituting aggressive collection strategies and establishing constructive dialogue with delinquent accounts.**
- **Negotiated and structured financing agreements, resulting in basis point reductions, easing/more favorable covenant restrictions and simplification of borrowing process.**
- **Saved over $2M through self-insurance strategy and an estimated $200K annually by positioning company to qualify to self-insure future workers' compensation claims.**
- **Designed executive and management reporting systems and tailored financial and operating reporting system to meet requirements of 100+ business units.**

RAYMOND MONROE • (555) 555-5555 • **Page 2**

Southington Company continued...

Note how every statement is results-oriented

③ *Technology Achievements*

- Turned around organization-wide resistance toward automation and streamlined procedures that significantly improved efficiency while reducing costs.
- Championed installation of leading-edge systems technology resolving long-standing profit measurement problems and created infrastructure to support corporate growth.
- Implemented automated cash management system in over 100 business unit locations and reduced daily idle cash by 50% ($750K).
- Recognized critical need and upgraded automated systems to track long-term assets which had increased from $28M to $48.8M in 5 years.

HAMDEN COMPANY • New York, New York • 1987-1991
Chief Financial Officer

Recruited for 3-year executive assignment to assume key role in building solid management infrastructure and positioning $15M company for its profitable sale in 1991. Directed general accounting, cash management, financial and tax reporting, banking relations, credit and collections, data processing, employee benefits, and administration. Managed and developed staff.

- Converted company to small business corporation saving $450K in taxes over 3-year period.
- Realized $195K in accumulated tax savings through strategies adopting LIFO inventory method, minimizing taxes on a continual basis.
- Secured 25% of company's major client base (50% of total sales volume) by leading design, installation and administration of computer-based EDI program.
- Reduced collection period from 3 weeks to 5 days by initiating new policies and procedures.

MADISON COMPANY • New York, New York • 1981-1987
Partner

Jointly acquired and managed public accounting firm serving privately held companies (up to $200M in revenues) in wholesale distribution, financial services and manufacturing industries. Concurrent responsibility for practice administration and providing accounting, business and MIS consulting services to corporate clients.

EDUCATION

B.S. in Accounting
New York University • New York, New York

Certified Public Accountant - New York

Submitted by Louise Garver

Home Health and Personal Care Aides

Susan J. Cascade

Each item in the Summary is very important to most employers. Emphasizing these attributes will give Susan an edge over other applicants.

1872 West Main Street
Appleton, Wisconsin 54914
(414) 830-7878

Summary of Attributes

- Excellent communication and interpersonal skills; demonstrate a compassionate and caring approach to patient care and assistance with activities of daily living.
- Enjoy providing care and assisting people to make them comfortable; particularly sensitive to the needs of elderly clients.
- Complete assignments with limited supervision.
- Excellent attendance record; always punctual.
- Accurately record information, paying close attention to details.
- Certified in C.P.R.

Experience

Homecare Specialists, Neenah, Wisconsin   1994-Present
Home Health Aide
- Assist clients in their homes with a variety of duties including meal preparation, daily living tasks, and housekeeping.
- Administer medications and carry out medical treatments as instructed by Registered Nurse.
- Participate in exercise and ambulation programs.

Bethel Home, Oshkosh, Wisconsin   1992-1994
Nursing Assistant
- Provided patient care, monitored and recorded vital signs, maintained patient charts, assisted with daily living skills, and administered range of motion therapy.

Education

Fox Valley Technical College, Appleton, Wisconsin
Certified Nursing Assistant   1992

Additional Training: CPR certified, July 1993

Oshkosh North High School, Oshkosh, Wisconsin; Diploma   1990

Submitted by Kathy Keshemberg

Librarians

Writer's comments: This resume is much improved over the original, with a solid summary, check marks for the strong experience sections, and other changes. Karen got a head librarian job.

Karen A. Librarian
000 Any Street • Anywhere, Michigan 00000 • (000) 000-0000

Summary of Qualifications

Over 10 years of Librarian experience with 8 years at the supervisory level, maintaining a positive working environment. Possess excellent verbal and written communications skills and significant knowledge in reference materials. Conscientious and detail-oriented with ability to plan, organize, and direct library services and programs. Substantial computer experience, including Internet support.

Strong opening

Professional Experience

Any Public Library – Anywhere, Michigan   *XXXX – Present*
Assistant to the Director
✓ Supervise, instruct, and schedule 11 staff members, including entire faculty in director's absence
✓ Automation Project Manager in regards to interlibrary loans, book status, and budgeting
✓ Administer reference and reader advisory services to patrons, provide outreach services to senior center, and schedule various meetings
✓ Lead adult book discussions including book selections and conduct library tours
✓ Assisted in library expansion, design, and construction (XXXX-XXXX)

Another Public Library – Anywhere, Michigan   *An effective,*   *XXXX – XXXX*
Assistant to the Director, (XXXX – XXXX)   *space-efficient*
✓ Supervised, instructed, and scheduled 9 staff members   *format*
✓ Maintained microfiche and microfilm storage
✓ Handled bookkeeping responsibilities and routine operations of the library

Children's and Young Adult Librarian, (XXXX – XXXX)
✓ Selected books, periodicals, and nonprint material for collection development
✓ Planned and implemented "Story Time" programs for preschool students, summer reading programs for grade school students, and "Computer Pix" for young adults
✓ Updated reference and library materials to exhibit most current information

Another Branch Library – Anywhere, California   *XXXX – XXXX*
Reference Librarian (Temporary)
✓ Examined ordered resources for collection development
✓ Assisted coworkers and patrons in microfiche operation and computer usage
✓ Handled book reservations and answered reference inquiries

Computer Experience

✓ Microsoft Word, Excel, and PowerPoint
✓ Michigan Occupational Information Systems (MOIS)
✓ Data Research Associates (DRA), Intelligent Catalog-Bibliofile, TDD, Magnifiers, RLIN, CLSI, OCLC, GEAC, ERIC Data Base, and Info Track – Magazine Index

Education

Texas Woman's University – Denton, Texas
• Master of Library Science, XXXX • Bachelor of Library Science, XXXX

Submitted by Maria E. Hebda

Manufacturers' and Wholesale Sales Representatives

A very clean, open format on one page. Good use of white space. Note how she is not limiting herself to one industry.

VIRGINIA S. GANT

1234 Lake Circle ♦ Burlingame, California 94222 ♦ vgant@gte.net
(415) 222-1222

QUALIFICATIONS

PROFIT-CONSCIOUS SALES MANAGER with proven success in building and motivating high-growth sales organizations. Equally competent in direct sales, including national/key account management. Career highlights:

Emphasis is on results

♦ **Sales Management** — Recruited, developed, and coached national distributor sales organization that more than doubled sales volume for six consecutive years. Led market expansion from local to national distribution, positioning company as the industry leader in recreational water treatment solutions.

♦ **Marketing** — Researched and identified target markets, selected channels of distribution, determined pricing structure, and developed packaging for new products. Successfully introduced new items that gained #1 market share in less than one year.

♦ **Technical Sales** — Strong technical background in sales of chemical products for recreational and industrial water uses. Led research and development functions for new treatment systems including label development, regulatory compliance, and market support. Excellent relationships with federal and state EPA officials.

PROFESSIONAL EXPERIENCE

CRAY COMPANY, BURLINGAME, CALIFORNIA   [date]–[date]

VICE PRESIDENT, MARKETING & SALES

Led this small, privately held company with sales in one western state through successful expansion into the national marketplace. Given complete autonomy for profit center reengineering and market alignment for the Recreational Chemical Division. Established and directed manufacturer's rep sales force. Established relationships with and serviced key national accounts. Directed advertising, merchandising, and account management strategies.

Accomplishments

A very effective visual

Emphasis is on results

▸ Recognized market opportunities and initiated expansion to build strong national market presence, achieving revenue growth of $100,000 in 1st year sales to more than $2 million in [date]:

Sales Growth

2,000,000
1,500,000
1,000,000
500,000
0

Year 1   Year 3   Year 5   Year 7

▸ Launched new products and line extension (R&D, EPA approval, pricing, market planning, sales presentations), capturing leading market share in less than six months.

▸ Secured new business with national accounts such as Wal★Mart (10 states), Home Depot, and Orchard Supply Hardware, negotiating prime retail space and capturing maximum distribution in accounts.

▸ Built number and quality of accounts from 100 to over 1,300.

▸ Maintained lucrative profit margins (7-8% over industry average) throughout rapid growth stage.

▸ Consulted clients such as The Disney Company and Caesar's Palace regarding above-ground water treatment.

STORE MANAGER, K&M COMPANY, BURLINGAME, CALIFORNIA   [date]–[date]

EDUCATION, AFFILIATIONS

Tom Hopkins Sales Seminar ... technical seminars on water treatment chemistry sponsored by Buckman Laboratories ... ongoing self-initiated study. Member, Association of Water Treaters and community service club.

♦ ♦ ♦

Submitted by Susan Britton Whitcomb
Résumé Magic

Pharmacists

JACK PATERSON
Licensed in New York and New Jersey
56 83rd Street · Brooklyn, NY 00000
(555) 555-5555

A well-designed format with bold headings, small bullets, and short statements make an attractive, uncrowded resume.

CAREER OBJECTIVE:

Experienced and accomplished professional seeks a position as a staff pharmacist.

DEMONSTRATED STRENGTHS:

DETAIL-ORIENTED · TIME MANAGEMENT · SUPERVISORY SKILLS · COMMUNICATIONS

PROFESSIONAL EXPERIENCE:

GENERAL ISRAEL HOSPITAL   Paramus, New Jersey
Staff Pharmacist   *1992 - Present*
· Supervises two registered pharmacists and two pharmacy technicians.
· Prepares IV solutions, chemotherapy and antibiotics.
· Maintains computer profiles of patients' medications.
· Ensures adequate inventory levels and places orders.
· Fills employee prescriptions.
· Member of the Chemotherapy Committee.
· Develops clinical guidelines for oncology therapies.
· Maintains DUEs for groups of medications used in patient population on assigned units.

HACKENSACK MEDICAL CENTER   Hackensack, New Jersey
Staff Pharmacist   *1987 - 1992*
·· Supervised four technicians and ensured high standards were maintained.
· Prepared IV solutions, chemotherapy and antibiotics.
·· Performed daily functions to ensure smooth operations.

MAIMONIDES MEDICAL CENTER   Brooklyn, New York
Pharmacy Intern   *1987*
· Performed daily functions under the supervision of a licensed pharmacist.
· Filled prescriptions and maintained computerized records.

EDUCATION:

Bachelor of Science in Pharmacy
College of Pharmacy and Health Sciences
Long Island University · Brooklyn, New York (1986)

Bachelor of Science in Biology
Long Island University · Brooklyn, New York

Submitted by Alesia Benedict

PROFESSIONAL MEMBERSHIPS:

NJ Society of Hospital Pharmacists
Society of Toxicology

Receptionists

Writer's comments: Mary's positive personality was an asset for the reception job she sought, so I contacted people who knew her work and included their comments.

MARY F. JOHNSON
12440 Miller Road
Clio, MI 48420   810-555-3299

PROFILE

"Mary takes the extra steps to assist her callers . . . she cares to make a difference."
—James Dunn, Chevrolet Representative

- Extensive successful experience dealing with the public. *Presents key adaptive skills*

- Possess many traits of an effective communicator:
  - Professional presence   - Patience
  - Warm, friendly demeanor   - Diplomacy
  - Outgoing personality   - Instinct
  - Sincerity   - Composure

- Front-line team player who presents a positive company image; committed to delivering top-quality service to all customers.

- Self-confident and level-headed; ability to remain poised even in demanding situations.

"She is polite and helpful, and has a wonderful personality . . . I would rate her a '10'!"
—Robert Maxwell, New Car Customer

- Keen ability to recognize voices and remember names.

- Skilled in intuitively assessing and relating to customers' moods and preferences while adapting to their diverse personalities.

HIGHLIGHTS OF EXPERIENCE

Her key job-related skills

- Single-handedly answer 25 phone lines and route calls (average volume: 100 per hour) to 30+ salespeople and departments.
- Manually track calls to generate informal statistical reports.
- Monitor disposition of calls to ensure satisfactory completion.
- Greet customers as they enter showroom.
- Provide support to sales staff as requested.
- Participated in the research process for new telephone system.
- Founded and operated dessert catering service; handled all aspects of business including marketing, purchasing, production, and delivery.

"The sound of Mary's voice can turn around anyone's bad mood. She can really perk you up."
—Susan Anthony, Car Conversions

EMPLOYMENT HISTORY

NIXON CHEVROLET-GEO • Pontiac, MI
Receptionist   xxxx-xxxx

A simple list works well here, since it shows a good work listing

ARMOUR SUPPLIES • Flint, MI   xxxx-xxxx
Receptionist

"Mary goes beyond just answering the telephone. She holds herself accountable for the calls she processes."
—Gil Baker, Manufacturers Representative

MID-MICHIGAN MOTORS • St. Johns, MI   xxxx-xxxx
Receptionist

MARY'S COOKIES • Lansing, MI   xxxx-xxxx
Owner/Founder

Excellent references available on request

Submitted by Janet L. Beckstrom

Retail Sales Worker Supervisors and Managers

Writer's comments: No education, overworked and underpaid in a dying industry (independent bookseller); Gloria was a real go-getter with impressive accomplishments that I highlighted with bullets and numbers. her customer service abilities because she did industry she was going to switch.

The summary stresses and general management not know to which

Gloria Gaughetter

999 Perky Street
Beautiful Vista, CA 99999
(666) 666-6666

Highly-motivated Customer Service / Operations Manager with strong commitment to achieving company goals.

Key adaptive and transferable Skills

- Hands-on manager who <u>leads by example</u> and develops well-trained, motivated staff.
- Excellent communication, interpersonal, and <u>customer service skills</u>.
- History of successfully <u>managing multiple operations</u> within tight deadlines, making <u>sound decisions</u>, and meeting and/or <u>surpassing sales objectives.</u>
- 10 years of experience within the Book Industry. Areas of experience and/or expertise include:

Purchasing	Customer Service
Staffing	Shipping & Receiving
Scheduling	Inventory Control
Organizing	Budget Management

← Positions she can handle

Manager, MOUNTAIN BOOKS, Beautiful Vista, CA   XXXX-Present

Direct operations, with P&L responsibility, for one of the few independent booksellers to achieve increased revenues in recent years.

Good use of numbers to emphasize her skills

- Purchase approximately <u>90,000</u> book titles plus a full line of accessories from <u>600</u> different vendors.
- Hire, train, and maintain high level of motivation for staff of <u>30.</u>
- Broke <u>$2 million</u> sales barrier in first year as Manager by gearing products for a largely high tech, business-oriented clientele and emphasizing customer service.
- Increased net profit by <u>11%</u> through controlling cost of goods and staff turnover.

Buyer, MOUNTAIN BOOKS, Sicily, CA   XXXX-XXXX

- Ensured optimal product supply and selection for highly academic clientele.
- In addition to purchasing, supervised staff of <u>35-40.</u>

Shift Manager, MOUNTAIN RECORDS, Sicily, CA   XXXX-XXXX

Based on reliability and results, was rapidly promoted to supervise shift employees.

COMPUTER SKILLS

Windows 98, MS Word, proprietary Inventory Control system, Internet

PROFESSIONAL AFFILIATIONS

Member, Northern California Independent Booksellers Association (NCIBA)

Submitted by Sydney J. Reuben

School Teachers—Kindergarten, Elementary, and Secondary

Writer's comments: This client held two long-term substitute teaching positions. This resume needed to minimize the short-lived assignments and emphasize her potential to be a dynamite teacher in a classroom of her own. The first page focuses on skills and achievements, so the reader gets a big dose of **Priscilla Dailey** *what this teacher can do before ever seeing the dates on page 2.*

69 Spruce Street
Boston, MA 02131

(617) 555–5555
pdailey@teacher.net

TEACHER, PreK–3

Energetic, enthusiastic teacher with unyielding commitment to educating children. Proven ability to foster trusting, cooperative environment that enables children to reach their full potential. Skilled in the design of challenging, enriching, and innovative activities that address the diverse interests and needs of students. Experience in multicultural and inclusion classrooms. Recognized for excellent interpersonal, organizational, and classroom management skills. Active member of school community. Master's Degree in Early Childhood Education.

> *"...a very effective teacher...a creative, organized, and energetic person who motivates students with exciting and interesting learning activities."*
> J. Franklin Thomas, Principal
> Russell P. Williams School, Boston, MA

An excellent addition!

This approach allows her to emphasize strengths better than a chronological format

SELECTED ACHIEVEMENTS

➤ Developed theme-based units that tie together different subject areas to reinforce learning of key concepts.

➤ Introduced a "peace table" strategy to assist students with conflict resolution and encouraged students to take responsibility for behaviors and their consequences.

➤ Tailored curriculum to engage students to learn most effectively by applying the concept of "multiple intelligences."

➤ Encouraged literacy with the creation of an author's corner for writing and reading activities.

➤ Engaged in school-wide activities: directed spring variety show; volunteered to chaperone week-long overnight trip for older students; participated in Home School Association that focused on long-range fiscal planning needs of school.

➤ Implemented Wellesley Social Competency Curriculum to teach students appropriate social and interpersonal skills.

➤ Participated in Core Evaluations and design and implementation of IEPs; adapted curriculum to accommodate a wide variety of special needs.

➤ Selected mid-year to take charge of unfocused classes in transition following teacher's departure; successfully managed behavior problems and directed children's energy toward new learning activities.

➤ Participated in scoring the Early Childhood writing samples for the Massachusetts Teachers Test.

Priscilla Dailey   **Page 2**

Makes the most of
her experience

TEACHING EXPERIENCE

Kindergarten Teacher – St. Catherine's School, Roslindale, MA   11/xx–6/xx
Taught full-day class of 20 kindergartners from multicultural backgrounds in private, parochial school. Developed and implemented curriculum in all subject areas, assessed student development, and made recommendations to implement services from outside sources, when necessary. Served as Faculty Representative to Home/School Association.

Kindergarten Teacher – Williams School, Roxbury, MA   1/xx–6/xx
Hired to take charge of full-day kindergarten class during teacher's extended absence. Established order and planned and taught lessons in all subject areas. Maintained ongoing communication with students' families.

Grade 2 Teacher (Clinical Practicum) – Curley School, Hyde Park, MA   9/xx–12/xx
Taught an inclusive, multicultural second grade classroom. Prepared lessons in reading, language arts, math, science, and social studies, using whole group and small group activities and tailoring curriculum to meet individual needs. Implemented objectives identified in IEP's.

Grade 1 Teacher (Provisional Practicum) – Fayerweather School, Cambridge, MA   1/xx–5/xx
Planned and implemented curriculum for reading, language arts, math, social studies, and science for students of varying abilities in multicultural setting.

Substitute Teacher – Boston and Lynn Public Schools   xxxx–xxxx

RELATED EXPERIENCE

Licensed Daycare Provider – Priscilla Dailey Child Care, Boston, MA   xxxx–xxxx
Community Trainer – Catholic Family and Children's Services, Boston, MA   xxxx–xxxx
Residential House Manager – Cambridge Children's Services, Cambridge, MA   xxxx–xxxx

EDUCATION / CERTIFICATION

MS, Early Childhood Education, Lesley College, Cambridge, MA   xxxx
BA, Political Science, Boston University, Boston, MA   xxxx

Certification: Standard, Early Childhood Education (PreK-3)

Submitted by Wendy Gelberg

School Teachers—Kindergarten, Elementary, and Secondary

Writer's comments: I revised this resume from a simple "just the facts" format to one that reflects his talents. The graphic and quote are perfect for the elementary grades.

The two-column format and use of white space present an attractive, orderly image

RANDY BEZ

123 E. Kids Circle
Fresno, CA 93711

(209) 234-2342

He lists four jobs then presents content for all of them—an effective way to handle this

The graphic and quote add considerable visual impact

> One hundred years from now it will not matter what my bank account was, the sort of house I lived in, or the kind of car I drove but the world may be different because I was important in the life of a child.
>
> —Anonymous

PROFESSION

Elementary Educator, Grades 2-5—highlights of 16-year career with Fresno Unified include the following:

♦ Three years' experience as Mentor Teacher.

♦ Experience as Master Teacher for CSUF Option IV Program.

♦ Strengths in science and math; effective classroom management skills; excellent rapport with multicultural, LEP, special needs, and at-risk students.

EDUCATION, CREDENTIAL

Language Development Specialist Certificate
Multiple Subject Credential—California State University, Fresno
B.A., Education/Biology Minor—University of Texas, Austin

PROFESSIONAL EXPERIENCE

FRESNO UNIFIED SCHOOL DISTRICT   [date]–Present

Teacher, 3/4 Combination—High Elementary (date-Present)
Literacy Summer School Teacher—Stars School (date)
Certificated Math Tutor—Ariana Elementary (date–date)
Summer School Teacher—Middleton School (date)

♦ Create an engaging, positive learning environment featuring integrated curriculum, hands-on lessons, computer applications, and use of portfolios to document students' growth and talents.

♦ Structure whole group, small group, and individual instruction to accommodate different academic levels and learning styles.

♦ Apply cooperative learning and cross-age tutoring to increase learning, self-esteem, and cross-cultural understanding.

♦ Employ C-SIN and AIMS in science and math to develop critical thinking skills and improve overall comprehension.

♦ Utilize SDAIE, Natural Approach, Language Experience Approach, and TPR to overcome language barriers.

♦ Selected by principal to develop special programs, such as Margaret Smith's MTA, TRIBES conflict resolution, and DBAE.

♦ Wrote and received community partnership minigrant "Walk Through California."

CONTINUING EDUCATION—Received training in and implemented the following:

Multi-Sensory Teaching Approach	Tribes
C-SIN (CA Science Implementation Network)	True Colors
Lee Canter's Assertive Discipline	FUSD Math Camp
Lee Canter's Beyond Assertive Discipline	Santillana
DBAE (Discipline-Based Art Education)	Cooperative Learning
Portfolio Assessment	Peer Coaching
Conducting Staff In-services	SDAIE
Parent Partnerships	Early Literacy

Submitted by Susan Britton Whitcomb Resume Magic

Secretaries

Writer's comments: For an older worker who does not plan on retiring, this resume hides her age and emphasizes her computer skills, productivity, and flexibility.

Mary O'Reilly

593 Maple Avenue • Brighton, MA 02135 • (617) 555-5555

OVERVIEW — *Most of the words here portray a very capable and results-driven person*

Hard-working and conscientious secretary with a broad range of experience in legal and corporate settings. Solid background maintaining the smooth flow of work in a busy office. Able to meet tight deadlines in fast-paced environment. Combination of strong administrative ability and excellent oral, written, and electronic communication skills. Team player with outstanding work ethic. Computer proficient. Eager to take on new challenges and learn new skills.

SECRETARIAL SKILLS

- 70+ wpm typing speed
- tape transcription
- telephone answering / screening
- statistical typing
- scheduling
- Corel / WordPerfect
- Microsoft Word / Excel
- editing

CAREER HIGHLIGHTS

Note the emphasis on high performance

- Edited, typed, and transcribed correspondence, legal documents, reports, proposals, and financial statements in various office settings, accurately and on time.
- Prioritized work flow to meet tight deadlines in busy departments.
- Rotated among different departments, filling in for secretaries who are on vacation or out sick; adapted to different formats, time constraints, work styles, and areas of specialization while keeping work flow on schedule.
- Answered and screened phone calls and scheduled appointments for up to 14 people.
- Set up and maintained filing systems to expedite tracking of documents.
- Performed overflow work to maintain work production timetables.
- Learned and used software upgrades, applying more sophisticated features to increase work efficiency.
- Interacted effectively with people at all levels of the organization as well as with the general public.

EXPERIENCE

Covers just the past 13 years, to help de-emphasize her age

LAW FIRM OF ANDERSON, THORNTON, SOCOLOVE & DOE, Boston, MA — xxxx–Present
    Floater Secretary (xxxx–Present)
    Overflow Secretary (xxxx–xxxx)
    Word Processor/Lead Operator (xxxx–xxxx)
    Word Processor (part-time) (xxxx–xxxx)

ERNST & YOUNG, Boston, MA — xxxx–xxxx
    Word Processor (part-time)

LAW OFFICES OF SMITH, JONES, JOHNSON & ANDREWS, Boston, MA — xxxx–xxxx
    Word Processor (part-time)

POLAROID CORPORATION, Cambridge, MA — xxxx–xxxx
    Secretary, Marketing Department (xxxx–xxxx)
    Secretary, Financial Planning Department (xxxx–xxxx)

EDUCATION — *No dates are included*

Coursework, University of Massachusetts, Boston, MA
Training in WordPerfect, E-mail

Submitted by Wendy Gelberg

Writers and Editors, including Technical Writers

Writer's comments: Lizzy was an extremely talented technical writer for a world-known computer company. But all her experience was in her most recent position for that company. So I separated her two positions by job title but did not list years in each position. Finally, rather than detract from recent accomplishments, pertinent accomplishments from previous jobs were bulleted under Previous Employment.

Lizzy B. Wright

8888 Calla Lily Lane
Mountain View, CA 99999

lbwright@batnet.com
(650) 999-9999

TECHNICAL WRITER — Highly Skilled, Technically Savvy, Energetic

A clean, disciplined format appropriate for a technical writer

- Award-winning writer and editor of highly technical documentation (print and online) for Silicon Valley giant. Documents include: manuals, guides, articles for trade journals, PR, proposals, course development, employee bulletins, technical reports.

- Strong communication, training and interviewing skills. Translate "engineer-ese" into users' language with a clear and accurate writing style.

- Excellent cross-organizational skills and teamwork. Work closely with engineers, editors, other departments and team members.

- History of learning applications with exceptional speed and handling multiple projects, from outline to finished product, within extremely tight schedules.

Systems:	UNIX, Windows, Macintosh, VMS, Solaris, OpenWindows, All-in-One, Netware
Applications:	Framemaker, Framemaker+ SGML, Interleaf, MS Office, MS Project, PhotoShop, Illustrator, Lotus 1-2-3, Sun's workstation tools, Filemaker Pro
Web Skills:	HTML, graphics design and layout, information mapping, content development

---

MAJOR SILICON PLAYER, INC., Computerville, CA   XXXX-Present

Technical Writer II

Promoted from Technical Writer I to Sustaining Project Lead, Illustration Project Lead and Technical Writer II within a year. Produce documentation for online and print at all testing stages.

- Maintain document sets and all revisions for 4 mid-range servers and wrote section of Well-Known Hardware Platform Notes.
- Currently developing document set (hardware and software) for next generation of servers.
- > Won *Touchstone Award* for Hardware Reference Category (one of three contributors) presented by Northern California Chapter of STC.

Global Project Coordinator

Developed/maintained documentation and communications for 3 worldwide projects. Organized international team meetings and coordinated projects, including budget and metrics tracking.

- Designed award-winning intranet web site. Served as web master and content developer for 50-page site containing Global Travel Policy (for 14 countries) and monthly Employee Newsletter.
- Designed user surveys, compiled information from hundreds of responses, and wrote 30-40 page recommendation reports used by Engineering in designing online tools.

PREVIOUS EMPLOYMENT

- Edited journal articles, wrote news releases and speeches, coordinated press relations for various contract positions, XXXX-XXXX.
- Fully computerized busy six-doctor practice using Alpha4 database system, Medical Center of Northeast, XXXX-XXXX.
- Developed information database used in health care reform initiatives, Regional Coalition for National Health Care, XXXX.

EDUCATION   *Related training*

BA, Sociology (Vocal Performance), Oberlin College and Conservatory, Oberlin, OH

Premed Certificate Program, University of Massachusetts, Boston, MA

Information Architecture; Advanced Technical Communications, UC Berkeley Extension

C Programming, Foothill College, Los Altos, Hills, CA

Languages: Conversational Spanish, French, Italian

Submitted by Sydney J. Reuben

Contact Information for Resume Contributors

The following professional resume writers contributed resumes to this section:

California

Fresno

Susan Britton Whitcomb
Alpha Omega Services
757 E. Hampton Way
Fresno, CA 93704
Phone: (559) 222-7474
Fax: (559) 222-9538
E-mail: topresume@aol.com
Web site: www.careerwriter.com
Member: PARW, NRWA
Certification: NCRW, CPRW

Menlo Park

Sydney J. Reuben
854 Coleman Avenue, #L
Menlo Park, CA 94025
Phone: (650) 321-3725
Fax: (650) 321-3725
E-mail: sreubenma@aol.com
Member: PARW, NRWA
Certification: CPRW, M.A.

Connecticut

Broad Brook

Louise Garver
Career Directions
P.O. Box 587
Broad Brook, CT 06016
Phone: (860) 623-9476
Fax: (860) 623-9473
E-mail: CAREERDIRS@aol.com
Web site: www.resumeimpact.com
Member: PARW, NRWA, IACMP, NCDA, ACA
Certification: CPRW, CMP, MA, JCTC

Massachusetts

Needham

Wendy Gelberg
Advantage Resume Services
21 Hawthorn Avenue
Needham, MA 02492
Phone: (781) 444-0778
Fax: (781) 444-2778
E-mail: wgelberg@aol.com
Member: NRWA
Certification: CPRW, JCTC

Michigan

Flint

Janet L. Beckstrom
Word Crafter
1717 Montclair Ave.
Flint, MI 48503
Voice/Fax: (800) 351-9818
Voice/Fax: (810) 232-9257
E-mail: wordcrafter@voyager.net
Member: PARW

Trenton

Maria Estela Hebda
Career Solutions, LLC
Trenton, MI 48183
Phone: (734) 676-9170
E-mail: maria@writingresumes.com
Web site: www.writingresumes.com
Member: PARW
Certification: CPRW

Minnesota

Rochester

Beverley Drake
CareerVision Resume & Job Search
Systems
1816 Baihly Hills Drive SW
Rochester, MN 55902
Phone: (507) 252-9825
Fax: (507) 252-1559
E-mail: bdcprw@aol.com
Member: PARW, AJST
Certification: CPRW, JCTC

New Jersey

Rochelle Park

Alesia Benedict
Career Objectives
151 West Passaic Street
Rochelle Park, NJ 07662
Phone: (800) 206-5353
Fax: (800) 206-5454
E-mail: Careerobj@aol.com
Web site: www.getinterviews.com
Member: PARW
Certification: CPRW, JCTC

Wisconsin

Appleton

Kathy Keshemberg
A Career Advantage
1615 E. Roeland, #3
Appleton, WI 54915
Phone: (920) 731-5167
Fax: (920) 739-6471
E-mail: kathyKC@aol.com
Web site: www.acareeradvantage.com
Member: NRWA
Certification: NCRW

SECTION THREE

IMPORTANT TRENDS IN JOBS AND INDUSTRIES

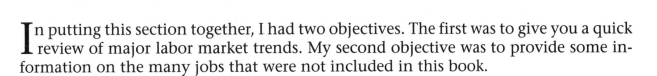

In putting this section together, I had two objectives. The first was to give you a quick review of major labor market trends. My second objective was to provide some information on the many jobs that were not included in this book.

To meet the first objective, I chose two excellent articles originally published in U.S. Department of Labor publications. The first article is "Tomorrow's Jobs: Important Labor Market Trends Through the Year 2008." It provides a superb—and short—review of the major trends that *will* affect your career in the years to come. Read it for ideas on selecting a career path for the long term. The second article is titled "Employment Trends in Major Industries." While you may not have thought much about it, the industry you work in is just as important as your occupational choice. This great article will help you learn about the major trends affecting various industries.

To meet the second objective, I included useful data on hundreds of jobs that are not described in this book. You may be working in one of these jobs now, so you may have more than passing interest in their projected growth and other details. Plus, among these many jobs, you may find one or more that interest you enough to consider them further. Many good jobs are not growing quickly, and the one you really want may be among them.

Tomorrow's Jobs: Important Labor Market Trends Through the Year 2008

Examining the past and projecting changes in these relationships are the foundation of the government's Occupational Outlook Program. This section presents highlights of Bureau of Labor Statistics projections of the labor force and occupational and industry employment that can help guide your career plans.

Comments

This article, with minor changes, comes from the *Occupational Outlook Handbook* and was written by U.S. Department of Labor staff. The material provides a good review of major labor market trends both for occupations and for industries.

Much of this article uses 1998 data, the most recent available at press time. Since labor market trends tend to be fairly predictable, the delay does not affect the material's usefulness.

You may notice that some job titles in this article differ from those used elsewhere in the book. This is not an error. The material that follows uses a different set of occupations than I used in choosing this book's described jobs.

Making informed career decisions requires reliable information about opportunities in the future. Opportunities result from the relationships between the population, labor force, and the demand for goods and services.

Population ultimately limits the size of the labor force—individuals working or looking for work—which constrains how much can be produced. Demand for various goods and services determines employment in the industries providing them. Occupational employment opportunities, in turn, result from skills needed within specific industries. Opportunities for computer engineers and other computer-related occupations, for example, have surged in response to rapid growth in demand for computer services.

Population

Population trends affect employment opportunities in a number of ways. Changes in population influence the demand for goods and services. For example, a growing and aging population has increased the demand for health services. Equally important, population changes produce corresponding changes in the size and demographic composition of the labor force.

The U.S. population is expected to increase by 23 million in the 10 years preceding 2008. This growth rate is about the same as during the 1988–98 period but much slower than during the 1978–88 period (chart 1). Continued growth will mean more consumers of goods and services, spurring demand for workers in a wide range of occupations and industries. The effects of population growth in various occupations will differ. The differences are partially accounted for by the age distribution of the future population.

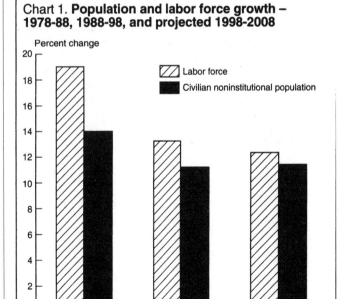

Chart 1. **Population and labor force growth – 1978-88, 1988-98, and projected 1998-2008**

The youth population, ages 16 to 24, is expected to increase as a share of the population for the first time since the 1970s. Overall, the 25-to-54 age group is expected to decrease as a share of the population. Within this group, however, the 45 and over age group will grow as a percent of the population. The 55-and-over age group will grow the fastest, increasing from 26.6 to 30 percent over the 1998–2008 period.

Minorities and immigrants will constitute a larger share of the U.S. population in 2008 than they do today. Substantial increases in the Hispanic, black, and Asian populations are forecasted, reflecting high birth rates as well as a continued flow of immigrants.

Labor Force

Population is the single most important factor in determining the size and composition of the labor force—comprised of people who are either working or looking for work. The civilian labor force is expected to increase by 17 million, or 12 percent, to 154.6 million over the 1998–2008 period. This increase is almost the same as the 13 percent increase during the 1988–98 period but much less than the 19 percent increase during the 1978–88 period.

The U.S. workforce will become more diverse by 2008. White, non-Hispanic persons will make up a decreasing share of the labor force, from 73.9 to 70.7 percent. Hispanics, non-Hispanic blacks, and Asians and other racial groups are projected to comprise an increasing share of the labor force by 2008— 10.4 to 12.7 percent, 11.6 to 12.4 percent, and 4.6 to 5.7 percent, respectively (chart 2). However, despite relatively slow growth, white non-Hispanics will have the largest numerical growth in the labor force between 1998 and 2008, reflecting the large size of this group.

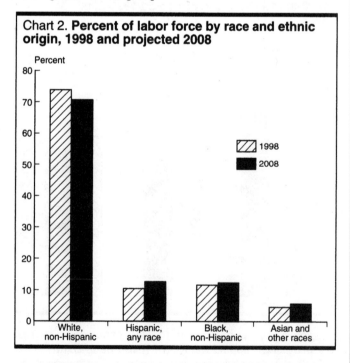

Chart 2. **Percent of labor force by race and ethnic origin, 1998 and projected 2008**

The number of men and women in the labor force will grow, but the number of men will grow at a slower rate than in the past. Between 1998 and 2008, men's share of the labor force is expected to decrease from 53.7 to 52.5 percent while women's share is expected to increase from 46.3 to 47.5 percent.

The youth labor force, ages 16 to 24, is expected to slightly increase its share of the labor force to 16 percent in 2008, growing more rapidly than the overall labor force for the first time in 25 years. The large group of workers 25-to-44 years old, who comprised 51 percent of the labor force in 1998, is projected to decline to 44 percent of the labor force by 2008. Workers 45 and older, on the other hand, are projected to increase from 33 to 40 percent of the labor force between 1998 and 2008, due to the aging baby-boom generation (chart 3).

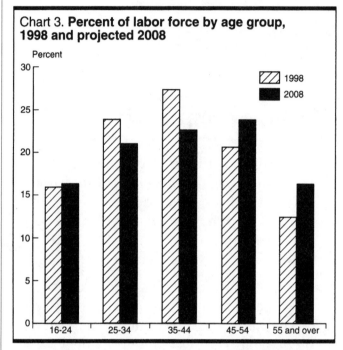

Chart 3. **Percent of labor force by age group, 1998 and projected 2008**

Education and Training

Projected job growth varies widely by education and training requirements. Five out of the six education and training categories projected to have the highest percent change require at least a bachelor's degree (chart 4). These five categories will account for one-third of all employment growth over the 1998-2008 period. Employment in occupations that do not require postsecondary education are projected to grow by about 12 percent while occupations that require at least a bachelor's degree are projected to grow by almost 22 percent, compared to 14 percent for all occupations combined.

Education is essential in getting a high-paying job. In fact, all but a few of the 50 highest-paying occupations require a college degree. However, a number of occupations—for example, blue-collar worker supervisors, electricians, and police patrol officers—do not require a college degree, yet offer higher-than-average earnings.

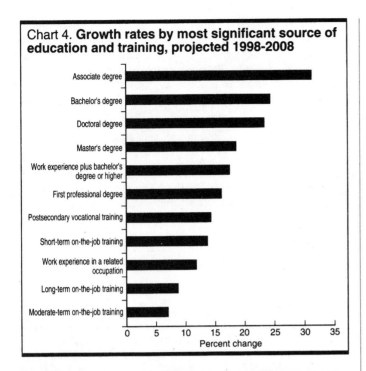

Chart 4. **Growth rates by most significant source of education and training, projected 1998-2008**

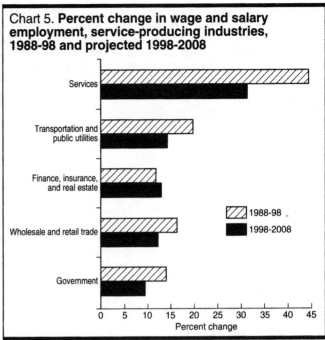

Chart 5. **Percent change in wage and salary employment, service-producing industries, 1988-98 and projected 1998-2008**

Employment

Total employment is expected to increase from 141 million in 1998 to 161 million in 2008, or by 14 percent. The 20 million jobs that will be added by 2008 will not be evenly distributed across major industrial and occupational groups. Changes in consumer demands, technology, and many other factors will contribute to the continually changing employment structure in the U.S. economy.

The following two segments examine projected employment change from both industrial and occupational perspectives. The industrial profile is discussed in terms of primary wage and salary employment; primary employment excludes secondary jobs for those who hold multiple jobs. The exception is agriculture, which includes self-employed and unpaid family workers in addition to salaried workers.

The occupational profile is viewed in terms of total employment—including primary and secondary jobs for wage and salary, self-employed, and unpaid family workers. Of the nearly 141 million jobs in the U.S. economy in 1998, wage and salary workers accounted for over 128 million; self-employed workers accounted for over 12 million; and unpaid family workers accounted for about 200,000. Of the nearly 141 million total jobs, secondary employment accounted for over 2 million. Self-employed workers held 9 out of 10 secondary jobs; wage and salary workers held most of the remainder.

Industry

The long-term shift from goods-producing to service-producing employment is expected to continue (chart 5).

Service-producing industries—including finance, insurance, and real estate; government; services; transportation and public utilities; and wholesale and retail trade—are expected to account for approximately 19.1 million of the 19.5 million new wage and salary jobs generated over the 1998–2008 period. The services and retail trade industry sectors will account for nearly three-fourths of total wage and salary job growth, a continuation of the employment growth pattern of the 1988–98 period.

Services. The largest and fastest-growing major industry group—services—is expected to add 11.8 million new jobs by 2008. Nearly three-fourths of this projected job growth is concentrated in three sectors of services—business, health, and professional and miscellaneous services. Business services—including personnel supply and computer and data processing services, among other detailed industries—will add 4.6 million jobs. Health services—including home health care services and nursing and personal care facilities, among other detailed industries—will add 2.8 million jobs. Professional and miscellaneous services—including management and public relations and research and testing services, among other detailed industries—will add 1.1 million jobs. Employment in computer and data processing services is projected to grow 117 percent between 1998 and 2008, ranking as the fastest-growing industry.

Transportation and public utilities. Overall employment is expected to increase by 674,000 jobs, or 14 percent. Employment in the transportation sector is expected to increase by 16 percent, from 4.3 to 5 million jobs. Air, truck, and local and interurban passenger transportation will account for 32, 30, and 23 percent, respectively, of the job growth in this industry. Employment in communications is expected to grow about as fast as average through 2008, adding about 300,000 new jobs. Employment in utilities is expected to decline by about 4 percent. However, faster-than-average growth is expected in water supply and sanitary services with the creation of about 67,000 jobs.

Finance, insurance, and real estate. Employment is expected to increase by 13 percent—adding 960,000 jobs to the 1998 level of 7.4 million. Demand for financial services is expected to continue. The security and commodity brokers segment of the industry is expected to grow by 40 percent, creating about 255,000 jobs. Nondepository institutions will add 193,000 jobs and have a growth rate of 29 percent, fueled by increased demand for nonbank corporations that offer bank-like services. Continued demand for real estate will create 179,000 new jobs, at a growth rate of about 12 percent. The insurance carriers segment is expected to grow by nearly 10 percent—adding 154,000 jobs.

Wholesale and retail trade. Employment is expected to increase by 7 and 14 percent, respectively, growing from 6.8 to 7.3 million in wholesale trade and from 22.3 to 25.4 million in retail trade. With the addition of 1.3 million jobs, the eating and drinking places segment of the retail industry is projected to have the largest numerical increase in employment.

Government. Between 1998 and 2008, government employment, including public education and public hospitals, is expected to increase by over 9 percent, from 19.8 to 21.7 million jobs. State and local government, particularly education, will drive employment growth. Federal government employment is expected to decline by 165,000 jobs.

Employment in the goods-producing industries has been relatively stagnant since the early 1980s. Overall, this sector is expected to grow by 1.6 percent over the 1998-2008 period. Although employment growth is expected to show little change, projected growth within the sector varies considerably (chart 6).

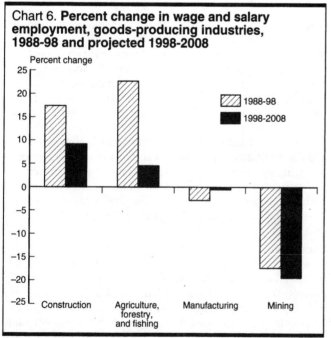

Chart 6. Percent change in wage and salary employment, goods-producing industries, 1988-98 and projected 1998-2008

Construction. Construction is expected to increase by 9 percent from 5.9 to 6.5 million. Demand for new housing and an increase in road, bridge, and tunnel construction will account for the bulk of employment growth in this industry.

Agriculture, forestry, and fishing. Overall employment in agriculture, forestry, and fishing is expected to increase by nearly 5 percent from 2.2 to 2.3 million. Strong growth in agricultural services will more than offset an expected continued decline in crops and livestock and livestock products.

Manufacturing. Manufacturing employment is expected to decline by less than 1 percent from the 1998 level of 18.8 million. The projected loss of jobs reflects improved production methods, advances in technology, and increased trade.

Mining. Mining employment is expected to decrease by 19 percent from 590,000 to 475,000. The continued decline is partly due to laborsaving machinery and increased imports.

Occupation

Expansion of the service-producing sector is expected to continue, creating demand for many occupations. However, projected job growth varies among major occupational groups (chart 7).

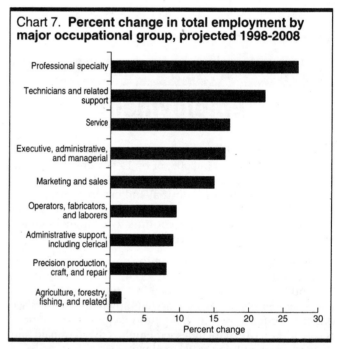

Chart 7. Percent change in total employment by major occupational group, projected 1998-2008

Professional specialty. Professional specialty occupations comprise the fastest-growing group. Over the 1998–2008 period, a 27-percent increase in the number of new professional specialty jobs is projected, an increase of 5.3 million. Professional specialty workers perform a wide variety of duties and are employed throughout private industry and government. Computer systems analysts, computer engineers and scientists, special education teachers, and social and recreation workers are among the fastest-growing occupations in this group.

Technicians and related support. Employment of technicians and related support occupations is projected to grow by 22 percent, adding 1.1 million jobs by 2008. Workers in this group provide technical assistance to engineers, scientists, physicians, and other professional specialty workers, and operate and program technical equipment. Over half of the projected employment growth among technicians—about 616,000 jobs—is among health technicians and technologists. Considerable growth is also expected among computer programmers and paralegals and legal assistants.

Service. Employment in service occupations is projected to increase by 3.9 million, or 17 percent, by 2008, the second largest numerical gain among the major occupational groups. Over half of the new jobs are in the rapidly growing services industry division, led by business services, health services, and social services.

Executive, administrative, and managerial. Executive, administrative, and managerial occupations are projected to increase by 16 percent, or 2.4 million, over the 1998–2008 period. Workers in this group establish policies, make plans, determine staffing requirements, and direct the activities of businesses, government agencies, and other organizations. The services industry division is expected to account for half of the job growth, adding 1.2 million jobs. The number of self-employed executive, administrative, and managerial workers is expected to increase by 361,000—more than any other major occupational group—to almost 2.5 million by 2008.

Marketing and sales. Workers in marketing and sales occupations sell goods and services, purchase commodities and property for resale, and stimulate consumer interest. Employment in this group is projected to increase by 15 percent, or 2.3 million, from 1998 to 2008. The services industry division is expected to add the most marketing and sales jobs—719,000—by 2008, followed by an additional 92,000 jobs in the transportation and public utilities industry division.

Operators, fabricators, and laborers. Employment of operators, fabricators, and laborers is expected to increase by 1.8 million workers, or 9.4 percent, from 1998 to 2008. Most new jobs in this group are expected among transportation and material moving machine and vehicle operators; helpers, laborers, and material movers; and hand workers, including assemblers and fabricators, adding 745,000; 626,000; and 290,000 jobs, respectively.

Administrative support, including clerical. The number of workers in administrative support occupations, including clerical, is projected to increase by 9 percent from 1998 to 2008, adding 2.2 million new jobs. With 24.5 million workers, this is the largest major occupational group. Workers perform a wide variety of administrative tasks necessary to keep organizations functioning efficiently. Due mostly to technological change, several large occupations within this group—for example, bookkeeping, accounting, and auditing clerks—are expected to decline. However, other occupations less affected by technological change are expected to increase. These occupations include teacher assistants, adding 375,000 jobs; office and administrative support supervisors and managers, adding 313,000 jobs; receptionists and information clerks, adding 305,000 jobs; and adjusters, investigators, and collectors, adding 302,000 jobs.

Precision production, craft, and repair. Employment in precision production, craft, and repair occupations is projected to grow 8 percent, creating almost 1.3 million new jobs, over the 1998–2008 period. Mechanics, installers, and repairers are expected to add 588,000 new jobs by 2008; construction trades workers are expected to add 390,000 new jobs; and blue-collar worker supervisors are expected to add 196,000 new jobs.

Agriculture, forestry, fishing, and related. Agriculture, forestry, fishing, and related occupations are projected to grow by only 2 percent, adding 71,000 new jobs. Workers in these occupations cultivate plants, breed and raise livestock, and catch animals. Within this major group, job losses are expected for farmers and farm workers. In contrast, landscaping, groundskeeping, nursery, greenhouse, and lawn service occupations are expected to add 262,000 new jobs by 2008.

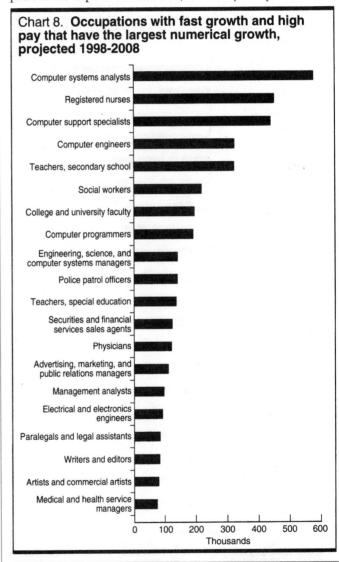

Chart 8. Occupations with fast growth and high pay that have the largest numerical growth, projected 1998-2008

Fast-Growing Jobs

The 20 occupations listed in chart 8 are among those projected to grow fast and produce large numbers of new jobs, in addition to having higher-than-average earnings. Half of these

occupations are involved with computer technology, health care, and education. Systems analysts top this list, adding over 577,000 jobs between 1998 and 2008, reflecting high demand for computer services. Among other computer-related occupations, computer support specialists and computer engineers are expected to add 439,000 and 323,000 new jobs, respectively. Similarly, strong demand for health care services will fuel growth among registered nurses, creating 451,000 new jobs. Among education-related occupations, secondary school teachers head the list, adding 322,000 jobs.

Computer-related jobs are expected to grow the fastest over the projection period (chart 9). In fact, these jobs make up the four fastest-growing occupations in the economy. Computer engi-

tivity and farm consolidations are expected to result in a decline of 173,000 farmers over the 1998–2008 period (chart 10). Office automation and the increased use of word processing equipment by professionals and managerial employees will lead to a decline among word processors and typists. Examples of occupations projected to lose jobs along with declining employment in the industries in which they are concentrated include farm workers; sewing machine operators, garment; and child-care workers, private household.

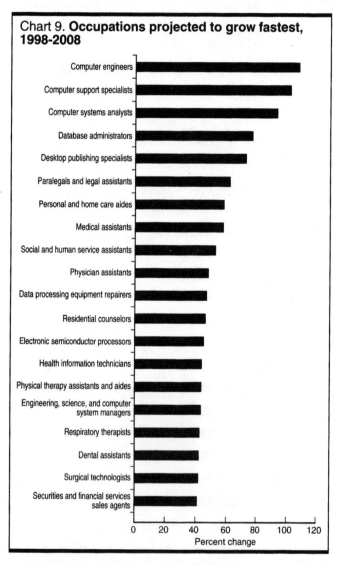

Chart 9. **Occupations projected to grow fastest, 1998-2008**

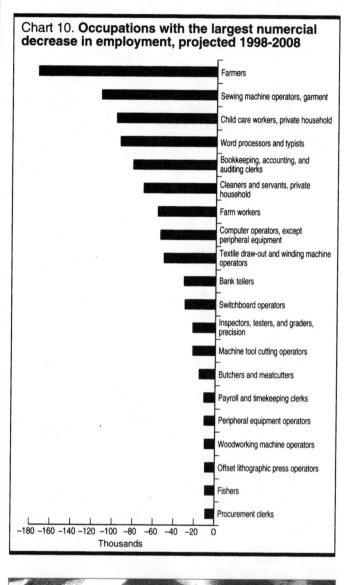

Chart 10. **Occupations with the largest numerical decrease in employment, projected 1998-2008**

neers, computer support specialists, computer systems analysts, and database administrators are expected to increase by 108, 102, 94, and 77 percent, respectively. Many other occupations projected to grow the fastest are in health care.

Declining occupational employment stems from declining industry employment, technological advances, organizational changes, and other factors. For example, increased produc-

Total Job Openings

Job openings stem from both employment growth and replacement needs (chart 11). Replacement needs arise as workers leave occupations. Some transfer to other occupations while others retire, return to school, or quit to assume household responsibilities. Replacement needs are projected to account for 63 percent of the approximately 55 million job openings between 1998 and 2008. Thus, even occupations with slower-than-average growth or little or no change in employment may still offer many job openings.

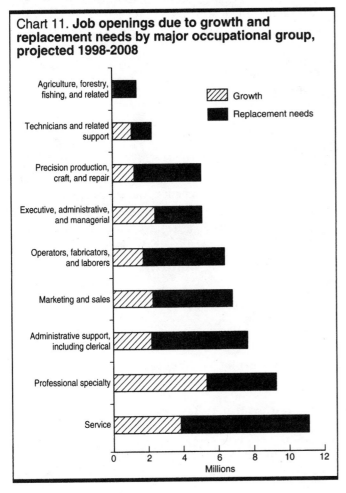

Chart 11. **Job openings due to growth and replacement needs by major occupational group, projected 1998-2008**

Professional specialty occupations are projected to grow faster and add more jobs than any major occupational group, with 5.3 million new jobs by 2008. Two-thirds of this job growth is expected among teachers, librarians, and counselors; computer, mathematical, and operations research occupations; and health assessment and treating occupations. With 3.9 million job openings due to replacement needs, professional specialty occupations comprise the only major group projected to generate more openings from job growth than from replacement needs.

Due to high replacement needs, service occupations are projected to have the largest number of total job openings, 11.1 million. A large number of replacements are expected to arise as young workers leave food preparation and service occupations. Replacement needs generally are greatest in the largest occupations and in those with relatively low pay or limited training requirements.

Office automation will significantly affect many individual administrative and clerical support occupations. Overall, these occupations are projected to grow more slowly than the average, while some are projected to decline. Administrative

support, including clerical occupations, are projected to create 7.7 million job openings over the 1998–2008 period, ranking third behind service and professional specialty occupations.

Precision production, craft, and repair occupations and operators, fabricators, and laborers are projected to grow more slowly than the average for all occupations through 2008, due mostly to advances in technology and changes in production methods. Replacement needs are projected to account for almost three-fourths of all the job openings in these groups.

Employment in occupations requiring an associate degree is projected to increase 31 percent, faster than any other occupational group categorized by education and training. However, this category only ranks seventh among the 11 education and training categories in terms of total job openings. The largest number of job openings will be among occupations requiring short-term on-the-job training, a bachelor's degree, and moderate-term on-the-job training (chart 12).

Almost two-thirds of the projected job openings over the 1998-2008 period will be in occupations that require on-the-job training, due mostly to replacement needs. These jobs will account for 34.5 million of the projected 55 million total job openings through 2008. However, many of these jobs typically offer low pay and benefits; this is particularly true of jobs requiring only short-term on-the-job training, which account for 24 million job openings, far more than any other occupational group.

Jobs requiring at least a bachelor's degree will account for about 12.7 million job openings through 2008. Most of these openings will result from job growth and usually offer higher pay and benefits.

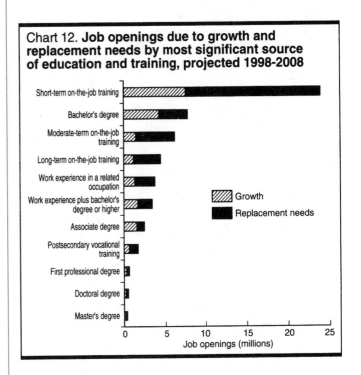

Chart 12. **Job openings due to growth and replacement needs by most significant source of education and training, projected 1998-2008**

Employment Trends in Major Industries

Comments

While hundreds of specialized industries exist, about 75 percent of all workers are employed in just 42 major ones. While space limitations do not allow us to provide you with detailed information on all industries, the article that follows presents a good overview of trends within industry types and gives important facts to consider in making career plans. The article comes, with minor changes, from a book published by the U.S. Department of Labor titled the *Career Guide to Industries, 2000-2001* edition.

While you may not have thought much about it, the industry you work in will often be as important as the career you choose. For example, some industries pay significantly higher wages. So, if you found your way back to this article, read it over carefully and consider the possibilities.

For more information on a specific industry, look for the *Career Guide to Industries* in your library. A more widely available version of the same book, published by JIST under the same title, is available through bookstores and many libraries. Here are the industries covered in the *Career Guide to Industries*:

Goods-Producing Industries

Agriculture, Mining, and Construction
Agricultural production
Agricultural services
Construction
Mining and quarrying
Oil and gas extraction

Manufacturing
Aerospace manufacturing
Apparel and other textile products
Chemical manufacturing, except drugs
Drug manufacturing
Electronic equipment manufacturing
Food processing
Motor vehicle and equipment manufacturing
Printing and publishing
Steel manufacturing
Textile mill products

Service-Producing Industries

Transportation, Communications, and Public Utilities
Air transportation
Cable and other pay television services
Public utilities
Radio and television broadcasting
Telecommunications
Trucking and warehousing

Wholesale and Retail Trade
Department, clothing, and accessory stores
Eating and drinking places
Grocery stores
Motor vehicle dealers
Wholesale trade

Finance and Insurance
Banking
Insurance
Securities and commodities

Services
Advertising
Amusement and recreation services
Child-care services
Computer and data processing services
Educational services
Health services
Hotels and other lodging places
Management and public relations services
Motion picture production and distribution
Personnel supply services
Social services, except child care

Government
Federal government
State and local government

Overview

The U.S. economy is comprised of industries with diverse characteristics. For each industry covered in the *Career Guide to Industries*, detailed information is provided about specific characteristics: the nature of the industry, working conditions, employment, occupational composition, training and advancement requirements, earnings, and job outlook. This article provides an overview of these characteristics for the economy as a whole.

Nature of the Industry

Industries are defined by the goods and services the industry provides. Because workers in the United States produce such a wide variety of products and services, industries in the U.S. economy range widely, from aerospace manufacturing to motion picture production. Although many of these industries are related, each industry contains a unique combination of occupations, production techniques, and business characteristics. Understanding the nature of the industry is important, because it is this unique combination that determines working conditions, educational requirements, and the job outlook for each industry.

Industries are comprised of many different places of work, called *establishments*, which range from large factories and office complexes employing thousands of workers to small businesses employing only a few workers. Not to be confused with "companies," which are legal entities, establishments are physical locations where people work, such as the branch office of a bank. Establishments that produce similar goods or services are grouped together into *industries*. Industries that produce related types of goods or services are, in turn, grouped together into *major industry divisions*. These are further grouped into the *goods-producing sector* (agriculture, forestry, and fishing; mining; construction; and manufacturing) or the *service-producing sector* (transportation, communications, and public utilities; wholesale and retail trade; finance, insurance, and real estate; services; and government).

Distinctions within industries are also varied. Each industry is comprised of a number of subdivisions, which are determined largely by differences in production processes. An easily recognized example of these distinctions is in the food processing industry, which is made up of subdivisions that produce meat products, preserved fruits and vegetables, bakery items, beverages, and dairy products, among others. Each of these subdivisions requires workers with varying skills and employs unique production techniques. Another example of these distinctions is in public utilities, which employs workers in establishments that provide electricity, sanitary services, water, and natural gas. Working conditions and establishment characteristics often differ widely in each of these smaller subdivisions.

There were nearly 7 million business establishments in the United States in 1997. The average size of these establishments varies widely across industries. Among industry divisions, manufacturing included many industries having among the highest employment per establishment in 1997. For example, the aerospace, motor vehicle, and steel manufacturing industries each averaged 150 or more employees per establishment.

Most establishments in the wholesale and retail trade, finance, and services industries are small, averaging fewer than 20 employees per establishment. Exceptions are the air transportation industry with 62 employees and educational services with 44. In addition, wide differences within industries can exist. Hospitals, for example, employ an average of 716 employees, while doctor's offices employ an average of 9. Similarly, despite an average of 14 employees per establishment for all of retail trade, department stores employ an average of 183 people.

Establishments in the United States are predominantly small; 55 percent of all establishments employed fewer than five workers in 1997. The medium to large establishments, however, employ a greater proportion of all workers. For example, establishments that employed 50 or more workers accounted for only 5 percent of all establishments, yet employed 58 percent of all workers. The large establishments—those with more than 500 workers—accounted for only 0.3 percent of all establishments, but employed 20 percent of all workers. Table 1 presents the percent distribution of employment according to establishment size.

TABLE 1

Percent Distribution of Establishments and Employment in All Industries by Establishment Size, 1997

Establishment Size (Number of Workers)	Establish- ments	Employ- ment
Total	100.0	100.0
1-4	54.5	6.1
5-9	19.6	8.5
10-19	12.4	10.9
20-49	8.3	16.4
50-99	2.8	12.7
100-249	1.7	16.2
250-499	0.4	9.4
500-999	0.2	7.0
1,000 or more	0.1	12.7

Source: Department of Commerce, *County Business Patterns, 1997*

Establishment size can play a role in the characteristics of each job. Large establishments generally offer workers greater occupational mobility and advancement potential, whereas small establishments may provide their employees with

broader experience by requiring them to assume a wider range of responsibilities. Also, small establishments are distributed throughout the nation; every locality has a few small businesses. Large establishments, in contrast, employ more workers and are less common, but they play a much more prominent role in the economies of the areas in which they are located.

Working Conditions

Just as the goods and services of each industry are different, working conditions in industries can vary significantly. In some industries, the work setting is quiet, temperature-controlled, and virtually hazard free. Other industries are characterized by noisy, uncomfortable, and sometimes dangerous work environments. Some industries require long workweeks and shift work; in many industries, standard 35- to 40-hour workweeks are common. Still other industries can be seasonal, requiring long hours during busy periods and abbreviated schedules during slower months. These varying conditions usually are determined by production processes, establishment size, and the physical location of work.

One of the most telling indicators of working conditions is an industry's injury and illness rate. Overexertion, being struck by an object, and falls on the same level were among the most common incidents causing injury or illness. In 1997, approximately 6.1 million nonfatal injuries and illnesses were reported throughout private industry. Among major industry divisions, manufacturing had the highest rate of injury and illness—10.3 cases for every 100 full-time workers—while finance, insurance, and real estate had the lowest rate—2.2 cases. About 6,000 work-related fatalities were reported in 1998; transportation accidents, violent acts, contact with objects and equipment, falls, and exposure to harmful substances or environments were among the most common events resulting in fatal injuries. Table 2 presents industries with the highest and lowest rates of nonfatal injury and illness.

TABLE 2

Nonfatal Injury and Illness Rates of Selected Industries, 1997

Industry	Cases Per 100 Full-Time Employees
All industries	7.1
High rates	
Motor vehicle manufacturing	25.5
Air transportation	16.4
Nursing and personal care facilities	16.2
Food processing	14.5
Trucking and warehousing	10.0

Industry	Cases Per 100 Full-Time Employees
Low rates	
Insurance	1.9
Banking	1.8
Radio and TV broadcasting	1.8
Computer and data processing	0.8
Securities and commodities	0.7

Work schedules are another important reflection of working conditions, and the operational requirements of each industry lead to large differences in hours worked and part-time versus full-time status. The contrast in an average workweek was notable between retail trade and manufacturing—29.1 hours and 41.7 hours, respectively, in 1998. More than 30 percent of workers in retail trade work part time (1 to 34 hours per week), compared to only 5 percent in manufacturing. Table 3 presents industries having relatively high and low percentages of part-time workers.

TABLE 3

Percent of Part-Time Workers in Selected Industries, 1998

Industry	Percent Part Time
All industries	15.9
Many part-time workers	
Apparel and accessory stores	38.6
Eating and drinking places	38.0
Department stores	33.0
Grocery stores	32.5
Child-care services	29.7
Few part-time workers	
Public utilities	3.0
Chemical manufacturing, except drugs	2.9
Textile mill products manufacturing	2.5
Motor vehicle and equipment manufacturing	1.8
Steel manufacturing	1.7

The low proportion of part-time workers in some manufacturing industries often reflects the continuity of the production processes and the specificity of skills. Once begun, it is costly to halt these processes; machinery and materials must be tended and moved continuously. For example, the chemical manufacturing industry produces many different chemical products through controlled chemical reactions. These processes require chemical operators to monitor and adjust the flow of materials into and out of the line of production. Production may continue 24 hours a day, 7 days a week under the watchful eyes of chemical operators who work in shifts.

Retail trade and service industries, on the other hand, have seasonal cycles marked by various events, such as school openings or important holidays, that affect the hours worked.

During busy times of the year, longer hours are common, whereas slack periods lead to cutbacks and shorter workweeks. Jobs in these industries are generally appealing to students and others who desire flexible, part-time schedules.

Employment

The number of wage and salary worker jobs in the United States totaled nearly 128 million in 1998, and it is projected to reach almost 148 million by 2008 (See Table 4). In addition to these workers, the U.S. economy also provided employment for nearly 12 million self-employed workers and about 182,000 unpaid family workers.

As shown in Table 4, employment is not evenly divided among the various industries. The services major industry division is the largest source of employment, with over 47 million workers, followed by wholesale and retail trade and manufacturing major industry divisions.

Among the industries covered in the *Career Guide,* wage and salary employment ranged from 181,000 in cable and other pay television services to 11.2 million in educational services.

Three industries—educational services, health services, and eating and drinking places—together accounted for about 30 million jobs, or nearly a quarter of the nation's employment.

TABLE 4

Wage and Salary Employment in Selected Industries, 1998, and Projected Change, 1998 to 2008

(Employment in thousands)

Industry	1998 Employment	1998 Percent Distribution	2008 Employment	1998-2008 Employment Change	1998-2008 Percent Change
All industries	128,008	100.0	147,543	19,535	15.3
Goods-producing industries	27,506	21.5	27,951	445	1.6
Agriculture, forestry, and fishing	2,159	1.7	2,257	98	4.6
Agricultural services	1,005	0.8	1,251	246	24.5
Agricultural production	1,106	0.9	968	-138	-12.5
Mining	590	0.5	475	-115	-19.4
Oil and gas extraction	339	0.3	283	-56	-16.7
Mining and quarrying	251	0.2	192	-59	-23.2
Construction	5,985	4.7	6,535	550	9.2
Manufacturing	18,772	14.7	18,684	-88	-0.5
Electronics manufacturing	1,564	1.2	1,701	137	8.8
Food processing	1,686	1.3	1,721	35	2.1
Printing and publishing	1,564	1.2	1,545	-19	-1.3
Motor vehicle and equipment manufacturing	990	0.7	940	50	-5.0
Chemicals manufacturing, except drugs	764	0.6	734	-30	-3.9
Apparel and other textile products manufacturing	763	0.6	586	-178	-23.3
Textile mill products manufacturing	598	0.5	501	-97	-16.2
Aerospace manufacturing	524	0.4	656	132	25.2
Drug manufacturing	279	0.2	308	29	10.7
Steel manufacturing	232	0.2	177	-55	-23.7

(continues)

Industry	1998 Employment	Percent Distribution	2008 Employment	1998-2008 Employment Change	Percent Change
Service-producing industries	100,501	78.5	119,590	19,089	19.0
Transportation, communications, and public utilities	6,600	5.2	7,540	940	14.3
Trucking and warehousing....................	1,745	1.4	1,944	199	11.4
Air transportation	1,183	0.9	1,400	217	18.3
Telecommunications	1,042	0.8	1,285	244	23.4
Public utilities	855	0.7	822	-33	-3.8
Radio and television broadcasting	247	0.1	253	6	2.5
Cable and other pay TV services	181	0.1	230	49	27.0
Wholesale and retail trade	29,128	22.8	32,693	3,565	12.2
Eating and drinking places	7,760	6.1	9,082	1,322	17.0
Wholesale trade	6,831	5.3	7,330	499	7.3
Department, clothing, and variety stores	3,872	3.0	4,101	228	5.9
Grocery stores	3,066	2.4	3,240	174	5.7
Motor vehicle dealers	1,145	0.9	1,277	132	11.6
Finance, insurance, and real estate	7,407	5.8	8,367	960	13.0
Insurance..	2,344	1.8	2,576	233	9.9
Banking	2,042	1.6	2,100	58	2.8
Securities and commodities	645	0.5	900	255	39.6
Services	47,528	37.1	60,445	12,917	27.2
Educational services	11,175	8.7	12,885	1,680	15.3
Health services	10,829	8.5	13,614	2,785	25.7
Personnel supply services	3,230	2.5	4,623	1,393	43.1
Social services...................................	2,039	1.6	2,878	839	41.1
Hotels and other lodging places	1,776	1.4	2,088	312	17.6
Amusement and recreation services	1,601	1.3	2,108	507	31.7
Computer and data processing services	1,599	1.2	3,471	1,872	117.1
Management and public relations services	1,034	0.8	1,500	466	45.1
Child-care services	605	0.5	800	196	32.3
Motion picture production and distribution	270	0.2	316	46	16.9
Advertising	268	0.2	323	55	20.5
Government	9,838	7.7	10,545	707	7.2
State and local government	7,152	5.6	7,996	844	11.8
Federal government	1,819	1.4	1,655	-164	-9.0

Although workers of all ages are employed in each industry, certain industries tend to possess workers of distinct age groups. For the reasons mentioned above, retail trade employs a relatively high proportion of younger workers to fill part-time and temporary positions. The manufacturing sector, on the other hand, has a relatively high median age because many jobs in the sector require a number of years to learn and rely on skills that do not easily transfer to other firms. Also, manu-facturing employment has been declining, providing fewer opportunities for younger workers to get jobs. As a result, almost one-third of the workers in retail trade were 24 years of age or younger, whereas only 10 percent of workers in manufacturing were 24 or younger. Table 5 contrasts the age distribution of workers in all industries with the distributions in retail trade and manufacturing.

TABLE 5

Percent Distribution of Industry Sector Employment by Age Group, 1998

Age Group	All Industries	Retail Trade	Manu-facturing
Total	100.0	100.0	100.0
16-24	15.0	32.5	9.9
25-54	72.3	56.9	78.2
55 and older	12.7	10.6	11.8

Employment in some industries is concentrated in one region of the country, and job opportunities in these industries should be best in the States in which their establishments are located. Such industries are often located near a source of raw materials upon which the industries rely. For example, oil and gas extraction jobs are concentrated in Texas, Louisiana, and Oklahoma; many textile mill products manufacturing jobs are found in North Carolina, Georgia, and South Carolina; and a significant proportion of motor vehicle and equipment manufacturing jobs are located in Michigan. On the other hand, some industries—such as grocery stores and educational services—have jobs distributed throughout the nation, reflecting population density in different areas.

Occupations in the Industry

As mentioned above, the occupations found in each industry depend on the types of services provided or goods produced. For example, construction companies require skilled trades workers to build and renovate buildings, so these companies employ a large number of carpenters, electricians, plumbers, painters, and sheet metal workers. Other occupations common to the construction sector include construction equipment operators and mechanics, installers, and repairers. Retail trade, on the other hand, displays and sells manufactured goods to consumers, so this sector hires numerous sales clerks and other workers, including nearly 5 out of 6 cashiers. Table 6 shows the major industry divisions and the occupational groups which predominate in the division.

TABLE 6

Industry Divisions and Largest Occupational Concentration, 1998

Industry Division	Largest Occupational Group	Percent of Wage and Salary Jobs
Agriculture, forestry, and fishing	Agriculture and related	78.8
Mining	Precision production	44.0
Construction	Precision production	55.5
Manufacturing	Operators, fabricators, and laborers	45.0
Transportation, communications, and public utilities	Operators, fabricators, and laborers	33.0
Wholesale and retail trade	Marketing and sales	32.7
Finance, insurance, and real estate	Administrative support	44.8
Services	Professional specialty	28.4
Government	Administrative support	26.1

The nation's occupational distribution clearly is influenced by its industrial structure, yet there are many occupations, such as general manager or secretary, which are found in all industries. In fact, some of the largest occupations in the U.S. economy are dispersed across many industries. Because nearly every industry relies on administrative support, for example, this occupational group is the largest in the nation (see Table 7). Other large occupational groups include service occupations, professional specialty workers, and operators, fabricators, and laborers.

TABLE 7

Total Employment in Broad Occupational Groups, 1998 and Projected Change, 1998-2008 (Employment in Thousands)

Occupational Group	1998 Employment	1998-2008 Percent Change
Total, all occupations	140,514	14.4
Executive, administrative, and managerial	14,770	16.4
Professional specialty	19,802	27.0
Technicians and related support	4,949	22.2
Marketing and sales	15,341	14.9
Administrative support, including clerical	24,461	9.0
Services	22,548	17.1
Agriculture, forestry, fishing, and related	4,435	1.6
Precision production, craft, and repair	15,619	8.0
Operators, fabricators, and laborers	18,588	9.4

Training and Advancement

Workers prepare for employment in many ways, but the most fundamental form of job training in the United States is a high school education. Fully 87 percent of the nation's workforce possessed a high school diploma or its equivalent in 1998. As the premium placed on education in today's economy increases, workers are responding by pursuing additional training. In 1998, 28 percent of the nation's workforce had some college or an associate's degree, while an additional 27 percent continued in their studies and attained a bachelor's degree or higher. In addition to these types of formal education, other sources of qualifying training include formal company training, informal on-the-job training, correspondence courses, the Armed Forces, and friends, relatives, and other nonwork-related training.

The unique combination of training required to succeed in each industry is determined largely by the industry's occupational composition. For example, machine operators in manufacturing generally need little formal education after high school, but sometimes complete considerable on-the-job training. These requirements by major industry division are clearly demonstrated in Table 8. Workers with no more than a high school diploma comprised about 67 percent of all workers in agriculture, forestry, and fishing; 65 percent in construction; 55 percent in manufacturing; and 57 percent in wholesale and retail trade. On the other hand, workers who had acquired at least some training at the college level comprised 73 percent of all workers in government; 69 percent in finance, insurance, and real estate; and 63 percent in services. Tables 9 and 10 provide further illustration of how greatly industries vary in their training requirements, which show industries having the highest percentages of college graduates and workers without education beyond high school.

TABLE 8

Percent Distribution of Highest Grade Completed or Degree Received by Industry Division, 1998

Industry Division	Bachelor's Degree or Higher	Some College or Associate Degree	High School Graduate or Equivalent	Less Than 12 Years or No Diploma
Agriculture, forestry, and fishing	13	20	34	33
Mining	24	22	39	15
Construction	10	25	44	21
Manufacturing	21	24	40	15
Transportation, communications, and public utilities	20	33	38	9
Wholesale and retail trade	14	29	37	20
Finance, insurance, and real estate	37	32	27	4
Services	39	24	28	9
Government, public administration	37	36	25	2

TABLE 9

Industries with the Highest Percentage of Workers Who Have a Bachelor's Degree or Higher, 1998

Industry	Percent
Management and public relations services	68.6
Securities and commodities	64.9
Elementary and secondary schools	62.8
Legal services	62.5
Accounting and auditing services	62.3

TABLE 10

Industries with the Highest Percentage of Workers Who Have 12 Years or Less of Schooling or No Diploma, 1998

Industry	Percent
Meat products processing	79.5
Apparel and other finished textile products manufacturing	74.4
Private households	74.4
Lumber and wood products manufacturing	74.2
Services to dwellings and other buildings	73.2
Agricultural production, crops	73.1

©2001 • JIST Works • Indianapolis, IN

Education and training are also important factors in the variety of advancement paths found in different industries. In general, workers who complete additional on-the-job training or education help their chances of being promoted. In much of the manufacturing sector, for example, production workers who receive training in management and computer skills increase their likelihood of being promoted to supervisors. Other factors which may figure prominently in the industries covered in the *Career Guide* include the size of the establishment or company, institutionalized career tracks, and the skills and aptitude of each worker. Each industry has some unique advancement paths, so persons who seek jobs in particular industries should be aware of how these paths may later shape their careers.

Earnings

Like other characteristics, earnings differ from industry to industry, the result of a highly complicated process that relies on a number of factors. For example, earnings may vary due to the occupations in the industry, average hours worked, geographical location, industry profits, union affiliation, and educational requirements. In general, wages are highest in metropolitan areas to compensate for the higher cost of living. And, as would be expected, industries that employ relatively few unskilled minimum-wage or part-time workers tend to have higher earnings.

A good illustration of these differences is shown by the earnings of production and nonsupervisory workers in coal mining, which averaged $858 a week in 1998, and those in eating and drinking places, where the weekly average was $162. These differences are so large because the coal mining industry employs a relatively highly skilled, highly unionized workforce, while eating and drinking places employ many relatively lower skilled, part-time workers, few of whom belong to unions. In addition, many workers in eating and drinking places are able to supplement their low wages with money they receive as tips, which are not included in the industry wages data. Table 11 highlights the industries with the highest and lowest average weekly earnings. Because these data exclude supervisors, they generally are lower than the average earnings for all workers in a given industry.

TABLE 11

Average Weekly Earnings of Nongovernment Production or Nonsupervisory Workers in Selected Industries, 1998

Industry	Earnings
All industries	$442
Industries with high earnings	
Coal mining	858
Railroad transportation	845
Aerospace manufacturing	845
Public utilities	843
Steel manufacturing	822
Computer and data processing services	815
Engineering services	810
Securities and commodities	800
Motion picture production and services	789
Motor vehicle production	780
Industries with low earnings	
Help supply services	330
Nursing and personal care services	318
Apparel and other textile products manufacturing	318
Hotels and other lodging places	279
Grocery stores	276
Amusement and recreation services	258
General merchandise stores	256
Child-care services	237
Apparel and accessory stores	226
Eating and drinking places	162

Employee benefits, once a minor addition to wages and salaries, continue to grow in diversity and cost. In addition to traditional benefits—including paid vacations, life and health insurance, and pensions—many employers now offer various benefits to accommodate the needs of a changing labor force. Such benefits are child care, employee assistance programs that provide counseling for personal problems, and wellness programs that encourage exercise, stress management, and self-improvement. Benefits vary among occupational groups, full- and part-time workers, public and private sector workers, regions, unionized and nonunionized workers, and small and large establishments. Data indicate that full-time workers and those in medium-size and large establishments—those with 100 or more workers—receive better benefits than part-time workers and those in smaller establishments.

Union affiliation may also play a role in earnings and benefits. In 1998, about 15 percent of workers throughout the nation were union members or covered by union contracts. As Table 12 demonstrates, union affiliation of workers varies widely by industry. Over a third of the workers in government and transportation, communications, and public utilities are union members or are covered by union contracts, compared to less than 4 percent in finance, insurance, and real estate and agriculture, forestry, and fishing.

TABLE 12

Percent of Workers Who Are Union Members or Covered by Union Contracts by Industry Division, 1998

Industry Division	Union Members Or Covered by Union Contracts
Total, all industries	15.4
Government, public administration	37.5
Transportation, communications, and public utilities	33.7
Construction	19.8
Manufacturing	16.8
Services	15.4
Mining	13.6
Wholesale and retail trade	5.8
Finance, insurance, and real estate	3.4
Agriculture, forestry, and fishing	2.3

Outlook

Total employment in the United States is projected to increase about 15 percent over the 1998-2008 period. Employment growth, however, is only one source of job openings; the total number of openings provided by any industry depends on its current employment level, its growth rate, and its need to replace workers who leave their jobs. Throughout the economy, in fact, replacement needs will create more job openings than employment growth. Employment size is a major determinant of job openings—larger industries generally provide more openings. The occupational composition of an industry is another factor. Industries with a high concentration of professional, technical, and other jobs that require more formal education—occupations in which workers tend to leave their jobs less frequently—generally have fewer openings resulting from replacement needs. On the other hand, industries with a high concentration of service, laborer, and other jobs that require little formal education and have lower wages generally have more replacement openings because these workers are more likely to leave their occupations.

Employment growth is determined largely by changes in the demand for the goods and services produced by an industry, worker productivity, and foreign competition. Each industry is affected by a different set of variables that impacts the number and composition of jobs that will be available. Even within an industry, employment in different occupations may grow at different rates. For example, changes in technology, production methods, and business practices in an industry might eliminate some jobs, while creating others. Some industries may be growing rapidly overall, yet opportunities for workers in occupations that are adversely affected by technological change could be stagnant. Similarly, employment of some occupations may be declining in the economy as a whole, yet may be increasing in a rapidly growing industry.

As shown in Table 4, employment growth rates over the next decade will vary widely among industries. Employment in goods-producing industries will increase slightly, as growth in construction and agriculture, forestry, and fishing is expected to be offset by declining employment in mining and manufacturing. Growth in construction employment will be driven by new factory construction as existing facilities are modernized; by new school construction, reflecting growth in the school-age population; and by infrastructure improvements, such as road and bridge construction. Overall employment in agriculture, forestry, and fishing will grow more slowly than average, with almost all new jobs occurring in the rapidly growing agricultural services industry—which includes landscaping, farm management, veterinary, soil preparation, and crop services. Employment in mining is expected to decline, due to the spread of labor-saving technology and increasing reliance on foreign sources of energy. Manufacturing employment also will decline slightly, as improvements in production technology and rising imports eliminate many production occupations. Apparel manufacturing is projected to lose about 178,000 jobs over the 1998-2008 period—more than any other manufacturing industry—due primarily to increasing imports. Some manufacturing industries with strong domestic markets and export potential, however, are expected to experience increases in employment. The drug manufacturing and aerospace manufacturing industries are two examples. Sales of drugs are expected to increase with the rise in the population, particularly the elderly, and the availability of new drugs on the market. An increase in air traffic, coupled with the need to replace aging aircraft will generate strong sales for commercial aircraft. Both industries have large export markets.

Growth in overall employment will result primarily from growth in service-producing industries over the 1998-2008 period, almost all of which are expected to witness increasing employment. Rising employment in these industries will be driven by services industries—the largest and fastest growing major industry sector—which is projected to provide more than 2 out of 3 new jobs across the nation. Health, education, and business services will account for almost 9 million of these new jobs. In addition, employment in the nation's fastest growing industry—computer and data processing services—is expected to more than double, adding another 1.8 million jobs. Job growth in the services sector will result from overall population growth, the rise in the elderly and school age population, and the trend toward contracting out for computer, personnel, and other business services.

Wholesale and retail trade is expected to add an additional 3.6 million jobs over the coming decade. Nearly 500,000 of these jobs will arise in wholesale trade, driven mostly by growth in trade and the overall economy. Retail trade is expected to add 3 million jobs over the 1998-2008 period, resulting largely from a greater population and increased personal income levels. Although most retail stores are expected to add employees, nonstore retailers will experience the fastest growth rate—55 percent—as electronic commerce and mail order sales account for an increasing portion of retail sales. Eating and drinking places will have the largest number of openings, over 1.3 million.

Employment in transportation, communications, and public utilities is projected to increase by nearly 940,000 new jobs. The telecommunications industry will have the biggest increase—244,000 jobs. Strong demand for new telecommunications services, such as Internet and wireless communications, will lead to an expansion of the telecommunications infrastructure and provide strong employment growth. Trucking and air transportation are expected to generate over 400,000 jobs. Trucking industry growth will be fueled by growth in the volume of goods that need to be shipped as the economy expands. Air transportation will expand as consumer and business demand increases, reflecting a rising population and increased business activity. Finally, while radio and television broadcasting will show little employment growth due to consolidations in the industry, cable and other pay television companies will increase by 27 percent as they upgrade their systems to deliver a wider array of communication and programming services.

Overall employment growth in finance, insurance, and real estate is expected to be around 13 percent, with close to 1 million jobs added by 2008. Securities and commodities will be the fastest growing industry in this sector, adding over 250,000 jobs. A growing interest in investing and the rising popularity of 401(k) and other pension plans are fueling increases in this industry. In contrast, the largest industry in this sector, banking, will grow by only 2.8 percent, or 58,000 jobs, as technological advances and the increasing use of electronic banking reduce the need for large administrative support staffs. Nondepository institutions—including personal and business credit institutions, as well as mortgage banks—are expected to grow at a rapid rate, and insurance will also expand, increasing by 232,000 jobs.

All 707,000 new government jobs are expected to arise in state and local government, reflecting growth in the population and its demand for public services. In contrast, the federal government is expected to lose more than 160,000 jobs over the 1998-2008 period, as efforts continue to cut costs by contracting out services and giving States more responsibility for administering federally funded programs.

In sum, recent changes in the economy are having far-reaching and complex effects on employment in each of the industries covered in the *Career Guide to Industries*. Jobseekers should be aware of these changes, keeping alert for developments that can affect job opportunities in industries and the variety of occupations which are found in each industry. For more detailed information on specific occupations, consult the 2000-2001 edition of the *Occupational Outlook Handbook*, which provides information on 250 occupations. (Note that both books mentioned above are available from JIST.)

Details on 500 Major Jobs: Earnings, Projected Growth, Education Required, Unemployment Rates, and Other Details

Comments

The table that follows provides a comprehensive picture of over 500 major jobs and makes it easier to compare the attributes of different occupations. The jobs are organized into clusters of related jobs, which helps you quickly identify occupations of interest.

In addition to statistics on employment and employment changes, growth rates, job openings, and self-employed workers, the table includes rankings from very low to very high for a number of variables. It also identifies the most significant source of education or training for each occupation.

The text that follows is from the U.S. Department of Labor and further explains the elements used in the table.

Selected Occupational Data, 1998 and Projected 2008

Every other year, the Bureau of Labor Statistics updates data on current and projected employment, employment change, self-employment, annual average job openings, and other characteristics for all national industry-occupation matrix occupations to ensure that the information is current.

The following table displays this data for 1998 and for projected 2008. Also presented are quartile rankings designating the relative magnitude of data for each detailed occupation. As a result, you can obtain specific data about several variables for any occupation and can use the rankings to determine how information for a specific occupation compares with that for other occupations.

Data Presented

Information about each variable's data source and potential use is presented below. The Occupational Employment Statistics (OES) survey and the Current Population Survey (CPS) provide almost all the employment data used in developing the 1998-2008 projections. These surveys also are the source of the other statistical information contained in the table.

Occupational data from the OES survey are not entirely comparable with those from the CPS because of differences in occupational classification systems, and differences in concepts and methods used in the two surveys. Information about worker characteristics that is based on CPS data is applied to industry-occupation matrix occupations based on judgments identifying the most comparable CPS occupations. Comparisons were excluded if they were based on CPS occupations with fewer than 50,000 workers in 1998 or on other occupations for which the data appeared unreliable; data for CPS proxy occupations were substituted. Where possible, larger, closely related CPS occupations were chosen as proxies. For example, data for purchasing agents and buyers, not elsewhere classified, were used to represent purchasing agents and buyers of farm products. When a detailed occupation could not be identified, a summary occupational group was used. For example, data about all therapists were substituted for those about inhalation therapists.

Rankings for data categories identify the relative magnitude of variables in terms of the distribution of employment. For example, to rank the projected percent change in employment, 1998 employment and projected 1998-2008 percent change in employment data were assembled for each occupation. Each occupation's employment as a percent of 1998 total employment was calculated. The occupations were sorted by employment change in descending order and the cumulative percent of 1998 employment for each was determined. Occupations within the group accounting for less than 25 percent of total employment are designated "VH" for a very high growth rate. Similarly, occupations sorted by descending order of employment change accounting for 25 to 50 percent of employment are "H" (high); 50 to 75 percent, "L" (low); and 75 to 100 percent, "VL" (very low). Occupations were sorted by other data elements, and rankings were determined in the same manner.

Employment, 1998 and 2008. (Source: Bureau of Labor Statistics, national industry-occupation matrixes for 1998 and 2008.) Employment information is a useful starting point for assessing opportunities, because large occupations usually have more openings than small ones, regardless of growth or replacement rates. The data include jobs in all industries.

Employment change, 1998-2008, numeric. (Source: Bureau of Labor Statistics, national industry-occupation matrixes for 1998 and 2008.) Information on numerical change provides an absolute measure of projected job gains or losses.

Employment change, 1998-2008, percent. (Source: Bureau of Labor Statistics, national industry-occupation matrixes for 1998 and 2008.) The percent change in employment measures the rate of change. A rapidly growing occupation usually indicates favorable prospects for employment. Moreover, the high demand for workers in a rapidly growing occupation improves their chances for advancement and mobility. A modest employment growth in a large occupation can result in many more job openings than rapidly growing employment growth in a small occupation.

Percent self-employed, 1998. (Source: Bureau of Labor Statistics, national industry-occupation matrixes for 1998 and 2008.) Individuals who are interested in creating and managing their own business may find it important to know the percentage of self-employed workers. This percentage is calculated from CPS data about unincorporated, self-employed persons in their primary or secondary job who are included in industry-occupation matrix employment data. Unincorporated, self-employed persons work for earnings or fees in their own business and, unlike self-employed persons in businesses that are incorporated, do not receive a wage or salary.

Job openings due to growth plus total replacement needs, 1998-2008. (Source: Bureau of Labor Statistics, *Occupational Projections and Training Data,* 2000-01 Edition.) These data provide the broadest measure of opportunities and identify the total number of additional employees needed annually in an occupation. Growth is calculated using data on increases in occupational employment from national industry-occupation matrixes for 1998-2008. These replacements refer to all job openings, regardless of experience level, and reflect the normal movements in the labor force. If employment declines,

job openings due to growth are zero. Total replacement needs are calculated from 1995-96 CPS data. Data from CPS proxy occupations are used to estimate replacement needs for some matrix occupations.

Job openings due to growth plus net replacement needs, 1998-2008. (Source: Bureau of Labor Statistics, *Occupational Projections and Training Data,* 2000-01 Edition.) These data estimate the number of new workers needed annually in an occupation and, if training is required, measure minimum training needs. Growth is calculated using data on increases in occupational employment from national industry-occupation matrixes for 1998-2008. If employment declines, job openings due to growth are zero. These net replacement job openings typically are due to experienced workers leaving the occupation or the labor force. Net replacement needs are calculated from CPS data. Data from CPS proxy occupations estimate replacement needs for some matrix occupations.

Median annual earnings, 1998. (Source: 1998 Occupational Employment Statistics survey, with some exceptions. OES data are not available for government chief executives and legislators. OES data also are not available for private household workers; farm operators and managers; captains and other officers, fishing vessels. Estimates developed from 1998 Current Population Survey annual average data for wage and salary employees provide information for child care workers, private household; and cleaners and servants, private household.) The table uses median annual earnings of workers to compare earnings among different occupations.

Unemployment rate. (Source: Average of 1996-98 Current Population Survey data.) Some occupations are more susceptible to factors that result in unemployment: seasonality, fluctuations in economic conditions, and individual business failures. A high unemployment rate indicates that individuals in that occupation are more likely to become unemployed than are those in occupations with a low rate. Data from CPS proxy occupations are used to estimate unemployment rates for some matrix occupations.

Percent part-time. (Source: Average of 1996-98 Current Population Survey data.) Persons who prefer part-time work may want to know the proportion of employees who work fewer than 35 hours per week. Data from CPS proxy occupations are used to estimate the proportion of part-time workers for some matrix occupations.

Most significant source of education or training. (Source: Bureau of Labor Statistics.) Occupations are classified into 1 of 11 categories that describe the education or training needed by most workers to become fully qualified. The categories are first professional degree, doctoral degree, master's degree, work experience in an occupation requiring a bachelor's or higher degree, bachelor's degree, associate degree, postsecondary vocational training, work experience in a related occupation, long-term on-the-job training, moderate-term on-the-job training, and short-term on-the-job training. The following are definitions of these categories:

Occupations that require a first professional degree. The first professional degree is the minimum preparation required for entry into several professions, including law, medicine, dentistry, and the clergy. Completion of this academic program usually requires at least 2 years of full-time academic study beyond a bachelor's degree.

Occupations that generally require a doctoral degree. The doctoral degree also can be easily related to specific occupations. It normally requires at least 3 years of full-time academic work beyond the bachelor's degree.

Occupations that generally require a master's degree. Completion of a master's degree program usually requires 1 or 2 years of full-time study beyond the bachelor's degree.

Occupations that generally require work experience in an occupation requiring a bachelor's or higher degree. Most occupations in this category are managerial occupations that require experience in a related nonmanagerial occupation. Jobs in these occupations usually are filled with experienced staff who are promoted into a managerial position, such as engineers who advance to engineering manager. It is very difficult to become a judge without first working as a lawyer, or to become a personnel, training, or labor relations manager without first gaining experience as a specialist in one of these fields.

Occupations that generally require a bachelor's degree. This is a degree program requiring at least 4 but not more than 5 years of full-time academic work after high school. The bachelor's degree is considered the minimum requirement for most professional occupations, such as mechanical engineer, pharmacist, recreational therapist, and landscape architect.

Occupations that generally require an associate degree. Completion of this degree program usually requires at least 2 years of full-time academic work after high school. Most occupations in this category are health related, such as registered nurse, respiratory therapist, and radiologic technologist. Also included are science and mathematics technicians and paralegals.

Occupations that generally require completion of vocational training provided in postsecondary vocational schools. Workers normally qualify for jobs by completing vocational training programs or by taking job-related college courses that do not result in a degree. Some programs take less than a year to complete and lead to a certificate or diploma. Others last longer than a year, but less than 4 years. Occupations in this category include some that require only the completion of a training program (such as a travel agent) and those that require individuals to pass a licensing exam after completion of the program before they can work (such as barber and cosmetologist).

Occupations that generally require skills developed through work experience in a related occupation. Jobs in this category require skills and experience gained in another occupation; the category also includes occupations in which skills may be developed from hobbies or other activities besides current or past employment or from service in the Armed Forces. Among the

occupations are cost estimators, who generally need prior work experience in one of the construction trades; police detectives, who are selected based on their experience as police patrol officers; and lawn service managers, who may be hired based on their experience as groundskeepers.

Long-term on-the-job training. This category includes occupations that usually require more than 12 months of on-the-job training or combined work experience and formal classroom instruction before workers develop the skills needed for average job performance. Among these are such occupations as electrician, bricklayer, and machinist that normally require formal or informal apprenticeships lasting up to 4 years. Long-term on-the-job training also includes intensive occupation-specific, employer-sponsored programs that workers must successfully complete before they can begin work. These include fire and police academies and schools for air traffic controllers and flight attendants. In other occupations—insurance sales and securities sales, for example—trainees take formal courses, often provided at the job site, to prepare for the required licensing exams. Individuals undergoing training usually are considered employed in the occupation. This group of occupations also includes musicians, athletes, actors, and other entertainers—occupations that require natural ability that must be developed over several years.

Moderate-term on-the-job training. Workers can achieve average job performance after 1 to 12 months of combined job experience and informal training, which can include observing experienced workers. Individuals undergoing training normally are considered employed in the occupation. This type of training is found among occupations such as dental assistants, drywall installers and finishers, operating engineers, and machine operators. The training involves trainees watching experienced workers and asking questions. Trainees are given progressively more difficult assignments as they demonstrate their mastery of lower level skills.

Short-term on-the-job training. Included are occupations like cashier, bank teller, messenger, highway maintenance worker, and veterinary assistant. In these occupations, workers usually can achieve average job performance in just a few days or weeks by working with and observing experienced employees and by asking questions.

Using Ranked Information

The table consolidates 1998 and 2008 projected employment data and also provides comparisons of occupational data. It ranks information about current and projected employment, projected job openings, earnings, unemployment rates, and the proportion of part-time workers. Except for the unemployment and part-time categories, a high rating indicates a favorable assessment. A high rating for the unemployment rate is considered undesirable. Unemployment rates in construction occupations, however, are inflated by the nature of the industry and distort comparisons. Construction workers typically incur periods of unemployment after completing a project and before starting work on a new project.

The rating for the part-time category also should not be used routinely in assessing the desirability of employment because the assessment depends on the perspective of the user. For example, high school students may consider a large proportion of part-time work desirable because they normally prefer not to work full time. A recent college graduate or anyone seeking full-time employment may reach the opposite conclusion.

The data in the table have many potential uses. At times, users may want to know how a particular occupation—cashiers, for example—compares with others. The "VH" (very high) rankings in the table for the increase in the number of jobs and for both categories of job openings point out that many jobs are available, certainly a favorable rating. The "VL" (very low) ranking for earnings and "VH" (very high) for unemployment, however, are unfavorable in comparison with other occupations, and these characteristics detract from the desirability of employment in the occupation. The table also shows that cashiers require only short-term on-the-job training.

Some readers might wish to identify occupations with favorable characteristics that jobseekers can pursue through a specific type of training. For example, a student might be interested in a technical occupation but not care to obtain a four-year college degree. In another instance, a planner might wish to ensure that training programs provided by junior colleges in the area are consistent with the needs of the national labor market. To obtain appropriate information, both the student and the planner could examine information for occupations placed in the associate degree educational or training category.

Although the table contains a great deal of information useful for career guidance, information about occupation comparisons should be used as an aid, not a sole source of information for making career choices. After using the table to identify occupations with favorable prospects, individuals should obtain additional information from other sources such as the *Occupational Outlook Handbook*, the *Occupational Outlook Quarterly,* and local sources, if available. Consideration should be given to individual aptitudes and preferences, and alternative sources of training available in the local area should be investigated. An electronic version of the table is available on the Internet at ftp://146.142.4.23/pub/special.requests/ep/OPTDData/.

America's Top White-Collar Jobs

Occupational employment and job openings data, 1998-2008, and worker characteristics, 1998

(Numbers in thousands)

| 1998 Matrix Occupation | Employment | | Employment change, 1998-2008 | | | | Percent self-employed, 1998 | Annual average job openings due to growth and total replacement needs, 1998-2008 | |
| | | | Numeric | | Percent | | | | |
	1998	2008	Number	Rank	Number	Rank		Number	Rank
Total, all occupations	140,514	160,795	20,281	-	14.4	-	8.7	28,351	-
Executive, administrative, and managerial occupations	14,770	17,196	2,426	-	16.4	-	14.3	2,090	-
Managerial and administrative occupations	10,139	11,823	1,684	-	16.6	-	16.2	1,402	-
Administrative services managers	364	430	66	L	18.1	H	.0	47	L
Advertising, marketing, promotions, public relations, and sales managers	485	597	112	L	23.0	VH	2.5	89	L
Communication, transportation, and utilities operations managers	196	234	38	L	19.3	VH	.0	25	VL
Construction managers	270	308	38	L	14.0	L	16.6	33	VL
Education administrators	447	505	58	L	13.0	L	8.7	60	L
Engineering, natural science, and computer and information systems managers	326	468	142	H	43.5	VH	.0	54	L
Financial managers	693	791	97	L	14.0	L	.8	78	L
Food service and lodging managers[1]	595	691	97	L	16.3	H	35.0	139	L
Funeral directors and morticians[1]	28	32	4	VL	16.1	H	8.8	4	VL
General managers and top executives	3,362	3,913	551	VH	16.4	H	.0	421	VH
Government chief executives and legislators[1]	80	82	2	VL	2.8	VL	.0	6	VL
Human resources managers	230	274	45	L	19.4	VH	.5	33	VL
Industrial production managers	208	207	-2	VL	-.9	VL	.0	21	VL
Medical and health services managers	222	297	74	L	33.3	VH	6.3	31	VL
Postmasters and mail superintendents[1]	26	27	1	VL	3.0	VL	.0	3	VL
Property, real estate, and community association managers[1]	315	359	43	L	13.7	L	47.6	48	L
Purchasing managers	176	188	13	VL	7.1	VL	.1	25	VL
All other managers and administrators[1]	2,114	2,420	305	VH	14.4	H	54.9	284	H
Management support occupations	4,631	5,374	743	-	16.0	-	10.3	688	-
Accountants and auditors	1,080	1,202	122	L	11.3	L	13.2	130	L
Assessors and real estate appraisers	70	78	8	-	11.3	-	18.1	9	-
Assessors	22	25	3	VL	11.8	L	.0	2	VL
Real estate appraisers	48	53	5	VL	11.2	L	26.6	6	VL
Budget analysts	59	67	8	VL	13.7	L	.0	10	VL
Buyers and purchasing agents	371	396	25	-	6.7	-	6.4	79	-
Purchasing agents and buyers, farm[1]	29	30	1	VL	5.0	VL	13.0	5	VL
Purchasing agents, except wholesale, retail, and farm products	224	248	24	L	10.8	L	1.2	42	VL
Wholesale and retail buyers, except farm products	118	118	0	VL	-.4	VL	14.6	31	VL
Construction and building inspectors	68	79	11	VL	15.7	H	6.0	4	VL
Cost estimators	152	171	20	VL	13.0	L	.0	28	VL
Credit analysts	42	50	8	VL	19.9	VH	.0	7	VL
Employment interviewers, private or public employment service	66	74	8	VL	12.9	L	.0	14	VL
Human resources, training, and labor relations specialists	367	433	66	L	17.9	H	3.9	83	L
Inspectors and compliance officers, except construction	176	195	19	VL	10.5	L	3.0	20	VL
Insurance claims adjusters, appraisers, examiners, and investigators	239	284	45	-	18.0	-	4.7	21	-
Insurance claims adjusters, examiners, and investigators	229	272	43	-	18.7	-	4.9	20	-
Claims examiners, property and casualty insurance	49	55	6	VL	12.5	L	.0	4	VL
Insurance adjusters, examiners, and investigators	180	217	37	L	20.4	VH	6.2	16	VL
Insurance appraisers, auto damage	10	12	2	VL	16.0	H	.0	1	VL
Insurance underwriters	97	100	3	VL	2.7	VL	1.1	4	VL
Loan counselors and officers	227	276	48	L	21.2	VH	.0	40	VL
Management analysts[1]	344	442	98	L	28.4	VH	53.5	24	VL
Tax examiners, collectors, and revenue agents	62	66	3	VL	5.4	VL	.0	5	VL
Tax preparers	79	95	15	VL	19.3	VH	33.1	14	VL
All other management support workers[1]	1,130	1,366	236	H	20.9	VH	4.4	199	H

[1] One or more Current Population Survey (CPS) proxy occupations are used to estimate CPS based data.
[2] Current Population Survey data are used to estimate median weekly earnings ranking.
[3] Bachelor's degree or higher.

NOTE: Rankings are based on employment in all detailed occupations in the National Industry-Occupation Matrix. For details, see "Data presented" section of text. Codes for describing the ranked variables are: VH = Very high, H = High, L = Low, VL = Very low, n. a. = Data not available. A dash indicates data are not applicable.

Occupational employment and job openings data, 1998-2008, and worker characteristics, 1998

(Numbers in thousands)

Annual average job openings due to growth and net replacement needs, 1998-2008		Median annual earnings		Ranking of:		Most significant source of education or training	1998 Matrix Occupation
Number	Rank	Dollars	Rank	Unemployment rate	Percent part-time		
5,462	-	-	-	-	-	-	**Total, all occupations**
511	-	-	-	-	-	-	**Executive, administrative, and managerial occupations**
348	-	-	-	-	-	-	Managerial and administrative occupations
13	L	44,370	VH	VL	L	Work experience plus degree[3]	Administrative services managers
18	L	57,300	VH	L	VL	Work experience plus degree[3]	Advertising, marketing, promotions, public relations, and sales managers
7	VL	52,810	VH	VL	L	Work experience plus degree[3]	Communication, transportation, and utilities operations managers
9	VL	47,610	VH	VL	L	Bachelor's degree	Construction managers
17	L	60,400	VH	VL	H	Work experience plus degree[3]	Education administrators
20	L	75,330	VH	VL	L	Work experience plus degree[3]	Engineering, natural science, and computer and information systems managers
21	L	55,070	VH	VL	VL	Work experience plus degree[3]	Financial managers
20	L	26,700	H	L	H	Related work experience	Food service and lodging managers[1]
1	VL	35,040	VH	VL	L	Associate degree	Funeral directors and morticians[1]
114	VH	55,890	VH	VL	L	Work experience plus degree[3]	General managers and top executives
2	VL	n.a.	-	VL	L	Work experience plus degree[3]	Government chief executives and legislators[1]
10	VL	49,010	VH	L	VL	Work experience plus degree[3]	Human resources managers
4	VL	56,320	VH	VL	L	Bachelor's degree	Industrial production managers
11	L	48,870	VH	L	H	Work experience plus degree[3]	Medical and health services managers
1	VL	44,730	VH	VL	L	Related work experience	Postmasters and mail superintendents[1]
9	VL	29,930	H	L	H	Bachelor's degree	Property, real estate, and community association managers[1]
5	VL	41,830	VH	VL	VL	Work experience plus degree[3]	Purchasing managers
68	H	49,300	VH	VL	L	Work experience plus degree[3]	All other managers and administrators[1]
162	-	-	-	-	-	-	Management support occupations
29	L	37,860	VH	VL	L	Bachelor's degree	Accountants and auditors
2	-	-	-	-	-	-	Assessors and real estate appraisers
1	VL	29,830	H	VL	L	Bachelor's degree	Assessors
2	VL	40,290	VH	VL	H	Bachelor's degree	Real estate appraisers
2	VL	44,950	VH	VL	L	Bachelor's degree	Budget analysts
12	-	-	-	-	-	-	Buyers and purchasing agents
1	VL	32,070	H	L	L	Bachelor's degree	Purchasing agents and buyers, farm[1]
8	VL	38,040	VH	L	L	Bachelor's degree	Purchasing agents, except wholesale, retail, and farm products
3	VL	31,560	H	L	H	Bachelor's degree	Wholesale and retail buyers, except farm products
3	VL	37,540	VH	L	L	Related work experience	Construction and building inspectors
4	VL	40,590	VH	L	H	Bachelor's degree	Cost estimators
2	VL	35,590	VH	VL	L	Bachelor's degree	Credit analysts
3	VL	29,800	H	L	L	Bachelor's degree	Employment interviewers, private or public employment service
16	L	37,710	VH	L	L	Bachelor's degree	Human resources, training, and labor relations specialists
5	VL	36,820	VH	VL	VL	Related work experience	Inspectors and compliance officers, except construction
8	-	-	-	-	-	-	Insurance claims adjusters, appraisers, examiners, and investigators
8	-	-	-	-	-	-	Insurance claims adjusters, examiners, and investigators
1	VL	40,110	VH	VL	L	Bachelor's degree	Claims examiners, property and casualty insurance
7	VL	38,290	VH	VL	L	Long-term on-the-job	Insurance adjusters, examiners, and investigators
0	VL	40,000	VH	VL	L	Long-term on-the-job	Insurance appraisers, auto damage
3	VL	38,710	VH	L	H	Bachelor's degree	Insurance underwriters
10	VL	35,340	VH	VL	L	Bachelor's degree	Loan counselors and officers
12	L	49,470	VH	L	H	Work experience plus degree[3]	Management analysts[1]
2	VL	39,540	VH	VL	VL	Bachelor's degree	Tax examiners, collectors, and revenue agents
3	VL	27,960	H	VL	L	Moderate-term on-the-job	Tax preparers
46	H	37,860	VH	VL	L	Bachelor's degree	All other management support workers[1]

[1] One or more Current Population Survey (CPS) proxy occupations are used to estimate CPS based data.

[2] Current Population Survey data are used to estimate median weekly earnings ranking.

[3] Bachelor's degree or higher.

NOTE: Rankings are based on employment in all detailed occupations in the National Industry-Occupation Matrix. For details, see "Data presented" section of text. Codes for describing the ranked variables are: VH = Very high, H = High, L = Low, VL = Very low, n. a. = Data not available. A dash indicates data are not applicable.

Occupational employment and job openings data, 1998-2008, and worker characteristics, 1998

(Numbers in thousands)

1998 Matrix Occupation	Employment		Employment change, 1998-2008				Per-cent self-emp-loyed, 1998	Annual average job openings due to growth and total replacement needs, 1998-2008	
			Numeric		Percent				
	1998	2008	Number	Rank	Number	Rank		Number	Rank
Professional specialty occupations	19,802	25,145	5,343	-	26.9	-	9.9	2,799	-
Engineers	1,462	1,752	290	-	19.8	-	3.4	133	-
Aerospace engineers	53	58	5	VL	8.8	L	.8	2	VL
Chemical engineers[1]	48	53	5	VL	9.5	L	2.3	4	VL
Civil engineers	195	236	41	L	20.9	VH	6.1	21	VL
Electrical and electronics engineers	357	450	93	L	25.9	VH	4.4	30	VL
Industrial engineers, except safety engineers	126	142	16	VL	12.8	L	2.6	13	VL
Materials engineers	20	21	2	VL	9.0	L	3.7	2	VL
Mechanical engineers	220	256	36	L	16.4	H	2.0	9	VL
Mining engineers, including mine safety engineers[1]	4	4	-1	VL	-12.6	VL	.0	0	VL
Nuclear engineers[1]	12	12	1	VL	5.8	VL	.0	1	VL
Petroleum engineers[1]	12	12	0	VL	-3.6	VL	15.0	1	VL
All other engineers[1]	415	509	94	L	22.6	VH	2.6	51	L
Architects and surveyors	163	185	23	-	13.8	-	25.1	17	-
Architects, except landscape and naval	99	118	19	VL	18.9	H	29.9	8	VL
Landscape architects	22	25	3	VL	14.5	H	40.7	2	VL
Surveyors, cartographers, and photogrammetrists[1]	41	42	1	VL	1.4	VL	5.4	7	VL
Life scientists	173	219	45	-	26.2	-	4.4	19	-
Agricultural and food scientists[1]	21	24	2	VL	10.9	L	17.4	2	VL
Biological scientists	81	109	28	L	35.0	VH	.9	10	VL
Conservation scientists and foresters[1]	39	46	7	VL	17.9	H	5.5	3	VL
Medical scientists	31	39	8	VL	24.6	VH	3.4	3	VL
All other life scientists	1	1	0	VL	16.5	H	.0	0	VL
Computer, mathematical, and operations research occupations	1,653	3,182	1,529	-	92.4	-	7.1	404	-
Actuaries[1]	16	17	1	VL	7.1	VL	14.2	2	VL
Computer systems analysts, engineers, and scientists	1,530	3,052	1,522	-	99.4	-	7.4	395	-
Computer engineers and scientists	914	1,858	944	-	103.3	-	4.7	241	-
Computer engineers	299	622	323	VH	107.9	VH	10.8	81	L
Computer support specialists	429	869	439	VH	102.3	VH	.0	113	L
Database administrators	87	155	67	L	77.2	VH	.0	19	VL
All other computer scientists	97	212	115	L	117.5	VH	11.0	28	VL
Systems analysts	617	1,194	577	VH	93.6	VH	11.5	154	L
Statisticians[1]	17	17	0	VL	2.3	VL	5.4	2	VL
Mathematicians and all other mathematical scientists[1]	14	13	-1	VL	-5.5	VL	.0	1	VL
Operations research analysts	76	83	7	VL	8.7	L	.7	5	VL
Physical scientists	200	229	29	-	14.6	-	4.0	17	-
Atmospheric scientists[1]	8	10	1	VL	14.6	H	.0	1	VL
Chemists	96	110	13	VL	13.9	L	1.6	8	VL
Geologists, geophysicists, and oceanographers[1]	44	51	7	VL	15.5	H	13.3	4	VL
Physicists and astronomers[1]	18	18	0	VL	2.2	VL	1.6	1	VL
All other physical scientists[1]	33	41	8	VL	22.7	VH	1.0	3	VL
Religious workers	304	356	53	-	17.2	-	1.2	32	-
Clergy	149	169	20	VL	13.4	L	.0	14	VL
Directors, religious activities and education[1]	112	140	28	L	25.1	VH	.0	13	VL
All other religious workers[1]	43	48	5	VL	10.7	L	8.7	4	VL
Social scientists	321	365	44	-	13.7	-	33.1	45	-
Economists and marketing research analysts	70	83	13	VL	18.4	H	25.7	12	VL
Psychologists	166	185	19	VL	11.4	L	49.8	21	VL
Urban and regional planners[1]	35	41	6	VL	17.4	H	.0	5	VL
All other social scientists[1]	50	56	6	VL	12.7	L	10.9	7	VL
Social and recreation workers	1,303	1,797	494	-	37.8	-	1.3	265	-
Recreation workers	241	287	46	L	19.2	H	.3	44	L
Residential counselors	190	278	88	L	46.3	VH	.0	28	VL
Social and human service assistants	268	410	141	H	52.7	VH	.0	92	L
Social workers	604	822	218	H	36.1	VH	2.6	103	L
Lawyers and judicial workers	752	871	119	-	15.8	-	32.4	41	-

[1] One or more Current Population Survey (CPS) proxy occupations are used to estimate CPS based data.

[2] Current Population Survey data are used to estimate median weekly earnings ranking.

[3] Bachelor's degree or higher.

NOTE: Rankings are based on employment in all detailed occupations in the National Industry-Occupation Matrix. For details, see "Data presented" section of text. Codes for describing the ranked variables are: VH = Very high, H = High, L = Low, VL = Very low, n. a. = Data not available. A dash indicates data are not applicable.

Occupational employment and job openings data, 1998-2008, and worker characteristics, 1998

(Numbers in thousands)

Annual average job openings due to growth and net replacement needs, 1998-2008		Median annual earnings		Ranking of:		Most significant source of education or training	1998 Matrix Occupation
Number	Rank	Dollars	Rank	Unemployment rate	Percent part-time		
915	-	-	-	-	-	-	**Professional specialty occupations**
61	-	-	-	-	-	-	Engineers
1	VL	66,950	VH	VL	VL	Bachelor's degree	Aerospace engineers
2	VL	64,760	VH	VL	VL	Bachelor's degree	Chemical engineers[1]
8	VL	53,450	VH	VL	VL	Bachelor's degree	Civil engineers
17	L	62,260	VH	VL	VL	Bachelor's degree	Electrical and electronics engineers
3	VL	52,610	VH	VL	VL	Bachelor's degree	Industrial engineers, except safety engineers
1	VL	57,970	VH	VL	VL	Bachelor's degree	Materials engineers
8	VL	53,290	VH	VL	VL	Bachelor's degree	Mechanical engineers
0	VL	56,090	VH	VL	VL	Bachelor's degree	Mining engineers, including mine safety engineers[1]
0	VL	71,310	VH	VL	VL	Bachelor's degree	Nuclear engineers[1]
0	VL	74,260	VH	VL	VL	Bachelor's degree	Petroleum engineers[1]
21	L	61,060	VH	VL	VL	Bachelor's degree	All other engineers[1]
5	-	-	-	-	-	-	Architects and surveyors
3	VL	47,710	VH	VL	L	Bachelor's degree	Architects, except landscape and naval
1	VL	37,930	VH	VL	L	Bachelor's degree	Landscape architects
1	VL	37,640	VH	L	L	Bachelor's degree	Surveyors, cartographers, and photogrammetrists[1]
9	-	-	-	-	-	-	Life scientists
1	VL	42,340	VH	VL	L	Bachelor's degree	Agricultural and food scientists[1]
5	VL	46,140	VH	VL	L	Doctoral degree	Biological scientists
2	VL	42,750	VH	VL	L	Bachelor's degree	Conservation scientists and foresters[1]
2	VL	50,410	VH	VL	L	Doctoral degree	Medical scientists
0	VL	41,320	VH	VL	L	Doctoral degree	All other life scientists
166	-	-	-	-	-	-	Computer, mathematical, and operations research occupations
0	VL	65,560	VH	VL	L	Bachelor's degree	Actuaries[1]
163	-	-	-	-	-	-	Computer systems analysts, engineers, and scientists
101	-	-	-	-	-	-	Computer engineers and scientists
34	H	61,910	VH	VL	L	Bachelor's degree	Computer engineers
47	H	37,120	VH	VL	L	Associate degree	Computer support specialists
8	VL	47,980	VH	VL	L	Bachelor's degree	Database administrators
12	L	46,670	VH	VL	L	Bachelor's degree	All other computer scientists
62	H	52,180	VH	VL	L	Bachelor's degree	Systems analysts
0	VL	48,540	VH	VL	L	Master's degree	Statisticians[1]
0	VL	49,120	VH	VL	L	Master's degree	Mathematicians and all other mathematical scientists[1]
3	VL	49,070	VH	VL	VL	Master's degree	Operations research analysts
8	-	-	-	-	-	-	Physical scientists
0	VL	54,430	VH	VL	L	Bachelor's degree	Atmospheric scientists[1]
3	VL	46,220	VH	VL	L	Bachelor's degree	Chemists
2	VL	53,890	VH	VL	L	Bachelor's degree	Geologists, geophysicists, and oceanographers[1]
1	VL	73,240	VH	VL	L	Doctoral degree	Physicists and astronomers[1]
2	VL	48,990	VH	VL	L	Bachelor's degree	All other physical scientists[1]
11	-	-	-	-	-	-	Religious workers
5	VL	28,890	H	VL	H	First professional degree	Clergy
5	VL	25,040	H	L	H	Bachelor's degree	Directors, religious activities and education[1]
1	VL	18,440	L	L	H	Bachelor's degree	All other religious workers[1]
11	-	-	-	-	-	-	Social scientists
3	VL	48,330	VH	VL	H	Bachelor's degree	Economists and marketing research analysts
5	VL	48,050	VH	VL	VH	Master's degree	Psychologists
1	VL	42,860	VH	VL	H	Master's degree	Urban and regional planners[1]
2	VL	38,990	VH	VL	H	Master's degree	All other social scientists[1]
75	-	-	-	-	-	-	Social and recreation workers
11	L	16,500	VL	L	H	Bachelor's degree	Recreation workers
13	L	18,840	L	VL	H	Bachelor's degree	Residential counselors
21	L	21,360	L	L	VH	Moderate-term on-the-job	Social and human service assistants
30	L	30,590	H	L	H	Bachelor's degree	Social workers
20	-	-	-	-	-	-	Lawyers and judicial workers

[1] One or more Current Population Survey (CPS) proxy occupations are used to estimate CPS based data.

[2] Current Population Survey data are used to estimate median weekly earnings ranking.

[3] Bachelor's degree or higher.

NOTE: Rankings are based on employment in all detailed occupations in the National Industry-Occupation Matrix. For details, see "Data presented" section of text. Codes for describing the ranked variables are: VH = Very high, H = High, L = Low, VL = Very low, n. a. = Data not available. A dash indicates data are not applicable.

Occupational employment and job openings data, 1998-2008, and worker characteristics, 1998
(Numbers in thousands)

1998 Matrix Occupation	Employment		Employment change, 1998-2008				Per-cent self-emp-loyed, 1998	Annual average job openings due to growth and total replacement needs, 1998-2008	
			Numeric		Percent				
	1998	2008	Number	Rank	Number	Rank		Number	Rank
Judges, magistrates, and other judicial workers[1]	71	73	2	VL	2.9	VL	.0	3	VL
Lawyers	681	798	117	L	17.2	H	35.8	38	VL
Teachers, librarians, and counselors	6,939	8,248	1,309	-	18.8	-	3.5	1,043	-
Teachers, preschool and kindergarten	529	645	116	-	21.9	-	1.0	61	-
Teachers, preschool	346	437	92	L	26.5	VH	1.5	42	VL
Teachers, kindergarten	184	208	25	L	13.4	L	.0	19	VL
Teachers, elementary school	1,754	1,959	205	H	11.7	L	.0	204	H
Teachers, secondary school	1,426	1,749	322	VH	22.6	VH	.0	134	L
Teachers, special education	406	543	137	H	33.8	VH	.0	37	VL
College and university faculty[1]	865	1,061	195	H	22.6	VH	.0	139	L
Other teachers and instructors	956	1,139	183	-	19.1	-	19.1	259	-
Farm and home management advisors	10	10	0	VL	-2.2	VL	.0	2	VL
Instructors and coaches, sports and physical training	359	460	102	L	28.4	VH	16.5	104	L
Adult and vocational education teachers	588	669	81	-	13.0	-	21.1	153	-
Instructors, adult (nonvocational) education	168	203	35	L	20.9	VH	20.5	46	L
Teachers and instructors, vocational education and training	420	466	46	L	11.0	L	21.3	106	L
All other teachers and instructors[1]	644	739	95	L	14.7	H	8.3	155	L
Librarians, archivists, curators, and related workers	175	186	10	-	5.8	-	.4	29	-
Archivists, curators, museum technicians, and conservators[1]	23	26	3	VL	12.6	L	3.1	4	VL
Librarians	152	159	7	VL	4.8	VL	.0	25	VL
Counselors	182	228	46	L	25.0	VH	.9	21	VL
Health diagnosing occupations	892	1,049	157	-	17.6	-	27.5	42	-
Chiropractors[1]	46	57	11	VL	22.8	VH	64.3	3	VL
Dentists	160	165	5	VL	3.1	VL	48.5	2	VL
Optometrists[1]	38	42	4	VL	10.6	L	33.6	2	VL
Physicians	577	699	122	L	21.2	VH	17.6	33	VL
Podiatrists[1]	14	15	1	VL	10.5	L	47.2	1	VL
Veterinarians[1]	57	71	14	VL	24.7	VH	29.9	3	VL
Health assessment and treating occupations	2,860	3,531	671	-	23.4	-	2.5	258	-
Dietitians and nutritionists	54	64	10	VL	19.1	H	10.4	8	VL
Pharmacists	185	199	14	VL	7.3	VL	3.9	6	VL
Physician assistants[1]	66	98	32	L	48.0	VH	.0	6	VL
Registered nurses	2,079	2,530	451	VH	21.7	VH	1.0	195	H
Therapists	476	640	164	-	34.5	-	8.1	42	-
Occupational therapists[1]	73	98	25	L	34.2	VH	10.6	6	VL
Physical therapists[1]	120	161	41	L	34.0	VH	5.3	11	VL
Radiation therapists[1]	12	14	2	VL	16.7	H	.0	1	VL
Recreational therapists[1]	39	44	5	VL	13.4	L	31.3	2	VL
Respiratory therapists[1]	86	123	37	L	42.6	VH	.9	9	VL
Speech-language pathologists and audiologists[1]	105	145	40	L	38.5	VH	10.3	10	VL
All other therapists[1]	40	54	14	VL	35.7	VH	2.3	4	VL
Writers, artists, and entertainers	1,996	2,409	413	-	20.0	-	39.6	352	-
Actors, directors, and producers[1]	160	198	38	L	23.8	VH	28.4	31	VL
Announcers	60	58	-3	VL	-4.3	VL	19.9	13	VL
Artists and commercial artists	308	388	79	L	25.7	VH	57.5	59	L
Athletes, coaches, umpires, and related workers	52	66	14	VL	27.9	VH	30.0	19	VL
Dancers and choreographers[1]	29	33	4	VL	13.6	L	30.8	5	VL
Designers	423	532	110	-	25.9	-	40.6	72	-
Designers, except interior designers	335	426	91	L	27.1	VH	44.0	58	L
Interior designers	53	68	15	VL	27.2	VH	44.9	9	VL
Merchandise displayers and window dressers	34	38	4	VL	12.7	L	.0	5	VL
Musicians, singers, and related workers	273	314	41	L	14.8	H	43.6	45	L
News analysts, reporters, and correspondents	67	68	2	VL	2.8	VL	7.1	8	VL
Photographers and camera operators	161	176	15	-	9.2	-	54.6	22	-
Camera operators, television, motion picture, video	11	15	3	VL	29.0	VH	8.1	2	VL
Photographers	149	161	12	VL	7.7	VL	58.1	20	VL

[1] One or more Current Population Survey (CPS) proxy occupations are used to estimate CPS based data.
[2] Current Population Survey data are used to estimate median weekly earnings ranking.
[3] Bachelor's degree or higher.

NOTE: Rankings are based on employment in all detailed occupations in the National Industry-Occupation Matrix. For details, see "Data presented" section of text. Codes for describing the ranked variables are: VH = Very high, H = High, L = Low, VL = Very low, n. a. = Data not available. A dash indicates data are not applicable.

Occupational employment and job openings data, 1998-2008, and worker characteristics, 1998

(Numbers in thousands)

Annual average job openings due to growth and net replacement needs, 1998-2008		Median annual earnings		Ranking of:		Most significant source of education or training	1998 Matrix Occupation
Number	Rank	Dollars	Rank	Unemployment rate	Percent part-time		
1	VL	35,630	VH	VL	L	Work experience plus degree[3]	Judges, magistrates, and other judicial workers[1]
19	L	78,170	VH	VL	L	First professional degree	Lawyers
283	-	-	-	-	-	-	Teachers, librarians, and counselors
23	-	-	-	-	-	-	Teachers, preschool and kindergarten
17	L	17,310	L	L	VH	Bachelor's degree	Teachers, preschool
6	VL	33,590	H	L	VH	Bachelor's degree	Teachers, kindergarten
61	H	36,110	VH	VL	H	Bachelor's degree	Teachers, elementary school
78	H	37,890	VH	VL	H	Bachelor's degree	Teachers, secondary school
17	L	37,850	VH	VL	H	Bachelor's degree	Teachers, special education
44	H	46,630	VH	L	VH	Doctoral degree	College and university faculty[1]
28	-	-	-	-	-	-	Other teachers and instructors
0	VL	37,200	VH	L	VH	Bachelor's degree	Farm and home management advisors
14	L	22,230	L	L	VH	Moderate-term on-the-job	Instructors and coaches, sports and physical training
14	-	-	-	-	-	-	Adult and vocational education teachers
5	VL	24,800	H	L	VH	Related work experience	Instructors, adult (nonvocational) education
9	VL	34,430	H	L	VH	Related work experience	Teachers and instructors, vocational education and training
18	L	27,180	H	L	VH	Bachelor's degree	All other teachers and instructors[1]
6	-	-	-	-	-	-	Librarians, archivists, curators, and related workers
1	VL	31,750	H	VL	VH	Master's degree	Archivists, curators, museum technicians, and conservators[1]
5	VL	38,470	VH	VL	VH	Master's degree	Librarians
9	VL	38,650	VH	VL	H	Master's degree	Counselors
31	-	-	-	-	-	-	Health diagnosing occupations
2	VL	63,930	VH	VL	H	First professional degree	Chiropractors[1]
4	VL	110,160	VH	VL	VH	First professional degree	Dentists
1	VL	68,500	VH	VL	H	First professional degree	Optometrists[1]
21	L	124,000	VH	VL	L	First professional degree	Physicians
0	VL	79,530	VH	VL	H	First professional degree	Podiatrists[1]
3	VL	50,950	VH	VL	H	First professional degree	Veterinarians[1]
116	-	-	-	-	-	-	Health assessment and treating occupations
2	VL	35,020	VH	L	VH	Bachelor's degree	Dietitians and nutritionists
6	VL	66,220	VH	VL	H	First professional degree	Pharmacists
4	VL	47,090	VH	VL	VH	Bachelor's degree	Physician assistants[1]
79	VH	40,690	VH	VL	VH	Associate degree	Registered nurses
24	-	-	-	-	-	-	Therapists
4	VL	48,230	VH	VL	VH	Bachelor's degree	Occupational therapists[1]
6	VL	56,600	VH	VL	VH	Master's degree	Physical therapists[1]
0	VL	39,640	VH	VL	VH	Associate degree	Radiation therapists[1]
1	VL	27,760	H	VL	VH	Bachelor's degree	Recreational therapists[1]
5	VL	34,830	VH	VL	VH	Associate degree	Respiratory therapists[1]
6	VL	43,080	VH	VL	VH	Master's degree	Speech-language pathologists and audiologists[1]
2	VL	30,270	H	VL	VH	Bachelor's degree	All other therapists[1]
83	-	-	-	-	-	-	Writers, artists, and entertainers
7	VL	27,400	H	H	VH	Long-term on-the-job	Actors, directors, and producers[1]
1	VL	17,930	L	H	VH	Moderate-term on-the-job	Announcers
14	L	31,690	H	H	VH	Work experience plus degree[3]	Artists and commercial artists
3	VL	22,210	L	H	VH	Long-term on-the-job	Athletes, coaches, umpires, and related workers
1	VL	21,430	L	H	VH	Postsecondary vocational	Dancers and choreographers[1]
17	-	-	-	-	-	-	Designers
14	L	29,200	H	L	H	Bachelor's degree	Designers, except interior designers
2	VL	31,760	H	L	H	Bachelor's degree	Interior designers
1	VL	18,180	L	L	H	Moderate-term on-the-job	Merchandise displayers and window dressers
9	VL	30,020	H	H	VH	Long-term on-the-job	Musicians, singers, and related workers
2	VL	26,470	H	L	H	Bachelor's degree	News analysts, reporters, and correspondents
4	-	-	-	-	-	-	Photographers and camera operators
0	VL	21,530	L	H	VH	Moderate-term on-the-job	Camera operators, television, motion picture, video
3	VL	20,940	L	H	VH	Postsecondary vocational	Photographers

[1] One or more Current Population Survey (CPS) proxy occupations are used to estimate CPS based data.
[2] Current Population Survey data are used to estimate median weekly earnings ranking.
[3] Bachelor's degree or higher.

NOTE: Rankings are based on employment in all detailed occupations in the National Industry-Occupation Matrix. For details, see "Data presented" section of text. Codes for describing the ranked variables are: VH = Very high, H = High, L = Low, VL = Very low, n. a. = Data not available. A dash indicates data are not applicable.

Occupational employment and job openings data, 1998-2008, and worker characteristics, 1998

(Numbers in thousands)

1998 Matrix Occupation	Employment		Employment change, 1998-2008				Percent self-employed, 1998	Annual average job openings due to growth and total replacement needs, 1998-2008	
			Numeric		Percent				
	1998	2008	Number	Rank	Number	Rank		Number	Rank
Public relations specialists	122	152	30	L	24.6	VH	10.4	25	VL
Writers and editors, including technical writers	341	424	83	L	24.4	VH	39.8	53	L
All other professional workers[1]	785	952	166	H	21.2	VH	1.3	136	L
Technicians and related support occupations	4,949	6,048	1,098	-	22.1	-	2.1	575	-
Health technicians and technologists	2,447	3,063	616	-	25.1	-	1.1	257	-
Cardiovascular technologists and technicians[1]	21	29	8	VL	39.4	VH	.0	3	VL
Clinical laboratory technologists and technicians	313	366	53	L	17.0	H	.2	20	VL
Dental hygienists	143	201	58	L	40.5	VH	.6	15	VL
EKG technicians[1]	12	10	-3	VL	-23.1	VL	.0	1	VL
Electroneurodiagnostic technologists[1]	5	6	0	VL	5.9	VL	.0	1	VL
Emergency medical technicians and paramedics[1]	150	197	47	L	31.6	VH	.0	23	VL
Licensed practical and licensed vocational nurses	692	828	136	H	19.7	VH	.3	43	L
Medical records and health information technicians[1]	92	133	41	L	43.9	VH	.7	11	VL
Nuclear medicine technologists	14	16	2	VL	11.6	L	.0	1	VL
Opticians, dispensing	71	81	10	VL	13.8	L	7.3	6	VL
Pharmacy technicians[1]	109	126	17	VL	15.7	H	.0	14	VL
Psychiatric technicians	66	73	7	VL	10.9	L	.0	15	VL
Radiologic technologists and technicians	162	194	32	L	20.1	VH	.4	11	VL
Surgical technologists[1]	54	77	23	L	41.8	VH	.0	9	VL
Veterinary technologists and technicians[1]	32	37	5	VL	16.2	H	.0	3	VL
All other health professionals and paraprofessionals[1]	510	688	178	H	35.0	VH	3.4	80	L
Engineering and science technicians and technologists	1,351	1,525	175	-	12.9	-	2.5	175	-
Engineering technicians	771	897	126	-	16.3	-	1.1	114	-
Electrical and electronic technicians and technologists	335	391	56	L	16.8	H	1.7	43	VL
All other engineering technicians and technologists	437	506	70	L	15.9	H	.6	71	L
Drafters	283	301	18	VL	6.4	VL	6.2	30	VL
Science and mathematics technicians[1]	227	243	16	VL	7.0	VL	1.3	17	VL
Surveying and mapping technicians	69	84	15	VL	21.8	VH	6.6	15	VL
Technicians, except health and engineering and science	1,152	1,460	308	-	26.7	-	3.8	142	-
Aircraft pilots and flight engineers	94	99	6	VL	5.9	VL	2.0	5	VL
Air traffic controllers[1]	30	30	1	VL	2.3	VL	.0	2	VL
Broadcast and sound technicians[1]	37	39	2	VL	6.0	VL	5.9	3	VL
Computer programmers	648	839	191	H	29.5	VH	4.8	75	L
Legal assistants and technicians, except clerical	252	346	94	-	37.4	-	3.2	47	-
Paralegals and legal assistants	136	220	84	L	62.0	VH	2.5	34	VL
Title examiners, abstractors, and searchers	30	29	0	VL	-.6	VL	11.1	4	VL
All other legal assistants, including law clerks	86	96	10	VL	11.6	L	1.7	9	VL
Library technicians[1]	72	85	13	VL	18.2	H	.0	9	VL
All other technicians[1]	20	21	1	VL	4.1	VL	1.9	2	VL
Marketing and sales occupations	15,341	17,627	2,287	-	14.9	-	13.4	4,285	-
Cashiers	3,198	3,754	556	VH	17.4	H	.8	1,290	VH
Counter and rental clerks	469	577	108	L	23.1	VH	3.3	199	H
Insurance sales agents	387	396	9	VL	2.2	VL	29.4	39	VL
Marketing and sales worker supervisors	2,584	2,847	263	H	10.2	L	33.9	411	H
Models, demonstrators, and product promoters	92	121	30	L	32.3	VH	6.1	28	VL
Parts salespersons	300	303	4	VL	1.2	VL	.7	35	VL
Real estate agents and brokers	347	382	34	-	9.8	-	70.5	46	-
Brokers, real estate	63	71	8	VL	13.5	L	65.1	9	VL
Sales agents, real estate	285	310	26	L	9.0	L	71.6	37	VL
Retail salespersons	4,056	4,620	563	VH	13.9	L	4.0	1,305	VH
Sales engineers	79	92	12	VL	15.7	H	1.2	3	VL
Securities, commodities, and financial services sales agents	303	427	124	L	41.0	VH	25.7	61	L
Travel agents[1]	138	163	25	L	18.4	H	12.5	17	VL
All other sales and related workers[1]	3,388	3,945	558	VH	16.5	H	15.0	865	VH

[1] One or more Current Population Survey (CPS) proxy occupations are used to estimate CPS based data.

[2] Current Population Survey data are used to estimate median weekly earnings ranking.

[3] Bachelor's degree or higher.

NOTE: Rankings are based on employment in all detailed occupations in the National Industry-Occupation Matrix. For details, see "Data presented" section of text. Codes for describing the ranked variables are: VH = Very high, H = High, L = Low, VL = Very low, n. a. = Data not available. A dash indicates data are not applicable.

Occupational employment and job openings data, 1998-2008, and worker characteristics, 1998

(Numbers in thousands)

Annual average job openings due to growth and net replacement needs, 1998-2008		Median annual earnings		Ranking of:		Most significant source of education or training	1998 Matrix Occupation
Number	Rank	Dollars	Rank	Unemployment rate	Percent part-time		
6	VL	34,550	H	L	H	Bachelor's degree	Public relations specialists
17	L	36,480	VH	L	H	Bachelor's degree	Writers and editors, including technical writers
36	H	36,730	VH	L	H	Bachelor's degree	All other professional workers[1]
220	-	-	-	-	-	-	**Technicians and related support occupations**
112	-	-	-	-	-	-	Health technicians and technologists
1	VL	35,770	VH	L	VH	Associate degree	Cardiovascular technologists and technicians[1]
9	VL	32,440	H	L	H	Bachelor's degree	Clinical laboratory technologists and technicians
9	VL	45,890	VH	L	VH	Associate degree	Dental hygienists
0	VL	24,360	H	L	VH	Moderate-term on-the-job	EKG technicians[1]
0	VL	32,070	H	L	VH	Moderate-term on-the-job	Electroneurodiagnostic technologists[1]
8	VL	20,290	L	L	VH	Postsecondary vocational	Emergency medical technicians and paramedics[1]
28	L	26,940	H	L	VH	Postsecondary vocational	Licensed practical and licensed vocational nurses
6	VL	20,590	L	L	VH	Associate degree	Medical records and health information technicians[1]
0	VL	39,610	VH	VL	VH	Associate degree	Nuclear medicine technologists
2	VL	22,440	L	VL	H	Moderate-term on-the-job	Opticians, dispensing
4	VL	17,770	L	L	VH	Moderate-term on-the-job	Pharmacy technicians[1]
2	VL	20,890	L	H	VH	Postsecondary vocational	Psychiatric technicians
5	VL	32,880	H	VL	VH	Associate degree	Radiologic technologists and technicians
4	VL	25,780	H	L	VH	Postsecondary vocational	Surgical technologists[1]
1	VL	19,870	L	L	H	Associate degree	Veterinary technologists and technicians[1]
30	L	26,940	H	L	VH	Associate degree	All other health professionals and paraprofessionals[1]
48	-	-	-	-	-	-	Engineering and science technicians and technologists
30	-	-	-	-	-	-	Engineering technicians
12	L	35,970	VH	L	L	Associate degree	Electrical and electronic technicians and technologists
18	L	37,310	VH	L	H	Associate degree	All other engineering technicians and technologists
9	VL	32,370	H	L	L	Postsecondary vocational	Drafters
7	VL	31,030	H	L	H	Associate degree	Science and mathematics technicians[1]
3	VL	25,940	H	L	L	Moderate-term on-the-job	Surveying and mapping technicians
59	-	-	-	-	-	-	Technicians, except health and engineering and science
3	VL	91,750	VH	VL	H	Bachelor's degree	Aircraft pilots and flight engineers
1	VL	64,880	VH	L	H	Long-term on-the-job	Air traffic controllers[1]
1	VL	25,270	H	L	H	Postsecondary vocational	Broadcast and sound technicians[1]
39	H	47,550	VH	VL	L	Bachelor's degree	Computer programmers
12	-	-	-	-	-	-	Legal assistants and technicians, except clerical
10	VL	32,760	H	L	H	Associate degree	Paralegals and legal assistants
0	VL	26,850	H	L	H	Moderate-term on-the-job	Title examiners, abstractors, and searchers
2	VL	29,520	H	VL	H	Associate degree	All other legal assistants, including law clerks
3	VL	21,730	L	L	H	Short-term on-the-job	Library technicians[1]
1	VL	27,200	H	L	H	Moderate-term on-the-job	All other technicians[1]
681	-	-	-	-	-	-	**Marketing and sales occupations**
195	VH	13,690	VL	VH	VH	Short-term on-the-job	Cashiers
31	L	14,510	VL	VH	VH	Short-term on-the-job	Counter and rental clerks
10	VL	34,370	H	VL	H	Bachelor's degree	Insurance sales agents
60	H	29,570	H	VL	L	Related work experience	Marketing and sales worker supervisors
5	VL	16,940	L	VH	VH	Moderate-term on-the-job	Models, demonstrators, and product promoters
9	VL	22,730	L	L	H	Moderate-term on-the-job	Parts salespersons
10	-	-	-	-	-	-	Real estate agents and brokers
2	VL	45,640	VH	VL	H	Related work experience	Brokers, real estate
8	VL	28,020	H	VL	H	Postsecondary vocational	Sales agents, real estate
194	VH	15,830	VL	H	VH	Short-term on-the-job	Retail salespersons
3	VL	54,600	VH	VL	VL	Bachelor's degree	Sales engineers
15	L	48,090	VH	VL	L	Bachelor's degree	Securities, commodities, and financial services sales agents
5	VL	23,010	L	L	H	Postsecondary vocational	Travel agents[1]
144	VH	31,140	H	H	VH	Moderate-term on-the-job	All other sales and related workers[1]

[1] One or more Current Population Survey (CPS) proxy occupations are used to estimate CPS based data.

[2] Current Population Survey data are used to estimate median weekly earnings ranking.

[3] Bachelor's degree or higher.

NOTE: Rankings are based on employment in all detailed occupations in the National Industry-Occupation Matrix. For details, see "Data presented" section of text. Codes for describing the ranked variables are: VH = Very high, H = High, L = Low, VL = Very low, n. a. = Data not available. A dash indicates data are not applicable.

Occupational employment and job openings data, 1998-2008, and worker characteristics, 1998

(Numbers in thousands)

1998 Matrix Occupation	Employment		Employment change, 1998-2008				Percent self-employed, 1998	Annual average job openings due to growth and total replacement needs, 1998-2008	
			Numeric		Percent				
	1998	2008	Number	Rank	Number	Rank		Number	Rank
Administrative support occupations, including clerical	24,461	26,659	2,198	-	8.9	-	1.8	4,986	-
Adjusters, investigators, and collectors	1,237	1,540	302	-	24.4	-	.2	292	-
Adjustment clerks	479	642	163	H	34.0	VH	.0	142	L
Bill and account collectors	311	420	110	L	35.3	VH	.6	106	L
Insurance claims, examining and policy processing clerks	339	377	38	-	11.2	-	.0	48	-
Insurance claims clerks	160	183	23	L	14.5	H	.0	13	VL
Insurance examining clerks	10	11	2	VL	17.3	H	.0	2	VL
Insurance policy processing clerks	170	183	13	VL	7.9	VL	.0	33	VL
Welfare eligibility workers and interviewers	109	100	-8	VL	-7.6	VL	.0	2	VL
Communications equipment operators	297	252	-46	-	-15.0	-	.2	64	-
Telephone operators	261	220	-41	-	-15.6	-	.2	57	-
Central office operators	23	19	-4	VL	-16.6	VL	.0	5	VL
Directory assistance operators	23	16	-7	VL	-31.1	VL	.0	5	VL
Switchboard operators	214	185	-30	VL	-13.9	VL	.2	47	L
All other communications equipment operators[1]	36	32	-5	VL	-13.6	VL	.0	8	VL
Computer operators	251	187	-64	-	-25.5	-	2.0	32	-
Peripheral equipment operators[1]	27	17	-10	VL	-37.6	VL	.0	3	VL
Computer operators, except peripheral equipment	224	170	-54	VL	-24.1	VL	2.2	29	VL
Information clerks	1,910	2,296	386	-	20.2	-	1.3	549	-
Hotel, motel, and resort desk clerks	159	180	21	L	13.5	L	.8	60	L
Interviewing clerks, except personnel and social welfare	128	158	30	L	23.3	VH	.4	44	L
New accounts clerks, banking	111	127	16	VL	14.7	H	.0	36	VL
Receptionists and information clerks	1,293	1,599	305	H	23.6	VH	1.8	387	H
Reservation and transportation ticket agents and travel clerks[1]	219	232	13	VL	6.0	VL	.0	23	VL
Mail clerks and messengers	247	270	23	-	9.1	-	4.2	62	-
Couriers and messengers	120	130	11	VL	8.8	L	7.6	35	VL
Mail clerks, except mail machine operators and postal service	128	140	12	VL	9.5	L	.9	26	VL
Postal clerks and mail carriers	405	434	30	-	7.3	-	.0	12	-
Postal mail carriers	332	357	25	L	7.4	VL	.0	7	VL
Postal service clerks	73	78	5	VL	6.8	VL	.0	5	VL
Material recording, scheduling, dispatching, and distributing occupations	4,183	4,382	199	-	4.7	-	.2	876	-
Dispatchers	248	278	30	-	12.1	-	1.2	48	-
Dispatchers, except police, fire, and ambulance	163	186	23	L	14.4	H	1.8	32	VL
Dispatchers, police, fire, and ambulance	85	92	7	VL	8.0	VL	.0	16	VL
Meter readers, utilities[1]	50	51	0	VL	.4	VL	.0	11	VL
Procurement clerks	58	49	-9	VL	-14.8	VL	.1	10	VL
Production, planning, and expediting clerks	248	249	1	VL	.4	VL	1.0	62	L
Shipping, receiving, and traffic clerks	1,000	1,031	31	L	3.1	VL	.2	243	H
Stock clerks and order fillers	2,331	2,462	131	H	5.6	VL	.1	442	VH
Weighers, measurers, checkers, and samplers, recordkeeping[1]	51	51	1	VL	1.5	VL	.4	12	VL
All other material recording, scheduling, and distribution workers[1]	196	210	13	VL	6.8	VL	.0	48	L
Records processing occupations	3,731	3,775	44	-	1.1	-	6.0	670	-
Advertising clerks[1]	14	14	1	VL	4.4	VL	.0	2	VL
Brokerage clerks	77	98	22	L	28.4	VH	.0	18	VL
Correspondence clerks[1]	25	28	3	VL	12.2	L	.0	4	VL
File clerks	272	298	26	L	9.6	L	1.2	117	L
Financial records processing occupations	2,698	2,653	-44	-	-1.6	-	8.1	415	-
Billing, cost, and rate clerks	342	392	50	L	14.6	H	1.1	63	L
Billing and posting clerks and machine operators[1]	107	104	-3	VL	-2.6	VL	3.0	11	VL
Bookkeeping, accounting, and auditing clerks	2,078	1,997	-81	VL	-3.9	VL	10.1	325	H
Payroll and timekeeping clerks	172	161	-11	VL	-6.2	VL	.9	15	VL
Library assistants and bookmobile drivers	127	148	21	L	16.5	H	.0	36	VL

[1] One or more Current Population Survey (CPS) proxy occupations are used to estimate CPS based data.
[2] Current Population Survey data are used to estimate median weekly earnings ranking.
[3] Bachelor's degree or higher.

NOTE: Rankings are based on employment in all detailed occupations in the National Industry-Occupation Matrix. For details, see "Data presented" section of text. Codes for describing the ranked variables are: VH = Very high, H = High, L = Low, VL = Very low, n. a. = Data not available. A dash indicates data are not applicable.

Occupational employment and job openings data, 1998-2008, and worker characteristics, 1998

(Numbers in thousands)

Annual average job openings due to growth and net replacement needs, 1998-2008		Median annual earnings		Ranking of:		Most significant source of education or training	1998 Matrix Occupation
Number	Rank	Dollars	Rank	Unemploy-ment rate	Per-cent part-time		
746	-	-	-	-	-	-	**Administrative support occupations, including clerical**
50	-	-	-	-	-	-	Adjusters, investigators, and collectors
19	L	22,040	L	L	H	Short-term on-the-job	Adjustment clerks
19	L	22,540	L	H	H	Short-term on-the-job	Bill and account collectors
9	-	-	-	-	-	-	Insurance claims, examining and policy processing clerks
5	VL	24,010	H	VL	L	Moderate-term on-the-job	Insurance claims clerks
0	VL	23,750	H	L	H	Moderate-term on-the-job	Insurance examining clerks
4	VL	23,960	H	L	H	Moderate-term on-the-job	Insurance policy processing clerks
2	VL	33,100	H	L	L	Moderate-term on-the-job	Welfare eligibility workers and interviewers
6	-	-	-	-	-	-	Communications equipment operators
6	-	-	-	-	-	-	Telephone operators
1	VL	26,220	H	H	VH	Moderate-term on-the-job	Central office operators
1	VL	30,530	H	H	VH	Moderate-term on-the-job	Directory assistance operators
5	VL	18,220	L	VH	VH	Short-term on-the-job	Switchboard operators
1	VL	26,400	H	H	VH	Moderate-term on-the-job	All other communications equipment operators[1]
4	-	-	-	-	-	-	Computer operators
0	VL	22,860	L	L	H	Moderate-term on-the-job	Peripheral equipment operators[1]
3	VL	25,030	H	L	H	Moderate-term on-the-job	Computer operators, except peripheral equipment
82	-	-	-	-	-	-	Information clerks
8	VL	15,160	VL	H	VH	Short-term on-the-job	Hotel, motel, and resort desk clerks
7	VL	18,540	L	VH	VH	Short-term on-the-job	Interviewing clerks, except personnel and social welfare
5	VL	21,340	L	VH	VH	Related work experience	New accounts clerks, banking
55	H	18,620	L	H	VH	Short-term on-the-job	Receptionists and information clerks
6	VL	22,120	L	L	H	Short-term on-the-job	Reservation and transportation ticket agents and travel clerks[1]
8	-	-	-	-	-	-	Mail clerks and messengers
4	VL	16,680	VL	H	VH	Short-term on-the-job	Couriers and messengers
4	VL	17,660	L	VH	H	Short-term on-the-job	Mail clerks, except mail machine operators and postal service
13	-	-	-	-	-	-	Postal clerks and mail carriers
12	L	34,840	VH	VL	L	Short-term on-the-job	Postal mail carriers
2	VL	35,100	VH	L	L	Short-term on-the-job	Postal service clerks
90	-	-	-	-	-	-	Material recording, scheduling, dispatching, and distributing occupations
7	-	-	-	-	-	-	Dispatchers
5	VL	26,370	H	L	L	Moderate-term on-the-job	Dispatchers, except police, fire, and ambulance
2	VL	23,670	H	L	L	Moderate-term on-the-job	Dispatchers, police, fire, and ambulance
1	VL	25,380	H	H	H	Short-term on-the-job	Meter readers, utilities[1]
1	VL	22,630	L	H	H	Short-term on-the-job	Procurement clerks
3	VL	29,270	H	L	VH	Short-term on-the-job	Production, planning, and expediting clerks
20	L	22,500	L	H	H	Short-term on-the-job	Shipping, receiving, and traffic clerks
50	H	16,520	VL	H	H	Short-term on-the-job	Stock clerks and order fillers
1	VL	22,310	L	VH	H	Short-term on-the-job	Weighers, measurers, checkers, and samplers, recordkeeping[1]
6	VL	21,070	L	H	H	Short-term on-the-job	All other material recording, scheduling, and distribution workers[1]
94	-	-	-	-	-	-	Records processing occupations
0	VL	20,550	L	L	H	Short-term on-the-job	Advertising clerks[1]
3	VL	27,920	H	L	H	Moderate-term on-the-job	Brokerage clerks
1	VL	22,270	L	L	H	Short-term on-the-job	Correspondence clerks[1]
12	L	16,830	L	VH	VH	Short-term on-the-job	File clerks
56	-	-	-	-	-	-	Financial records processing occupations
12	L	22,670	L	L	H	Short-term on-the-job	Billing, cost, and rate clerks
2	VL	20,560	L	L	H	Short-term on-the-job	Billing and posting clerks and machine operators[1]
39	H	23,190	L	L	VH	Moderate-term on-the-job	Bookkeeping, accounting, and auditing clerks
3	VL	24,560	H	L	H	Short-term on-the-job	Payroll and timekeeping clerks
8	VL	16,980	L	H	VH	Short-term on-the-job	Library assistants and bookmobile drivers

[1] One or more Current Population Survey (CPS) proxy occupations are used to estimate CPS based data.

[2] Current Population Survey data are used to estimate median weekly earnings ranking.

[3] Bachelor's degree or higher.

NOTE: Rankings are based on employment in all detailed occupations in the National Industry-Occupation Matrix. For details, see "Data presented" section of text. Codes for describing the ranked variables are: VH = Very high, H = High, L = Low, VL = Very low, n. a. = Data not available. A dash indicates data are not applicable.

Occupational employment and job openings data, 1998-2008, and worker characteristics, 1998

Table 2. Occupational employment and job openings data, 1998-2008, and worker characterisitcs, 1998 — Continued

(Numbers in thousands)

1998 Matrix Occupation	Employment		Employment change, 1998-2008				Per-cent self-emp-loyed, 1998	Annual average job openings due to growth and total replacement needs, 1998-2008	
			Numeric		Percent				
	1998	2008	Number	Rank	Number	Rank		Number	Rank
Order clerks	362	378	17	VL	4.6	VL	.5	57	L
Human resources assistants, except payroll and timekeeping[1]	142	145	3	VL	2.0	VL	.0	22	VL
Statement clerks	16	12	-3	VL	-22.3	VL	10.2	3	VL
Secretaries, stenographers, and typists	3,764	3,744	-19	-	-.5	-	3.0	518	-
Court reporters, medical transcriptionists, and stenographers[1]	110	121	11	VL	9.7	L	31.4	16	VL
Secretaries	3,195	3,258	63	-	1.9	-	1.8	436	-
Legal secretaries	285	322	37	L	13.0	L	.2	44	L
Medical secretaries	219	246	26	L	12.0	L	1.6	34	VL
Secretaries, except legal and medical	2,690	2,691	0	VL	.0	VL	1.9	358	H
Word processors and typists	459	365	-93	VL	-20.4	VL	4.9	65	L
Other clerical and administrative support workers	8,436	9,780	1,344	-	15.9	-	.6	1,931	-
Bank tellers	560	529	-31	VL	-5.5	VL	.0	107	L
Court, municipal, and license clerks	100	112	12	-	11.6	-	.0	26	-
Court clerks	51	57	6	VL	10.8	L	.0	13	VL
License clerks	24	27	3	VL	13.1	L	.0	6	VL
Municipal clerks	25	28	3	VL	11.9	L	.0	7	VL
Credit and loan authorizers, checkers, and clerks	254	271	17	-	6.7	-	.0	63	-
Credit authorizers	17	15	-2	VL	-10.7	VL	.0	4	VL
Credit checkers	41	42	1	VL	1.5	VL	.0	9	VL
Loan and credit clerks	179	200	21	L	11.8	L	.0	47	L
Loan interviewers	16	14	-3	VL	-17.0	VL	.0	4	VL
Data entry keyers	435	474	39	L	9.0	L	2.1	107	L
Duplicating, mail, and other office machine operators[1]	197	201	4	VL	1.9	VL	.2	43	L
Office and administrative support supervisors and managers	1,611	1,924	313	VH	19.4	VH	.1	238	H
Office clerks, general	3,021	3,484	463	VH	15.3	H	.3	745	VH
Proofreaders and copy markers[1]	41	34	-7	VL	-17.1	VL	3.1	9	VL
Statistical clerks	72	69	-3	VL	-4.5	VL	.1	5	VL
Teacher assistants	1,192	1,567	375	VH	31.5	VH	.2	344	H
All other clerical and administrative support workers	953	1,116	162	H	17.0	H	3.1	243	H
Service occupations	22,548	26,401	3,853	-	17.0	-	5.7	6,720	-
Cleaning and building service occupations, except private household	3,623	4,031	408	-	11.2	-	5.0	822	-
Institutional cleaning supervisors	87	97	9	VL	10.5	L	1.8	9	VL
Janitors and cleaners, including maids and housekeeping cleaners	3,184	3,549	365	VH	11.5	L	4.8	736	VH
Pest control workers[1]	52	65	13	VL	25.4	VH	9.0	8	VL
All other cleaning and building service workers[1]	300	320	20	VL	6.7	VL	8.1	68	L
Food preparation and service occupations	8,735	9,831	1,096	-	12.5	-	.9	3,392	-
Chefs, cooks, and other kitchen workers	3,306	3,748	442	-	13.3	-	1.7	1,201	-
Cooks, except short order	1,373	1,560	187	-	13.6	-	3.6	443	-
Bakers, bread and pastry	171	200	28	L	16.6	H	5.2	57	L
Cooks, institution or cafeteria	418	431	12	VL	2.9	VL	.0	124	L
Cooks, restaurant	783	929	146	H	18.7	H	5.1	263	H
Cooks, short order and fast food	677	801	124	H	18.4	H	1.0	226	H
Food preparation workers[1]	1,256	1,387	131	H	10.4	L	.0	529	VH
Food and beverage service occupations	5,150	5,778	628	-	12.0	-	.4	2,081	-
Bartenders	404	412	8	VL	1.9	VL	1.5	86	L
Dining room and cafeteria attendants and bar helpers	405	422	16	VL	4.0	VL	.6	182	H
Food counter, fountain, and related workers[1]	2,025	2,272	247	H	12.2	L	.1	945	VH
Hosts and hostesses, restaurant, lounge, or coffee shop	297	351	54	H	18.2	H	1.1	111	L
Waiters and waitresses	2,019	2,322	303	H	15.0	H	.4	758	VH
All other food preparation and service workers	280	306	26	L	9.4	L	.8	110	L
Health service occupations	2,309	2,984	676	-	29.2	-	1.8	547	-
Ambulance drivers and attendants, except EMTs	19	26	7	VL	35.0	VH	.0	4	VL
Dental assistants	229	325	97	L	42.2	VH	.0	56	L

[1] One or more Current Population Survey (CPS) proxy occupations are used to estimate CPS based data.

[2] Current Population Survey data are used to estimate median weekly earnings ranking.

NOTE: Rankings are based on employment in all detailed occupations in the National Industry-Occupation Matrix. For details, see "Data presented" section of text. Codes for describing the ranked variables are: VH = Very high, H = High, L = Low, VL = Very low, n. a. = Data not available. A dash

Occupational employment and job openings data, 1998-2008, and worker characteristics, 1998

(Numbers in thousands)

Annual average job openings due to growth and net replacement needs, 1998-2008		Median annual earnings		Ranking of:		Most significant source of education or training	1998 Matrix Occupation
Number	Rank	Dollars	Rank	Unemployment rate	Percent part-time		
10	L	21,550	L	L	H	Short-term on-the-job	Order clerks
3	VL	24,360	H	L	H	Short-term on-the-job	Human resources assistants, except payroll and timekeeping[1]
0	VL	18,640	L	L	H	Short-term on-the-job	Statement clerks
70	-	-	-	-	-	-	Secretaries, stenographers, and typists
3	VL	25,430	H	L	VH	Postsecondary vocational	Court reporters, medical transciptionists, and stenographers[1]
58	-	-	-	-	-	-	Secretaries
8	VL	30,050	H	L	VH	Postsecondary vocational	Legal secretaries
6	VL	22,390	L	L	VH	Postsecondary vocational	Medical secretaries
44	H	23,560	H	L	VH	Moderate-term on-the-job	Secretaries, except legal and medical
9	VL	22,590	L	H	VH	Moderate-term on-the-job	Word processors and typists
329	-	-	-	-	-		Other clerical and administrative support workers
24	L	17,200	L	L	VH	Short-term on-the-job	Bank tellers
3	-	-	-	-	-	-	Court, municipal, and license clerks
1	VL	22,960	L	L	H	Short-term on-the-job	Court clerks
1	VL	22,900	L	L	H	Short-term on-the-job	License clerks
1	VL	22,810	L	L	H	Short-term on-the-job	Municipal clerks
5	-	-	-	-	-		Credit and loan authorizers, checkers, and clerks
0	VL	22,990	L	L	H	Short-term on-the-job	Credit authorizers
0	VL	21,550	L	L	H	Short-term on-the-job	Credit checkers
4	VL	22,580	L	L	H	Short-term on-the-job	Loan and credit clerks
0	VL	23,190	L	L	H	Short-term on-the-job	Loan interviewers
7	VL	19,190	L	H	VH	Moderate-term on-the-job	Data entry keyers
6	VL	20,370	L	H	VH	Short-term on-the-job	Duplicating, mail, and other office machine operators[1]
68	H	31,090	H	VL	VL	Related work experience	Office and administrative support supervisors and managers
130	VH	19,580	L	H	VH	Short-term on-the-job	Office clerks, general
1	VL	18,620	L	H	VH	Short-term on-the-job	Proofreaders and copy markers[1]
1	VL	23,380	L	L	H	Moderate-term on-the-job	Statistical clerks
51	H	15,830	VL	H	VH	Short-term on-the-job	Teacher assistants
33	L	23,520	L	L	H	Short-term on-the-job	All other clerical and administrative support workers
1,111	-	-	-	-	-	-	**Service occupations**
116	-	-	-	-	-		Cleaning and building service occupations, except private household
3	VL	19,600	L	L	L	Related work experience	Institutional cleaning supervisors
103	VH	15,340	VL	VH	VH	Short-term on-the-job	Janitors and cleaners, including maids and housekeeping cleaners
2	VL	22,490	L	VH	VH	Moderate-term on-the-job	Pest control workers[1]
8	VL	17,910	L	VH	VH	Short-term on-the-job	All other cleaning and building service workers[1]
516	-	-	-	-	-		Food preparation and service occupations
167	-	-	-	-	-		Chefs, cooks, and other kitchen workers
55	-	-	-	-	-		Cooks, except short order
7	VL	16,990	L	VH	VH	Moderate-term on-the-job	Bakers, bread and pastry
12	L	16,090	VL	VH	VH	Long-term on-the-job	Cooks, institution or cafeteria
35	H	16,250	VL	VH	VH	Long-term on-the-job	Cooks, restaurant
30	L	12,720	VL	VH	VH	Short-term on-the-job	Cooks, short order and fast food
82	VH	13,710	VL	VH	VH	Short-term on-the-job	Food preparation workers[1]
336	-	-	-	-	-		Food and beverage service occupations
18	L	13,000	VL	H	VH	Short-term on-the-job	Bartenders
14	L	12,550	VL	VH	VH	Short-term on-the-job	Dining room and cafeteria attendants and bar helpers
148	VH	12,600	VL	VH	VH	Short-term on-the-job	Food counter, fountain, and related workers[1]
14	L	13,410	VL	H	VH	Short-term on-the-job	Hosts and hostesses, restaurant, lounge, or coffee shop
142	VH	12,170	VL	VH	VH	Short-term on-the-job	Waiters and waitresses
13	L	14,560	VL	VH	VH	Short-term on-the-job	All other food preparation and service workers
106	-	-	-	-	-		Health service occupations
1	VL	16,970	L	L	VH	Short-term on-the-job	Ambulance drivers and attendants, except EMTs
13	L	22,640	L	L	VH	Moderate-term on-the-job	Dental assistants

[1] One or more Current Population Survey (CPS) proxy occupations are used to estimate CPS based data.
[2] Current Population Survey data are used to estimate median weekly earnings ranking.
[3] Bachelor's degree or higher.

NOTE: Rankings are based on employment in all detailed occupations in the National Industry-Occupation Matrix. For details, see "Data presented" section of text. Codes for describing the ranked variables are: VH = Very high, H = High, L = Low, VL = Very low, n. a. = Data not available. A dash indicates data are not applicable.

Occupational employment and job openings data, 1998-2008, and worker characteristics, 1998

(Numbers in thousands)

1998 Matrix Occupation	Employment		Employment change, 1998-2008				Per-cent self-emp-loyed, 1998	Annual average job openings due to growth and total replacement needs, 1998-2008	
			Numeric		Percent				
	1998	2008	Number	Rank	Number	Rank		Number	Rank
Medical assistants[1]	252	398	146	H	57.8	VH	.0	49	L
Nursing and psychiatric aides	1,461	1,794	332	-	22.7	-	2.9	371	-
Nursing aides, orderlies, and attendants	1,367	1,692	325	VH	23.8	VH	3.1	350	H
Psychiatric aides	95	102	7	VL	7.7	VL	.0	21	VL
Occupational therapy assistants and aides[1]	19	26	7	VL	39.8	VH	.0	3	VL
Pharmacy aides[1]	61	71	10	VL	15.9	H	.0	9	VL
Physical therapy assistants and aides	82	118	36	L	43.7	VH	.0	14	VL
All other health service workers	185	226	41	L	22.3	VH	.0	36	VL
Personal service occupations	2,934	3,828	894	-	30.4	-	28.9	835	-
Amusement and recreation attendants	337	439	102	L	30.2	VH	.8	142	L
Baggage porters and bellhops[1]	40	45	5	VL	13.7	L	.0	10	VL
Child care workers	905	1,141	236	H	26.1	VH	54.6	329	H
Barbers, cosmetologists, and related workers	723	796	73	-	10.0	-	46.6	84	-
Barbers	54	50	-4	VL	-7.3	VL	76.7	2	VL
Hairdressers, hairstylists, and cosmetologists	605	667	62	L	10.2	L	45.4	73	L
Manicurists	49	62	13	VL	26.0	VH	42.3	7	VL
Shampooers	15	17	2	VL	14.5	H	.0	2	VL
Flight attendants	99	129	30	L	30.1	VH	1.5	5	VL
Personal care and home health aides[1]	746	1,179	433	VH	58.1	VH	1.9	250	H
Ushers, lobby attendants, and ticket takers[1]	84	99	15	VL	17.6	H	.0	23	VL
Private household workers	928	751	-178	-	-19.1	-	.0	280	-
Child care workers, private household[2]	306	209	-97	VL	-31.7	VL	.0	115	L
Cleaners and servants, private household[1,2]	600	530	-71	VL	-11.8	VL	.0	157	L
Cooks, private household[1,2]	5	2	-2	VL	-51.3	VL	.0	1	VL
Housekeepers and butlers[1,2]	17	10	-7	VL	-42.4	VL	.0	4	VL
Protective service occupations	2,769	3,486	717	-	25.8	-	.9	465	-
Fire fighting occupations	314	334	20	-	6.4	-	.7	20	-
Firefighters	239	251	11	VL	4.7	VL	.0	10	VL
Fire fighting and prevention supervisors[1]	60	66	6	VL	10.7	L	.5	9	VL
Fire inspection occupations[1]	15	17	2	VL	17.2	H	12.9	1	VL
Law enforcement occupations	1,147	1,501	354	-	30.8	-	.0	143	-
Correctional officers	383	532	148	H	38.7	VH	.0	65	L
Police and detectives	727	929	202	-	27.7	-	.0	77	-
Detectives and criminal investigators	79	96	17	VL	21.0	VH	.0	8	VL
Police and detective supervisors	111	124	13	VL	12.0	L	.0	14	VL
Police patrol officers	446	586	141	H	31.6	VH	.0	52	L
Sheriffs and deputy sheriffs	91	123	31	L	34.2	VH	.0	3	VL
Other law enforcement occupations	37	40	3	VL	9.4	L	.0	1	VL
Other protective service workers	1,308	1,651	343	-	26.1	-	1.8	304	-
Crossing guards[1]	54	57	2	VL	4.0	VL	.0	10	VL
Guards	1,027	1,321	294	H	28.6	VH	.2	257	H
Private detectives and investigators	61	76	15	VL	24.3	VH	34.8	15	VL
All other protective service workers	166	198	32	L	19.0	H	.0	23	VL
All other service workers[1]	1,249	1,490	241	H	19.3	H	8.6	319	H
Agriculture, forestry, fishing, and related occupations	4,435	4,506	71	-	1.0	-	38.3	767	-
Farm operators and managers	1,483	1,309	-174	-	-11.7	-	88.4	145	-
Farmers[2]	1,308	1,135	-173	VL	-13.2	VL	99.5	133	L
Farm managers[2]	175	174	-1	VL	-.8	VL	5.3	11	VL
Farm workers	851	794	-57	VL	-6.6	VL	3.0	157	L
Fishers and fishing vessel operators	51	40	-11	-	-21.7	-	58.3	10	-
Captains and other officers, fishing vessels[1,2]	11	9	-2	VL	-18.6	VL	41.1	2	VL
Fishers[1,2]	40	31	-9	VL	-22.7	VL	63.2	8	VL
Forestry, conservation, and logging occupations	120	116	-4	-	-3.1	-	27.8	18	-
Forest and conservation workers[1]	33	33	0	VL	.7	VL	9.7	5	VL
Timber cutting and logging occupations	87	83	-4	-	-4.5	-	34.6	13	-

[1] One or more Current Population Survey (CPS) proxy occupations are used to estimate CPS based data.
[2] Current Population Survey data are used to estimate median weekly earnings ranking.
[3] Bachelor's degree or higher.

NOTE: Rankings are based on employment in all detailed occupations in the National Industry-Occupation Matrix. For details, see "Data presented" section of text. Codes for describing the ranked variables are: VH = Very high, H = High, L = Low, VL = Very low, n. a. = Data not available. A dash indicates data are not applicable.

Occupational employment and job openings data, 1998-2008, and worker characteristics, 1998

(Numbers in thousands)

Annual average job openings due to growth and net replacement needs, 1998-2008		Median annual earnings		Ranking of:		Most significant source of education or training	1998 Matrix Occupation
Number	Rank	Dollars	Rank	Unemployment rate	Percent part-time		
21	L	20,680	L	L	VH	Moderate-term on-the-job	Medical assistants[1]
54	-	-	-	-	-		Nursing and psychiatric aides
52	H	16,620	VL	H	VH	Short-term on-the-job	Nursing aides, orderlies, and attendants
2	VL	22,170	L	H	VH	Short-term on-the-job	Psychiatric aides
1	VL	28,690	H	L	VH	Associate degree	Occupational therapy assistants and aides[1]
2	VL	18,480	L	L	VH	Short-term on-the-job	Pharmacy aides[1]
6	VL	21,870	L	L	VH	Associate degree	Physical therapy assistants and aides
8	VL	19,160	L	L	VH	Short-term on-the-job	All other health service workers
141	-	-	-	-	-	-	Personal service occupations
16	L	12,860	VL	VH	VH	Short-term on-the-job	Amusement and recreation attendants
1	VL	13,340	VL	H	VH	Short-term on-the-job	Baggage porters and bellhops[1]
32	L	13,760	VL	H	VH	Short-term on-the-job	Child care workers
26	-	-	-	-	-		Barbers, cosmetologists, and related workers
2	VL	18,470	L	L	VH	Postsecondary vocational	Barbers
22	L	15,150	VL	L	VH	Postsecondary vocational	Hairdressers, hairstylists, and cosmetologists
3	VL	13,490	VL	L	VH	Postsecondary vocational	Manicurists
1	VL	12,570	VL	L	VH	Short-term on-the-job	Shampooers
5	VL	37,800	VH	VL	VH	Long-term on-the-job	Flight attendants
57	H	15,760	VL	H	VH	Short-term on-the-job	Personal care and home health aides[1]
3	VL	12,480	VL	VH	VH	Short-term on-the-job	Ushers, lobby attendants, and ticket takers[1]
28	-	-	-	-	-	-	Private household workers
14	L	10,733	VL	VH	VH	Short-term on-the-job	Child care workers, private household[2]
13	L	14,435	VL	VH	VH	Short-term on-the-job	Cleaners and servants, private household[1,2]
0	VL	n.a.	-	VH	VH	Moderate-term on-the-job	Cooks, private household[1,2]
0	VL	n.a.	-	VH	VH	Moderate-term on-the-job	Housekeepers and butlers[1,2]
149	-	-	-	-	-	-	Protective service occupations
10	-	-	-	-	-		Fire fighting occupations
7	VL	31,170	H	VL	VL	Long-term on-the-job	Firefighters
3	VL	44,830	VH	VL	VL	Related work experience	Fire fighting and prevention supervisors[1]
1	VL	40,040	VH	L	VL	Related work experience	Fire inspection occupations[1]
64	-	-	-	-	-	-	Law enforcement occupations
25	L	28,540	H	VL	VL	Long-term on-the-job	Correctional officers
38	-	-	-	-	-		Police and detectives
4	VL	46,180	VH	VL	VL	Related work experience	Detectives and criminal investigators
5	VL	48,700	VH	VL	VL	Related work experience	Police and detective supervisors
26	L	37,710	VH	VL	VL	Long-term on-the-job	Police patrol officers
4	VL	28,270	H	VL	VL	Long-term on-the-job	Sheriffs and deputy sheriffs
1	VL	28,830	H	VL	L	Long-term on-the-job	Other law enforcement occupations
74	-	-	-	-	-	-	Other protective service workers
2	VL	14,940	VL	VH	VH	Short-term on-the-job	Crossing guards[1]
55	H	16,240	VL	VH	H	Short-term on-the-job	Guards
3	VL	21,020	L	VH	H	Related work experience	Private detectives and investigators
15	L	17,470	L	VH	VH	Short-term on-the-job	All other protective service workers
55	H	20,360	L	H	VH	Related work experience	All other service workers[1]
136	-					-	**Agriculture, forestry, fishing, and related occupations**
23	-			-	-		Farm operators and managers
20	L	n.a.	-	VL	H	Long-term on-the-job	Farmers[2]
3	VL	n.a.	-	VL	H	Work experience plus degree[3]	Farm managers[2]
26	L	12,570	VL	VH	H	Short-term on-the-job	Farm workers
1	-			-	-	-	Fishers and fishing vessel operators
0	VL	n.a.	-	VH	L	Related work experience	Captains and other officers, fishing vessels[1,2]
1	VL	n.a.	-	VH	L	Short-term on-the-job	Fishers[1,2]
3	-	-	-	-	-	-	Forestry, conservation, and logging occupations
1	VL	23,140	L	VH	L	Short-term on-the-job	Forest and conservation workers[1]
2	-	-	-	-	-	-	Timber cutting and logging occupations

[1] One or more Current Population Survey (CPS) proxy occupations are used to estimate CPS based data.

[2] Current Population Survey data are used to estimate median weekly earnings ranking.

[3] Bachelor's degree or higher.

NOTE: Rankings are based on employment in all detailed occupations in the National Industry-Occupation Matrix. For details, see "Data presented" section of text. Codes for describing the ranked variables are: VH = Very high, H = High, L = Low, VL = Very low, n. a. = Data not available. A dash indicates data are not applicable.

Occupational employment and job openings data, 1998-2008, and worker characteristics, 1998
(Numbers in thousands)

1998 Matrix Occupation	Employment		Employment change, 1998-2008				Per-cent self-emp-loyed, 1998	Annual average job openings due to growth and total replacement needs, 1998-2008	
			Numeric		Percent				
	1998	2008	Number	Rank	Number	Rank		Number	Rank
Fallers and buckers	18	16	-2	VL	-11.5	VL	37.5	2	VL
Logging equipment operators	56	55	-1	VL	-2.0	VL	37.2	8	VL
All other timber cutting and related logging workers	13	12	-1	VL	-6.0	VL	19.2	2	VL
Landscaping, groundskeeping, nursery, greenhouse, and lawn service occupations	1,285	1,548	262	-	20.4	-	19.0	310	-
Laborers, landscaping and groundskeeping[1]	1,130	1,364	234	H	20.7	VH	16.1	283	H
Lawn service managers[1]	86	104	17	VL	20.0	VH	71.1	10	VL
Nursery and greenhouse managers[1]	5	6	1	VL	15.1	H	19.5	1	VL
Pruners	45	50	5	VL	12.1	L	.0	11	VL
Sprayers/applicators	19	23	4	VL	23.6	VH	.0	5	VL
Supervisors, farming, forestry, and agricultural related occupations[1]	92	97	6	VL	6.2	VL	13.9	12	VL
Veterinary assistants and nonfarm animal caretakers	181	223	42	-	23.0	-	19.4	58	-
Animal caretakers, except farm	137	166	30	L	21.6	VH	25.7	43	L
Veterinary assistants	45	57	12	VL	28.0	VH	.0	15	VL
All other agricultural, forestry, fishing, and related workers[1]	373	379	6	VL	1.7	VL	1.7	71	L
Precision production, craft, and repair occupations	15,619	16,871	1,252	-	8.0	-	12.1	2,118	-
Blue-collar worker supervisors[1]	2,198	2,394	196	H	8.9	L	10.4	216	H
Construction trades	4,628	5,018	390	-	8.4	-	21.3	762	-
Boilermakers[1]	18	19	0	VL	1.6	VL	6.6	2	VL
Bricklayers, blockmasons, and stonemasons[1]	157	176	19	VL	12.3	L	27.6	30	VL
Carpenters	1,071	1,145	74	L	6.9	VL	32.1	236	H
Carpet, floor, and tile installers and finishers	138	147	8	-	6.0	-	53.2	21	-
Carpet installers	85	88	3	VL	3.6	VL	64.0	11	VL
Hard tile setters[1]	29	31	3	VL	8.7	L	39.0	5	VL
All other carpet, floor, and tile installers and finishers	25	28	3	VL	11.0	L	33.0	4	VL
Ceiling tile installers and acoustical carpenters	16	17	1	VL	8.9	L	.0	3	VL
Concrete finishers, cement masons, and terrazzo workers	139	148	9	VL	6.1	VL	5.0	14	VL
Construction equipment operators	321	346	25	-	7.0	-	6.3	39	-
Grader, bulldozer, and scraper operators	122	129	7	VL	5.7	VL	6.5	6	VL
Operating engineers	126	135	10	VL	7.9	VL	8.7	20	VL
Paving, surfacing, and tamping equipment operators[1]	74	82	8	VL	10.6	L	2.0	14	VL
Drywall installers and finishers	163	175	12	VL	7.5	VL	25.6	33	VL
Electricians	656	724	68	L	10.3	L	10.5	93	L
Elevator installers and repairers	30	33	4	VL	12.2	L	1.1	5	VL
Glaziers[1]	44	46	2	VL	3.9	VL	12.9	8	VL
Hazardous materials removal workers	38	45	7	VL	19.3	VH	.0	5	VL
Highway maintenance workers	155	173	17	VL	11.1	L	.0	21	VL
Insulation workers	67	72	5	VL	7.5	VL	4.1	7	VL
Painters and paperhangers	476	517	41	L	8.6	L	43.7	87	L
Pipelayers and pipelaying fitters	57	60	3	VL	4.9	VL	11.0	7	VL
Plasterers and stucco masons[1]	40	47	7	VL	17.1	H	16.9	8	VL
Plumbers, pipefitters, and steamfitters	426	449	22	L	5.3	VL	19.5	58	L
Roofers	158	177	19	VL	12.0	L	31.9	29	VL
Sheet metal workers and duct installers[1]	230	262	32	L	14.1	H	2.2	23	VL
Structural and reinforcing metal workers	81	87	6	VL	8.0	VL	1.9	14	VL
All other construction trades workers[1]	146	155	8	VL	5.7	VL	11.0	18	VL
Extractive and related workers, including blasters	244	255	11	-	4.4	-	1.7	19	-
Oil and gas extraction occupations	69	63	-6	-	-9.0	-	.0	4	-
Roustabouts, oil and gas[1]	30	23	-6	VL	-21.1	VL	.0	2	VL
All other oil and gas extraction occupations[1]	40	40	0	VL	.0	VL	.0	2	VL
Mining, quarrying, and tunneling occupations[1]	23	18	-4	VL	-19.1	VL	2.2	1	VL
All other extraction and related workers[1]	152	173	21	L	14.1	H	2.4	14	VL
Mechanics, installers, and repairers	5,176	5,763	588	-	11.3	-	8.8	690	-

[1] One or more Current Population Survey (CPS) proxy occupations are used to estimate CPS based data.
[2] Current Population Survey data are used to estimate median weekly earnings ranking.
[3] Bachelor's degree or higher.

NOTE: Rankings are based on employment in all detailed occupations in the National Industry-Occupation Matrix. For details, see "Data presented" section of text. Codes for describing the ranked variables are: VH = Very high, H = High, L = Low, VL = Very low, n. a. = Data not available. A dash indicates data are not applicable.

Occupational employment and job openings data, 1998-2008, and worker characteristics, 1998

(Numbers in thousands)

Annual average job openings due to growth and net replacement needs, 1998-2008		Median annual earnings		Ranking of:		Most significant source of education or training	1998 Matrix Occupation
Number	Rank	Dollars	Rank	Unemployment rate	Percent part-time		
0	VL	23,510	L	VH	L	Short-term on-the-job	Fallers and buckers
1	VL	23,150	L	VH	L	Moderate-term on-the-job	Logging equipment operators
0	VL	24,230	H	VH	L	Short-term on-the-job	All other timber cutting and related logging workers
63	-	-	-	-	-	-	Landscaping, groundskeeping, nursery, greenhouse, and lawn service occupations
57	H	17,140	L	VH	H	Short-term on-the-job	Laborers, landscaping and groundskeeping[1]
2	VL	25,420	H	VL	H	Related work experience	Lawn service managers[1]
0	VL	25,360	H	VL	H	Related work experience	Nursery and greenhouse managers[1]
2	VL	22,070	L	VH	H	Short-term on-the-job	Pruners
1	VL	21,650	L	VH	H	Moderate-term on-the-job	Sprayers/applicators
2	VL	24,560	H	VL	H	Related work experience	Supervisors, farming, forestry, and agricutural related occupations[1]
7	-	-	-	-	-	-	Veterinary assistants and nonfarm animal caretakers
5	VL	14,820	VL	H	VH	Short-term on-the-job	Animal caretakers, except farm
2	VL	16,200	VL	H	VH	Short-term on-the-job	Veterinary assistants
11	L	15,760	VL	VH	H	Short-term on-the-job	All other agricultural, forestry, fishing, and related workers[1]
505	-	-	-	-	-	-	**Precision production, craft, and repair occupations**
80	VH	37,180	VH	L	VL	Related work experience	Blue-collar worker supervisors[1]
143	-	-	-	-	-	-	Construction trades
0	VL	38,380	VH	L	VL	Long-term on-the-job	Boilermakers[1]
5	VL	35,200	VH	VH	L	Long-term on-the-job	Bricklayers, blockmasons, and stonemasons[1]
36	H	28,740	H	VH	L	Long-term on-the-job	Carpenters
4	-	-	-	-	-	-	Carpet, floor, and tile installers and finishers
2	VL	26,480	H	H	H	Moderate-term on-the-job	Carpet installers
1	VL	33,810	H	VH	L	Long-term on-the-job	Hard tile setters[1]
1	VL	25,840	H	VH	L	Moderate-term on-the-job	All other carpet, floor, and tile installers and finishers
1	VL	31,750	H	VH	L	Moderate-term on-the-job	Ceiling tile installers and acoustical carpenters
3	VL	25,770	H	VH	L	Long-term on-the-job	Concrete finishers, cement masons, and terrazzo workers
8	-	-	-	-	-	-	Construction equipment operators
2	VL	26,920	H	VH	VL	Moderate-term on-the-job	Grader, bulldozer, and scraper operators
3	VL	35,260	VH	VH	VL	Moderate-term on-the-job	Operating engineers
3	VL	24,510	H	VH	L	Moderate-term on-the-job	Paving, surfacing, and tamping equipment operators[1]
3	VL	29,920	H	VH	L	Moderate-term on-the-job	Drywall installers and finishers
20	L	35,310	VH	L	VL	Long-term on-the-job	Electricians
1	VL	47,860	VH	L	L	Long-term on-the-job	Elevator installers and repairers
1	VL	26,410	H	VH	L	Long-term on-the-job	Glaziers[1]
2	VL	27,620	H	VH	L	Moderate-term on-the-job	Hazardous materials removal workers
5	VL	24,490	H	VH	L	Short-term on-the-job	Highway maintenance workers
3	VL	25,490	H	VH	L	Moderate-term on-the-job	Insulation workers
16	L	25,110	H	VH	L	Moderate-term on-the-job	Painters and paperhangers
2	VL	25,690	H	VH	L	Moderate-term on-the-job	Pipelayers and pipelaying fitters
2	VL	29,390	H	VH	L	Long-term on-the-job	Plasterers and stucco masons[1]
8	VL	34,670	H	H	VL	Long-term on-the-job	Plumbers, pipefitters, and steamfitters
7	VL	25,340	H	VH	H	Moderate-term on-the-job	Roofers
9	VL	28,030	H	H	VL	Moderate-term on-the-job	Sheet metal workers and duct installers[1]
3	VL	32,880	H	VH	L	Long-term on-the-job	Structural and reinforcing metal workers
4	VL	25,390	H	VH	L	Moderate-term on-the-job	All other construction trades workers[1]
8	-	-	-	-	-	-	Extractive and related workers, including blasters
2	-	-	-	-	-	-	Oil and gas extraction occupations
1	VL	19,780	L	H	VL	Short-term on-the-job	Roustabouts, oil and gas[1]
1	VL	25,540	H	H	VL	Moderate-term on-the-job	All other oil and gas extraction occupations[1]
1	VL	32,660	H	H	VL	Long-term on-the-job	Mining, quarrying, and tunneling occupations[1]
6	VL	27,270	H	H	VL	Moderate-term on-the-job	All other extraction and related workers[1]
184	-	-	-	-	-	-	Mechanics, installers, and repairers

[1] One or more Current Population Survey (CPS) proxy occupations are used to estimate CPS based data.
[2] Current Population Survey data are used to estimate median weekly earnings ranking.
[3] Bachelor's degree or higher.

NOTE: Rankings are based on employment in all detailed occupations in the National Industry-Occupation Matrix. For details, see "Data presented" section of text. Codes for describing the ranked variables are: VH = Very high, H = High, L = Low, VL = Very low, n. a. = Data not available. A dash indicates data are not applicable.

Occupational employment and job openings data, 1998-2008, and worker characteristics, 1998

(Numbers in thousands)

1998 Matrix Occupation	Employment		Employment change, 1998-2008				Per-cent self-emp-loyed, 1998	Annual average job openings due to growth and total replacement needs, 1998-2008	
			Numeric		Percent				
	1998	2008	Number	Rank	Number	Rank		Number	Rank
Electrical and electronic equipment mechanics, installers, and repairers	409	472	63	-	15.3	-	8.5	52	-
Computer, automated teller, and office machine repairers	138	184	46	-	33.7	-	11.6	22	-
Data processing equipment repairers	79	117	37	L	47.0	VH	17.9	20	VL
Office machine and cash register servicers	58	67	9	VL	15.6	H	3.2	3	VL
Telecommunications equipment mechanics, installers, and repairers	125	138	13	-	10.0	-	1.3	13	-
Radio mechanics	7	7	0	VL	-1.4	VL	.0	1	VL
Telephone equipment installers and repairers	69	75	6	-	8.8	-	2.4	6	-
Central office and PBX installers and repairers[1]	44	59	14	VL	32.3	VH	3.8	5	VL
Station installers and repairers, telephone[1]	24	16	-8	VL	-33.8	VL	.0	1	VL
All other telecommunications equipment mechanics, installers, and repairers[1]	49	56	7	VL	13.3	L	.0	6	VL
Miscellaneous electrical and electronic equipment mechanics, installers, and repairers	146	150	4	-	2.6	-	11.7	17	-
Electronic home entertainment equipment repairers	36	31	-4	VL	-11.9	VL	21.3	4	VL
Electronics repairers, commercial and industrial equipment	72	81	9	VL	12.7	L	10.6	10	VL
All other electrical and electronic equipment mechanics, installers, and repairers	39	38	-1	VL	-2.4	VL	4.7	3	VL
Machinery mechanics, installers, and repairers	1,850	1,967	117	-	6.3	-	3.8	222	-
Industrial machinery mechanics[1]	535	559	24	L	4.4	VL	3.4	37	VL
Maintenance repairers, general utility	1,232	1,327	95	L	7.7	VL	4.2	181	H
Millwrights	82	81	-2	VL	-1.9	VL	.1	5	VL
Vehicle and mobile equipment mechanics and repairers	1,612	1,828	216	-	13.4	-	15.7	219	-
Aircraft mechanics and service technicians[1]	133	147	14	VL	10.4	L	.4	11	VL
Automotive body and related repairers	227	263	36	L	15.8	H	16.0	33	VL
Automotive mechanics and service technicians[1]	790	922	132	H	16.7	H	22.2	119	L
Bus and truck mechanics and diesel engine specialists	255	280	25	L	9.8	L	5.8	22	VL
Farm equipment mechanics[1]	49	47	-3	VL	-5.2	VL	10.6	8	VL
Mobile heavy equipment mechanics	106	116	10	VL	9.3	L	5.0	19	VL
Motorcycle, boat, and small engine mechanics	52	54	2	-	4.7	-	30.5	8	-
Motorcycle mechanics[1]	14	14	1	VL	3.9	VL	30.4	2	VL
Small engine mechanics[1]	38	40	2	VL	5.0	VL	30.5	6	VL
Other mechanics, installers, and repairers	1,305	1,496	191	-	14.6	-	7.6	197	-
Bicycle repairers	11	13	2	VL	22.6	VH	24.5	2	VL
Camera and photographic equipment repairers[1]	9	10	1	VL	8.2	VL	63.9	1	VL
Coin, vending, and amusement machine servicers and repairers	27	31	4	VL	15.6	H	.0	4	VL
Heating, air conditioning, and refrigeration mechanics and installers	286	334	48	L	16.9	H	15.0	30	VL
Home appliance and power tool repairers[1]	51	54	3	VL	5.6	VL	15.0	8	VL
Line installers and repairers	279	335	56	-	19.9	-	.7	24	-
Electrical powerline installers and repairers	99	100	1	VL	1.1	VL	1.4	6	VL
Telephone and cable TV line installers and repairers[1]	180	235	55	L	30.3	VH	.3	18	VL
Locksmiths and safe repairers[1]	27	30	3	VL	10.0	L	32.2	5	VL
Medical equipment repairers	11	12	1	VL	13.5	L	.0	2	VL
Musical instrument repairers and tuners[1]	13	13	1	VL	6.5	VL	64.1	2	VL
Precision instrument repairers[1]	33	32	-1	VL	-4.0	VL	8.4	5	VL
Riggers	11	11	0	VL	.5	VL	.0	2	VL
Tire repairers and changers	83	92	9	VL	10.4	L	3.1	26	VL
Watch repairers[1]	8	8	0	VL	-4.2	VL	63.7	1	VL
All other mechanics, installers, and repairers[1]	455	520	65	L	14.3	H	2.3	85	L
Production occupations, precision	2,971	3,010	39	-	1.3	-	6.9	395	-
Assemblers, precision	422	442	20	-	4.6	-	.8	68	-
Aircraft assemblers, precision[1]	17	20	3	VL	19.3	VH	.0	2	VL
Electrical and electronic equipment assemblers, precision	201	213	12	VL	6.0	VL	1.7	39	VL

[1] One or more Current Population Survey (CPS) proxy occupations are used to estimate CPS based data.
[2] Current Population Survey data are used to estimate median weekly earnings ranking.
[3] Bachelor's degree or higher.

NOTE: Rankings are based on employment in all detailed occupations in the National Industry-Occupation Matrix. For details, see "Data presented" section of text. Codes for describing the ranked variables are: VH = Very high, H = High, L = Low, VL = Very low, n. a. = Data not available. A dash indicates data are not applicable.

Occupational employment and job openings data, 1998-2008, and worker characteristics, 1998

(Numbers in thousands)

Annual average job openings due to growth and net replacement needs, 1998-2008		Median annual earnings		Ranking of:		Most significant source of education or training	1998 Matrix Occupation
Number	Rank	Dollars	Rank	Unemployment rate	Percent part-time		
18	-	-	-	-	-	-	Electrical and electronic equipment mechanics, installers, and repairers
7	-	-	-	-	-	-	Computer, automated teller, and office machine repairers
5	VL	29,340	H	L	L	Postsecondary vocational	Data processing equipment repairers
2	VL	27,830	H	H	L	Long-term on-the-job	Office machine and cash register servicers
6	-	-	-	-	-	-	Telecommunications equipment mechanics, installers, and repairers
0	VL	30,590	H	L	L	Postsecondary vocational	Radio mechanics
4	-	-	-	-	-	-	Telephone equipment installers and repairers
3	VL	43,680	VH	VL	VL	Postsecondary vocational	Central office and PBX installers and repairers[1]
1	VL	39,630	VH	VL	VL	Postsecondary vocational	Station installers and repairers, telephone[1]
2	VL	42,850	VH	L	L	Postsecondary vocational	All other telecommunications equipment mechanics, installers, and repairers[1]
5	-	-	-	-	-	-	Miscellaneous electrical and electronic equipment mechanics, installers, and repairers
1	VL	23,540	L	L	L	Postsecondary vocational	Electronic home entertainment equipment repairers
3	VL	35,590	VH	L	L	Postsecondary vocational	Electronics repairers, commercial and industrial equipment
1	VL	31,300	H	L	VL	Postsecondary vocational	All other electrical and electronic equipment mechanics, installers, and repairers
54	-	-	-	-	-		Machinery mechanics, installers, and repairers
14	L	31,850	H	L	VL	Long-term on-the-job	Industrial machinery mechanics[1]
37	H	23,290	L	L	L	Long-term on-the-job	Maintenance repairers, general utility
2	VL	36,940	VH	VH	VL	Long-term on-the-job	Millwrights
62	-	-	-	-	-	-	Vehicle and mobile equipment mechanics and repairers
4	VL	38,060	VH	VL	VL	Postsecondary vocational	Aircraft mechanics and service technicians[1]
10	VL	27,400	H	H	L	Long-term on-the-job	Automotive body and related repairers
33	L	27,360	H	H	L	Postsecondary vocational	Automotive mechanics and service technicians[1]
8	VL	29,340	H	L	VL	Long-term on-the-job	Bus and truck mechanics and diesel engine specialists
1	VL	22,750	L	L	VL	Long-term on-the-job	Farm equipment mechanics[1]
4	VL	31,520	H	L	VL	Long-term on-the-job	Mobile heavy equipment mechanics
2	-	-	-	-	-	-	Motorcycle, boat, and small engine mechanics
0	VL	23,440	L	L	VL	Long-term on-the-job	Motorcycle mechanics[1]
1	VL	21,580	L	L	VL	Long-term on-the-job	Small engine mechanics[1]
51	-	-	-	-	-	-	Other mechanics, installers, and repairers
0	VL	15,700	VL	L	L	Moderate-term on-the-job	Bicycle repairers
0	VL	28,320	H	L	L	Moderate-term on-the-job	Camera and photographic equipment repairers[1]
1	VL	23,260	L	L	L	Long-term on-the-job	Coin, vending, and amusement machine servicers and repairers
10	VL	29,160	H	L	VL	Long-term on-the-job	Heating, air conditioning, and refrigeration mechanics and installers
2	VL	26,010	H	L	L	Long-term on-the-job	Home appliance and power tool repairers[1]
14	-	-	-	-	-	-	Line installers and repairers
2	VL	42,600	VH	VL	VL	Long-term on-the-job	Electrical powerline installers and repairers
11	L	32,750	H	VL	VL	Long-term on-the-job	Telephone and cable TV line installers and repairers[1]
1	VL	24,890	H	L	L	Moderate-term on-the-job	Locksmiths and safe repairers[1]
0	VL	34,190	H	L	L	Long-term on-the-job	Medical equipment repairers
0	VL	23,010	L	L	L	Long-term on-the-job	Musical instrument repairers and tuners[1]
1	VL	39,580	VH	L	L	Long-term on-the-job	Precision instrument repairers[1]
0	VL	31,770	H	L	L	Long-term on-the-job	Riggers
5	VL	16,810	VL	VH	VH	Short-term on-the-job	Tire repairers and changers
0	VL	24,590	H	L	L	Long-term on-the-job	Watch repairers[1]
16	L	29,240	H	L	L	Long-term on-the-job	All other mechanics, installers, and repairers[1]
74	-	-	-	-	-	-	Production occupations, precision
12	-	-	-	-	-	-	Assemblers, precision
1	VL	38,400	VH	L	VL	Related work experience	Aircraft assemblers, precision[1]
6	VL	21,740	L	VH	VL	Related work experience	Electrical and electronic equipment assemblers, precision

[1] One or more Current Population Survey (CPS) proxy occupations are used to estimate CPS based data.

[2] Current Population Survey data are used to estimate median weekly earnings ranking.

[3] Bachelor's degree or higher.

NOTE: Rankings are based on employment in all detailed occupations in the National Industry-Occupation Matrix. For details, see "Data presented" section of text. Codes for describing the ranked variables are: VH = Very high, H = High, L = Low, VL = Very low, n. a. = Data not available. A dash indicates data are not applicable.

Occupational employment and job openings data, 1998-2008, and worker characteristics, 1998

(Numbers in thousands)

1998 Matrix Occupation	Employment		Employment change, 1998-2008				Per-cent self-emp-loyed, 1998	Annual average job openings due to growth and total replacement needs, 1998-2008	
	1998	2008	Numeric		Percent			Number	Rank
			Number	Rank	Number	Rank			
Electromechanical equipment assemblers, precision	50	52	3	VL	5.7	VL	.0	10	VL
Fitters, structural metal, precision[1]	17	15	-2	VL	-13.0	VL	.0	2	VL
Machine builders and other precision machine assemblers[1] ...	74	76	1	VL	1.7	VL	.0	9	VL
All other precision assemblers[1]	64	66	2	VL	3.7	VL	.0	8	VL
Food workers, precision	310	303	-7	-	-2.3	-	7.9	36	-
Bakers, manufacturing	55	60	5	VL	8.5	L	28.8	11	VL
Butchers and meatcutters	216	201	-15	VL	-7.1	VL	3.3	18	VL
All other precision food and tobacco workers[1]	39	42	3	VL	8.5	L	3.5	7	VL
Inspectors, testers, and graders, precision	689	667	-22	VL	-3.2	VL	.6	96	L
Metal workers, precision[1]	707	734	27	-	3.7	-	4.4	74	-
Jewelers and precious stone and metal workers[1]	30	28	-2	VL	-6.0	VL	32.1	3	VL
Machinists	426	452	26	L	6.2	VL	2.5	42	VL
Numerical control machine tool programmers	8	9	1	VL	6.1	VL	.0	1	VL
Shipfitters[1]	9	8	0	VL	-4.5	VL	.0	1	VL
Tool and die makers	138	136	-2	VL	-1.5	VL	1.1	15	VL
All other precision metal workers[1]	97	101	4	VL	4.0	VL	9.8	11	VL
Printing workers, precision	138	137	-1	-	-1.0	-	4.0	24	-
Bookbinders[1]	7	6	-1	VL	-15.2	VL	5.2	1	VL
Prepress printing workers, precision	115	114	0	-	-.4	-	4.6	20	-
Camera operators[1]	9	6	-3	VL	-31.4	VL	.0	1	VL
Compositors and typesetters, precision[1]	14	11	-3	VL	-18.9	VL	38.2	2	VL
Desktop publishing specialists[1]	26	44	19	VL	72.6	VH	.0	8	VL
Film strippers, printing[1]	23	15	-8	VL	-33.0	VL	.0	3	VL
Job printers	17	18	1	VL	4.3	VL	.0	3	VL
Paste-up workers[1]	9	4	-5	VL	-51.2	VL	.0	1	VL
Photoengravers[1]	3	1	-1	VL	-51.5	VL	.0	0	VL
Platemakers[1]	15	14	-1	VL	-5.2	VL	.0	2	VL
All other printing workers, precision[1]	17	17	0	VL	.2	VL	.0	3	VL
Textile, apparel, and furnishings workers, precision	234	226	-8	-	-3.3	-	31.3	23	-
Custom tailors and sewers	74	67	-6	VL	-8.4	VL	56.5	6	VL
Patternmakers and layout workers, fabric and apparel[1]	16	15	-1	VL	-3.8	VL	.0	1	VL
Shoe and leather workers and repairers, precision[1]	23	19	-4	VL	-17.6	VL	24.3	2	VL
Upholsterers[1]	66	67	1	VL	.9	VL	36.2	5	VL
All other precision textile, apparel, and furnishings workers[1] ...	55	58	2	VL	4.4	VL	3.7	9	VL
Woodworkers, precision	229	236	7	-	2.8	-	15.1	35	-
Cabinetmakers and bench carpenters	123	129	6	VL	5.2	VL	18.9	20	VL
Furniture finishers[1]	38	38	0	VL	-1.0	VL	27.1	5	VL
Wood machinists	40	41	1	VL	3.2	VL	.0	6	VL
All other precision woodworkers[1]	27	27	-1	VL	-2.5	VL	3.2	4	VL
Other precision workers	242	266	25	-	10.2	-	12.2	38	-
Dental laboratory technicians, precision	44	44	0	VL	1.0	VL	20.1	3	VL
Ophthalmic laboratory technicians	23	24	1	VL	4.7	VL	.0	2	VL
Photographic process workers, precision	18	19	1	VL	7.0	VL	51.2	4	VL
All other precision workers	157	179	22	L	14.0	L	7.3	29	VL
Plant and system occupations	403	431	28	-	6.0	-	.7	35	-
Chemical plant and system operators[1]	43	48	5	VL	11.0	L	.0	3	VL
Electric power generating plant operators, distributors, and dispatchers	45	44	-1	-	-1.5	-	.0	3	-
Power distributors and dispatchers[1]	14	12	-2	VL	-12.2	VL	.0	1	VL
Power generating and reactor plant operators[1]	31	32	1	VL	3.1	VL	.0	2	VL
Gas and petroleum plant and system occupations[1]	38	33	-5	VL	-12.6	VL	.0	2	VL
Stationary engineers	31	29	-2	VL	-5.7	VL	3.8	2	VL
Water and liquid waste treatment plant and system operators ..	98	112	14	VL	14.2	H	.0	13	VL
All other plant and system operators[1]	148	164	16	VL	11.1	L	1.2	12	VL

[1] One or more Current Population Survey (CPS) proxy occupations are used to estimate CPS based data.
[2] Current Population Survey data are used to estimate median weekly earnings ranking.
[3] Bachelor's degree or higher.

NOTE: Rankings are based on employment in all detailed occupations in the National Industry-Occupation Matrix. For details, see "Data presented" section of text. Codes for describing the ranked variables are: VH = Very high, H = High, L = Low, VL = Very low, n. a. = Data not available. A dash indicates data are not applicable.

Occupational employment and job openings data, 1998-2008, and worker characteristics, 1998

(Numbers in thousands)

Annual average job openings due to growth and net replacement needs, 1998-2008		Median annual earnings		Ranking of:		Most significant source of education or training	1998 Matrix Occupation
Number	Rank	Dollars	Rank	Unemploy-ment rate	Percent part-time		
1	VL	23,250	L	VH	VL	Related work experience	Electromechanical equipment assemblers, precision
0	VL	26,180	H	L	VL	Related work experience	Fitters, structural metal, precision[1]
2	VL	29,250	H	L	VL	Related work experience	Machine builders and other precision machine assemblers[1]
2	VL	22,110	L	L	VL	Related work experience	All other precision assemblers[1]
8	-	-	-	-	-	-	Food workers, precision
1	VL	22,030	L	H	VH	Moderate-term on-the-job	Bakers, manufacturing
5	VL	20,420	L	H	L	Long-term on-the-job	Butchers and meatcutters
2	VL	22,400	L	H	H	Long-term on-the-job	All other precision food and tobacco workers[1]
15	L	23,470	L	H	L	Related work experience	Inspectors, testers, and graders, precision
18	-	-	-	-	-	-	Metal workers, precision[1]
1	VL	23,820	H	L	VL	Postsecondary vocational	Jewelers and precious stone and metal workers[1]
11	L	28,860	H	L	VL	Long-term on-the-job	Machinists
0	VL	40,490	VH	L	H	Related work experience	Numerical control machine tool programmers
0	VL	28,840	H	L	VL	Long-term on-the-job	Shipfitters[1]
3	VL	37,250	VH	VL	VL	Long-term on-the-job	Tool and die makers
3	VL	26,300	H	L	VL	Long-term on-the-job	All other precision metal workers[1]
4	-	-	-	-	-	-	Printing workers, precision
0	VL	20,690	L	H	L	Moderate-term on-the-job	Bookbinders[1]
4	-	-	-	-	-	-	Prepress printing workers, precision
0	VL	24,370	H	L	L	Long-term on-the-job	Camera operators[1]
0	VL	22,560	L	L	L	Long-term on-the-job	Compositors and typesetters, precision[1]
2	VL	29,130	H	L	L	Long-term on-the-job	Desktop publishing specialists[1]
0	VL	32,300	H	L	L	Long-term on-the-job	Film strippers, printing[1]
0	VL	24,100	H	L	L	Long-term on-the-job	Job printers
0	VL	19,830	L	L	L	Long-term on-the-job	Paste-up workers[1]
0	VL	28,430	H	L	L	Long-term on-the-job	Photoengravers[1]
0	VL	28,600	H	L	L	Long-term on-the-job	Platemakers[1]
0	VL	30,420	H	L	L	Long-term on-the-job	All other printing workers, precision[1]
5	-	-	-	-	-	-	Textile, apparel, and furnishings workers, precision
1	VL	18,630	L	H	VH	Related work experience	Custom tailors and sewers
0	VL	21,580	L	H	H	Long-term on-the-job	Patternmakers and layout workers, fabric and apparel[1]
0	VL	16,610	VL	H	H	Long-term on-the-job	Shoe and leather workers and repairers, precision[1]
1	VL	22,050	L	L	H	Long-term on-the-job	Upholsterers[1]
1	VL	16,790	VL	VH	VH	Long-term on-the-job	All other precision textile, apparel, and furnishings workers[1]
4	-	-	-	-	-	-	Woodworkers, precision
2	VL	22,390	L	L	L	Long-term on-the-job	Cabinetmakers and bench carpenters
1	VL	19,880	L	L	L	Long-term on-the-job	Furniture finishers[1]
1	VL	19,980	L	L	L	Long-term on-the-job	Wood machinists
1	VL	22,430	L	L	L	Long-term on-the-job	All other precision woodworkers[1]
8	-	-	-	-	-	-	Other precision workers
1	VL	25,660	H	VL	H	Long-term on-the-job	Dental laboratory technicians, precision
0	VL	19,530	L	VL	H	Long-term on-the-job	Ophthalmic laboratory technicians
1	VL	21,620	L	H	VH	Moderate-term on-the-job	Photographic process workers, precision
6	VL	22,720	L	H	L	Long-term on-the-job	All other precision workers
15	-	-	-	-	-	-	Plant and system occupations
2	VL	39,030	VH	VL	VL	Long-term on-the-job	Chemical plant and system operators[1]
2	-	-	-	-	-	-	Electric power generating plant operators, distributors, and dispatchers
0	VL	45,690	VH	VL	VL	Long-term on-the-job	Power distributors and dispatchers[1]
1	VL	44,840	VH	VL	VL	Long-term on-the-job	Power generating and reactor plant operators[1]
1	VL	43,820	VH	VL	VL	Long-term on-the-job	Gas and petroleum plant and system occupations[1]
1	VL	38,270	VH	VL	VL	Long-term on-the-job	Stationary engineers
4	VL	29,660	H	VL	VL	Long-term on-the-job	Water and liquid waste treatment plant and system operators
6	VL	22,580	L	VL	VL	Long-term on-the-job	All other plant and system operators[1]

[1] One or more Current Population Survey (CPS) proxy occupations are used to estimate CPS based data.

[2] Current Population Survey data are used to estimate median weekly earnings ranking.

[3] Bachelor's degree or higher.

NOTE: Rankings are based on employment in all detailed occupations in the National Industry-Occupation Matrix. For details, see "Data presented" section of text. Codes for describing the ranked variables are: VH = Very high, H = High, L = Low, VL = Very low, n. a. = Data not available. A dash indicates data are not applicable.

Occupational employment and job openings data, 1998-2008, and worker characteristics, 1998

(Numbers in thousands)

1998 Matrix Occupation	Employment		Employment change, 1998-2008				Per-cent self-emp-loyed, 1998	Annual average job openings due to growth and total replacement needs, 1998-2008	
			Numeric		Percent				
	1998	2008	Number	Rank	Number	Rank		Number	Rank
Operators, fabricators, and laborers	18,588	20,341	1,753	-	9.4	-	3.4	3,941	-
Machine setters, set-up operators, operators, and tenders	5,139	5,230	91	-	1.7	-	1.8	812	-
Numerical control machine tool operators and tenders, metal and plastic[1]	88	108	20	VL	22.6	VH	.0	19	VL
Combination machine tool setters, set-up operators, operators, and tenders, metal and plastic[1]	107	122	15	VL	13.8	L	.0	21	VL
Machine tool cut and form setters, operators, and tenders, metal and plastic	726	690	-36	-	-4.9	-	.7	83	-
Drilling and boring machine tool setters and set-up operators, metal and plastic[1]	42	34	-8	VL	-18.3	VL	.0	7	VL
Grinding, lapping, and buffing machine tool setters and set-up operators, metal and plastic	75	68	-7	VL	-9.6	VL	4.6	4	VL
Lathe and turning machine tool setters and set-up operators, metal and plastic[1]	72	66	-6	VL	-8.4	VL	.0	12	VL
Machine forming operators and tenders, metal and plastic	163	157	-6	VL	-3.9	VL	.0	16	VL
Machine tool cutting operators and tenders, metal and plastic	109	88	-22	VL	-19.9	VL	.0	6	VL
Punching machine setters and set-up operators, metal and plastic	47	44	-4	VL	-7.5	VL	.2	6	VL
All other machine tool setters, set-up operators, metal and plastic[1]	218	235	17	VL	7.7	VL	.6	34	VL
Metal fabricating machine setters, operators, and related workers	167	178	10	-	6.1	-	.0	22	-
Metal fabricators, structural metal products[1]	46	49	3	VL	7.5	VL	.0	9	VL
Soldering and brazing machine operators and tenders[1]	12	13	1	VL	8.2	VL	.0	2	VL
Welding machine setters, operators, and tenders	110	116	6	VL	5.4	VL	.0	11	VL
Metal and plastic processing machine setters, operators, and related workers	478	528	50	-	10.5	-	.0	55	-
Electrolytic plating machine setters, set-up operators, operators, and tenders, metal and plastic[1]	45	49	4	VL	9.6	L	.0	5	VL
Foundry mold assembly and shake out workers	9	10	0	VL	2.5	VL	.0	1	VL
Furnace operators and tenders[1]	23	22	-1	VL	-5.0	VL	.0	2	VL
Heat treating, annealing, and tempering machine operators and tenders, metal and plastic[1]	23	22	-1	VL	-4.1	VL	.0	2	VL
Metal molding machine setters, set-up operators, operators, and tenders	58	63	5	VL	9.0	L	.0	6	VL
Plastic molding machine setters, set-up operators, operators, and tenders	171	196	25	L	14.7	H	.0	21	VL
All other metal and plastic machine setters, operators, and related workers[1]	148	166	18	VL	11.9	L	.0	17	VL
Printing, binding, and related workers	406	410	4	-	1.0	-	2.1	64	-
Bindery machine operators and set-up operators[1]	90	100	10	VL	11.5	L	.0	16	VL
Prepress printing workers, production	20	11	-9	-	-44.7	-	.0	3	-
Photoengraving and lithographic machine operators and tenders[1]	7	6	-1	VL	-15.0	VL	.0	1	VL
Typesetting and composing machine operators and tenders[1]	13	5	-8	VL	-59.8	VL	.0	2	VL
Printing press operators	225	225	0	-	.1	-	3.8	33	-
Letterpress operators	10	8	-2	VL	-18.2	VL	.0	1	VL
Offset lithographic press operators	63	54	-9	VL	-14.7	VL	4.5	8	VL
Printing press machine setters, operators and tenders	142	154	12	VL	8.3	VL	4.1	22	VL
All other printing press setters and set-up operators	10	9	0	VL	-4.5	VL	.0	1	VL
Screen printing machine setters and set-up operators	28	29	1	VL	3.0	VL	.0	4	VL
All other printing, binding, and related workers[1]	43	45	2	VL	4.1	VL	.0	7	VL
Textile and related setters, operators, and related workers	851	687	-164	-	-19.2	-	2.5	108	-
Extruding and forming machine operators and tenders, synthetic or glass fibers[1]	33	35	3	VL	7.9	VL	.0	6	VL
Pressing machine operators and tenders, textile, garment, and related materials	69	66	-3	VL	-4.0	VL	.0	10	VL
Sewing machine operators, garment	369	257	-112	VL	-30.3	VL	3.6	42	VL

[1] One or more Current Population Survey (CPS) proxy occupations are used to estimate CPS based data.
[2] Current Population Survey data are used to estimate median weekly earnings ranking.
[3] Bachelor's degree or higher.

NOTE: Rankings are based on employment in all detailed occupations in the National Industry-Occupation Matrix. For details, see "Data presented" section of text. Codes for describing the ranked variables are: VH = Very high, H = High, L = Low, VL = Very low, n. a. = Data not available. A dash indicates data are not applicable.

Occupational employment and job openings data, 1998-2008, and worker characteristics, 1998

(Numbers in thousands)

Annual average job openings due to growth and net replacement needs, 1998-2008		Median annual earnings		Ranking of:		Most significant source of education or training	1998 Matrix Occupation
Number	Rank	Dollars	Rank	Unemployment rate	Percent part-time		
637	-	-	-	-	-	-	**Operators, fabricators, and laborers**
146	-	-	-	-	-	-	Machine setters, set-up operators, operators, and tenders
							Numerical control machine tool operators and tenders, metal and plastic[1]
4	VL	27,110	H	H	VL	Moderate-term on-the-job	
4	VL	23,860	H	H	VL	Moderate-term on-the-job	Combination machine tool setters, set-up operators, operators, and tenders, metal and plastic[1]
19	-	-	-	-	-	-	Machine tool cut and form setters, operators, and tenders, metal and plastic
1	VL	25,630	H	H	VL	Moderate-term on-the-job	Drilling and boring machine tool setters and set-up operators, metal and plastic[1]
2	VL	24,740	H	H	VL	Moderate-term on-the-job	Grinding, lapping, and buffing machine tool setters and set-up operators, metal and plastic
2	VL	28,250	H	H	VL	Moderate-term on-the-job	Lathe and turning machine tool setters and set-up operators, metal and plastic[1]
4	VL	20,170	L	H	VL	Moderate-term on-the-job	Machine forming operators and tenders, metal and plastic
3	VL	24,510	H	H	VL	Moderate-term on-the-job	Machine tool cutting operators and tenders, metal and plastic
1	VL	23,270	L	VH	VL	Moderate-term on-the-job	Punching machine setters and set-up operators, metal and plastic
7	VL	25,020	H	H	VL	Moderate-term on-the-job	All other machine tool setters, set-up operators, metal and plastic[1]
5	-	-	-	H	-	-	Metal fabricating machine setters, operators, and related workers
1	VL	24,070	H	H	VL	Moderate-term on-the-job	Metal fabricators, structural metal products[1]
0	VL	20,950	L	VH	L	Moderate-term on-the-job	Soldering and brazing machine operators and tenders[1]
3	VL	25,010	H	H	VL	Moderate-term on-the-job	Welding machine setters, operators, and tenders
17	-	-	-	-	-	-	Metal and plastic processing machine setters, operators, and related workers
2	VL	21,210	L	VH	VL	Moderate-term on-the-job	Electrolytic plating machine setters, set-up operators, operators, and tenders, metal and plastic[1]
0	VL	21,910	L	H	VL	Moderate-term on-the-job	Foundry mold assembly and shake out workers
0	VL	25,870	H	H	VL	Moderate-term on-the-job	Furnace operators and tenders[1]
1	VL	25,160	H	VH	VL	Moderate-term on-the-job	Heat treating, annealing, and tempering machine operators and tenders, metal and plastic[1]
2	VL	24,870	H	H	VL	Moderate-term on-the-job	Metal molding machine setters, set-up operators, operators, and tenders
7	VL	18,580	L	H	VL	Moderate-term on-the-job	Plastic molding machine setters, set-up operators, operators, and tenders
5	VL	22,780	L	VH	VL	Moderate-term on-the-job	All other metal and plastic machine setters, operators, and related workers[1]
11	-	-	-	-	-	-	Printing, binding, and related workers
3	VL	20,610	L	L	L	Moderate-term on-the-job	Bindery machine operators and set-up operators[1]
0	-	-	-	-	-	-	Prepress printing workers, production
0	VL	23,960	H	L	L	Moderate-term on-the-job	Photoengraving and lithographic machine operators and tenders[1]
0	VL	23,050	L	L	L	Moderate-term on-the-job	Typesetting and composing machine operators and tenders[1]
6	-	-	-	-	-	-	Printing press operators
0	VL	28,620	H	L	VL	Moderate-term on-the-job	Letterpress operators
1	VL	31,000	H	L	VL	Moderate-term on-the-job	Offset lithographic press operators
4	VL	26,030	H	L	VL	Moderate-term on-the-job	Printing press machine setters, operators and tenders
0	VL	27,720	H	L	L	Moderate-term on-the-job	All other printing press setters and set-up operators
1	VL	18,880	L	L	L	Moderate-term on-the-job	Screen printing machine setters and set-up operators
1	VL	22,950	L	L	L	Moderate-term on-the-job	All other printing, binding, and related workers[1]
13	-	-	-	-	-	-	Textile and related setters, operators, and related workers
1	VL	27,940	H	VH	L	Moderate-term on-the-job	Extruding and forming machine operators and tenders, synthetic or glass fibers[1]
1	VL	15,150	VL	VH	VH	Moderate-term on-the-job	Pressing machine operators and tenders, textile, garment, and related materials
5	VL	14,740	VL	VH	L	Moderate-term on-the-job	Sewing machine operators, garment

[1] One or more Current Population Survey (CPS) proxy occupations are used to estimate CPS based data.

[2] Current Population Survey data are used to estimate median weekly earnings ranking.

[3] Bachelor's degree or higher.

NOTE: Rankings are based on employment in all detailed occupations in the National Industry-Occupation Matrix. For details, see "Data presented" section of text. Codes for describing the ranked variables are: VH = Very high, H = High, L = Low, VL = Very low, n. a. = Data not available. A dash indicates data are not applicable.

Occupational employment and job openings data, 1998-2008, and worker characteristics, 1998

(Numbers in thousands)

1998 Matrix Occupation	Employment		Employment change, 1998-2008				Per-cent self-emp-loyed, 1998	Annual average job openings due to growth and total replacement needs, 1998-2008	
			Numeric		Percent				
	1998	2008	Number	Rank	Number	Rank		Number	Rank
Sewing machine operators, non-garment	137	140	3	VL	2.5	VL	3.8	19	VL
Textile bleaching and dyeing machine operators and tenders[1]	24	22	-2	VL	-9.0	VL	3.2	4	VL
Textile draw-out and winding machine operators and tenders[1]	192	141	-50	VL	-26.3	VL	.9	23	VL
Textile machine setters and set-up operators	28	26	-3	VL	-9.6	VL	.0	4	VL
Woodworking machine setters, operators, and other related workers	143	130	-14	-	-9.4	-	5.6	45	-
Head sawyers and sawing machine operators and tenders, setters and set-up operators	64	61	-4	VL	-5.7	VL	2.0	24	VL
Woodworking machine operators and tenders, setters and set-up operators[1]	79	69	-10	VL	-12.5	VL	8.5	21	VL
Other machine setters, set-up operators, operators, and tenders	2,172	2,377	205	-	9.4	-	2.3	396	-
Boiler operators and tenders, low pressure	16	14	-2	VL	-11.0	VL	.0	1	VL
Cement and gluing machine operators and tenders[1]	32	27	-5	VL	-15.6	VL	.0	5	VL
Chemical equipment controllers, operators and tenders[1]	100	111	11	VL	11.4	L	.0	20	VL
Cooking and roasting machine operators and tenders, food and tobacco[1]	31	28	-3	VL	-8.5	VL	1.6	4	VL
Crushing, grinding, mixing, and blending machine operators and tenders	150	154	4	VL	2.8	VL	1.6	27	VL
Cutting and slicing machine setters, operators and tenders	96	102	6	VL	6.4	VL	2.5	18	VL
Dairy processing equipment operators, including setters[1]	15	12	-3	VL	-20.4	VL	6.8	2	VL
Electronic semiconductor processors	63	92	29	L	45.2	VH	.0	11	VL
Extruding and forming machine setters, operators and tenders[1]	126	132	6	VL	5.0	VL	.0	23	VL
Furnace, kiln, oven, drier, or kettle operators and tenders[1]	25	24	-1	VL	-5.6	VL	.0	2	VL
Laundry and dry-cleaning machine operators and tenders, except pressing	167	184	16	VL	9.8	L	14.7	38	VL
Motion picture projectionists[1]	9	7	-2	VL	-21.8	VL	6.4	1	VL
Packaging and filling machine operators and tenders	377	425	49	L	12.9	L	.0	88	L
Painting and coating machine operators	171	186	15	-	8.7	-	5.5	35	-
Coating, painting, and spraying machine operators, tenders, setters, and set-up operators	129	140	11	VL	8.7	L	2.3	26	VL
Painters, transportation equipment	42	46	4	VL	9.0	L	15.4	9	VL
Paper goods machine setters and set-up operators[1]	62	59	-3	VL	-4.1	VL	.0	9	VL
Photographic processing machine operators and tenders	46	41	-5	VL	-11.4	VL	.0	10	VL
Separating, filtering, clarifying, precipitating, and still machine operators and tenders[1]	28	26	-2	VL	-7.2	VL	.0	5	VL
Shoe sewing machine operators and tenders[1]	7	4	-2	VL	-35.8	VL	.0	1	VL
Tire building machine operators	18	17	0	VL	-1.4	VL	.0	2	VL
All other machine operators, tenders, setters, and set-up operators[1]	635	732	97	L	15.2	H	1.4	92	L
Hand workers, including assemblers and fabricators	3,092	3,382	290	-	9.3	-	3.6	636	-
Cannery workers	50	44	-6	VL	-12.0	VL	.0	10	VL
Coil winders, tapers, and finishers	22	22	1	VL	2.5	VL	.0	5	VL
Cutters and trimmers, hand[1]	42	39	-4	VL	-8.3	VL	1.2	7	VL
Electrical and electronic assemblers	246	265	19	VL	7.7	VL	.0	59	L
Grinders and polishers, hand	81	84	3	VL	4.3	VL	.0	13	VL
Machine assemblers	67	71	4	VL	5.5	VL	.0	16	VL
Meat, poultry, and fish cutters and trimmers, hand[1]	143	178	35	L	24.2	VH	.0	33	VL
Painting, coating, and decorating workers, hand[1]	39	46	7	VL	17.7	H	18.4	9	VL
Pressers, hand	13	12	-2	VL	-11.4	VL	.0	2	VL
Sewers, hand	10	8	-1	VL	-14.8	VL	.0	1	VL
Solderers and brazers[1]	35	40	5	VL	14.4	H	.0	8	VL
Welders and cutters	368	398	31	L	8.3	L	5.2	38	VL
All other assemblers, fabricators, and hand workers[1]	1,976	2,175	198	H	10.0	L	4.2	437	VH

[1] One or more Current Population Survey (CPS) proxy occupations are used to estimate CPS based data.
[2] Current Population Survey data are used to estimate median weekly earnings ranking.
[3] Bachelor's degree or higher.

NOTE: Rankings are based on employment in all detailed occupations in the National Industry-Occupation Matrix. For details, see "Data presented" section of text. Codes for describing the ranked variables are: VH = Very high, H = High, L = Low, VL = Very low, n. a. = Data not available. A dash indicates data are not applicable.

Occupational employment and job openings data, 1998-2008, and worker characteristics, 1998

(Numbers in thousands)

Annual average job openings due to growth and net replacement needs, 1998-2008		Median annual earnings		Ranking of:		Most significant source of education or training	1998 Matrix Occupation
Number	Rank	Dollars	Rank	Unemployment rate	Percent part-time		
2	VL	16,990	L	VH	H	Moderate-term on-the-job	Sewing machine operators, non-garment
0	VL	19,350	L	VH	L	Moderate-term on-the-job	Textile bleaching and dyeing machine operators and tenders[1]
3	VL	19,480	L	VH	H	Moderate-term on-the-job	Textile draw-out and winding machine operators and tenders[1]
0	VL	21,620	L	VH	H	Moderate-term on-the-job	Textile machine setters and set-up operators
4	-	-	-	-	-	-	Woodworking machine setters, operators, and other related workers
2	VL	19,490	L	VH	L	Moderate-term on-the-job	Head sawyers and sawing machine operators and tenders, setters and set-up operators
2	VL	19,260	L	VH	L	Moderate-term on-the-job	Woodworking machine operators and tenders, setters and set-up operators[1]
69	-	-	-	-	-	-	Other machine setters, set-up operators, operators, and tenders
0	VL	30,320	H	VL	VL	Moderate-term on-the-job	Boiler operators and tenders, low pressure
1	VL	20,720	L	H	L	Moderate-term on-the-job	Cement and gluing machine operators and tenders[1]
4	VL	32,180	H	VL	VL	Moderate-term on-the-job	Chemical equipment controllers, operators and tenders[1]
1	VL	21,710	L	H	VL	Moderate-term on-the-job	Cooking and roasting machine operators and tenders, food and tobacco[1]
4	VL	23,350	L	H	L	Moderate-term on-the-job	Crushing, grinding, mixing, and blending machine operators and tenders
3	VL	21,680	L	H	L	Moderate-term on-the-job	Cutting and slicing machine setters, operators and tenders
0	VL	25,800	H	VL	VL	Moderate-term on-the-job	Dairy processing equipment operators, including setters[1]
4	VL	24,810	H	H	VL	Moderate-term on-the-job	Electronic semiconductor processors
4	VL	23,180	L	H	L	Moderate-term on-the-job	Extruding and forming machine setters, operators and tenders[1]
0	VL	25,110	H	H	VL	Moderate-term on-the-job	Furnace, kiln, oven, drier, or kettle operators and tenders[1]
6	VL	14,670	VL	VH	VH	Moderate-term on-the-job	Laundry and dry-cleaning machine operators and tenders, except pressing
0	VL	15,420	VL	H	L	Short-term on-the-job	Motion picture projectionists[1]
15	L	20,060	L	VH	L	Moderate-term on-the-job	Packaging and filling machine operators and tenders
5	-	-	-	-	-	-	Painting and coating machine operators
4	VL	21,820	L	VH	VL	Moderate-term on-the-job	Coating, painting, and spraying machine operators, tenders, setters, and set-up operators
1	VL	29,120	H	VH	VL	Moderate-term on-the-job	Painters, transportation equipment
1	VL	25,990	H	H	VL	Moderate-term on-the-job	Paper goods machine setters and set-up operators[1]
2	VL	17,810	L	H	VH	Short-term on-the-job	Photographic processing machine operators and tenders
1	VL	29,600	H	VL	VL	Moderate-term on-the-job	Separating, filtering, clarifying, precipitating, and still machine operators and tenders[1]
0	VL	16,230	VL	VH	VL	Moderate-term on-the-job	Shoe sewing machine operators and tenders[1]
0	VL	36,430	VH	H	VL	Moderate-term on-the-job	Tire building machine operators
19	L	22,170	L	H	VL	Moderate-term on-the-job	All other machine operators, tenders, setters, and set-up operators[1]
97	-	-	-	-	-	-	Hand workers, including assemblers and fabricators
1	VL	15,720	VL	VH	L	Short-term on-the-job	Cannery workers
0	VL	18,660	L	VH	L	Short-term on-the-job	Coil winders, tapers, and finishers
1	VL	17,130	L	VH	L	Short-term on-the-job	Cutters and trimmers, hand[1]
6	VL	18,800	L	VH	L	Short-term on-the-job	Electrical and electronic assemblers
3	VL	20,450	L	VH	L	Short-term on-the-job	Grinders and polishers, hand
2	VL	22,640	L	VH	L	Short-term on-the-job	Machine assemblers
7	VL	16,270	VL	VH	L	Short-term on-the-job	Meat, poultry, and fish cutters and trimmers, hand[1]
2	VL	19,060	L	VH	L	Short-term on-the-job	Painting, coating, and decorating workers, hand[1]
0	VL	14,750	VL	VH	L	Short-term on-the-job	Pressers, hand
0	VL	15,520	VL	H	VH	Short-term on-the-job	Sewers, hand
1	VL	17,610	L	VH	L	Short-term on-the-job	Solderers and brazers[1]
12	L	25,810	H	H	VL	Long-term on-the-job	Welders and cutters
61	H	18,770	L	VH	L	Short-term on-the-job	All other assemblers, fabricators, and hand workers[1]

[1] One or more Current Population Survey (CPS) proxy occupations are used to estimate CPS based data.
[2] Current Population Survey data are used to estimate median weekly earnings ranking.
[3] Bachelor's degree or higher.

NOTE: Rankings are based on employment in all detailed occupations in the National Industry-Occupation Matrix. For details, see "Data presented" section of text. Codes for describing the ranked variables are: VH = Very high, H = High, L = Low, VL = Very low, n. a. = Data not available. A dash indicates data are not applicable.

Occupational employment and job openings data, 1998-2008, and worker characteristics, 1998

(Numbers in thousands)

1998 Matrix Occupation	Employment		Employment change, 1998-2008				Per-cent self-emp-loyed, 1998	Annual average job openings due to growth and total replacement needs, 1998-2008	
			Numeric		Percent				
	1998	2008	Number	Rank	Number	Rank		Number	Rank
Transportation and material moving machine and vehicle operators	5,215	5,960	745	-	14.2	-	6.8	866	-
Motor vehicle operators	4,084	4,723	639	-	15.6	-	8.1	685	-
Bus drivers	638	747	108	-	1.0	-	1.1	95	-
Bus drivers, transit and intercity	203	235	32	L	15.8	H	3.3	30	VL
Bus drivers, school	435	511	76	L	17.6	H	.0	65	L
Taxi drivers and chauffeurs	132	158	26	L	20.0	VH	34.4	27	VL
Truck drivers	3,274	3,782	507	-	15.4	-	8.6	557	-
Driver/sales workers	305	319	14	VL	4.7	VL	4.5	23	VL
Truck drivers light and heavy	2,970	3,463	493	VH	16.6	H	9.0	535	VH
All other motor vehicle operators[1]	40	37	-3	VL	-8.5	VL	.0	6	VL
Rail transportation workers	85	75	-10	-	-11.0	-	.0	5	-
Locomotive engineers[1]	33	35	2	VL	4.8	VL	.0	2	VL
Railroad brake, signal, and switch operators[1]	14	7	-7	VL	-47.8	VL	.0	1	VL
Railroad conductors and yardmasters[1]	25	24	-2	VL	-6.7	VL	.0	2	VL
Subway and streetcar operators[1]	3	4	0	VL	7.1	VL	.0	0	VL
All other rail transportation workers[1]	8	5	-3	VL	-35.6	VL	.0	0	VL
Water transportation and related workers	56	58	3	-	4.7	-	5.5	11	-
Able seamen, ordinary seamen, and marine oilers[1]	23	24	1	VL	5.1	VL	.6	4	VL
Captains and pilots, water vessels[1]	19	19	1	VL	3.0	VL	15.7	4	VL
Mates, ship, boat, and barge[1]	8	9	1	VL	7.9	VL	.0	2	VL
Ship engineers[1]	6	7	0	VL	4.3	VL	.0	1	VL
Material moving equipment operators	808	883	74	-	9.0	-	2.2	131	-
Crane and tower operators	49	49	0	VL	.5	VL	.0	6	VL
Excavation and loading machine operators[1]	106	122	16	VL	15.3	H	14.4	6	VL
Hoist and winch operators[1]	11	11	1	VL	6.0	VL	6.1	2	VL
Industrial truck and tractor operators	415	454	38	L	9.2	L	.2	81	L
All other material moving equipment operators	228	247	19	VL	8.3	L	.4	36	VL
All other transportation and material moving equipment operators[1]	183	222	39	L	21.5	VH	.0	35	VL
Helpers, laborers, and material movers, hand	5,142	5,768	626	-	12.1	-	1.4	1,636	-
Cleaners of vehicles and equipment	288	360	72	L	25.0	VH	8.2	117	L
Freight, stock, and material movers, hand[1]	822	834	12	VL	1.5	VL	1.7	307	H
Hand packers and packagers	984	1,197	213	H	21.7	VH	.8	249	H
Helpers, construction trades	576	618	42	L	7.3	VL	.4	167	L
Machine feeders and offbearers	213	211	-2	VL	-.9	VL	.0	40	VL
Parking lot attendants[1]	86	113	27	L	31.2	VH	.0	18	VL
Refuse and recyclable material collectors[1]	99	103	4	VL	3.9	VL	1.7	39	VL
Service station attendants	141	139	-2	VL	-1.2	VL	3.0	40	VL
All other helpers, laborers, and material movers, hand[1]	1,934	2,194	260	H	13.4	L	.9	654	VH

[1] One or more Current Population Survey (CPS) proxy occupations are used to estimate CPS based data.

[2] Current Population Survey data are used to estimate median weekly earnings ranking.

[3] Bachelor's degree or higher.

NOTE: Rankings are based on employment in all detailed occupations in the National Industry-Occupation Matrix. For details, see "Data presented" section of text. Codes for describing the ranked variables are: VH = Very high, H = High, L = Low, VL = Very low, n. a. = Data not available. A dash indicates data are not applicable.

Occupational employment and job openings data, 1998-2008, and worker characteristics, 1998

(Numbers in thousands)

Annual average job openings due to growth and net replacement needs, 1998-2008		Median annual earnings		Ranking of:		Most significant source of education or training	1998 Matrix Occupation
Number	Rank	Dollars	Rank	Unemployment rate	Percent part-time		
161	-	-	-	-	-	-	Transportation and material moving machine and vehicle operators
127	-	-	-	-	-	-	Motor vehicle operators
22	-	-	-	-	-	-	Bus drivers
7	VL	24,380	H	L	VH	Moderate-term on-the-job	Bus drivers, transit and intercity
15	L	18,820	L	L	VH	Short-term on-the-job	Bus drivers, school
5	VL	15,550	VL	H	H	Short-term on-the-job	Taxi drivers and chauffeurs
99	-	-	-	-	-	-	Truck drivers
7	VL	19,330	L	VL	L	Short-term on-the-job	Driver/sales workers
92	VH	24,260	H	H	L	Short-term on-the-job	Truck drivers light and heavy
1	VL	18,330	L	H	H	Short-term on-the-job	All other motor vehicle operators[1]
3	-	-	-	-	-	-	Rail transportation workers
1	VL	39,800	VH	VL	VL	Related work experience	Locomotive engineers[1]
0	VL	36,550	VH	VL	VL	Related work experience	Railroad brake, signal, and switch operators[1]
1	VL	38,500	VH	VL	VL	Related work experience	Railroad conductors and yardmasters[1]
0	VL	43,330	VH	VL	VL	Moderate-term on-the-job	Subway and streetcar operators[1]
0	VL	35,600	VH	VL	VL	Moderate-term on-the-job	All other rail transportation workers[1]
2	-	-	-	-	-	-	Water transportation and related workers
1	VL	23,700	H	L	VL	Short-term on-the-job	Able seamen, ordinary seamen, and marine oilers[1]
1	VL	41,210	VH	L	VL	Related work experience	Captains and pilots, water vessels[1]
0	VL	29,310	H	L	VL	Related work experience	Mates, ship, boat, and barge[1]
0	VL	40,150	VH	L	VL	Related work experience	Ship engineers[1]
21	-	-	-	-	-	-	Material moving equipment operators
1	VL	30,510	H	H	VL	Moderate-term on-the-job	Crane and tower operators
4	VL	27,090	H	H	VL	Moderate-term on-the-job	Excavation and loading machine operators[1]
0	VL	28,030	H	VH	VL	Moderate-term on-the-job	Hoist and winch operators[1]
9	VL	23,360	L	H	VL	Short-term on-the-job	Industrial truck and tractor operators
7	VL	23,970	H	VH	L	Moderate-term on-the-job	All other material moving equipment operators
7	VL	24,120	H	H	H	Moderate-term on-the-job	All other transportation and material moving equipment operators[1]
234	-	-	-	-	-	-	Helpers, laborers, and material movers, hand
16	L	14,540	VL	VH	VH	Short-term on-the-job	Cleaners of vehicles and equipment
31	L	18,460	L	VH	VH	Short-term on-the-job	Freight, stock, and material movers, hand[1]
46	H	14,550	VL	VH	H	Short-term on-the-job	Hand packers and packagers
31	L	19,510	L	VH	H	Short-term on-the-job	Helpers, construction trades
6	VL	18,810	L	VH	H	Short-term on-the-job	Machine feeders and offbearers
4	VL	13,920	VL	H	H	Short-term on-the-job	Parking lot attendants[1]
4	VL	21,860	L	VH	H	Short-term on-the-job	Refuse and recyclable material collectors[1]
6	VL	14,350	VL	VH	VH	Short-term on-the-job	Service station attendants
89	VH	17,920	L	VH	H	Short-term on-the-job	All other helpers, laborers, and material movers, hand[1]

[1] One or more Current Population Survey (CPS) proxy occupations are used to estimate CPS based data.

[2] Current Population Survey data are used to estimate median weekly earnings ranking.

[3] Bachelor's degree or higher.

NOTE: Rankings are based on employment in all detailed occupations in the National Industry-Occupation Matrix. For details, see "Data presented" section of text. Codes for describing the ranked variables are: VH = Very high, H = High, L = Low, VL = Very low, n. a. = Data not available. A dash indicates data are not applicable.

252 Major Jobs, Sorted by Percent of Projected Growth

Comments

America's Top White-Collar Jobs is part of JIST's America's Top Jobs series. I update the books in this series every two years in response to new data from the U.S. Department of Labor. The DOL provides data on 252 major occupations that account for about 90 percent of the American workforce.

I created the following list by sorting these 252 occupations in descending order by their percent of projected growth through 2008. I thought you would find this list interesting. It is the basis for *America's Fastest Growing Jobs*, another book in the America's Top Jobs series.

If you are interested in a job that is not described in this book, you can find a description for it in one of the other books in the America's Top Jobs series, which are referenced on page ii. Descriptions for all the jobs can be found in the *Occupational Outlook Handbook*, which is published by the U.S. Department of Labor. You can order the America's Top Jobs books or the *Occupational Outlook Handbook* from a bookstore or from JIST. You can also find them in your local library.

252 Major Jobs, in Order of Projected Percent Growth

Order of Projected Percent Growth	Occupation	Percent Growth in Employment, 1998-2008	Employment 1998	Numerical Change in Employment, 1998-2008
1	Computer systems analysts, engineers, and scientists	99	1,530,000	1,522,000
2	Paralegals	62	136,000	84,000
3	Medical assistants	58	252,000	146,000
4	Home health and personal care aides	58	746,000	433,000
5	Human service workers and assistants	53	268,000	141,000
6	Services sales representatives	51	841,000	429,000
7	Physician assistants	48	66,000	32,000
8	Electronic semiconductor processors	45	63,000	29,000
9	Health information technicians	44	92,000	41,000
10	Physical therapist assistants and aides	44	82,000	36,000
11	Engineering, natural science, and computer and information systems managers	43	326,000	142,000
12	Respiratory therapists	43	86,000	37,000
13	Surgical technologists	42	54,000	23,000
14	Dental assistants	42	229,000	97,000
15	Dental hygienists	41	143,000	58,000
16	Securities, commodities, and financial services sales representatives	41	303,000	124,000
17	Occupational therapy assistant and aides	40	19,000	7,400

Order of Projected Percent Growth	Occupation	Percent Growth in Employment, 1998-2008	Employment 1998	Numerical Change in Employment, 1998-2008
18	Correctional officers	39	383,000	148,000
19	Speech-language pathologists and audiologists	38	105,000	40,000
20	Social workers	36	604,000	218,000
21	Special education teachers	34	406,000	137,000
22	Occupational therapists	34	73,000	25,000
23	Physical therapists	34	120,000	41,000
24	Computer, automated teller, and office machine repairers	34	138,000	46,000
25	Health services managers	33	222,000	74,000
26	Biological and medical scientists	32	112,000	36,000
27	Emergency medical technicians and paramedics	32	150,000	47,000
28	Demonstrators, product promoters, and models	32	92,000	30,000
29	Teacher assistants	31	1,192,000	375,000
30	Computer programmers	30	648,000	191,000
31	Flight attendants	30	99,000	30,000
32	Guards	29	1,027,000	294,000
33	Management analysts	28	344,000	98,000
34	Instructors and coaches, sports and physical training	28	359,000	102,000
35	Police and detectives	27	764,000	205,000
36	Electrical and electronics engineers	26	357,000	93,000
37	Designers	26	423,000	110,000
38	Visual artists	26	308,000	79,000
39	Preschool teachers and child-care workers	26	1,250,000	328,000
40	Sheet metal workers and duct installers	26	122,000	32,000
41	Counselors	25	182,000	46,000
42	Veterinarians	25	57,000	14,000
43	Pest controllers	25	52,000	13,000
44	Public relations specialists	24	122,000	30,000
45	Writers and editors, including technical writers	24	341,000	83,000
46	Actors, directors, and producers	24	160,000	38,000
47	Adjusters, investigators, and collectors	24	1,466,000	345,000
48	Receptionists	24	1,293,000	305,000
49	Private detectives and investigators	24	61,000	15,000
50	Advertising, marketing, and public relations managers	23	485,000	112,000
51	College and university faculty	23	865,000	195,000
52	Chiropractors	23	46,000	11,000
53	Counter and rental clerks	23	469,000	108,000
54	Nursing and psychiatric aides	23	1,461,000	332,000
55	Veterinary assistants and nonfarm animal caretakers	23	181,000	42,000
56	Registered nurses	22	2,079,000	451,000
57	Loan officers and counselors	21	227,000	48,000
58	Civil engineers	21	195,000	41,000
59	Physicians	21	577,000	122,000

Order of Projected Percent Growth	Occupation	Percent Growth in Employment, 1998-2008	Employment 1998	Numerical Change in Employment, 1998-2008
60	Engineers	20	1,462,000	290,000
61	Licensed practical nurses	20	692,000	136,000
62	Radiologic technologists	20	162,000	32,000
63	Information clerks	20	1,910,000	386,000
64	Brokerage clerks and statement clerks	20	92,000	18,000
65	Landscaping, groundskeeping, nursery, greenhouse, and lawn service occupations	20	1,285,000	262,000
66	Line installers and repairers	20	279,000	56,000
67	Taxi drivers and chauffeurs	20	132,000	26,000
68	Architects, except landscape and naval	19	99,000	19,000
69	Recreation workers	19	241,000	46,000
70	Dietitians and nutritionists	19	54,000	10,000
71	Interviewing and new accounts clerks	19	239,000	46,000
72	Office and administrative support supervisors and managers	19	1,611,000	313,000
73	Hazardous materials removal workers	19	38,000	7,300
74	Administrative services and facility managers	18	364,000	66,000
75	Human resources, training, and labor relations specialists and managers	18	597,000	110,000
76	Restaurant and food service managers	18	518,000	92,000
77	Conservation scientists and foresters	18	39,000	7,000
78	Economists and marketing research analysts	18	70,000	13,000
79	Library technicians	18	72,000	13,000
80	Travel agents	18	138,000	25,000
81	Urban and regional planners	17	35,000	6,100
82	Clinical laboratory technologists and technicians	17	313,000	53,000
83	Cashiers	17	3,198,000	556,000
84	Automotive mechanics and service technicians	17	790,000	132,000
85	Heating, air-conditioning, and refrigeration mechanics and installers	17	286,000	48,000
86	Plasterers and stucco masons	17	40,000	6,900
87	Busdrivers	17	638,000	108,000
88	Construction and building inspectors	16	68,000	11,000
89	Funeral directors and morticians	16	28,000	4,400
90	General managers and top executives	16	3,362,000	551,000
91	Mechanical engineers	16	220,000	36,000
92	Engineering technicians	16	771,000	126,000
93	Geologists, geophysicists, and oceanographers	16	44,000	6,800
94	Lawyers and judicial workers	16	752,000	119,000
95	School teachers—kindergarten, elementary, and secondary	16	3,364,000	552,000
96	Cardiovascular technologists and technicians	16	33,000	5,300
97	Pharmacy technicians and assistants	16	170,000	27,000
98	Library assistants and bookmobile drivers	16	127,000	21,000
99	Automotive body repairers	16	227,000	36,000

Order of Projected Percent Growth	Occupation	Percent Growth in Employment, 1998-2008	Employment 1998	Numerical Change in Employment, 1998-2008
100	Coin, vending, and amusement machine servicers and repairers	16	27,000	4,200
101	Landscape architects	15	22,000	3,200
102	Atmospheric scientists	15	8,400	1,200
103	Musicians, singers, and related workers	15	273,000	41,000
104	Office clerks, general	15	3,021,000	463,000
105	Truckdrivers	15	3,274,000	507,000
106	Budget analysts	14	59,000	8,100
107	Construction managers	14	270,000	38,000
108	Financial managers	14	693,000	97,000
109	Property, real estate, and community association managers	14	315,000	43,000
110	Surveyors, cartographers, photogrammetrists, and surveying technicians	14	110,000	16,000
111	Chemists	14	96,000	13,000
112	Adult and vocational education teachers	14	588,000	81,000
113	Opticians, dispensing	14	71,000	9,800
114	Dancers and choreographers	14	29,000	3,900
115	Water and wastewater treatment plant operators	14	98,000	14,000
116	Cost estimators	13	152,000	20,000
117	Education administrators	13	447,000	58,000
118	Employment interviewers, private or public employment service	13	66,000	8,500
119	Industrial engineers, except safety engineers	13	126,000	16,000
120	Social scientists, other	13	50,000	6,400
121	Archivists, curators, museum technicians, and conservators	13	23,000	2,900
122	Recreational therapists	13	39,000	5,200
123	Hotel, motel, and resort desk clerks	13	159,000	21,000
124	Chefs, cooks, and other kitchen workers	13	3,306,000	442,000
125	Electronics repairers, commercial and industrial equipment	13	72,000	9,100
126	Nuclear medicine technologists	12	14,000	1,600
127	Retail salespersons	12	4,582,000	565,000
128	Dispatchers	12	248,000	30,000
129	Food and beverage service occupations	12	5,429,000	655,000
130	Bricklayers and stonemasons	12	157,000	19,000
131	Elevator installers and repairers	12	30,000	3,600
132	Roofers	12	158,000	19,000
133	Handlers, equipment cleaners, helpers, and laborers	12	5,142,000	626,000
134	Accountants and auditors	11	1,080,000	122,000
135	Inspectors and compliance officers, except construction	11	176,000	19,000
136	Agricultural and food scientists	11	21,000	2,300
137	Psychologists	11	166,000	19,000
138	Optometrists	11	38,000	4,000

Order of Projected Percent Growth	Occupation	Percent Growth in Employment, 1998-2008	Employment 1998	Numerical Change in Employment, 1998-2008
139	Podiatrists	11	14,000	1,500
140	Billing clerks and billing machine operators	11	449,000	47,000
141	Janitors and cleaners and institutional cleaning supervisors	11	3,271,000	374,000
142	Chemical engineers	10	48,000	4,600
143	Real estate agents and brokers	10	347,000	34,000
144	Court reporters, medical transcriptionists, and stenographers	10	110,000	11,000
145	File clerks	10	272,000	26,000
146	Barbers, cosmetologists, and related workers	10	723,000	73,000
147	Telecommunications equipment mechanics, installers, and repairers	10	125,000	13,000
148	Aircraft mechanics and service technicians	10	133,000	14,000
149	Diesel mechanics and service technicians	10	255,000	25,000
150	Electricians	10	656,000	68,000
151	Bindery workers	10	96,000	9,300
152	Aerospace engineers	9	53,000	4,600
153	Materials engineers	9	20,000	1,800
154	Operations research analysts	9	76,000	6,700
155	Photographers and camera operators	9	161,000	15,000
156	Mail clerks and messengers	9	247,000	23,000
157	Mobile heavy equipment mechanics	9	106,000	9,900
158	Painters and paperhangers	9	476,000	41,000
159	Blue-collar worker supervisors	9	2,198,000	196,000
160	Painting and coating machine operators	9	171,000	15,000
161	Material moving equipment operators	9	808,000	74,000
162	Retail sales worker supervisors and managers	8	1,675,000	134,000
163	Maintenance mechanics, general utility	8	1,232,000	95,000
164	Construction equipment operators	8	321,000	25,000
165	Structural and reinforcing metal workers	8	87,000	7,300
166	Welders, cutters, and welding machine operators	8	477,000	37,000
167	Purchasing managers, buyers, and purchasing agents	7	547,000	38,000
168	Actuaries	7	16,000	1,100
169	Science technicians	7	227,000	16,000
170	Pharmacists	7	185,000	14,000
171	Loan clerks and credit authorizers, checkers, and clerks	7	254,000	17,000
172	Carpenters	7	1,086,000	76,000
173	Drywall installers and finishers	7	163,000	12,000
174	Insulation workers	7	67,000	5,000
175	Hotel managers and assistants	6	76,000	4,500
176	Aircraft pilots and flight engineers	6	94,000	5,500
177	Nuclear engineers	6	12,000	700
178	Drafters	6	283,000	18,000
179	Electroneurodiagnostic technologists	6	5,400	300

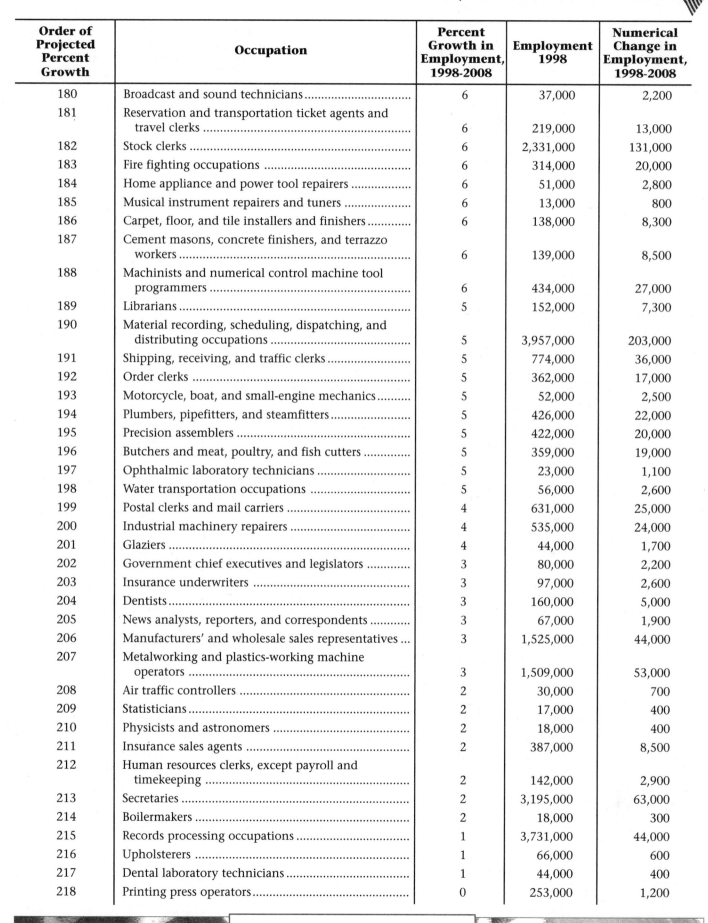

Order of Projected Percent Growth	Occupation	Percent Growth in Employment, 1998-2008	Employment 1998	Numerical Change in Employment, 1998-2008
180	Broadcast and sound technicians	6	37,000	2,200
181	Reservation and transportation ticket agents and travel clerks	6	219,000	13,000
182	Stock clerks	6	2,331,000	131,000
183	Fire fighting occupations	6	314,000	20,000
184	Home appliance and power tool repairers	6	51,000	2,800
185	Musical instrument repairers and tuners	6	13,000	800
186	Carpet, floor, and tile installers and finishers	6	138,000	8,300
187	Cement masons, concrete finishers, and terrazzo workers	6	139,000	8,500
188	Machinists and numerical control machine tool programmers	6	434,000	27,000
189	Librarians	5	152,000	7,300
190	Material recording, scheduling, dispatching, and distributing occupations	5	3,957,000	203,000
191	Shipping, receiving, and traffic clerks	5	774,000	36,000
192	Order clerks	5	362,000	17,000
193	Motorcycle, boat, and small-engine mechanics	5	52,000	2,500
194	Plumbers, pipefitters, and steamfitters	5	426,000	22,000
195	Precision assemblers	5	422,000	20,000
196	Butchers and meat, poultry, and fish cutters	5	359,000	19,000
197	Ophthalmic laboratory technicians	5	23,000	1,100
198	Water transportation occupations	5	56,000	2,600
199	Postal clerks and mail carriers	4	631,000	25,000
200	Industrial machinery repairers	4	535,000	24,000
201	Glaziers	4	44,000	1,700
202	Government chief executives and legislators	3	80,000	2,200
203	Insurance underwriters	3	97,000	2,600
204	Dentists	3	160,000	5,000
205	News analysts, reporters, and correspondents	3	67,000	1,900
206	Manufacturers' and wholesale sales representatives	3	1,525,000	44,000
207	Metalworking and plastics-working machine operators	3	1,509,000	53,000
208	Air traffic controllers	2	30,000	700
209	Statisticians	2	17,000	400
210	Physicists and astronomers	2	18,000	400
211	Insurance sales agents	2	387,000	8,500
212	Human resources clerks, except payroll and timekeeping	2	142,000	2,900
213	Secretaries	2	3,195,000	63,000
214	Boilermakers	2	18,000	300
215	Records processing occupations	1	3,731,000	44,000
216	Upholsterers	1	66,000	600
217	Dental laboratory technicians	1	44,000	400
218	Printing press operators	0	253,000	1,200

Order of Projected Percent Growth	Occupation	Percent Growth in Employment, 1998-2008	Employment 1998	Numerical Change in Employment, 1998-2008
219	Industrial production managers	-1	208,000	-1,800
220	Millwrights	-2	82,000	-1,500
221	Tool and die makers	-2	138,000	-2,100
222	Electric power generating plant operators and power distributors and dispatchers	-2	45,000	-700
223	Woodworking	-2	372,000	-6,900
224	Forestry, conservation, and logging	-3	120,000	-3,800
225	Inspectors, testers, and graders	-3	689,000	-22,000
226	Petroleum engineers	-4	12,000	-400
227	Announcers	-4	60,000	-2,600
228	Bookkeeping, accounting, and auditing clerks	-4	2,078,000	-81,000
229	Mathematicians	-5	14,000	-800
230	Bank tellers	-5	560,000	-31,000
231	Farm equipment mechanics	-5	49,000	-2,600
232	Payroll and timekeeping clerks	-6	172,000	-11,000
233	Word processors, typists, and data entry keyers	-6	894,000	-54,000
234	Jewelers and precious stone and metal workers	-6	30,000	-1,800
235	Stationary engineers	-6	31,000	-1,800
236	Prepress workers	-6	152,000	-9,400
237	Photographic process workers	-6	63,000	-4,000
238	Rail transportation occupations	-11	85,000	-9,600
239	Farmers and farm managers	-12	1,483,000	-174,000
240	Electronic home entertainment equipment repairers..	-12	36,000	-4,300
241	Mining engineers, including mine safety engineers	-13	4,400	-600
242	Communications equipment operators	-15	297,000	-46,000
243	Apparel workers	-17	729,000	-124,000
244	Shoe and leather workers and repairers	-18	23,000	-4,000
245	Private household workers	-19	928,000	-178,000
246	Textile machinery operators	-19	277,000	-53,000
247	Fishers and fishing vessel operators	-22	51,000	-11,000
248	Computer operators	-26	251,000	-64,000
249	Job opportunities in the Armed Forces	(1)	1,238,000	(1)
250	Protestant ministers	(2)	400,000	(2)
251	Rabbis	(2)	5,000	(2)
252	Roman Catholic priests	(2)	47,000	(2)

[1] Projections not available from the Bureau of Labor Statistics
[2] Estimates not available

Here Are Just Some of Our Products!

JIST publishes hundreds of books, videos, software products, and other items. Some of our best-selling career and educational reference books are presented here, followed by an order form. You can also order these books through any bookstore or Internet bookseller's site.

Check out JIST's Web site at www.jist.com for tables of contents and free chapters on these and other products.

Guide for Occupational Exploration, Third Edition

J. Michael Farr; LaVerne L. Ludden, Ed.D., and Laurence Shatkin, Ph.D.

The first major revision since the *GOE* was released in 1979 by the U.S. Department of Labor! It still uses the same approach of exploration based on major interest areas but is updated to reflect the many changes in our labor market. The new *GOE* also uses the recently released O*NET database of occupational information developed by the U.S. Department of Labor. An essential career reference!

ISBN 1-56370-636-9 / Order Code LP-J6369 / **$39.95** Softcover
ISBN 1-56370-826-4 / Order Code LP-J8264 / **$49.95** Hardcover

Occupational Outlook Handbook, 2000-2001 Edition

U.S. Department of Labor

We will meet or beat ANY price on the OOH!

The *Occupational Outlook Handbook* is the most widely used career exploration resource. This is a quality reprint of the government's *OOH,* only at a less-expensive price. It describes 250 jobs–jobs held by almost 90 percent of the U.S. workforce–making it ideal for students, counselors, teachers, librarians, and job seekers. Job descriptions cover the nature of the work, working conditions, training, job outlook, and earnings. Well-written narrative with many charts and photos. New edition every two years.

ISBN 1-56370-676-8 / Order Code LP-J6768 / **$18.95** Softcover
ISBN 1-56370-677-6 / Order Code LP-J6776 / **$22.95** Hardcover

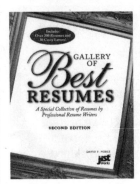

Young Person's Occupational Outlook Handbook, Third Edition

Compiled by JIST Editors from U.S. government data

Based on the *Occupational Outlook Handbook,* this text is ideal for helping young people explore careers. This book covers 250 jobs–each on one page–held by 85 percent of the workforce. It clusters job descriptions, making it easy to explore job options based on interest. It also makes direct connections between school subjects and the skills needed for jobs.

ISBN 1-56370-731-4 / Order Code LP-J7314
$19.95

The College Majors Handbook

The Actual Jobs, Earnings, and Trends for Graduates of 60 College Majors

Neeta P. Fogg, Paul E. Harrington, and Thomas F. Harrington

Faced with the college decision? This book details what actually happened to more than 15,000 undergraduates from 60 college majors. This is the only college planning guide with the perspective of what actually happened to college undergraduates. It identifies jobs in which the graduates now work and their earnings on those jobs.

ISBN 1-56370-518-4 / Order Code LP-J5184
$24.95

The Kids' College Almanac, Second Edition

A first Look at College

Barbara C. Greenfeld and Robert A. Weinstein

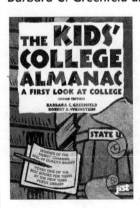

Selected by the New York Public Library as one of the best books for teens and preteens, it provides helpful information about going to college and encourages career and educational planning.

ISBN 1-56370-730-6 / Order Code LP-J7306
$16.95

Health-Care Careers for the 21ˢᵗ Century

Saul Wischnitzer, Ph.D., and Edith Wischnitzer

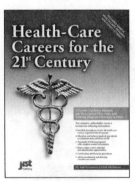

This three-in-one book is a career guidance manual, job description overview, and training program directory. It provides detailed descriptions of over 80 health-care careers, organized into five groups. It lists thousands of training programs with complete contact information. And it offers career guidance on everything from self-assessment to the interview process. Sample resumes and cover letters are included.

ISBN 1-56370-667-9 / Order Code LP-J6679
$24.95

JIST Ordering Information

JIST specializes in publishing the very best results-oriented career and self-directed job search material. Since 1981 we have been a leading publisher in career assessment devices, books, videos, and software. We continue to strive to make our materials the best there are, so that people can stay abreast of what's happening in the labor market, and so they can clarify and articulate their skills and experiences for themselves as well as for prospective employers. **Our products are widely available through your local bookstores, wholesalers, and distributors.**

The World Wide Web

For more occupational or book information, get online and see our Web site at **www.jist.com**. Advance information about new products, services, and training events is continually updated.

Quantity Discounts Available!

Quantity discounts are available for businesses, schools, and other organizations.

The JIST Guarantee

We want you to be happy with everything you buy from JIST. If you aren't satisfied with a product, return it to us within 30 days of purchase along with the reason for the return. Please include a copy of the packing list or invoice to guarantee quick credit to your order.

How to Order

For your convenience, the last page of this book contains an order form.

24-Hour Consumer Order Line:
Call toll free 1-800-648-JIST
Please have your credit card (VISA, MC, or AMEX) information ready!

Mail your order to:

JIST Publishing, Inc.
8902 Otis Avenue
Indianapolis, IN 46216-1033
Fax: Toll free 1-800-JIST-FAX

JIST Order and Catalog Request Form

Purchase Order #: _____ (Required by some organizations)

Billing Information

Organization Name: _____

Accounting Contact: _____

Street Address: _____

_____

City, State, Zip: _____

Phone Number: (_____) _____

Shipping Information with Street Address (If Different from Above)

Organization Name: _____

Contact: _____

Street Address: (We *cannot* ship to P.O. boxes) _____

_____

City, State, Zip: _____

Phone Number: (_____) _____

Please copy this form if you need more lines for your order.

Phone: 1-800-648-JIST
Fax: 1-800-JIST-FAX
World Wide Web Address:
http://www.jist.com

Credit Card Purchases: VISA_____ MC_____ AMEX_____

Card Number: _____

Exp. Date: _____

Name As on Card: _____

Signature: _____

Quantity	Order Code	Product Title	Unit Price	Total
	———	**Free JIST Catalog**	**Free**	———

jist ®
Publishing

8902 Otis Avenue
Indianapolis, IN 46216

Shipping / Handling / Insurance Fees

In the continental U.S. add 7% of subtotal:
- Minimum amount charged = $4.00
- Maximum amount charged = $100.00
- FREE shipping and handling on any prepaid orders over $40.00

Above pricing is for regular ground shipment only. For rush or special delivery, call JIST Customer Service at 1-800-648-JIST for the correct shipping fee.

Outside the continental U.S. call JIST Customer Service at 1-800-648-JIST for an estimate of these fees.

Payment in U.S. funds only!

Subtotal	
+5% Sales Tax *Indiana Residents*	
+Shipping / Handling / Ins. (See left)	
TOTAL	

JIST thanks you for your order!